BOOK

The Philip E. Lilienthal imprint
honors special books
in commemoration of a man whose work
at the University of California Press from 1954 to 1979
was marked by dedication to young authors
and to high standards in the field of Asian Studies.
Friends, family, authors, and foundations have together
endowed the Lilienthal Fund, which enables the Press
to publish under this imprint selected books
in a way that reflects the taste and judgment
of a great and beloved editor.

The Monster That Is History

The Monster That Is History

History, Violence, and Fictional Writing in Twentieth-Century China

David Der-wei Wang

UNIVERSITY OF CALIFORNIA PRESS
Berkeley Los Angeles London

University of California Press
Berkeley and Los Angeles, California

University of California Press, Ltd.
London, England

Library of Congress Cataloging-in-Publication Data

Wang, Dewei.
The monster that is history : history, violence, and fictional writing in twentieth-century China / David Der-wei Wang.
p. cm.
Includes bibliographical references and index.
ISBN 0-520-23140-6 (alk. paper)—ISBN 0-520-23873-7 (pbk. : alk. paper)
1. Chinese fiction—20th century—History and criticism. 2. Chinese fiction—Taiwan—History and criticism. 3. Violence in literature. I. Title.

PL2443.W.244 2004
895.1'35093552—dc22 2003026337

Manufactured in the United States of America
13 12 11 10 09 08 07 06 05 04
10 9 8 7 6 5 4 3 2 1

The paper used in this publication is both acid-free and totally chlorine-free (TCF). It meets the minimum requirements of ANSI/NISO Z39.48–1992 (R 1997) *(Permanence of Paper).*

CONTENTS

ACKNOWLEDGMENTS / *vii*
INTRODUCTION / *1*

1. Invitation to a Beheading / *15*
2. Crime or Punishment? / *41*
3. An Undesired Revolution / *77*
4. Three Hungry Women / *117*
5. Of Scars and National Memory / *148*
6. The Monster That Is History / *183*
7. The End of the Line / *224*
8. Second Haunting / *262*

NOTES / *293*
BIBLIOGRAPHY / *343*
GLOSSARY / *371*
INDEX / *383*

ACKNOWLEDGMENTS

I am most grateful to my colleagues in China, Taiwan, Japan, and the States, Yung-fa Chen, Rey Chow, Amy Dooling, Howard Goldblatt, Shirinaga Jun, Martin Kern, Ch'ing-ming Ko, Leo Ou-fan Lee, Feng Li, Liu Zaifu, Jianmei Liu, Chia-ling Mei, Shang Wei, Shen Weiwei, Cheng-sheng Tu, Ban Wang, Fan-sen Wang, Wang Hui, and Chin-lung Yang, for their advice, comments, and support at the various stages of the writing of this book. Above all, I am deeply indebted to the works and ideas of Professor C. T. Hsia. I particularly thank Carlos Rojas for reading the first draft of the book and making insightful suggestions. I would also like to thank my students Mingwei Song and Enhua Zhang and my research assistant Kamloon Woo for their assistance in the preparation of the manuscript.

Special thanks go to Elizabeth Berg, Randy Heyman, and Mary Severance of the University of California Press for their editing expertise and professionalism.

Portions of Chapter 1 appeared in *Ideology and Politics in Modern Chinese Literature,* ed. Liu Kang and Xiaobing Tang (Durham, N.C.: Duke University Press, 1993), 174–87, under the title "Lu Xun, Shen Congwen, and Decapitation." Chapter 2 appeared in *Becoming Chinese: Passages to Modernity and Beyond: 1900–1950,* ed. Wen-hsin Yeh (Berkeley: University of California Press, 1999), 260–97, under the title "Crime or Punishment? The Forensic Discourse of Modern Chinese Literature." Chapter 4 appeared in *Modern Chinese Literary and Cultural Studies in the Age of Theory: Reimagining the Field,* ed. Rey Chow (Durham, N.C.: Duke University Press, 2000), 48–77. Parts of Chapter 5 appeared in *Chinese Literature in the Second Half of a Modern Century,* ed. Pang-yuan Ch'i and David Der-wei Wang (Bloomington: Indiana University Press, 2000), 39–64, under the title "Reinventing National History: Communist and Anti-Communist Fiction from 1946 to 1955." All have been extensively revised for this book.

Introduction

This book represents an effort to integrate my engagement over the past decade with literature and history. In studying fiction, poetry, and drama drawn from various periods, this book delineates the multivalence of Chinese violence across the past century and inquires into its ethical and technological consequences. It extends its arguments between two related axes: history and representation, modernity and monstrosity.

I understand that I have undertaken a difficult task. Most of the subjects that occupy the following pages, from decapitation to suicide, from hunger to scarring, are not pleasant. But I feel compelled to write about them because they constitute a major portion of twentieth-century Chinese history, a history whose poignant beginnings and atrocious outcomes cannot be overstressed. And, given my background, I must admit to personal motivations. The literature to be discussed, particularly that which describes the 1949 Communist takeover, the diaspora of Chinese mainlanders to Taiwan and overseas, and the breakdown of family ties, with a concomitant dissipation of cultural legacies, inhabits a dark niche in the architecture of familial and communal memory. Fiction may be able to speak where history has fallen silent.

Along the pathway of my research, I became increasingly alert to the pitfalls of such a project, both personal and impersonal. I hasten to emphasize that I am writing neither a testimonial to Chinese suffering nor an exposé of Chinese cruelty. More than enough fictional and nonfictional writing has been published about the pains and sorrows of modern China, and one can even postulate the existence today of cultural industries nurtured upon Chinese atrocity, Maoist oppression, or simply the adolescent vandalism of the Cultural Revolution. These writings, while bearing witness to the horror of recent Chinese history, have led the rest of us to a dilemma:

outcries of "j'accuse" or "call to arms" may ignite a justice that is as cruel and unnecessary as the original crimes, and one person's account of "tears and blood" may achieve nothing more than a second person's undeserved catharsis. In my study of modern Chinese history and literature about violence and suffering, I address these ambivalent endings. But I do hope that I have confronted some hard issues. I believe, for example, that suffering does not translate directly into virtue; that surviving a calamity does not authorize one to speak for those who perished in it; that justice, either as a concept or as an institution, is overdetermined and therefore subject to continued contestation.

At the beginning of modern Chinese literature, Lu Xun (1881–1936) already noted the ambiguity of writing and reading (or hearing and watching) violence and pain. He observes how the bloody punishment of beheading could be transformed into public entertainment ("The True Story of Ah Q," 1921), and how a peasant woman's report of her misfortune could first induce tears and, after several repetitions, end up inciting laughter, mockery, and finally total indifference ("New Year's Sacrifice," 1924). The line between the self-defense mechanisms that are operative in surviving and recollecting brutalities and the need to consume bloody spectacles has never been so thin as in Lu Xun's world.

But stories about how Chinese civilization has been maimed and distorted across the century must be told and retold so as to be remembered. The dialectic of historical violence and its (impossible) representation should not serve as an impediment to, but rather as an impetus for, "the morality of form."[1] This is where my book starts. In my view, modern Chinese historiography has not sufficiently addressed the scale or the moral and psychological aftermath of China's violence and pain, and I contend that literature, particularly fiction in my case, can be drawn on as a complementing *and* contesting discourse.

One can hardly read modern Chinese history without noticing a seemingly endless brutality totted up in dishearteningly large figures. For instance, at least one million Chinese lost their lives during the Warlord and Nationalist periods, and more than fourteen million were killed during the Second Sino-Japanese War. More than two million fled China after the Communist seizure of power, while almost five million perished during the same period. After the founding of the People's Republic, at least thirty million perished during Mao's Great Leap Forward, which was followed by the Great Famine and Retrenchment period, and an estimated fifteen million were persecuted and executed every year between those famously bloody wars, campaigns, and movements.[2] While these facts can be gathered, screened, analyzed, and analyzed away in historical accounts, literature perhaps does more by resurrecting individual lives from the oblivion of collective memory and public documentation in reenacting the affective intensities of private and inadmissible truth.

There has always been a mutual implication of historicity and narrativity, to be sure, in Chinese historiographical and literary studies. But never have we seen such a moment as we have in modern times, when official history has been so dictated by the ideological and institutional imaginary as to verge on a discourse of make-believe, a discourse often associated with traditional fiction, and fiction so arrested by a desire to reflect the past *and* future as to appropriate the functions of traditional history with respect to completed fact. Hence the genesis of the peculiar double-bind of Chinese literary modernity.

With this in mind, I tackle the ways Chinese writers register the man-made and natural disasters that forged a century of violence: foreign aggression, civil war, revolution, riots, clan conflict, famine, floods, and the cataclysmic collapse of time-honored establishments. These signs of palpable violence were compounded by contending ideological totems and taboos, which ravaged Chinese life with unprecedented efficiency and resulted in mental and behavioral wounds far beyond familiar diagnosis. Transcribing both the visible and invisible forms of violence poses a lasting challenge to mimesis.

I also call attention to the fact that the modern Chinese representation of violence can be underwritten as a violence of representation.[3] For Chinese writers and readers alike, to represent pain and suffering is not merely to reflect external instances of violence; rather it demands to be appreciated and enlisted as a radical agency of change. Chinese literary history from the Literary Revolution to Revolutionary Literature has left ample evidence of the imaginary and actualized power of literature. Literature thus presents itself as a meeting ground where poetic justice contends with legal justice, or in more volatile terms, where ink demands blood. Writing and reading are taken as juridical events capable of transforming symbolic victims into social rebels and figurative humiliation into moral passion.

Modern Chinese writers and readers have learned to write and read in spite of the most capricious censorship, defamation, bowdlerization, propaganda, purges, confiscation, incarceration, "rehabilitation," exile, suicide, and execution. The most menacing challenge to literature is the imposition (or self-imposition) of silence. These decades saw a large number of writers either choosing or being forced to give up writing. Few were those determined against all odds to make their voices heard. There were cases of writers remaining silent when the name of injustice could have been spoken or, worse, becoming exuberant on behalf of that injustice, thereby revealing literature's complicity with all master narratives, old or new. This, I argue, is the worst form of "the violence of representation."[4]

In view of the plentiful writing about violence and suffering, there must be an irony in the paucity of critical, or diacritical, engagements with the issues that are raised. Zheng Zhenduo's (1898–1958) invocation of a literature of "tears and blood" in the 1920s first established the content and desired effect of the modern Chinese "literature of engagement."[5] Zheng's concept was echoed in the 1970s, not without a touch of sarcasm, by Joseph Lau as a literature of "tears and sniveling."[6] Whereas writing for "the insulted and the injured" prevailed in the 1930s, C. T. Hsia finds in it and its successors a penchant for "hard-core realism," which flaunts its raw materials and practices unabashed moral exhibitionism.[7] And in the wake of "scar writing"—a powerful literature indicting the Cultural Revolution, as critics such as Liu Zaifu have pointed out, Chinese literature under the auspices of leftist aesthetics started out as "a literature against violence" and became mere "literary violence."[8] Meanwhile, the premodern Chinese tradition of writing violence and pain—from the descriptions of war and the hardship of life in the *Shijing* to the testimonials to national crisis in Du Fu's poetry, from the late Ming chronicles of dynastic cataclysm to the late Qing recollection of the "history of pain"[9]—has been overlooked by modern critics.

When the representation of violence is at issue, we have tended to resort to Western paradigms,[10] among which the critique of the Holocaust usually takes the most prominent position. Among other provocations, there is Theodor Adorno's famous statement that "after Auschwitz, it is no longer possible to write poems."[11] By this, Adorno indicates the unbridgeable gap between suffering and writing about suffering, between the articulated testimonials of those who survived the Holocaust and the eternally muted protests of those who were killed. From a psychoanalytical perspective, theorists of trauma have taken up where Adorno left off. What should have never happened had happened. These critics ask whether it is possible to find any literary rhetoric or clinical analysis to properly explain this unlikely historical wound.[12]

Beyond these models, it will be recalled, Georges Bataille directs one's attention to the dark, violent undercurrent of the social and political unconsciousness. Violence and death wishes take on ambiguous dimensions in his idiosyncratic observation of rituals, religions, and polities, so much so as to generate an "erotics" of annihilation and ecstasy. René Girard offers a triangular diagram of sacrificial ritual, violence, and mimesis for the human agency that contains the inscrutable and undesirable forces in society.[13] Exercising an alternation of Jewish mysticism and apocalyptic Marxism, Walter Benjamin imagines a Violence that could subsume all forms of violence.[14]

Equally intriguing is Mikhail Bakhtin, who highlighted carnivalesque festivity as a way in which a society parodies and critiques, indulges and transcends, its deep-seated impulses for disorder and violence.[15]

One must bear in mind the debate over the modern technology of violence in all its recognized forms, from totalitarian control to totalistic revolution, from colonial rule to ubiquitous micro- and macro-power. Whereas Hannah Arendt launches her attack on modern violence and its political sanctification in totalitarian regimes, Jean Baudrillard contemplates the illusory nature of the spectacle of terrorism in postmodern society.[16] And who can improve on Michel Foucault in drawing a genealogy of Western modernity in lockstep with a progression of violence from the "theater of bloodshed" to the super-vision of the body?[17]

Finally, in the deadly aftermath of every form of violence, the task of mourning is analyzed and imposed. Using the controversy over the "death of Marxism" as a case in point, Jacques Derrida imagines a "hauntology" to replace conventional ontological thought: when the dead do not rest peacefully and threaten repeatedly to return to life, Derrida suggests, history reveals its ties with its spectral other. "Haunting is historical . . . but it is not dated, it is never docilely given a date in the chain of precedents . . . according to the instituted order of the calendar."[18] There is no shortage of modern forms of violence—and there is no shortage of modern theories either.

While acknowledging and indeed utilizing these and other models of violence, this book is directed toward opening a new critical dimension by looking into the rich repository of Chinese historiographical imagination. I pay special attention to a strain of historical discourse that stresses history's potential to witness, and sometimes even instantiate, what is violent and potentially undesirable in humanity. Numerous historical accounts have been inscribed to testify to, indict, and repair the evil consequences of man-made, natural, and supernatural disasters. It is said that Confucius compiled the *Chunqiu* to curb malicious schemes by treacherous officials and evil-doers.[19] The *Zuozhuan* and the *Shiji,* two of the most prominent ancient Chinese histories, incorporate abundant materials on tyrannical rulers and brutal administrators, underscored by a project of condemning evil and honoring virtue. The call to appease evil and violence in deference to moral rectification remained strong among premodern Chinese historians, amid echoes of Confucius's wishful remark that: "If a state could be ruled by those who have virtue continuously for one hundred years, brutality might well be overcome and slaughter might well be done away with."[20]

Of course, history since Confucius's time has proven to be otherwise. Evil has continued to proliferate from one generation to another despite the presumed vindictive power of history, so much so that with a twist of logic, one may even ponder if evil and the violence it entails have not become part of the raison d'être of history. More menacing are the moments when writing history as such risks violence. I am thinking of the numerous historians who chronicle facts and preserve their vocational integrity against all adversity. The legendary Histor Dong Hu of the Jin and the Histor Jian of the Qi, who risked their lives by transcribing facts as they were, have been hailed as model historians.[21] And who can forget how violence and suffering served as the motivation for the arch-historian, arch-castrato, and thereby arch-singer-of-tales, Sima Qian (145 or 135 B.C.–?), to complete the *Shiji*?[22]

While official historiography derived its legitimacy from moral determinism, skeptical voices, however minor and wayward, were heard all along. By the late Ming and early Qing period, there had arisen a counterdiscourse regarding violence as an intrinsic component of history and writing about history. Among the more remarkable examples are Ding Yaokang (1599–1669), who wrote *Tianshi* (History of heaven) to study the irredeemable atrocities of bygone periods; Li Zhi (1527–1602), who framed his *Fenshu* (Burning books) with a foreknowledge of the lethal consequences his recalcitrant writing would entail; and Aina, who concluded his storytelling collection *Doupeng xianhua* (Casual talks under the bean arbor) by contemplating the complementary relationship between violence and humanity.

I further suggest that the intertwined relations of violence and historicity have their mythopoetic counterparts. The title of this book, *The Monster That Is History,* draws on the ancient Chinese concept of the monster *taowu,* known for both its ferocious nature and its divinatory power. In classics such as the *Shenyi jing* (The classic of the fantastic and the strange), the *taowu* is described as a creature that "looks like tiger, with hair two feet long. It has a human face, a tiger's feet, a pig's teeth, and a tail as long as eighteen feet."[23] From such menacing origins, the *taowu* underwent various incarnations over the centuries, to the point where it was identifiable with humans of evil inclination, as evinced by accounts in the *Zuozhuan, Shangshu,* and *Shiji.*[24] It is said that Prince Zhuanxu's son, Guen, was of such wayward nature that he earned himself the monstrous name of *Taowu.*[25] Together with three other evils of the time, this human *taowu* was tamed and exiled to the frontiers, where it scares away ghostly mountain spirits, or *chimei,* since only something evil can withstand other evils.

Even more pertinent is the fact that the *taowu* was known for its power to see the past and the future, so as to make the best of its own life.[26] As scholars have noted, in the Xia, Shang, and particularly Chu mythological traditions, the *taowu* is a creature with divinatory powers and was therefore worshipped as a tribal totem.[27] Because of its ferocious nature and mysterious visionary ability, the *taowu* was made a guardian of the imperial tombs in the Chu region.[28] Most significantly, somewhere along the way, the *taowu* acquired cognitive identity with history itself; hence the *taowu* is an animal that can foresee the future, so it can always run away before the hunters arrive. Since history reveals both past and future, it is referred to as the *taowu*.[29] Thus one finds in *Mencius* the following statement:

> The *Sheng* of the Chin [Jin], the *T'ao U* [Taowu] of Ch'u [Chu], and the *Spring and Autumn Annals* of Lu are the same kind of work . . . and the style is that of the official historian.[30]

The metamorphosis of the *taowu* from monster to historical account, while indicative of the amorphous power of the ancient Chinese imaginary, points to one way in which Chinese history took form. As the *Zuozhuan* indicates, because of its fiendish nature, the *taowu* compels the ancients to "remember and recount its wickedness so as to take precaution."[31] In other words, the monster is invoked as an objective correlative, so to speak, to the human account of past experience, registering what is immemorial and yet unforgettable in Chinese collective memory, and cautioning against any similar mishaps in the future.

Ambiguity abounds when one looks into the way by which *Taowu* the monster is translated into *Taowu* the diviner, and when *taowu* as *history* is folded into *taowu* as divination. In view of the incessant outbursts of violence and brutality from one generation to another, one has to ponder: could history be regarded as both an embodiment and an indictment of monstrosity? If so, to what extent has the contemplation of history entailed insight as well as indifference? This paradox becomes all the more poignant in modern times, when monstrosity has taken on an unprecedented multitude of forms. Particularly in view of the massive scale of violence and pain that the Chinese administered to China in the name of enlightenment, rationality, and utopian plenitude, one senses that the line between understanding and complicity had never been so difficult to discern.

My genealogical foray into the ancestry of the *taowu* was inspired by the novelist Jiang Gui's (1908–1981) *Jin taowu zhuan*, or *A Tale of Modern Monsters* (1952). For Jiang Gui, the function of *taowu*, or history, is to "record evil so as to admonish." He sees in the image of *taowu* a liminal zone where the inhuman and the human mingle, a region that is politically and morally anomalous. Evil monster and evil human are seen as overlapping in behavior and appearance, a confusion that blurs the cultural and moral boundaries that humanity would draw around itself. History, Jiang Gui holds, is an inscription of the acts and consequences of evildoers; it is meant to recount the past in such a way as to caution subsequent generations against immorality and aberration.

Extrapolating Jiang Gui's logic, one can argue that though the professed goal of history lies in promoting virtue to the exclusion of evil, the act of writing history is made possible ironically by the continued accumulation—the inclusion—of what is immoral and therefore excludable. This historiographical vision generates its own antithesis: insofar as its moral telos holds true and valid in the long run, history, as a narrated account of bygone events, performs its function negatively, as an agency revealing vice, waste, and anomaly. Walter Benjamin's statement resounds: "There is no documentation of civilization which is not at the same time a document of barbarism."[32]

More discussion of the *taowu* as monster and history will be provided in Chapter 6, which deals with Jiang Gui's novel and its late Ming and late Qing counterparts. What I would emphasize here is the way that Jiang Gui invokes the term "taowu" as constitutive of his fiction. He thus adds a modern layer to the many definitions of the ancient creature. Jiang Gui and his contemporaries seem to suggest that at a time when history has failed to convey the meaning of the past in the present, fiction becomes its substitute. But insofar as it is by definition an amorphous, rootless representation of human experience, can fiction transcribe and impeach evil and violence without betraying its own suspect, malleable nature? When fiction is written under the name of *taowu,* hasn't it already intimated the subversion of civilization by its own discontents?

With the anomalous and polymorphous mediation of the *taowu*—as monster, as outlaw, as historical account of evil, and as fictional representation of that historical account—we may find ourselves imagining past inhumanity in the hope of a future in which such inhumanity can scarcely be imagined. And yet at any fold of time we may come to realize that without imagining past evil we are unprepared to recognize it in its future incarnations, and for this reason all modernities bear the imprint of primitive savagery. A monster haunts the human struggle for self-betterment. Coming to terms with this monstrosity by teasing out its hidden divinatory force remains a task as urgent in our millennium as it was in ancient times.

The eight chapters of the book represent eight entry points to modern Chinese history in its literary manifestation. These chapters form a timeline that covers almost all the notable events in modern China, including the Boxer Rebellion (1900), the May Fourth Movement (1919), the First Chinese Communist Revolution (1927), the Second Sino-Japanese War (1936–1945), the Yan'an period (1940s), the Nationalist and Communist "Divide" (1949), the Taiwan White Terror (1950s), the Great Leap Forward (1958–1962), the Cultural Revolution (1966–1976), the Post-Tian'anmen Diaspora (1989), and the Return of Hong Kong (1997).

But my intention is not to reinstate modern Chinese literature in the traditional linear, monolithic chronology. Instead of reifying a selected moment (such as the Communist takeover) or incident (such as the Cultural Revolution), I use each of the eight entry points to explore and depict a multiple configuration of temporalities. I mingle public events with personal adventures, view canonical works side by side with marginal undertakings, and reshuffle the premodern, modern, and postmodern timetables. Therefore, Lu Xun's account of the Japanese decapitation of a Chinese man is read against the late Qing writer Youhuan Yusheng's relation of Yuan Shikai's beheading of Boxers in the Boxers' Rebellion and the contemporary Taiwanese writer Wuhe's rewriting of Taiwanese aborigines' beheading of Japanese colonizers in the Musha Incident. The leftist discourse of revolutionary hunger is discussed in light of works by Lu Ling, the mainland leftist writer of the 1940s, Eileen Chang, the expatriate noncommittal writer of the 1950s, and Chen Yingzhen, the Taiwanese leftist writer of the 1980s.

Nor do I intend to adopt mainland-centered geopolitics in mapping the terrain of modern Chinese literature. The twentieth century saw a China in constant shift among political, historical, and literary entities, each reciting its own self-narrative and pursuing its own idea of (post)modernity. As a result of this historical fragmentation and dispersal, writers have come to interpret the Chinese experience in ways that could never have been marshalled into a stifling unity. While the canon of one community is the taboo of another, apparently antagonistic discourses may share an uncannily similar premise. One can find no better example than the confrontation and complicity of pro- and anti-communist fiction of the 1950s, in terms of stylistics, thematics, and modes of production. When speaking of "revolution plus love," the formula subject of leftist literature in the 1930s, how often do we think of its residual traces in Taiwan or even in the Chinese community of Malaysia in the postmodern era? As the book's last chapter indicates, it is a welcome surprise to see ghosts of various temporal-spatial, cultural, and social zones travelling across late-twentieth-century Chinese literature, on the mainland as well as overseas.

By describing a network of histories continuously cutting across one another, I hope the book will have provided a critique of conventional paradigms of modern Chinese literature. When Zheng Zhenduo pronounced a "literature of tears and blood" in the 1930s and when C. T. Hsia commented on Chinese writers' "obsession with China" in the 1960s, each sought a distinct notion of what makes modern Chinese literature "modern." Today critics are able to read modern Chinese literature and history using a multiplicity of global tools and theories. Yet it is a paradox that critics pursue a "politics of marginality" and a "polemics of intervention," or seek "global contextualization" with "local articulation," while rigidly marginalizing all forms of Chinese modernity (and historicity) that have not emerged within some preconceived mainstream, and resolutely refusing to articulate the local contexts of modern Chinese creativity. In this sense, the familiar statement "always historicize!" can best be understood as self-parody. If one of the most important lessons one can learn from modern Chinese literature and history is the tortuous nature of Chinese writers' attempt to grapple with polymorphous reality, this knowledge can be appreciated in full only by a criticism equally exempt from any form of formulaic and ideological dogmatism. One has to genuinely believe that Chinese writers have always been capable of complex and even contradictory thoughts, even in moments of political suppression. I argue that any critical task in the name of "modernity" must look unafraid at this monstrous fact of contested modernities.

Chapter 1 deals with decapitation as the "primal scene" of the twentieth-century Chinese imagination of national, ethnic, and personal trauma. Taking Lu Xun's decapitation complex as a point of reference, I observe the advent of Chinese literary modernity in tandem with the eruption of violence. This argument is contested by writers such as Youhuan Yusheng of the late Qing, Shen Congwen of the post–May Fourth era, and Wuhe of fin-de-siècle Taiwan; each writes to address a different view of modern Chinese body politics. The beheading syndrome is seen as a source of century-long debates on civility versus savagery, and nationalism versus colonialism.

As a follow-up to my discussion of decapitation, Chapter 2 looks into the dialectic of justice, which is crucial to any survey of violence and its representation. I describe how a forensic discourse—a discourse formed by open debate, in the courtroom or in any other public space, regarding the legal consequences of a narrated event—has arisen and evolved in modern Chinese literature. Taking examples drawn from four historical moments—the late Qing era, the post–May Fourth era, the 1930s, and the Yan'an era—I show how, at a time when the old political, judicial, and moral order had collapsed and new orders were yet to be established, literature provided a textual space in which legal cases were presented for debate and deliberation. As such, legal justice and poetic justice, crime and punishment, were brought into play.

Chapter 3 zeros in on one particular form of justice-driven violence—revolution—and examines its ideological and affective impact. The "revolution plus love" fiction of the 1930s has often been dismissed as a genre nurtured on blind political and romantic passion. I find in it nevertheless a manifestation of how one generation of avant-garde writers came to terms with their political and erotic capacities. I focus on the life and works of three leftist writers, Mao Dun, Jiang Guangci, and Bai Wei, during the 1927 Communist Revolution and the period immediately following. I depict their political engagements as if they were romantic adventures and vice versa, and in so doing I ponder the mutual implication of polis and eros, and reality and fiction.

Chapter 4 takes the politics of revolution and desire in a different direction—gender, materiality, and the gendered representation of national identity. The hungry woman was emblematic of a nation in material and spiritual impoverishment as early as Lu Xun's time. This image took on a political profile when incorporated in the leftist discourse of the hunger revolution in the late 1930s. In the next decades, I argue, it fostered a corporeal symbolism through which the Communist Revolution was sanctioned or critiqued. I discuss works by three writers, Lu Ling during the Second Sino-Japanese War, Eileen Chang of the Cold War era, and Chen Yingzhen during the post–Cultural Revolution time. Each of these writers observes how hunger affects a woman's fate and, more poignantly, how writing about hunger entails a tension between the digestive and diegetic imagination, and metabolic and metaphoric actions.

The year 1949 witnessed the Chinese Communist takeover of the mainland, followed by the retreat of the Nationalist regime to Taiwan and the diaspora of more than two million Chinese people to Taiwan, Hong Kong, and overseas. Along with geopolitical shifts came radical changes in the geopoetic configuration of Chinese literature, whose impact is still felt. Chapter 5 examines the volatile circumstances of the 1950s, when Chinese writers from the two sides of the Taiwan Straits were engaged in reforging the nation's past and future. Their textual confrontations were just as treacherous as their political crusades or military campaigns. Taking examples from Taiwan, Hong Kong, and the mainland, this chapter reviews the twists and turns of revolutionary poetics up until the 1960s, observing the rise of a new national myth on either side of China and chronicling the way this national myth was transformed into a nationalized myth.

Chapter 6, from which the title of this book is derived, analyzes the novel *Jin taowu zhuan,* or *A Tale of Modern Monsters,* by Jiang Gui, a Chinese émigré writer in Taiwan after 1949. My purpose, however, goes beyond elucidating the ideological complexities of the novel. Instead I link it with two other novels employing the same monstrous symbolism, *Taowu cuibian,* or *A Compendium of Monsters,* of the late Qing (ca. 1905) and *Taowu xianping,* or *An Idle Commentary on Monsters,* of the late Ming (1629). These works were produced during the most menacing of man-made disasters: dynastic cataclysm, political upheaval, and civil war. In their efforts to construe and configure the irrationalities of these moments, all three writers call on the ancient monster *taowu,* which in one of its many etymological transformations is related to the genre of historical writing. *Taowu* is invoked to bear not only on the monstrosity of human experience at a certain moment but also on the moral urgency of making sense of the monstrous. By conjuring the various *taowu* of their own times, I argue, these writings renew the haunting question of the intelligibility of history and historical fiction.

Chapters 5 and 6 touch on the "typology of the scarred," which registers the physical and psychological brutalities perpetrated by Nationalist and Communist regimes. Chapter 7 takes the survey of Chinese body politics one step further, examining the fact that certain writers ended their work by ending their life. I discuss the suicide of three poets: Wen Jie during the Cultural Revolution; Shi Mingzheng in the midst of Taiwan's democratic campaign of the late 1980s, and Gu Cheng in exile in New Zealand in the early 1990s. These three poets came from very different backgrounds and committed suicide for very different reasons. By putting them side by side, one grasps the ominous dialectic of the "death of poetry," the most crystallized form of literature, as the modern century reached its end. Significantly enough, these suicides were either anticipated in the authors' writings or written about posthumously by others. Hovering over these works is an enigma: was this writing in order to prepare for death? Or was it dying in order to be able to have written?

To conclude my investigation of history, monstrosity, and representation, the last chapter tackles the phantom poetics that permeates late-twentieth-century Chinese writing, first in Taiwan and overseas, and then on the mainland. After the century-long pursuit of realism, "a literature for the sake of life," and an "aesthetics of corporeality," fin-de-siècle Chinese writers seemed finally ready to critique and appreciate an apparitional turn. This trend of ghostly writing may represent a Chinese response to the circulation of postmodern phantasmagoria, but my chapter pays equal attention to the return of premodern spectrality. History is that which haunts. The ghostly narrative leads us to the task of memory and mourning. Across corporeal and temporal-spatial barriers, ghosts reappear like vanishing memories and perished relations, while they "embody" the hiatus between the dead and the living, the unreal and the real, the unthinkable and the admissible.

In the main, these eight chapters touch on four general areas: the interaction between grand history and "historical detail"; the corporeal infliction of pain and its textual representation; the writing of violence and writing as violence; and history as testimony and history as plot. But, as I hope I have made clear, these chapters do not pursue any specific critical or temporal program, any more than they guide us into the multitude of Chinese experiences and efforts at construing these experiences. Looking back at China's century-long search for modernity and modernization, what comes to mind is Francisco Goya's (1746–1828) enigmatic and disturbing caption to *Los Caprichos:* "The dream of reason produces monsters."[33] Goya's pronouncement, from the end of the Age of Reason, has generated many interpretations, and when interpreted in the perspective of Chinese history, it suggests that monstrosity *(taowu)* may serve as the precondition of all civilized self-understanding. Such an understanding prods one to face the fearsome nature of the Chinese modern, which is as much a revolt against as it is a recapitulation of its historical monstrosity. What I hope this book accomplishes, accordingly, is to project the ferocious anomaly of contemporary intellectual life back upon historicity itself, sighting but not necessarily taming the monster that is Chinese history.

Chapter 1

Invitation to a Beheading

Linnü yu, or *Women's Words Overheard* (1902–1904), by Youhuan Yusheng (Survivor of calamities, pseudonym of Lian Mengqing, 18??–after 1914), is one of the first late Qing narratives about the atrocities of the Boxer Rebellion. This novel describes the experiences of Jin Bumo, a scholar from Jiangsu, in the aftermath of the rebellion. Upon learning of the fall of Beijing and adjacent provinces to the foreign forces, Jin is so concerned about the well-being of the refugees that he sells everything to undertake a one-man rescue mission. While thousands of Chinese flee to the south, Jin Bumo, we are told, is the only one traveling in the opposite direction.

On the road, Jin witnesses repeated scenes of massacre, robbery, rape, famine, and family separation—violence perpetrated by both foreign troops and the Boxers. However, none of these scenes is more horrible than the one he encounters in Shandong on a snowy late afternoon:

> As Jin Bumo approaches the area of Dongguang, he sees in the woods countless heads hung on the trees: heads of old and young, male and female, fat and skinny; some with eyes open and some with eyes closed, some with hair and some without; some with nothing but a skull and some with deep, sunken eye sockets. Big and small, high and low, the heads are all hung on trees, all with red turbans on which the character "Buddha" is still recognizable. . . . Riding through the woods, Jin looks at the numerous red-turbaned heads against the snowy background and feels as if he is visiting a peach-blossom grove.[1]

Jin Bumo learns from the locals that these heads are those of Boxers killed by one Commander Mei at the order of Yuan Shikai (1859–1916). A strongman who rose to power during the Boxer Rebellion, Yuan is said to have administered such mass decapitation for two purposes: "To show the Chinese people that Boxers are not bulletproof, and to demonstrate to the foreign allied forces that regions under his control do not share the same stance as the imperial court."[2] While admitting that the Boxers deserve beheading for their misdeeds, Jin concludes that the real villains to be condemned are the rulers of the Qing Empire. "What knowledge could these rustic people have? What good deeds could they do [without knowledge]? They have never been educated by officials and teachers to do good; and yet they were made to undergo such gruesome punishment by their superiors. Confucius says: 'To execute people without enlightening them first is to brutalize them.'"[3]

Women's Words Overheard is an obscure late Qing novel, and its description of a head-studded "peach-blossom grove," striking as it is, has rarely been noted by critics.[4] This bloody scene, however, is a poignant moment in the rise of modern Chinese literature. It dramatizes the tensions of Chinese reality after the Boxer Rebellion: tensions between an enlightened intellectual of the south and the conservative political and religious leaders of the north; between a lonely, chivalric scholar and the fanatical masses; between a philanthropist ever ready to give away his fortune for humanitarian ends and an underclass that has nothing to lose but their lives; and finally, between a privileged narratorial subject capable of thinking and speaking and a multitude of heads forever denied the right to think or speak for themselves.

Above all, this episode anticipates the decapitation scene made famous by Lu Xun. In 1906, Lu Xun (1881–1936) saw a slide show in Japan, in which a Chinese crowd idly watched as one of their compatriots was beheaded for spying on the Japanese army in the Russo-Japanese war.[5] What ensued is now a familiar story. Dumbfounded by this scene of decapitation, Lu Xun realized that before saving Chinese people's bodies, he had first to save their souls; hence, before practicing ordinary medicine, he had first to cure the spirit of China with the medicine of literature. A slide show of decapitation triggered the crucial moment in Lu Xun's life, and thereby the direction of modern Chinese literature.

But Lu Xun is not the only post–May Fourth Chinese writer attracted to the political and literary implications of decapitation. Shen Congwen (1902–1988) also wrote extensively about this bloody form of capital punishment. Dwelling on his benign, lyrical presentation of life in southwestern China, critics have hardly ever discussed why or how Shen Congwen wrote about the cruel penal practice. The subject nevertheless merits attention, not only because it contributes significantly to Shen's repertoire of "imaginary nostalgia," but also because it provides an entry point into his radical lyricism.

Put side by side, narratives of decapitation by Youhuan Yusheng, Lu Xun, and Shen Congwen form a powerful triumvirate within early modern Chinese literature, delineating the politics of the Chinese body within the aesthetic and moral boundaries of realism. This *decapitation syndrome* was to haunt Chinese literature throughout the remainder of the twentieth century. While Wang Luyan's (1901–1943) "Youzi" (Grapefruit) depicted the public beheading of revolutionaries with Lu Xunesque sarcasm, Shi Zhecun's (b. 1905) "Jiangjun de tou" (The general's head), in the form of "old stories retold," explored the sexual and ethnic ambiguities of a Tang dynasty general's romantic adventures, which end in self-decapitation. Other prominent examples include Ba Jin's (b. 1904) *Miewang* (Destruction) and *Xinsheng* (New birth), in which the protagonist Du Daxin's turbulent life as an anarchist ends with decapitation by the warlords; Luo Guangbin (1924–1967) and Yang Yiyan's (b. 1925) *Hong Yan* (Red rock), in which the heads of decapitated leftist revolutionaries become emblems of Marxist martyrdom; Zong Pu's (b.1928) "Nizhao zhong de toulu" (Heads in the mire), in which the heads of intellectuals are seen rolling in a surrealist mire; Jiang Xun's (b.1947) "Gundong de toulu" (Rolling heads), in which amputated heads enact a postmodernist, headless Chinese existence; and Long Yingtai's (b. 1952) "Zai Haidebao duoru qingwang" (Falling in love in Heidelberg), in which an accidental, exotic romance culminates in a horrible ritual of decapitation.

The latest literary manifestation of this decapitation theme, and arguably the most polemical since the time of Lu Xun and Shen Congwen, is to be found in the novel *Yusheng* (Remains of life, 2000) by the Taiwanese writer Wuhe (Chen Guocheng, b. 1952). This novel is based on the 1930 Musha Incident (Wushe shijian), in which more than one hundred Japanese colonizers were beheaded by aboriginal Tayal rebels in the mountain village of Musha in central Taiwan. In his analysis of the incident, Wuhe challenges official accounts, both colonialist and nationalist, and ponders the moral status of decapitation in relation to the aboriginal tradition of headhunting. By the end of his deliberations, the line between savagery and civility has become imperceptible. Insofar as it deals with issues ranging from the politics of (post)colonial resistance to the ethics of writing violence, *Remains of Life* serves as a belated rejoinder to Youhuan Yusheng, Lu Xun, and Shen Congwen. More importantly, while treating a subject that apparently bears little relevance to mainstream, mainland-directed discourse, Wuhe nevertheless speaks to all Chinese realism.

DECAPITATING CHINA

Women's Words Overheard features a string of episodes in which its protagonist, Jin Bumo, overhears women talking wherever he stays on his way north.[6] These women include nuns, ballad singers, and store proprietors. Through their private conversations, Jin, as male eavesdropper, learns otherwise inaccessible truths about the plight of the Chinese people after the Boxer Rebellion. In contrast to these feminine murmurs collected through eavesdropping, Jin's intrusion into the "peach-blossom grove" of decapitated heads is a revelation of speechlessness. This scene of deadly silence points to unspeakable aspects of late Qing life involving native power struggles, foreign imperialism, epistemological confusion, and multiple layers of ignorance, self-deception, and betrayal.

The dead Boxer heads are of various physiognomies, appearances, ages, and genders. By and large, they appear to be people from the lower social strata. They rose to challenge foreigners, buoyed by superstition and fanaticism, only to die, proving that the foreign devils were far more dangerous than native fantasies of demonic power. Although he blames the Boxers for almost ruining the Qing empire, Jin Bumo holds the Qing monarchy and ruling class accountable for the rebellion. As mentioned above, Jin is disheartened by the fact that these Boxers were killed not by the foreign invaders but by Yuan Shikai's troops. Yuan ordered the massive decapitation to intimidate Boxer sympathizers and to demonstrate his independence from the Qing court. In so doing, Yuan fostered his own power, and in that sense, the Boxers were killed only to further one man's ambition. The Boxers' heads are therefore evidence not so much of justice as of traditional political maneuvering.

Its intended connotation notwithstanding, the Boxers' decapitation leads Jin Bumo to contemplate its legal *and* pedagogical implications. For Jin, the Boxers are people of the lower classes led astray by xenophobic impulses and superstitious beliefs. Under normal circumstances, they should have been guided—taught, or *jiao*—by the rulers to harness their unruly natures. But instead of edifying them, the Qing court willingly chose to believe in the Boxers' magic powers and indulged their fanaticism as part of a strategy against the foreigners. Thus imperial power appears to support mass hysteria, and Confucian edification has given way to popular superstition: disaster is inevitable.

In his preference for tutelage, or *jiao,* over forms of punishment, Jin Bumo, or his creator, Youhuan Yusheng, invokes a deep-seated Confucianism. This ideology preaches a benevolent kingship, in which ordinary people are ruled by awakening and reinforcing their innate virtues. But the events of the Boxer Rebellion show the failure of this traditional belief. The legend of benevolent kingship turns out to be a sham. Before the foreign forces entered Beijing, the empress dowager and the emperor had already fled the Forbidden City, leaving its ordinary citizens to be looted, humiliated, and killed by the Boxers or the foreigners. As the narrator observes, after the fall of Beijing, few officials had risen up against the invaders, and next to none sacrificed their lives for the government. Instead, on the doors of high-ranking officials' residences were banners inscribed with characters that proclaimed "'Submissive Surrender to Great Japan,'" while "inside and outside Beijing, all big and small households displayed foreign flags, as if everyone had become foreigners overnight."[7] Echoing Jin's questions, one thinks: If Confucian teachings were so deeply rooted in the Chinese mentality, how could Chinese, especially elite Chinese, so easily sell themselves to the first conqueror? If the rulers fail to recognize superstition, how could they be expected to enlighten the masses? If Heaven had selected a Yuan Shikai to put down the Boxers and overthrow the Qing, did he have the capacity to understand and defeat the foreigners? Confucius's words, "to execute people without enlightening them first is to brutalize them," echo ironically.

For Jin Bumo as for Youhuan Yusheng, therefore, the Boxer Rebellion is more than a political fiasco. Rather, it is an event that exposes the barbarism inherent in Chinese civilization, something that, in accordance with Confucian theory, can be and should have been held in check by able dynastic rulers. The savageries perpetrated by both the foreign invasions and the Boxer uprisings constitute merely a surface symptom of this crisis. Something far more sinister nurtures Chinese civilization, most dangerously when it invokes the name of virtue. The Chinese ruling classes repeatedly misguide, or simply ignore, the Chinese people, and yet have continually made them the scapegoats of their own errors. Those who are presumably best informed on the subject of virtue—benevolence and loyalty, righteousness and compassion—have turned out to be the least committed to these virtues when put to the test. But they are empowered to penalize in the name of law and order. Each of the decapitated heads in the bloody "peach-blossom grove," therefore, embodies brutal betrayal; each testifies to the failure of a system of meaning and understanding.

As Youhuan Yusheng suggests, a scholar like Jin Bumo is a rarity. Chances are he will never be able to rescue enough Chinese refugees from the national disaster, to say nothing of fulfilling his dream of a people cultivated after the Confucian model, in which the rulers cultivate themselves first so that they are able to cultivate the ruled. That the novel remains unfinished reflects Youhuan Yusheng's incapacity to narrate, or complete, such a poetics of enlightenment. And so, as the dynastic "chain-of-beings" falls apart, the dismembered bodies of Boxer believers and bits and pieces of women's wisdom are all that can be remembered.

Along with Li Boyuan's (1867–1906) *Gengzi guobian tanci* (A ballad about the national calamity of the Boxer Rebellion, 1902), Wu Jianren's (1866–1910) *Henhai* (The sea of regret, 1906), and Liu E's (1857–1909) *Lao Can youji* (The travels of Lao Can, 1907), *Women's Words Overheard* represents the first wave of modern Chinese literature dedicated to narrating national crises. They are the earliest examples of what C. T. Hsia calls an "obsession with China."[8] In particular, Youhuan Yusheng shares with Liu E a Confucian desire to rescue China though civilized means, but to no avail. (It is said that Liu E, a close friend of Youhuan Yusheng, was motivated to write *The Trav-*

els of Lao Can to raise money for this friend beset by financial problems.)[9] I have discussed elsewhere the modernity of *The Travels of Lao Can* in terms of bringing a new polemic of *narrative order* and *poetic justice* to bear on Chinese reality.[10] In what sense can *Women's Words Overheard* be read as another early modern testimonial to the representational crisis of writing China? Was Youhuan Yusheng entitled to speak on behalf of the speechless heads? Can writing fill the emptiness left where the (national) body was once whole?

Youhuan Yusheng's questions were echoed by Lu Xun just a couple of years later. In the reported slide show of 1906, Lu Xun saw the more despicable side of the Chinese character. Lu Xun asks how Japan and Russia could wage a war against each other, but choose China as their battlefield. Why were Chinese willing to serve as spies for foreign troops at the risk of decapitation? Why did Chinese show more curiosity than indignation when they were brought to witness the beheading of one of their compatriots? Sixteen years after he first saw the slide show, Lu Xun stated in *Nahan* (A call to arms): "The people of a weak, backward country, even though they may enjoy sturdy health, can only serve as the senseless material of an audience for public executions. . . . Our first task was surely to transform their spirits, and I thought at that time that literature could best meet the task of spiritual transformation. I then began to think about promoting literary activities."[11]

The moment of seeing decapitation in the slide show thus triggered the most crucial turn in Lu Xun's life, changing him from a modern student of medicine into a traditional member of the literati. No longer would he adopt the viewpoint of clinical anatomy when faced with a Chinese person about to be beheaded; instead he views the moment as an allegorical scene in which China's fate is illuminated.

This is where one sees an intriguing dialogue between Youhuan Yusheng and Lu Xun. Both are accidental spectators of a cruel conventional penal technology in practice, and both see in the maimed Chinese body a representational chain linking mind and body, body and language, re-form and reform. However, a "quirk" appears in their depictions of the representational chain. In Youhuan Yusheng's case, the Boxers vow to "support the Qing and destroy the foreigners" *(fuqing mieyang)*, and yet they are beheaded by a Qing general because of their excessive loyalty. In Lu Xun's case, the Chinese spy loses his head for an act of espionage that turns out to have little to do with China's interests. The Boxers and the Chinese spy are punished either for total resistance to or for total collaboration with foreign forces. Yet in both cases, the decapitation is meant to be a "lesson" for the Chinese.

The difference between Youhuan Yusheng and Lu Xun lies in their responses to the consequences of decapitation. Youhuan Yusheng recognizes in the amputated heads the crisis of China, and yet he chooses to cling to a Confucian paradigm as the way to heal the wound. By contrast, Lu Xun turns the paradigm inside out so as to flaunt his radical iconoclasm. Accordingly, whereas Youhuan Yusheng indicts the rulers and elite intellectuals in the hope that they might edify themselves and then the masses, Lu Xun forgoes any hope of either educating Chinese people or educating their educators. For Lu Xun, hidden in the four thousand years of Chinese civilization is an ongoing barbarism—a cannibalistic banquet. Relishing decapitation constitutes merely one of the many ways the Chinese participate in this banquet.

Lu Xun's radicalism can be appreciated only as part of his ambivalent interaction with tradition. In his project to reform the Chinese mind, he demonstrates a case of what Yü-sheng Lin calls a "cultural, intellectualistic approach" to Chinese problems: a prevalent conviction that China's problems stem solely from a break in cultural and intellectual coherence and can be approached only in immanent, holistic terms.[12] Lu Xun, to be sure, sets out to take issue with such an approach; for him, the sanctioned Chinese civilization has long been lost, or worse, it never existed except as a pretext for a highly developed cannibalism. But in spite of his iconoclastic intent, he betrays time and again a longing to regain a coherent meaning, at the same time as a skepticism regarding this longing.[13] His desire to "transform the spirits" of the Chinese people and his subsequent denial of such a possibility result in a basic dilemma in his search for modernity.

The *aporia* in Lu Xun's project of reforming China finds vivid testimony in the way he narrates the project. Can Chinese reality be reflected, critiqued, and even reformed in literary terms? I have pointed out in my earlier study of modern Chinese realism that Lu Xun's decapitation complex may have created an ontological vacuity, which nevertheless necessitated a desire to write and reinstate reality.[14] I would again call attention to a narratological crack in the way by which Lu Xun writes about the decapitation event. His statement as to how he came to engage in literature as a result of watching the 1906 slide show of decapitation only appeared in the 1923 foreword to his collection *Nahan* (A call to arms). This belated reminiscence already partakes of a figurative meaning, dramatizing his anxiety about the primordial loss of origin—meaning and life symbolized by the head, loss symbolized by the mutilated body. His effort to retrospectively add a beginning, a head, to his literary career suggests such an anxiety.

Critics like Leo Lee have pointed out that the fact that the traumatic slide has never been found suggests that Lu Xun fabricated the whole incident,[15] giving allegorical form to his abstract conception. Lu Xun is known to have manufactured or refashioned personal experience for literary purposes. The case of the decapitation suggests that fiction and (private and public) history might have become inextricably confused, at the (textual) beginning of modern Chinese (literary) history.[16]

The final twist is the fact that Lu Xun's anxiety over decapitation or rupture of meaning did not prevent him from capitalizing on decapitation and rupture in his literary imaginings. Critics have repeatedly noticed that Lu

Xun's most engaging works deal not with his reasoning about China's fate but with the "dark side" of reason,[17] not with coherent social and epistemological systems in prospect or retrospect, but rather with the rupture of those systems. When the representational order of the world he establishes for himself breaks loose, demons, superstitions, and macabre fantasies haunt him in the form of a spectral carnival. In other words, beneath his project of edification and enlightenment, something ghostly always looms. And strangely, before these dark forces can be exorcised, he is first hopelessly deceived or even charmed by them. Lu Xun's anxiety over decapitation and headlessness serves as the secret fountainhead of his literary inspiration.[18]

One notices an ambivalent adherence to the imagery of dismemberment or mutilation in both the fiction and essays of Lu Xun. For instance, "Yao" (Medicine), reportedly motivated by the decapitation of the woman revolutionary Qiu Jin, points out the bloody cost of revolution and its gratuitous rewards. Yet the story also betrays Lu Xun's strange fascination with the macabre ritual and cannibalistic superstitions that form part of the ceremony of beheading. Decapitation is one of the leitmotifs in another famous Lu Xun short story, "Ah Q zhengzhuan" (The true story of Ah Q). Public beheading represents for Ah Q and his fellow villagers both a "heroic" death and the most thrilling form of entertainment. But the action culminates in an anticlimactic nonbeheading, a last blow to Ah Q's logic of spiritual victory as well as his audience's "nostalgic" desires. Stranger yet is "Zhujian" (Forging swords), Lu Xun's rewriting of the classical tale about Mei Jianchi's revenge of his parents' murder by the Prince of Qin. In the story, beheading and self-beheading are depicted in such a way that they suggest not so much a necessary means of revenge as a decadent sport participated in by both the heroes and the villains, in search of sadomasochistic pain and pleasure.

While criticizing the convict about to be decapitated, Lu Xun was even more upset by the Chinese in the slide who simply watched the execution. Lu Xun's onlookers were admitted to the scene to be taught a lesson, to be scared, by the death of "one of them," but Lu Xun cannot but notice with resentment that the audience is equally excited by the rare spectacle, and that they share a secret sense of carnival. In an essay entitled "Changong daguan" (A spectacle of chopping Communists), Lu Xun shows how the crowds in Hunan relish the decapitation of several young women communists with a fervor almost akin to sexual ecstasy: "One 'crowd' ran from south to north [of the town], another from north to south. In the hustle and bustle, they screamed and yelled . . . , their facial expressions showed either that they were longing for a scene of decapitation or that they had already been satisfied by the ones they had seen."[19] Literally and symbolically, modern China was a "head"-less country, crowded by spiritually decapitated people whose life was intensified only by watching beheadings or waiting to be beheaded.

Lu Xun would have shared Michel Foucault's view that classical punishments were often designed with a strong theatrical dimension.[20] By performing corporal mutilation in public, authorities not only impose torture and humiliation on the convicted victim, but also extend their power to those who are watching the execution. But for Foucault, there always lurks a threat in the public show of corporal punishment. Besides fear, the bloody spectacle gives its audience an unexpected thrill, which upsets the solemnity of the execution and may even threaten to turn it into a festive occasion. At its extreme, the audience's deviant response to public corporal punishment may endanger the authorities, since it implies either an indifference to or a rebellious consciousness of the power displayed by the mutilated body.[21]

If Foucault has a point in revealing the mixed ideological and psychological outcomes of the public spectacle of punishment, we can then take note of the "crisis" involved in Lu Xun's treatment of decapitation. Insofar as he expects his readers to read the meaning of beheading more "seriously" than the immediate audience of decapitation does—that is to say, to realize the tyrannical power at work behind the scenes—he recapitulates better than anyone else the representational meaning imposed by authorities on the body. Though conceptually against the authorities that legitimize the cruel decapitation, Lu Xun shares the same moral and penal episteme. On the other hand, Lu Xun reveals his secret alliance with the cannibalistic audience he openly condemns when he indulges his ironic fascination with the theatrical turmoil and spectacular bloodshed of public beheadings and with the cynical knowledge that whatever happens, things remain the same. Stretched between these two contradictory and complementary roles, Lu Xun has put himself in a state no better than that of poor Xianglin's wife in "Zhufu" (New Year's sacrifice), who is haunted by the possibility of being dismembered by her two dead husbands in hell, yet finds no plausible means of escape.

The way Lu Xun handles decapitation leads us to reconsider the problematic of realism. The anguish Lu Xun suffers at the scene of beheading is underlain by an imaginative encounter with a primordial emptiness. Decapitation must signal not only a barbaric form of punishment handed down from previous generations and a powerful symbol of Chinese people's state of spiritual dehumanization, but also the mutilated condition of the system of meaning that makes reality what it is not. Watching the slide show in which the Chinese crowd watched a decapitation, where did Lu Xun situate his own standpoint? Reading (watching) Lu Xun watching the Chinese crowd watching the decapitation, how should we readers modulate our moral and intellectual distance from the narrated subject? This vertiginous interplay between authors' and readers' engagement in and detachment from "reality" would become one of the major issues of modern Chinese critical realism.

Marston Anderson once suggested that the realist discourse initiated by Lu Xun prefigures its own formal/ideological gap.[22] Lu Xun (and his followers) explored a discursive form in which the gaps between the text and the world, self and others, narrated truth and historical reality, are supposed to be bridged. Lu Xun led his contemporaries in demonstrating the mimetic power of realism, but his "confirmation" of social abuses and inertia soon proved to be a vicious circle, making him just as much a critic as an accomplice of the forces he had vowed to overthrow. In an effort to reform and "re-form" Chinese reality, Lu Xun's own writing remains "severed" from the outset.

But more paradoxical is the ideological mandate that looms ever larger behind Lu Xun's realist discourse. As suggested by his preface to *A Call to Arms* quoted above, Lu Xun declares that the task for intellectual reformers is to take over people's minds, and the best way to accomplish this is to inscribe in them a new consciousness, as if they were naked writing tablets. But judging by his decapitation complex, what really fascinates Lu Xun is the representational power of the body and the head. The new, sophisticated rhetorical power of literature in place of the ritual anatomy of torture and decapitation is, after all, derived from the politics of bodies and is to take effect on bodies. The spiritual lessons have to find somatic manifestations. At its best, the mind serves as a surface for the submission of bodies to the control of ideas.

As mentioned above, implied in Lu Xun's writing about decapitation is a theory of literature that emphasizes the representational link between mind and body, body and language, referents and referentiality. But Lu Xun's longing for a full-fledged representation of the real ironically nurtures itself on the "break" in this chain of referentiality, as emphatically symbolized by a beheaded body, a split personality ("Diary of a Madman," "New Year's Sacrifice"), a living dead man ("Zai jiuloushang" [In the tavern]), or a "speaking" head on a deformed or decayed body ("Mujie wen" [Tomb tablet], "Cong baicaoyuan dao sanwei shuwu" [From Baicao Garden to Sanwei Study]). This break drives home Lu Xun's imaginary nostalgia for the semantic and somatic plenitude of China. Given Lu Xun's iconoclastic pose, what Yü-sheng Lin calls the traditional "totalistic" mode of thinking permeates Lu Xun's writing, only now as the negative cause, postponing the presence of the Real.

Lu Xun's anxiety about the break between body and soul motivated a long line of writings in the 1930s. In the 1940s, leftist ideologues took up where Lu Xun left off, giving his realist problematic a crude and abrupt solution. When Mao Zedong and his literary cohorts asserted that literature should and can openly serve political purposes, writing about reality did bring about bodily discipline or punishment. A literature almost without rupture or anxiety replaced Lu Xun's literature of rupture and anxiety, invoking Lu Xun's name and suppressing Lu Xun's voice.

RE-MEMBERING CHINA

Shen Congwen's references to decapitation are found in works like *Wode jiaoyu* (My education), "Huanghun" (Twilight), "Xin yu jiu" (The old and new), "Qian xiaojing" (Little scene in Guizhou), "Sange nanren yu yige nüren" (Three men and one woman), *Congwen zizhuan* (Autobiography of Congwen), and *Xiangxi* (West Hunan). Decapitation is described as a common form of penalty practiced by rural authorities in late Qing and early Republican days, despite the fact that advanced penal technology was already accessible. In *Autobiography of Congwen,* Shen relates how the Miao aborigines were beheaded by the thousands after the failure of their rebellions in the late Qing period, how on the eve of the Republican revolution, local agitators were arrested and put to death by chopping off their head, and how this cruel form of execution still went on whenever warlords came to seize local power.[23]

As a child, Shen saw thousands of heads hung out for display on the city wall or simply dumped on the riverbank for family members to sort out. More appalling is his recollection that soldiers often arrested innocent peasants to fulfill their daily quota, and after too many killings, they let their captives gamble for their lives in a lottery-like religious ritual. The winners were set free, while the losers had to resign their lives to fate.[24] Thus it was not unusual to see an unlucky peasant bid farewell to his cellmates and ask them to settle for him things unfinished at home ("Twilight"), a sad child carrying baskets containing the heads of his father and his brother, walking home along a mountain path ("Little Scene in Guizhou," *Autobiography of Congwen*), or more gruesomely, dogs fighting for decomposed bodies left on the riverbank *(Autobiography of Congwen).* What Youhuan Yusheng would have described as a stunning massacre in *Women's Words Overheard* becomes a daily routine in Shen's world.

Given the cruelty of public decapitation, one would have expected a post–May Fourth writer either to lash out at the backwardness of the Chinese penal system or to deplore the callousness of those who participate in such bloody spectacles. Besides Lu Xun, Wang Luyan represents such a case. In his short story "Grapefruit," he bitterly criticizes the "shows" of public beheading in Hunan and ridicules the onlookers as grapefruit buyers.[25] But Shen Congwen must have witnessed far more scenes of decapitation than his peers, and he may well have been a more qualified judge, testifying to the injustice and inhumanity of the killings. In the works under discussion, nevertheless, one has the feeling that his attitude toward decapitation is ambiguous, if not weak. Besides muted humanitarian comments, he always seems to have "something else" to say about the old capital punishments.

Take the highly autobiographical novella *My Education* as an example. The novella deals with Shen Congwen's early experience as a soldier, when watching decapitation was one highlight. The novella contains twenty-three sections; twelve of them contain explicit descriptions of scenes of decapitation. Shen Congwen writes, "Army life is too monotonous, only scenes of decapitation can make strong soldiers excited." After the beheading, some of the soldiers climb to the top of the tower where the heads are hung, playing with the eyes of the dead, some throwing heads at each other for fun. Even Shen Congwen kicks at the hard skulls and hurts his toes. At night, the soldiers get together. They kill and cook dogs using the same knife they kill people with in the daytime and boast about what they see and do on the execution grounds. But as the days go by, Shen Congwen feels bored even with the spectacle of decapitation. One morning, he walks to the bridge near the execution site. Four headless bodies are still there. "A handful of ashes of paper money look like a blue chrysanthemum flecked with dark red traces of congealed blood."[26] Everything is quiet.

Insofar as tutelage constitutes an important apparatus of civilization, we find a difference between Youhuan Yusheng, Lu Xun, and Shen Congwen, in that Shen is far less worried about attaching any inherent meaning to decapitation and headlessness. Whereas Youhuan Yusheng sees in the Boxers' heads a failure of Confucian edification, Shen Congwen questions the limitation of conventional pedagogy and legality; whereas Lu Xun deplores the Chinese spy's decapitation as the last sign of his compatriots' stupidity and cannibalism, Shen Congwen finds a complex of coexisting human motives. In the decapitation scenes he narrates in *My Education,* Shen Congwen is a member of the heartless audience, as Lu Xun would have it, scared and thrilled by the bloody scenes. But Shen is also the young soldier dutifully observing daily routine as part of the "war," and the young, sensitive artist, saddened by the meaningless waste of human life.

In "Little Scene in Guizhou," the scene about decapitation is like a vignette inserted into a broader picture that is itself an impressionistic slice of life in Guizhou. In "The Old and New," Shen uses black humor in describing how a professional decapitator loses his sense of value after the technique he has mastered so well is replaced by a more modern method of execution. It is the decapitator, not the decapitated, who wins sympathy. And in *Autobiography of Congwen* and *West Hunan,* despite the massive number of people killed, Shen maintains a retrospective posture that combines ironic curiosity and a sense of intellectual and emotional distance.

I am not saying that Shen Congwen lyricizes the horrible decapitation at the cost of social conscience or conferring on Shen Congwen a privileged, transhistorical position. At the readerly level, when a lyrical tone is applied to a scene of cannibalism, or when legal injustice and bloody punishment are integrated into casual daily routines like eating and sleeping, we are induced to question the moral consequences both of the political system that legitimizes decapitation and of a literary mode like lyricism that is used to describe such a political system. But this is not where the charm (or horror) of Shen's art lies.

I am emphasizing the rhetorical strategy through which Shen Congwen makes the subject appear and "disappear" on the surface of his narrative, creating a discordant harmony among things. In Shen's lyrical agenda, ugly things are neither erased nor reversed as a supplement of the real, but only "displaced," as it were, from their roots, to enact a dreamlike simulacrum. The most human part of his story (like decapitation) is rendered in the most literal way, whereas the most insensible part may prove the most allegorical.

If one senses a strong irony here, it stems not so much from Shen Congwen's reversal of the cognitive hierarchy of referents in reality as from his exposure of the figurativeness of referentiality itself in presenting the real. In his decapitation stories, Shen does not erect a symbolic system around the head alone; instead he builds associative relations between likes and unlikes, what exists and what does not.[27] There is an essential simultaneity embedded in his poetic vision of the world that forces his reader to take multiple perspectives and weave together the sensory impressions. The result is a fundamental undecidability of meaning in his stories. But such a nondefinitiveness, or *aporia,* should not be understood in contemporary critical terms. It takes on a moral and historical dimension, ironically by refusing to add another dogmatic voice to the ideology-ridden discourse of modern Chinese literature.

The best example of Shen's view of decapitation is found in "Twilight." Lacking a clear plotline, "Twilight" recounts the daily routine of decapitation in a "small town in the mid-Yangtze valley." It opens with an overview of the serene life of a shabby city at sunset: sunshine reflecting the last spectrum of colors in the darkening sky, smoke of cooking fires coming out of the chimneys, and children winding up their games before supper. As part of the late afternoon city scene, a decapitation is soon to be conducted in a detention center. Hearing soldiers' footsteps approach, the prisoners become anxious. Names of those who will be executed are then announced, followed by sighs, cries, and noises of feeble resistance, dragging, and beating. An old warden is standing by, watching the daily turmoil of his job. Moments ago, he was absorbed in thinking of the gains and losses of his own life, necessary preparations for his own death, and the wanton adventures of his youth. He can do little with these innocent victims. Shortly, their heads will be cut off and scattered over the execution site, becoming toys for children to kick around.

What baffles us here is Shen Congwen's narrator, who describes the scenes in a familiar, casual tone. His use of the iterative style in describing the procedure of decapitation and the onlookers' responses risks dissolving the temporal and psychological urgency of the round of executions about to take place. In addition, the narrator's voice refuses to stay with the core of the narrative—the prisoners to be beheaded—and shifts from one consciousness to another. The reader will not forget a prisoner who, when asked for his last words before death, earnestly wishes for his fellow villagers to pay on his behalf a small bill he owes to a painter, nor the supervisor of the execution, who loses his temper over the delay of the daily routine by a soldier's misdeed, thinking of the pot of braised pork already well heated on his stove.

Shen Congwen's narrative weaves varied sensory images from natural and human environments into a fabric, establishing correspondences between them. The ever-changing colors in the darkening sky, mothers' dinner calls, a romantic flashback in an old prison warden's mind, prisoners' anguished cries, and the smell of pork on the supervisor's stove are all presented at the same level of narrative proportion, calling for equal attention. As the night finally falls at the end of the story, the narrator gives himself over to the embrace of the impending darkness. Human and nonhuman activities gradually blur together. What is important and what is not are no longer distinguishable in the realm of twilight.

One can, of course, speak of Shen Congwen's ironic intention, which reveals the absurdities of the real world by understating rather than exaggerating them. But I suspect that the real polemical problem with a story like "Twilight" is that it draws the attention of readers without any specific interest in the subject matter supposedly at issue, and without giving them any confidence that the work is a definitive treatment of anything.

To conjure up a story where things and creatures *seem* to exist nakedly and resist interpretation, Shen Congwen must have learned a lot from Turgenev. Even his description of the prisoner's last wish that was mentioned above reminds us of the farmer Maxim in "Death," from *Sketches from a Hunter's Album,* who, before dying from a logging accident, asks his wife and friends to return money he owes to others.[28] Still, since Shen is not bound to a conscious viewpoint like the Russian's gentleman-hunter, he has more freedom to disorient his narratorial position in exchange for an indefinite expansion of perspective. He removes and scatters, as it were, the objects of his storyline, and consequently offers his reader a mystically "graphic" construction of the scene of decapitation, in that the narrated "event" is described literally and the "narrative" event, the language as displayed by Shen Congwen, demands equal attention.

As previously discussed, this antidefinitiveness, or *aporia,* that outlines Shen's lyrical vision takes on a moral dimension, since it refuses to impose a new dogmatic view on Chinese society, which is already in disorder, while revealing its own expression as a literary/linguistic and therefore partial, culture-bound practice. Shen Congwen's belief in and "fear of" the pure form of language and its poetic performance should not be seen merely as a predilection for stylistic craftsmanship; rather it provides a key to his artistic vision of reality. His poetic (or lyrical) worldview demands paying just as much attention to the linguistic surface of a work as to the "deep" meanings behind it.

An arguable "reality" does not represent itself; it is represented. If a literary presentation of life is substantially a rhetorical performance, a formal display of language rather than the outcome of logical or ideological prefiguration (such as the canons underlining "hard-core" realism), then the text can be liberated from the Lu Xunesque "iron prison-house" of referential determinism and gain the freedom to express its figurations of the real. By describing Chinese reality in terms of a *lyrical* realism, Shen Congwen questions the privileged position of Lu Xun's and Youhuan Yusheng's kind of realism in representing the world. Shen also redraws the conventional boundary of lyricism. Emphasis on language and poetic expression is also confirmation of a writer's choice in "figuring" out the world. At its peak, Shen's ironic view of text and world dissolves the distinction between realism and lyricism, between prose and poetry, and asserts the fundamentally figured—that is to say, poetic—nature of all language. This may well explain why, even when Shen Congwen confronts a pathetic subject directly, he can still manage to transmit a sense of poetic composure.

This special mode is not a Chinese strain of Mallarméan nihilism, nor does it leave its stories *en abîme,* as a poststructuralist might have. Shen never lets irony overpower other modes, as, say, Lao She (1896–1966) tends to do in his finest writings. One always has to understand the deep ethical concern behind Shen Congwen's mixed lyricism and irony, however different his "ethical" pose might look from that of other May Fourth writers. This ethical bearing stems from the long Chinese tradition that stresses the ethical dimensions of rhetoric (*shi yanzhi,* or poetry expressing one's intent), and it is reinforced by Shen's own existential consciousness of human absurdity and the need to affirm choice against psychological and sociopolitical determinism.

In welding incongruities of rhetorical form and subject matter, Shen melds man's immensely complex emotional capacity to cope with contradiction and the built-in contradictions of any ideal moral/political order. Lyricism enables him to emphasize the creative force of language and the freedom of human perception, while his sense of irony leads him to bracket, but not do away with, any lyrical indulgence in life. Only by allowing these narrative modes to illuminate each other, while putting them "under erasure," as conventional critics would have it, can we appreciate that, in a most subtle way, Shen's art expresses the humanism of the May Fourth movement.

SURVIVING CHINA

In 2000, almost one century after the appearance of *Women's Words Overheard,* the Taiwanese writer Wuhe (pseudonym of Chen Guocheng, b. 1952) published a novel entitled *Yusheng* (Remains of life). In the novel, the first-person narrator, Wuhe, recounts a two-year residential experience (1997–1998) in Musha (Wushe), a small mountain town in central Taiwan inhabited by the Tayal aborigines. Musha is a popular resort nowadays, famous for its idyllic scenery, spa, and cherry blossoms. What tourists tend to ignore is that Musha was the site of the 1930 Musha Incident *(Wushe shijian),* one of the bloodiest anti-Japanese riots in Taiwanese colonial history (1895–1945).

As a self-styled ethnographer, Wuhe claims that his " fieldwork" has enabled him to deal with three things in the novel: "1. the legitimacy and feasibility of the Musha Incident, which was led by Monarudao, and a follow-up riot called 'The Second Musha Incident'; 2. a spiritual pilgrimage led by [a Tayal called] Girl next door to where [Wuhe] was staying; 3. the people [Wuhe] interviewed or encountered in Musha, people who are the 'remains of life.'"[29] These three subjects are intertwined in *Remains of Life,* forming a sprawling narrative in a single paragraph more than 250 pages long. For Wuhe, such a narrative design highlights the "synchronicity" of the three subjects under one rubric of "remains of life."[30]

Wuhe started writing in the late 1970s but only became known in the early 1990s, when he reemerged from a thirteen-year seclusion with a series of stories on the maimed personalities of Taiwan. These stories, which mix grotesque events, carnivalesque sensualities, neurotic imagery, and a "spasmatic" style, deserve critical appraisal in their own right.[31] *Remains of Life* represents Wuhe's most ambitious project to date. What concerns me here is the novel's treatment of decapitation, the subject that haunted late Qing and May Fourth writers, such as Youhuan Yusheng, Lu Xun, and Shen Congwen.

On the morning of October 27, 1930, Tayal aborigines, Japanese and Han Chinese settlers, provincial colonial officials and police and their families, and guests, numbering four hundred or so, gathered in the primary school of Musha for a sports competition—a most important annual social event in the mountain village. As the participants were about to sing the Japanese national anthem and raise the Japanese flag, three hundred or so aboriginal men, in native attire, surged onto the school ground as if from nowhere. With rifles, guns, and swords, they stormed into the crowd and in no time at all the head of Sugano Masae, the commissioner of the Taichushu Police Bureau, was catapulted into midair. What followed was a horrific killing field. The Tayal warriors chased Japanese men, women, and children, stabbed or shot them, and hewed off many heads. By the end, 134 Japanese had been slain, making this one of the largest and most notorious uprisings in Japanese colonial history.[32]

The Musha Incident has been attributed to causes as diverse as labor grievances, romantic scandals between Japanese officers and settlers and Tayals, the inherent bloodthirstiness of "savages," and the laxity of local colonial rule.[33] By all accounts, Monarudao, chief of the Mahebo tribe, appears to have masterminded the bloody ambush.[34] To quell the uprising, the Japanese government sent in more than seven thousand police and soldiers equipped with machine guns, cannons, and poison gas. Monarudao and his followers were driven into the mountains and, after a twenty-three-day holdout, all either were killed or committed suicide. Many of their family members followed the same fatal path. The final death toll came to 644, more than half of the total population of the six rebelling Tayal tribes.[35]

In his fictional survey of the Musha Incident, the first issue Wuhe raises is none other than the decapitation of the Japanese by the Tayal people. He notes that the decapitations resulted in two types of interpretations. For the Japanese, because of their spectacular cruelty, the decapitations mark the most bitter moment in Japanese rule over Taiwan; they signal the unfathomable chasm between the colonizers and the colonized. Although the Japanese government took severe measures in response to the uprising, the following years saw a substantive change in its colonial policy, from segregation and oppression to assimilation and containment.[36] Scholars have pointed out that this policy change indicates not the colonizers' reconciliation with the recalcitrant aborigines, but rather Japanese renegotiation of the ethnic *and* moral boundaries between colonizers and colonized, between "civility" and "savagery."[37] The policy worked. In ten years, many of the descendents of the aboriginal mutineers would join Japanese "volunteer" troops and fight the Pacific War in the name of the Meiji emperor.

For mainstream Chinese historians, the decapitations in the Musha Incident represent a heroic Chinese retaliation against Japanese oppression. Monarudao and his fellow rebels were enshrined as martyrs by the Nationalist government in 1953, and a statue was erected in his memory in 1974.[38] Nevertheless, these gestures have done little good for the Tayal people. They still suffer from a low economic and political status compared to the Han Chinese. Their situation has remained more or less the same even after Taiwanese Nativists, who are mostly Han Chinese by origin, took power at the turn of the millennium. Recast as the "original inhabitants" *(yuan zhumin)* of Taiwan, they have been treated at best as tokens to be invoked whenever the slogan of nativism is invoked.

Wuhe takes issue with both colonial and nationalist interpretations of the Musha Incident, regarding them as products of the same hegemonic structure. He proposes instead to examine the incident anew by reopening the case of decapitation and witnessing its lingering impacts on the Tayal people. Through interviews with survivors of the incident and their descendents, Wuhe comes to the conclusion that the event cannot be understood as a violent form of colonial resistance any more than it was an enactment of the time-honored aboriginal "headhunt." In the words of an aboriginal character, "Our ancestors would have acknowledged a headhunt headed by Monarudao, but they would not have cared about the so-called Musha Incident."[39]

The more compelling motive for Wuhe to rewrite the Musha Incident is to make known the "remains of life" after the incident. For him, the ways in which the Tayal people suffered from the incident in subsequent decades, undergoing coercion, humiliation, and cooptation, are more chilling than the incident itself. Wuhe's intent is already indicated by the title, *Remains of Life,* or *Yusheng.* The title, writes Wuhe, is taken from the inscription on a humble "tablet for the survivors," or *yusheng jinian bei,* erected by the Tayal people after the Musha Incident, as opposed to the grandiose official one mandated by the Nationalist government. To the Tayal people, "the governmental tablet is erected for the dead; the tribal tablet is erected for the survivors, who, upon being born, are already 'remains of life.'"[40] The deadliness of the past cannot be resurrected until the work of mourning is undertaken by its survivors. In this sense, Wuhe is engaged in a task akin to Adorno's description of Benjamin's in a different historical context: "He is driven not merely to awaken congealed life in petrified objects—as in allegory—but also to scrutinize living things so that they present themselves as being ancient, 'Ur-historical' and abruptly release their significance."[41]

In what sense can Wuhe's *Remains of Life* lend a different light to the decapitation discourse underwritten by early modern Chinese writers, such as Youhuan Yusheng, Lu Xun, and Sheng Congwen? It will be recalled that Youhuan Yusheng's *Women's Words Overheard* starts with a scene of Beijing residents hurrying to raise Japanese flags for protection after the fall of the Forbidden City, and that Lu Xun's literary career was reportedly motivated by seeing a slide of a Chinese being beheaded by the Japanese. In both accounts, the Chinese are described as fanatics, traitors, hypocrites, cowards, or callous onlookers, unworthy of "spiritual" rescue. By the time of the Musha Incident, Taiwan had been ruled by Japan for thirty-five years, and Han Chinese resistance activities had all but disappeared. That the Tayal aborigines rose up against the Japanese colonizers was, therefore, unusual. Although situated on the margins of the margins of China, these aborigines carried out what Han Chinese may have imagined but failed to do. In terms of Lu Xun's terminology, they turned the tables in the Musha Incident by decapitating the decapitators.

But, as Wuhe makes clear in the beginning of his novel, the Musha Incident engages him not because it illustrates either a nationalist or postcolonialist agenda, but because it manifests a juncture where tribal subjectivity and colonial/national sovereignty are brought together. In what sense do we call the Tayal aborigines Chinese? To what extent can their attack on the Japanese be interpreted as an anticolonial event? How can an aboriginal ritual of headhunting be reconciled with the colonial trauma of decapitation? If Lu Xun and Youhuan Yusheng are obsessed with a China torn apart by modern forces, Wuhe at the outset questions the validity of China as such. In terms of corporeal symbolism, where Lu Xun and Youhuan Yusheng find in decapitation a break on behalf of a holistic China, Wuhe associates it with the continuity of a local (Chinese?) culture called headhunters.

This brings us to the most polemical point of the novel, where Wuhe calls attention to another mass decapitation that happened five months after the Musha Incident. By then, the survivors of the six rebellious Tayal tribes, totaling 564, had been placed in Japanese custody at several locations. On April 25, 1931, they were attacked by warriors of the rival Toda tribe, which had sided with the Japanese in the Musha Incident, and as a result, 266 Tayal were killed. Many of the dead were beheaded. Generally called the Second Musha Incident, this massacre has often been ignored or downplayed by scholars because, unlike the Musha Incident proper, it appears to be a tribal clash (though possibly instigated by the Japanese) and therefore lacking in immediate colonial/national relevance.[42]

For Wuhe, nevertheless, the Second Musha Incident deserves more of our attention precisely because of its apparent lack of direct colonial or national motivation. It suggests that even in the aftermath of the Japanese crackdown, the aboriginal peoples did not form a unified resistance, as would have been expected in the patriotic scenario; instead, they carried on internecine struggles among themselves as before, perhaps somewhat impeded by the Japanese presence. Politically correct historians would see this Second Musha Incident as an unwelcome appendix to the first, an embarrassing revelation of untamed human barbarism. But Wuhe argues, in language almost reminiscent of deconstructive rhetoric, that the Second Musha Incident serves as the key to demythifying the "original" incident. As he maintains, only through the prism of the redundant second massacre can one understand the complex significance of the first.

At the climax of his "investigation," Wuhe suspects that the Tayal tribes fought the Japanese colonizers in the same way as they fought among themselves. In both cases, "headhunting" was performed in such a way as to obfuscate the distinction between condemnation of colonial rule and consummation of tribal feuding. In the words of a senior tribal member, if the Japanese had treated it not as a riot but as a conventional headhunt and "reciprocated" with another headhunt—as did the Toda tribe in the Second Musha Incident—the Japanese could have avoided the bloody incident. Wuhe presents evidence in support of his investigation. The rival tribes who once decapitated each other also marry each other's daughters, as if headhunts were both exception to and part of the taxonomy of kinship systems. Lévi-Strauss would have loved investigating the deep structure of reciprocity and exchange among these tribes.

Wuhe's defense of the Tayal people's headhunting admittedly betrays a penchant for primitivism. But he is not a romantic merely yearning for the return of the noble savage. Any history predicated on a linear development, either progressive or regressive, bespeaks reductionism in his view. He would instead conceive a "synchronic" view *(gongshi xing)* of history, a view that allows him to synthesize past and ongoing events, Han Chinese and aboriginal subjectivities, public and private concerns. In his own words, "there is no history about history; truth lies only in the present that is history."[43]

Thus, while parading his characters, Wuhe asks: if Monarudao and his fellow rioters are deemed savage for decapitating the Japanese, aren't the Japanese who slaughtered hundreds of Tayal people with modern military weapons ten times more savage than the savages? If the Tayal people's decapitation of the Japanese was once honored nationwide, why did the Nationalist government at the same time denigrate headhunting as a most barbaric custom? (For years, the Nationalist regime promoted the story of Wu Feng, a benevolent Qing official who allegedly taught the aborigines to give up headhunting by letting them decapitate him. It should be noted that this fable was first concocted by Japanese colonialists after the Musha Incident.)[44] Most intriguingly, if the Tayal people were immersed in their own cultural heritage and tribal pride, with the headhunt at its apex, why were the descendents of the Musha rioters so easily converted to colonial imperialism within the decade after the incident?

With an anachronistic twist, Wuhe's questions prod us to rethink the "primitive" impulses embedded in Youhuan Yusheng and Lu Xun's decapitation episodes. Both Youhuan Yusheng and Lu Xun bring decapitation to bear on something monstrous in China's quest for modernity. In their efforts to reconcile the savage nature of decapitation with its legal and ethical claims, they are compelled to invoke a ghostly duplicity of history: the past and the present, the barbarous and the civilized, are intertwined, contrary to those prefigurations of history in which humanity moves via edification to revolution.

At their most polemical, Youhuan Yusheng and Lu Xun grudgingly realize that savagery may always have been built into Chinese civilization, and that the decapitation in question may serve as an unwelcome reminder of the Chinese variant of a human heart of darkness. In Youhuan Yusheng's case, decapitation is administered by a Chinese general to Chinese people *in the absence* of foreigners. In Lu Xun's case, decapitation is perpetrated by the Japanese for the sake of battling Russia, but its "effect" is actualized in Chinese criminals and Chinese spectators. In other words, both writers start out to indict foreign aggression against the Chinese, and yet both indictments end up taking an inward turn—they discern in decapitation a barbarism that circulates within indigenous civilization.

To carry the argument further, consider again Lu Xun's sweeping charge that ancient Chinese civilization is nothing but an endless cannibalistic banquet. For the master, behind the façade of virtues and proprieties, an obscene ritual of man-eating is played out. Enter the back door of rationality, and one finds a bloodthirsty impulse being enacted. Whereas Youhuan Yusheng tries to salvage China by making a last nostalgic effort to retrieve salvation through Confucian enlightenment, Lu Xun simply concludes that Confucianism functions as the perpetrator and protector of institutionalized savagery.

Barbarism and civilization are thus seen as two sides of a coin. It is at this juncture that Michael Taussig's idea of "mimetic excess" becomes relevant: the way the civilized tame the primitives may reveal nothing more than their appropriation, however intricately and unwittingly, of the "savage mind" they meant to abolish.[45] A horrible double vision indeed. But perhaps more horrible is the fact that, having recognized such a double vision, Lu Xun and his followers alike were to sanctify a new, more powerful form of cannibalism—revolutionism—and treat it as the remedy for the evils of the old, enfeebled one.

Given their exegesis of its allegorical meaning, neither Youhuan Yusheng nor Lu Xun shows enough concern about the consequences of decapitation and the tactics of *surviving* it. Youhuan Yusheng seems to find a glimmering hope in the women's words about the atrocities of the Boxer Rebellion; traditionally denied access to the male-centered discourse of education and politics, women's voices are now treated as the only sober commentaries on the national crisis. Youhuan Yusheng particularly excels at having his male protagonist overhear women's next-door murmurings, but for unknown reasons this profitable format comes to a sudden halt after the first six chapters. Meanwhile, the protagonist continues to dream the impossible dream of benevolent rule. As we have seen, Lu Xun is infuriated by the Chinese happily watching the decapitation, and concludes that before any reform to his liking takes place, "the people of a weak and backward country, however strong and healthy they may be, can only serve to be made examples of, or to witness such futile spectacles [of decapitation]."[46] He is so obsessed with the rupture represented by the decapitation that he is unable, or unwilling, to look into the multitude of ways in which Chinese struggle to carry on their lives, however infamously.

This is where Shen Congwen's project of re-membering China is worth revisiting. Shen's project, it will be recalled, starts with a disavowal of any authentic heritage in either familial or historical terms. Shen comes from a region that Han and various ethnic tribes such as the Miao and Tujia peoples cohabit, and he is part Tujia on his grandmother's side.[47] Many of his works, particularly early tales, such as those from *Fengzi* and *Shenwu zhiai* (The romance of a shaman), bear clear imprints of aboriginal influence.[48] Shen cherishes his hometown culture, but he understands only too well that for every invocation of the "noble savage," there goes unheeded a multitude of violent and irrational elements of aboriginality. As he notes, his home region is the alleged site of the ultimate Chinese utopia, the Peach Blossom Grove, while in reality it is known for banditry, superstition, voodoo, and tribal warfare.[49]

Insofar as he tries to trace the reciprocal relations between primitivism and modernity, Wuhe could find in Shen a congenial voice. Both venture to synchronize aboriginal and Han cultures and to expound on their mutual implications, and both are concerned about how writing—or any human form of inscription—can bear witness to man-made and natural atrocities. At their most compelling, both seek the meaningfulness of history and memory by calling on "the remains of life."

How to "survive China," a land brutalized by modernity, constitutes the core of Shen Congwen's and Wuhe's fictional ethics. There is a difference between the two writers' approaches, however. As I have argued elsewhere, Shen Congwen draws the power of his writing from an "imaginary nostalgia," a poetic mechanism enabling him to preempt his sense of loss when viewing the past *as well as* the future.[50] By contrast, Wuhe comes across as a practitioner of literary melancholia. If Shen Congwen can still salvage his sense of loss by conjuring up a lyrical vision of the world on the eve of its dismemberment, Wuhe dwells on a world already torn asunder.

In Shen's writings, however grisly or obscure the subject, there is always a worldly narrator standing by as our point of reference. This narrator may not always be reliable, but because of his familiarity with West Hunan, he helps mediate between the mystical region and the world of his implied readers. Wuhe never endows his narrator with such a privileged stance. Language signifies to the Taiwan writer the primary sign of historical and cultural artifice rather than an easy vehicle of redemption. As the title of one of his most acclaimed short stories, "Shigu zhe" (The bone collector, 1992), suggests, Wuhe sees himself as a caretaker of the relics of a bygone age.

Wuhe thus plays out the other side of the dialectic through which Shen Congwen re-members his youthful experience of witnessing decapitation. While Shen is capable of "transforming whatever is obscene into something fantastic,"[51] Wuhe seems determined to bring whatever Shen Congwen made fantastic, in colonial, nationalist, or aboriginal terms, back to the domain of the brutal and "obscene."

The first-person narrator of *Remains of Life* has come to Musha to cure his own psychological malaise. Having lived a life of mishaps, thanks above all to coercive Nationalist control, this narrator appears to be a wounded soul, and he feels he cannot address the magnitude of his pain without searching a historical locus for a trauma of similar scope. His decision to stay in Musha is therefore not a coincidence: "I stayed [in Musha] because I was touched by the term 'remains of life.' I want to experience the meaning of life after atrocities, and the Musha Incident served as a lead-in to that exploration."[52] In other words, the Musha Incident is treated by Wushe as both a historical site and a psychological coordinate where historical violence and personal trauma, however disparate in appearance, are made to elucidate each other's meaning.

Perhaps for this reason, *Remains of Life* does not have a plot by conventional standards. Rather it features a parade of characters encountered by Wuhe the narrator during his stay in Musha. These characters include an old warrior who relishes the Musha headhunt; a survivor of the incident who has since withdrawn into the "Zen of *Bushido*"; a Tayal scholar eager to rewrite colonial history; a human rights campaigner working to restore Tayal "tribal consciousness"; a retired Tayal soldier who volunteered to fight with the Japanese army in the Pacific War; a Han grocery store owner; a Christian minister; a group of nuns going on a retreat in the woods; a Tayal ne'er-do-well nicknamed Wanderer; and another nicknamed Weirdo. These characters' stories constitute a constellation of voices which may or may not be relevant to the incident. For Wuhe, to juxtapose these voices has become the only viable way to recapitulate the fractured circumstances of the Tayal people since the incident.

The Musha Incidents represent a point of *no* return for the Tayal people; following the two bloody decapitation incidents, they have been thrown into a state of prolonged disgrace and disorientation. To Wuhe the listener and transcriber, whether these characters' stories of how they survived the incidents are "true" is no longer important. What matters is that these stories are tributaries of a shared trauma—the Tayal people's and Wuhe's own. The result is an array of genres, taken at random from reportage, ethnography, sketch, anecdote, interview, hearsay, fantasy, interior monologue, and others, relating the abject life of Tayal people. These genres, rendered as if they were remnants from various sources, form a peculiar aesthetics of the "remains of life."

One of the most touching episodes in the *Remains of Life* relates the life of Monamahong, daughter of Monarudao. Monamahong was miraculously spared in the Japanese crackdown after the incident, while all her family members died, either at the hands of Japanese or by suicide. Her survival becomes a curse. She tries to kill herself many times, but in vain. As years pass by, she becomes increasingly haunted by the dead, and whenever she is left unattended, she sneaks into the deep valley where her father and other family members perished. Only when meeting with the ghosts of her family, she holds, can she find some peace of mind.

In another episode, Wuhe runs into an old man named Daya, who claims to be the son of Monamahong, grandson of Monarudao. Daya tells an incredible story of surviving the incident. Still a baby when the Japanese slaughtered the Tayal rebels, Daya was smuggled out of Musha and entrusted to a Christian missionary family in Puli, a small city in central Taiwan. Daya became an apprentice Christian minister, only to be sent on a ship bound for Latin America at the age of eighteen, when "a riot happened outside the church."[53] He spent most of his adult life on women and wine, and at one point married the widow of a Latin American merchant and fathered a daughter. In old age, however, Daya came to be haunted by his ethnic origin, and he returned to Musha to rediscover the family tragedy:

> Most people took him as a madman returning to Musha. He kept asking about his mother, Monamahong, and every time he heard that Mother tried to walk [to the mystery valley] to hang herself, he wept so much as to lose his voice. His sorrowful weeping induced many others' tears, to the point that his weeping had become a nuisance. He was asked to leave by the tribal elders, because no one can afford to constantly live in trauma; they have to plough the field, raise pigs, feed the chickens. Most importantly, "children born in trauma are children condemned by ancestral spirits."[54]

Finally, to round out his theory of the "remains of life," Wuhe introduces a woman character nicknamed Girl. Girl is a young Tayal woman who, having survived a failed marriage and a disreputable life in the city, has come back to resettle in Musha. Indulging in drink and promiscuous sex, Girl appears to be a fallen woman, someone who has wasted her life. Wuhe, however, sees in Girl a poignant embodiment of "the remains of life" and, to his surprise, Girl is not unaware of the symbolism in her downfall. Claiming that "I am the granddaughter of Monarudao,"[55] Girl feels destined to bear both the pride and shame of the Musha Incident like all other Tayal offspring: no more headhunting. Girl experiences an excess of life, as if enacting the disastrous consequences of the final, massive headhunt in the premature decline of her body and an overly mature communion with her past.

At the end of the novel, Wuhe is seen following Girl, travelling upstream along a river in search of the home of the Tayal spirits. In a way, Girl acts like a medium, ushering Wuhe into the maze of her Tayal legacy. But we know from the outset that Wuhe is a disqualified searcher and Girl an unreliable guide. Can they really locate the origin of Tayal history? If so, what would that primitive origin mean in a time of postmodernity? Musha at the end of the twentieth century, notes Wuhe, thrives on tourists' consumption of the cherry blossoms planted by the Japanese colonizers, on its spa, and on its proprietary "legend" of anticolonial resentment culminating in spectacularly bloody vengeance. The Tayal custom of headhunting has gone extinct; in its place is a modern scavenger hunt presided over by tourists. We thus come full circle in the debate over savagery and modernity. Walking the narrow streets of Musha, Wuhe almost has the sensation that the Musha Incident might as well have never happened—a fin-de-siècle specter haunting the remains of life.

This chapter describes a dialectic of modernity versus monstrosity in twentieth-century Chinese literature, first by rereading writings on decapitation by Youhuan Yusheng, Lu Xun, and Shen Congwen. These three writers share the same repulsion from sociopolitical abuses and feel the same pathos over the follies and cruelty of humanity. For them, modernity has left its imprint on Chinese experience in the form of a bodily rupture: decapitation. Both literally and symbolically, China is invoked as a site of trauma.

But in their search for artistic expression of their feelings, these writers employ different methods. Youhuan Yusheng empathizes with the dead from a Confucian perspective, with the hope, however minimal, of reforming the Chinese through Confucian pedagogical means. Lu Xun is both horrified by and obsessed with the spectacle of decapitation; the severed body paradoxically "embodies" for him a world broken into pieces. Shen Congwen's rewriting of decapitation with a displaced lyricism proposes an alternative to Lu Xun and Youhuan Yusheng's treatment, a treatment that had become overloaded with guilty conscience and moral anxiety. A writer who had seen thousands more decapitations than either Lu Xun or Youhuan Yusheng, Shen is engaged not in what the beheading "means" in itself, but in how it can be written about so as to let us remember and "re-member" the rest of the world.

The question of how to survive China as trauma is asked by Wuhe at the beginning of the new millennium. In my view, Wuhe echoes Lu Xun in critiquing the authenticity of Chinese culture, but he surpasses the master by problematizing the premise of "Chineseness" that makes the latter's critique possible. On the other hand, Wuhe concurs with Shen Congwen in that he cannot provide any "real" solution to human misery; instead he tries to negotiate a way to live with it. Wuhe betrays a far gloomier stance when he comes to terms with lyrical narrativity, which is sanctioned by Shen, as the final resting place for suffering and injustice. The "remains" of (Chinese) life, as he would have it, constitute the first and foremost condition of modern Chinese civilization.

But it is with Youhuan Yusheng that Wuhe would have been able to engage the most intriguing dialogue. Incidentally, the second part of the name of the author of *Women's Words Overheard,* Yusheng, is identical with the Chinese title of Wuhe's *Remains of Life.* Literally meaning "survivor of calamities," Youhuan Yusheng understands the harshness of his time and yet writes quixotically on behalf of a utopian plan. It takes almost one hundred years for someone like Wuhe to bring about the menacing ambivalence nurtured by the Confucian-minded writer.

Women's Words Overheard highlights women as the last recourse when national disaster has engulfed all *man*-made discourses. In a déjà-vu, Wuhe invokes Girl as the last witness to the Musha Incident. With her peculiarly feminine vision, Girl is expected to usher Wuhe into the origin of the Tayal culture, where, from time immemorial, headhunting has played a sacred role. As Wuhe follows Girl along a valley to locate the head-spring of Tayal culture, uncannily the scene in *Women's Words Overheard* comes to mind: the "peach blossoms" into which Jin Bumo ventures, which, when looked at from closer in, turn out to be the bloody fruit of myriad beheadings.

Chapter 2

Crime or Punishment?

In Yokohama, Japan, in 1902, Liang Qichao (1873–1929) launched the magazine *Xin xiaoshuo*, or *New Fiction*. Of possible methods of reform, Liang and like-minded enlightened intellectuals held that "fictional revolution" must be regarded as foremost, as it could exert an impact of "incredible magnitude."[1] In that same year, the Qing court decreed a reform whose goal was to update China's increasingly obsolete legal system. The Institute for Legal Revision (Xiuding Falü Guan) was established to carry out this mission. Under Shen Jiaben and Yu Liansan, a comprehensive overhaul of Chinese legal structure took place in the next couple of years. Foreign experts were consulted; selected constitutional and legal documents from Germany, Russia, and Japan were translated; criminal, commercial, and civil law was renewed; cruel forms of punishment, including decapitation, were abolished; a renewed judicial system was instituted; and rules concerning police, household status, and nationality, among others, were introduced.[2] Most of these reforms were put forward by the court as a way to ease the dynastic crisis, and they were barely implemented when the Qing dynasty fell. The reforms nevertheless constituted the foundational work of modern Chinese legal discourse.[3]

The simultaneous rise of new fiction and new legal discourse in 1902 may not be entirely coincidence. The call to revamp Chinese reality had become increasingly urgent since the Boxer Rebellion. The fictional and legal reforms, one generated by exiled intellectuals, the other mandated by monarchical power, constitute two sides of a dialectic of national self-renewal. Insofar as "Law is associated with Literature from its inception as a formalized attempt to structure reality through language,"[4] the fictional and legal renovations reciprocated control over the task of reforming, and re-forming, China.

There exists, to be sure, a tremendous difference between law and literature in terms of hermeneutic claims, ethical prerequisites, power dispositions, and physical and affective consequences, among other things. I am nevertheless calling attention to the fact that, in the given circumstances of China in the first half of the twentieth century, law and literature continued to infiltrate each other's territory, recasting the perennial struggle of legal and poetic justice. While the weakened implementation of the new legal discourse was attributable to ongoing sociopolitical and axiological chaos, that new literature could lay a claim to juridical agency reflects the belief of Chinese writers, and their readership, in the punitive power of writing—a belief that can be traced back to premodern times.

The dialogics of law and literature in early modern China gave rise to a unique *nomos*—a normative universe in which right and wrong, lawful and unlawful, and valid and invalid are deliberated and sanctioned in a narrative form.[5] In this *nomos,* one of the most frequently debated issues is the distinction between violence and justice. The entangled relations between violence and justice can be found in the legal literary discourse of earlier eras.[6] What concerns me here is the way in which inquiries by modern Chinese writers into the meaning of violence and justice have served as a poignant index to the rise (and premature decline?) of a new consciousness called Chinese modernity. I consider justice to be a social institution that is implemented in many ways—from legal codes to administrative norms, from consensual conventions to mythical taboos, and from disciplinary measures to revolutionary action—so as to define and curb natural and human forms of violence.[7] By extension, violence is understood as a demonstration of natural, social, or individual power that crosses the consensual boundary of the rational and results in physical or psychological damage to the victim.[8] These are working definitions and are admittedly provisional. As will be demonstrated by the following examples, these two definitions tend to collapse into one, as dramatized in some of the most intriguing moments in modern Chinese legal-literary representation.

A high-strung, contentious call for justice permeated modern Chinese literature from the start; it obliged writers to write in order to indict social evils, right wrongs, and prefigure a world of equality and order. This discourse originated in the late Qing and May Fourth eras, when literati promulgated the "new literature" as a total rejection of the old, and it reached a climax in the 1940s, in the wake of Mao's Yan'an talks. Chen Duxiu's advocacy of "a literature for the common people" and the leftist writers' slogan "literature for the insulted and the injured" are but the most blatant examples.[9] Under the dictate of modern Chinese writers, traditional norms, from imperial mandate to familial patriarchy, are shown to have lost their claim to legitimacy and, worse, to be nothing but excuses for systematic coercion. In Lu Xun's words, the Chinese had been attending a spectacular banquet that was nothing but "cannibalism."[10] In revulsion, modern Chinese literature set about to demolish an obsolete system in which oppression had been invisible, even if it took acts of representational violence to stop the old "cannibalism" and make the Chinese see the horrible truth. As critics such as Liu Zaifu have pointed out, Chinese literature under the auspices of leftist aesthetics starts out as "a literature against violence" but becomes a "violence of literature."[11]

After all, in understanding modern China, one sees that violence is not just a theoretical issue.[12] The mutual implication of violence and justice can never be understood as simply what happened "out there" and why some activity had to be punished.[13] One must understand justice as a discourse in which some forms of violence are condemned while others are taken for granted. Insofar as it constituted a major cultural premise in modern China, "violence of representation" presented literature as the meeting ground where poetic justice contested with legal justice, where ink demanded blood. Instead of merely reflecting external instances of violence, literature would demand to be appreciated and enlisted as a radical agency of change. In other words, writing and reading were taken as juridical events capable of transforming symbolic victims into social rebels and figurative humiliations into moral passions.

Long before politically correct scholars began to trumpet the power of language and rhetoric, Chinese literary discourse emphasized the politics of literature, and the late Qing had only to substitute European terms in the traditional discourse of the Way. The changing images of the modern Chinese writer, from the "scholarly knight-errant" *(ruxia)* promoted by Zhang Taiyan (1869–1936) in the late Qing, to the "revolutionary vanguard" sanctioned by the Communist Party in the late 1940s, bespoke writers' persistent attempts to retain their traditional role as arbiters of social order and moral chaos.[14] But Chinese literary history from Literary Revolution to Revolutionary Literature has left ample evidence that such representational claims might backfire. By this I do not mean merely that language might "instigate" criminal activity or that literature might contain false "indictments." I mean that the Way may be silenced because of censorship or external coercion, and when the name of injustice should be spoken, literature may remain silent, thereby betraying its complicity with all master narratives, old and new. This, I argue, is the worst form of "the violence of representation."[15]

When dealing with the dialectic of violence and justice in modern Chinese literature, critics tend to highlight a "literature of tears and blood," a tradition that commemorates the physical and emotional pain of the Chinese people. What remains to be explored is an equally compelling, if not so famous, literature of "crime and punishment."[16] To further my argument, I will describe how forensic discourse—a discourse formed by open debate in the courtroom or in any other public space regarding the legal consequences of a narrated event—has arisen and evolved in modern Chinese literature. With examples drawn from four historical moments, the late Qing era, the post–May Fourth era, the 1930s, and the Yan'an era, I will show how, at a time when the old political, judicial, and moral order had collapsed and new orders were yet to be established, literature provided a textual space in which legal cases were presented for debate and deliberation. In each of the examples to be discussed, a crime has been committed, followed by a call for due punishment as a form of revenge, retribution, or discipline. But close reading suggests that the narrated crime and punishment may have penetrated each other's realm, violating rather than vindicating each other's legal or moral presumptions. These examples reveal a practice of justice that is as vulnerable as it is violent. Meanwhile, as a transmitter of these debatable cases of crime and punishment, literature itself comes to be questioned as an accomplice of criminals or executioners.

JUSTICE UNDONE

For readers of late Qing fiction, one of the most memorable scenes is perhaps the intrusion of Lao Can into the hall of justice in Liu E's *Lao Can youji* (The travels of Lao Can, 1907). In chapter sixteen of *The Travels of Lao Can,* Prefect Gangbi is cross-examining a woman prisoner named Jia Wei, who had been wrongly indicted for the murder of the family of her father-in-law—a total of thirteen people—after her alleged adultery was exposed. Exasperated by the woman's response that she could not give the name of her lover-accomplice because she had never had one, Gangbi orders thumbscrews placed on her. At this crucial moment, Lao Can walks into the middle of the courtroom and stops the torture.

Lao Can had learned of the misjudged case from a friend. Outraged by Gangbi's bigotry and cruelty, Lao Can had volunteered to send a letter of impeachment to Governor Zhuang and Judge Bai, Gangbi's superiors, so as to save the innocent defendant, and he had received positive responses from Zhuang and Bai. As there was no time to deliver the letters to Gangbi through normal channels, in the crucial scene described above, Lao Can has walked into the hall of justice without permission, carrying the letters.

The illegal intrusion of Lao Can into the hall of justice brings together two strands from competing themes that have been manifested from the beginning of the novel. The confrontation between Lao Can and Gangbi is not merely a showdown between a chivalrous traveling doctor and a haughty judge-investigator over a misjudged case. Rather, it represents the dramatic moment in which the incipient issues of legal praxis and its transgression, governmental mandate and individual agency, social justice and poetic justice, are finally laid on the table for negotiation. Through the travels of its protagonist, Lao Can, *The Travels of Lao Can* introduces a China caught in an array of crises from the Boxer Rebellion to local riots, from natural disaster to impending revolution. But in his diagnosis of the national malaise, what most troubles Lao Can (and Liu E) is the injustice that prevails throughout the governmental system, a condition that Lao Can believes is symptomatic of the final sickness of the dynasty.

Despite conventional wisdom, however, Liu E does not hold corrupt officials responsible for the collapse of law and justice. As many scholars have pointed out, what makes the novel polemical is that it condemns apparently good, incorruptible judges, not the corruptible ones, as the real source of evil. In the episode cited above, Judge Gangbi is not a classically "bad" judge but rather one famous for his sense of integrity. In a judicial system in which buying oneself out of indictments has become the norm, Gangbi is known for taking no bribes, and to that extent he has reason to be proud of himself. But as he struggles to maintain his clean image, he turns this virtue into a vice. He is so proud of his virtuous reputation that he has become an intolerant puritan, as his Chinese name, homophonous with the word for bigotry, indicates.

When Jia Wei was put in jail, her family had followed the normal rules of the game by paying a sizable sum of money to the court. Instead of returning the money right away, however, Gangbi keeps it to use as evidence against Jia Wei; he believes that the family of an innocent defendant would not bribe a judge. He tortures the woman with all kinds of penal instruments, forcing her to confess in accordance with a scenario that jumps to the worst conclusion. Gangbi's behavior leads Liu E to make the famous commentary at the end of chapter sixteen: "All men know that corrupt officials are bad, but few know that incorruptible officials are even worse. Whereas a corrupt official knows his own faults and dares not play the tyrant openly, an incorruptible official imagines that since he never takes bribes, he is free to do whatever he likes. Then self-confidence and personal prejudice may lead him to kill the innocent or even endanger the state."[17]

Gangbi's perpetration of "pious violence" posits an uncanny challenge to the conventional practice of justice. To scare people away from transgressing the law, or to demonstrate the absolute power of justice over evil, Gangbi can impose a punishment that is crueler and more spectacular than the crime for which the punishment is imposed. The effect of Gangbi's law resorts to a penal technology that comes from the very transgression it aims to eliminate. Liu E described this paradox of justice earlier in the novel in relation to another incorruptible judge, Yuxian.[18] Under his rule, a part of Shandong has become a model region free of crime. But Yuxian has achieved this temporary miracle by instituting a regime of horror; he mercilessly kills not only bandits but also innocent suspects. The citizens under Yuxian's governorship enjoy a communal life safe from bandits, their lives safe until they themselves are accused of banditry. That the justice system is legalized crime, so to speak, becomes apparent when the state, in a moment of fanatical self-affirmation, decides that it can eliminate crime at any cost.

By exposing the violence concealed behind the facade of "benevolent" governorship, Liu E means to do more than criticize local judicial errors. He sees this hidden injustice as a most dangerous malady that, left unchecked, would eventually jeopardize national well-being. A historically verifiable figure, Yuxian was later promoted to a high position because of his judicial impartiality. He nevertheless became one of the most vehement supporters of the Boxer Rebellion, which led to national disaster. The final irony is that, in the wake of the invasion by eight foreign armies, Yuxian found himself indicted by his own government as a war criminal for having instigated a rebellion aimed at "punishing" foreigners. The incorruptible judge was finally sentenced as a traitor and beheaded.[19]

Back to the episode of Gangbi and Jia Wei. When he is planning to save the woman, Lao Can at the same time involves himself in ransoming a prostitute named Cuihuan, who otherwise would be resold to a lower-class brothel. The girl survived a massive flood of the Yellow River in Shandong Province. She came from a rich farm family from the fertile land between the government dikes along the Yellow River.[20] As the Yellow River was about to flood one year, Governor Zhuang of Shandong took the advice of a scholar to sacrifice some land bordering the government dikes so as to ease the peak of the flood. But the area between the government dikes was densely populated and rimmed by smaller dikes built by farmers to protect their land. For fear that these people would object to his policy, Zhuang was urged to keep it a secret until the last moment. Governor Zhuang was an official well known for his benevolence and fair-mindedness: a "good judge," in other words.[21] In the case of the Yellow River flood, nevertheless, he knowingly let thousands of people be drowned and their properties washed away, as the wisest and most effective policy.

Governor Zhuang, it will be recalled, is the fictional force whose last-minute intervention rescues Jia Wei from the hands of Gangbi. He serves as the deus ex machina whose power supports Lao Can in his intrusion in the courtroom scene. But Lao Can is not unaware of the fact that it is this same Governor Zhuang who has indirectly killed thousands. One innocent has been saved by a merciful man, the governor; thousands of innocents have been killed by that same merciful man. If the criminal in the mystery of thirteen deaths is guilty of murder, what can be said about a "good" judge like Gangbi or Yuxian who has handed down so many wrongful convictions and unjust capital punishments before this case? If a small-scale "good judge"

(Gangbi or Yuxian) is to be condemned for harming dozens, how about a higher-ranking "good judge" (Governor Zhuang), who is responsible for annulling thousands of innocent lives? No Lao Can turns up to "expose" the governor; indeed, all Lao Can does is to salvage a few victims from the thousands sacrificed to the public good and manipulate a small "good judge" with the help of a large "good judge," whose crimes are also on a much grander scale.

In volume two of *The Travels of Lao Can,* Lao Can has a dream. He travels to Hell and witnesses thousands of condemned souls undergoing various forms of punishment: they are scourged by nail-studded clubs till their flesh falls off their bones, deep-fried in a huge cauldron full of boiling oil, or ground into powder with grindstones.[22] These souls are paying the price for their misdeeds, however trivial, during their lifetime. As for those who were virtuous when alive, they have been rewarded with a smooth transmigration into their next life. The dream visit to Hell reinforces Lao Can's belief that some supernatural agency is at work handing out retribution.

One wonders if Lao Can's dream visit to hell in volume two is not to be taken as a belated act of poetic justice, written to counterbalance the numerous episodes of misjudged cases and undeserved sufferings in volume one. Although the secular judicial system fails, Liu E tells us, a higher judicial system still works. The eternal wheel of fortune still turns, at least in Lao Can's dreams. But for a reader alerted by the first volume of Liu E's novel to the fact that incorruptible judges can be more dangerous than corruptible ones, and that justice on earthly China is only an expensive fantasy, questions remain. Given the way that hell is visualized as a gigantic, rigid bureaucracy handing out gory punishments by the book, one can only see it as an extension of, rather than a contrast to, human courtrooms. When the earthly "incorruptible" judge is seen as culpable, one cannot help questioning the "incorruptibility" of the judge of judges, Yama, the ruler of hell. And the other side of a rigid and abacus-like system of rewards and punishments in heaven and hell can be the corrupt and careless system of divine whims and tantrums.[23]

Whereas Liu E takes pains to distinguish between divine and human agencies of justice and their violent consequences, only to call attention to the collusive relation between them, Li Boyuan, Liu's contemporary, approaches the issue from a different angle. Li tells his readers that hell is neither worse nor better than this world; as a matter of fact, hell *is* this world. In his preface to his *Huo Diyu* (Living hell, 1906), he says:

> At the trial in the grand hall of justice, the magistrate is the king of Hades; the clerks and underlings are the judges who demand the death penalty; the run-

> ners and servants . . . are like the ox-headed and horse-faced demon messengers from purgatory; and the flat bamboo canes and instruments of torture designed to hurt people are like the two-edged sword-leaf trees and the hill of knives in hell. Before the prisoner has been assigned to his quarters or incarcerated, he has suffered more than enough! Alas! Heaven is above us and hell is below! Although I have never seen this hell of "judges of hell," I am afraid there is nowhere one will not find such a hell on earth.[24]

Living Hell is a novel featuring fourteen misjudged cases and cruel tortures presided over by corrupt judges. It has never been a popular work within Li's oeuvre.[25] Among the few critics who appreciated it, the novel was regarded as "the first book written in Chinese which sought to expose malpractice and corruption in the Chinese penal system."[26] In terms of unveiling the most inhuman aspects of the Chinese legal system, the novel is indeed a chilling success. Such a reading, however, overlooks the real "virtue" of *Living Hell* by making it merely another example of late Qing exposé.

A relentless parody of the genre of chivalric and court-case fiction, *Living Hell* questions the concept of justice and its violation (most exposé novels assume or reaffirm a concept of it). *Justice,* as I am using the word, is not just the implementation of a human or divine law by human or divine judges; it is also the process of questioning and remaking the laws themselves.[27] It contains a dimension in which narrative praxis figures importantly, because there it does not assume an originary concept of justice by which human or celestial laws can be evaluated. Liu E in *The Travels of Lao Can* still betrays a lingering nostalgia about the lost world of chivalry and justice. With all his cynical observations on contemporary society, Li Boyuan makes abuses of law and order the *pretext* of his novel; his is a world in which chivalry is nullified and justice turned upside down, but there is still a perspective from which abuse is clearly *abuse.* If Liu E still worries about why justice can be so generally violated, Li Boyuan is surprised to see any justice being done anywhere.

What kinds of cases does Li Boyuan examine in his novel? In one story, local officers provoke two feuding families in Shanxi to sue each other. As more and more of their members are put in jail, both families are forced to spend thousands of dollars to buy the magistrate's favor; the case comes to a sudden halt as the magistrate moves to a new position (chapters 1–8). In another, a highway robber known for his capacity to endure any form of punishment finally succumbs to the tools of torture invented by a cruel judge (chapter 12). More than half of the episodes in the novel deal with the suffering of the innocent, however. A chaste woman turns down the sexual advances of a local official, only to find herself charged with murdering her husband, who is actually away on business. The woman suffers horribly in jail and is acquitted only because her husband returns from his trip (chapters 13–18). In a similar case, a man who loses all his property in an accidental fire is accused of arson. Without money to buy himself out of the charge and unable to stand police torture, he drowns himself (chapter 33).

In Li Boyuan's world, corruptible judges and incorruptible judges are alike in administering inhuman punishments; innocent people and bandits are tortured equally once they fall into the hands of the judges. In sharp contrast to Liu E, who doggedly searches against all odds for a way of rectifying the social order, Li Boyuan tells us that any effort to amend the way things are will prove to be too little too late. If good judges never exist, neither do "good" outlaws. As if ridiculing such popular late Qing chivalric novels as *Sanxia wuyi* (Three knights-errant and five sworn brothers, 1878), in which former lawbreakers are persuaded by loyal judges to serve the emperor, Li Boyuan introduces in *Living Hell* bandits and officials cooperating like business partners in setting up innocent people and cheating them of their money. Business is so good that one highway robber becomes rich enough to buy himself a position as county magistrate. This bandit-judge appoints his cohorts as officers and attendants in his court and runs a lucrative business taking bribes from the innocent and guilty alike (chapters 38–39). All of the fourteen cases narrated in the novel end with a non-ending, the narrator's moral commentary at the end of each case being at best perfunctory. No justice, not even the dream of divine justice, appears in the novel.

This is where Li Boyuan shows that his novel can at the same time be more conservative and more radical than *The Travels of Lao Can*. One may conclude that Li Boyuan views the total breakdown of the judicial system from a conventional perspective, that of the dynastic cycle. By comparing the world to hell, he reveals his reliance on conventional wisdom without either questioning its premises or stating the resolution in traditional terms. His cynicism partakes less of skeptical rigor, such as Liu E's, than of noncommittal play. Nonetheless, Li Boyuan's portrayal of the late Qing courtroom as a bloody circus marks a radical departure from the traditional aesthetics of spectatorship. Just as Liu E's narrative innovations shed an ambiguous light on his politics of writing, Li Boyuan's relentless narratives of bodily torture chart new ground in the morality of reading.

One cannot overlook the possibility that Li Boyuan (and his intended readers) may actually enjoy the blood and pain, in a kind of philosophical schadenfreude. What he ultimately provides in the novel is not an account of misjudged cases but, rather, a *spectacle* of punishments. Few readers will fail to be impressed by Li's meticulous descriptions of the tools and paraphernalia used to torture the indicted. Women are often among the first group of victims in this circus of cruelty. A woman charged with adultery is treated with a "nippled iron": stripped of her clothes, she is ironed by a burning-hot metal instrument with nipple-like points.[28] Another woman culprit with tender bound feet is forced to stand barefoot on bricks for hours. Because her feet are already deformed from foot binding, she can hardly stand straight for a moment. Some penal devices are so ingenious that they are even given patented names. "Red embroidered shoes" are shoes made from iron. Prisoners put on the shoes only when they are red hot. "Big red gown" refers to a kind of glue as thick as ox hide. After being heated to a liquid, it is applied to the prisoner's body. The courtroom attendants wait until it dries and then peel it off together with the prisoner's skin. Judged by the ingenuity of these devices, one may well imagine what other punishments hide behind such euphemisms as "Dragon flying amid mountains," "Five sons pass the civil service examination," and "Three immortals make a visit to a cave."[29]

Li Boyuan scrupulously catalogues the variety of courtroom punishments, so much so that the report takes on an aesthetic of its own. A mock-encyclopedic form of narrative, of course, is a familiar trait of late Qing exposé novels. *Living Hell* stands out as the exposé that relates social justice to bodily pain in the most direct and systematic way (like the judges it exposes). It features a penal technology that resorts heavily to the presentation of a bloody corporeal theater, and in this sense it is almost a textbook illustration of Michel Foucault's notion of the relation between disciplining and punishing, power and law, in premodern society.[30] Pain and confession are supposed to come together; fragments of information can be pieced together at the cost of torn limbs. Through performing physical torture and mutilation in public, the authorities make sure that the law has been literally implicated into body politics.

Besides offering lip service to the institution of justice, Li shows little sympathy for his victims. No matter how he justifies his narrative stance, he cannot hide his thirst for sensationalism. Following the Foucauldian argument, one can say that Li's elaborate description of punishment betrays a sadomasochistic penchant, something that upsets the solemnity of justice and turns it into an excuse for a macabre carnival. In a similar manner, the novel anticipates a reader who may be as much provoked as he or she is excited by the bloody cases. Twice removed from the scene of punishment, the implied reader occupies a safe position and may attentively observe limbs torn apart and bodies charred into pieces. With a quivering sigh, the reader may experience a quick catharsis, accompanied by a puff of reassuring indignation.

These Foucauldian observations lead us back to the question: how can justice be represented as such? One remembers that in *The Travels of Lao Can,* Liu E scandalizes his readers by declaring that incorruptible judges are more dangerous than corruptible judges. While it blurs the distinction between good and bad judges sanctioned by conventional wisdom, Liu E's discovery is nevertheless based on a belief that there is an essential system for judging the goodness of a "good" judge; hence he experiments with various forms of poetic justice, from appropriating new Sherlock Holmes techniques of investigation to invoking old Buddhist consolations of Heaven and Hell.[31]

Li Boyuan answers the question by telling us that there is no distinction between good and bad judges, because there are no good judges. Li envisions in *Living Hell* a state of legal and bureaucratic anarchy, one that celebrates the complicity between corruptible and incorruptible judges and shows no sympathy for the fate of either the innocent or the criminal in custody of the law. Li Boyuan does not solve the dilemma generated by this vision. If Earth is merely hell, then Li Boyuan is plainly one of the cruel, incompetent, and greedy inhabitants. As an earthly devil, he enjoys staging punishments, the bloodier the better. And as a minion of Yama, his opinions on justice are those of a devil: they question nothing of the divine order. If Earth is hell, then judges are devils, and writers who judge the judges are also devils. Liu E puts institutions into question; Li Boyuan puts intuitions into question.

MISOGYNY AND MISANDRY, FILICIDE AND PARRICIDE

Questions arising in *Living Hell,* as in *The Travels of Lao Can,* about the equivocal relationship between law and violence, between the cynical and carnivalesque responses to judicial anarchy, continue to occupy the minds of Chinese writers of the post–May Fourth era. As a matter of fact, modern Chinese literature has been described as originating with a bloody scene. As I discussed in Chapter 1, Lu Xun was allegedly so traumatized by the slide show he saw in Japan in 1906 that he gave up medical school to become a writer.[32]

Violence and "modern" literature erupted at the same time, as Chinese literati set out to gaze at the bloody consequences of their cultural heritage.[33] Modern Chinese literature is not a medium employed passively to reflect extant social abuses. As implied by the dramatic case of Lu Xun, it was instead provoked into existence by a drastic jolt at both the emotive and ideological levels, when the author confronted his national status, symbolized by a decapitated body. This literature arose as part of the search by the radical Lu Xun and his contemporaries for the source of Chinese "original sin," which is projected by the spectacle of decapitation.

For Lu Xun, the Chinese spy he saw in the slide show might as well be killed for collaborating in a war that nominally had nothing to do with China. Moreover, just as the spy deserves capital punishment, so are his fellow Chinese spectators unworthy of mercy.[34] Lu Xun sees in these Chinese a readiness to transform themselves from spectators to practitioners at every cannibalistic rite, though the cost is everyone's blood. Lu Xun's condemnation could extend even further, to the Japanese and Russians, who manipulated the Chinese into humiliating themselves. Finally, Lu Xun must have tortured himself with this question: if all Chinese are culpable for bringing shame upon their nation, what about Lu Xun, the spectator who stands gaping at a slide show of Chinese being humiliated? Is he the last conscience of China, privileged with a superhuman vision and voice? Or does he after all share in this collective Chinese original sin?

Lu Xun's "Diary of a Madman" (1918) invites one more reading. Insofar as his madman launches a one-man investigation of social evils, only to discover that Chinese society as a whole is guilty of cannibalism, Lu Xun has told a story about justice lost and refound, the most cynical version. The origin of social evil—cannibalism—can be named by the madman only at the cost of his being confined, censored, clinically (mal)treated, imprisoned, and finally "eaten up" by his closest family members. The story is full of penal and carceral imagery, such as quarantine, persecution, rehabilitation, and a stifling iron house. All these forms of punishment, as the ending of the story tells us, prove to be nothing but preludes to yet another round of cannibalistic banqueting.

Lu Xun's predicament as a justice seeker, together with the cynical, self-deprecating bent of his imagination, may not be completely original, however. An apparently "modern" writer, Lu Xun has a temperament that betrays many fixations inherited from "premodern" writers. What comes to mind are Liu E's elite yearning for justice in *The Travels of Lao Can* and Li Boyuan's cynical spectatorship in *Living Hell.* One recalls that in the imagined hell of Lao Can's dream, Liu E can still see justice done in another world; in the realistic hell that is contemporary China, Li Boyuan simply scoffs at any attempt to restore justice. Lu Xun appears as the self-imposed tragic fighter standing at the threshold of hell, unable, or unwilling, to cross over to either side. As T. A. Hsia speculates, one of the most prominent images Lu Xun employs as a modern writer is that of a chivalric hero in a dynastic cycle, a hero who holds open the "gate of darkness" to let his comrades and other innocent people flee disaster, only to be crushed by the gate when he falls exhausted.[35]

Straddling the threshold of the "gate of darkness," Lu Xun, as a "scholarly knight-errant," must have sensed the uncertainties in his re-visioning of justice. Like Liu E, Lu Xun wishes to imagine himself as a chivalrous literatus, standing alone against the "gate of darkness" while dreaming a late Qing dream of true justice on the other side; but, like Li Boyuan, Lu Xun cannot take his gaze away from the nightmarish injustice on this side of the gate. Lu Xun must also have known from his predecessors that the "gate of darkness" may stand not between the old and the new China, between injustice and justice, but rather between the world of institutionalized cannibalism on this side and its phantom replica on the other. Lu Xun cannot indict the "living hell" of China without demonstrating that his power derives from the hell of which he is a part. A Liu E–like champion protesting against social injustice, Lu Xun was no less a connoisseur, à la Li Boyuan, of the dark aspect of humanity, a fact well attested by the ghastly imagery of his essays, memoirs, and stories. Though it is said to be savored in the modern world, the new justice conceived by Lu Xun still has a taste for blood from the old, cannibalistic world.[36]

Two more examples can be cited from Lu Xun's short stories to illuminate the uncanny affinity between the concept of justice and its denial. For instance, the climax of "New Year's Sacrifice" is preceded by an argument about the innocent suffering in this world and its redress in the other. In that episode, Xianglin's ill-fated wife, now reduced to a beggar, stops the narrator, Lu Xun, on his way home and asks him if the soul survives death. Earlier, Xianglin's wife was told that since she had been twice widowed and was now deprived of her only son, her body would be sentenced to be torn apart by her dead husbands in hell. She was advised to donate a threshold at a nearby Buddhist temple, to be trampled on as her substitute so that her sin would be atoned for. In their encounter, the dying woman intends to seek from the narrator, Lu Xun, a reason for her plight in this life. To her question, the narrator responds, "I am not sure."

The reference to hell and afterlife brings to mind, again, the dialectic formed by two of the late Qing novels discussed in the last section. Hell, in Lu Xun's narrative, may suggest the underworld courtroom of Liu E's *Travels of Lao Can,* in which retribution is carried out in the most fastidious way; at the same time, it may also correspond to the secular judicial institutions of *Living Hell,* which prove to be hideous replicas of the other world. After her donation of the threshold, Xianglin's wife was still treated by her fellow villagers as if under a curse. Neither the justice of this world nor the justice of hell applies to her. With her question still unanswered, Xianglin's wife dies, presumably in fear that she will be eternally tortured in hell.

But, as she dies, Xianglin's wife leaves behind another hell, so to speak, in which our narrator-author will be eternally tortured. In his failure to either stand by the poor woman or deny collusion with society, narrator Lu Xun carries in himself an everlasting sense of guilt. One question remains, however. Given his obsession with crime and punishment, could it be possible that his vision of hell is that which Lu Xun fears *and* desires? Not unlike Xianglin's wife, who resigns herself to an imagined perpetual condemnation, Lu Xun may have created and inhabited a literary hell of his own, from which he is unable, and perhaps unwilling, to escape. The psychological drama of self-imposed crime and punishment constitutes the most treacherous aspect of Lu Xun's, and his followers', image of justice. As will be argued later, this psychological mechanism would eventually be appropriated by the communists in forming their discourse of crime and punishment.

At the other end of Lu Xun's gallery of characters stands the ne'er-do-well Ah Q. In the earlier part of the story, Ah Q dreams of becoming a bandit-hero who, even when he is arrested and sentenced to capital punishment, would die a fearless man. This dream is reinforced after he watches the spectacle of a beheading at a city theater. For Ah Q and his rustic fellow villagers, the bloody punishment has been romanticized into an exotic event. Ah Q's "death wish" is finally realized, but in the most ironic manner. Ah Q is executed for a crime of which he believes himself to be largely innocent; for the crowd coming to see his execution, the much-anticipated decapitation turns out to be an anticlimax. Thanks to advances in modern technology, Ah Q is not ceremoniously beheaded but shot.

As a parody of a society nurtured on insatiable cannibalistic desires, the story easily impresses one with its violent potential. At issue here is how the violence and its punishment are described so as to become a fatal comedy of errors. Although he has previously committed crimes that result in no legal punishment, Ah Q is now executed for a felony he did not commit. He is transformed from an enthusiastic onlooker at a bloody spectacle to the devastated scapegoat in that spectacle; his tragedy, if there is one at all, lies in his complacency as a cruel but empathetic spectator. But if Ah Q's bloody desire was aroused by watching the beheading scene in the folk theater, how does one describe the arousal in Lu Xun's writing about Chinese cannibalism, a result of watching the legendary slide show? As a chronicler-spectator of Ah Q's tragicomedy, does Lu Xun hide a cannibalistic impulse behind his indignant posturing? If so, has Lu Xun done justice to Ah Q in the literary world?

For the revolution-minded writers of the post–May Fourth era, drama became an important venue of the debate over justice versus violence. With its mandate to be "acted" out in a public space peopled with viewers, drama appeared to more readily approximate the locus of the courtroom, prodding its implied audience to deliberate over a human case reenacted on the stage. Courtroom drama, just like its fictional counterpart, had been one of the major genres of traditional Chinese literature since the Yuan dynasty.[37] For centuries, Chinese audiences have watched judge-investigators preside over difficult cases on stage, with the denunciation of the villain and the rehabilitation of justice as the climax of the play. In what sense has the modern theater opened up a new horizon in this old genre?

Two early modern plays, *Pan Jinlian* (1928) by Ouyang Yuqian (1889–1962) and *Dachu youling ta* (Fight out of the Ghost Tower, 1928) by Bai Wei (1894–1987), may serve as examples. As its title indicates, *Pan Jinlian* is based on the life and death of Pan Jinlian, one of the most notorious femmes fatales in classical Chinese literature. As one of the earliest modern efforts to rewrite the "bad woman," Ouyang Yuqian's play takes a sympathetic view of

Jinlian's motives for committing adultery and murder. Instead of viewing Pan Jinlian as a licentious shrew and bloodthirsty villainess, Ouyang Yuqian casts her as the archetype of the free-spirited Chinese woman sacrificed to a rigid, male-centered social system. After having been humiliated and sold by her first master, married to an impotent dwarf, and spurned by the brother-in-law she had fallen in love with, Pan Jinlian turns to adultery and murder, as if these extreme deeds were the only remaining means by which she could express her desire.

A feminist might very well develop this theme into a reading of Pan Jinlian's sexual politics. However, also at stake here is Ouyang Yuqian's introduction of a dynamic, critical dramaturgy representing traditional justice held at bay. Here I have in mind particularly the final act, in which Pan Jinlian and her brother-in-law Wu Song come face-to-face at the funerary meal in memory of her dwarf husband, Wu Da. Cross-examined by Wu Song regarding the murder, Pan Jinlian retorts that while she may be the person who poisoned her husband, the genuine murderers are none other than Wu Song and the other men in her life. As for Ximen Qing, the archvillain of the play and Jinlian's lover, Jinlian defiantly argues that she "has been willing to serve as his plaything" because, unlike other men, Ximen Qing "would treat [her] as nothing less than a plaything."[38] Doubly infuriated by Jinlian's confession, Wu Song demands Jinlian's heart as compensation for the death of his brother. To the murderous demand, Jinlian responds, "I gave you my heart a long time ago."[39]

Pan Jinlian sounds more like the victim than the principal suspect, whereas Wu Song is less the avenger than the perpetrator of the whole family tragedy. As Wu Song thrusts his sword into the chest of his sister-in-law, justice *seems* to have been done, with Jinlian's protesting words still lingering in the air. Rarely has one seen in traditional court-case drama such a gripping debate between two parties to a murder case, to say nothing of the alleged murderer rising to bring charges against the prosecutor. Crime and punishment threaten to switch roles.

Still, what primarily distinguishes Ouyang Yuqian's *Pan Jinlian* is that he has turned a play *about* a court case into a play *as* a court case. In a conventional courtroom play, the courtroom provides the central chronotope in which evidence is presented, testimony is heard, and a conviction is handed down. None of these elements is to be found in *Pan Jinlian;* missing from the stage is not only the courtroom but also the judge-investigator in charge of the courtroom. A different dramatic effect is thus generated. One is given to feel that as Pan Jinlian delivers her testimony on stage, she cannot mean to persuade those unsympathetic characters around her; rather she argues as if she were addressing across space and time an audience ready to renegotiate moral and legal conventions. Ouyang Yuqian has turned the theater into a substitute courtroom and the audience into the jury-judge.

This implied forensic scene must have indicated a significant change in the way modern Chinese writers and audience imagined justice at the time. Ouyang Yuqian's play is as much a violation of the law of verisimilitude constituted by conventional court-case drama as it is a defiant rewriting of the law sanctioned by moral and political authorities. As will be argued in the following sections, this new "theatrics" of justice and violence would eventually become a major trope in Chinese Communist revolutionary discourse. When the function of the formal courtroom has been handicapped by wayward political and legal forces, a public space like the stage can be used as its phantom substitute; the stage reenacts cases denied access to the courtroom, thus challenging the monolithic institutionalization of judicial procedure.

In Bai Wei's *Fight Out of the Ghost Tower,* a different kind of family tragedy bears witness to the tyranny of Chinese cannibalism. In the play, a cruel landlord cum opium dealer, Master Rongsheng, is about to marry Yuelin, a servant girl whom Rongsheng bought years before and later adopted as his foster daughter. This despite the fact that Rongsheng has seven concubines and Yuelin has fallen in love with Rongsheng's son, Qiaoming. In the meantime, Rongsheng has to cope with his rebellious tenants, whose recent riots have been reinforced by the support of local revolutionaries. The plot is complicated by the appearance of a woman revolutionary named Xiao Sen, who was once impregnated by Rongsheng. On a visit to Rongsheng's mansion, Xiao Sen is shocked to discover that Yuelin is her long-lost illegitimate daughter, and so the real father of Yuelin is none other than Rongsheng!

The play's central symbolism develops around the "tower of ghosts" *(youling ta),* the site of a ruined tower where Rongsheng cages women who refuse to submit to his lust. Shrouded in a deadly atmosphere, the tower site is a "living hell" for these women. The tower of ghosts reminds us of the famous essay by Lu Xun, "Lun leifeng ta de daodiao" (On the collapse of Leifeng Tower, 1926).[40] As legend goes, the monk Fahai incarcerated the beautiful White Snake in Leifeng Tower forever—an eternal condemnation of the snake for having fallen in love with a human. The collapse of the tower, after having stood for hundreds of years, represents for Lu Xun a belated natural justice supplanting the punishment meted out by a male-centered justice system.

Bai Wei makes clear reference to the collapse of Leifeng Tower in her play and adds a bitter note. Although the tower of ghosts no longer exists physically, the old male power structure still rules women by invoking the coercive system of the tower. At one point in the play, Bai Wei has a woman servant articulate the fact that the tower site is not haunted by ghosts; it is Master Rongsheng who fakes ghostly sounds from time to time to sustain the terrifying old myth. Moreover, Bai Wei suggests that the "ghosts" of the tower not only persecute women but also their own young male descendants. Hence, "the tower of ghosts is referred to by the young master as the [patriarchal tyranny of the] old master. Master Rongsheng may not look like a ghost, but in view of the way he oppresses his young male descendants, isn't he comparable to the Leifeng Tower that crushed the White Snake spirit?"[41]

The archvillain Master Rongsheng is described as a fiendish landlord, an unscrupulous merchant, a heartless father, and a sex maniac. His evil forces have undermined the political, economic, ethical, and sexual foundations of Chinese society and could let it fall into anarchy at any time. Yet, until his final moment comes, Master Rongsheng manages to hold on to his power, a pillar of his society. As the play develops, Rongsheng's son, Qiaoming, comes forward to challenge his father's wish to marry Yuelin, and the father takes out his pistol and slays his son. Not content with this, Rongsheng captures the leader of the tenants, jailing him under false charges of murder, kills an old servant, who at the last minute reveals that he has been Rongsheng's best friend and romantic rival.

Loaded with creaking plots, improbable characters, and sentimental tears, *Fight Out of the Ghost Tower* may well be an example of bad melodrama, indicating the immaturity of the playwright. However, precisely because these dramatic elements are so "unnaturally" blended, they call attention to the play's contesting of ideological powers. For Bai Wei, crime on such a horrific scale goes beyond the control of any imaginable legality. It can only be put down by even more outrageous deeds of violence. In the final moment of the play, when the woman revolutionary Xiao Sen returns and reveals to Master Rongsheng that she was the girl once seduced by him and that Yuelin is their daughter, Rongsheng, in fury, shoots at her. To protect her mother, Yuelin rushes to Xiao Sen with another pistol and fires back at her father. The attempted incest-plus-rape ends with the concomitant crime of patricide-plus-filicide. Yuelin dies in the arms of her mother, deliriously singing celebrations of her pathetic life: a baby deserted by both parents, a child-servant abused by her master, a foster daughter almost raped by her foster father, and a daughter killed by her own father.

What strikes us is that when she is delivering her crazed dying remarks, Yuelin directly addresses the implied audience, as if the surplus of anger, madness, and pathos can no longer be contained by the enclosure of the stage, but must spill over into the audience. As in the case of Ouyang Yuqian's *Pan Jinlian,* the theater is turned into a site where a different kind of justice is being sought. To her audience, Yuelin cries,

> Shame, shame, . . . unbearable shame, revenge, revenge, only to be acknowledged by the sea. Ah! What a world it would be like! *(addressed to the audience)* Red, yellow, green . . . all colors! (crazier, driven to dance) Ha ha ha! . . . Upside down! . . . All is upside down! The world has been turned over! . . . Fresh,

beautiful! . . . Ha ha ha, all is upside down—this is the gift of death.[42] [Stage directions in parentheses; emphasis mine.]

Critics in the Communist camp have praised *Fight Out of the Ghost Tower* as a model drama for women's liberation. The theme of class struggle has been highlighted in view of the deadly conflict between landlord and proletariat, father and children, man and woman.[43] A feminist of the fundamentalist persuasion would praise the play for its focus on misandry and its celebration of sisterhood and mother-daughter coalition.[44] These critics may have underestimated the (self-)destructive power embedded in the play. Close reading shows that in Bai Wei's world, revolutionary leaders turn out to be either burdened by their dark past or disabled by unforeseeable contingencies. The woman revolutionary Xiao Sen, for instance, has been so busy with her adventures that she has had no time for the baby, which she left in the hands of cruel and rapacious foster parents; hence the daughter's protest that she never had a real mother. The peasant protest does triumph in the end, but only as the result of landlord Rongsheng's death at the hands of his own daughter. Moreover, Yuelin is never portrayed as a feminist heroine; she appears instead as a girl troubled by chronic manic depression, and the root of her psychological instability is traceable to being abandoned by her mother. Whereas the incestuous relationship between father and daughter is prevented by the timely death of the father, the much-anticipated reunion between mother and daughter comes only at the cost of the daughter's life. Finally, Yuelin has fallen in love with her own half-brother, so that even if she had had her (unnatural) way, she would still have committed incest.

The political, ethical, and emotional irrationalities in the play, once unleashed among the characters, are never really resolved as the curtain drops. These irrationalities, which manifest themselves in the expedient form of madness, I argue, constitute the most equivocal force in the play. As Yuelin tries to address her listeners beyond the stage, the other characters and the stage directions describe her as having gone mad. Bai Wei may never have achieved the kind of self-irony attained by Lu Xun in his story about an equally confused mind, "Diary of a Madman." In spite of her difficult personal life (described in Chapter 3), however, Bai Wei manages to showcase a gendered, compulsive soul in desperate quest of a just way out, both within and without the play.

The play takes on another dimension when one looks at its extratextual context. Bai Wei writes in her postscript to the play that the extant version of *Fight Out of the Ghost Tower* is actually a rewrite based on an original that had been rudely "taken away" by a male colleague, Xiang Peiliang (1905–1961).[45] This violence in the literary world adds yet another dimension to the risks that a writing woman has to face while she is writing about the risks her female characters encounter in the male world. Finally, Bai Wei's play lends itself to a parallel reading with Cao Yu's (1910–1996) *Leiyu* (Thunderstorm, 1934), a melodrama also dealing with oppressed children, incestuous marriage, forbidden love, mistaken identity, murder, and revolution. Cao Yu's play was an immediate success when premiered in 1935, and would be staged numerous times in the decades to come. Bai Wei may not be the playwright that Cao Yu was, but the eclipse of her play, despite its striking resemblance to *Thunderstorm,* serves as one more example of a woman writer's vulnerability when searching for literary power in a male-dominated world.

A LITERATURE OF BLOOD AND TEARS

I have described the way in which the modern Chinese concepts of justice and violence evolved along with the genres of fiction and drama. With a series of short stories and sketches, Lu Xun launched a narrative inquiry into the ambiguous terms of crime and punishment in a society bereft of political and ethical order. In a new dramatic form, Ouyang Yuqian and Bai Wei dealt with the polemic of justice by staging the crime scene in such a way as to stimulate a debate not only among characters but also among theater audiences.

By the beginning of the 1930s, these two genres—the narrative deliberation and the theatrical reenactment of crime and punishment—had converged to become a powerful discourse, demanding and instantiating a new definition of social and poetic justice. This discourse was further consolidated as the Communist trope of "mass revolution" gained currency. To show their solidarity with the "insulted and the wounded" and to promote a body politics of revolutionary writing, progressive writers united under the banner of a "literature of blood and tears."

This slogan, as well as the works produced in its name, derives its power from a renegotiation of the arts of telling and of showing. The literature of blood and tears is believed to possess such demonstrative force as to both *evoke* the blood and tears repressed in the objects of narration and to *induce* blood and tears at the site of writing and representing. Instead of catharsis, as would have been expected of these Europeanized intellectuals, the new poetics aims to incite action (blood) and indignation (tears). Hence Marston Anderson's comment, "The new fiction was to possess the palpable reality of fluids exuded by the body. But significantly the fluids to which the expression refers are released only when the body is physically wounded (blood) or when the spirit is bruised by empathy (tears)."[46]

What Anderson does not mention is that in the name of displaying blood and tears, this literature offers a discursive format akin to the forensic debate over the nature of violence and its containment. Tears and blood are corporeal clues that need to be reconstituted so as to testify for or against a given defendant. Its performative inclination is expected to be the first step leading to the final call to justice. As such, the works of "blood and tears" are really not too far away from the two late Qing court-case novels discussed above, in the sense that the realization of crime and justice presupposes staging in a corporeal theater.

There are, nevertheless, moments in which tears and blood are called on, only to confuse the issue instead of settling it. These moments give rise to the theoretical double bind in legal or ethical disputes. In *Paoxiao lede tudi* (Roaring earth, 1931) by Jiang Guangci (1901–1931), for example, the young leftist revolutionary Li Jie is forced to make a painful decision as his comrades propose to burn down buildings owned by local landlord families. As a leader of the local proletariat organization, Li Jie is obliged to see to the implementation of this plan. He is, however, beset by several worries. Li happens to be the son of the richest landlord in town; should the peasants' riot include burning and looting, it would mean total devastation of the Li family estate. Moreover, even though he could not care less about his father's life and fortune, Li is worried about the well-being of his bedridden mother and his younger sister, still a mere child. Should these two females be sacrificed to the cause of justice as part of the peasant rebellion?

Throughout his short career, Jiang Guangci had been known as a writer with a corpus of works promoting contemporary revolution in a most sentimental way. Jiang's narcissism and romantic eccentricities nevertheless gave him a literary imagination useful to Communist literature, despite its superficial call for altruism and scientific historicism. It is the romantic yearning for a lost originary communal state that makes it easy for a writer like Jiang Guangci to be taken in by Communist myths about the return to a lost origin. There is good reason that he has been regarded as the forerunner of the "revolution plus love" formula of Chinese leftist fiction (discussed in Chapter 3). This fact, ironically, may very well be one of the reasons for his ejection from the party in 1930.[47] But in the above-mentioned episode of *Roaring Earth*, Jiang demonstrates an acute sensitivity when dramatizing the personal dilemma of a revolutionary.

After years under the tyrannical rule of Li Jie's father, the rioting tenants finally prove that they have the will and capacity to overthrow a landlord. Li Jie shows no qualms about the tenants' plan to kill his father and burn down his family properties. Patricide is necessary as a young revolutionary's clearest act of defiance against a feudal patriarchal system. But Li cherishes deep feeling for his mother and is much troubled by the likelihood of her death in the proposed riots. At one of the most gripping moments in his interior monologue, Li cries:

> I have no father now. I have only an enemy. It is only on the battlefield that I can meet the enemy, but I hear that my mother is at home sick. . . . Mother! Please forgive your rebellious son! . . . There is a duty much more important, much greater than filial piety. To live up to this duty, I am willing to bear the bad name of rebel. Mother, you have lost your son! . . .
>
> Alas! A man after all has his feelings. You know how distressed I am! I love my innocent, darling little sister.[48]

In pain and despair, Li Jie falls unconscious. When he comes to, the burning and killing have taken place.

Insofar as it endorses "rebel justice" at the expense of an existing social order, *Roaring Earth* must be regarded as one of the most important models for Chinese Communist fiction of the 1940s and 1950s, a model that celebrates a "spontaneous" uprising of the proletariat against the ruling class. By forgoing personal and familial attachments, Li Jie has passed the harsh test of his Communist convictions. He may be guilty of a family murder, but for the advancement of revolution and history, he understands that the end justifies the means.

There are irksome factors, however, looming behind such a (self-)righteous reading of this episode. Even before the fire starts, we are told, Li's father, the archvillain of the novel, has run away to a nearby town. To avenge their suffering, the peasants should presumably have tracked him down and punished him in person. Instead, they choose to set fire to the Li family compound *in the absence* of the villain. The fire thus works more like a symbol, or staged effect, signaling the end of landlord rule. Moreover, by burning to death a very ill woman and her child, for the reason that they are immediate family members of the villain, these peasant heroes show a decided preference for justice in the form of theater, for acts of symbolic terrorism. By "theater," I do not mean that the riot or killing is unreal, but that it is acted out in such a way as to gesture toward a "real" revolution that has yet to happen. The revolutionaries appropriate for themselves the landlords' power to oppress, punish, and destroy at will. At best, the symbolic justice mimics the peasants' desire to throw off oppression; at worst, the theatrical terror enacts the peasants' desire to replace and imitate their oppressors.

After pushing Li Jie to the center of the terrorist stage, the tenants wait and watch to see whether their leader will play his role the right way. Li Jie could have prevented the murder from happening, as he well understood that his sick mother and weak sister should not have been held responsible for his father's misdeeds. But he lets the fire engulf his family compound so as to make a point to his fellow revolutionaries as well as to himself, to show that he relinquishes all ties to the past. Li Jie's mother and sister thus die an undeserved and cruel death, ultimately for the sake of Li Jie's accreditation as one who is more a revolutionary than a son. By killing them for crimes they never committed, Li Jie can purge his own crime, that of being a descendant of a landlord family, though it is a crime Li Jie never committed.

Only in feudalism are individuals held to be guilty of the sins of their ancestors; here Li Jie offers a feudal proof that he no longer is the property of his father, by destroying the father's other feudal property—buildings, women, and children—convincing himself that he has rid himself of feudal consciousness. And only in feudalism can one purge oneself of the guilt acquired from one's original clan by submitting utterly to the will of one's new clan. The ultimate proof of new cult loyalty is always the ability to destroy the old clan, to put aside one's individual feelings and become as one with the new clan. Jiang Guangci could not have been unaware of the ironies underlying this violent code of self-abnegation. This is most emphatically indicated by Li Jie's monologue: "I have read Turgenev's *Fathers and Sons* and always felt the conflict between the fathers and sons in the novel is too commonplace. It is far less exciting than the antagonism between my father and me. I wonder if there will be a writer who can write out this father-son struggle of mine. I truly hope that such a writer exists."[49] Even before the crime has been committed, the hero of the patricide is already contemplating his status in comparison to famous examples. This is the narcissistic, romantic side of the would-be revolutionary hero, the side that makes him more than ordinarily vulnerable to group shame and group praise.

One is now supposed to read Jiang Guangci's works in a negative way, treating it as a "historical phenomenon."[50] T. A. Hsia, for instance, doubts Jiang Guangci's sincerity, even at Jiang's seemingly most pained moment. Having seen too many melodramatic gestures in Jiang's works and life, Hsia rightly suspects the veracity of *Roaring Earth*. My argument is that, given his indulgence in role playing, Jiang's posture as a writer and as a revolutionary may have given rise to a crucial trope in Chinese Communist poetics and politics alike. When theater and violence, mutual spectatorship, and reciprocal surveillance are mixed, a dangerous discourse—of romanticism but not necessarily of revolution—is born. The question has to be whether this discourse has significantly rewritten the discourse of feudalism or is merely its reiteration, disguised by its romantic, European clothing. One suspects the killing is performed as a bloody public spectacle so as to renew, rather than subvert, the kind of hell of crime and punishment these romantic revolutionaries wish to overthrow.

As one of the best interpreters of Lu Xun's ethics of writing, Wu Zuxiang (1908–1994) may well have intended in his stories a 1930s version of cannibalism, indicting a society devoid of all moral and legal resources. Indeed, in the famous "Guanguan de bupin" (Young master gets his tonic, 1932),

Wu literally takes on cannibalism, by writing how the young master of a landlord family is nurtured on the milk and blood of a peasant couple during his recovery from a car crash. The story ends by recapitulating another of Lu Xun's favorite images, as the peasant husband is sentenced to decapitation after being convicted as a bandit courier. Few readers of the story can forget the gory execution scene, when the dying convict "suddenly struggles and stands up, raising his hands and screaming like a demon."[51]

The execution scene can be treated as a neat reversal of the ending of "The True Story of Ah Q," in which Ah Q is quickly shot to death while the crowd looks on. For Wu Zuxiang, a proletarian convict of the 1930s would struggle against his oppressors right up to the moment of extinction, registering one last protest against the injustices done to him. Still, "Young Master Gets His Tonic" is a story couched in the rhetoric that marked Lu Xun's tributes to the "insulted and the injured." It is in works such as "Fanjia pu" (Fan family village, 1934) and *Yiqian babai dan* (Eighteen hundred piculs of rice, 1934) that the terms of crime and punishment are polemically reexamined.

In "Fan Family Village," a village woman named Xianzi is subject to increasing humiliation and pain as her village is beset by drought, civil war, and changes in the rural economic structure. The final blow comes when Xianzi's husband, Gouzi, whose love is her only remaining source of stability, is arrested on a charge of robbing and murdering a nun, and a cunning intermediary comes to demand a bribe for the local magistrate. Xianzi turns for help to her mother, who has recently won a considerable amount of money in a lottery, but she is refused. In desperation, Xianzi kills her mother by clubbing the old woman with a sacrificial candlestick.[52]

I need not belabor the multiple layers of plight surrounding the woman: drought, civil war, religious fraud, superstition, judicial malpractice, murder, robbery, parental cruelty, and burgeoning capitalism, each making its contribution to the matricide. Critics from C. T. Hsia to Philip Williams have had a lot to say about the ethical dilemma involved in the final bloody scene of the novella.[53] Matricide, which used to be considered a quintessential taboo, is justified in given historical circumstances. Xianzi's mother used to be a rustic peasant woman. After working for years as a servant to a rich family in the city, she has developed a monstrous desire for money. Ironically, this old woman's acquisitiveness, which makes her value money more than kinship, augments in proportion to her Buddhist convictions about spiritual transcendence. Instead of helping her daughter out, she would prefer to donate money to the nunnery run by a nun who will later be accidentally killed by Xianzi's husband.

Xianzi's mother intends to purge her sins from this and previous lives by donating money to the nunnery, money she has made by participating in the new mode of production in the city. Xianzi's husband robs the nunnery in the belief that the gods should return part of their worshipers' donation so as to reduce the pain these worshipers are undergoing. In either case, there is a mounting conflict between different systems of justice. The laws of the human world and the ordinances of supernatural beings, the imperative of blood kinship and the rule of monetary ownership, the God of Mercy and the God of Mammon—all are presented in a radical clash, with each axis of the contested values demanding a new judgment. Caught right in the middle of these conflicts, Xianzi is driven to maintain her own "moral sanity," in C. T Hsia's words, by committing matricide.[54]

Just as in *Roaring Earth,* a horrific crime has to be committed in "Fan Family Village" so as to make life less inhuman and underline the necessity of revolution. Whereas the young, educated, landlord-turned-revolutionary Li Jie completes his initiation into revolution by countenancing the killing of his mother and younger sister, an illiterate peasant woman such as Xianzi is now made to go through a similar ordeal of parricide so as to reach her moment of political awakening. Bai Wei's *Fight Out of the Ghost Tower* can be regarded as the predecessor of both works in terms of parricide, but her play differs in trying to exonerate its patricidal heroine by recourse to the old device of hysteria and madness. However, for Jiang Guangci and Wu Zuxiang, at a time when the whole world verges on moral and economic bankruptcy, nobody can have clean hands.

In this sense, Lu Xun's vision of cannibalism must be reinterpreted. Lu Xun sees in the Chinese an instinctual need for mutual persecution that will drive them to catastrophe. Violence, in the form of parricide, is treated by Wu Zuxiang, Jiang Guangci, and like-minded leftist writers as capable of generating positive consequences. Revolution is nothing if not a justifiable form of violence, enacted to subvert the traditional form of tyranny. Chinese political theory, from the earliest times to the Qing, justifies popular violence—if it overthrows a cruel and decadent dynasty and replaces it with the dynasty that is historically destined to loot, kill, and defy authority until it secures imperial power. The morbid strain of cannibalism that upset Lu Xun in the Chinese character is legitimated, so to speak, in the hands of Jiang Guangci and Wu Zuxiang. As either would agree, at the right historical moment, for the right ideological cause, even the most victimized social being can be, and should be, motivated to walk over any remnants of social and moral law. What distinguishes Jiang and Wu from other writers, at least in the examples being discussed here, is that they are not unaware of the terrible freedom implied by the group violence newly sanctioned in the name of revolution. These two writers have dramatized criminal cases in their works so as to warrant not a hasty verdict but a prolonged legal debate.

This leads us to the juxtaposition of two forensic scenes in Wu's acclaimed novella *Eighteen Hundred Piculs of Rice.* As the novella opens, representatives of the various houses of the powerful Song clan meet, after a drought, to determine what to do with the eighteen hundred piculs of rice they have reserved from the last harvest. The meeting soon deteriorates into a series of squabbles indicative of the conflicting interests among the houses. It is suggested that the rice be sold to pay for irrigation, local militia reinforcement, or educational improvement; or that the proceeds be used to pay off outstanding loans or be given to charity. Behind all these noble causes, however, are generations of corruption and self-interest that have driven the houses farther and farther apart. As the debate continues on endlessly, one important factor has been neglected: the starving tenants who produced the rice. These tenants are waiting outside the clan temple to demand their share of the rice so as to survive.

The central scene of the novella takes place in the clan temple where the meeting is being held. Long overdue for refurbishment, the clan temple is in dreadful dilapidation, a most telling sign of the decline of the Song clan. The clan temple used to be where social functions were performed, the most important of which was the execution of familial justice and order. For this reason the meeting is being held at the temple, but, as Wu Zuxiang tells us, just as the temple can no longer properly accommodate a family meeting, the continued squabble under the leaking roof of the temple signals the disintegration of the doomed houses. Meanwhile, the angry peasants have run out of patience. They break into the clan temple, grab the representatives, and steal the rice.

The novella does not stop there, however. In the uprising, the peasants carry gongs and drums, wear devil masks, and "shriek, jump, and whistle like demons."[55] They drag the district head to an abandoned platform, where the community once prayed to the rain deity for relief from the drought, and use the site to act out the ritualized destruction of the old order and its superstitions. For a writer as careful as Wu Zuxiang, the fact that the mock trial is performed on a ritual stage cannot be coincidence. Taking justice in their own hands, the peasants still need to return to the site of clan ritual to enact the destruction of the old order.

The eerie, carnivalesque atmosphere of the uprising, with a cacophony of peasants dressed as demons and devils, suggests not so much the beginning of a new historical moment—in which a different or at least reinvigorated justice will begin—as a return to the mood of late Qing novels such as *The Travels of Lao Can* and *Living Hell,* where the image of hell is displayed. Violence perpetrated in the name of "modern" justice is tellingly reinstated here in its premodern, even prefeudal form. Wu Zuxiang may have attempted to realistically record the way peasants conceive of justice, but his realistic representation of the revolutionary scene betrays a romantic longing for the fiendish and brutal pleasures of originary communal life.

LIVING HELL REVISITED

The year 1942 marks a turning point in both the Nationalist and Communist versions of modern Chinese literary history. In response to the increasingly recalcitrant postures among the writers in the "liberated area," Mao gave a series of talks that prescribed the format of Communist literature for the next four decades.[56] Much has been written about the hegemonic status of Mao's talks as well as their consequences. Two things command our attention at this juncture. First, as the call for justice expanded to become a national campaign, on behalf either of a regime or a class, the debate about crime and punishment entered a more tendentious stage. For Communist writers, two wars had to be fought at the same time, the war against the national enemy, the Japanese, and the war against the class enemy, the Nationalist regime. Mutilated bodies and broken families became regular themes of the time; but they were treated in such a way as to be subsumed into the national, or Nationalist, symbolism of a China ravished and lacerated by both external and internal wounds. As I will argue in Chapter 6, a corporeal typology of "the scarred" was inaugurated at this time, as a climax to the tears and blood flowing through Chinese literature from previous ages and an (unfortunate) anticipation of more tears and blood to come in the next few decades.[57]

Second, as far as leftist literature was concerned, there appeared a decisive inward turn, so to speak, as writers came to terms with the new definition of violence. The quarrel between Hu Feng (1902–1985) and Mao Zedong as to how reality was to be represented, with all its ideological turmoil, mirrors the disturbed etiological state of Chinese Communist discourse. Hu Feng and his followers depict in their critical treatise a people seriously maimed by an inhuman history, so much so that it cannot be rehabilitated until its inherently primitive, individual power is called forth. Mao and his cohorts acknowledge the suffering of the people but argue that to do justice to "the insulted and the injured," they first have to subordinate individual subjectivity—which seemed to have gone out of control in Hu Feng's hands—to a collective, historical subjectivity.[58]

The debate cannot be adequately characterized here, but let it be said that the two sides concurred in a diagnosis of the self as beset by *storms*. As will be discussed, whereas Lu Ling (1923–1994), Hu Feng's protégé, features a gallery of grotesques trapped in a losing war against their own ferocious ressentiment, Ding Ling (1904–1986), a grudging follower of Mao, moves her drama of revolution toward a portrait of individual passion that has submitted itself to the will of the masses and found its true vocation in self-discipline.[59] If Lu Ling aims at a negative dialectic of the soul caught in its libidinous desire to be free, Ding Ling intends to show how that soul can truly liberate itself through intense acts of continual submission. Set side by side, the two form an unexpected dialogue pointing to how, before the final revolution happens, the mindscape of China has already become a battleground of furious impulses.

This changing configuration of national, international, and "intentional" factors results in a significant reform of the discourse of justice and violence. My first case in point is the well-known short story by Ding Ling, "Wo zai xiacun de shihou" (When I was in Xia village, 1941). In this story, a girl named Zhenzhen (literally meaning "chastity-chastity"), who had defiantly rejected an arranged marriage, was raped when the Japanese invaded her village. To avenge herself, Zhenzhen secretly signs up for a Communist mission requiring her to spy on the Japanese army while serving as prostitute. As the story opens, Zhenzhen has returned from the front lines to cure her venereal disease, which she contracted while "serving" the Japanese and, in that way, China. Her situation nevertheless induces more contempt than sympathy among her fellow villagers.

Zhenzhen's rape embodies a fear any Chinese woman might entertain during wartime; her mission as a prostitute-spy exemplifies total patriotism. But as Ding Ling has it, Zhenzhen's fellow villagers, who mostly remain ignorant of her mission, think of her otherwise. For these villagers, a girl like Zhenzhen, who defied an arranged marriage and then failed to safeguard her virginity, is already quite detestable; that she should have capitalized on her misfortune and become a prostitute *and* traitor amounts to nothing less than outrage. Meanwhile, Zhenzhen suffers submissively, her venereal disease becoming a physical token of both her patriotic fervor and her irredeemable shame.

Feminist critics have argued forcefully that Zhenzhen's story indicates as much the cruelty of the Japanese invaders as the callousness of Chinese defense forces. As Yi-tsi Mei Feuerwerker puts it, the sufferings of Zhenzhen are "fully 'available' only to women: arranged marriage, rape by enemy soldiers, exploitation of her body by both armies and, after her return to the village, ostracism for violating the chastity code."[60] Zhenzhen's story is built on the paradox that she can derive self-esteem only through willful self-abandon. For her patriotic contribution, she is rewarded with the most humiliating of diseases. To this one may add one more point: Zhenzhen joins the secret mission supposedly at the call of the Communist United Front. In the cause of liberating the collective body of Chinese, first her own body must be taken and ruined by the enemy. But when she returns home, it is those "people" whom she has vowed to save that ostracize her, in accordance with a most unliberated code of chastity.

Even more striking is the fact that, for all the physical illness and torture she has suffered, Zhenzhen appears in the story as a rather healthy-looking person. As the I-narrator puts it, "There was no outward sign of her disease. Her complexion was ruddy. Her voice was clear. She showed no signs of inhibition or rudeness. She did not exaggerate. She gave the impression that she had never had any complaints or sad thoughts."[61] That Zhenzhen appears undisturbed by her painful experience would have indicated to a romantic reader a personality of nunlike goodness and saintly self-control. Her ideological (or religious?) commitment is stronger than her still-hidden physical degeneration. But I wonder if one can take Ding Ling's narrative at face value. Zhenzhen's natural, healthy look is, after all, a front, hiding a body that is rapidly deteriorating. The contrast between how Zhenzhen's body looks and how it feels invites an allegorical reading; it is symptomatic of a reality or realism that turns against itself. As such, it may very well point to the dilemma that beset Ding Ling as a writer in the "liberated area."[62]

For Ding Ling, to write a story like "When I Was in Xia Village" meant to indict the evil forces of reality: the Nationalist regime, the feudal forces, class enemies, and the Japanese invaders. But as her narrative develops, she cannot celebrate the power of justice represented by the party without pondering its newly installed system of coercion and discipline. Zhenzhen's "crime" of being a free-spirited girl opposed to a prearranged marriage should be treated as a virtue in the new society; however, this virtue is later both rewarded and punished. Zhenzhen is persuaded to sacrifice for her party and nation because she had already been raped by the Japanese and belittled by her fellow villagers. Later, she proclaims that she accepted the mission of prostitution of her own free will and that she harbors neither hatred nor regret. Zhenzhen's total submission to the party reveals a revolutionary zeal tantamount to religious fanaticism, her healthy appearance a suspicious sign of her deteriorating capacity to judge.

As expected, the story has a bright, formulaic ending. Zhenzhen will go to another city, presumably Yan'an, for medical treatment and rehabilitation. But with her inglorious past as a raped woman and a Japanese army prostitute, will Zhenzhen be treated fairly by the puritanical party cadres? Knowing that "illness" and "rehabilitation" are terms characteristic of Chinese Communist literary and political discourse, one wonders whether Zhenzhen's disease can be cured, even in medical terms.[63] One recalls that the story started with a frame in which the narrator, Ding Ling, is sent to Xia Village for "rehabilitation . . . because of the turmoil of the department of politics."[64] Even if she could recover from her physical ailment, chances are that Zhenzhen would end up like her creator, Ding Ling, spending the rest of her life in a cycle of political illness and rehabilitation.

"When I Was in Xia Village" thus appears to be a Communist retelling of Christian-Buddhist hagiography, while providing a chilling subtext regarding the continuing usefulness and disposability of the female body. A dimension of violence and justice in modern Chinese literature has been touched on here by a woman cadre and author. The case of Zhenzhen demonstrates the advent of an intricate technology of violence that inflicts pain on its victim only to win the victim's wholehearted support. By writing her story in this way, Ding Ling proves that she is not as naïve as Zhenzhen. Allegedly because of publications like "When I Was in Xia Village," Mao put forth his literary policy in 1942, followed by the first rectification *(zhengfeng)* movement.[65] In the next few years, Ding Ling, together with other outspoken writers, would disappear from the scene for "rehabilitation." Despite the nostalgic mood of its narrative, "When I Was in Xia Village" is both a nostalgic posture and an ominous warning indicating the end of an age of innocence.

Far away from Yan'an, a young writer named Lu Ling wrote *Ji'e de Guo Su'e* (Hungry Guo Su'e, 1943) in Chongqing, Sichuan, to bear witness to the atrocities of the war. Instead of ordinary patriotic themes, Lu Ling exhibits the primitive psychological landscape of a group of people who have been condemned to the pit of life. At the center of the novel is Guo Su'e, a woman who was driven out of her hometown by famine and banditry, only to be taken as wife by a sleazy opium addict. Ever discontented with her circumstances, Guo carries on sexual liaisons with local miners. Her adulterous behavior finally results in her death at the hands of her husband and his clan.

I will give a detailed discussion of *Hungry Guo Su'e* in the context of Communist hunger discourse in Chapter 4. What concerns me here is the extent to which the novel sheds light on an internalized form of violence. In the case of "When I Was in Xia Village," Ding Ling witnesses the transformation of the village girl Zhenzhen into an obedient servant of the people. By contrast, Lu Ling sees in the life and death of Guo Su'e a (self-)destructive impulse that calls for rebellion—against reality itself, if necessary.

Guo Su'e's tortured soul can never find peace with itself, let alone submit to discipline. Her "hunger" is caused by her need for food and sex and by her innate yearning for spiritual redemption, which will happen only if there is a Communist revolution. But just as in the case of Ding Ling, Lu Ling can find no way to convey the gospel of revolution without first questioning, however involuntarily, the "hygienic" preoccupation of that gospel. Moreover, because of Lu Ling's obsession with the sadomasochistic forces propelling human desire, he sees in Guo Su'e's downfall a strange mixture of creation and destruction, a libidinous chasm that cannot be filled by sociopolitical institutions.

This fuels the crucial but ambiguous moment of the novel, in which the adulterous Guo Su'e is caught by her husband and relatives and put on trial in the back room of a Daoist temple. They tie her to a board, humiliating and beating her at will, and burn her thighs with red-hot pokers until she loses her consciousness.[66] One thug rapes her after the trial is over. Guo Su'e is left alone, dying three days later from lack of food and medical care.

If the scene of Guo Su'e's punishment seems familiar to us, it is perhaps because it first appears to be a parody of courtroom scenes from late Qing novels, such as *Living Hell* and *The Travels of Lao Can*. Nevertheless, while the bloody punishments in the two late Qing novels are attributed to officials, Guo Su'e's death is a spectacle put on strictly under the direction of the masses. The predictable charges against the evil of male-centered feudalism notwithstanding, the scene reveals how cruelly the social underdogs can be to each other, before they unite to stand against their class enemy. As Lu Ling puts it, there is almost a sense of festivity as Guo Su'e's torturers engage in mutilating her body, as if their own repressed desire had found a final vicarious consummation.[67]

This leads us to reconsider the crime Guo Su'e committed. As a deserted child, a beggar, an abused wife, and a sexual object, Guo Su'e is the stereotypical suffering woman of socialist fiction. As the story develops, her vulgar, militant manners and her seemingly insatiable sexual desire appear to constitute her new identity, which must have raised the eyebrows of many Communists. Compared with Zhenzhen in "When I Was in Xia Village," who willingly donates her soiled body to her country while managing to look healthier than ever, Guo Su'e commits adultery for a much humbler reason: after her body, she has nothing to lose. In any case, if Communist critics found it irksome to diagnose Zhenzhen's dubious health, it must have been more difficult for them to explain Guo Sue's eternal hunger. In the most ironic sense, the death of Guo Sue might well be the solution to her problem: eternally "repressed," Guo Su'e can no longer stir up trouble and, perhaps because of this fact, her corpse can be safely displayed in the gallery of victims in the Communist hall of justice.

In 1948, seven years after her visit to "Xia Village," Ding Ling reemerged with a novel about another village experience. Entitled *Taiyang zhaozai Sanggan heshang* (The sun shines over the Sanggan River), the novel deals with the land reform movement in a village of northern China, Nuanshuicun. The transformation of Ding Ling into a cadre writer is clearly indicated in the new book. In a humble, almost self-effacing manner, Ding Ling describes the drastically changing ethical and economic structure of the village after the arrival of a land reform team. Though winner of a Stalin Literary Prize in the early 1950s, the novel suffered a sudden eclipse when its author was purged in 1956.[68]

Ding Ling's ups and downs notwithstanding, the novel represents in many ways the climax of the dialectic of violence and justice discussed in this chapter. Despite its economic initiatives, the land reform movement as Ding Ling describes it was never a mere attempt to overhaul the infrastructure of rural China; rather, it had a superstructural dimension, as the land reform contributed to, and was conditioned by, changes in traditional Chinese ethical, cultural, and legal systems. To that extent, Yi-tsi Mei Feuerwerker makes an important point when she calls the novel a "historical novel."[69]

With such built-in epic implications, *The Sun Shines over the Sanggan River* can no longer be treated as a mere account of the transfer of land ownership from landlords to poor peasants. Instead, it tries to capture an apocalyptic moment of history, when a new moral machinery has been activated: the revolution finally has begun. When Ding Ling's peasants demand justice, they are uttering outrage that has been stored up in the Chinese soul for hundreds of years; and when the villain—the landlord—is captured, he must be indicted as a *lishi de zuiren,* or a "criminal of History."[70] It should be noted that systems such as "public trial" *(qunzhong gongshen)* and "on-location trial" *(jiudi gongshen)* were widely promoted in Communist regions at this time.[71] As Ding Ling and her colleagues would have it, real "people" have finally seized the power from those inhuman beings who have always oppressed the "people"; thus the transfer of the control of justice from the ruling class to the ruled is set in motion.

In *The Sun Shines over the Sanggan River,* Liu Zaifu observes the rise of a new dialectic of violence and justice. Based on Roland Barthes's typological approach to the forms of revolution, Liu argues that the Chinese Communist revolution was a hybrid, inspired by both the "bloody ritual" of the French Revolution and the teleological imperative of the Stalinist Revolution.[72] In other words, the Chinese Communist revolution, as manifested in Ding Ling's novel, takes on a doubly grandiose form, combining both spectacular purgation and predestined fulfillment.[73]

While acknowledging Liu Zaifu's observation, I would call attention to an indigenous dimension of the Chinese form of revolution. The legal motifs of Ding Ling's novel, from public trial to communal ostracism, from the theater of blood to the invention of penal technology, could hardly have been new to twentieth-century Chinese readers and writers. When class enemies are judged by the arbitrary will of the newly empowered and punishments are performed with a view to arousing bloody festivity, even actual cannibalism, one cannot help recalling how "Chinese" these modes of imagining justice are. After almost half a century of debate on the feasibility of justice and its manifestation, one sees in a novel such as *The Sun Shines over the Sanggan River* not a leap over, but an uncanny return to the premodern discourse of crime and punishment.

Take the prosecution of Qian Wengui, the archvillain of Ding Ling's novel, for example. For years Qian has joined with other local notables to persecute tenants. Upon hearing of the impending land reform movement, Qian sends his son to the Communist army and marries his daughter to the local cadre, with the hope of forestalling possible charges. Qian's scheme fails. At the climax of the novel, appropriately subtitled "The Final Combat" *(Jue-*

zhan), Qian and his wife are paraded in public, humiliated, beaten, and almost clawed to death by the angry masses. Even the cannibalistic impulse comes close to consciousness, as the peasants converge to punish the hated landlord: "One feeling animated them all—vengeance! They wanted vengeance! They wanted to give vent to their hatred, the sufferings of the oppressed since their ancestors' times, the hatred and loathing of thousands of years; all this resentment they directed against him. *They would have liked to tear him with their teeth* [italics mine]."[74]

It is not coincidental that such a ferocious scene appears in Communist fiction of this time. Zhou Libo's (1908–1979) *Baofeng zouyu* (Hurricane, 1948), another novel about the land reform movement, which was published about the same time as *The Sun Shines over the Sanggan River,* features a similar scene with a similar suggestion of cannibalism. At the public trial of the landlord Han Laoliu, the angry masses raise clubs and sticks to beat the villain. Widow Zhang, a weak old woman, also raises her club and cries to Han Laoliu,

> "You, you killed my son!"
>
> Her elm stick falls on Han Laoliu's shoulders. As she is about to hit Han Laoliu again, she finds herself short of energy. She drops the stick, jumps over to Han Laoliu, biting his shoulders and arms with her teeth. Nothing else can relieve the hatred in her mind.[75]

If the two public trial scenes are still shocking to us today, it is perhaps due not to the questionable modes of popular justice but to the capacity of humans to be so possessed by bloodlust that they jump about and bite like beasts. The sensational language and bloody descriptions that permeate the texts are reminiscent of the revolutionary works of an earlier generation, such as Jiang Guangci's *Roaring Earth* and Wu Zuxiang's "Fan Family Village" and *Eighteen Hundred Piculs of Rice.* Ding Ling's work differs in that it programs all the motivations that Wu's and Jiang's peasants would have felt in such a way as to present animality as a logical outcome rather than a momentary human reversion to the bestial.

Incidentally, one must bear in mind that the Communist government made it illegal to impose physical torture on the indicted in the land reform movement.[76] The public trial is planned as if in accordance with a court procedure, the difference being that this court scene takes place in an open space that demands everybody's attendance and, ostensibly, everybody's judgment. The fusion of the theater, the courtroom, and the site of punishment, long embedded in early revolutionary plays and fiction, such as *Pan Jinlian* and "The True Story of Ah Q," are finally officialized as an integral part of Communist legality.

The old questions regarding the way the late Qing novel *Living Hell* represents justice remain pertinent. Whereas *Living Hell* presents a closed courtroom in which suspects are punished and paraded about as if in a variety show, a novel like *The Sun Shines over the Sanggan River* introduces an open courtroom where suspects are served up in a mock cannibalistic feast. Lu Xun and Lu Ling's cynical vision of the cruel human capacity to humiliate and persecute is enthusiastically endorsed in a model Communist novel. One could argue that the Communist masses are not the corrupt judges of the late Qing, and that they inflict punishment on the wicked as a necessary step toward long-awaited social justice. Liu E's paradoxical warning in *The Travels of Lao Can* is relevant: self-righteous, incorruptible judges are far more dangerous than corruptible ones.[77] Believing that they are acting at the behest of a new mandate, the Communist masses are more dangerous when they torture the villains and their families indiscriminately than the self-righteous, incorruptible judges of the Qing dynasty, not because the technology of torture has advanced but because there is now a vast number of self-righteous, incorruptible judges.[78]

I would further argue that the discourse of violence and justice demonstrated in a novel like *The Sun Shines over the Sanggan River* can also be more cruel than that offered in the two late Qing novels. Liu E and Li Boyuan describe in one way or another the corruption of the late Qing judicial system, pointing out or merely insinuating that there are cracks between what the law means to achieve and what it really achieves. Despite their righteous or cynical undertones, the two novels contain a measure of self-reflection, which compels the writers and their implied readers to demand a judicial and penal system other than what is practiced in the novels. By contrast, *The Sun Shines over the Sanggan River* celebrates the mixture of rites of torture and rites of cannibalism and sees it as the final *solution* to the problem of justice. Ding Ling takes for granted what Liu E and Li Boyuan would have either condemned or parodied, if they had not died first.

There is another aspect of violence in *The Sun Shines over the Sanggan River* that has been less discussed by critics. The land reform movement does not end with the redistribution of the land and properties that used to belong to the rural ruling class. Reform of the Chinese landscape prefigures the reform of the Chinese mindscape. Behind the confrontation between the landlords and the peasants stand the land reformers; their task is to mobilize the long-oppressed peasants to rise against local authorities. Throughout the novel, one witnesses how the reformers carefully plan to arouse anger among the peasants and channel that anger into action. The peasants, at the opening of the novel, are shown to be so intimidated by Qian Wengui's power that they dare not articulate their suffering in public. After they have been worked on by the reformers, however, they cannot talk enough about their hatred and vengeful desire. Insofar as they undergo group-therapeutic personality changes designed and initiated by the reformers, the peasants' liberation inaugurates a new, advanced form of serfdom; land reform is the outward form of mind reform.[79]

This psychological re-education of the peasants is closely related to the so-called violence of language that is imposed on them. Xiaobing Tang has argued, taking Zhou Libo's *Hurricane* as an example, that language in Communist literature at this time has been reduced to its most primitive level, and can make sense only through recourse to the invocation of physical scars.[80] Tang sees a dangerous reduction of a symbolic system of linguistic signs to that of bodily spectacle.[81]

One should, however, never take the apparent Communist vulgarization of language for a simplification of figural symbolism. The obsession with the reciprocity of ink and blood is not an invention of Communist writers. Lu Xun's "decapitation complex" still has to be regarded as one of the origins of the "scarred" discourse that later prevails in leftist and rightist literature. As argued above, the new violent language can be a well-orchestrated linguistic system, couched in a deep cultural and literary subtext traceable as far back as to late Qing literature. While evoking an immediate, bodily spectacle, this language functions not as a means to do away with a richly encoded discourse of violence but as a way to revitalize it. Thus, as David Apter and Tony Saich observe, the violence of language is an intricate figural mechanism rather than a raw abuse of words, which manages to evoke an exegetical bonding among the party members.[82]

My final point is about the way in which some forms of suffering and punishment, horrific as they are, have been written *as a result of* the new Communist discourse of justice. I have in mind cases where the debate over crime and punishment is least expected, such as the love affair between Heini, Qian Wengui's niece, and Cheng Ren, the newly appointed local leader of the land reform. Before the reform took place, the two were lovers despite their class difference. Now, under the new legal terms that distinguish the lawful from the unlawful, they have to redefine their relations.

Though closely related to Qian Wengui, Heini has been treated as a free laborer by Qian and his wife. After discovering Cheng Ren's position in the new power structure, the couple suddenly change their attitude toward their niece, hoping to use her to win Cheng Ren's favor. Heini is despised by the villagers for a scheme she is innocent of. Although she is later accepted as part of the oppressed class and enlisted to join the rally against her uncle, her romance with Cheng Ren is indefinitely suspended by public will and by self-abnegation.

Cheng Ren is no better off. That Cheng Ren should have transgressed social taboos and fallen in love with a landlord's niece before the land reform is a sign of his genuine courage and revolutionary consciousness. But in the new society, Cheng Ren becomes conscious of his newly won class status, which carries with it a new taboo as severe as the old one. The romance proves even more trying than before. When he finally decides to pick out Qian Wengui as the chief target of a public trial, Cheng Ren recognizes that he has been less than resolute in facing up to that reality: "He felt as if *he had committed a crime, and done something wrong to others, and could not hold up his head.* This was something he had never felt before. . . . He had forgiven [Qian Wengui] everything for the sake of his niece. . . . In his heart he had been secretly protecting her, that is, protecting them, the interests of the landowning class [italics mine]."[83] Torn between his dedication to the party and his love for Qian Wengui's niece, Cheng Ren finally sacrifices all personal feelings for the sake of the revolution. And the motive that compels him to do so is a deeply rooted sense of prohibition and guilt.

In Cheng Ren's self-sacrifice there lurks a gender politics crucial to the Chinese Communist way of disciplining the "new" citizen. In "When I Was in Xia Village," Zhenzhen suffered under the old regime because she had lost her virginity, but she was allowed to prove her worth by sacrificing her body again, as a prostitute. Now, under Communist rule, Cheng Ren has lost his ideological purity by falling in love with a class enemy, and to prove his worth he must dedicate himself physically and emotionally to the party. As such, the man of the new era has been reduced to playing the role of the woman of the prerevolutionary era. Both men and women will take up the old "feminine" role, so to speak, in the new society, a role in which the taint of evil is acquired by rape or by association, and can be removed only by continual acts of selfless penitence, if at all. The emasculation of Cheng Ren thus completes the dialectic of gender already started in "When I Was in Xia Village."

Above all, as the homonyms of his name suggest, "Cheng Ren" means both "becoming human" and "dying as a martyr." Humanity can be attained only through a self-willed nullification of separate humanity. Lu Xunesque cannibalism—institutionalized oppression in the name of social virtue—has reappeared on a grander scale. If Qian Wengui is condemned for his lack of humanity, Cheng Ren is honored because he has chosen to lose his humanity. Qian Wengui tries to bribe his way out of punishment; Cheng Ren condemns himself and carries out his own punishment.

The case of Ding Ling brings us back to the beginning of this chapter. Late Qing writers like Liu E and Li Boyuan modernized conventional court-case literature by providing venues in which the terms of justice and violence were radically renegotiated. What had seemed complete, divine law and human law, was revealed as incapable of addressing either morality or equity. Their indictments of legal justice led to restatements of poetic justice; hence the beginnings of a new forensic discourse.

While they look into social abuses and political atrocities, writers since Lu Xun's generation have excoriated social evils and called for the implementation of individual punishment; they have usually come to the conclusion that justice cannot be done without violence—in the form of a revolution in the self. The consummation of the Qing desire for true forensic discourse was a massive network of self-censorship and mutual surveillance, and the Communist scene of justice shifted from the physical courthouse to the interior monologue. This inward turn of policing would prove to be far more "advanced" than any moment illustrated in the late Qing novels, both in penal technology and juridical efficacy. With violence finally stabilized in the form of self-imposed crimes and self-inflicted punishments, the moral and legal machinery of a new justice was in full operation.

Chapter 3

An Undesired Revolution

On August 19, 1927, a poem entitled "Liubie" (Farewell) appeared in the literary supplement to *Zhongyang zhibao* (Central daily news) of Wuhan:

> Sister Cloud:
> Half a pound of black tea has been finished,
> Five hundred cigarettes have been finished,
> Translation of the forty-thousand-character novel has been finished,
> . . . .
> Envelopes, stationary, draft sheets, also used up;
> So is the Agfa film.
> Summer is almost over,
> Fun is long gone,
> All the paths have been trodden,
> All the words have been spoken,
> All the money has been spent,
> All is over, over.
> It is time to leave.
>
> When shall we be reunited?
> How could I tell?[1]

This poem reads like a love poem, about a romance turning sour. After having spent a summer in some resort area with his beloved, Sister Cloud, the poet realizes that their affair has come to an end. In a pensive tone, he looks back at the barren consequences and bids farewell to Sister Cloud. What is left for him to feel is nothing but "deep disillusionment."

The author of this poem is Mao Dun (Shen Yanbing, 1896–1981), one of the most prominent leftist writers in modern Chinese literature. While the poem's romantic allusions remain opaque, its political motivation has been elucidated. On July 25, 1927, Mao Dun and several friends arrived in the summer resort of Lushan, in Jiangxi Province. Earlier that month, the Nationalist and Communist coalition government in Wuhan had collapsed in the face of warlord attacks, local riots, and Nationalist "liquidations."[2] The fate of the Wuhan government had been decided since the Shanghai massacre[3] masterminded by Chiang Kai-shek and his supporters in early April and the founding of a new Nationalist government in Nanjing.[4] A Communist veteran who had worked for the Wuhan regime, Mao Dun was among those named to be hunted down. On July 24, bearing a check for two thousand dollars entrusted to him by the party, he fled Wuhan for Jiujiang, a harbor city on the Yangtze River. In Jiujiang, Mao Dun met his contact and was told to travel to Nanchang, the capital of Jiangxi.[5] The Chinese Communists had decided on a mass uprising in Nanchang, and the money was intended to support it.

But Mao Dun never made it to the Nanchang Uprising, which took place, underfunded, on August 1, 1927. Instead, he took a detour to Lushan and stayed there until mid-August, long after the uprising was over. Why Mao Dun failed in this mission is a riddle in his life story.[6] In his autobiography, Mao Dun stated that he had contracted diarrhea in Lushan, so severe that it prevented him from leaving the resort in time.[7] But his physical condition did not prevent him from vigorously writing and translating, the poem "Farewell" being one notable product. And curiously, for all the turmoil that was happening not too far away, Mao Dun showed in these works little sign of agitation or regret. Rather he appears disillusioned over a failed romantic affair. "All is over, over," sighs the poet in "Farewell."

In view of the fact that Mao Dun's works are always implicated in political message-sending, "Farewell" invites an allegorical reading. The romance Mao Dun refers to may euphemistically invoke his period of revolutionary engagement, and beloved Sister Cloud may be none other than the seductive Communist Party.[8] Thus, when he bids farewell to his lover in the poem, Mao Dun may be signaling the end of his devotion to the party.

This, of course, is a serious charge against someone who joined the party in its founding days in 1921. But there is evidence that Mao Dun's prolonged sojourn in Lushan coincided with a "temporary loss of contact" with the party. He was in fact denied party membership till the end of his days. Neither Mao Dun nor the party was able to explain this incident to anyone's satisfaction, leaving his farewell poem, and his diarrhea, as suspicious blemishes on a literary career otherwise known for its revolutionary zeal. Historical hindsight allows us to observe that Mao Dun might have been hasty in calling it quits at the moment when he wrote, "All is over, over" in Lushan. The collapse of the Wuhan government was but a prelude to the combat between the Nationalist and the Communist Parties, and Mao Dun's poetic disavowal of his romantic and political commitment would mark the beginning of a tortuous revolutionary adventure. For this premature gesture of farewell and its accompanying abdominal unease, Mao Dun would spend the rest of his life in unfulfilled repentance.

Revolution and romance—punctuated by frequent outbreaks of disease—constitute major phenomena in the literary etiology of the First Chinese Communist Revolution of 1927,[9] and the case of Mao Dun becomes significant only when read in conjunction with those of his contemporaries. This is a time when the Nationalist Party, the Communist Party, imperialist aggressors, and warlord forces played treacherous games of collaboration and confrontation, disrupting and distracting the young republic. This is also a time when a younger generation of literati, inspired by the May Fourth agenda, were ready to participate in politics. Compared to their predecessors, these writers were more committed to ideological agendas, which in turn induced them to practice a more volatile literary discourse. They produced an "engaged literature" in the sense not only of literature as politics but also of literature as sentimental education.

From the outset, the 1927 Communist Revolution—or in the Nationalist version, the 1927 Nationalist Party Liquidation *(qingdang)*—was a mixture of contesting political platforms and actions. For the Communists, it had resulted in the first mass movement to establish Chinese proletarian solidarity with the leadership of the Third International. For the Nationalists, it represented a project of nation building held in abeyance since 1911, which aimed at the consolidation of a Nationalist regime. In spite of their antagonistic goals, the Nationalist and Communist Parties had collaborated from 1924 to 1927. Many Communists, Mao Dun included, joined the Nationalist Party and played active roles in the Northern Expedition—the Nationalist campaign against the warlords. Meanwhile, leftists within the Nationalist Party sought to extend their power by cooperation with the Communists. The anomalous relations between the two parties broke up when Chiang Kai-shek launched the coup in Shanghai, followed by the Nationalist liquidation of leftists in Nanjing and Wuhan.

The failure of the 1927 Communist Revolution nevertheless gave rise to the first wave of full-length modern Chinese novels. Through the intermediary of the novel, many writers cum revolutionaries delineated their searches for social actions that would reform China, and pondered the consequences. Ye Shaojun's *Ni Huanzhi* (1929), Ba Jin's *Miewang* (Destruction, 1928), Jiang Guangci's *Duanku dang* (Des Sans-culottes, 1927), Bai Wei's *Zhadan yu zhengniao* (The bomb and the expeditionary bird, 1928) are among the most conspicuous examples. Modeled after nineteenth-century European realist novels, these works feature long, slow narratives and sweeping views of a society in crisis. They highlight ordinary characters personally confronting historical stimuli in terms of their own passions, and chronicle their development of a certain moral, emotional, or ideological idea against the linear progression of history.[10] Above all, the two realms of revolution and love are called on to inform reality through different modes of representation.[11] In Stephen Chan's words, if "love can be considered the inner, emotional symbol for an eternal, social revolution, then Eros in this sense may be taken to signify the Life-energy that propels the wheel of the ultimate Revolution."[12]

Thus revolution and romance did not merely lend the raw material to the Chinese novel of the late 1920s; rather they constituted its raison d'être. These writers find in the realist novel a viable form for expressing their "desire for plot," to borrow Peter Brooks's terminology, with regard to their revolutionary and romantic experiences.[13] This desire for plot has two meanings, in my definition. It indicates the writers' use of a narrative ploy to render the fragmented postrevolutionary realities as a unified whole, to have a go at making sense of what has gone wrong. At the same time, it demonstrates a propensity among these writers to resist any form of closure. Before their romantic and revolutionary desires are consummated, their "plotting" must carry on. Between these two narrative poles exists a tension, one addressing the need for coherence and closure, and the other subverting such a need; hence more storytelling and more plotting to fill the expanding space.

This tension sustains the dilemma that once beset the writers to be discussed in the following pages. If the revolutionary romance novel sets the reader on a trajectory toward an apocalyptic moment that reveals the final fulfillment of historical subjectivity, acts of writing occur by maintaining and projecting that imminent revelatory moment. Writing becomes an act of anticipation, a gesture of desiring revolution. Nevertheless, writing can also be an act of procrastination, because by foretelling the future, it also inscribes the prolonged stay of the "present," which should long ago have receded into the anteriority of all dissatisfaction. A negative dialectic is implied in such writing. This dialectic suggests that the more a writer writes, the more he or she articulates his or her incapacity to reach the ideal state of rationality accessible only through revolution. Revolution, which will abolish unsatisfied desire, may not after all be desired by writers who practice the imagination of its postponement. The realist novel in the post-1927 era thus best addresses what Reality is by delaying and subverting its Revolutionary fulfillment. No surprise then that model works by writers such as Mao Dun and Ding Ling should have provoked much controversy.

With this argument in mind, I focus in this chapter on selected works by three leftist writers, Mao Dun, Jiang Guangci (Jiang Ruheng, 1900–1931), and Bai Wei (Huang Zhang, 1894–1987), in the post-1927 era. Mao Dun and Jiang Guangci were Communist Party members. Mao Dun was hailed as one of the most accomplished leftist literati in the 1920s, but it was Jiang Guangci who initiated the trend toward "Revolution plus Love" fiction after the 1927 Revolution. Bai Wei was a prominent woman writer from Hunan, like Ding Ling and Xie Bingying (1907–2000). A dedicated revolutionary novelist and playwright, Bai Wei is perhaps better remembered for her stormy romance with the poet Yang Sao (1900–1957).

These three writers participate in a coincidence: for the sake of revolution, they were all drawn to Wuhan during the last months of the coalition government. Mao Dun worked as the editor of *Guomin ribao* (Citizens' news) in Hankou, Bai Wei served as a Japanese translator in the Bureau of International Information, and Jiang Guangci was about to start his career when the Nationalist Liquidation took place. All three writers witnessed the bloody confrontation between leftists and rightists. After the fall of the coalition government, they all returned to Shanghai and in one way or another took up the novel as a way of negotiating their revolutionary idealism. More notably, in so doing they each invoked romance as a symbol of the revolution.

But is romance a mere rhetorical figure? The three writers' personal love stories prove more polemical, and revolutionary, than what is described in their fiction. And it is through their romantic adventures, in textual and extratextual terms, that they bring home the nature of utopian desire. Because they shuffled between revolutionary action and romantic sport, between lived historical experience and imaginary romance, I argue, these writers did not merely write down but rather personally acted out modern Chinese fictional realism.

THE REVOLUTIONARY DISCOURSES

There is no revolution when revolutionary writers appear in large numbers.

LU XUN

In late August of 1927, Mao Dun left Lushan and took a Japanese ship heading for Shanghai, where his mother and his wife lived. To avoid the secret police in the Shanghai port, he landed in Zhenjiang, but was snared for a customs investigation. On the spur of the moment, Mao Dun bribed them with the two-thousand dollar check he was supposed to bring to the party for the Nanchang Uprising, and he was released.[14]

Back in Shanghai, Mao Dun maintained contact only with selected friends on the left. Alienated from the circles he used to be familiar with and inspired by the traumatic events he had just been through, he decided to try his hand at fictional writing. The result was a series of three novellas, *Huanmie* (Disillusionment, 1927), *Dongyao* (Vacillation, 1927), and *Zhuiqiu* (Pursuit, 1928). Later published under the title *Shi* (Eclipse, 1930), the trilogy marked the beginning of Mao Dun's career as a novelist.[15]

In *Disillusionment,* Mao Dun illustrates through two girls' vain pursuit of love and revolution how, for those who are eager to find a way out of murky reality, history unfolds as a deceptive circle. The two girls, Jing and Hui, alternately undertake romantic and political causes—the May Thirtieth Incident, the Northern Expedition, the Nanchang Uprising, and so on—throughout the story, yet find themselves ending up nowhere.

Vacillation takes an even more equivocal look at the paradox of conceptions of revolution under way and revolution in stagnation. All the characters are seen as vacillating between different categories of values, in such a way as to give rise to an anarchist blank that nullifies any logic of action. Meanwhile, the outbreak of local riots have turned all revolutionary agendas into a bloody circus.

In *Pursuit,* young revolutionaries who have survived the revolution are reunited again, fittingly in Shanghai. They are searching for something meaningful with which to restart their lives. But whatever they do, they are doomed to fall back into the predestined trap of their environment. Most noticeable is Zhang Qiuliu. A high-spirited, flamboyant woman, Zhang wants to rekindle her political passion by rescuing an old classmate, Shi Xun, from his suicidal tendency. Zhang never succeeds. Shi Xun dies at the end of the novella, not from suicide, but from tuberculosis, while Zhang finds after his death that she has contracted syphilis from him.[16]

Mao Dun: The Politics of Realism

In my previous study on Mao Dun's fiction, I pointed out how Mao Dun disputes the legitimacy of historiography with reference to a newly conceived concept of realism.[17] Yu-shi Chen and Marston Anderson have done their own exegeses of Mao Dun's early fiction.[18] What concerns me here is how the trilogy *Eclipse* ignited the debate among leftist critics regarding the representability of revolution, a debate crucial to the transformation of the *literary revolution* of the May Fourth into the *revolutionary literature* of the 1930s.

After the completion of *Eclipse* in early July 1928, Mao Dun took a ship to Kobe, Japan. By then, his trilogy had already received various criticisms, of which the most vehement were from the radical leftist writers associated with the Creation Society (Chuangzao she) and the Sun Society (Taiyang she).[19] He was faulted with casting a nihilist eye on the revolution, indulging petit bourgeois sentimentalism, and most seriously, resorting to dubious realist aesthetics of distance and noncommitment.

In response to his critics, Mao Dun wrote "Cong Guling dao Dongjing" (From Guling to Tokyo, 1928). In the essay he argued that his characters' romantic exaltation and abjection underscored the complex facets of the revolution and that his role as a writer was to present reality as it was. He highlighted three issues he believed to be integral to revolutionary literature. First, revolutionary literature must hold on to its aesthetic imperative and not devolve into propaganda; second, it should address the issues that most concern its intended readers, the petite bourgeoisie, its goal being to enlighten these readers and convert them to Marxism; third, it should avoid all the tendentious rhetoric originating from "Western formulism, neologism, excessive symbolism, didacticism and propaganda."[20]

Mao Dun's essay soon came under severe attack from critics such as Pan Zinian, Fu Kexing, and Qian Xingcun. Qian Xingcun (1900–1977), the most vociferous among the Sun Society members, wrote a series of essays denouncing Mao Dun's ideological defects, calling him a spokesman for decadent bourgeois literature. In "Cong Dongjing huidao Wuhan" (From Tokyo back to Wuhan, 1928), Qian started his attack with Mao Dun's poem "Farewell." For Qian, the poem is a blatant example of Mao Dun's opportunistic mentality: "In the heyday, when the White Terror was demolishing revolutionary forces, our Mr. Mao Dun was touring the waterfalls in Lushan and chatting about lice with Miss Cloud, completely drenched in the luxury of disillusionment."[21] Moreover, Qian holds that *Eclipse* was written by Mao Dun not as a revolutionary but as someone "on the run," "full of nostalgia" and "morbidities": "morbid characters, morbid thoughts, morbid actions—all are morbid; all are unhealthy."[22] If proletarian literature is an institution that "utilizes language as a weapon, organizes mass consciousness and life, and promotes social trends," argues Qian, Mao Dun must be treated as a traitor.[23]

Qian Xingcun concludes his criticism by calling for a "new realism" *(xin xieshi zhuyi)* or "proletarian realism." For Qian and his fellow critics, this "new realism" has four characteristics: an "objective viewpoint," a "scientific method," a "militant posture," and a subject relevant to proletarian liberation. Its aim is to project the dynamism of revolution and future success rather than mirroring the status quo, which will soon become passé anyway.[24]

As a literary theory, "new realism" was borrowed from the Japanese Marxist Kurahara Korehito, who derived his theory from at least two sources. It was a modification of Fukumotoism, the radical Japanese Communist discourse that promotes the principles of "separation as a way to reorganize party members" and "theoretical struggle."[25] It was also an adaptation of the theory of RAPP (All Russian Association of Proletarian Writers), which aimed to absorb "other cultural organizations, eliminate liberal tendencies in culture and prepare the path for socialist realism."[26] In practice, "new realism" maintains the class nature and propaganda function of proletarian literature, while toning down its inherent exclusivism and dogmatism in favor of a more comprehensive embrace of reality.

Looking back at the fight between Mao Dun and his opponents in the late 1920s, one may view it simply as a squabble over dreadfully tendentious slogans and doctrines. However, close reading reveals a context that is far more complicated. The term "new realism" would have amused Mao Dun, for just a few years earlier, he had been praised for introducing (nineteenth-century European) realism and naturalism to China as something new. Concepts such as "objective viewpoint" and "scientific method" were hailed as the two bases of inscribing reality.[27] Nor was Mao Dun, as a believer in Communist revolution, ignorant of proletarian literature's mandate to arouse mass consciousness and action. What Mao Dun could not agree to was the unmediated equation of revolution and literature. In particular, having become a fiction writer in his own right after 1927, Mao Dun was all the more vigilant about the feasibility of revolutionary literature in terms of production and readership. He thus maintained that the most needed realism was that which best addressed the circumstances of its intended readers—the bourgeoisie. This position was further consolidated in his critique of Ye Shaojun's novel *Ni Huanzhi*.[28]

Qian Xingcun's criticism and Mao Dun's rebuttal point to the equivocal nature of the novel as a revolutionary apparatus. As mentioned above, Mao Dun made it clear that he was driven to write novels as a result of the failure of the 1927 revolution, and that, for him, the novel served as a way of reconciling what should have happened with what did happen. By contrast, Qian Xingcun and his colleagues regarded the novel as a new form of propaganda that anticipated the success of revolution. While Mao Dun may win more of our sympathy owing to his respect for the aesthetic value of literature, however qualified it was, one has to recognize that his viewpoint differed from that of his opponents in degree rather than in kind. For both parties, between the miserable past and the fantastic future, a fold in time had occurred, and it is in that parallel time that the novel was called on to witness the suspension of history and project its fulfillment in the long run. The novel therefore plays a contradictory role. It chronicles the temporal duration in which the revolution has arisen and come to a momentary halt, whereas its existence as such embodies the residual factor that alienates individual talent from collective volition, history from History. The novel is a symptom, or, in Qian Xingcun's word, a sign of "morbidities." How to overcome the historical and narrative incongruity, as symbolized by the appearance of the modern Chinese realist novel, constitutes the core of the debate between Mao Dun and his leftist colleagues.

Mao Dun's dilemma was not specific to him. In a larger context, he carried on the quarrel between Lu Xun and the radical leftists over the direction of revolutionary literature.[29] Lu Xun had taken a serious interest in the relation between literature and revolution since the mid-1920s, but his skeptical nature kept him from endorsing the burgeoning revolutionary literature movement. On April 8, 1927, he made his first open utterance on revolutionary literature at the Whampoa Military Academy, less than a week before

Chiang Kai-shek's coup in Shanghai. In the speech, Lu Xun acknowledged the importance of literature only on the condition that the purpose of revolution first be served. He suggested a three-stage progression regarding literature and revolution: first, a literature protesting social inequalities in the prerevolution days; second, a silent literature during the revolution, as people would all be engaged in revolutionary action; third, a literature of either eulogizing the revolution or bemoaning the past after the success of revolution, in preparation for the rise of the people's literature.

Lu Xun denied that literature could truly propel revolution; instead he held that "for revolution, we need revolutionaries, but revolutionary literature can wait, for only when revolutionaries start writing can there be revolutionary literature."[30] This is a remark typical of Lu Xun's polemical posture. It indicates both his skepticism about literary formulism and his concern about the dialectic between revolutionary writing and revolutionary action. Thus for him literature may as well be silenced in the midst of revolution, when blood, rather than ink, is spilt. As Lu Xun reiterated in "Geming wenxue" (Revolutionary literature) later that year, "There is no revolution when revolutionary writers appear in large numbers."[31]

The literary scene of 1928 proved Lu Xun right: the revolution was at an ebb while revolutionary writers prevailed. These young writers, affiliated either with the Creation Society or with its rival, the Sun Society, campaigned for a shakeup of Chinese literature in the name of proletarian liberation. They sneered at Lu Xun and other like-minded literati for their bourgeois taste and political opportunism. Feng Naichao, for instance, caricatured Lu Xun as a senior citizen longing for the past,[32] Li Chuli likened Lu Xun to Don Quixote, and Qian Xingcun ridiculed Lu Xun as lagging behind his time and announced that "the era of Ah Q has passed."[33] The most devastating charge came from one Du Quan, who labeled Lu Xun a double counterrevolutionary, a feudal remnant, and a fascist. Only recently did we find out that Du Quan was a pseudonym of Guo Moruo (1892–1978).[34]

In view of the attacks Lu Xun endured, it is little surprise that Mao Dun should have become the next target of radical critics. For, like Lu Xun, Mao Dun never hesitated to point out the gap between the theory and the practice of revolutionary literature; his *Eclipse* illustrated everything the Creationists and the Sun Society members were opposed to. While the confrontation among these writers testified to the fanatic sectarianism within leftist circles, more intriguing was the covert interaction among Lu Xun, Mao Dun, their enemies, and the invisible political machine. Scholars have long observed that Lu Xun was not always consistent in his fight against his critics. The latter's charge against him, unfair as it may be, must have deepened his sense of urgency. All along he had been a diligent reader of Soviet literary criticism (via Japanese translations) by such "liberal" Marxists as Leon Trotsky and Aleksandr Voronsky. While battling his critics, he became increasingly convinced of the class nature of art and the imperative of maintaining a united front in proletarian literature. In other words, despite the apparent scuffles, he and his opponents were moving closer together. One of his sources, the Japanese Marxist Kurahara Korehito, was a proponent of "new realism," the canon Qian Xingcun resorted to in denigrating Mao Dun. By the end of 1928, Lu Xun had turned his attention to such "orthodox" Marxist theoreticians as Plekhanov and Lunacharsky, and was ready to embark on his pilgrimage to the far left.[35]

The debate among the literati would not have become so volatile had it not been orchestrated, at least to a certain degree, by the party machine. Critics have called attention to the close ties between the Sun Society and the Communist Party. All the members of the Sun Society were affiliated with the Chinese Communist Party. Qu Qiubai (1899–1935), head secretary of the party at the time, was in charge of the affairs of the Sun Society. With Commitern theoreticians behind him, Qu was able to mobilize a "general intensification of revolutionary policy," as manifested by confrontations on social as well as literary fronts.[36] But the invincible "machine" was set in motion not by the party so much as by the revolutionary writers themselves. As Leo Lee notes, "In the welter of personal scuffles and doctrinal division in the literary circles, the urgent task was to clarify theoretical confusion and forge organizational unity."[37] Hence Guo Moruo's claim (under the pseudonym Mai Keang) in 1928 that revolutionary writers "should do away with their broken bugles—they should serve as a megaphone [to arouse the masses]."[38]

By replacing the "broken bugle" with the "megaphone," Qian Xingcun and Guo Moruo proposed a literary machinery capable of both mystical calls to arms and modern incantations. The megaphone symbolizes a loud, persistent sound capable of drowning out the cacophony of individual revolutionary buglers. The ancient instruments are no match for the mass-produced modern device, which, aware of its historical role, blares away with a single tune. Perhaps with such an understanding, Lu Xun and Mao Dun, among others, decided to tone down their independent theorizing on revolutionary literature. And, under the banner of the united front, they and their opponents joined the Chinese League of Left-Wing Writers, which was formed on March 2, 1930.

Jiang Guangci: The Poetics of Revolutionary Romanticism

One of the key figures in Mao Dun and Lu Xun's skirmishes with the members of the Creation Society and the Sun Society was Jiang Guangci. Jiang Guangci met Mao Dun in 1925, when both were teaching at Shanghai College (Shanghai Daxue), the training school for leftist youth. Even at that time, the two showed conflicting literary concepts despite their shared commitment to Communism. Jiang, then a member of the Creation Society, favored the imperative of "literature for the preliterate," while Mao Dun, a pillar of the Society of Literary Studies (Wenxue Yanjiuhui), upheld the tenet of literature in the service of humanity.[39] The disagreement between the two encapsulated the theoretical confrontation of the two largest literary cliques of the post–May Fourth era. Jiang Guangci also played a subtle role in the last decade of Lu Xun's career. As Guo Moruo noted, at Jiang Guangci and Zheng Boqi's invitation, Lu Xun left Guangzhuo for Shanghai in the fall of 1927, entering the belligerent circles of leftist literature.[40]

Jiang Guangci was among the first recruits of the Chinese Communist Youth League in 1920. In 1921, together with some ten other members, he was sent to study Marxism and revolutionary tactics at the Oriental University in Moscow. It was during this time that he made the acquaintance of Qu Qiubai, who in 1928 became party secretary and the head of the Sun Society. Life in the new Soviet Union was harsh, yet it never affected Jiang's ideological convictions. When he returned to China in early summer 1924, Jiang was a professional revolutionary.

Jiang already showed a strong predilection for literature during his Moscow years. He presented in his poetry collection *Xinmeng* (New dream, 1925) a persona fervently yearning for nation, motherhood, and selfhood, and he gushed over his admiration for such Western romantics as Byron, Pushkin, and Blok.[41] Jiang's first breakthrough came in 1926, with the publication of his semi-autobiographical novel *Shaonian piaopozhe* (The youthful tramp). In a picaresque form, the novel depicts how an orphan survives as a beggar, a robber, an apprentice, and a worker, among others, in a society in deep crisis. This young man finally makes his way to the Whampoa Military Academy, becoming a revolutionary cadet. We are told in the epilogue that he was killed during the antiwarlord campaign in Huizhou.[42]

In May 1927, just two weeks after the fiasco of the Communist insurrection in Shanghai, Jiang wrote *Duanku dang* (Des Sans-culottes, 1928), a roman à clef about party members involved in a failed revolution. The novel is replete with dichotomized moral values, exemplary figures, high-strung rhetoric, and the celebration of a death wish, all in the name of proletarian emancipation. Again, the novel was well received despite its artistic flaws. Together with *The Youthful Tramp, Des Sans-culottes* anticipated the Communist literary discourse of the years to come. Whereas *The Youthful Tramp* transformed the post–May Fourth decadent hero—the melancholy, superfluous loner who dies an untimely death, perfected by writers such as Yu Dafu—into a revolutionary martyr, *Des Sans-culottes* filled out this new revolutionary subjectivity with a melodramatic repertoire.

But Jiang Guangci gained fame, or notoriety, primarily for a series of works that maximized the tension between revolution and romance. In *Yeji* (A sacrifice in the wild, 1927), a young revolutionary literatus, Jixia, is torn between two girls, the beautiful and innocent Yuxian and the plain and independent Shujun. Jixia chooses Yuxian; in disappointment, Shujun entrusts her love to revolution.[43] As the revolution becomes increasingly perilous, Yuxian deserts Jixia; meanwhile, Shujun is arrested and put to death. The climax finds Jixia holding a personal commemoration of Shujun facing the sea and vowing to carry on her unfinished mission.

The novella's plot is hackneyed, but it scores by adding to the love-triangle convention a fourth factor, revolution. Revolution is described as a test of the moral capacities of the young characters. It functions as the absent cause through whose displacement, romance, the young characters negotiate their own libidinous yearnings. Feminists can of course argue about the secondary roles the two women characters play in the service of Jixia's political awakening. The point is nevertheless that revolution and love are invoked as reciprocal terms in the sentimental education of post–May Fourth youth.

The success of *Sacrifice in the Wild* initiated a wave of "revolution plus love" fiction. Ding Ling's *Weihu,* Ba Jin's *Aiqing sanbuqu* (Trilogy of love), Hu Yepin's (1905–1931) *Dao Mosike qu* (Go to Moscow), Bai Wei's *The Bomb and the Expeditionary Bird,* and Mao Dun's *Eclipse,* among others, can all be read in the light of this formula. By 1930, Jiang Guangci was equated with "revolution and love." His *Chongchu yunwei de yueliang* (The moon forces its way through the clouds) went through six printings in a year after its publication in early 1930.[44] The protagonist, Wang Manying, is a girl student who becomes a woman soldier during the revolutionary period. The Communist fiasco in Shanghai shatters her faith and hurls her into the abyss of nihilism. To avenge the failed revolution, she quits the army and becomes a prostitute. "Instead of changing the world, I may as well ruin the world; instead of reforming the world, I may as well destroy humanity."[45] With her body, Wang corrupts one man after another. Meanwhile, she finds she has contracted syphilis.

What made *The Moon Forces Its Way through the Clouds* controversial was its striking analogies between failed revolution and sexual depravity, and between ideological malaise and venereal disease. Seductive *and* destructive, the revolution helps elucidate the "true" object of desire among Wang and her lovers. As Jiang Guangci sees it, when revolution is eclipsed by ressentiment, love degenerates into promiscuity. That Wang Manying contracts syphilis is not a mere medical problem; rather the disease is traceable to her emotional dissipation, which is in turn born of her ideological crisis. A short circuit has occurred in the circulation of revolutionary and romantic desire, releasing powerful currents that corrode not only the individual components of society but also their infrastructure of political hope.

In Mao Dun's *Pursuit,* it will be recalled, the heroine, Zhang Qiuliu, also suffers from syphilis as a result of an affair with fellow revolutionary Shi Xun.

The parallel between the two females' venereal cases will be discussed later. My concern here is that while Mao Dun observes Zhang Qiuliu's fall from a distance, Jiang Guangci feels obliged to intervene in his heroine's degeneration. Thus, midway through the novel, Wang's ex-lover Li Shangzhi comes to her rescue. Ashamed of her disease, Wang at first turns him down and considers suicide. She is nevertheless enlightened by the "primitive power of nature" on her way to death and decides to start life over as a factory worker. Happily, at this moment she learns that her venereal disease was actually a misdiagnosis and that she is therefore again entitled to seek revolution and love.

Critics of Jiang Guangci's time already noticed the forbidden attractions in his works. In 1932, Qu Qiubai criticized the novel *Diquan* (Earth spring) by Hua Han (Yang Hansheng, 1902–1990), Jiang Guangci's colleague and follower, as an example of "revolutionary romanticism" *(geming de langman dike).*[46] For Qu Qiubai, Hua Han had concocted a world of revolution and romance based on self-delusion, allowing his romantic sentiment to mystify reality. Hua Han's problem, as Qu would have it, stems from Jiang Guangci, since Hua Han inherited all the characteristics of Jiang's fiction, from hyperbole to sentimentality.[47]

Mao Dun was also involved in this critique of Jiang. In his essay "Geming yu lian'ai de gongshi" (On the formula of revolution and love, 1935), Mao Dun called attention to the wave of revolution plus love fiction and sarcastically summarized its three formulas. When writers first took up the formula, they often focused on *conflict* between the revolutionary cause and the romantic drive, and they concluded their works with a call to relinquish love for the sake of revolution. Next to this "conflict" formula was the *reciprocation* formula. That is, instead of being an impediment, revolution served to bring forth the true romantic feelings between the revolutionaries. Finally, this reciprocation formula progressed to the *nurturing* formula, which saw love emanating from the comradeship and compassion of revolutionaries. In other words, revolution was no longer the antagonistic factor in one's pursuit of love; revolution was love.[48]

Mao Dun's criticism must lead us to the question: wasn't Mao Dun himself among the practitioners of revolution plus love fiction he attacked? His first two novels, *Eclipse* and *Hong* (Rainbow, 1930), both deal with young men and women's struggle with the ever-entangled relations between revolution and love. When Ms. Jing and Ms. Hui of *Disillusionment* alternate between their pursuit of love and revolution, they remind us of Jiang Guangci's characters, like Jixia in *Sacrifice in the Wild.* And when Zhang Qiuliu tries to cure the postrevolutionary syndrome through carnal games, she behaves like a predecessor of Wang Manying in *The Moon Forces Its Way through the Clouds.*

If Jiang Guangci was culpable for exaggerating the conflict between revolution and love, why shouldn't Mao Dun equally be held responsible for spreading this decadence? Hadn't Qian Xingcun, Jiang Guangci's colleague, already blamed Mao Dun's fiction for depicting nothing but a world of decadent bourgeois love games?

Significantly enough, the revolution and love issue did not concern only leftists. As early as April 1928, *Geming yu lianai* (Revolution and love) was published under the aegis of the Nationalist Party. Its author, Hong Ruizhao, a sociologist and cultural critic, began his study by observing that romantic love had become the most "worrisome problem" within the Nationalist revolutionary campaign. The problem was intensified, as Hong observed, by the boom in literature dealing with "modern-style love": "The conflict between revolutionary fever and romantic passion has become such a serious issue that it demands an immediate solution."[49] Hong then pointed his finger at the Communists affiliated with the Wuhan government, accusing them of promoting a dubious reconciliation between one's romantic instinct and revolutionary commitment. For Hong, although the Communists cautioned the revolutionaries on the harmful consequences of romance, they secretly encouraged sexual desires among revolutionary youth so as to undermine their political convictions. He therefore called for a more engaged Nationalist Revolution, which he believed promised genuine freedom and equality in economy and education, and a total emancipation of the force of love.

Hong Ruizhao's argument, for all its partisan rhetoric, sounds uncannily similar to that of Communist critics. But unlike his leftist colleagues, who mostly resorted to the mandates of Marxian ideology, Hong drew his argument from theories of psychoanalysis and sociology. Citing Sigmund Freud, Auguste Comte, Ellen Key, and Havelock Ellis, among others, Hong acknowledged that love cannot be separated from sexuality, and that individual desires must be addressed in regard to the welfare of the social body at large. He nevertheless suggested that, at a time of national crisis, a strong revolutionary must subordinate his personal yearning to the public good; he must modulate his desires, avoiding the pitfalls of either stoicism or promiscuity, so as to facilitate a successful revolution. "For those who do not wish to be trapped by lack of sexual fulfillment, they had better heighten their desire to a love for truth, good, and beauty, to a love for family, society, and nation, so that they will contribute to academic construction and Nationalist Revolution."[50]

It remains to be discovered whether Mao Dun, Jiang Guangci, and other leftist literati were aware of Hong Ruizhao's *Revolution and Love.* For our purposes, the book provides a unique perspective from which to revisit the quarrel not only between rightists and leftists but also among the leftists themselves. The leftists would have agreed with Hong that romantic love derives its force from the libidinous realm of sexuality, and that it works both as an impetus for and an impediment to revolution. Change the label Hong cited from Nationalist to Communist, and one discerns an almost identical set of syndromes befalling revolutionary youth.

What distinguishes the leftists, however, is their willingness to push the dialectic between love and revolution a step further by deliberating on the agency of literature. Both Mao Dun and Jiang Guangci ground their literary concepts in a pseudoscientific methodology. Mao Dun treats the tension between revolution and love as a sign of social crisis, a generation's pathological incapacity to cope with their predicament. If "weak human beings under the pressure of environment and determinism" are facts of life, argues Mao Dun, a novelist is obliged to present these facts. By contrast, Jiang sees in revolution plus love a coherent agenda through which the revolutionary subjectivity progresses from the domain of eros to that of polis. He endorses the immediate link between the revolutionary imaginary and revolutionary action, and harbors no qualms about turning literature into propaganda. Accordingly, whereas revolution plus love is for Mao Dun a symptom of a larger social malaise, for Jiang Guangci it serves as a treatment for the malaise.

The danger in Mao Dun's brand of realist/naturalist fiction has been much discussed. His exposé may risk demoralizing his intended readers before reassuring them about the future revolution. Moreover, in dwelling on the morbidity of the status quo, Mao Dun tends to betray his own fascination with that which he claims to reject. He thus demonstrates what Marston Anderson calls the "limits of realism": the more he exposes the social predicament, the more he proliferates the problems and thus insinuates, however unwittingly, the impossibility of any reform.[51]

It might be with such a misgiving about the "old" realism that Jiang Guangci labeled his "new realism" one of "simplicity and sincerity." He believed it should provide a "way out" *(chulu)* of Mao Dun's no-exit world. As one of his followers writes, "A way out! A way out! This is the difference between new realism and naturalism. Precisely because the writers are able to observe the society with a proletarian consciousness, there appears such a way out for them. Not only do they depict the symptoms of society, they also prescribe the medicine."[52]

But one finds in Jiang Guangci's approach to revolution and love an equally dangerous, if not more dangerous, problem. When he proffers a program sublimating lovesick revolutionaries' desire for a higher, sacrificial passion for the masses, Jiang at the same time cultivates a romantic solipsism. With the pretext of fusing with the masses, his romantic subjectivity becomes magnified to a cosmic scale. As he proclaims,

> Revolution is art. The true poet cannot help feeling the same grounds he shares with revolution. The poet—the romantic—is more capable of understanding revolution than anybody else! . . . His romantic heart oftentimes crosses the boundaries of ordinary life, demanding to be united with the cosmos. . . . He loves the power and the lightning, the blizzard and the waves of revolution.[53]

Here Jiang describes an almost apocalyptic delirium in the embrace of revolution, through which a poetic transcendence of the mundane rises to a state of supernal ecstasy. "Only the genuine romantic can capture the soul of revolution, and solicit from revolution its magnificent poetry."[54] Action and language are seen as mutually complementary in the blessed moment of writing revolution. Thus he asks, "Is there anything that can be more interesting, and more romantic, than revolution?"[55]

The question has to be asked: did Jiang Guangci's fictional theory and practice really provide a way out for him and his readers? When he tries to yoke together the tenets of "new realism" with his romantic yearnings, Jiang reveals no fewer contradictions than did Mao Dun in dealing with his (old) realism. If "new realism" indicates a literature that subordinates individual talent to proletarian needs and equates historical contingency with historical necessity, Jiang's romantic subject, with its stress on self-expression, creativity, and innate sovereignty, can hardly serve the purpose. Love and poetry cannot always compensate for the cruelties of actual revolution. When he apologizes for the "crudeness and violence" of his fiction, therefore, Jiang might not merely be referring to the paucity of his rhetorical skill. Rather, he might, to his own chagrin, be revealing the inconsistencies that occur when two literary programs, European romanticism and European realism, are brought simultaneously to China.

One also notices that Jiang prefers to define revolutionary literature in terms of poetry rather than fiction. This again brings us to the issue of the feasibility of narrating revolution in the post-1927 era. Striking a typically romantic posture, Jiang sees poetry as the genre that lifts everyday life into a state of imaginative plenitude. He compares revolution to the political actualization of a romantic poet's desire. In practice, however, Jiang found in the novel a form necessitated by historical opportunity: before the poetics of revolution can be made accessible to everyone, narrative is called on to occupy the historical space opened for it. Given his capacity, it became impossible for Jiang to reconcile his rhapsodic celebration of revolution and his narrative account of a reality full of nonrevolutionary or counterrevolutionary elements. Circling through the revolving doors of poetic vision and novelistic vocation, ideological fanaticism and romantic narcissism, Jiang comes out as a revolutionary writer more encumbered by reactionary impulses than his opponent Mao Dun.

In his pioneering study of Jiang Guangci, T. A. Hsia describes him as shallow, sentimental, self-congratulatory, and "romanticism's loudest advocate and its most pathetic caricature."[56] That Jiang Guangci became a popular writer in the late 1920s is a poignant symptom of his times, a moment when earnest readers and writers highlighted "spontaneity" and "frankness" as the gist of progressive literature. For Hsia, Jiang stands at best as "a gigantic 'negative lesson' to the readers of 'revolutionary literature' and its would-be practitioners"; Jiang's "contribution was his failure, and his worth is found in his worthlessness."[57]

Hsia may have underestimated the significance of Jiang Guangci's failure. Compared to Mao Dun, Jiang Guangci is indeed a failure. Few people, including liberal and not-so-liberal leftist critics, read his works nowadays. But "failure" makes better sense applied not to his works particularly, but rather to his unsuccessful struggle to defend those works. In early 1930, in connection with the founding of the League of Left-Wing Writers, Jiang Guangci and his radical colleagues were made to reconcile with erstwhile opponents such as Mao Dun and Lu Xun. Midway through that year, however, Jiang Guangci had become increasingly impatient with the party leadership. He rose up against the party's order that all writers must participate in mass movements. For him, a writer could do his best by churning out propagandist works at home rather than fomenting demonstrations in the streets. For someone who just a couple of years before celebrated the unification of revolutionary writing and revolutionary action, such a recalcitrant attitude was indeed self-contradictory. It indicates that the romantic poet inside Jiang finally refused to yield more ground to the party's single-minded realism.

Vexed by the callous party leadership, Jiang Guangci decided to give up his membership. But no sooner did he submit his statement of resignation than he was expelled by the party as a "traitor."[58] His ten-year "romance" with his party ended in bitter mutual rejection. Jiang Guangci died in the fall of 1931; the attacks on his revolution plus love writings were yet to begin. But where Jiang failed, another poet cum revolutionary would succeed. In 1957, when Mao Zedong decreed that revolutionary romanticism was part of the new literary campaign, he and his cohorts were conjuring Jiang Guangci's ghost. Next to Jiang, who else was more eager, and more ruthless, than Mao in draping the proletarian engine of history with poetic sentiments? But perhaps Jiang Guangci was fortunate to have missed this resurrection of his slogans, because Mao's successful appropriation of romantic décor would soon bring even greater disaster to those who continued to practice literary romanticism.

Bai Wei: The Ethics of Gendered Revolution

Looking back at the debate over revolution plus love, one notices that women played a much less prominent role in it. This is ironic in that the revolution plus love formula highlighted women's emancipation and equal freedom in romance. Writers such as Mao Dun and Jiang Guangci, to be sure, spared no effort in depicting women's romantic and revolutionary pursuits. Mao Dun was particularly acclaimed for his inquiry into female ideological and sexual complexities of the revolution. But as feminist critics have long argued, Mao Dun tended to make an allegory of his gender politics, so as to obscure more pressing issues such as the agency of womanhood vis-à-vis historical crisis.[59] Similar criticism applies to Jiang Guangci's creation of women characters.

The critic Hong Ruizhao may well have summarized a view shared by many male literati, left and right alike:

> Evidence has it that women's thought and behavior are in general subject to the manipulation of emotions, and at least half of their emotional faculties belong to the realm of sexuality. . . . Therefore, it is indeed not an easy matter to expect women to keep firm grounds in revolution and other public activities.[60]

> Particularly those who are of neurotic and melancholy temperament, when in tense emotional circumstances, tend to fail to recognize the nature of their lovers. Aroused by momentary encounters, they throw themselves in the arms of their beloved, . . . ignoring all other works.[61]

It is at this juncture that I would revisit the case of Bai Wei. Bai Wei joined the Wuhan regime in March 1927, as a Japanese translator while moonlighting as a teacher at Sun Yat-sen University. An independent woman revolutionary in appearance, Bai Wei nevertheless kept to herself a life already bearing too many scars. The dark side of Bai Wei found expression in her writings, which best demonstrated the "neurotic and melancholy" style disapproved by her male colleagues. This "neurotic and melancholy" tendency, however, brings one to an aspect of revolution plus love that male writers fail to address.

Bai Wei was the eldest daughter of an enlightened gentry scholar who had participated in the 1911 Republican Revolution. The father's revolutionary principles never benefited his daughter, however. Instead, he forced Bai Wei to marry the only son of a household run by a tyrannical widow. After countless beatings, starvation, sexual abuse, and public humiliation, Bai Wei ran away and took shelter in normal school. One day in the summer of 1918, just when she was about to graduate, Bai Wei found her husband's family members waiting outside the school to take her home. With the assistance of her classmates, she barely made it to Shanghai, later traveling alone to Japan.

In Japan, Bai Wei worked as a maid and waitress until she received a scholarship to study biology at a women's college. It was at this time that she fell in love with Yang Sao, a poet six years her junior. The romance was volatile from the start, and it continued through quarrels, breakups, and reunions in the next decade. In 1925, without any forewarning, Yang Sao left for Southeast Asia, leaving Bai Wei totally devastated. She returned to China in the winter of 1926, and after a short trip home, she went to Wuhan to join the revolutionary government.

Bai Wei's ambivalent feelings toward her father and her lover constitute the two strains of her works. And it is through her continued struggle against and compromise with these two male figures that she comes to terms with the meaning of "woman" and "revolution." After her escape to Japan, Bai Wei found out that her sister had been the next to suffer from an arranged marriage. Infuriated, she wrote more than twenty letters in a few days challenging her father:

> Let me step aside from my position as your daughter and talk to you like a sister to a brother. You have allowed mother to take charge of everything at the cost of your daughters' fate. Is this right? You forced them to marry in such a pathetic way, leading to one tragedy after another. Is this what your conscience is all about? You were once a revolutionary, how could you have done such a thing totally against humanity? . . . Are you entitled to do so simply because we are your daughters?[62]

Amid her father's furious charges that she was a traitor and a "family revolutionary," Bai Wei cut her ties to her family.[63]

Notice how "revolution" serves as a keyword for both father and daughter, sanctifying each other's ethical position. Situated at the juncture of ethical (father versus daughter), gendered (man versus woman), and generational (the old versus the young) trajectories, Bai Wei's "j'accuse" anticipated the quarrels of many leftist women writers, not only with their fathers but also with the paternalistic revolutionary machine. Nevertheless, the intriguing fact in Bai Wei's career is not that she was a radical woman revolutionary, but that she was never a consistent feminist revolutionary. In 1926, when Bai Wei made her first trip home to Hunan since her escape, what she sought most anxiously was her father's forgiveness.[64]

Revolution and the (indecisive) disavowal of patriarchy form an intertwined polemic in Bai Wei's early works. I discussed in Chapter 2 Bai Wei's *Fight out of the Ghost Tower,* a play saturated with incest, rape, oppression, and murder, ending with the father and daughter killing one another. As if trying to balance the moribund obsessions of *The Ghost Tower,* Bai Wei wrote *Geming shen shounan* (The revolutionary god is in danger) in 1928.[65] The play foregrounds a girl's heroic combat, with the assistance of supernatural powers, against a monstrous general who had just crushed a revolution. Bai Wei frames her feminist idealism in a fantastic context, dreaming of a revolution carried out by superwomen. Nevertheless, as its title suggests, at the center of the play is the revolutionary god in danger, and this god is also our heroine's father. The daughter's rebellion thus becomes a contradictory task, indicating as much a defiance of the patriarchal force in the political world as a longing for its return in the familial realm.

Just as it brought an ambiguous solution to Bai Wei's encounter with paternal power, revolution serves as a dubious deus ex machina when her romance reaches a dead end. As her confessional novel *Beiju shengya* (My tragic life, 1936) notes, Bai Wei turned to revolution after Yang Sao's first betrayal. In her dialectic of desire, frustrated romantic yearning and an unfulfilled revolutionary mandate become interchangeable entities. When she discovers that she has been deserted by Yang Sao, she exclaims:

> Humanity loses its heart, and the universe is in chaos. I can no longer stand the blows of a stormy life. I am going crazy. I felt suffocated, I wept, I jumped, I wanted to die. Death, no! I want to declare war against all the evils in the world. I want revolution![66]

Both leftist and rightist critics of her time might have sneered at Bai Wei's easy enactment of her erotic and political capacities. A critic like Qian Xingcun might have concluded that Bai Wei behaved just like those jaded bourgeois women in Mao Dun's fiction who found in revolution a substitute for lost objects of love. Judged by Hong Ruizhao's analysis, Bai Wei serves as a perfect illustration of women revolutionaries' changeable, "neurotic and melancholy" inclinations. From her vantage point, however, Bai Wei could have retorted: what is revolution if not an action propelled by one's innermost desire to break through established boundaries? What is revolutionary literature if it cannot mediate between one's yearning for bodily fulfillment and one's aspiration for the public good?

We therefore turn to this question: how "realistic" can a realist novel be in regard to a young woman writer's search for a truthful representation of revolution and love? Bai Wei's life/story reminds us of female characters under Mao Dun's pen. But where Mao Dun creates an allegory of woman's desire and political commitment, Bai Wei substitutes an exposé of female suffering and its failed political redemption. On the other hand, Bai Wei sounds like Jiang Guangci when cultivating an autobiographical alter ego and declaiming fanatical lines, such as

> I want to dedicate my life to revolution! My hot revolutionary blood can no longer be cooled. The fire of revolution is burning in my heart. . . . I just can-

not wait to fly to Canton, to learn the skills of riding, shooting, and fighting in the front ranks.[67]

Nevertheless, whereas one can talk about Jiang Guangci's sublation of revolutionary desire from an erotic dimension to an ideological dimension, one can hardly find such optimism in Bai Wei's writing. Instead, she and her characters are seen as cast into a labyrinth of desire, revolutionary or not, searching fruitlessly for ways out.

Between conventional realism and "new realism," championed respectively by Mao Dun and Jiang Guangci, Bai Wei's works represent an (unwelcome) alternative. This does not merely mean that her feminist stance lends a gendered perspective to the revolution plus love formula. She goes far beyond this. As if mixing Mao Dun's allegorical maneuvering and Jiang Guangci's confessional impulse, Bai Wei creates a narrative that questions the realist repertoire her male colleagues inherited. On the one hand, her works cut into the nightmarish fear and fantasy shared by revolutionary youth, so haunting as to be denied by many. On the other, her works appear to have laid bare subjects so raw as to offend the decorum of verisimilitude. Either way her writings manifest a wide range of affective responses—from neurosis to catharsis, and from paranoia to euphoria—according to the revolutionary circumstances.

Take, for example, Bai Wei's poetic drama *Linli* (1926). In the play, two sisters, Linli and Lili, are involved in a rivalry for the love of a young musician, Qinlan. Linli first captures Qinlan's heart, but her sister, a more passionate girl, soon wins the upper hand. Qinlan hesitates between the two girls until he finds that Lili is pregnant with their child. In despair, Linli commits suicide by drowning herself. Soon after her death, Qinlan's body is found ripped to shreds by a trio of chimpanzees.

The play's dialogue is rendered in poetic language, which, together with the highly expressionist stage directions, calls forth an eerie, dreamlike effect. That the goddesses of Flower, Time, and Death intervene in the love triangle and the unfaithful Qinlan is killed by chimpanzees further emphasizes the fantastic element of Bai Wei's dramaturgy. But for those who are familiar with Bai Wei's biography, *Linli* is all too personal a testimony. Bai Wei completed the play in 1925, after chasing Yang Sao back to Hangzhou following a breakup. The two competing sisters may refer to Bai Wei and another woman who fell in love with Yang Sao at the same time; they could equally be the double projection of a Bai Wei torn between conflicting virtue and desire. The two sisters alternate in singing their desperate need to love and communicate, while the play, propelled by irresistible death wishes, moves toward the bloody spectacle of its ending.

With contrived plot, hysterical characterization, and convoluted rhetoric,

Bai Wei's style has often been regarded as a failed attempt to grasp the real. But insofar as realism is still just a narrative artifice that negatively projects (male) writers' unrealized desire for revolution and romance, Bai Wei's arguable failure to render a more "realistic" writing is significant.

Stephen Chan once used the term "discourse of despair" to describe the aesthetic and ideological dilemmas of post–May Fourth realism. Often associated with the character of a "new woman" in crisis, the discourse of despair indicates "the specific tendency in literary discourse to deal with the extinction of hope, the utter loss of the will to discourse, and the disbelief in action and ideas of any positive value."[68] Bai Wei's "realism," therefore, may point to a narrative stance of "despair" twice removed from the position occupied by her male colleagues. Or, more poignantly, it may indicate a grammatology of her own, which defies any truth-claims, including the truthful representation of reality.

In 1928, Bai Wei published her first full-length novel, *The Bomb and the Expeditionary Bird.* The title refers to the nicknames of two sisters of contradictory temperaments, Yu Yue and Yu Bin, both runaways from arranged marriages and both involved in the Wuhan coalition. Bai Wei must have based her story on firsthand observation of the Wuhan government. Yue's unhappy marriage, lonely adventures, and political fanaticism all find identical imprints in Bai Wei's own life. Sensuous and opportunistic, Bin is contrasted to her sister, who represents the decadent inclination of select women revolutionaries. While in Guangzhou, Yue had a brief romance with a young officer, Shaofang. Now in Wuhan, Yue is amazed at her sister Bin's skill in the sport of love, but the real shock comes as she finds out that one of Bin's lovers, Shifu, is her old sweetheart Shaofang in guise! Yue never knows why Shifu has assumed a different identity in Wuhan; rumors are that he is acting as an agent for the "reactionary party."

While its aesthetic merits remain debatable, *The Bomb and the Expeditionary Bird* teaches us something neither Mao Dun nor Jiang Guangci understands. In appearance, Yue is portrayed like a model revolutionary who forsakes love at the call of revolution. But when called by duty, she utilizes her body in a special mission for the party. In contrast, her sister, Bin, lets her sensual instincts override her political volition. Close reading reveals that the two characters do not conflict so much as represent two distinct responses to revolutionary power. For all her sacrifices, Yue is not blind to the fact that the revolutionary government is full of corruption and chaos. Bin, on the other hand, becomes indifferent to revolution only after realizing that women play no role in the revolution other than that of sexual stimulus for revolutionary men. Between a degenerate political campaign and a degenerate love game, the two sisters' different choices lead to the same outcome.

Bai Wei moves us more when she features not the illusory nature of revolution as such but the tenacity of women revolutionaries holding onto the revolution despite its illusoriness. There seems to be something addictive in revolution plus love that disables the women revolutionaries' capacity to judge, all the while inducing them to dwell on what they have gained, or lost. This is a "discourse of despair" at its most polemical. Jianmei Liu points out that "Bai Wei's rewriting of 'revolution and love' shows a frantic interest in imitating the same fashion, yet her suspicious attitude interrogates the whole mutual identification and empathy of love and revolutionary discourse. By questioning both love's and revolution's power over women, she actually challenges the formula [of revolution and love] itself, reducing the myth of love and revolution to an empty alternation of performance."[69] In other words, Bai Wei is interested in dealing with something more "existential" than that promised by revolution and romance. It is this deep-seated disquiet that hollows out the plentitude and rationality implied in the formula of realism, conventional or new. And it is this disquiet that drives Bai Wei to seek a gendered ethic and rhetoric during the revolutionary time, however futilely. Hence the title *The Bomb and the Expeditionary Bird,* which suggests the explosive force of revolution as opposed to the trial of romantic longing of any sort.

THE LOVE STORIES

The more intense the revolution appears, the more immense the romantic heart becomes.

JIANG GUANGCI

In the last section I discussed the rise of revolution plus love fiction as a literary syndrome in the aftermath of the 1927 Communist Revolution. With Mao Dun, Jiang Guangci, and Bai Wei as my points of departure, I delineated the discursive network through which writers and critics tried to figure out the ideological and emotive consequences of the revolution. In this section, I move my survey in a different direction. In addition to discussing their theoretical treatises and fictional works, I argue that the love stories of Mao Dun, Jiang Guangci, and Bai Wei "in reality" complement as well as undercut their discursive endeavors. Revolution and romance were not constituted merely in imagined fiction, they were consubstantiated in lived intention. Only through the act of reading lives as willed fictions and fictions as imagined lives can one understand the meanings of "revolution" and "love" in modern Chinese literary history.

With this in mind, we revisit Mao Dun's world in 1928. Mao Dun finished *Eclipse* in April of that year. Hard work and perilous political circumstances had greatly affected his health. At a friend's suggestion, Mao Dun took a boat trip to Japan in July. On board was a woman passenger whose true identity has only recently been revealed. The woman was Qin Dejun (1905–1993). The two quickly fell in love and, in the next two years in Japan, they lived as a couple despite the fact that Mao Dun was still legally married and Qin Dejun had yet to divorce her estranged husband.[70]

In his autobiography and almost all other accounts of his life, we are left with the impression that Mao Dun spent his Japan days by himself.[71] That he and his biographers "forgot" this romance does not surprise us. Since the 1940s, Chinese Communist revolutionary discourse has become ever more vigilant about suppressing unsuitable romantic elements. The affair between Mao Dun and Qin Dejun must have been deemed politically inappropriate by both the master and his biographers, and the figure of Qin Dejun was airbrushed out of the scenes from Japan.

The affair is significant to us, however, because it happened at a turning point in Mao Dun's career. More importantly, the way Mao Dun dealt with the affair dramatizes the impossibilities of writing revolution and love in terms of the realism of the time.

Mao Dun and Qin Dejun: Love As Betrayal

Up until the summer of 1928, Mao Dun had remained a faithful married man, though works such as "Farewell" seem to imply certain extramarital excursions. He married Kong Dezhi (1897–1969) in 1918 at his mother's request. Although she came from a small merchant's family, Kong Dezhi had been denied access to education; she was illiterate before marrying Mao Dun.[72] Unlike many of his peers, Mao Dun accepted the arranged marriage and tried to make the best of it. He taught Kong and introduced her to the world of Communist revolution. In his early essays on feminine issues, he maintained that enlightened men are obligated to enlighten their underprivileged spouses; instead of divorce, education might well be a way to improve marriage.[73] His first short story, "Chuangzao" (Creation, 1930), deals with the Pygmalion theme, recounting a male intellectual's effort to educate his wife and his fear of falling victim to his new creation.[74]

But there must have been an unfulfilled desire gnawing at Mao Dun when he wrote about liberated women in *Eclipse.* Although Kong Dezhi became more and more involved in revolutionary activities, she was basically a traditional woman with a strong personality. Thus, when Mao Dun had a chance to travel with a woman like Qin Dejun, he was understandably overwhelmed by her charm and most unusual life.

Mao Dun had met Qin in 1922, but he did not learn of her background until they were on the trip to Japan. The illegitimate daughter of a rich man in Sichuan, Qin Dejun grew up an independent girl. When the May Fourth Movement broke out in Chengdu, she was among the first three female students to bob their hair. Through student movements, she came to know Mu Jibo and Liu Bojian (1895–1935). Mu followed Qin to Chongqing after her expulsion from school and raped her one night. Barely fifteen, Qin was ashamed of her violation and tried to commit suicide, only to be rescued and sent to Wuhan. After a period of intensive travel, Qin enrolled as a high school student in Shanghai; meanwhile Mu Jibo had come to Shanghai, and the two were reconciled. The couple led a very unstable life in 1921 and 1922. During this period, Qin gave birth to two children while becoming ever more engaged in the leftist-feminist movement. She joined the Communist Party in 1923.[75]

Qin Dejun seemed to have undergone experiences that would have taken many women half a lifetime, but she was only turning eighteen. If one considers her teen years melodramatic, more was to come. In 1925, Qin was assigned to conduct underground work in Xi'an. There she again encountered Liu Bojian, who had just returned from the Soviet Union and become a military officer. The two fell in love despite the fact that Qin was still married and Liu was engaged to another woman, an engagement Qin had arranged. As their romantic and revolutionary companionship reached a new high point, Qin Dejun deserted her two children and husband and joined Liu's antiwarlord expedition. Both were in Wuhan when the coalition government fell, and Qin Dejun was pregnant with Liu's child. Liu Bojian later took part in the Nanchang Uprising, which Mao Dun missed.[76]

In November 1927, Qin Dejun gave birth to a girl in Wuhan. With her newborn daughter, she traveled in the spring of 1928 from Wuhan to Nanjing, but her connection had been taken into custody and the secret police were waiting for her. In haste, she left her daughter with a friend and fled to Shanghai alone. When she embarked on the ship to Japan, she had planned to transfer from there to the Soviet Union, but her encounter with Mao Dun changed her revolutionary itinerary.[77]

I summarize Qin Dejun's story at length because, except for select Japanese and Chinese scholars, her life has remained obscure to general readers.[78] In the first decade of Chinese Communist history, Qin Dejun acted out a woman revolutionary's fate at its most dramatic. But she has been denied entrance to the pantheon of virtuous women Communists, due no doubt to her checkered life. In 1928, however, Mao Dun was enchanted by this woman who, at twenty-three, had been through affairs with two men and borne them three children, while still maintaining her personal independence and dynamism. Presumably inspired by Qin's first romance and suicide attempt, Mao Dun wrote "Zisha" (Suicide), in which a young girl kills herself after her boyfriend, a revolutionary, leaves her on a mission and she finds she is pregnant. For the next two years, Qin continued to play Mao

Dun's muse, inspiring him to write criticism and fiction, including his second novel, *Hong* (Rainbow).[79]

Qin Dejun inadvertently stepped into a crucial role in Mao Dun's debate with the radical leftist writers over realism and revolutionary literature. In "From Guling to Tokyo," Mao Dun conceded the decadent inclination in his works and vowed to renew himself:

> I have decided to change my life and reinvigorate my spirits.
>
> I am already doing so. I hope I will rise up and not fall listless; I believe I can do so. The second of the Scandinavian goddesses of fate solemnly stands before me, encouraging and guiding me to march forward. Her eternally struggling spirit draws me forward. . . . The pessimism and despondency in *Pursuit* has been swept away by the ocean breeze. Now I have a courageous Scandinavian goddess of fate as my guiding force.[80]

In his autobiography, Mao Dun took pains to explain the mythological origin of the Scandinavian goddess of fate and her impact on his literary and political vision. Not only did she symbolize perseverance and courage, virtues a dejected revolutionary needed most, but she also embodied the attraction of the Soviet Union.[81] What Mao Dun did not mention is that in reality his newly found goddess of fate was Qin Dejun, a fact known to many of their friends in Japan.[82]

Qin Dejun's entrance into Mao Dun's literary world is of more than anecdotal interest. She was so taken in by her beloved's career that she even joined the dispute over *Eclipse.* Her literary debut was an essay on the woman character Zhang Qiuliu of *Pursuit.* Zhang Qiuliu continues the fight when most of her friends suffer from postrevolution disillusionment. Qin Dejun may have found many similarities between this woman character and herself. Under the pseudonym Xinyi, she wrote "*Zhuiqiu zhongde* Zhang Qiuliu" (Zhang Qiuliu in *Pursuit*), in which she held that Zhang Qiuliu, despite all her bourgeois defects, is commendable for defying the limitations of her class inheritance. Zhang may appear self-indulgent and addicted to sensuous pleasures, argues Qin, but deep inside she has always struggled to redefine her political stance.[83]

Even decades later, Qin Dejun relished her role as the Zhang Qiuliu–like woman who reinvigorated Mao Dun's life with her vitality and sensuousness. She came into Mao Dun's life to enact what he had dreamed of in his fiction. Indeed, at this time Mao Dun and Qin Dejun found in their cohabitation an ideal union between revolution and romance, so much so that they even entertained the thought of going to Moscow together. For a while, Mao Dun wanted to write a novel with Qin Dejun as his model, but he was eventually persuaded to create a composite character based on the life of Qin Dejun and her equally adventurous friend, Hu Lanqi (1900–1995).[84]

The result was *Rainbow.* A novel tracing a young woman's growing sexual and political awareness during the period from the May Fourth to the May Thirtieth Incident, *Rainbow* appeared as a landmark piece in modern Chinese literature. Its heroine, Mei, a rebellious and sensuous woman, bears a clear resemblance to Qin Dejun. In the wake of the controversy over the ideological shortcomings of *Eclipse*, *Rainbow* indicated Mao Dun's adaptation to his leftist peers' demand that fiction resonate with a political agenda. Mei is portrayed as struggling amid the forces of arranged marriage and sexual liberation, bourgeois habits and revolutionary calls, all the while keeping to her search for ideological truth. The novel culminates in Mei's joining the May Thirtieth mass rally against the imperialist invasion, her romantic yearning suspended in deference to her patriotic passion.

Whereas *Rainbow* dramatized the delicate balance of revolution and love as Mao Dun imagined it, the scenario of his lived experience took a different turn at this time. In the summer of 1929, just when his writing of *Rainbow* was half done, Mao Dun learned that Qin Dejun was pregnant. By then, their affair had reached the ears of Kong Dezhi in Shanghai. Outraged, Kong retaliated by spreading the news of her husband's infidelity among friends, maltreating their children, and demanding a divorce on terms so harsh that Mao Dun was unable to accept. In late July, Qin Dejun agreed to go back to Shanghai, have an abortion, and test the winds on both the political and domestic fronts. Upon Qin's return to Japan, Mao Dun might still have harbored some hope that he could divorce Kong and start a new marriage, but he obviously was no longer so certain. Qin Dejun's revolutionary bearing made her a model new woman, but in daily life it translated into a resolute and feisty personality, quite unlike Mao Dun. What ended their romance was politics. Starting in late 1929, the Japanese government launched a series of crackdowns on exiled Chinese Communists; under this mounting pressure Mao Dun and Qin Dejun, among many other leftists, were forced to leave. The couple returned to Shanghai in early April 1930.

The love story was now approaching its end, still charged with drama. Back in Shanghai, Mao Dun continued to live with Qin Dejun, but the "reality" he was so good at capturing in fiction became uncontrollable in real life. He had to deal with problems from at least four sources: Kong Dezhi's irrational divorce proposal; the support of his children and his mother; continued pressure from the Nationalist secret police; and, most cumbersome, the Communist Party's suspicion of his loyalty. It had been two years since his "loss of contact" with the party, and he had yet to provide a strong excuse for his behavior. Adding to these problems was Mao Dun's sentimental and reconciliatory character and his frail health.[85] All along he had been troubled by insomnia and other diseases.

The last straw came when Mao Dun found that Qin was pregnant with their second child. He negotiated with Qin Dejun, asking her to have another abortion and to allow him four years to settle his divorce problem; he needed the time to write and earn royalties to pay off Kong Dezhi. Qin agreed. But after having the abortion, she came back to the apartment she shared with Mao Dun to find that Mao Dun had moved out for good. The "Scandinavian goddess of fate" failed to foresee her own fate.

In *Vacillation,* the second part of his trilogy, *Eclipse,* Mao Dun describes Fang Luolan as trapped between the leftist and rightist wings of the Wuhan government, between revolutionary causes and local interests, and between his wife and his lover. Little could he have imagined that in two years he would find himself in a situation even more awkward than his character's. The early 1930s found Mao Dun torn between his shrewish wife and his demanding lover, and between his desire to carry on his literary career and his fear of deepening the party's suspicion of him as a traitor. The master of Chinese naturalism/realism seemed to have fallen prey to the environment and heredity many of his characters managed to escape. Meanwhile, thanks to the success of *Rainbow,* Mao Dun's position as the leading practitioner of modern Chinese realism became more solid than ever. He joined the newly founded League of Left-Wing Writers and made peace with erstwhile opponents such as Jiang Guangci and Qian Xingcun. Most significantly, having barely settled his real-life troubles with revolution plus love, he was more ready than ever to critique the shortcomings of revolution plus love fiction by Jiang Guangci and Hua Han.

I recount Mao Dun's love affair not for the purpose of exposé, still less as a moral indictment. The material I have drawn on comes largely from Qin Dejun's reminiscences, and they may be biased. Still, I suggest that this love affair, so cliché-ridden and yet so *realistic,* encapsulates the circulation of the textual and extratextual powers of revolution plus love discourse. For progressive readers and writers, revolution plus love functioned both as a literary trope, titillating and sustaining a society's desire for self-reform, and as a political mandate, calling for the redisposition of the social body in both public and personal spheres. Mao Dun's case, however, manifests how a writer tried to actualize the literary trope and the political mandate in words as well as in the world, only to reveal an elusive property that was not so obvious in the fiction.

This *maodun,* or contradiction, constituted the motivation for, rather than an impediment to, the proliferation of the realist novel at this time. Mao Dun understood well the tenets of the realist novel in Tolstoy and Zola's tradition: to pin down the fluidity of life, lend a form to that which otherwise runs amorphously, and name a (political) desire for plenitude. But one wonders, as he was struggling through the Scylla and Charybdis of his own life, if he ever had second thoughts about the theoretical claims made on behalf of the genre. With his own thwarted revolutionary and romantic experiences, Mao Dun may have come to realize earlier than others that realism has so many triumphs because it instantiates the fluidity of life, reveals the contingencies behind any effort to re-form life, and sustains a desire whose fulfillment conveniently recedes as soon as it comes clearly into view.

The gap that appeared within Mao Dun's practice of revolution and love continued to widen in the 1930s, when he churned out one realist piece after another, ranging from the "Village Trilogy" to *Ziye* (Midnight). He had been reunited with Kong Dezhi, but deep inside he could not have forgotten the scars he had left on Qin Dejun. He may have learned from friends that, right after he left her, Qin tried to end her life (by taking all the sleeping pills he had left behind) and that she had a hard time reestablishing her revolutionary career. On her side, Qin never forgot Mao Dun's promise to marry her in four years. In 1932, she published an essay in Sichuan, reminding Mao Dun of his promise. This essay was soon reprinted in a Shanghai tabloid. The revolution plus love Mao Dun once so cherished had now come full circle, returning to its roots in prurience and ressentiment.[86]

In 1941, with the Second Sino-Japanese War becoming ever more tense, Mao Dun published *Fushi* (Putrefaction), a novel based allegedly on a Nationalist woman spy's confession. In her diary, this woman spy, Zhao Huiming, indicates that she participated in the Nationalist network not because of her political commitment so much as her desire to avenge her unhappy family life and her impregnation and desertion by an irresponsible man. Zhao's hardest assignment comes when she is ordered to investigate a Communist leader, who turns out to be her first love. Vacillating between the classical dilemma of love and duty, Zhao fails both.

Mao Dun claimed that *Putrefaction* was motivated by the Nationalist attack on the New Fourth Army in 1941.[87] Its plot nevertheless tells otherwise. It sounds like a twisted version of Mao Dun's affair with Qin Dejun, so much so that Bai Wei (!), upon reading the novel, rushed to check with her friend Qin Dejun about its validity.[88] Before starting the novel, Mao Dun had learned that Qin Dejun had married two more times after their breakup, and that her current husband was the high-ranking Nationalist military officer Guo Chuntao (1898–1950). Qin Dejun's reemergence in the high society of the wartime capital, Chongqing, must have stunned Mao Dun. From Communist revolutionary to Nationalist socialite, her metamorphosis left too many riddles for Mao Dun to resolve. Mao Dun made *Putrefaction* a spy novel for good reason. What other formula, with its presumptions of endless cheating, espionage, and betrayal, could explain, and explain away, all the intricacies of human destiny? But one has to ask: is the novel Mao Dun's paranoid fantasy or wish fulfillment? Is it Mao Dun's autobiographical alibi or a fictional confession?

The novel's diary part begins:

> The greatest pain I have felt recently is that I cannot find a person to speak to. My mind is full of things to be let out, but I cannot find the right person so that I can pour out what I have in mind. . . . My memories . . . make me unable to forget my past. These memories suck my blood like poisonous snakes, driving me to the verge of nervous breakdown.[89]

Through a novel about betrayal, Mao Dun played with his own politics of betrayal. "To betray" means both to turn back on a cause (ideology, party, love, contract, etc.) and to reveal unknowingly what would otherwise be concealed. This is, of course, a double-edged tactic, for in seemingly laying bare the fact, Mao Dun sets in motion endless guesswork of intention and its representation. In any case, with a novel such as *Putrefaction,* the revolution plus love formula has exhausted its utopian potential, and Mao Dun's realism has become a literary recipe erasing instead of revealing the truth.

Jiang Guangci and Song Ruoyu: Love As Sickness

We now turn to Jiang Guangci, the progenitor of revolution plus love fiction and Mao Dun's vehement critic. Judged by the passion he injected into his literary and political writings, one may assume that in personal life Jiang must have been equally susceptible to romantic stimuli. Byron and Pushkin, two of Jiang's models, were known for their supreme capacities at both works of poetry and games of love.

True, Jiang Guangci resisted the marriage arranged by his parents and proceeded to engage in "free love." But this was a common practice in the post–May Fourth days. What makes Jiang so different is that given his desire to revolt, love, and write, his love story comes across as surprisingly simple, at least when compared with other famous pairs of his time, such as Mao Dun and Qin Dejun, Yu Dafu and Wang Yingxia, or Xu Zhimo and Lu Xiaoman. The simplicity of Jiang Guangci's love story is deceptive, however, for it contains a passion that points to the other extreme of the dialectic of revolution and love.

Unlike Mao Dun, who found himself entangled in twisted transactions of revolution and love, Jiang Guangci fell in love because of revolution. His political consciousness and sexual awakening seemed to bloom simultaneously and to complement each other till the end of his life. As he proclaims, "The more intense the revolution appears, the more immense the romantic heart becomes."[90] In 1920, while still a high school student, Jiang Guangci was already a famous name among the new youth in central China. His poem on Li Chao—the young woman who was immortalized by Hu Shi owing to her death in a protest against feudal family pressure—reached a girl student in Henan Province, Song Ruoyu (1903–1926). Song was so moved by the poem that she wrote Jiang to express her admiration. Jiang responded warmly and yet, because of his preoccupation with revolution, it took him three more years to reciprocate Song's good will. Not until 1924 did Jiang send Song a second letter, from far-off Moscow, pouring out his patriotism, loneliness, and need for love. Hence the beginning of the voluminous exchange of love letters between the two.[91]

Critics have often called attention to the narcissistic inclination in Jiang Guangci's work and life. As Leo Lee suggests, "It was on the basis of this ideal that he managed to win the heart of [Song Ruoyu]: feminine adulation embellishes a poet's life and inspires his poetic imagination; love springs from his own self-love."[92] Lee never pursues the other half of the love story, however. Evidence indicates that Song Ruoyu was never a mere sounding board for Jiang's calls for love. Song took the initiative in writing to Jiang and, later on, despite her failing health as a result of tuberculosis, traveled to Shanghai to marry him. Read their correspondence, and one realizes that Song was a woman as passionate as Jiang. And as far as narcissism is concerned, Song Ruoyu showed no less a need for love to complete her own romantic self-esteem. Perhaps because the two loved each other, nay, themselves, too much, they were able to create, and sustain, through letters, their own image as well the image of a beloved other. Correspondence enabled them elaborate feelings at an intimate pitch while keeping the real person at a hygienically safe distance.

Jiang Guangci's romantic and revolutionary passion could not be consummated without bringing with it its malignant traditional counterpart, tuberculosis, the "romantic disease." In the summer of 1925, almost five years after their initial exchange of letters, Jiang Guangci and Song Ruoyu met in Peking for the first time, and they soon decided to get married despite their families' opposition. But one dark factor loomed. Song Ruoyu's tuberculosis was worsening rapidly. Jiang was well aware of the danger of the disease, yet he was determined to risk his luck.

We need not belabor the romantic implication of tuberculosis in both Western and Chinese literature. Its contagious nature and vicious symptoms, coupled with its alleged side-effect of sexual arousal, have long been associated with the romantic invocation of love and death. At the outbreak of the disease, libidinous consummation and physical consumption are seen as inseparable. Tuberculosis, however, partakes of an additional implication in Jiang's case. When they plunged into the fatal last step of their epistolary romance, Jiang Guangci and Song Ruoyu did not only recapitulate the classical paragon of love and death; they also achieved a new kind of martyrdom.

Jiang and Song were married in mid-August 1926 in Shanghai. One month after their marriage, Song's disease could no longer be controlled. She was hurried to Guling, the summer resort Mao Dun would visit the following year, for treatment and rest, and she died there in early November. Worse, after Song's death, Jiang found he had contracted the disease from his wife.

One year after Song Ruoyu's death, Jiang brought their love letters to his friend Wang Mengzou, tearfully offering to burn them in memory of his wife. Wang, who worked for the East Asia Bookstore, persuaded Jiang to publish the letters in a collection called *Jinianbei* (Monument).[93] On the second anniversary of Song Ruoyu's death (November 1928), Jiang wrote a long poem entitled "Guling yihen"(Everlasting regrets in Guling):

> Amid the peaks of the cloudy Lushan,
> There is a lonely, quiet tomb,
> Wherein she lies eternally—
> My beloved who unfortunately died so soon.
>
> Let me live the rest of my life all by myself,
> Keeping only my memories of you.
> For the sake of remembering you,
> Let me keep my oath as a revolutionary poet forever.[94]

The symbolic connection between disease and Chinese modern imaginary has become a popular topic in recent years. Huang Ziping, Su Wei, Andrew Schonebaum, Xiaobing Tang, and others have all called attention to the poetics of disease as a key to the politics of national etiology.[95] In one way or the other, they echo Karatani Kojin's study of disease and the rise of Japanese literary modernity. Karatani observes the metaphorical use of sickness in the formation of modern Japanese national consciousness. Because of the institutionalization of the Western medicinal episteme and its practice, argues Karatani, a disease like tuberculosis was "discovered" as both an index to an emerging interiority and an indictment of the ailing national body.[96] In the Chinese context, before Jiang Guangci came along, Zeng Pu, Lu Xun, and Yu Dafu had already described disease, particularly tuberculosis, as symptomatic of national weakness. Implied in their critique of the weak Chinese body is a shared desire for a national subjectivity free of malaise.[97]

Accordingly, Jiang Guangci's tuberculosis invokes a reading along the lines of vintage romantic pathology and modern revolutionary body politics. All along, Jiang had yearned for an immaculate form of self-expression that might facilitate dialogue between poetry and politics, love and revolution. Then tuberculosis crept into his world. The disease cut short his marriage, weakened his health, and might be thought to contradict idealized images of revolutionary heroism and romantic passion. But if one can sacrifice oneself for revolution or for love, why not sacrifice oneself for "revolution and love" in one grand romantic gesture? Dying sadly of *the* romantic disease adds to an ongoing revolution a medical pathos, endowing revolutionary heroes and heroines with a grotesque glory, as they cough out their spirits in the noblest of causes. A heroism of the absurd was thus made manifest, as disease and death were laid bare as modes of revolutionary happiness. Jiang Guangci in this way dramatizes the inherent contradiction—or complicity—between the modern romantic body of self-consumption and the Communist vision of somatic solidarity.

One witnesses a swift exchange between love, revolution, disease, and writing in Jiang Guangci's life between 1925 and 1927, the heyday of the First Communist Revolution. When he threw himself into the romantic vortex with Song Ruoyu, Jiang was at the same time busy with revolutionary literary activities. He had joined the Communist Party just two months before meeting Song Ruoyu in the summer of 1925, and his first novel, *The Youthful Tramp,* was published later that year. Meanwhile, he was increasingly involved in students' and workers' activities in Shanghai. He completed his collection of short stories *Yalu jiangshang* (On the Yalu River) by the bedside of his dying wife in the fall of 1926; a couple of months after Song's death, he published his poetry collection *Ai zhongguo* (Lamenting China). Jiang finished *Des Sans-culottes* on the eve of the Shanghai massacre, and the novel was published on the same date as his love letter collection *Monument* in late 1927. It was also at this time Jiang met with Lu Xun to discuss the revival of the *Creation Weekly,* while he, Meng Chao, Yang Cunren, and others were working on the inaugural issue of *Taiyang yuekan* (Sun monthly).

Jiang's career took a new turn in 1928. With the founding of the Sun Society and *Sun Monthly,* he became the spokesman for the radical leftist front, in opposition to people like Mao Dun and Lu Xun. As if fully aware of the parallel between his love for Song Ruoyu and his love of the revolution, he set to work doubly hard for leftist causes, and his health deteriorated rapidly. So much so that in the summer of 1929 he had to quit work and travel to Japan for a rest. Even then, he never stopped writing. His bestseller, *The Moon That Breaks through the Clouds,* was finished at this time. As Jiang's ideological fever carried him further and further from the party line, the disease bequeathed to him by his beloved wife was consuming the last strength of his body.

In early 1930, Jiang Guangci fell in love with a young girl student-turned-actress Wu Sihong, and they soon married. But before their honeymoon was over, their relations became strained.[98] In November of that year, Jiang finished his last novel, *Paoxiaole de tudi* (Roaring earth), and his deviations from the party line resulted in his expulsion from the party. Jiang spent the early part of the next year pursued by Nationalist police. Worse, his unloved young wife, Wu Sihong, was diagnosed with tuberculosis too. She had of course contracted the disease from Jiang. Tuberculosis, poverty, and persecution finally overcame Jiang, and he died on August 31, 1931, at the age of thirty-one.

The marriage of Jiang Guangci to Song Ruoyu and of Wu Sihong to Jiang Guangci may read like case studies of how tuberculosis is transmitted through intimate contact between lovers, or comrades, living under the same roof. Jiang Guangci's death was foreseeable when he decided to marry Song Ruoyu, and yet he was willing to do it, as it fit beautifully into his romantic ideology. Both biographically and ideologically, his second marriage to Wu Sihong came as a redundant action that tipped the delicate balance between sanctioned romanticism and sanctioned revolutionism. Song had died consummating a love postponed for the sake of the revolution; Wu struggled and survived the disease, an undesired reminder of Jiang's attempt to outlive his moment of revolutionary/romantic transfiguration.

From the perspective of party historiography, the chain of infection was symbolic of Jiang's career. Ever a recalcitrant figure, Jiang had played a temporary role in the debate with Lu Xun and Mao Dun and in the founding of the Sun Society. His days as an independent cultural hero were numbered, however, when the party intervened in the internecine leftist wars, ordering all factions to unite under the League of Left-Wing Writers. Meanwhile, tuberculosis had greatly weakened his health. In any event, history had no place for the kind of unhealthful element that Jiang Guangci had become, and in late 1930, the dying Jiang Guangci was expelled from the party. Jiang's problem was not that he died too soon but that he did not die soon enough. He could have been honored as a hero had he died in a timely and exemplary fashion. He had too long outlived Song Ruoyu, appended a tempestuous second marriage to the love and death scenes of the first, and distressed the party by pursuing an ideal after pragmatism had come into fashion.

Bai Wei and Yang Sao: Love As Despair

Bai Wei joined the League of Left-Wing Writers right after it was founded in spring 1930. At that time, she was teaching literature at Chinese Public College (Zhongguo Gongxue) through the recommendation of Shen Congwen. The publication of her works, including *Fight out of the Ghost Tower* and *The Bomb and the Expeditionary Bird,* had won her recognition among literature lovers and critics, including Lu Xun. Despite her growing reputation, however, Bai Wei was an unhappy woman. Her romance with Yang Sao had by then become nightmarish torture, and yet she could not bring herself to end it. In Bai Wei we seem to discern a perfect example of how love can undermine one's will to revolt. The reverse side of this argument tells more about the antinomy embedded in the case: Bai Wei's painful romance, however unworthy of her talent and energy, served as the motivation for her political and literary engagement.

Bai Wei came to know Yang Sao in Japan in 1924, when the latter was suffering from a recent split with his girlfriend. They were introduced by mutual friends in the hope that she, six years his senior, would become his confidante. The two fell in love right away. For Bai Wei, who had been through a failed arranged marriage and many other hardships, Yang Sao's youth, talent, and gentle manners must have made a deep impression. In a letter to Yang Sao she wrote,

> I am nothing but a ghost emerging from a deserted tomb. . . . I don't know how long I have been here and what year this is. I meant to forget all humanity, pretty or ugly, resisting all hope of redemption. Whom do you take me for? What do you see in me? You may have made a mistake. Are you in a dream? The difference between you and me is that between life and death. . . . Even before we met each other, I had been dreaming that you would become my friend, a friend with an angelic heart.[99]

This "friend with an angelic heart" would turn out to be a romantic demon. From the outset, the relationship between Bai Wei and Yang Sao was continuously disrupted by the latter's unfaithfulness, and yet after every quarrel and separation they returned to each other's embrace. In the spring of 1925, without any advance notice, Yang Sao suddenly returned to China and then left for Southeast Asia. Bai Wei tracked him down in Hangzhou but could not dissuade him from his plan. Heartbroken, she turned for solace to literature and revolution. Bai Wei came back to China in late 1926, and subsequently found a way to work for the Wuhan government. She returned to Shanghai after the fall of the Wuhan regime.

In October 1927, just as Bai Wei's career was about to take off, Yang Sao showed up at her apartment like a prodigal son. But no sooner had the lovers reunited than Yang Sao resumed his old habits. According to the translator Zhang Yousong, Bai Wei and Yang Sao decided to marry in late 1928 and invited all their close friends to their wedding banquet. But Yang Sao never turned up, on account of yet another female conquest.[100] By the end of 1929, the couple's relations had become irreparable. Even then, Bai Wei still indulged Yang Sao, serving as his financial benefactor and "spiritual" companion whenever they were not actually fighting.

Although traumatized by her father's tyrannical rule and her lover's unfaithfulness, Bai Wei seemed to maintain an almost masochistic attachment to these two men. She was compelled to return to them and claim their care as a means of justifying her suffering. As a result, she trapped herself in a cycle of humiliation, revenge, and unwarranted reconciliation. Bai Wei's pain, nevertheless, cannot be generalized as mere psychological torture. Rather, it was manifested in a stunning physical degradation. Yang Sao did not just torture Bai Wei's spirit; he afflicted her with gonorrhea, a venereal disease he had contracted from prostitutes in Singapore.

Gonorrhea is caused by gonococci acquired through sexual intercourse. It is characterized by inflammation of the mucous membrane of the genitourinary tract and a discharge of mucus and pus. Without proper treatment, it can seriously affect other mucous membranes. Soon after their reunion in 1927, symptoms of gonorrhea started to manifest in Bai Wei's body. She suffered from excruciating pain in her genitourinary system, crippling her and making it impossible to walk. Bai Wei then found that other parts of her body were being directly or indirectly affected by the venereal disease. In the next couple of years, she underwent attacks of pneumonia, rheumatism, cholera, chronic abdominal pain, and nasal reconstruction (nine surgeries). Owing to her impoverishment, she received only minimal medical treatment. As she put it in a poem, she had become "a good museum specimen of all known human diseases."[101] And yet Bai Wei still lived with Yang Sao. The two agreed to have no sexual relations but found it difficult to carry it out. Torn between desire and disease, they had developed a most bizarre mode of cohabitation.

In the cases of Jiang Guangci, Song Ruoyu, and Wu Sihong, I discussed tuberculosis as a metaphor that motivates a circulatory relationship between revolution and love, and between love and death. Granting its deadly threat to the Chinese body, tuberculosis takes on a romantic dimension because of conventional literary devices and medicinal mythology. Thus Jiang and Song's death from tuberculosis, however unromantic in reality, symbolized their mutual love as well as their dedication to revolution. By contrast, gonorrhea, like syphilis, induces public fear and contempt because it is a disease transmitted through a decadent lifestyle and promiscuous intercourse, and as such is morally disapproved by society. Bai Wei was an innocent victim of gonorrhea, but the way she contracted the disease from Yang Sao, who in turn had gotten it from prostitutes in Singapore, bespeaks most emphatically her vulnerable position as a (modern) woman in love. In particular, in a society where revolutionary women were regarded by the traditionalists as nothing if not promiscuous, Bai Wei was bound to be stereotyped as a living example of the pathological consequences of revolution.

Bai Wei's case brings to mind two women characters who suffer from venereal disease. In Mao Dun's *Pursuit,* Zhang Qiuliu tries to rescue her peer Shi Xun from his suicidal inclination by starting an affair with him. Shi Xun dies not from suicide but from tuberculosis, and Zhang Qiuliu contracts syphilis from him. In Jiang Guangci's *The Moon That Breaks through the Clouds,* Wang Mangying is afflicted with syphilis as a result of an unsolicited romantic advance. She then decides to avenge the failure of revolution and love by poisoning as many men as possible. In both instances, venereal disease is treated as a physical symptom of the characters' ideological defects. Thus Zhang Qiuliu's high-strung idealism has to be deflated by her syphilis, and Wang Mangying's revolutionary status is reinstated only after she is authoritatively declared never to have had the infamous disease.

Bai Wei's case reads like a harsh counterpart to Zhang Qiuliu's because, like the latter, she tries to rehabilitate her ex-lover by offering her own body, only to be rewarded with an incurable disease. But perhaps she is more of a parody of Wang Mangying: whereas Wang Manying undergoes a miraculous cure by being simply told that the syphilis she thought she had never existed, Bai Wei finds no such miraculous cure in reality. The ghostly disease *(guibing),* as she calls it, haunts and pains her day and night, as a physical reminder of her failure as a woman, and a revolutionary, in love.

We learn of Bai Wei's story primarily from her autobiographical novel, *My Tragic Life,* a work she wrote in 1935, when she was undergoing medical treatment and saw little hope of survival. By all standards, this nine-hundred-page novel (Shenghuo Bookstore edition, 1936) must be regarded as one of the most poignant female confessional narratives in twentieth-century Chinese literature. In the novel, Bai Wei delineates in detail her ten-year romance with Yang Sao, from their first encounter to her contraction of gonorrhea and other diseases, and to being hospitalized alone to have her ovaries removed. Although the surgery is necessitated by her worsening venereal disease, for Bai Wei, it is a symbolic deprivation of her womanhood. And when the novel comes to a close, the fate of its protagonist is left in suspense.

In her reading of *My Tragic Life,* Amy Dooling gives a succinct analysis of Bai Wei's renovation of female autobiographical fiction, a genre popular among post–May Fourth women writers.[102] Dooling argues that, by altering the narrative stance and rhetorical tropes, Bai Wei challenges the verisimilitude of autobiographical narrative and relates a most disturbing story about writing women in love. What concerns me here is how the novel serves as Bai Wei's testimony to her betrayed revolution *as* romance and vice versa, and how, through a "discourse of despair," it reveals the schizophrenic nature of a woman relating reality.

In parallel to her personal "tragic life," Bai Wei describes the 1927 revolution as if it were a romance on a national scale. In the "revolutionary stage of the Wuhan coalition government," writes Bai Wei, "China was flowering, like the red begonia in full bloom. . . . People were in revelry, their souls were jumping and the national soul was jumping too."[103] Revolutionary youth drove away foreign imperialists, occupied consulate buildings, took over catholic churches, and opened new schools. Women were liberated, peasants arose, students were mobilized, and troops of soldiers were on their way to quell warlords. Meanwhile, young men and women revolutionaries were seen walking hand in hand along the banks of the Yangtze River, singing in the summer night. They enthusiastically talked about the future of the nation, they laughed and joked around, and they fell in love. "Everyone knew this was the bliss of revolution, the luxury of revolution."[104]

Nowhere else in the writings by these three writers in discussion can one find such an explicit celebration of the sensuous power of revolution over Chinese youth. But in just a few months, the revolution that promised a New China crumbled. In its second stage, the stage of "literary boom," "numerous promising lives were drowned in the sea of blood while many others were driven to write down their ressentiment. They brought to the fore the Chinese people's melancholy. From 1928 to 1930, they roared out a new Chinese literature like awakening lions."[105] Terms such as "revolutionary literature," "socialist literature," and "new realist literature" were proposed in the place of May Fourth "enlightenment literature" and "new romantic literature," and literature became a shared goal of revolutionaries.

Bai Wei and Yang Sao were part of this new literary trend. Neither, however, could fully devote themselves to revolutionary literature for reasons of sexual distraction, poverty, and disease. Under the banner of literature for the mass, they were more involved in a traditional battle of bourgeois individuals. As Bai Wei puts it, Yang Sao was so possessive of her that he forbade her from accepting any public engagements. He was infuriated when he discovered her participation in the League of Left-Wing Writers and the League of Drama Workers *(julian);* he did everything to damage her career, to the extent of exposing her political alliance in public, still taboo in the early 1930s. But Bai Wei never revealed the fact that Yao Sao too had joined the League of Left-Wing Writers in its founding days.

What infuriated Bai Wei most was her disease. However she wanted to join in political activities, she ended up a burden to others because of her physical limitations. She was forced "to leave any group activity. Disease terminated all her hopes. The sorrow of loneliness always followed her."[106]

Bai Wei called the third stage of the revolution "the stage of cultural hegemony." This is a period when national crises, from the Mukden Incident to the Japanese attack on Shanghai, came one after another, while the literati underwent censorship and surveillance more severe than ever before. This period saw Bai Wei's love and health completely destroyed by her beloved. In her study, Dooling vividly describes how in 1933, when Bai Wei was hospitalized for gonorrhea and other diseases, Yang Sao rushed to publish a collection of love letters between Bai Wei and himself, *Zuoye* (Last night), to "lay bare" their romance, which had become a tabloid sensation.[107] He did so to capitalize on his residual relations with Bai Wei and to renew his own image. Compared to Jiang Guangci and Song Ruoyu's love correspondence, *Last Night* was a farce. Worse, in anticipation of Bai Wei's impending death, Yang

Sao even prepared a "posthumous" edition of her diary, with entries mostly concocted by himself.[108]

My Tragic Life impresses one as more than a woman writer's confession of her sexual frustrations. It also serves as a revelation of her failed love affair with revolution. At the end of her novel, Bai Wei reminisces about her days in the Wuhan government. She worked with a Mr. K, a noble gentleman who cherished her talent and treated her with extreme kindness. Bai Wei kept a distance from Mr. K; "she did not want to be in love with anyone, because she was a woman in love with revolution."[109] We cannot identify this Mr. K (he might even be the personification of the Nationalist Party, or *Kuomintang*). In just seven years, this high-minded woman revolutionary was to find herself struggling to survive her venereal disease, a disease derived from a highly risky romance. If "desire," or the force of the political and romantic unconscious, once drove revolutionary youth to pursue hope and action, this desire has come full circle in Bai Wei's case, now manifesting itself as despair. "The dejection of love, the dejection of disease, the dejection of time, constitute this multifaceted tragedy and fell on her. . . . History brought her melancholy, love destroyed her health and strength, and disease shortened her life. However she tried to turn over, she failed to do so. Despair, despair, triple despair."[110]

CODA

The revolution plus love discourse came to a halt on the eve of the Second Sino-Japanese War. The end of this discourse represented both the changing national ethos and the increasingly tightened control of revolutionary correctness. But it also marked a generation of revolutionary writers coming to maturity and ready to settle with their destiny. Gone were the days when love and revolution could mean an irreconcilable struggle and result in such intense pain and joy to the revolution youth. Amid the national propaganda against foreign invasion and the Communist Party's call for a united front, individual desire was to be put aside in favor of patriotic alliance. Although "revolution and love" was still to serve as an important theme of leftist literature in the years to come, it no longer retained the thrust that once galvanized restless youth in the post–1927 Revolution days.

The "revolution" yearned for by the 1927 revolutionaries was supposed to end when the People's Republic was founded in 1949. But as the party fought one power struggle after another, the whole nation was mobilized to "continue the revolution." Love was continuously invoked, too, but only in the name of Chairman Mao. In retrospect, the 1931 death of Jiang Guangci, the spokesman for revolution plus love fiction, became the most dramatic moment of the discourse. In Jiang, life (or death?) and fiction penetrated each other's realms, fully enacting the power and threat of the discourse.

Jiang Guangci was rehabilitated in 1956 as a party member, his revolutionary romanticism finally enshrined as a major inspiration of the new literary campaign.

Bai Wei, on the other hand, survived the surgery she described in *My Tragic Life,* as well as subsequent operations. Her pathetic situation and despairing confession drew national attention, and she severed her relation with Yang Sao. When the war broke out, she joined the anti-Japanese campaign and entrusted her love to the nation. She "sublimated" her love for the sake of the masses, as Jiang Guangci would have it, but became an increasingly isolated woman in real life. In the 1950s, Bai Wei volunteered to work in northern Manchuria and Xinjiang, as if exiling herself in pursuit of mental peace. She suffered a great deal during the Cultural Revolution but miraculously survived.[111] She remained unmarried until her death in 1987.

Mao Dun continued to write and remained active in political and literary circles after the 1949 Revolution, serving as minister of culture in the 1950s and 1960s. As his reputation mounted, was there any moment when he suddenly cringed at the thought of his romantic adventure? Mao Dun never divorced his wife, Kong Dezhi, their relations becoming ever more estranged in their last years. Kong died in 1969. Mao Dun ran into Qin Dejun once in 1976, but not a single word was exchanged between them. He died on March 27, 1981, allegedly working on his autobiographical notes on how he wrote *Rainbow,* a novel inspired by Qin, his "Scandinavian goddess of fate."[112] At his funeral, he was vindicated as a loyal party member, his party membership made traceable to 1921.

Qin Dejun was jailed for eight years during the Cultural Revolution, living long enough to witness the Tiananmen Incident, the last revolutionary attempt by Chinese youth in the twentieth century. In an interview in May 1989, she talked about her and Mao Dun's joint revolutionary adventures sixty years before. Instead of love, she remembered Mao Dun's betrayals, the betrayal of his party and of her. Or was this her way of asserting negatively a lingering love for Mao Dun? As a final gesture of revenge, she revealed in the interview one more secret: with *Putrefaction,* Mao Dun imagined Qin as a Nationalist spy ever ready to set him up. He never knew that Qin, though appearing to be a Nationalist general's wife, was, she said, actually working for the Communist revolution.[113] In the game of revolution plus love, Mao Dun's "goddess of fate" had the last laugh.

Chapter 4

Three Hungry Women

Women and hunger are most peculiarly linked in the configuration of gender, materiality, and revolution in modern Chinese fiction. Shortages of food, with their grave implications for national politics, economics, and even eugenics, have, of course, appeared all too often in China's quest for modernization.[1] But when hunger is treated in literary terms, it manifests itself in a wide variety of typologies, from famines caused by nature to "hunger revolutions" dictated by ideology. For Chinese writers since the May Fourth era, "having nothing to eat" not only reflects the agricultural crisis of an ancient nation whose roots are in the countryside *(yinong liguo),* but also concentrates the minds of a modern people who argue over "social welfare versus cultural nourishment" and "the survival instinct versus body politics."[2] Above all, national hunger has been imagined in feminine terms, owing perhaps to women's somatic vulnerability during natural and man-made famines, or to women's conventional role in the semiotics of victimology. Hunger is a recurrent theme throughout modern Chinese history, and hungry women are recurrent protagonists in modern Chinese fiction.

The genealogy of literary hungry women can be traced to works by Lu Xun. For example, in the short story "Zhufu" (New Year's sacrifice), the most memorable moment occurs when the narrator encounters the ill-fated wife of Xianglin on New Year's Eve. Ostracized by the townsfolk of Luzhen, Xianglin's wife has been living as a beggar (*yaofande,* literally, a food beggar) as the story opens. Upon meeting the narrator, however, this poor woman begs not for food but for an answer to her question, "After a person dies, does he turn into a ghost or not?" Caught completely off guard by this question, the narrator can respond only by murmuring, "I am not sure."[3]

On this festive occasion, marked by the reunion of families and an abundance of edibles, Xianglin's wife impresses the narrator as a woman hungry for something other than food. But she readily swallows the narrator's empty contribution and eventually dies a pitiful death. Ironically, the pathetic situation of Xianglin's wife arouses the narrator's appetite: he may have failed to provide the hungry woman with a satisfactory answer, but, we are told, perhaps a bowl of shark fin soup will give him peace of mind and satisfy his stomach. Where food is expected, meaning is requested; the words given are meaningless to the giver, but his emptiness can be filled with food.

Between Xianglin's wife and the narrator, there exists a cluster of images around the double functions of orality: eating and speaking. Beggar though she is, Xianglin's wife refuses to be fed with mere food and tries instead to articulate her puzzlement. Her attempt to speak out and obtain some response is nevertheless thwarted by the narrator, who, as Lu Xun insinuates, can contribute to the woman neither something edible nor something thinkable. Drawing on Freudian theory, critics have argued about the shared motivational structure in eating and speaking: "Language is nothing other than the praxis of eating transposed to the semiosis of speaking: both are fundamentally communicative acts by which man appropriates and incorporates the world."[4] In "The New Year's Sacrifice," one finds a short-circuiting of these two functions of orality. Xianglin's wife dies a mute woman, while the townsfolk consume their New Year's Eve banquet with a happy clamor. As Lu Xun would have it, she is the New Year's sacrifice served up at a cannibalistic banquet in honor of ancestors and deities.

As far as writings with alimentary motifs are concerned, Lu Xun is more famous for his short story "Kuangren riji" (The diary of a madman), a story replete with symbolical food, eating, banquets, and cannibalism.[5] But in celebrating the madman as the spokesperson for the modern Chinese imagination of orality, one tends to ignore the existence of Xianglin's wife—a hungry woman—who is the madman's gendered counterpart. Although a social outcast, the madman is saturated with thoughts new and old, and thereby capable of observing and lashing out at social malaise in gastronomic terms. By contrast, Xianglin's wife appears to have been deprived of any chance of making a living, let alone a capacity for reasoning through or speaking of her predicaments. Lu Xun's madman is a classical sage who sees the classically horrible truth about a food/word culture based on classical institutions. But Xianglin's wife has been thrown into a zero state from the outset (no food, no home, no meaning, and no self-assurance), and as such can only be treated classically as a token of lack and passivity, with her encounter with the narrator seen as a painful communication between woman, who "has naught," and man, who "has."

As the archetypal hungry woman in modern Chinese literature, a long line of sisters follows Xianglin's wife. For instance, in Rou Shi's (1902–1931) short story "Wei nuli de muqin" (A slave's mother, 1930), a hungry woman is sold as a surrogate mother by her husband to save the family from starving to death. In Wang Jingzhi's (1902–1994) "Renrou" (Human flesh, 1925), a hungry woman is literally cut into pieces and consumed by a group of hungry men. In Wu Zuxiang's (1908–1994) "Fanjia pu" (Fan family village, 1934), another hungry woman commits matricide after her mother refuses to lend her money to survive a drought. And in Xiao Hong's (1911–1942) *Shengsi chang* (The field of life and death, 1935), hungry peasant women follow their men and resist Japanese oppression. The gallery of hungry women was well furnished by the early 1940s, culminating in Lu Ling's (1923–1994) novel *Ji'e de Guo Su'e* (Hungry Guo Su'e, 1943).

For Lu Xun, as for those authors who followed him, hungry women are powerful tokens who inscribe the misery of the powerless in a cannibalistic society. The exuberance of these writers' words on behalf of hungry women, however, leads us to consider issues beyond a simple typology of social injustice and cannibalism. As indicated by the previous discussion of Xianglin's wife, one has to assess the following aspects of female subjectivity and its manifestation in modern Chinese literature: (1) the consumptive and enunciative capacities of women in quest of social and economic selfhood; (2) the deployment of biological and gender resources in both the public and private spheres; (3) the mythification of hunger and femininity as an arguably male imaginary of the physical and metaphysical destitution that besets modern China.

These assessments take on a polemical dimension to the degree that they occur in a revolutionary discourse sanctioned by Chinese leftist politicians and progressive writers since the 1920s. It is the juncture of biological and ideological hunger in Chinese Communist revolutionary discourse that renders the above issues all the more provocative. To exemplify my assessment, I will focus on three of these hungry women: Guo Su'e in *Hungry Guo Su'e;* Tan Yuexiang in *Yangge* (The rice-sprout song, 1954), by Zhang Ailing (Eileen Chang, 1920–1995); and Cai Qianhui in "Shanlu" (Mountain path, 1983), by Chen Yingzhen (Ch'en Ying-chen, b. 1939). In each of these works, the writers observe how hunger affects a woman's fate, and, more poignantly, how writing about hunger entails a tension between digestive and diegetic imagination, and metabolic and metaphoric action.

GUO SU'E

In 1942, as Mao Zedong laid down the rules for a new Communist literature in his Yan'an talks, nineteen-year-old Lu Ling was creating an independent piece of leftist fiction in Chongqing, Sichuan.[6] This work, which would bring him fame—and notoriety—was *Hungry Guo Su'e.* Published in 1943, the novel generated immediate controversy for its daring revelations about wartime life at the lower depths and its stylized, almost self-indulgent description of sex, violence, and irrationality. Far from the stereotypical innocent victims of leftist literature, its characters suffer *and* practice sham, malice, and depravity. Life's misery is so overwhelming that their response is to join in and propagate it further.

At the center of the novel is Guo Su'e, a woman who is driven out of her hometown by famine and banditry, and, against her will, becomes the wife of a degenerate opium addict, Liu Shouchun, twenty-four years her senior. Barely nourished, Su'e comes to realize that she has fallen into an even more unbearable situation. In response, she develops a new appetite—an appetite for men. The title of the novel, *Hungry Guo Su'e,* therefore invites the interpretation that hunger for food is merely a prelude to hunger for the unspeakable.

Guo Su'e carries on an affair with a local worker, Zhang Zhenshan, while another worker, Wei Haiqing, secretly falls in love with her. But it does not take long for Guo's husband to discover his wife's adulterous behavior; he and other clan members catch her in flagrante delicto one night and put her on private trial. They humiliate and abuse her in a most horrific way until she loses consciousness. Later, a thug from the crowd takes advantage of her helplessness and rapes her. Guo is left alone in a temple and dies three days later from lack of medicine and food.

The death of Guo Su'e takes place in the middle of the novel. In the second half, Zhang Zhenshan disappears from town, presumably shamed by his failure to stand up to Guo's persecutors, while Wei Haiqing vows to avenge Guo's death. Wei eventually tracks down the thug who raped Guo, but he loses his life fighting him.

Spiritual Hunger, Spiritual Food

In deciphering the mysterious etiology of Guo Su'e's hunger, an answer can be found in Lu Ling's commentary. For him, given all the miseries she has been through, Guo Su'e is not "a woman crushed by the old society"; rather, what he wants to "wastefully search for" in this woman is "the primitive strength of the people and the active liberation of personality."[7] But Lu Ling wonders whether the "base aspect of ancient China" can be easily reformed; hence his note that before any hope of liberation comes in sight, "Guo Su'e will continue to degenerate, however temporarily, into promiscuous inertia and selfish stupor."[8]

In the same spirit, Lu Ling's mentor, Hu Feng (1902–1985), wrote this famous comment in his preface to the 1943 edition of the novel: "Guo Su'e is a sort of woman from the old, feudal kingdom; but physical hunger not only cannot be numbed by moral prescriptions handed down from the ancestors, it also produces an even stronger spiritual hunger, hunger for a profound liberation, hunger for a firm and unyielding human nature. She uses a primitive fierceness to knock against the iron wall of this society, but she pays the price and her life is tragically sacrificed."[9]

Hu Feng, it will be recalled, was one of the most vociferous advocates of a "subjective" Chinese Marxism. At the risk of oversimplification, let us say that Hu and his followers in the July (Qiyue) school, of whom Lu Ling was the most promising, envision a humanity seriously maimed by the atrocities of inhuman history, so much so that it cannot be rehabilitated until its primitive, individual power is stimulated. Hu Feng's view is different from Mao's. Mao and his cohorts acknowledge the suffering of humanity but argue that, to do justice to "the insulted and the injured," they first have to subordinate individual subjectivity, which seemed to them to have gotten out of control in Hu Feng's hands, to a collective, historical subjectivity.[10]

Hu Feng's quest for the spiritual rejuvenation of the Chinese national body in turn smacks of the contentiousness of his mentor, Lu Xun, as illustrated by his preface to *A Call to Arms*.[11] But, together with Lu Ling and other July school writers, Hu Feng would have suggested that Guo Su'e differentiates herself from women in Lu Xun's fiction—such as Xianglin's wife—in that Guo is capable of feeling not only a physical hunger but "an even stronger spiritual hunger."[12] This spiritual hunger is ingrained in Guo Su'e's political unconscious like a primitive drive, ever ready to surface when provoked by dissatisfaction. Hu Feng's comment is reinforced by contemporary critics, such as Shao Quanlin (1906–1971), who suggests that people like Guo Su'e are not just beset by physical shortages of food; rather they are "morbid and starved in spiritual terms. . . . Precisely they are so oppressed by life and tradition that they undergo a strong contradiction and combat in their mind. This combat, hundreds of times more painful than physical hunger, gives rise to these people's rough character."[13] Since his rehabilitation in the late 1970s, Hu Feng has again become respected as a forerunner of the humanitarian vein of Chinese Communist revolutionism, and his comment on *Hungry Guo Su'e* finds echoes among late-twentieth-century critics such as Yang Yi and Qian Liqun.[14]

Insofar as she is a symbol both of a China trapped in social and natural devastation and of a "primitive" life force that would rejuvenate China from such a state, Guo Su'e personifies what Rey Chow calls "primitive passions." For Chow, the interest in the primitive emerges at a moment of cultural crisis; when the master narrative of traditional culture can no longer monopolize signification, fantasies of an origin arise. These fantasies are played out with recourse to invocations of the culturally backward and the naturally primitive, which stand in "for that 'original' something that has been lost."[15] Moreover, women have often been brought to express such a desire for the primitive for the paradoxical reason that they are socially underprivileged, and as such, they are "obscene."[16] Feminists may push this and argue that

Guo's suffering and death at the hands of a male group readily indicate male sadomasochistic spectatorship vis-à-vis woman's (dead) body. Guo above all is amplified as a signifier for the suffering of general humanity, while her erotic pursuit is staged as a feminine spectacle, promising less salvation from than subordination to the gaze of male subjectivity.

Given its provocative female character, its experimental narrative format, and its polemical debate over ideological orientations, *Hungry Guo Su'e* has curiously not drawn much attention from scholars in the English-speaking world. Among the handful of studies, Kirk Denton calls attention to the mythological themes evoked in Guo's delirium and desire, and puts these themes in the context of Chinese Daoist dynamics. Liu Kang highlights the Lacanian "imaginary" inherent in Guo Su'e's psychological makeup and the drama of Bakhtinian heteroglossia that informs the rhetorical gesture of the novel. Yunzhong Shu refers Guo Su'e's characterization to the revolutionary poetics conceived by Hu Feng and argues that by creating such a female figure, Lu Ling has taken issue with the formula Mao prescribed for leftist writers in 1942.[17]

I would offer a reading of *Hungry Guo Su'e* that places the novel in the context of leftist corporeal discourse and argues that, for all its conformist premises, it can best be seen as an unexpected response to the hungry dialectics of Chinese Marxism. Historians have repeatedly pointed out that hunger, a result of both natural and man-made disasters, constituted one of the main causes of the Chinese Communist Revolution, particularly in the countryside.[18] As early as 1926, Mao declares in his "Zhongguo shehui jieduan de fenxi" (Analysis of class in Chinese society) that social disparity is often described in terms of unequal food distribution. In 1927, in his famous "Hunan nongmin yundong kaocha baogao" (Report on an investigation of the peasant movement in Hunan), he stipulates that "we must create a short reign of terror in all parts of the countryside. A revolution is not like having a dinner party, or composing an article, or doing embroidery, a revolution is an uprising."[19] Mao enumerates fourteen tactics that rebellious peasants used against the landlords, of which "eat the rich" *(chi dahu)*—eating the landlords' grain and livestock—stands out as an action that asserts most symbolically the proletariat's immediate needs.[20]

Beginning in the late 1920s, hunger was a popular theme in Chinese Communist literature, testifying to the writers' ideological commitment to recording reality and instigating extreme measures to change it. In Jiang Guangci's *Roaring Earth* (see Chapter 3), Ding Ling's "Shui" (Flood, 1931), Mao Dun's *Village Trilogy* (Spring silkworms, Autumn harvest, Winter ruins, 1932–1934), and Wu Zuxiang's *Eighteen Hundred Piculs of Rice* (see Chapter 2), poor, hungry peasants are portrayed as being driven to violence by an ever-mounting threat of starvation, thus providing a major impetus for the oncoming revolution.

Whereas in an ordinary sense hunger represents a lack of physical resources—food, nutrition, and access to the normal circulation of foodstuffs—in Communist terms, it can mean something quite different. Under revolutionary circumstances, hunger drives one to an acute awareness of one's class status in the social hierarchy, thereby opening the way for radical solutions. On the other hand, in the same revolutionary circumstances, one's capacity to withstand hunger becomes a sign through which one demonstrates one's physical and moral strength. From bodily destitution to political institution, hunger, as a spiritual state, has been reified, so to speak, in the discourse of revolution. For those who are willing to suffer for the truth of history, hunger is not only a cause of revolutions; it is a mark of the true revolutionary, the outward demonstration of political virtue. Revolution, as Mao defines it, is not a "dinner party"; one must cease self-indulgence and begin a life of resolute action. If such arguments sound familiar, it is because they recapitulate the Confucian call for spiritual rectification at the price of bodily deprivation.[21] The well-known statement by Mencius comes to mind: when Heaven "is about to place a great burden on a man, [it] first tests his resolution, exhausts his frame and makes him suffer starvation and hardship, frustrates his efforts so as to shake him from his mental lassitude, toughen his nature and make good his deficiencies."[22]

But in Mao's and his literary cohorts' hands, the hunger motif acquires even greater superstructural significance. Instead of *lack,* hunger comes to indicate its opposite, *excess.* Hunger is comparable to a libidinous drive—for revolution and for Communism—that remains insatiable. It is easy to fill a body with physical food, but the spirit can never have enough ideological food. After the revolution, Mao is equally deft at playing the politics of hunger on the level of the imaginary. The still unsolved but merely finite problem of physical satisfaction is superseded by the infinite problem of spiritual satisfaction. He constructs a mythology in which one's utopian desire cannot and should not be satisfied; hence the necessity of continued revolution. Ban Wang describes such power in terms of the "Maoist sublime," a range of figurative capacities by which "whatever smacks too much of the human creature—appetite, feeling, sensibility, sensuality, imagination, fear, passion, lust, self-interest, etc.—is purged and repressed so that the all-too-human is sublimated with violence into the superhuman and even inhuman realms."[23]

As early as 1940, Mao made it a crucial part of his policy to feed his "people" with proper "cultural food,"[24] and almost at the same time, the term "spiritual food" *(jingshen shiliang)* appeared in Communist publications.[25] In the following decades, his literary workers raised endless crops of "spiritual food" to be harvested for mass consumption on the pretext that, in the cornucopia of Maoist discourse, there can be no limit to the people's hunger. By the late 1940s, "anti-hunger" *(fanji'e)* had become one of the most popular slogans of urban leftist intellectuals and students. And though they might never have experienced the food shortages firsthand, the intelligentsia felt no less strongly about spiritual hunger: Anti-hunger meant an effort both to prevent a lack of material food (attention: farm managers) and to ensure a limitless supply of spiritual food (attention: urban intellectuals).

Hungry Guo Su'e appeared as a most intriguing dedication to, and deviation from, the hunger discourse of the 1940s, and to that effect, it dramatized the intricate relations between Hu Feng's "spiritual hunger" and Mao's "spiritual food." Lu Ling created the character Guo Su'e presumably to illuminate Hu Feng's observation that Chinese civilization was experiencing spiritual hunger, a hunger that calls for a special remedy beyond mere edible food. He (or even Hu Feng) would have concurred with Mao that, to satisfy her spiritual hunger, Guo would need an abundant supply of "spiritual food," best represented by revolutionary yearning and utopian vision. It is now apparent, however, that in the search for that spiritual food, Lu Ling has taken a narrative path so idiosyncratic that it digresses from the set course approved by Mao—or even by Hu Feng. And in so doing, Lu Ling manages to push Chinese literature to a new stage in the assimilation of modern literary consciousness.

Language of Desire, Desire for Language

The characters in *Hungry Guo Su'e* yearn for fulfillment of an unidentifiable desire. They suffer from symptoms such as hysteria, manic depression, nymphomania, and sadomasochism—presumably bodily signs of their ressentiment. But physical and psychological ailments only intensify their pursuit of the unattainable. Lu Ling's description of Guo Su'e's husband, Liu Shouchun, also applies to other characters: through his wayward behavior, he "does not mean to have people feel that he suffers doubly for faking the intensity of his pain so much as he wants to unnerve them by letting them think they are actually confronting a sham."[26] C. T. Hsia finds in *Hungry Guo Su'e* "hard-core realism," a depiction of low life so raw as to turn aside all humanitarian concern.[27] But when Lu Ling reveals the obduracy of suffering by taking life's hard-core aspect literally, the most dismal circumstances are bound up into a sensuous escapade that is both repugnant and seductive.

This is the juncture where Guo Su'e's sexual appetite meets her spiritual hunger and thus results in a murky interpretation of Mao's (and Hu Feng's) body politics. Guo Su'e pursues erotic satisfaction, but she is only temporarily satiated and experiences a deeper sense of vacuity. She is trapped in cyclical elevation and depression, while her body succumbs to every external stimulus. She cries and laughs vulgarly, and she quarrels, shouts, cheats, and backbites as if possessed. A mood of macabre excitement prevails as Guo's mysterious hunger becomes more desperate.

Thus Guo Su'e acts out the "irrational" aspect of spiritual hunger, as she shuffles back and forth between apocalyptic visions and psychotic hallucinations, between erotic appetite and political hunger. In the arms of her lover, Zhang Zhenshan, Guo Su'e is described as "transported; all her worries, sadness, fear and anguish are gone"; she experiences "a foggy and ebullient sensation of ecstasy"; her "vision blur[s] and she gasp[s], feeling delight . . . her soul [is] completely immersed in beatitude." When she waits for another tryst with Zhang, she is "absorbed in her desires and aspirations,"[28] and the uncertain future submerges her alternately in moods of "bitterness and ecstasy."[29]

> The abrupt appearance of Zhang Zhenshan made her cry out in ecstatic pain. . . . The ecstasy aroused by pain and despair is an ecstasy that verges upon insanity. Zhang Zhenshan was lying next to her once again. Though he had never promised her hope of life and escape, Guo Su'e did demonstrate to her own satisfaction, under the momentary light of the moon, that Zhang, a rough and stubborn man with burning breath and open heart, would never fool her or rudely run away from her and withdraw into a private world of malice and indifference.[30]

In his study of the deep structure of Chinese collective psychology, Sun Longki describes the Chinese as fixated on the oral stage, a stage characterized by (male) infantile nostalgia and fear of adult sexuality.[31] Sun can find no better example than *Hungry Guo Su'e.* The novel is irksome precisely because it enacts a confrontation between orality and sexuality and projects it onto a new ideological plane. Before Lu Ling came along, to be sure, an array of Communist writers had written about sexuality as either an incentive or an impediment to revolution, Mao Dun being one of the most frequently cited.[32] What makes Lu Ling's voice more polemical is that sexuality in his novel bears no clear, logical relevance to the cause of revolution, other than serving as a bodily index to an unpredictable and violent force, in deference to the impending revolution.

Take, for instance, a figure such as Yang Xi'er in the play *Baimao nü* (The white-haired girl, 1946), one of the most celebrated heroines of Chinese Communist literature of the Yan'an period. In the original version of *The White-Haired Girl,* Yang Xi'er, after being raped, impregnated, and deserted by an evil landlord, runs to hide in the local mountains. To keep her newborn baby and herself alive, she steals food from a monastery and is accidentally mistaken by the superstitious village folk for the immortal White-Haired Girl. When the revolution reaches her village, Xi'er is eventually rescued and becomes a token figure who bears witness to the cruelties of the old society.[33] Whatever the nature of Xi'er's hunger, her tortured metabolism is easily understood as a metaphor for feudal suffering, which is, when seen from the point of view of Marxist metaphysics, the necessary precondition for human progress.

Guo Su'e is a counterexample to model heroine Yang Xi'er, in terms of both characterization and the implied timetable ascribed to her salvation (or its absence). Yang Xi'er undergoes a metamorphosis that fits easily into the classic linear, progressive format, which delineates how she is "transformed from a ghost into a human being" by the new society, as the most famous statement about the play puts it.[34] By sharp contrast, Guo Su'e's story fails to provide such familiar, progressive significance. Where Mao and his followers establish a symbolic linkage among material need, somatic constitution, revolution, and spiritual transcendence, Lu Ling reveals the ambiguous fissures in such "chains of being"; where Mao enshrines ideal Communist womanhood in terms of saintly magnanimity, Lu Ling instead lodges souls tempted and engulfed by worldly desires. Hence Guo Su'e's ambiguous thoughts about her salvation:

> She has been thirsty to attain a new life through sexual desire, and most of the time this thirst elevates her to dreams that she could revolt and thus leave her past behind. Although she works hard and appears extremely kind to neighbors, she cannot help displaying the look of a criminal, for which she is still considered to be a uniquely bad woman. But she ignores this and entertains a fastidious determination: she hurriedly takes a stand on the shore of the sea of labor. No matter how unfathomable and horrible the sea is, the faster the strong wind blows behind her, the sooner she will jump into the sea.[35]

Of note here is the way Lu Ling (or Guo Su'e) renders the Communist cliché "the sea of labor" through a sequence of metaphoric shifts. Guo fantasizes about salvation in the sea of labor as if she were yearning for her next depraved adventure, and she qualifies her final rescue in terms of an eternal fall. As a result, she leaves the reader wondering whether her thoughts are an eruption of fleeting impressions, subject to continued verbal and emotive displacement, or the emanation of a telos that will sublate all rhetorical contingencies.

This language of desire finds its preliminary expression in the desire for language. As Guo Su'e and other characters' psychiatric symptoms surface as verbal symptoms, they signal that the linguistic process of representation becomes possible only when these problems can no longer be contained within the order of reality and rationality. At the textual level, Lu Ling matches his characters' volatile fits and writes "wastefully" about their syndromes. His images, metaphors, and other rhetorical devices, from free indirect style to narrated monologue, proliferate in such a way that the whole narration dramatizes the frustration, rather than the fulfillment, of his characters' efforts to satisfy deep-seated desires. His infatuation with language corresponds to an unexpected surplus of meaning, anathema to the Maoist economy of literature, in which there is only one true meaning.[36]

If Maoist hunger discourse aims to solicit from literal and symbolic lack of food the "sublime" effect, an emotive response that overwhelms any human effort at corporeal and linguistic representation,[37] Lu Ling's may be seen as directed toward a subliminal realm, where language evolves amorphously in approximation of libidinal turbulence.[38] This subliminal realm can be understood in terms of Julia Kristeva's description of abjection, or repugnance, as a reaction to the inability to transcend the base associations of the corporeal, such as food, waste, and gender differences. In contrast to the Maoist sublime, which hinges on the transcendence of the symbolic system of language and sign systems, the abject focuses attention on "thresholds," which are manifested, among other ways, in those bodily orifices that blur the distinction between the inside and the outside, attraction and repulsion, Eros and Thanatos. Abjection appears, as one critic puts it, "where boundaries are traversed and unity punctured so that the resultant breach threatens to widen and overtake the whole."[39]

Kristeva's theory appears relevant to Hungry *Guo Su'e* in that it locates the site of abjection in women and links such a feminine abject state to the formation of a language system, on the one hand, and of the psychosomatic condition, on the other. If language is that which is predetermined by the patriarchal symbolic order, the feminine presents itself as an amorphous semiotic force coming from outside the male order. Contrary to the rational distinction based on the chain of language and naming, the feminine reestablishes these distinctions "by inscribing itself in sites of the body, particularly those bodily holes which confuse the boundary between inside and outside, and therefore between the Self and Other."[40]

Lu Ling's straddling of the realms of the sublime and the abject enables him to project Guo Su'e at the "threshold," so to speak, of the Communist somatic/semiotic system. Guo's unpleasant appearance embodies the ambiguous zone one has to cross over in negotiating metabolic hunger and metaphysical hunger. Incidentally, to redeem her sins, Xianglin's wife, in Lu Xun's "New Year's Sacrifice," is taught to donate a threshold, as her own bodily substitute, at a local Buddhist temple, to be trampled on by people. Whereas Xianglin's wife falls at the threshold of feudal ideology, Guo Su'e fights a fatal battle before the edifice of Chinese Communism. That she dies in the middle of the narrative is therefore highly suggestive. Instead of providing an apotheosis, Guo Su'e's death resolves neither the novel nor the problem of hunger.

In the final hours of her life, when Guo Su'e is taken to the back room of Zhang Fei Temple, she cries, "Don't touch me! I am a woman!" and "You scum who eat human flesh and don't spit bones!" She is forced into one corner of the room and her clothes torn to pieces, but her look is still defiant. As one of the clan women approaches her, "a devil suddenly comes out [of Guo Su'e]. This devil dishevels her hair, spits saliva, and jumps fiendishly onto the old woman, strangling the old woman [by seizing her] tender throat."[41] Infuriated by this unexpected move, Guo's husband and others tie her to a plank and sear her thighs with red-hot pokers, until, in excruciating pain, she loses consciousness. Then, "three days after that fearful night in Zhang Fei Temple, she regained consciousness and groped her way out through the hall door. She could move because . . . she felt she could live, and in the end, because she was hungry. But when she had groped her way to the courtyard, she let out a shriek and fell to the ground as white pus oozed out from below her belly."[42]

Guo Su'e's struggle to live thus ends in slow and horrific degeneration to a state of total nullification; she dies after her voice fails to reach anybody and her need for food is left unfilled. Through the fatal denial of the fundamental needs of female orality, Lu Ling unveils the cannibalistic nature of the old society, while at the same time undermining, however unwittingly, the call of the new Communist society for a new, higher hunger. The corpse of Guo Su'e, rotting on the grounds of the feudal temple, induces one to question whether hers is just another heroic body to be added to the mausoleum of leftist victimology or, more pointedly, whether it is an abject reminder of the figural and figurative inadequacies of Stalinist/Maoist hunger symbolism.

An Avant-Garde Hunger Narratology

We can now return to the issue of what makes *Hungry Guo Su'e* so modern in a literary discourse heavily influenced by nineteenth-century European realist doctrines. Critics like to quote Lu Ling's comment that Guo Su'e's search for spiritual salvation is handicapped by her weak will and her infamous desire. What has been overlooked is Lu Ling's claim that he wants to "wastefully search for . . . the primitive strength of the people and the active liberation of personality" in this woman. This claim was repeated by Hu Feng in his preface to *Hungry Guo Su'e,* quoting from Lu Ling's 1942 letter to him. Not until recently have critics noticed an oversight on Hu Feng's part. The term "langfeide" (wasteful; sometimes translated as "gratuitous") was a misquote; Lu Ling's original statement was "lang*man*de" (romantic).[43] By taking "romantic" for "wasteful," Hu Feng demonstrates a Freudian slip that, ironically, brings to the fore the problem of excess in Lu Ling's style.

Implied in Lu Ling's "wastefully romantic" style is the rationale that, without a full exposé of her predicament and consequent fall, Guo Su'e's need for salvation cannot be so urgently presented to the reader. Ironically, whereas Lu Ling engages with the subject of hunger and lack, his style impresses one as being saturated with abundant, "indigestible" syntax, numerous narrated interior monologues, overflowing free-indirect speeches, and rich symbolism in the vein of synesthesia. In other words, Lu Ling seems to have furnished his novel with a style that suggests anything but lack. One must therefore ask: what does Lu Ling's narrative expenditure mean vis-à-vis a narratology based on stoicism and simplicity? Has Lu Ling violated the "morality of form" when he interprets material and spiritual destitution using a linguistic extravaganza? Most intriguingly, how does such a narrative expenditure bear on the hidden vision of Mao's hunger discourse, which promises infinitude and abundance?

Emphasis on the congruence between theme and its formal manifestation, the world and the word, is one of the oldest literary concepts, and it retained its currency in nineteenth-century Europe, despite the actual practice of the great realists. When Mao launched in 1942 his campaign for a new literature to reflect and instruct the general public, he did not break any new ground, merely putting conventional realism to his own uses. With plebeian subject matter, modest language, skeletal structure, and popular imagery, Chinese literature in the wake of the Yan'an talk was charged with the double duty of fleshing out the insufficiencies of reality and embodying the spirit by which reality would at last become sufficient. Literature was treated as an extension of life; practice and theory, lived and imagined experience, became one.

Following Mao's logic, one might conclude that *Hungry Guo Su'e* is flawed by a discrepancy between form and content, as a result of the mode of production to which it was bound. Created in Chongqing, the wartime Nationalist capital and an ideologically reactionary environment compared to Yan'an, the novel is inevitably less informed by the new aura of revolutionary literature. And to that extent, one can even suggest that the novel's (capitalist?) fixation on formal expenditure recaptured the spirit that occupied nineteenth-century European realists from Walter Scott to Emile Zola. Georg Lukács once contended that this fixation enabled the writers to look fully into the dark niches of reality, while still manifesting itself as one of the problems of that reality.[44] Indeed, Lu Ling's relentless depiction of the animalistic undercurrents of humanity reminds one of Zola's famed naturalism, the last, inevitable stage in the Lukácsian timetable of "classical" realism. What remains implicit in Lukács's comment is the irony that, despite his avowed intent as an experimentalist in literary science, Zola exhibits in his works a highly impressionist predilection; subjects such as poverty, sickness, crime, and hunger are treated in such a sensuous and exuberant manner that they exude the same unlikely charm as in the paintings of his impressionist contemporaries, Manet, Renoir, and Toulouse-Lautrec.

This is where Lu Ling's problem becomes pertinent. Not unlike Zola, who unwittingly turned his scientific enterprise into a parade of subjective spectacles, Lu Ling injects in his works an eccentric style quite resistant to Communist aesthetic formulae. Referring to Hu Feng's theory, Lu Ling could have retorted that, while Guo Su'e under his treatment is not a Communist female paragon, she nevertheless undergoes a most horrible degradation and death to enact a "negative dialectic" in regard to the prospective revolution. Guo Su'e's infamous hunger instantiates *both* the cause *and* the effect of a society bereft of any "spiritual" nourishment; thus it emphasizes all the more the need for revolution. Insofar as Lu Ling believes China's final salvation "presupposes" the total degradation of someone like Guo, history can be seen as a regressive movement, with each stage deteriorating more than the preceding one, until revolution reveals its true progressive course in one great leap forward. The logic of *Hungry Guo Su'e* is that depravity and purification are like the winding and release of a cosmic spring; hence the intensified pursuit of decadence in the absence, or service, of redemption.[45]

I do not mean that Lu Ling is more appealing to us than other leftist writers of his time merely because he has betrayed salvationist narratology. Although one may twist Lukácsian logic and conclude that Lu Ling derives his linguistic charm ironically from his inability to unite reality and Reality, language and Truth, the flip side of the argument may also be valid. As in the case of Zola's total conviction of his own empiricism, the lack of any positive promise in Lu Ling's work, instead of hinting at the author's ideological slippage, may prove to be a most tendentious way of pledging his faith in Communist salvation—a faith that need not be rewarded by either miracle or deus ex machina. A dangerous faith, too, because to prove its total imperative, it demands a total test of temptations, including the loss of faith.

Thus, if orthodox Communist literature calls for an immediate and intelligible resolution, through which decadence and revolution are melodramatically displayed, Lu Ling's novel appears far more radical, because it is underlain by a cluster of semantic axes as contradictory as immanent faith and absurdist whim, fanatic aspiration and sensuous desire. It is with such depth behind his political vision, I argue, that Lu Ling can risk ambiguity, or wasteful expenditure, in language, characterization, and plot, which is inhibited—or sublimated—by Mao's discourse.

Historical hindsight tempts one to read an allegory into Guo Su'e's hunger and death. Lu Ling was purged from the new Communist society, together with other members of the Hu Feng gang, in the mid-1950s, *Hungry Guo Su'e* being only one example of his ideological impurity. One recalcitrant fictional hungry woman had to be sacrificed so that postrevolutionary men and women could be nourished on more soothing fictional formulas. In the late 1950s, as the country was happily digesting Mao's words—his spiritual food—rampant physical starvation was already under way. During the Great Leap Forward (1959–1962), millions of people paid their respects to Mao by dying, or killing and eating each other, in the name of spiritual truth.[46]

When Lu Ling was at last rehabilitated in the 1980s, he was already a schizophrenic old man, thoroughly reformed and unable to write anything measuring up to the standard set by his early works.[47] Although his novels were altogether unknown to the general reader, the language revolution he had quietly launched inspired a new generation of writers in the 1980s, including modernists such as Ge Fei, Bei Cun, and Yu Hua. Responding to a new kind of self-indulgent hunger that spread across post-Maoist China, these young writers scandalize orthodox Chinese readers with a literature that threatens to devour all certainties and encourage feasting on possibility: they took up where Lu Ling left off.

TAN YUEXIANG

Tan Yuexiang is the female protagonist of *The Rice-Sprout Song* by Eileen Chang, one of the most important writers of modern Chinese fiction. When she turned up in occupied Shanghai during the Second World War, Chang was welcomed and simultaneously condemned as a popular romance writer who was turning her back on the cause of national salvation. Her inquiries into human frailties and trivialities, stylized portraits of Chinese mannerisms, and "celebrations" of historical contingencies make her a perfect contrast to the discourse of orthodoxy represented by such writers as Lu Xun, Mao Dun, and Ding Ling. But, as the century came to its end, Chang proved to be far more observant than most of her peers in depicting China's tragicomic search for the modern.

After the Communist liberation in 1949, Chang first decided to stay in her beloved Shanghai, but political circumstances were so unpredictable that in 1952 she left for Hong Kong. During her 1952–55 stay in Hong Kong, she was commissioned by the United States Information Service to write two novels in English, *The Rice-Sprout Song* and *Naked Earth;* she later rewrote them in Chinese (*Yangge* and *Chidi zhilian*). Both novels have clear anti-Communist themes, and to that extent they can easily be taken as examples of cold war propaganda. Neither *The Rice-Sprout Song* nor *Naked Earth* has ever been popular with her fans because Chang seemed to have dropped her familiar subject matter for something more epic. They also raised the eyebrows of those who insisted that high literature must transcend politics.

As I have argued elsewhere, Chang is cynical about the myth of national salvation, a firm believer in individualism, and a connoisseur of fin-de-siècle aesthetics.[48] During her three years living under a Communist regime, she witnessed the ever-tightening control of Maoist policy and sensed the rapid decline of her own creativity. In Hong Kong, she might have been equally skeptical of the goals of the anti-Communist front, but felt nonetheless more compelled than ever to articulate her own politics. In the formulaic closure of the political novel, she manages to lay bare the constraints of propaganda literature, left and right, and to set up a play between them, such as to expose the volatile relations between politics and literature.

The Rice-Sprout Song conveys the horror and absurdity that the land reform movement brought to a southern village in China in the early 1950s. The victorious revolution, followed by the redistribution of land, is supposed to "liberate" the peasants of the village. But, contrary to their hopes, life does not change. As a result of both natural and man-made disasters, the peasants face yet another threat of famine, and China's involvement in the Korean War only deepens their misery. When they can no longer endure the pressure from local leaders to produce grain, the peasants take to bloody rioting. The local people's militia intervenes, massacring the rioters and further tightening their control in the village. At the end of the novel, the survivors are forced to parade and take part in the New Year's celebrations.

Instituted as early as the 1940s, land reform was among the most important policies of the Chinese Communist Revolution in its early stages. At first glance, land reform appeared to be nothing more than a radical agricultural-economic policy. But, as argued in Chapter 2, the movement was never a mere attempt to revamp the rural infrastructure; rather, it was always given a superstructural dimension, as its implementation contributed to and was conditioned by a program of drastic changes in traditional Chinese morality, legality, and psychology. As early as the mid-1940s, leftist writers such as Zhao Shuli (1906–1970), Zhou Libo (1908–1979), and Ding Ling were already engaged in writing about the triumphant consequences of the movement in northern China.[49] Their works do not stop at describing the redistribution to the many of the land that once belonged to the few. For them, reform of the Chinese landscape would lead to the reform of the Chinese mindscape.

The Rice-Sprout Song rewrites this land reform discourse. As if parodying the jubilant tone of Communist land reform novels, Chang maintains a festive atmosphere in *The Rice-Sprout Song*. But as her story develops, this festive atmosphere turns out to be a celebration of something ghastly, the prelude to a danse macabre. Chang details the chilling food shortages in the newly liberated south, traditionally the richest agricultural area of China, and reveals the desperate measures peasants took to survive the famine. Her critique of Communist abuses, however, is accompanied by a deep sympathy with, and curiosity about, the human endeavor to undergo the test of life, however absurd. In her moral schemata, villains are detestable not because they are inhuman but because they are only too human. Hence the paradox that the most anti-Communist moment of *The Rice-Sprout Song* occurs when the two major Communist villains win our sympathy rather than our hatred.

Fighting Hunger

Hu Shi (1891–1962), a leader of the modern Chinese literary revolution, was among the first scholars to praise *The Rice-Sprout Song.*[50] He sees hunger as the theme of the novel and credits Chang for her verbal subtlety and emotive control, a far cry from the "tears-and-blood" style of propaganda literature, Communist or anti-Communist. Following Hu Shi, critics have praised Chang's understated yet powerful narrative, but little has been said about the way she elaborates on the politics of hunger.[51]

The disproportionate growth in population and food supply has long threatened China's modernization. When Mao launched the land reform movement in the 1940s, he was aware of the fundamental problem of Chinese agricultural economy and tried to tackle it with radical measures. Together with land reform, "hunger revolution" had been the slogan of one of the most enticing Communist campaigns of the 1930s and 1940s.

Chang's questions are: if the hunger revolution has been successfully implemented, why do the Chinese still suffer from hunger? Could it be possible that a new famine has taken place as a result of the successful revolution? The average grain harvest between 1949 and 1958 was less than those of 1931–1937, and the peasants were better off between 1929 and 1933, when annual per capita grain production was higher.[52] In the early 1930s, the leftist writer Mao Dun had published the *Village Trilogy,* in which he made famous a paradox of production: the harder the farmers work, the less they earn; the more grain they produce, the hungrier they are. By means of this paradox, Mao Dun's *Trilogy* pointed to the irrationality of the prerevolutionary mode of agricultural production. *The Rice-Sprout Song* insinuates that the same paradox applies to the new mode of agricultural production.

According to Chang, the old landlords may have been liquidated, but the Communist government has become the single new landlord, with proportionately increased power and greed. Jin'gen and his wife, Yuexiang, the protagonists of the novel, work hard to meet the increasing demands of local cadres, only to realize that, however hard they work, they will never have enough to eat.

As the famine becomes more serious, Yuexiang, and not her husband, Jin'gen, emerges as the stronger one in the household. Before the land reform, Yuexiang worked as a maid in Shanghai and is therefore more worldly than her husband and most villagers. She returns home in response to the government's call to support rural work, realizing too late that life in the village is far worse than she had imagined. A pragmatic woman, Yuexiang understands that to survive hunger she has to store and ration food strictly; to that effect, she cheats cadres, turns down her sister-in-law's requests, and even denies her own daughter's request for a bowl of rice. But Yuexiang cannot prevent her husband from rioting. After learning that Jin'gen has been killed by the cadres, she sets the barn on fire and burns to death.

From Lu Xun's Xianglin's wife to Lu Ling's Guo Su'e, the "hungry woman" has been made into an archetype of modern Chinese literature; more often than not, these hungry women are treated as passive victims characterized by physical weakness and gender inferiority. They are symbols of a certain "victimology," projecting the suffering of the Chinese people. Through these characters, the writers are able to address the polemics of lack—lack of food, justice, humanity, and revolution. Yuexiang is quite different from the stereotypical hungry woman. She is the most resourceful member of her family; after her husband's death, she does not lack the courage to act out her anger. Whereas Guo Su'e defies the archetype of the hungry woman through her excessive sexual appetite, Yuxiang distinguishes herself by her shrewdness and resilience in "cutting down" her appetites, of whatever kind.

In his reading of *The Rice-Sprout Song,* C. T. Hsia calls attention to Yuexiang's endurance and deep feeling for her husband and family. Hsia puts this female character in the humanitarian context of modern Chinese writing.[53] Granting its humanitarian context, however, I would argue that the novel's power is derived not so much from Chang's compassion as from her lack of confidence in humanity and her idiosyncratic notion of individualism. For her, individualism is a euphemism for self-interest and self-protection; "selfish" as it may be to others, it is nonetheless the only way one can survive in a time of crisis. This unique individualism gives meaning to Chang's embrace of the material world, her aestheticization of eschatology, and her play of irony, which subverts everything hailed as solid, including her own writings. And she does not hesitate to generalize these traits and associate them with her vision of femininity.

Yuexiang is a creditable female only by Eileen Chang's definition of femininity: selfish, earthy, and material. Although she may not appear as slick and sophisticated as those Shanghai ladies who crowd Chang's earlier fiction, she proves herself worthy of citizenship in Chang's female republic by fully representing what Chang calls "the most universal, the most basic of humanity: the cyclical movement of the four seasons; the earth; life, age, illness, and death; recreation and food."[54] Compared to the agenda of other feminist writers of her time, Chang's understanding of femininity may seem rather passive, if not reactionary. She is nevertheless a most somber guardian of her space as a woman and as a writer. She knows well the importance of being not too earnest—or not too politically correct, in contemporary terms—whatever the cause.

At a time when most male and female Chinese writers were eager to exchange individual subjectivities for a collective, national subjectivity, Chang's brand of selfish and feminine mannerisms are a genuinely defiant gesture. As *The Rice-Sprout Song* develops, it is Yuexiang who sees through the myth of spiritual food and dares to cross political guidelines in pursuit of her family's livelihood. Reading Yuexiang against other Communist figures in the novel, one wonders who is more sensitive to the material basis of life. Ironically, Yuexiang has to be killed, in the produce barn, to ensure Communist spiritual abundance.

Writing Hunger

The significance of Yuexiang as a hungry woman takes on an extra dimension in the subplot of *The Rice-Sprout Song*. While the villagers are increasingly threatened by the shortage of food, Gu Gang, a scriptwriter, is sent from Shanghai to the country to "experience life." His mission is none other than to witness the "success" of land reform and write a movie script about the alleged abundance to be found in the new rural life. Gu Gang, however, soon suffers from writer's block because of his isolation in the village and his discovery of the discrepancies between what he sees and what he is supposed to see, between what he can write and what he is supposed to write. But an even more immediate and embarrassing reason is that, once settled in the village, he too must deal with the lack of food, in spite of his privileged class. Driven by the constant fear of hunger, Gu Gang more often racks his brain in search of food than for cinematic inspiration.

Gu's story drives home Eileen Chang's sarcasm about the myth of Maoist spiritual gastronomy. Before he can produce Communist "cultural food," Gu Gang needs to feed himself—in the first place, with material food. He finds temporary solace in Yuexiang, since she has been to Shanghai and appreciates his "culture"; even so, he cannot fully understand Yuexiang's need. As a self-conscious revolutionary artist, Gu hews to the party line regardless of the visible evidence in the village. In the most ironic twist of the novel, he finally completes his manuscript, finding inspiration in the villagers' food riots.

Thus, the peasant riot against the land reform movement provides the idea, in Gu's script, for a peasant riot scene against Nationalist landlords. In the script, the reactionary landlords are seen "eating and drinking ferociously" behind closed doors, and there, in the midst of the secret banquet, stands a young woman who looks like Yuexiang: "Her main function in the scene is to lean against the table . . . thus lending an eerie and sensual atmosphere to the secret meeting among the landlords. Her appearance and dress look very much like Yuexiang's."[55] Nowhere else has Chang shown more bitter sarcasm about Communist morality than in describing Gu Gang's final submission to the formulaic, feudal convention: a woman in reality recklessly seeking food has been demonized in light of the traditional stereotype of the femme fatale, a woman relentlessly hungry for sex, in Communist fiction.

Moreover, Gu Gang is so fascinated by the dazzling visual effect of the barn fire set by Yuexiang that he makes it the climax of his script, rewriting it as a fire set by Nationalist spies. From hungry woman to lustful femme fatale, Yuexiang's transformation in Gu Gang's script bespeaks a gynophobia in feudal Chinese wisdom that has now been transplanted to the revolutionary Communist imagination. Gu Gang's experience of hunger and his writing about hunger betray a woman he thought he had understood and appreciated.

The story of Gu Gang illustrates the tension between the oppressiveness of a totalitarian party and the creative freedom of a writer. But Eileen Chang gives this tension one more twist. Gu may have betrayed his political conscience by writing what he did not see and did not believe. He nevertheless settles with his artistic conscience because, party line notwithstanding, he has organized words, images, and symbolism into a verbal and visual extravaganza that meets his own satisfaction. Is Gu's script a decadent testimonial to or tendentious propaganda for a certain ideology? Has he acted out the cause of "art for art's sake" under a regime that despises "art for art's sake"? Has he become a despicable accomplice in the collaboration of art with politics? And what is "art for art's sake," after all, if not the insatiable Maoist desire for ideological perfection?

In the afterword to the Chinese edition of the novel, Chang wryly tells us that *The Rice-Sprout Song* was inspired by a "reported" confession by a Communist leader admitting his failure to prevent a peasant riot during the land reform movement, and by a Communist movie that featured a barn fire set by Nationalist spies. She turned these pro-Communist materials against themselves. But a follow-up question is: what about Chang herself as an anti-Communist writer?

Not unlike her character, Eileen Chang has enacted, on the scene of writing, a cluster of self-reflexive ironies on the mutual implication of history and fiction, imagined truth and materialized myth. Her sarcasm about Gu Gang's mission to rewrite history reverberates in her own work, throwing open the question of its intentions. A writer who had been stranded in early 1950s Hong Kong, Chang was commissioned to write anti-Communist literature—a genre thought not to be her strong suit. She nevertheless managed to work out her own version of anti-Communist literature, a version that has unexpected depths but may not be welcome to the propaganda machine. Thus, in Gu Gang's story and her own afterword, Chang has written an allegory about the vulnerable situation of Chinese writers of the time, Communist and anti-Communist alike.

The final irony, perhaps, is that, forty years after the first publication of the novel, the hunger motif it so vividly portrayed has acquired a retrospective poignancy. Recent studies by historians such as Jasper Becker have revealed that, between 1958 and 1962, at least thirty million Chinese perished in perhaps the worst famine in Chinese history, one caused not by nature but by Mao's ideological vanity.[56] This man-made disaster was hardly acknowledged at the time, partly because of tight government censorship and partly because of the self-censoring of China experts. When Chang wrote *The Rice-Sprout Song* in the mid-1950s, she had neither the intention nor the resources to predict the forthcoming horrors, but in an uncanny way, her novel foretold the cruel absurdities that Chinese would experience. A China watcher she was not, and yet she saw something inherently ominous by resorting to her "material," commonsensical vision. "Our age plunges forward and is already well on its way to collapse, while a bigger catastrophe looms."[57] A connoisseur of eschatology, Chang made this sober prediction in regard to the China of the 1940s; with *The Rice-Sprout Song*, the prediction proved all too true and came to pass all too quickly, despite (or because of) official proclamations of an age of plenty.

CAI QIANHUI

"When I first came to your family, I was ready to eat bitterness," the fifty-year-old Cai Qianhui, who lies in a hospital bed, recalls to her brother-in-law, Li Guomu.[58] Struck down by a mysterious illness, Cai Qianhui has been hospitalized for two months and is getting increasingly weak in spite of the nourishment and medical care she has received. She eventually dies, and the cause of her death is revealed by a letter she leaves behind.

Cai Qianhui is the protagonist of "Mountain Path," by Chen Yingzhen, arguably the most important leftist writer from Taiwan. First published in 1983, "Mountain Path" is the second story in a trilogy Chen wrote in memory of the "White Terror" of the 1950s, an era that witnessed an increase in underground Taiwanese socialist activities followed by massive crackdowns and bloody purges by the Nationalist party.

In Chen Yingzhen's narration, we are not fully informed of the historical background of the story until the end, when Cai Qianhui's letter is posthumously disclosed. Of the clues provided in the first part of the story, the most intriguing is Cai Qianhui's revelation to her brother-in-law, "When I first came to your family, I was ready to eat bitterness." "Eat bitterness" *(chiku)*, a figure of speech that means "to endure hardships," suggests the life that Cai Qianhui must have lived. Indeed, as her letter details, for almost thirty years, she had helped the Li family survive all sorts of adversity, bringing it from the verge of starvation to the status of a comfortable urban middle-class household. Why, then, dying in a first-class hospital room, does she reiterate, nostalgically, her capacity to eat bitterness?

Unlike the two hungry women discussed above, Cai Qianhui appears well fed. Though widowed when she came to the Li household, she is well respected by the family of her brother-in-law and is almost like a mother to them; now, in the hospital, she is surrounded by doctors and all the food and medical supplies one could hope for to cure her mysterious disease. Yet Cai Qianhui lacks any appetite for food or anything else that might sustain her life. "She just became weak all of a sudden. Such a healthy person to become weak like that so suddenly."[59] When she dies, it is as a woman remembering those hungry days she had with her family.

Chen Yingzhen has invested the story of this enigmatic figure with a touching allegory about political idealism and its betrayal and, as I will argue below, about the treacherous conditions of Communist hunger politics. Chen Yingzhen's career may appear no less tortuous than those of some of the characters in his fiction. He was born into a pious Christian minister's family in northern Taiwan but grew up searching for his own beliefs. In 1967, Chen was arrested by the Nationalist party on a charge of pro-Communist activities, and he spent the next seven years in jail. After his release in 1973, he resumed his career as a writer, focusing mostly on the consequences of Taiwan's newfound economic prosperity, which resulted, Chen concluded, from American-Japanese capitalist imperialism beginning in the 1960s. As he continued to hold on to his leftist idealism, the gradual revelation of the atrocities of the Great Cultural Revolution must have struck him as an unbearable departure from the expected course of global Communist revolution. In the meantime, the death of Chiang Kai-shek in 1975 triggered a cluster of political metamorphoses in Taiwan, particularly the outburst of the Taiwanese independence movement. Chen Yingzhen was faced with multiple challenges: how could a once noble revolutionary ideal have turned rotten so fast in the fresh air of history? How could unconditional dedication entail falsehood, betrayal, and self-destruction? Should a Taiwanese leftist writer still endorse a Marxist regime that had caused such disaster in China?

An Anorexic Logic

"Mountain Path" is a remarkable effort on the part of Chen Yingzhen to respond to these questions. From Cai Qianhui's posthumous letter, one learns that, as a teenage girl, she was involved in a Communist organization in northern Taiwan, of which both her brother and her fiancé, Huang Zhenbo, were members. Through this connection, Cai came to know the leader of the organization, Li Guokun, who stole her heart through his unconditional idealism. The organization was later suppressed by the Nationalist government. Li Guokun was put to death and Huang Zhenbo sentenced to life in prison; the informant was none other than Qianhui's brother. To compensate for her brother's betrayal and sustain her own revolutionary romanticism, Cai Qianhui decided to "marry" into the family, oddly, not of her fiancé, Huang Zhenbo, but of Li Guokun. She went to the poverty-stricken Li family, making up a story that she and Li had been secretly married, and vowed, as Li's widow, to endure with them all hardships, or "eat bitterness," for the years to come.

Thirty years after arriving on the Li doorstep, Cai Qianhui, seated one morning in the comfortable living room of Li Guomu, her supposed brother-in-law, read in the newspaper that Huang Zhenbo, her real fiancé, had been released from prison. Shamed by her betrayal of Huang and his comrades, and even more by her ideological amnesia in recent years owing to changes in Taiwanese lifestyle, Cai collapsed and thereafter lost her will to live.

I summarize the story at length because it is full of melodramatic surprises. But to anyone who criticizes its hackneyed plot, Chen Yingzhen would perhaps have retorted that the outrageous history of the White Terror, which affected so many families, would seem only more "unlikely" than the story. By the same logic, he could also have argued that if for Cai Qianhui or Li Guokun "revolution" meant acting to make the impossible possible, it ought to demand an extraordinary sacrifice on the part of ordinary humanity. Thus the characterization of Cai Qianhui is credible precisely because she is capable of an incredible sacrifice; her story is a small-scale example of Communist hagiography.

My reading suggests that Cai Qianhui be regarded as one of the last hungry heroines of modern Chinese Communist discourse. Her appearance in Chen Yingzhen's fiction, across the Taiwan Straits and in the aftermath of the Cultural Revolution, recapitulates the metaphorics and metaphysics of hunger that have either enshrouded or enshrined so many modern Chinese female characters. There exists, however, a fundamental difference between Cai Qianhui and her other hungry sisters. Whereas characters such as Guo Su'e and Tan Yuexiang suffer egregiously from a lack of food, Cai Qianhui has more than enough, were it not for her antipathy to food and her inability to absorb nutrition. In the story, she is fed and dutifully eats, but she cannot help the deterioration of her body, as if she had no control over it anymore.

In Cai Qianhui's mysterious withering away, one discerns an "anorexic logic." By this I do not mean merely an eating disorder that results from a physical and psychological repugnance to food, a disease from which the term "anorexic" derives its primary definition. Rather, I mean a mode of thinking that compels one to configure one's body so as to express one's real relations to the world, in which consumption of food constitutes an embarrassment. At the core of such an anorexic logic is a tendency toward self-negation that drives one to despise or ignore one's corporeal constitution in anticipation of a higher, sanctified state of existence.

The medical and imagined symptoms of anorexia and their consequences have become a popular topic in recent years. Leslie Haywood, for instance, delineates how anorexia has been borrowed as a trope to describe the "bony," "self-destructive" aesthetics of European high modernism and its inherent phallocentric agenda.[60] In her study of the phenomena of "fasting girls" in the Victorian period, Joan Brumberg differentiates two types of anorexic women: *anorexia mirabilis* and *anorexia nervosa.* Whereas the former is seen as the result of divine immanence and thus calls for religious sanction, the latter is associated with a hysteria that requires medical examination.[61] From *anorexia mirabilis* to *anorexia nervosa,* or from religious miracle to clinical illness, argues Brumberg among others, there is a process of rhetorical ambiguity, and it is this process of ambiguity that informs the shift of episteme as well as the changed image of the modern woman at the turn of the century.[62]

Inspired by, but not limited to, these critical approaches, I find in the Chinese Communist hunger discourse an uncanny counterpart to the medical, gendered symptoms of anorexia: a self-willed hunger motivated (possibly first) by historical circumstances but reinforced, and finally sanctioned, by ideological goals. The Chinese Communist hunger discourse has always entertained a component of self-willed hunger as a physical testimony to ideological strength. In theory, it reminds one of traditional religious fasting as a trial of self-purgation through self-negation, but in practice, it echoes more the (neo-)Confucian tenet of curbing one's corporeal welfare while asserting one's moral rectitude.[63] From the case of Boyi and Shuqi in the early Zhou dynasty to Liu Zongzhou (1578–1645) of the late Ming, Chinese historiography is full of accounts of model figures who have starved to death to assert their moral or political integrity. And in terms of moralizing the relations between women and food, what can be more telling than the statement by Song scholar Cheng Yi (1033–1107): "To die from hunger is an extremely trivial matter; to lose one's chastity is an extremely grave shame"?[64]

Cai Qianhui's case is challenging because at first glance she is neither anorexic in the strict Western medical sense nor a self-willed hunger heroine in the Chinese ideological sense. Her death, presumably from her body's resistance to nutrition, comes, at best, too late (and too gratuitously) to serve the revolution that failed. What is more, one finds in Cai Qianhui a cluster of ambiguities: a girl in the guise of the widow of someone other than her fiancé; a virgin who assumes the role of "mother of the revolution" and is sustained by "eating bitterness"; and a woman who denies her womanly qualities in the name of Communist fraternity. This cluster of ambiguities culminates in her mysterious death, where the lines between medical pathology and ideological fanaticism, regret and bliss, alimentary nutrition and spiritual hemorrhage are blurred. Cai Qianhui never demonstrates the medical symptom of turning away food, but the point is precisely that she has developed such contempt for her body that food simply becomes a superficial reminder of the gap between what she is eating and what she wants to be fed.

Thus it may not be coincidence that in the story Cai Qianhui first utters the words "eating bitterness" as her brother-in-law offers her a bowl of the Taiwanese delicacy perch soup. As Chen Yingzhen writes, "She obediently ate the perch Yuexiang [Guomu's wife] fed her, spoonful by spoonful, chewing it very attentively."[65] The way Cai Qianhui eats

> suddenly mak[es] Li Guomu think of his own mother. . . . Sister-in-law had done just what [Li's wife is] doing now—feeding mother spoonful by spoonful. What's different, however, is that now Sister-in-law is in a private room in the hospital; Mother had to lie in a damp, dark room, full of the smell of urine from the toilet bucket. Also, when Mother's sickness became worse, her spirits changed. . . . Once, when Sister-in-law was spoon-feeding Mother rice porridge, she deliberately spat it out, dirtying the quilt and the edge of the bed.
>
> "My life is already too miserable, don't make me eat any more," she sobbed without tears. . . . "I'll die and get it all over with. Let me die and get it all over with. . . ."[66]

In this scene, the Li family's past and present are linked together through two old women's complex responses to food. Cai Qianhui's mother-in-law spat out rice porridge presumably because she had suffered enough and wished only to die; she knew well that to sustain her life, much food had to be wasted on her at the cost of younger family members. Thirty years later, Cai Qianhui too has lost the will to live, for the opposite reason, that she has not suffered enough. She despises herself as "a tamed animal" in an illusory progressive environment of capitalism and, as there is no other way to express her repentance and protest, she turns to her own body as the last purgatory.

Cai Qianhui's desire to relinquish her body nevertheless should be regarded as the climax of an entire life dedicated to self-sacrifice. Taking another look at the "anorexic logic" implied in the Chinese Communist hunger discourse, one realizes that throughout her life, Cai has lived to denounce her corporeal well-being. Over the three decades of "eating bitterness" at the Li's, she undertook ordeals unthinkable to a woman who had grown up in a well-to-do family. As she puts it in her letter to Huang Zhenbo, she "worked furiously . . . making a slave of [her] body and soul. . . . Whenever [she] was physically and emotionally exhausted, [she] thought of those men who had died . . . and those . . . exiled . . . to endure endless punishment. *Whenever [she] bathed and saw [her] body, once as young and fresh as a flower, wither day by day from the heavy manual labor, [she] thought of [Guokun] . . . and of those . . . whose lonely aging bodies and souls were imprisoned and completely forgotten by the outside.* With such thoughts, [she] relished [her hardship] with a sweet taste [my emphasis]."[67]

Cai Qianhui has all along seen the withering away of her virginal body as a way to live out the saintly bliss of the hunger revolution. But in the 1980s in Taiwan, she cannot understand why her revolutionary life of "eating bitterness" has brought the family to a heaven of capitalist expenditure. Material things have made her and her family "tame animals" of capitalism, yet she thinks back to her days of hardship, in search of the "proper" outcome: Communist utopian life. Finally, as Cai Qianhui writes in her letter, "If the revolution fails on the mainland, does that mean [Li Guokun's] death and [Huang Zhenbo's] long-term imprisonment have turned into meaningless punishments more cruel than death or life in prison?"[68] For Cai, the only way to assure the meaning of life as it should be, as prescribed by the Communist Revolution, is to cut life (and time) short by losing her body, an act that could at least freeze her own history into the crystallized narrative form of History.

A "No-Body" Aesthetics

Chen Yingzhen's negotiation with Chinese Marxist revolutionism does not end with his rewriting of the hunger motif. Before he is an ideologue, he is first and foremost a strong writer. As in the case of Lu Xun, Lu Ling, and Eileen Chang, Chen has always been self-conscious about the conditions of literature vis-à-vis the conditions of politics. In what sense, then, can we read "Mountain Path" not simply as a political allegory but as an allegory about the politics of writing?

Lu Xun and Lu Ling wrote about hungry women as a way of conveying their own political yearning, or hunger, for national reform. Whatever their miseries, these hungry women are expected to inform a national aspiration for revolution, which would help feed Chinese with material and spiritual food. In "Mountain Path," however, Chen Yingzhen struggles to find a rationale after the Communist revolution has come to a disastrous halt and such a noble hunger discourse has acquired the expected validation. If *Hungry Guo Su'e* marks the outbreak of the libidinous political unconscious that knows no limits, "Mountain Path" faces the challenge of recalling, elegiacally, the bygone days of political fervor amid the ruins of revolutionary praxis. Instead of the primitive force driving Guo Su'e to consume and consummate her desire in the shadow of total destruction, Chen Yingzhen invests in Cai Qianhui's body politics a deep sense of irony: her anorexic gesture is a retrospective visitation of the hunger spirit, and her suicidal motive is the result of her historical hindsight. She has experienced both hunger and revolution, but these have resulted in a quite unexpected outcome. Hence Cai Qianhui's apprehension in her letter: "I have a feeling of desperate waste."[69]

What worries Cai Qianhui is not the bloody waste of the life and idealism of one generation of Taiwanese revolutionaries, but the threatening "meaninglessness" of that waste viewed in retrospect. Strangely enough, to act out her resistance to the wasted revolution, she chooses to waste her own body, as if only through the relinquishment of the body could she regain the pristine nature of her revolutionary selfhood.

Given Chen Yingzhen's Christian background, one can talk about a kind of religious martyrdom that underlies Cai Qianhui's political fanaticism. Feminists can charge Chen Yingzhen with indulging the idea of female self-effacement in support of a male-centered revolutionary cause, to the point where woman is transformed from a nobody in the revolution to a literal *no body* after the revolution. I suspect, nevertheless, that Chen Yingzhen is no more an ideological fanatic or a misogynist than he is a modernist informed by the (anti-)heroism of the absurd. Although allegedly dying for a revolutionary cause that has been invalidated in the postrevolutionary days, Cai Qianhui shows more determination to hold on to an idealism on her own terms. Her insistence intimates a mixture of self-assertion and self-abandon, thereby introducing the absurdist double bind Chen Yingzhen describes as a "desperate waste."[70]

We then come to one last, poignant fact: instead of private but violent measures of suicide, Cai Qianhui dies in a slow and semipublic exhibition—the spectacle of a body wasting away. In this regard, she brings to mind Franz Kafka's "Hunger Artist." The hunger artist, the reader will recall, cages himself as an art exhibit, and the subject of his performance art is the withering away of his own subjectivity. In other words, he acts out an art of deduction through his own self-deduction. With such a self-deductive and self-destructive character, as critics suggest, Kafka announces the coming of the age of modernism.[71] But in light of the Judaic mysticism behind Kafka's writing, this self-deduction may very well be regarded as the first step toward the plenitude of divine grace.

I have yet to find evidence of Chen Yingzhen's indebtedness to the hunger artist, although, considering his education, he should have been aware of the work. My point is rather that by describing Cai Qianhui's death in the manner of hunger-artist-cum-ideologue, Chen has presented a provocative mixture of modernist aesthetics and Chinese Marxist ethics.

But Chen's story has something more to tell us about history and its artistic inscription. If writing can be treated as a "trace" in the poststructuralist sense, removed from the primal, logocentric scene, which in its own turn is an *écriture* of the regressive ontological meaning, the fact that Cai Qianhui leaves behind a letter strikes a final ironic note. Written in a lyrical, nostalgic tone, the letter appears as a relic, something that will survive the erosion of time and bear witness to the truth that Cai Qianhui was unable to speak in her lifetime. But as remnants of the past, relics cannot retroactivate history per se but can only reaffirm the irretrievability of history. A sense of futility pervades the end of this story, which aims to be the remainder and reminder of past revolutionism. Questions must be asked: hasn't Chen Yingzhen himself become a ghostlike chronicler of the glory of revolutionism? Would the meaning of Chen's corpus end up like Cai Qianhui's skeletal corpse, which asserts its protest against history by canceling its own existence?

THE DAUGHTERS OF HUNGER

I have described the polemics of hunger in modern Chinese literature in terms of three "hungry women" portrayed by Lu Ling, Eileen Chang, and Chen Yingzhen. By depicting the causes of these women's hunger and the way in which each one deals with the material consequences of hunger, these writers have achieved a special perspective from which to survey the revolutionary discourse of modern China. Behind these women, moreover, lies the writers' own desire—hunger—for a better understanding of the metaphoric and metaphysical dimensions of hunger, as proffered by Chinese Marxist discourse.

Thus, though a dedicated follower of Hu Feng's theory of Marxist spiritual food, Lu Ling reveals an eccentric self-indulgence when he "wastefully" parades the depraved deeds of hungry Guo Su'e and the people around her. His extravagant style betrays a textual desire that appears to contradict the stylistic manual prescribed by Mao. Eileen Chang, by paralleling Tan Yuexiang's desperate effort to survive the rural famine with Gu Gang's desperate effort to churn up cultural food for mass consumption, takes issue with the circulation of superstructural nourishment, which had been deemed unquestionable in an ideological system that otherwise favored infrastructural work. Chen Yingzhen, in a story about the waste of recollecting things past, ponders the authenticity of remembering and writing when political dedication had become a thing of the past.

All three writers start with a hard-core realist style by mimicking reality and comparing truth claims to linguistic make-believe. But while depicting hunger, they cannot help taking up the "side issues" of the aesthetics of hunger writing, which can be so polemical as to offend the political authorities. Hunger is no longer merely a theme or subject matter but a formal challenge, a body politics demanding its own literary politic. In Lu Ling's indulgence in textual desire, Eileen Chang's flirtation with metafiction (a novel about the writing of a movie script about hunger), and Chen Yingzhen's posthumous epistolary confession, one witnesses a most engaging dialogue between Chinese (anti-)Communist writing and modernist sensibilities.

The hunger motif has remained a popular subject since the 1980s. Zhang Xianliang's (b. 1939) *Luhua shu sanbuqu* (Mimosa trilogy, 1983) and *Wo de putishu* (My own Bodhi tree, 1995) and Wang Ruowang's (1918–2001) *Ji'e sanbuqu* (A trilogy of hunger, 1981) use hunger as a point of reference for chronicling the Maoist coercion of intellectuals. Lu Wenfu's (b. 1928) "Meishijia" (The gourmet, 1984) and Ah Cheng's (b. 1949) "Qiwang" (The chess king, 1984), on the other hand, approach hunger from the vantage point of either ironic recollection or critical lyricism. Liu Zhenyun's (b. 1959) *Wengu 1942* (Remembering 1942, 1992) chronicles the famine of 1942, which took the lives of millions, using a complex of genres including reportage, newsreel, fictional reconstruction, and contemplative essay, whereas Yu Hua's (b. 1964) *Huozhe* (To live, 1992) portrays the forty years of PRC history as nothing but a record of survivalism.[72] And in Mo Yan's (b. 1957) *Jiuguo* (The wine republic, 1992), Chinese cannibalistic desire comes full circle; instead of the Lu Xunesque "save the children," one hears the hungry calls of gourmets to "cook the children."

What about the fate of hungry women in end-of-the-century Chinese literature? The most unforgettable case, perhaps, is *Shafu* (The butcher's wife, 1983) by the Taiwanese writer Li Ang (b. 1952). In this novella, a woman is forced to have sex with her husband, a pig butcher, in exchange for food. Driven by humiliation and hunger, she finally butchers her husband like one of his pigs. In Yu Hua's "Gudian aiqing" (A classical love story, 1987), a dark parody of the classical talent-beauty *(caizi jiaren)* romance, the beauty ends up becoming an "edible human" *(cairen)* in a year of famine, her limbs chopped off and sold to the highest bidder. In Li Rui's (b. 1951) *Wufeng Zhishu* (Trees without wind, 1993), hungry women are sold as late as 1963 in the back country of Shan'xi to poor and deformed peasants as "public" wives. Across the Taiwan Straits, Tan Zhongdao (b. 1964) publishes an equally ghoulish account of famine, "Canghai zhi yisu" (A tiny grain in the world, 1994), in which the hungry woman protagonist runs away from her husband's family, who was conspiring to eat her, only to be consumed by her own parents once she arrives home.

The latest addition to the century-long gallery of hungry women is the heroine in the London-based writer Hongying's (b. 1962) novel, *Ji'e de nüer* (The daughter of hunger, 1997). *The Daughter of Hunger* should be regarded as one of the rare fictional accounts to confront the national famine during the Great Leap Forward, whose atrocities still remain taboo today. More importantly, it relates in autobiographical form a woman writer's painful experience of growing up during the time.

Hongying was born in the heyday of the Great Leap Forward, the illegitimate daughter of an illiterate woman. Hongying tells how her mother ran away from an arranged marriage, but could not evade fate's blows in the years to come, including her husband being jailed on political charges. During the Great Famine, she and her children were close to starvation when a young man came to their rescue and then fell in love with her. The affair was soon disclosed, but by then Hongying's mother had already become pregnant with her.

The story of Hongying's mother provides a striking parallel to Lu Ling's Guo Su'e. Both are hungry women who harbor a desire that cannot be settled by mere food. Given the horrible life Hongying's mother led after her adultery was revealed, one can well imagine what would have happened to Guo Su'e even if she had survived the private trial and lived to see the establishment of the People's Republic. Hongying's own experience of growing up "almost" repeats her mother's. Her foster father is never able to convey his concern about her; her birth father never gets the chance to meet her until she is eighteen; and her first lover, her history teacher twice her age, introduces her to sex but soon commits suicide because of his own historical burden. "All three of my fathers—my foster father, my natural father, and my history teacher—betrayed me."[73]

Her tumultuous life notwithstanding, "the daughter of hunger" grows up to become a chronicler of the famine that devastated China and that preceded the even more disastrous Cultural Revolution. Like thousands of women her age, Hongying has all along been troubled by a deep-seated hunger: she is fed up with the revolutionary spiritual food and starving for more sensuous kinds of food: a full meal, love, sex. Even years after the hunger years, she can never forget the deficiency and desolation. In both the literal and the symbolic sense, hunger embodies her experience of becoming a woman.

Unlike Xianglin's wife, Guo Su'e, Tan Yuexiang, and even her own mother, all of whom were silenced by their society and denied basic survival needs, Hongying cries out and writes down, however painfully, the fears and desires, anxieties and aspirations shared by the new generation of daughters of hunger. Hongying's writing career starts where her early life story ends; in contrast to the conventional male bildungsroman, her novel concerns not her acquisition of social knowledge but its relinquishment, not her initiation into society but her self-chosen exile.

"Perhaps someday, my innate feeling of hunger can be cured by writing,"[74] Hongying writes at the end of *The Daughter of Hunger*. While one is not sure whether writing will ever exorcise the hunger demon that has haunted her life, Hongying has at least made known her capacity to produce her own kind of "spiritual food." By inscribing in her own way memories of the days of utter destitution, she has managed to turn the tables on the formidable hunger discourse. Eighty years after Xiangling's wife falls down on a snowy New Year's Eve and dies a silent death, a hungry woman at the end of the twentieth century can at last write a story of her own, answering some of the unpalatable questions posed by a cannibalistic century.

Chapter 5

Of Scars and National Memory

Literature of the late 1940s to the early 1960s emerged during one of the most volatile moments in modern Chinese cultural history. In the wake of the Communist takeover of mainland China and the Nationalist retreat to Taiwan in 1949, Chinese literature bifurcated into two traditions, each flaunting a distinct political and aesthetic program. Although politics and literature had been closely tied since the rise of "new fiction" in the late Qing era, it was in the midcentury that writing finally transformed itself into political action and became a vocation that regularly demanded as much blood as ink.

When registering the physical and psychological consequences of the splitting of China, mid-twentieth-century Chinese writers reenacted a typology of scars. In Chapter 1 I described the scar in association with the truncated condition of a nation in search of (literary) modernity as it was understood in the era before 1949. In Lu Xun's recollection of viewing a Chinese spy being decapitated, I argued, a scar is invoked both as physical evidence of violence and as a "textual" memento of the violence. As the physical trace of a wound, a scar is the body's way of simultaneously affirming and denying a man-made or accidental injury. The scar is a sign of the healing, and sealing, of that which has been unnaturally opened and exposed. But so long as the line of laceration remains, it is a reminder of the moment of violence. Implied in the scar is its corporeal testimony, pointing to the infliction upon the body of intrusion, to the passage of time, and to a contested desire to deny, while revisiting, the scene of violence. Upon examination of one's scars, memories are brought back and an implicit narrative takes shape.[1]

This scar typology was to take on a national dimension during the 1950s, when it was brought to bear on a new, lacerated state of Chinese geopolitics. For émigré mainland writers in Taiwan and Hong Kong, to write at this historical moment was to commemorate the loss of the motherland as well as the trauma of diaspora. For writers supporting the new Communist regime, on the other hand, to write was to remember the suffering under the old Nationalist regime and to anticipate recovery in the socialist utopia. In either case the physical wound—the scar—is frequently invoked to flesh out the historical reality of a split nation and a deeply injured semantic system.

For instance, in 1954, Duanmu Fang (b. 1922), a mainland émigré writer living in Taiwan, wrote a novel entitled *Ba xunzhang* (A badge of scars). In the novel, the protagonist, a young Nationalist soldier, recalls his experience in the second Sino-Japanese war and the civil war between 1946 and 1949. In combat with the Japanese, the soldier's right cheek is pierced by an enemy bayonet, leaving an eternally grotesque scar across his face. After his recovery, the protagonist joins a group of anti-Japanese guerrillas in Shandong, only to find that he has to fight a second unexpected enemy—the Communists.

The end of the anti-Japanese war does not bring the protagonist joy, as the Communists are winning more and more support despite their subversive role in the war period. When confronted by friends sympathetic to the Communist revolution, the soldier can protest only by opening his shirt to show the scars on his body, scars all inflicted by Communist bullets, during the anti-Japanese war.

Duanmu Fang was not alone in depicting the recent national crisis in terms of scar symbolism. Across the Taiwan Straits, Luo Guangbin (1924–1967) and Yang Yiyan (b. 1925) also wrote emphatically in *Hongyan* (Red rock, 1961) about the bodily ordeal Chinese Communist revolutionaries and their sympathizers underwent on the eve of the 1949 victory. It will be recalled that the novel's first climax takes place when Sister Jiang, an underground agent and one of the most unforgettable figures in the Communist gallery of heroines, runs into a display of decapitated heads on entering a city in northern Sichuan. The heads belong to revolutionaries recently put to death by the Nationalists. Sister Jiang is startled by the bloody scene, yet upon closer examination, she realizes, to her devastation, that among the heads is that of her beloved husband![2] Nevertheless, in sharp contrast to the decapitation scene in Lu Xun's preface to *A Call to Arms,* viewing her husband-cum-comrade's head only deepens Sister Jiang's determination to fight the Nationalist tyrants, and she eventually dies a martyr.

Even more pertinent is a Nationalist jail scene in *Red Rock,* in which a young Communist soldier is found inscribing on the cell wall a poem by his commander, General Ye Ting (1896–1946). The soldier describes to cellmates how he was wounded and arrested in a recent battle against Nationalist troops, revealing "a huge scar on his right shoulder as he removed his uniform."[3] His will to die for a cause is only reinforced by this scar, a physical wound that serves as an objective correlative to the poem he has inscribed on the wall:

> I wish the day to come
> When the infernal fire
> Burns me together with the coffin-like jail into ashes,
> And I should win eternity in blood and flame.[4]

Thus, long before the appearance of *shanghen wenxue,* or "literature of the scarred," in the late 1970s—a literature about the sorrow caused by the Chinese Communist rule that had culminated in the Cultural Revolution—midcentury Chinese writers from the two sides of the Taiwan Straits had already written profusely of their scar experiences. These writers wrote from mutually hostile stances, to bear witness to the three-decade-long fight between the Nationalists and the Communists and project competing visions of the meaning of early modern Chinese history. At a time when writing was equated with fighting, such textual confrontations could be judged no less treacherous than political oppression or military atrocity.

Nevertheless, more than half a century after this great historical divide, these works about scars have gradually lost the edge that once made them acute testimonials to a national trauma. As a matter of fact, they themselves have become traces—scars—of a brand of modern Chinese literature that (meant to) *hurt.* Few readers of today would read a novel like *A Badge of Scars* or *Red Rock* for ideological guidance or historical inculcation. Yet one cannot help asking: has time healed, or merely concealed, the pain that was once deemed so horrible it could not be related often enough? To reread these literary works, therefore, is not unlike reexamining physical scars: it is a ceremony, in which one remembers the mutilated reality of the past, diagnoses the erstwhile wound beneath the apparent sign of healing, and most importantly, traces out a story, nay, a history, that seems to have receded into oblivion along with the originating physical and psychological laceration.

With such scar symbolism in mind, I will examine the capricious conditions in which twentieth-century political fiction rose and fell. In Section 1 I take issue with two tendencies in the current paradigm of mid-twentieth-century Chinese literary criticism: that this literature appeared as a break with the pre-1949 tradition and that, thanks to their respective claims to ideological legitimacy, writers of the Communist and anti-Communist camps displayed rigid antagonism on all issues. I argue that, insofar as fiction is regarded as charged with "a power of incalculable magnitude," to borrow Liang Qichao's words,[5] mid-twentieth-century Chinese fiction must represent not an aberration but an (unfortunate?) actualization of the old revolutionary poetics, conceived by writers from the late Qing to the 1940s. Moreover, as a result of their shared roots and despite their mutual recriminations, both

Communist and anti-Communist writers may well have been locked in unacknowledged dialogue.

In Section 2 I describe the way in which midcentury Chinese writers intensified the dialectic between fictional narrative and national history, a rhetoric also first enunciated by late Qing and May Fourth literati. In relating how a modern China had come about, writers constructed or repaired the national myths. In so doing they not only lent support to one regime or the other but also worked out a rationale for their own and their readers' existence in an age of chaos and violence. These writers still believe that ideological truth claims can be validated in fiction, and that national histories can be legitimated by national mythologies. I conclude that the midcentury Chinese writers' commitments to narrating the scar begot a cluster of paradoxical tensions; these tensions would eventually surface as major themes of Chinese fiction after 1980.[6]

These two sections prepare my inquiry into the subject of scars and writing in Section 3. With sample works from Taiwan, the mainland, and Hong Kong, I examine how a writing about pain could end up becoming a writing in pain, and how a literature of trauma and a literature of propaganda could infiltrate each other's domains. I describe a "technology" that helped make the scar a palpable sign of public awareness; this technology prods one to ponder the moral imperative, and impasse, within such a form of writing. As will be illustrated, writers on both sides of China wrote to register the scar and anticipate its healing. Little did they know, however, that their visions of public redemption would cause them so much private pain, or that a literature about healing old wounds could soon turn itself into an instrument for opening new ones.

WRITING HISTORY AFTER THE GREAT DIVIDE

Literary historians have tended to see Chinese literature after 1949 as a clear break from the May Fourth tradition.[7] With the founding of the People's Republic on the mainland, a new literary paradigm is said to have been established in the place of the old one, which had by then completed its "historical mission." In Taiwan, the literature of 1919 to 1949 was regarded by the Nationalist government as one reason for the loss of the mainland; it had allegedly lured thousands of young, innocent readers to the Communist heresy. Except for works by writers who had fled to Taiwan, such as Liang Shiqiu, Xie Bingying, and Su Xuelin, or who had died before 1949, such as Xu Zhimo and Yu Dafu, literature of the May Fourth tradition was banned. Both regimes were eager to cultivate a new literature in the service of politics, and to that effect, both were responsible for numerous disposable pieces of propagandist writing. Little wonder that historians should have juxtaposed midcentury and May Fourth literature on such axes as individualism versus conformism, humanitarianism versus dogmatism, and critical vigor versus ideological rigor.

This practice must be subjected to closer examination. I argue that midcentury literature in Taiwan, as in mainland China, cannot be appreciated without referring to the legacy of the May Fourth tradition. Historians have characterized the external causes that led to the rise of the Maoist literary tradition.[8] Little, however, has been discussed about the gradual *implosion* of a Chinese revolutionary poetics, which was initiated by late Qing and May Fourth literati and reached its logical (dead) end in the hands of Mao and his literary cohorts. This revolutionary poetics manifests itself in the conviction of an immediate link between fictional rhetoric and national policy, a Promethian symbolism of rebellion and sacrifice,[9] an "obsession with China,"[10] and an apocalyptic vision of national rejuvenation through revolution. Writing becomes the textual manifestation of revolution. Through writing, accordingly, social and political evils can be exposed, new and progressive thoughts can be propagated, and a bright future for a new China can be mapped out. Mao and his followers belong to the generation inspired by the May Fourth spirit; they carried on, rather than terminated, this established revolutionary poetics.

The Implosion of Revolutionary Poetics

The "revolution of fiction" *(xiaoshuo geming)* advocated by late Qing intellectuals such as Yan Fu and Liang Qichao comes to mind; its furor is best summarized by Liang Qichao's famous announcement that "to renew people's hearts and remold their character, one must first renovate fiction."[11] Despite their antitraditionalist pose, intellectuals of the May Fourth era primly reiterated the calls of their late Qing predecessors for a new, revolutionary literature. Chen Duxiu's militant manifesto for a new literature, Hu Shi's proposal for a literary revolution, and Lu Xun's "call for arms" are but the most prominent examples.[12] Starting in the late 1920s, leftist writers and critics from Qu Qiubai to Mao Dun equipped this revolutionary literature with Marxist-oriented theories, debates, campaigns, creative writing, and translations.[13] Their contributions should be seen as a consequence of, not the cause of, campaigns to remold China through literature.

From the "literary revolution" to "revolutionary literature," writers pursued a modern China free from the old, cannibalistic shackles, a China that would finally attain humanism, equality, and enlightenment. Realism, whether labeled critical, revolutionary, or socialist, became the primary format for this discourse, not merely because of its mimetic presupposition but also because of its adherence to a rationalist agenda and total truth claims. Nevertheless, close analysis reveals that the end and means of this poetics did not coalesce; realism's inherent "rationalist" agenda calls for justice and humanity, but its practice was subject to spells of fanaticism and radical mannerism. The intelligentsia adopted attitudes as readers that they readily contradicted as writers. As readers, they celebrated the immanent power of literature to reveal the nature and destiny of all humanity, while as writers they counted on the capacity of literature to obey the whims and purposes of every propagandist. Their rationales both downplayed and overestimated language and literature as cultural institutions.[14]

Mao Zedong's Yan'an talks and the literature that arose in the wake of the talks should be regarded as a radical outcome of this revolutionary poetics. The talks brought out literature's authoritarian potential, in that they confirm the mystical "power of an incalculable magnitude" of literature, while believing that this power cannot be fully played out unless it has been disciplined.[15] At its most utopian level, Maoist literature is said to bridge the gap between elite writers and illiterate audience, the "literary" subject and the "everyday" event, individual talents and dogmatic tradition, deplorable past and irresistible future. Writing and revolution, ink and blood, are mixed to produce a most powerful literary agency. Had it ever been realized, this ideal literature would have been a (con)fusion of all horizons.

Implied here is a vision of revolution as revelation. In the Maoist literary formula, "ideal" literature can finally be imagined and even written once the success of revolution is in sight. Thus, by the late 1940s, a new image of writers had been shaped. Zhao Shuli (1906–1970) was an amateur raconteur before he was trained to be a writer; Ma Feng (b. 1922) and Xi Rong (b. 1922) never finished their primary education. Veteran "new youth" such as Ding Ling and Zhou Libo vowed to leave behind their urban, intellectual fixations and bourgeois aesthetics in support of the new discourse. Also arising was a new ethics of writing that demanded that writers descend to the proletarian world, mingling with "the people" they were delegated to portray, so as to tell "the people's" stories firsthand—a most literal practice of realism. One discerns a new narrative typology, which merges fiction with politics, pedagogy with entertainment, and allegory with truth.

With the founding of the new republic, it was logical to expect that writers could finally put into practice a discourse they had long yearned for. The fact that the majority of writers, despite widely divergent political stances, chose to stay on the mainland is hardly a coincidence. It indicates less the writers' ideological endorsement of the new regime than logical reasoning based on a shared expectation that the golden age for literature would come with a regime representing humanity and rationality.

The fact is, however, that 1949 marked the beginning of a rapid degradation of literature in both vitality and variety. In July 1949, three months before the formal establishment of the regime, the first National Conference of Writers and Artists was held in Beijing, followed by the founding of the United Association of Chinese Literature and the Arts and the Association of Literary Workers. In 1953, the Association of Literary Workers was renamed the Chinese Writers' Association. As the highest organization for writers, it resolved to make Chinese Marxism the guideline of literature and the arts, and socialist realism the method of creativity and criticism.[16] The Leninist/Maoist concept that literature should serve as a "cog and screw in the revolutionary machinery" was finally realized nationwide, as seen in the rapid emergence of writers' associations and party-sponsored magazines and activities all over China.

This most rationalist move to organize writers into leagues of mouthpieces on behalf of party policies nevertheless proved to be a devastating blow to their creativity. Numerous accounts have been written about the suffocating atmosphere of the early 1950s.[17] Things went so badly that, on the eve of the Hundred Flowers Movement, Mao Dun, then culture minister of the PRC, summarized the new nation's literary production of the first six years as "too dry, every piece alike. This dryness surely stems from the general adherence to stereotyped concepts; this uniform monotony from formulism, from arbitrary confinement to a narrow range of themes and ideas."[18] Meanwhile, the purging of recalcitrant intellectuals, a tradition dating back to the Yan'an days, had become ever more gruesome. The fall of the "gang" of Ding Ling and Chen Qixia and the persecution of Hu Feng and his circle were merely the most spectacular cases.[19]

Chinese writers since the turn of the century had written under the pressure of governmental coercion as well as factional struggles; history from the literary revolution to revolutionary literature was punctuated by numerous accounts of censorship, arrest, imprisonment, confiscation, and execution. The tension between artistic freedom and ideological constraint concerned writers, especially those from the leftist camp, as early as the 1920s. Modern Chinese writers did not have to wait until the Communist era to acquire their first lesson on the dangers of writing. If this is the case, what made writing in the early PRC era and the following decades an impossible vocation? What made the rational agenda of revolutionary poetics an incubator of all the irrationalities already seen in PRC literature at its earliest stage? To be sure, government surveillance was the primary cause; the new regime enforced the law of literary practice and censorship so severely that, by contrast, the Nationalist days seemed like heaven. Beyond these extratextual reasons, one must inquire into the problems arising from the core of revolutionary poetics now formally installed by the authorities.

If the bottom line of revolutionary poetics is to see to the arrival of an apocalyptic moment that reveals the final truth of history, writing—for modern Chinese writers in the May Fourth and post–May Fourth eras—means a yearning for that imminent revelatory moment. Writing becomes an act of anticipation. Paradoxically, writing can also be an act of procrastination, because in foretelling the future revolution, it inscribes the prolonged stay of the "present," which should have long ago receded into the past. However popular, post–May Fourth writings by a master such as Lu Xun or Mao Dun entailed a negative dialectic. This dialectic indicates that the more a writer wrote, the more he or she articulated his or her incapacity to reach the ideal state of rationality accessible only through revolution. Writing in the prerevolution days thus can best be defined as an act of self-denial—a desperate naming of what Reality is not.[20]

Now that the much anticipated revolution had taken place and, as a result, a new society had been founded, writers were told that they could finally inhabit the new discourse their earlier writings had promised but failed to achieve. However, this new discourse turned out to contain a double bind. On the one hand, it informed the writers that the revolution had succeeded, and thus conditions for the existence of prerevolutionary literature had disappeared. Although it was first occasioned by social and political injustice before 1949, modern writing had become redundant in the new society, except to recall the bad old days and reaffirm the happy status quo. On the other hand, this new discourse informed writers that the revolution was still going on; more class enemies were yet to be overthrown, and more anticapitalist wars were yet to be fought. But if writers resumed their critical positions of prerevolutionary days, according to the argument above, they would postpone rather than hasten the completion of the revolution. Either way, the writers were forced into a corner, where they had to submit to the role prepared for them by the party. The result was a hollowing out of the rationale that substantiated the moral courage and theoretical rigor of "literature for revolution" before 1949. While deploring the fact that the literature of the 1950s had been totally tamed, one has to bear in mind that writers half a century before, if not even earlier, had begun the construction of their own literary zoo.

By the mid-1950s, a literature that presumably had sublated all previous revolutionary writings had been well on its way to becoming an absurd praxis. Absurd not in the sense of contemporary European thinkers' and writers' self-reflexive observation of barren humanity, but in the sense of the forced collective practice of a poetics that had turned against itself, while parading itself under the old labels of modernity, rationality, and emancipation.[21] The "master plot" of this Chinese brand of absurd literature cannot sound more noble—a literature for the people—but once en route, it kept turning onto sidetracks, stopping at the least expected stations, and taking on fictional and actual cargoes that were never in any plan. Its rhetoric was marked by redundancy and hyperbole, which amounted to nonsensical extravaganza, while what was really at stake was always beyond verbal transmission. Its melodramatic goal—fighting class enemies such as the Nationalists and the

Americans—was soon replaced by an even more melodramatic goal, fighting class enemies hiding at the very center of the party.[22] Heroes and villains of this literature were shown as combating not only within but also without the text; more surprisingly, they could exchange roles right in the middle of action. Speaking of the neohistoricist "circulation" of political and poetic power,[23] or of the neo-Marxist "critique" of and "intervention" in reality,[24] can there be a more blatant example than the early PRC literature? But all this is only an overture. A more bloody literary politics was yet to come, followed by a more spectacular waste of talent and life.

For those who discerned the irrational quality of this new literature, they either willingly suspended disbelief, hoping that things would take a turn for the better, or mutely protested by going into inner exile. There were writers, however, who engaged in Quixotic combat, at the expense of their careers and lives. It is their resistance to hegemonic literary doctrine, which would be renamed "Maoist discourse" three decades later,[25] that lends a tragic dimension to these Chinese literati of the absurd. Despite these writers' moral integrity, nevertheless, questions must be raised as to whether their critique was predicated on the same May Fourth/Maoist tautology of politicized literature and fictionalized politics, and whether their protests disrupted, as scholars have usually held, or simply reaffirmed, the old revolutionary poetics.

Historical hindsight shows that it would be many years before these writers realized that the collective "we" was not the historically assigned subjectivity of a socialist regime, any more than the "I" had been a singular transcendental myth of every presocialist regime, or merely that Chinese literature did not have to have the mission of saving China. Postponement, silence, and protest were not the only postures taken. There were also cases like Ding Ling and Zhou Libo, who made the transition from the vanguard of the early revolution to the palace guard of the post–Cultural Revolution, carrying their ever-renewed belief with them to their graves. In any case, the fixity of their "bitter love" for the party and the people (to borrow the title of Bai Hua's play) is a fitting emblem of the rigidity and death of the revolutionary poetics born in the early twentieth century.

"A Call to Arms"—The Rightist Edition

Before Chiang Kai-shek resumed his position as president of Nationalist China in 1950, a campaign against the Communist regime had started in Taiwan, the last Nationalist bastion. On October 18, 1949, the literary supplement of *Xinsheng Bao* (New life daily) carried an essay by Ba Ren (1905–1967) entitled "Xiou'shou pangguan lun" (On the theory of noncommital spectatorship). In the essay, Ba Ren compared the Nationalist anti-Communist campaign to an abject theatrical performance; he advised readers to hold a noncommittal attitude, as spectators of a hopeless show. Ba Ren, it will be recalled, was an established leftist writer; he would eventually play a crucial role in the PRC literary politics of the mid-1950s.[26] The essay triggered a cluster of bitter counterattacks. Sun Ling (1914–1983), editor-in-chief of the literary supplement of *Minzu Bao* (People's news) retaliated by advocating a "literature for the sake of the war";[27] echoing Sun Ling, Feng Fangmin (b. 1919), the new editor-in-chief of the literary supplement of *New Life Daily*, promulgated another slogan in support of anti-Communist literature, "First comes fight, second comes delight."[28]

Amid these "calls to arms," the Association of Chinese Literature was established in 1950 as the official organization implementing governmental literary policy. Zhang Daofan (1897–1968), veteran Nationalist party liner, was commissioned to found the Committee of Chinese Literature and the Arts in 1949. Before it was abolished in 1956, the committee was the most important official organization in sponsoring and supervising the development of anti-Communist literature. A similar organization was founded for writers in the military service in 1954.[29] Through literary contests and awards, the two organizations, among others, enlisted a large number of writers to serve the mission of anti-Communism.

For all the ideological antagonism between the two regimes, one finds striking similarities in Nationalist and Communist ways of administering literary activities. The Nationalist Party, after all, was structured on the Soviet model, its literary policy schooled by the same Leninist concepts that inspired the Chinese Communists. Learning from the painful experiences of the past, the Nationalist government tried hard to enhance the pedagogical and military function of literature; this policy was theoretically backed up in 1953 by Chiang Kai-shek's "Supplementary Treatises on Education and Recreation," written to accompany Sun Yatsen's "Principle of Livelihood" *(Minsheng zhuyi yule liangpian bushu)*, and by Chiang's call for "literature for the sake of war" *(zhandou wenyi)* in 1955. The government also saw to aesthetic hygiene by launching movements such as the Chu Sanhai campaign (eradicating the three killers of leftist, pornographic, and decadent literature) to clean out the poisonous elements of literary practice. It aimed to create a literary sanatorium, ensuring its own Nationalist brand of health.

The most extreme measure was the total ban of Chinese literature written between 1919 and 1949. Removed from the market were not only names like Lu Xun, Guo Moruo, and Ba Jin, for their support of the leftist cause, but also writers such as Shen Congwen and Qian Zhongshu, for staying on the mainland after its fall.[30] Despite the ban, however, writers largely followed the narrative models first perfected by post–May Fourth fiction. Chen Jiying's (1908–1997) *Dicun zhuang* (Fool in the reeds, 1950), for example, skillfully rewrote Lu Xun's "The True Story of Ah Q" in an anti-Communist context. One finds in his *Chidi* (Red land, 1954) the return of the family saga, as illustrated by works such as Ba Jin's *Jia* (Family, 1932). Both Pan Lei's (b. 1927) *Honghe sanbuqu* (Red river trilogy, 1954) and Pan Renmu's (b. 1920) *Lianyi biaomei* (Cousin Lianyi, 1952) deal with the trials intellectual youth undergo in search of a political ideal; they both reflect a deep indebtedness to the revolutionary bildungsroman, such as *Family* and Lu Ling's *Caizhu de ernü men* (Children of the rich, 1947). In Jiang Gui's (1908–1980) *Jin taowu zhuan* (A tale of modern monsters, 1952; retitled *Xuanfeng* [The whirlwind] in 1957), one sees the revival of grotesquery and satire, a May Fourth legacy that was completely dismissed by the Communist novel.

Next to Taiwan, Hong Kong was a haven for writers who did not want to live under Communist rule. Of the so-called writers coming to the south *(nanlai zuojia),*[31] the most remarkable case was Eileen Chang, the princess of the (pre)mature fin-de-siècle cult in 1940s Shanghai. Chang chose to stay in Shanghai after 1949, and even published two works displaying tongue-in-cheek pro-Communism, *Shiba chun* (Eighteen springs, 1951) and *Xiao Ai* (Little Ai, 1951).[32] But Chang's cynical view of Chinese sociopolitical dynamics and her persistent inquiry into the dark aspects of Chinese culture finally forced her to leave her beloved Shanghai in 1952. Chang stayed in Hong Kong until 1955. Motivated both by personal experience under Communist rule and by immediate economic pressure, she published two anti-Communist novels, *Yangge* (The rice-sprout song, 1954) and *Chidi zhilian* (Naked earth, 1954), under the sponsorship of the United States Information Service. Both novels are characterized by Chang's personal vision of China as a desolate theater and her sympathetic study of the psychology of the oppressor as well as the oppressed. From "decadent" writer to reluctant pro-Communist writer, and then to nonconformist anti-Communist writer, Chang's trajectory testifies to the writer's difficult position in a disturbed decade.

Driven by indignation at the bloody Communist takeover and the pathos of exile, anti-Communist writers developed a literature of nostalgia about their homeland and the questionable good old days. Understandably, all their pathos, indignation, and nostalgia is directed toward supporting the anti-Communist cause, in the hope that the Nationalist government would soon reclaim its legitimate position. A discourse arose that was later ridiculed as "anti-Communist eight-legged literature,"[33] a literature loaded with Communism-bashing, extreme sentimentalism, melodramatic plotting, and simple, polarized characterizations. This, however, should not keep one from speculating on the logic of writing that preoccupied such writers. Inasmuch as literary production is part of the military campaign through which the government counterattacked Communist evils, the formulaic, repetitive quality of literature may not have been entirely a defect. Its "virtue" may lie precisely in its easy, recyclable features. As long as the anti-Communist war was going on, one could never produce enough literary ammunition to fight the enemy. According to a conservative estimate, more than fifteen hundred writers wrote vigorously in the 1950s, producing over seventy million words, or literary bullets, in the service of the anti-Communist crusade.[34]

This logic of a militant anti-Communist literature would not have sounded strange to writers of the period, especially those who had been practitioners or consumers of literature produced during the previous war, the Second Sino-Japanese war. Many critics related this literature to the revolutionary poetics mentioned above. Situ Wei (b. 1921), one of the leading theoreticians, interpreted literature of 1950s Taiwan as a continuation of the May Fourth spirit, though most of May Fourth literature had been banned as ideologically incorrect.[35] Another critic, Ge Xianning (1906–1961), echoed Situ Wei's argument by asking *all* writers to write literature with anti-Communist themes. What will a writer be, Ge queries, if he avoids writing about the war with the excuse that he is unfamiliar with the front and life on the occupied mainland? Failing to write an anti-Communist novel is insignificant, but failing to write about the anti-Communist cause is significant.[36]

As if reflecting the inner predicament of Communist literature of the time, anti-Communist literature developed revolutionary poetics to a parallel theoretical impasse. One may well discern a "suicidal" tendency in its discourse. Since the anti-Communist war had become the raison d'être for writing, there was simply no way for a writer to carry on if he did not take up the ultimate theme. Writers were encouraged to write about the new war, even if their artistic failure was foreseeable. Just as warriors must gamble their lives on the battlefield, so writers must pay the price of heroism through a daring literary death.

Underneath the call for "art for war's sake" are two dark possibilities. If anti-Communist literature succeeded in carrying out its mission, namely, helping to defeat the Communists, it would lose its reason to exist, except as historical remnant; but if it failed to carry out its mission, and the Communists won, then too it would lose its reason to exist. Vacillating between these two poles, anti-Communist literature became caught in existential indeterminacy; either its success or its failure would obliterate it. The most ironic turn, of course, would come years later, when the two hostile regimes started to reconcile. Negotiations between the two regimes in the 1990s have contravened the basis of the anti-Communist literary campaign, forcing us to reconsider its historical role.

In view of the uncanny parallel between Communist and anti-Communist literature of the early 1950s, a cynic might conclude that the two regimes produced the same type of literature. Take off their tendentious, militant labels, and one finds twin traditions. Their difference is in degree, not in kind. Nevertheless, these subtle differences should not be ignored, as they resulted in very different Taiwanese and mainland Chinese literature in the following three decades.

The year 1956 is a crucial moment in Chinese Communist literary and political history. To ease tensions from within the party, and to test the water in preparation for more efficient control over intellectuals and literati, Mao launched the Hundred Flowers movement. It marks the end of the first stage of Communist literature, which began with Mao's Yan'an talks. Under the illusion that they were finally being allowed to speak their minds, writers like Liu Binyan (b. 1925), Wang Meng (b. 1934), Qin Zhaoyang (1916–1994), and Liu Shaotang (b. 1921) created works rich in critical spirit and reformist intent. A literary springtime seemed to be coming, but it was soon overtaken by a chilly season of purges.

The year 1956 is significant for Chinese literature in Taiwan, too. It saw the founding of the Modernist Poetry Society (Xiandai Shishe) by Ji Xian (b. 1912), a poet who first emerged in 1940s Shanghai. Although anti-Communism was listed as one of the goals in its manifesto,[37] the society nevertheless encouraged poetic writings that are anything but "eight-legged" anti-Communist literature. It represented the revival of the modernist movement that first took root in China in the 1930s. In the same year, a literary journal entitled *Wenxue Zazhi* (Literary magazine, 1956–1960) was founded by T. A. Hsia, then literature professor of National Taiwan University, and his friends and students. It featured translations of foreign literature and creative writings with little overt political intent. The magazine lasted only four years. When it closed, it had trained a group of young writers and critics who would vitalize Taiwan's literature of the next decade with a modernist movement.

The Nationalist government was culpable for interfering with many cultural and literary activities of liberal tenor in the 1950s and on, the crackdown on the magazine *Ziyou Zhongguo* (Liberal China, 1949–1960) being one of the most notorious cases, but it was not as adept as its Communist counterpart at policing writers' imagination and activities. Thanks to this new Nationalist failure, limited though it was, literature thrived in 1960s Taiwan.[38] Works by writers such as Huang Chunming, Wang Zhenhe, and Bai Xianyong filled the gap left in Chinese literature as more and more fearsome movements extinguished the last spark of mainland writers' creativity.

FROM NATIONAL HISTORY TO NATIONALIZED HISTORY

The Nationalist regime's retreat to Taiwan in 1949 represented a low point in its almost three-decade-long combat with the Chinese Communist Party.

Driven to the smallest province of China, the Nationalist government had lost not only its control over the immense mainland and millions of Chinese people, but also its mandate as the sole legitimate power over the Chinese nation. For the defeated regime, this historical crisis led to a historiographical crisis. Insofar as history always involves a narrative sequence through which discrete, tangible data are organized in an intelligible discourse, how would the Nationalist government explain, or explain away, the causes of its mainland debacle? How would the government reclaim its legitimacy over the mainland, if not in political terms, at least in narrative terms? How would it mobilize a pedagogical apparatus through which a "correct" national history could be taught to the Chinese citizens in Taiwan?

Along with the founding of a new People's Republic, the Communist Party also needed to establish its own historical discourse, one that reviewed how the new nation had come about and where it would take its people. In less than half a century, Chinese people had seen their country invaded by foreigners, torn apart by warlords, and turned upside down by revolutions. How were they to believe that the new Communist government was the final, legitimate force, whose ascent to power validated a historically predetermined judgment?

Close ties between the new fiction and the new nation had been established since the late Qing, so it is no surprise that narrative fiction, especially the full-length historical novel, was employed by writers of both mainland China and Taiwan as a particularly apt model for narrating the nation. This mode derives its power as much from the nineteenth-century European historical novel as from the dynastic saga of classical Chinese fiction, especially that which deals with the rise of a new regime, such as *Suitang yanyi* (The saga of the Sui and Tang dynasties). With its slow, linear temporality, built-in cognitive sequence from chaos to order, gradual integration of individual characters into a communal whole, and conviction in the total communicative function of language, the full-length novel provided an ideal model to substantiate a national narrative.[39] It provided an ideal simulated context through which a national community would recall its past and project its future. For all their sharp ideological conflicts in denying or rewriting each other's history, both Chinese Communist and anti-Communist novelists shared a single belief that history provides a neutral ground on which truth can be tested and reality sanctioned.

Romancing Revolution and History

Communist novels of the late 1940s and early 1950s demonstrate an affinity with the emerging national discourse in two thematic directions. On the one hand, writers looked backward, chronicling the rise of the Communist revolution against great adversity, from Nationalist oppression to the

Japanese invasion. On the other hand, they depicted the drastic changes brought by the land reform movement, beginning in northern and northeastern Chinese villages. The overthrowing of local landlords, followed by the redistribution of their property, is treated as more than implementation of a Communist policy; rather it appears as a most dramatic shakeup of traditional Chinese society in economic production, power structure, and ethical relationship.

Given their apparently different themes, the two novelistic trends are relevant to the remaking of national history. The anti-Japanese and anti-Nationalist saga constructs a dark past that had almost engulfed Chinese people when a new political power came to the rescue. The land-reform melodrama prefigures the bright future guaranteed by the new regime. At the center of these two novelistic trends is an intricate spatial symbolism evoked by the loss, recovery, and redistribution of the homeland at both national and personal levels, and a well-orchestrated temporal scheme that advocates the inevitable triumph of the future over the past and the eternal return of lost justice.

Before the nation is built and the official historiography can be written, fiction serves as a surrogate form of history, relating not just what has happened but what should have happened. This tradition has its roots in the leftist fiction of earlier times. In the late 1920s, writers like Mao Dun had employed fiction as a defiant challenge to the truth claims of Nationalist historiography, a phantom voice that doubled the monolithic text controlled by government historians.[40] This dialogical relation between historical fiction and historiography was downplayed in the 1940s, as the Communist Party tried to authenticate a literary canon of its own. Mao Zedong and his followers envisioned a literature that did not argue with reality, but rather spoke on behalf of reality. To read and write fiction was accordingly to endorse a prescribed narrative of history. Hidden behind this seemingly progressive definition of literature is a reactionary move. As Yi-tsi Mei Feuerwerker points out, insofar as traditional historiography conceives the notion that truth is what is consensual or officially sanctioned, "it is tempting to see the Marxist novel's claim to be contemporary history as a return, albeit with a difference, to the Chinese narrative tradition in which historiography served as the central model of narration."[41]

War novels of the late 1940s, such as *Xin ernü yingxiong zhuan* (New tale of heroes and lovers, 1949) and *Lüliang Yingxiong zhuan* (Heroes of Lüliang Mountain, 1948) prefigure a national discourse by addressing a nationalist thematic.[42] They introduce groups of Communist heroes and heroines who dedicated themselves to guarding the Chinese land against foreign invasion, while the Nationalists are depicted as opportunists or even collaborators, who seek individual gain at the cost of the nation's future. Although they are comparable to popular Russian masterpieces, such as *The Rout* by Fadeyev, which was translated by Lu Xun,[43] and earlier leftist war narratives, such as *Bayue de xiangcun* (August in the village, 1935) by Xiao Jun, these novels were largely modeled after classical Chinese vernacular narratives like *Shuihu zhuan* (The water margin).[44] Responding to Mao's Yan'an talks, these novels renewed modern Chinese literature by reviving folk narrative forms. The immediate question is how in so doing they had initiated their readers into "progressive consciousness" by refamiliarizing them with, instead of detaching them from, the "feudal unconscious" inherent in traditional fiction.

The Water Margin was valorized by Communist writers on account of its indictment of official abuses and its endorsement of peasant rebellion. The new Communist virtues of fraternity and comradeship are supported by the old feudal notions of sworn brotherhood and bandit morality. More intriguing is the fact that these writers derived their narrative format from the ideologically incorrect models of the late Qing era, such as *Sanxia wuyi* (Three knights-errant and five sworn brothers, 1889) and *Ernü yingxiong zhuan* (Tale of heroes and lovers, 1878). In these novels, chivalric knight-errantry and group heroism are celebrated only on the condition that they be subordinated to total loyalism. Through endless tests and combats, the heroes and heroines complete the chivalric ideal by serving the supreme authority—the emperor. They have been transformed from individualistic warriors fighting for self-sufficient moral causes, into obedient citizens guarding established political values. Communist war novels did not merely borrow plots, characters, or even titles (*New Tale of Heroes and Lovers,* for instance) from the late Qing chivalric novel. When these "new" novels highlight heroes and heroines who forgo individual concerns in the interest of a total(itarian) goal, they have grafted revolutionary altruism onto reactionary loyalism.

Guarding the land continued to serve as a central theme of Communist fiction of the 1950s. Although the mainland was already in the hands of the Communist regime, the fear that foreign invaders would join the Nationalists in starting a new war clearly haunted the national discourse. This fear was emphatically projected by works on the Korean War, such as Yang Shuo's (1913–1968) *Sanqianli jiangshan* (Three-thousand-mile mountain, 1952). The writing of national history through national "geopoetics" reached its apex in Du Pengcheng's (b. 1921) *Baowei Yan'an* (Guarding Yan'an, 1954). The novel depicts the 1948 battle between Nationalist and Communist troops in northwestern China, when the former launched a desperate final attack on Yan'an. Though far outnumbered by the enemy, Communist troops won a hard victory thanks to the leadership of General Peng Dehuai (1898–1974).

A small group of soldiers, led by a superman sergeant, Zhou Dayong, are highlighted in the novel. By relating these soldiers' bravery, perseverance, wisdom, and other saintly virtues, Du Pengcheng perfected the Communist hagiography, which had already been practiced by Communists in the 1940s. In reading Wu Qiang's (1910–?) *Hongri* (Red sun, 1957), T. A. Hsia has commented that Communist war fiction is crowded with larger-than-life heroic figures, so much so that it ends up becoming a parody of heroism.[45] Hsia's comment also applies to *Guarding Yan'an*. These noble soldiers fight, cook, mend, philosophize, and sleep together. They take care of each other's emotional as well as physical wounds. When Du Pengcheng takes great pains to describe how Zhou Dayong helps a wounded fellow soldier urinate, the homosocial bonding among them verges on the heroically homoerotic.[46] His soldiers are fictional predecessors of the Lei Feng cult of the 1960s.

For these saintly soldiers, can there be a better cause than fighting and dying for Yan'an, the mecca of Chinese Communism? In the novel, Yan'an is more than the geopolitical center of the Chinese Communist revolution; it is a locus where history meets myth and fiction crystallizes into Truth. Guarding Yan'an is not just a military mission but a crusade. As Yan'an is transformed into the earthly equivalent of the Western paradise, the novel's narrative becomes more and more religious, demanding unconditional sacrifice from all believers. The mythologized space of Yan'an in particular and mainland China in general is best described by Commander Chen:

> We Communists love our birthplace and people more than anybody else in the world. People ask, "What is so good about the barren mountainous area of northern Shanxi?" But we devote our lives to every inch of land of this place . . . every inch of the Chinese land was opened with the blood and sweat of our heroic ancestors. Fighters of our People's Liberation Army have trod this land with their feet. We know there are inexhaustible treasures in this immense place.[47]

Published in 1954, *Guarding Yan'an* is a retrospective account of a historical event and concerns a revolutionary paradise *almost* lost to the enemy. Though relating a bygone event, the ambiance of the past is cultivated as if it were not yet over; it generates a sense of crisis in continuum. Recollection of the nation's past serves as a way to ensure anticipation of her future. As such, *Guarding Yan'an* became a salient instance of a PRC fictional genre, the revolutionary historical novel *(geming lishi xiaoshuo)*, a genre that covers heroic Communist activities from 1921 to 1949. Through retelling the painful but glorious wars and resurrections of the past, the revolutionary historical novel teaches readers a lesson about how nations are made and remade. It employs a peculiar temporal scheme, too, which regards (continued) revolution not as the means but as the end of history. Other prominent titles in this genre include Yang Mo's (1914–1995) *Qingchun zhige* (The song of youth, 1958), about a group of young men and women's political tests and ideological transformation in the 1930s, Feng Deying's (b. 1935) *Ku caihua* (Bitter endive flower, 1958), about the hardship and sacrifice of a mother and her children during the anti-Japanese aggression era, and the aforementioned *Red Rock.*

Indeed, in the peculiar historical context of the PRC, no account of the past can be finalized till the revolution completes itself. A so-called historical revolutionary novel like *Guarding Yan'an* brings to the fore the contradictory goals of PRC historiographical narrative: it aims both to remember the historical dimension of the past, settling the meaning of a given period, and to reenact the revolutionary dimension of the past, destabilizing the meaning of the given period.[48] To meet the needs of history, Du Pengcheng was extremely cautious in preparing his manuscript. In his own words, he interviewed numerous battle witnesses, the manuscript going through several major rewritings before it was completed.[49] The complete version could not, however, withstand the treacherous, "revolutionary" turn of history. In 1958, when General Peng Dehuai was purged, *Guarding Yan'an* was banned, its historical rendition of Peng's crucial role in the Yan'an battle being judged antihistorical. Du Pengcheng became a casualty on the ideological front as the meaning of history was once again remade.

The second trend closely related to the formation of PRC national historiography is the land reform novel. At first glance, the land reform movement appeared to be nothing more than a radical Communist economic and agricultural policy of the late 1940s and early 1950s.[50] But the movement was never a mere attempt to revamp the infrastructure of rural China; rather it took on a superstructural dimension from the outset as its implementation contributed to, and was conditioned by, drastic changes in traditional Chinese ethical, legal, and cultural systems.

The land reform novel does not only describe the redistribution of the land that once belonged to a few landlords. Reform of the Chinese landscape results in reform of the Chinese mindscape. A national discourse cannot be complete until its human components, the people, are redefined. At the center of the land reform novel is the confrontation between the landlord and his tenants, while the members of the reform team remain skillful organizers behind the confrontation. The poor peasants always first appear as silent, inactive victims. Inspired (or instigated) by the land reformers, they challenge local authorities from landlords to gentry families. They are told they are the chosen subjects of the regime to come, while in practice they are subject to the will and power of the revolutionaries.

Critics have pointed out the inherent contradictions of land reform novels in characterization and plot. From an anti-Communist viewpoint, C. T. Hsia contends that, in promoting the ideal of equalization of land ownership, members of the Communist land reform teams brought to a halt the conventional ethical system that would have maintained social stability at a minimum level.[51] Moreover, the reformers could be as scheming and cruel as their enemies in arousing the peasants' vengeful consciousness and organizing riots. Critics from the PRC like Liu Zaifu and Tang Xiaobin call attention to a dialectic of violence in both the form and content of land reform novels.[52] If Ding Ling's *The Sun Shines over the Sanggan River* (1949) and Zhou Libo's *Hurricane* (1949), both winners of Stalin literary prizes in 1951, are still compelling to us today, it is not because of their celebration of the way in which farmers brought down the traditional agricultural system but because of their unexpected revelation of the violence and chaos in the reform process.

In Chapter 2, I discussed the dubious dialectic of justice and violence in *The Sun Shines over the Sanggan River.* I particularly call attention to the internalization of violence as a result of the land form movement. At her most polemical, Ding Ling argues that humanity can be attained only through a self-willed nullification of various aspects of humanity. If villains are condemned because of their lack of humanity, heroes are honored because they can afford to lose their humanity—as the old Chinese saying goes, to achieve a greater magnanimity of justice, familial personal ties can be sacrificed *(dayi mieqin).* Heroes and villains share a strange type of (self-)alienation by the end of the novel, thereby revealing the most irrational capacity of the new Communist mechanism of rationality.

In Zhou Libo's *Hurricane,* a novel about land reform in a village of northeastern China, poor peasants are mobilized by the revolutionaries to fight local landlords. Three times they are challenged by the landlords, and three times they overcome the challenges. By the end of the first part of the novel, unsurprisingly, the peasants have won their preordained victory. What distinguishes *Hurricane*'s characterization is that its peasant heroes, once injected with revolutionary zeal, act like robots whose continued motion can only be stopped when they have run out of power. Death becomes their destiny. Thus, when Zhao Yulin, the impoverished peasant who rises in the movement to become a brave and virtuous proletarian hero, dies a heroic death fighting against an attack by local bandits at the end of the first part of *Hurricane,* one feels less grief than relief.

Rudolf Wagner has shown how the narration of *Hurricane* projects the "faceless image" of the Communist writer. The novel's deceptively neutral style, according to Wagner, reflects an omniscient, authoritarian discourse at work.[53] A more remarkable feature of the novel's narrative format, however, is its repetitive structure. Close reading of the two parts of *Hurricane* reveals that Zhou Libo tells the same story twice. In part one, the poor peasants are united by the leader of the land reform team, Xiao Xiang, to overthrow the landlords. In part two, a weary but no less shrewd Xiao Xiang returns to the village, organizing another campaign against a new group of villains, opportunists who had capitalized on the victory of the first reform movement. A new proletarian hero, Guo Quanhai, is introduced to fight the villains; the peasants win. Guo has by the end of the novel joined the army to fight against the Nationalists, leaving behind his wife of less than a month. Judging by Zhao Yulin's fate in part one, one fears that Liang may never rejoin his wife.

This repetitive structure, while highlighting the revolutionary fervor shared by the tireless party members and the newly awakened proletarians, is ominous, and will surface over and again in later PRC narrative fiction. In contrast to the concept of revolution, which is an irretrievable act of overcoming the old and reactionary, repeated revolution, in narrative as well as in political action, hints that no sooner has a reform or revolution been completed than the evil elements are reborn. A revolution thus envisioned becomes not a progressive project leading to a teleological end, but a redundant task aimed at an ever-receding goal. The return of Xiao Xiang to the village and the repeated fights between revolutionaries and antirevolutionaries constitute an unlikely Sisyphean task, a Chinese form of the absurd. Lu Xun's words reverberate: "Revolution, counterrevolution, antirevolution, . . . revolution, revolutionize the revolution, revolutionize, revolutionize, revolutionize."[54]

In compliance with government policy, land reform novels were replaced in the mid-1950s with novels about the land co-op movement. Both Li Zhun's (b. 1928) *Buneng zou zhetiaolu* (Do not take this path, 1953) and Zhao Shuli's *Sanli wan* (Three-mile bay, 1955), for instance, tell of the problems of a emerging new landowner class in confrontation with the co-op system. Only a few years after being given land, these farmers have amassed a fortune and are strongly resisting the new policy of sharing their newly won property with "the people."

Neither novel features the archenemies of conventional Communist fiction, such as Nationalist spies, landlords, foreign invaders, and villains who cannot be rehabilitated in a new society. Instead, moral and ideological conflicts break out within the socialist utopia, among social strata whose purity should not have been suspect. In *Do Not Take This Path,* peasants who had obtained land in the recent land reform movement have developed among themselves an unexpected class struggle. Owing to shrewd management and hard work, a peasant named Song Laoding, for example, has accumulated a small fortune in a few years and is now ready to buy more land from those who have failed to do so. In *Three-Mile Bay,* a veteran party member, Fan Denggao, who had fought heroically in the Sino-Japanese War, emerges as a major barrier to the land co-op movement. Through a sequence of predictable conflicts and reconciliations, both novels end with the repentance of the characters with questionable ideological consciousness, followed by a festive anticipation of the benefits of the co-op system.

The land reform novel describes the difficult process through which the bad elements of a society are eradicated by means of exile, expulsion, incarceration, and execution. The land co-op novel puts its focus elsewhere. Instead of hunting down evil landlords or Nationalist traitors, the new genre presents a huge gallery of characters who are pro-Communist by nature and susceptible to any prescribed regime of citizenship. As the uncooperative elements of the society are all co-opted rather than eradicated, a new system of surveillance emerges. This new system is introduced in a benign, pastoral rhetoric, as illustrated by the two novels in discussion, while it is more "violent" in its determination to socialize Chinese minds as well as Chinese bodies and Chinese land.

The two novels raise more questions. If the proletariat and the party cadres are supposed to be pillars of the new nation, why, only a couple of years after the land reform movement and the founding of the co-op system, are there signs of (self-)betrayal? If the cadres and peasants have to be reeducated to meet the progressive historical mission, shouldn't the rest of the Chinese people be even more closely watched and disciplined? Obediently following government policy, Li Zhun and Zhao Shuli write "innocently" about what history should be. The pastoral tone of their two novels is the most flagrant of signs, reminding one of what is missing from the new countryside. The Yan'an leaders have won, and the city boundaries of Yan'an are now the boundaries of all China. Land is to be rationalized by party fiat, and history too is to be nationally controlled. Through promulgating the Communist policy of land nationalization, the land co-op novels expose, however unwittingly, the extent to which the innocent writing of national history is to be replaced by a deliberate nationalization of history.

(Nationalist) Paradise Lost

Across the Taiwan Straits, anti-Communist writers were engaged in a novelistic discourse to narrate and therefore rationalize the loss of the national land. "Fangong dalu, shoufu shitu," or "Fight back to the mainland, restoring the lost land," one of the most prominent slogans, spells out the central imagery of historiography: the national land and national time lost and regained. Compared with their Communist colleagues, anti-Communist writers had a more difficult task to cope with, however. Whereas Communist writers built their discourse on a moral logic that the new and revolutionary had overthrown the old and corrupt, and that the mandate had been handed over to "the people's" liberator, anti-Communist writers had to prove that the loss of the mainland was only a temporary sidetrack on the set course of history. To restore the lost land meant to also redeem lost national(ist) history.

Two interrelated themes, diaspora and nostalgia, prevailed in the anti-Communist fiction of this time. More than one million mainlanders, the majority of whom were related politically or economically to the Nationalist regime, escaped to Taiwan in 1949 and the years immediately after. To these émigré mainlanders, the forced exile was a traumatic experience, their nation having been broken up, families torn apart, and familiar value systems turned upside down. Looking across the Taiwan Straits, they felt compelled to write about their past and their lost land. Diaspora indicates a temporary evacuation from a cultural and geographical space that authenticates one's identity as Chinese, whereas nostalgia suggests an effort of remembering and reclaiming a lost golden time. Both themes are incorporated into a higher discourse about the re-forming of national history.

Two novels by Chen Jiying, *Fool in the Reeds* and *Red Land,* best represent this point. One of the earliest examples of anti-Communist fiction, *Fool in the Reeds* explores the rise of Chinese Communists by tracing the changes in a northern Chinese village from the Boxer Rebellion to the fall of the mainland to the Communists. The novel's central figure is an illiterate, good-for-nothing social outcast named Changshun the Fool. This Ah Q–like figure has a hard early life. Miraculously, he rises to become the head of his village when the Communists come. Together with local rascals, he brings horrible chaos to the village. But when his value is exhausted, he is buried alive by his comrades. *Red Land* investigates the causes of the Communist takeover by turning to another social level. Starting with the victory over the Japanese in 1945 and ending with the fall of Peking in 1948, the novel depicts how two old gentry families struggle to recover from the atrocities of the Japanese invasion before they are totally ruined by the Communist takeover.

Sampling the turmoil in the country and in the city, Chen Jiying conjures up a national allegory about established political, economic, and cultural traditions in crisis. While condemning Communist conspiracies that had brainwashed intellectuals and peasants alike, both *Fool in the Reeds* and *Red Land* cultivate local color by accumulating linguistic data, customs, and figures supposedly reminiscent of the mainland but not of Taiwan. Despite the man-made and natural disasters they describe, Chen's novels manage to create a fantastic landscape called "the homeland," a landscape that substantiates the reader's imaginary nostalgia. The land reform novel, it can be argued, also couches its political agenda in a nativist topos. But an anti-Communist novel like *Fool in the Reeds* differs in that, even if the narrated facts indicate a past of pain and suffering, the narration serves an opposite purpose by creating in its readers an eternal yearning for that past, for going home.

As I have argued elsewhere, taking writers such as Lu Xun and Shen Congwen as examples, imaginary nostalgia is one of the most important features of modern Chinese nativist fiction. Imaginary, in the sense that nativist writers came forth to write about what they had failed to experience in reality; their imagination is just as important as their lived experience. In my definition, imaginary nostalgia is characterized by a temporal scheme of anachronism. Writers reconstruct the past in terms of the present, and they see in the present a residue of the past. On the other hand, imaginary nostalgia is underlain by a spatial scheme of displacement, which means not only a writer's physical dislocation from his homeland but also a relocation of his social status and intellectual/emotional capacity. Moreover, displacement "points to a narrative device or psychic mechanism that makes possible the (re)definition of something either irretrievable or unspeakable, and to the eternally regressive state of such a narrative and psychological quest."[55]

Chen Jiying's novels "nationalize" this nostalgic discourse of the 1930s, turning individual homesickness into a communal desire for the lost homeland. For him, only the Nationalist regime can serve as the agency through which imaginary nostalgia can be cured. Chen has been denounced by Communists and Taiwanese dissidents for his close ties to the Nationalist Party.[56] His politicized nostalgia novels, however, anticipated a trend of nativist fiction in Taiwan by émigré mainland writers of the 1950s and 1960s. Anachronism and displacement motivated the nostalgia novel, but they would eventually become its limitations. As time went by and hopes of recovering the mainland waned, the genre was gradually appropriated by native Taiwanese writers. They had had plenty of lessons on how to imagine the loss and recovery of a homeland—in this case, Taiwan.

Closely intertwined with the themes of nostalgia and diaspora is that of a belated initiation. Consider Pan Renmu's *Cousin Lianyi* and Pan Lei's *Red River Trilogy*, two acclaimed works of this type. The protagonists of these novels first appear as innocent youths in search of a political ideal. They are blinded either by vanity or by political fanaticism and thus fall prey to Communist temptations. They do not realize the destructive nature of Communism until they have wasted the better part of their life and been driven out of their homeland. For their ignorance, they pay the highest price. Both novels thus tell a story of paradise lost, a fall from naiveté into broken (national) time and space. From Manchuria to Hong Kong, from Saigon to Shanghai, these novels make their hero or heroine travel through the immense land of China, physically bearing witness to the harsh trials of history. Communist reality makes them long for a lost humanity, redirecting them toward the bright path of anti-Communism. The tragicomedy of the two protagonists' ideological initiation is best appreciated as a morality play.

For Chen Jiying, as for most other anti-Communist writers, given all the external contingencies, something quintessentially (Nationalist) Chinese remains intact. Whether it is called "tradition," "orthodoxy," or "humanity," this treasured essence of Chinese culture has been temporarily demolished by the Communists, its rehabilitation hinging on the recovery of the mainland by the Nationalist Party. One finds in Communist literature a mirror image of this rationale, enshrining a different yet parallel set of concepts, such as "revolution," "liberation," or "the people." These key terms are the mythical bedrock upon which national history can be built. As far as anti-Communist fiction is concerned, nevertheless, one must ask, if tradition and orthodoxy enjoy an immanent and transhistorical quality, how could they have been destroyed by the Communists? Is it possible that they contain the seeds of their own destruction? If tradition, orthodoxy, and humanity need to be reestablished, they are historical constructs based on a program of temporal, rather than transcendental, omnipresent givens. If there is no quintessential imperative that enshrines history, why does the Nationalist Party have to be the vehicle of that history? The same set of questions, with appropriate substitutions, to be sure, applies to Communist literature.

It is in this context that Jiang Gui and Eileen Chang deserve special attention. Both are severely critical of the Chinese Communist revolution. But when writing their political view in fictional terms, they refuse to submit to any predetermined, monological scheme. Jiang Gui's *A Tale of Modern Monsters* (or *Whirlwind*) will be discussed in full in the next chapter. Suffice it to say here that this novel chronicles the rise of Communist activities that engulf both leftists and rightists in a northern Chinese town. While he ridicules the leftist revolutionaries and likens them to monsters, Jiang Gui has little confidence in the orthodox rightist forces, old and new, despite the fact that he was a dedicated Nationalist Party member. For him, those who suffer from the Communist devastation might be ignorant of leftist radicalism; they are not innocent victims, however, in that they are nurtured by the same cannibalistic tradition that begot Communism. That the novel was never a favorite of anti-Communist establishments bespeaks its (self-)subverting potential.

Eileen Chang published two anti-Communist novels, *The Rice-Sprout Song* and *Naked Earth,* during her stay in Hong Kong from 1952 to 1955. An arch-cynic, Chang holds a desolate, "comic" view of nationalism, which is a far cry from the "tears and sniveling" strategy favored by mainstream anti-Communist literature. Her skepticism nevertheless is accompanied by a deep sympathy with and curiosity about the human endeavor to fight a losing war, whatever the cause. I have already discussed *The Rice-Sprout Song* in the context of Communist hunger discourse in the previous chapter; I will focus here on *Naked Earth.*

Naked Earth covers three crucial events in the early era of People's Republic of China: land reform, the Three Antis (antibribery; anticorruption; antibureaucracy) movement, and the Korean War. The hero of the novel is a young college graduate named Liu Quan. A political activist, Liu Quan sympathizes with the Communist cause and, after the founding of the new China, volunteers to participate in the land reform movement in the countryside. His revolutionary fervor, however, falters as he witnesses the bloody land reform in the country and the grotesque power struggles in the city. Liu finds solace with a female coworker, Huang Juan, but their burgeoning romance can hardly survive the surveillance of the party on the one hand and the temptation of a veteran woman cadre on the other. Like a Balzacian hero, Liu Quan is both ambitious and vulnerable, both unscrupulous and innocent. He is finally set up by his opponents, put in jail, and sent as a "volunteer" soldier to Korea.

Chang is never an optimist in regard to intimate human relations, romantic or familial. Even so, she cannot help feeling surprised by a political system that bases its claim to solidarity on the "technology" of betrayal. It is against such a treacherous human landscape that the love and sacrifice between Liu Quan and Huang Juan appear particularly risky and gratuitous. I hasten to add that these two figures are not committed to love for any lofty reasons; they find shelter in each other's embrace merely because they believe that to maintain their own sanity in a chaotic time this is the last thing over which they have some control. This humble, selfish wish is destined to be crushed. As the novel develops, Liu Quan and Huan Juan are among the first victims of Communist campaigns.

The last part of *Naked Earth* recounts Liu Quan's adventures on the Korean battlefield. The theme of the Korean War cannot appear more politically motivated. One recalls how Yang Shuo, in *Three-Thousand-Mile Mountain,* depicts a romantic couple who cannot consummate their love until they dedicate themselves to the war of "fighting America and supporting Korea." In *Naked Earth,* the Korean battlefield is reserved for those who have already exhausted themselves in political and romantic games. Having already been a loser in both games, Liu Quan has nothing more to lose, and so is sent off to war. Eileen Chang makes Liu Quan a most selfish soldier in the sense that he personalizes the Korean War, as if it broke out only to provide him with a convenient excuse to die. She thus subordinates the grand call for Communist patriotism to a moribund romantic motive.

Liu Quan wants to die on the Korean battlefield, but he survives. When captured by the Americans, Liu turns down the option of going to Taiwan; he wants to go back to China so as to subvert the regime from within. "As long as one man like him remained alive and out of jail, the men who ruled China would never be safe."[57]

This must be the most blatantly propagandist statement in *Naked Earth.* Such a tendentious moment, however, cannot overcome its decadent undertone. By sending Liu Quan back to China and making him a political dissident or even a spy in the "red land," Chang seems to have played the most heroic card in the anti-Communist repertoire. But questions remain. Isn't

Liu Quan volunteering to go back to China for the same unspeakable reason that made him volunteer to go to Korea? Given his past record, could he really hope to carry out his suddenly acquired mission? Liu may well be a three-time loser, unless deliberately choosing failure is considered a kind of heroism.

In 1955, Eileen Chang left China for good, but she sent the protagonist of her last major novel back to China.[58] Liu Quan would presumably have gone underground, but chances are that he would not join any anti-Communist network, but rather would tend the remnants of his passion alone in an environment hostile to loneliness. In a sense, Liu Quan went back to China on behalf of Eileen Chang and lived out a possibility she had had the foresight to avoid. Liu Quan would not be lonely in the sense that many other Shanghai characters created by Chang are lonely, hanging around somewhere, quietly withering away in silent protest. It would be thirty years before these characters surfaced and fascinated a new generation of Chinese readers with their stubborn and desolate philosophies of life.

In the person of her ideologically unhealthy characters, or as herself, Chang might have achieved more than countless anti-Communist heroes in undermining the literary discourse of Maoism. But perhaps she would not have done so without a sneer at the dreams of the free society in which she took shelter. After all, Eileen Chang was found dead, like her unhappy characters, an exile, old and alone, having lived in self-imposed seclusion in a barren apartment on the borders of Hollywood.

LITERATURE OF THE SCARRED, LITERATURE OF THE HEALED

Mid-twentieth-century Chinese fiction did not merely rationalize the rise and fall of a certain regime; it committed itself no less to inscribing the pains and sorrows that millions of Chinese experienced in wars, purges, exiles, and other contingencies. The split in the nation cannot be more emphatically signified than by the physical and mental wounds that afflicted millions of Chinese. Insofar as it investigates the traumatic experiences induced by rampant party politics and the moral and psychological consequence of these experiences, midcentury pro- and anti-Communist fiction predates the literature of the scarred *(shanghen wenxue)* by almost thirty years.

I used the term "scar" in my reading of Lu Xun's works in Chapter 1. The official term, literature of the scarred, however, originated with the short story "Shanghen" (The scar), by a young Shanghai writer, Lu Xinhua (b. 1953), in 1978. Written in the aftermath of the Cultural Revolution, the story depicts a family tragedy resulting from a decade when all China went mad. With its crude style and melodramatic plot, the story touched on a wide range of issues, such as political commitment versus familial ties, communal hysteria versus individual pain, and abused trust versus wasted youth. It moved millions of

Chinese readers, triggering a phenomenal trend toward soul-searching through writing about the atrocities of the revolution.

By invoking a physical scar as a testimonial of a bygone experience of misery, "The Scar" lends itself to a reading grounded in the politics of the body. Thousands of Chinese were cruelly beaten, paraded, deformed, incarcerated, exiled, enslaved, and put to death during the Cultural Revolution, to say nothing of those who were either driven mad or suffered from endless psychological agony. Political violence manifests itself by maneuvering and violating human bodies. Thus, the scar imagery partakes of a symbolic dimension. It serves as an emblem through which the past can be remembered and the lost memory restored. Marian Gálik has a point in comparing the scar symbolism of Lu Xinhua's story with Odysseus's scar in the *Odyssey,* however different the two works may be. In both cases, Gálik argues, the physical trace of an old wound is brought forth, either to vindicate obscured human relations or to reestablish the tie between the past and the present.[59]

But the Chinese example of the scar leads to more questions. Is the scar a sign of rehabilitation, indicating an alleviation of the pain of the past? Or is it a reminder of injury, pointing to a past that, once lacerated, can no longer be fully healed? Does writing about scars let the author and reader face the past, or does it represent the "irrepresentability" of the past, which can only be recovered as a trace? If the scar refers to a body inscribed with an eternal sign of injury, can writings about the scar present the broken body of history in complete form? Finally, has the literature of the scarred of the late 1970s found a new way to recount the horror and suffering undergone by the Chinese, or was it a bitter reenactment of scars already revealed in mid-century Chinese fiction?

A Genealogy of Scars

As I pointed out at the beginning of this chapter, twenty-five years before the appearance of the literature of the scarred, Duanmu Fang had already written blatantly about the politics of scars in *The Badge of Scars.* A political novel, *The Badge of Scars* cannot be more propagandist. Of importance here is that its tendentious message is predicated on the evocation of scars, both literal and symbolic, caused by the Japanese and the Communists. We are told that while physical wounds may have deformed the surface of the soldier's body, emotional and ideological wounds have hurt him to the bone. The image of a scar generates a cluster of images: a disfigured body, a broken heart, a separated family, a disjointed society, and a severed country. These images form the major trope of the anti-Communist novel. Hence Zhang Daofan's remarks in the preface that the youth of free China should "read this novel with a humble heart, thereby reflecting on the past. [They should] accept the lesson of failure . . . having bravely engaged in combat with the enemy. A scar left from tearing and bleeding is the most honorable badge of revolutionary youth."[60]

In Pan Renmu's *Cousin Lianyi,* Lianyi is portrayed as a romantic girl who is encouraged by her progressive classmates to join Communist activities. Though knowing little of Marxist/Maoist doctrine, Lianyi is deeply attracted to the heroism and mystique implied in the idea of revolution; moreover, as a fashion-conscious girl, she must prove that she can lead in thought as well as in clothing. Lianyi eventually pays a most painful price for her revolutionary enthusiasm. By the time she runs away from the mainland, she has lost her child, her family, her youth, and her political beliefs.

If the story sounds familiar to us, it is partially because Lu Xinhua's "The Scar" relates a shorter but similar plot about an innocent girl who is driven by the cause of the Cultural Revolution to overthrow any establishment that stands in the way of her and her fellow Red Guards. Her fanaticism leads her to persecute her own mother and "volunteer" to a farm in northeastern China. When she realizes how wrong she has been, she has wasted her youth and missed the last chance to express her regret to her mother.

I am not suggesting that an anti-Communist writer like Pan Renmu had such foresight about Communist evils as to prefigure the thesis of literature of the scarred almost three decades before Lu Xinhua. Given the extremely tense situation across the Taiwan Straits at the time, it must have been a final gamble for Lianyi (as well as her author) to denounce one ideological camp for another.[61] What I want to stress is that, political labels aside, Chinese writers of the 1950s had started a narrative typology of the scarred to describe the irrationalities of the ongoing war and political struggle, as if bodily torture could serve as the final testimonial to a political catastrophe. The reemergence of a similar "scar" typology in late 1970s China does mean not the belated victory of anti-Communist literature but the continued precipitation of literary politics since the 1950s; not the renewed outburst of writers' creativity but the prolonged pain and confusion of their lived experience.

With this argument in mind, one may enumerate more examples of scars from both Nationalist and Communist discourses of the midcentury. Chen Jiying's *Fool in the Reeds* describes how the Communists enlist support from the lower classes and underworld, manipulating them in such a way as to ruin established social and ethical orders. The Communist revolution succeeded, as Chen sees it, not by advocacy of any noble goal but by cultivation of the most debased aspect of humanity. The revolution is nothing but a circus of fools, the most dedicated participants often becoming the first victims.

Eileen Chang provides more gruesome pictures of the horror in the Communist land reform movement. In *The Rice-Sprout Song,* the peasant woman Yuexiang burns the village barn to avenge her husband's death, but she is driven into the fire by local soldiers and burns to death. In *Naked Earth,* a modest landlord is accused of maltreating his tenants, although all evidence proves otherwise. He is tied to the end of a horse carriage with barbed wire, then pulled around behind a galloping horse until his body is torn into pieces. His daughter-in-law, an innocent eight-month-pregnant woman, is hung upside down from the top of a flag pole and dies after her screaming and wailing has upset everyone.

Mid-twentieth-century Chinese Communist literature derives its scar consciousness from the leftist traditions of earlier decades. Before Mao's Yan'an talks, revolutionary literature had been known as a literature of rebellion, by and for those who had been "insulted and injured." This tradition was reinforced by Mao's advocacy of literature as a tool of class struggle. Accordingly, to write fiction in the wake of Mao's talks was to commemorate the proletariat's suffering under Nationalist rule, while anticipating their recovery through Communist revolution.

One must not forget that Hu Feng and his followers developed their poetics at the same time as Mao did, viewing literature as that which inscribes those who are "spiritually scarred."[62] Though sharing Mao's call for a literature in the service of revolution, Hu Feng's emphasis on the wounded subjectivity and its recovery through ideological sublation betrays a different theoretical heritage from Mao's; this heritage includes at least elements of Hegelian and Lukácsian aesthetics, May Fourth critical realism, and a Dionysian penchant for decadence and destruction.[63] Hu Feng's thesis on "the spiritually scarred" was forcefully put to use by his protégé Lu Ling, one of the most talented writers of the 1940s. In Lu Ling's fiction of the late 1940s and early 1950s, such as *Children of the Rich* and *Zai tielian zhong* (In the midst of the shackles, 1951), spiritual scars, from psychological trauma to ideological ressentiment, are treated as a contagious ailment afflicting rich and poor, rightists and leftists.

In any case, revolution was seen by midcentury Communist writers as the crucial means by which to cure the national body and revitalize a dying culture. If scars are described profusely in Chinese literature, it is because they are tangible signs pointing to the national malaise caused by the Nationalist Party and the remedy of the Communist Party. The Communist seizure of the mainland in 1949 formally substantiated the promise that the new regime would prescribe a magical medicine healing both the inner and outer wounds of the people. In contrast to the anti-Communist literature of this time, which is motivated solely by scar symbolism, Communist literature accentuated the scars so as to flaunt the availability of their cure. It claimed to be a literature of healing.

As if competing with their anti-Communist counterparts in presenting graphic violence and its resultant scars, Communist fiction of the late 1940s is loaded with miserable pictures of life under Nationalist rule. Zhao Shuli's *Changes in Li Village,* for instance, tells how a village in northwestern China had been ravished by feudal powers, landlords, foreigners, warlords, and Nationalists before being liberated by Communist troops. In Zhou Libo's *Hurricane,* peasants are extorted, overburdened with work, beaten, jailed, raped, and deprived of food until the land reform team comes to their rescue. In both *Hurricane* and Ding Ling's *The Sun Shines over the Sanggan River,* the pain and fear of the peasants are so deep that the land reformers have to serve as their psychiatrists, helping them remember and talk through the past. Only after they revisit the primal scenes of their pain can the peasants be mobilized to fight back against the landlords and Nationalist devils.

Revolutionaries also have their role in the theater of corporeal suffering. In Yuan Jing and Kong Jue's *New Tale of Heroes and Lovers,* both the hero and heroine are arrested and tortured in a most inhuman way. But their firm belief in Communism helps them put up with all the trials without releasing any information to the investigators. Later, they manage to run away from the Nationalist jail, personal suffering making them only more brave in carrying out their missions. Those who support the revolutionary cause in *Changes in Li Village* are not so lucky, though. When their insurrection fails, more than one hundred members of the Li village have their hands cut off and their eyes plucked out by the Nationalists. Their Communist leader is buried alive. In war novels of the 1950s, such as *Guarding Yan'an, Tiedao youji dui* (Railroad guerrillas, 1954), and *Bitter Endive Flower,* soldiers are uniformly ex-victims of the Nationalists and foreign invaders; they appear like avengers whose wrath can be pacified only after they either kill off their immediate enemies or lose their own lives in the attempt to kill.

The Technology of Writing Scars

I am aware of the anachronism in my application of the term "scar" to works produced in the early 1950s. Writers of the late 1970s and writers of the mid-century, after all, created works under different political circumstances and for different kinds of readers. What concerns me, to repeat, is a consistent typology in Chinese literature from both the mainland and Taiwan after the mid-twentieth century, which claims to testify to manmade disasters resulting from political struggles *among the Chinese themselves.* This literature is related to the "hard-core" realism of the May Fourth tradition, to use C. T. Hsia's term,[64] in that it renders a raw, bloody picture of Chinese people in misery. But whereas "hard-core" realism envisages a narrative that spurns ideological and philosophical pretensions, thus driving home its humanitarian concern, the literature of the scarred since the 1950s has clear political agendas.

Involved here is a much more complicated issue about the politicized body in pain and the "technology" of writing and reading the pain and scars of this body. Since both Communist and anti-Communist fiction claim to represent innocent people's suffering, it became a challenge to writers to articulate the pain on behalf of those who could not utter their feelings. From *Changes in Li Village* to *The Sun Shines over the Sanggan River,* one notices that the peasants were either so inhibited by evil forces or so numbed by their hard life that they could not say anything to the Communist liberators. Once properly "encouraged," however, these peasants could not say enough about their sufferings, to the point of becoming dreadfully redundant and hyperbolic.

Hyperbole and redundancy, the two major rhetorical traits of Communist and anti-Communist fiction, must be examined carefully. From an ideological viewpoint, hyperbole and redundancy are the prerequisites of a grammar of propaganda literature. Through excessive, repetitive linguistic expressions, the authoritarian power machine makes sure that its people accurately receive a precoded message. Violent language is supposed to incite violent action; linguistic excess can generate mass behavioral hysteria.[65] As the scar is turned into a totem, writing becomes a prelude to more wounds.

The first part of *Hurricane* culminates in the indictment of the landlord Han Laoliu at a public trial.[66] The peasants are so infuriated by the collective remembrance of their suffering under the cruel landlord that they finally come forward and surround Han, grabbing and biting him. In the climax of *Changes in Li Village,* the angry masses are encouraged to humiliate the evil landlord Li Ruchen and then beat him to death. When asked if they have gone too far, a farmer retorts: "You call this too bloody? When they killed us, our blood flowed into the sewer like a flood!"[67] Similarly, a cannibalistic impulse finally erupts in Ding Ling's *The Sun Shines over the Sanggan River,* as the peasants are incited to beat the landlord Qian Wengui.[68]

However, hyperbole and redundancy can be seen as signs of a desperate effort at communicating a pain beyond normal rhetorical capacity. In view of the aftermath of the Holocaust, Theodor Adorno writes, "After Auschwitz, it is no longer possible to write poems."[69] In this way, Adorno points out the unbridgeable gap between suffering and writing about suffering, between the articulated testimonials of those who survived the holocaust and the eternally silenced protests of those who were killed. What should have never happened had happened. Can one find any rhetoric to properly explain this unlikely historical wound? A conscientious writer thus faces an impossible challenge: while he is compelled to continuously write for the dead and the inarticulate, he can best do so by writing about the irrepresentability of the pain and death he sets out to pin down.[70]

To stretch Adorno's reasoning a little, one might argue that excessive, repetitive linguistic expressions may not always serve as a propagandist device, reiterating a certain ideological truism. Rather they may indicate a continued failed attempt to name something whose implied poignancy is beyond verbal transmission. For anti-Communist as for Communist writers, the wounds caused by the inner war between the Nationalists and the Communists are so deep that they can be conveyed, paradoxically, only through unsuccessful repetition and exaggeration. Under these circumstances, the inflated rhetoric of redundancy and hyperbole takes on a moralistic dimension. It defers any conclusive act of remembering of the past by denying any proper form of re-membering the past.

For writers who were driven to Taiwan, this argument may have even greater relevance. After the land of the Republic of China had been mutilated, could their personal scars be exaggerated to surpass the national wound?[71] "Do not shed tears for those who are dead, feel sorrow for those who are alive," writes Zhao Zifan (1924–1986) in his *Banxialiu shehui* (Semi-lower class society, 1954). The novel provides a pathetic picture of a group of mainlanders stranded in early 1950s Hong Kong. These people deserve more sympathy than those who were killed by the Communists, Zhao argues, not only because they are faced with an unknown future but also because they are burdened with a moral responsibility for the past, and for the dead. How can the survivors effectively tell the story of the Communist evil without usurping the voices of those who have been eternally silenced? In what way can they atone with words for the bloodshed during the Communist takeover? Traditional criticism has sneered at anti-Communist fiction as empty propaganda. This emptiness, I suggest, stems as much from the writers' deep-seated awareness of having been severed from the motherland and their unfathomable sense of loss as from ideological dogmatism.

In contrast to conventional wisdom, I argue that, vacillating between ideological excess and psychological vacuity in narrating the suffering of Chinese people, Communist and anti-Communist writers have generated in their works some of the most philosophically perplexing moments in modern Chinese literature. But our investigation does not stop here. Insofar as literature sustains its literary effect by means of defamiliarization, the question must be raised as to how anti- and pro-Communist fiction keeps its audience's interest by aesthetically renewing the form by which the scar can be conveyed. Does even the most excruciating human misery need a new packaging after being recycled only a few times?

Coming to mind is the lesson drawn from Lu Xun's short story "New Year's Sacrifice." When the main character, Xianglin's wife, first tells her story to a group of curious auditors, its pathos induces a profusion of tears. Her story becomes such a wonderful tearjerker that it draws listeners from distant villages. Both the narrated subject and the narration become a spectacle of plight, which leads to a cheap catharsis for the audiences if not for the teller. But the audiences soon tire of Xianglin's mechanical retelling of the very same story; soon she becomes a butt of jokes and then is totally forgotten by society.

The story about Xianglin's wife and her tale of misery has been used by Lu Xun and his followers to illustrate the cannibalistic nature of the Chinese people. Lu Xun, however, may have unwittingly constructed an allegory of the grotesque consequences of turning scars into moral lessons. In repeating and elaborating the pain and bloody facts of the Communist or Nationalist persecution, majority writers of the 1950s were faced with a predicament. Whether ideologically or psychologically motivated, their redundant, exaggerated, and above all overly familiar narratives exhaust their audience's curiosity and patience. A ritual account of the most repugnant crime can degenerate into a most boring pastime and ultimately trivialize the crime itself. A constant literature of engagement will produce the effect promised by a literature of alienation.

Hence Eileen Chang's story about narrating the scar. In *The Rice-Sprout Song,* an ideologically progressive old woman has been well trained to talk about her misery in the Nationalist days. After repeating her rhetoric too many times, she is so inattentive as to let her tongue slip, making Communists into Nationalist enemies.

This leads to a most cynical question. If a good "effect" is all that is needed, why not just make up the scars? In Eileen Chang's *Naked Earth,* the protagonist Liu Quan is assigned to work on a newspaper in Shanghai after the liberation. His first mission is to work on a photo in which a blond woman's breasts are mutilated by a Nazi soldier. He is asked to darken the woman's hair and smear the insignia of the Nazi uniform so as to make him look like an American soldier. The purpose of this is to show American cruelty in the Korean War. Liu's superior, a woman cadre, sees the young man's hesitation. She explains that the distortion is justifiable because the Chinese people already know the evil "essence" of the Americans but the newspaper needs something concrete, an objective correlative, so to speak, to bolster this inherent knowledge among the people. Liu is to erase the identity of the woman and the soldier in the picture and to replace the original disfiguration by disfiguring its representation; in so doing, he can rely on the inherent Chinese knowledge of evil, which is so easy to invoke that a cheap trick will suffice. Or so the cadre says, believing as she does in the efficacy of propagandistic tricks; thus the cadre defines the potential and limitation of scar literature.

This chapter has tried to reassess the significance of Communist and anti-Communist fiction of the mid-twentieth century seen from three aspects. First, I argued that fiction of this period, while carrying all the traces of contemporary politics, cannot be fully understood without referring to the May Fourth literary tradition. Despite their claims of starting modern Chinese literature anew, Communist and anti-Communist writers carried on with the revolutionary poetics initiated by the first generation of modern Chinese literati. They are the inheritors of the dark power of the late Qing and May Fourth tradition. Discernible political interventions aside, the implosion of this revolutionary poetics constitutes the most important fact of midcentury Chinese literature.

Second, in the wake of the dialogics between "new fiction" and "new nation" first proposed by late Qing intelligentsia, narrative fiction again demonstrated its affinity to the (re)making of national history in the mid-twentieth century. In one way or another, pro- and anti-Communist writers retold the history of the rise, fall, and rebirth of modern China. Their fiction aims to redefine the space, time, and human agents forming a national narrative to the point where the mythical mandate took charge; hence a national history written as if one could nationalize history.

Third, Communist and anti-Communist fiction formulated a "scar" typology to describe the sorrow of the Chinese people torn by political struggles. This scar discourse, manifested more as a "hard-core" account of the human body in pain, triggers a cluster of ideological, moralistic, and formal debates about the body politics of narrative literature. The inextricable debate about the political significance of human suffering and its textual manifestation anticipated the rise of the literature of the scarred in the late 1970s.

To conclude my fictive reconstruction of the most chaotic moments of modern Chinese history, let us glance at how midcentury mainland and Taiwanese fiction has been inscribed by history since the early 1950s. For Nationalist writers, the fall of mainland China implied a loss of control over the master narrative of Chinese history. They have therefore written so as to imagine the recovery of a complete, perhaps Nationalist, China. But, as argued above, continued writing about rupture, dispersed families, mutilated bodies, and lost master narratives can bring about only incompleteness, even incompleteness of effect. As years passed by, anti-Communist literature became increasingly trapped in the predictability of its historical mission. It retreated to the backstage of history, when the consciousness of Taiwan as a de facto political state was occupying stage front, even more so when the Communist and Nationalist regimes began to open doors to each other for cultural, economic, and political exchange.

Communist literature of the midcentury unfailingly starts with an account of the scars left in 1949 and ends with a promise or even realization of a cure. PRC history since 1956, however, showed us a different story. Writing of the old scar does not close off the memory of the painful past; rather there are new wounds, and new scars. Almost all the writers mentioned in this chapter were cruelly persecuted. Ding Ling fell dramatically in 1955 with her cohorts, as a result of a fearsome internecine power struggle among cadre writers. Du Pengcheng's *Guarding Yan'an* was banned in 1958, during the purge of Peng Dehuai; Du was to be cruelly charged of conspiring against Mao in the Cultural Revolution. Zhou Libo's *Hurricane* was cited as a negative example in the late 1960s for highlighting individual heroism;[72] Zhao Shuli died a miserable death in 1970 for supporting an incorrect party line.[73] The scenes of public trials, mass riots, and ruthless physical persecutions these writers so vividly described in their novels were acted out by the revolutionary crowds and red guards; those who survived the violent decades would come back to write about their scars in the late 1970s. The literature of the healed became only a preparation for more literature of the scarred.

Chapter 6

The Monster That Is History

The dream of reason produces monsters.
FRANCISCO GOYA, *Los Caprichos*

In Taiwan in the fall of 1957, the Chinese émigré writer Jiang Gui (Wang Yijian, 1908–1980) published a novel entitled *Jin taowu zhuan* (A tale of modern monsters). This novel chronicles Communist activities in a small town in Shandong Province from the 1920s through the 1940s, culminating in a macabre riot costing hundreds of lives. At the center of the novel is a pair of amateur revolutionaries, Fang Xiangqian, a Confucian literatus turned Marxist ideologue, and his nephew, Fang Peilan, a local militia chieftain with a dubious past as a highway bandit. In their yearning for reform, their revolutionary action, and their downfall amid internecine party struggles, Jiang Gui describes how the utopian project of the two Fangs ends up producing a monstrous machine that engulfs its makers.

With such a plot, *A Tale of Modern Monsters* can be read as an example of anti-Communist fiction, the major literary genre in Taiwan in the 1950s. This genre comprises works that lash out at Communist evils while projecting an imminent Nationalist restoration. It was either produced spontaneously by newly exiled mainland writers or concocted by the ruling party's propaganda machine; many cases show an interplay of both factors.[1] As a dedicated Nationalist Party member, Jiang Gui made it clear that he wrote *A Tale of Modern Monsters* to bear witness to Communist atrocity,[2] and he would have had no qualms about the novel serving the purposes of propaganda. However, perhaps for the reasons to be discussed shortly, the novel never drew much official attention. The novel, at first titled Xuanfeng (The whirlwind), was completed as early as January 1952, but in the next six years it was rejected by at least ten publishers. This was unusual at a time when the government tried every method—from prize contests to publicity stunts—to solicit anti-Communist works and sponsor their publication.[3] In 1957, the disillusioned Jiang Gui retitled the novel *A Tale of Modern Monsters* and printed five hundred copies at his own expense. As he later admitted, besides about two hundred copies given away to friends and scholars, the novel hardly reached the market.[4]

Critics nevertheless responded warmly to *A Tale of Modern Monsters.* Both Jiang Mengling (1886–1964) and Hu Shi, literary giants at the time, welcomed the novel as a powerful testimony to the horror of the Chinese Communist revolution.[5] Rightist critics, such as Wang Jicong and Liu Xinhuang, also paid due respect to Jiang Gui's political stance and narrative skill.[6] Of the contemporary reviews, the one by the historical fiction writer Gao Yang (1922–1992) stands out for its perceptive analysis of the novel's rhetorical and psychological nuances.[7] With the sponsorship of the United States Information Service, *A Tale of Modern Monsters* was formally published by a commercial press in 1959, with its title changed back to *The Whirlwind.* When C. T. Hsia discussed *The Whirlwind* in his 1971 revised edition of *A History of Modern Chinese Fiction,* he added the novel to the canon of modern Chinese fiction.[8]

C. T. Hsia praised *The Whirlwind* as the work that best encapsulated the modern Chinese literary tradition from the Late Qing to the post–May Fourth Era. By this, Hsia meant that Jiang Gui captured both the satirical and humanitarian strains of modern Chinese fiction since the turn of the century, yet never fell prey to either sentimentalism or propagandizing, as did most of his contemporaries.[9] Hsia highlights the novel's critique of Chinese politics at both micro and macro levels, and he concludes that "among the host of cliché-ridden anti-Communist novels published in Taiwan, [Jiang Gui's] work stands out as a gripping chronicle of the rise of Communism, masterly told against the complex background of Chinese life—with all its corruption and horror—from the May Fourth period to the early years of the Sino-Japanese War."[10]

The readings by Hsia and other critics, perceptive as they are, have focused on the linkage between the novel and ongoing national politics. But today, when the debate between pro-Communist and anti-Communist literature is just another costly quarrel from the past century, such comments have limitations. The lasting power of *The Whirlwind* has to be sought elsewhere: in the multiple trajectories of Chinese history and their fictional representations, and Jiang Gui's ability to configure history. If the novel is still compelling to us, it is not so much because Jiang Gui tells a more truthful anti-Communist story as because he manages to address issues that also concern us, such as: how did political calamity and personal trauma during the Great Divide of 1949 affect the imaging and inscribing of history? How can we make sense of a modernity that is so full of irrationalities and contradictions as to preclude any coherent, rational "emplotment"? How can we negotiate the relations between historiography, ideology, and the literary representation of scars? And above all, what drives one to seek an ethical and intellectual heritage in a century that purports to break with tradition and reach the end of history?

I suggest a first answer to these questions about *The Whirlwind* by reinvoking the title of its second incarnation, *Jin taowu zhuan*, or *A Tale of Modern Monsters*. Behind this obscure title lies Jiang Gui's indebtedness to a premodern Chinese fiction trope crucial to an understanding of his vision of modern Chinese history. As he puts it, *Jin taowu zhuan* was adopted as the title because the novel was inspired by a late Ming novel, *Taowu xianping* (An idle commentary on monsters, 1629).[11] Allegedly by the late Ming literatus and official Li Qing (1602–1683), this novel deals in fifty chapters with the rise and fall of Wei Zhongxian (1568–1627), the vicious eunuch of the Tianqi reign of the Ming (1621–1627), and Madame Ke (d. 1627), the wet nurse of the emperor, who together almost brought down the dynasty. Jiang Gui links his novel to the late Ming work because both aim at "recounting evils so as to admonish" *(ji'e yiwei jie)*.[12] He sees *A Tale of Modern Monsters* as resuming the moral intent of the late Ming novel.

But why *taowu*? In his preface to *A Tale of Modern Monsters* Jiang Gui offers the following explanation:

> Legend has it that Zhuanxu had a wayward son named Taowu. *Taowu* also refers to broken wood, which in my judgment is as despicable as the *shu* [useless wood] in the *Zhuangzi*. Both references thus partake of the allegorical meaning. By association, *taowu* also indicates a monster. Moreover, the historiography of the ancient Chu Kingdom is called *taowu*, meaning to "recount evils so as to admonish". In fiction, there is a work entitled *Taowu xianping*, which tells of the evildoings of Wei Zhongxian and Madame Ke, in service of the goal of moral improvement.[13]

With the clues in this passage as a point of departure, one can trace the etymological origins of "taowu," among which the following are most suggestive. "Taowu" appears in the *Shenyi jing* (Classic of the supernatural and the strange) as a monster of ancient times:

> [The monster Taowu] looks like a tiger, with hair two feet long. It has a human face, a tiger's feet, a pig's teeth, and a tail as long as eighteen feet. It likes to fight and will never withdraw.[14]

In the *Shiji*, Sima Qian writes,

> Prince Zhuanxu has a wayward son who turns his back on any moral teachings and is incorrigible. This son is called Taowu by the world.[15]

Identified as Zhuanxu's son Guen, Taowu is said to be among the four major evils of the ancient times who were tamed and exiled by Prince Shun to withstand *Chimei,* the ghostly mountain spirits, on the frontiers. Similar references can also be found in the classics *Zuozhuan, Zhouli,* and *Shangshu.*[16]

Yet equally important is the fact that *taowu* is identified with history as a narrative account of bygone events, which "records the evil deeds of the monstrous and the invincible."[17] This usage can best be illustrated in *Mencius:*

> When the wooden clappers [used by officials who went around collecting ballads] of the true king fell into disuse, songs were no longer collected. When songs were no longer collected, the *Spring and Autumn Annals* were written. The *Sheng* of the Chin, the *T'ao U [Taowu]* of Ch'u [Chu], and the *Spring and Autumn Annals* of Lu are the same kind of work. The events recorded concern Duke Huan of Ch'i [Qi] and Duke Wen of Chin [Qin], and the style is that of official historian.[18]

The association of the *taowu* with history may have something to do with the divinatory power with which the monster is endowed. Anthropologists have pointed out that, in the ancient Chu region, the *taowu* was taken as a creature of auspicious nature because it had the capacity to foresee the future. *Xiangdong jiwen* (Accounts of the eastern Hunan region) recounts that

> the *taowu* is an animal that can foresee the future, so it can always run away before the hunters arrive. Since history reveals both past and future, it is referred to as the *taowu.*[19]

Because of its ferocious nature and mysterious visionary ability, the *taowu* became a guardian of the imperial tombs.[20] "As a creature against evil, the *taowu* can withstand ghosts and monsters; as a creature of good omen, wisdom, and totem, it can direct one to meet with good fortune and avoid danger, help resurrect the dead, guide ghosts in ascending to heaven, and serve as a medium for the transmigration of the dead."[21]

In his study, Tu Cheng-sheng points out that the imagination, invocation, and categorization of monsters, generalized as *wuguai,* constitute the incipient signs of civilization in ancient China. According to Tu, the naming of a certain monster is crucial to the formation of tribal and state identity. Moreover, the knowledge system emanating from the worship, deciphering, and institutionalization of *wuguai* can be associated with the formation of ritual, bureaucracy, and the legal system of a state. In the Zhou dynasty, Tu argues, *wuguai* was still referred to as an externalization of the virtue or *de*—or "humor" of the social body—of a state. Above all, *wuguai* serves as an integral part of the rise of ancient historiography.[22]

With these references in mind, we can take a look at Jiang Gui's apologia in his novel, which is reminiscent of Cao Xueqin in the opening chapter of his *Hongloumeng* (The dream of the red chamber):

> The author of *A Tale of Modern Monsters* is in his forties. Recollecting the way he led the first half of his life, he cannot express enough remorse over his degeneration. He wrote the novel with the honest and sincere purpose inherent in all good literature; he harbors no wish to publicize sordid deeds. The novel is based on the goal of "recounting evils so as to admonish".[23]

It is striking that Jiang Gui has retrieved the rhetorical *and* ethical roots of classical historiography. "Taowu" denotes a monster from ancient times known for its bizarre appearance and ferocious nature, like a tiger with a human face, who loves to fight and is reluctant to stop. (Or should that be a human with a tiger body who loves to fight and is reluctant to stop?) Even when bracketed as a familial black sheep or a social outlaw, the *taowu* is humanized, and vice versa: specimens of humanity have been enlisted in the armies of bestiality. There exists in the image of the *taowu* a liminal zone where the inhuman and the human mingle, a region that is legally and morally anomalous. Evil monster and evil human intersect in looks and deeds, blurring the cultural and natural boundaries that humanity would draw around itself.

More intriguingly, history, or *taowu*, as Jiang Gui describes it, is none other than an inscription of the acts and consequences of evildoers; it is meant to recount the past in such a way as to caution subsequent generations against immorality and aberration. Chinese historiography, to be sure, comprises a full range of views on how history makes sense to us. The one Jiang Gui holds contemplates humanity as an ambiguous existence, forever subject to the test of good and evil; as such, it calls for either an inner awakening to or the external enforcement of the moral constitution of humanity so as to avoid deviation. Extrapolating Jiang Gui's logic, one can argue that although the professed goal of history is to reveal virtue to the exclusion of evil, the act of historical writing is ironically made possible by the continued accumulation—inclusion—of that which is immoral and therefore excludable. This historiographical vision generates its own antithesis: insofar as its moral telos holds true and valid in the long run, history, as a narrated account of bygone events, performs its function negatively, as an agency revealing only vice, waste, and anomaly. In other words, history admonishes the good only by adducing elements that prolong, or even belie, the search for the good.

Therefore, when fiction is written under the name of *taowu*, it bespeaks the complicity of civilization in its own discontent. This is a pessimistic brand of historiography and, in the case of Jiang Gui, it threatens to turn into a sinister irony at every turn of its narrativization of the human past. According to Jiang Gui and his predecessors, each generation witnesses, withstands, and helps produce the monster of its own times. With the anomalous and polymorphous mediation of the *taowu*—as monster, as broken timber, as outlaw, or as a record of evil—we find ourselves still coping with the inhumanity of the past in the hope of its eradication in the future. And yet at any point in time, the inhuman may prove to be that which is all too human. A monster looms over the human struggle for self-betterment. Because of its cruelty and ambiguity, *taowu* intensifies our motivation to remember the past. Inherent in the making of history is the shared memory of its monstrosity.

With Jiang Gui's contemplation of history as my point of reference, I will trace a preliminary fictional genealogy of the *taowu* from the late Ming to the modern period. I will discuss how Li Qing's *Idle Commentary on Monsters* renewed the fictional imaginary of history versus evil in late imperial China, and how the novel inspires Jiang Gui's *Tale of Modern Monsters,* thematically as well as discursively. In the historical space between these two works, I find a little-known late Qing/early Republican novel, *Taowu cuibian* (A compendium of monsters, 1916) by Qian Xibao (?–?). Evidence is yet to be found regarding Jiang Gui's knowledge of it. In terms of its ambiguous laughter at clowns who turn the late Qing empire upside down and its biting sarcasm on social absurdities, *A Compendium of Monsters* no doubt belongs to the tradition of late Qing exposés, in which Jiang Gui was well versed. In linking these three works, I am not attempting to establish verifiable relations of influence and reception. Rather I want to look into how each work responds to its own crisis by reawakening the ancient monster from its historical slumber. These works share a posture of depicting the violence and grotesquerie in—and of—history, but they do not necessarily establish a coherent dialogue among themselves. They call attention to the menacing changeability of history, in which the form of monstrosity cannot be predicted, only its persistence.

A TALE OF MODERN MONSTERS

Like many writers of his generation, Jiang Gui had a life and career intertwined with the historical turmoil of modern China. His hometown, Zhucheng County in Shandong Province, is associated with many other modern literary and political figures, such as Wang Tongzhao (1897–1957), Wang Yuanjian (1929–1991), Zang Kejia (b. 1905), Kang Sheng (1898–1975), and most notably, Mao Zedong's wife, Jiang Qing (1914–1991).[24] Jiang Gui was the posthumously adopted son of Wang Mingzhao, a Republican revolutionary who died in a local insurrection in 1911.[25] As early as 1924, when he was still a high school student, Jiang Gui left Shandong for Guangzhou to join the Nationalist Party; he was subsequently involved in almost all the major historical events from the late 1920s to the late 1940s, including the Northern Expedition, the collaboration and resultant split of the Nationalist and Communist Parties, the Anti-Japanese Aggression War, and the Nationalist campaign to prevent a Communist revolution.[26] In late 1948, Jiang Gui and his family followed the defeated Nationalist government to Taiwan. By then, he had retired from the army and started his own business, but in the next two years he lost all his investments.[27]

When he came to Taiwan, Jiang Gui had already tried his hand at creative writing. One of the four novels he produced in the 1930s and 1940s, *Tuwei* (Breaking free, 1939), was published during wartime under the aegis of Mao Dun and Ba Ren.[28] Thus Jiang Gui was a latecomer to the post–May Fourth fictional tradition. Jiang Gui resumed his writing career in the late 1950s. At that time, in his own words, with "my business failed and my wife fallen ill and confined to bed, my life was trapped in the most disorienting conditions I had ever experienced. Looking back at all that had happened in the previous years, I felt as if I had had a dream, and my gravest pain stemmed from having to cope with a broken nation and a collapsed family, a fate I shared with many other [Chinese émigrés]. Given what I have witnessed over the past thirty years, I believe I know the true nature of the Chinese Communist Party. By rearranging and editing my personal memories, I thus had a complete story."[29]

Such motives are representative of most mainland Chinese émigré writers in the 1950s. For Jiang Gui as for his fellow writers, the Communist takeover of the mainland was an event so catastrophic as to constitute a breakdown of Chinese society at both public and personal levels. As he puts it, the Nationalist exodus triggered a cluster of disasters in his life: his political allegiance was spurned, his commercial investments went bankrupt, his wife fell victim to chronic disease, his family fell apart, and he felt himself trapped in an insoluble riddle. Empirical adversities nevertheless constituted only the surface outcome of the national calamity. What really beset Jiang Gui and like-minded writers was the loss of a set of rationales that had seemingly put their lives in perspective. These writers' condemnation of Chinese Communism betrays an existential crisis: for them, the loss of the mainland would take on a symbolic dimension as a flaw in history and the origin of trauma.

One may argue that before the Communist takeover, modern China already suffered from endless natural and man-made disasters, so the Communist Revolution could not have been the cause any more than the effect—perhaps a fortunate effect from the leftist perspective—of a history that had gone awry. Jiang Gui would have retorted that, granting the incessant turmoil in recent Chinese history, what had remained intact was the lineage of *zhengtong*—the cultural, intellectual, and political orthodoxy that sanctions the present in terms of the past. For him, this *zhengtong* was represented by the Nationalist regime. Following his logic, even if the Nationalist Party was culpable for having failed to renew China efficiently, it at least had safeguarded the "authentic" continuum of Chinese historicity. By contrast, the Communist Party must be treated as a temporary aberration from this lineage—just like the dynastic usurpers of the past.

Although modern critics may consider it a mere pretext for hegemonic sovereignty, the notion of *zhengtong* points to a deep-seated tradition within Chinese historiography. The current study cannot look into the subject in detail.[30] What concerns me here are two issues: the temporal and spatial implications of *zhengtong* in regard to the legitimacy of power, and the ethical thrust behind the valorization of *zhengtong* as such. Scholars have pointed out that *zhengtong* is traceable to the calendric principle by which ancient historians judge the legitimacy of dynastic transitions; by the Qin dynasty its meaning has expanded to indicate total territorial annexation by a certain ruler.[31] From chronological coherence to geographical unification, the two meanings of *zhengtong* coalesce when employed to assert the mandate of an imperial power. Time and space are seen as united in such a way as to substantiate the plenitude of a political entity. But embedded in these temporal and spatial principles is the moral representation of political power; time and space are unified as a site from which the polity emanates its quintessential "moral occult."[32] Thus, despite all the dynasties' claims to orthodoxy, *zhengtong* is said to have been accorded only to that which exerts the greatest moral edification.[33]

Reinstating Orthodoxy

In *A Tale of Modern Monsters,* Jiang Gui's indebtedness to such a historical discourse of orthodoxy can be seen in the way he links temporal-spatiality, morality, and politics to the Great Divide of 1949. For him the 1949 fall of the mainland reflects not merely a changing of parties in power; it indicates a break in the unified imaginary of Chinese history and geography and, as a result, a dissipation of the "moral occult" inherent in Chinese experience. When the *zhengtong* falls, the forces of anomaly, abnormality, and amorphism go rampant. These forces manifest themselves at human, natural, and supernatural levels, and they must be contained before history can return to its proper course. Writing in 1950s Taiwan, Jiang Gui believed that he had been thrown into the latest struggle between orthodoxy and its deviations and that his mission lay in identifying the wayward forces and chronicling their rise and (anticipated) fall. He writes to "recount evils so as to admonish." As such, Jiang Gui sees himself not much differently from premodern historians, and he addresses this role most vividly by calling attention to the rich imagery of *taowu*.[34]

By reinvoking the ancient monster *taowu* to register the human evils of his time, Jiang Gui brings an additional polemic to his survey of history and orthodoxy. It is not difficult to see that Jiang Gui follows the format of conventional historical fiction in depicting the ebb and flow of the Republican regime in combat with the Communist evil. But there is something unconventional embedded in this notion of history as a cycle. *A Tale of Modern Monsters* opens with all established institutions already in shambles and ends with the ejection of the virtuous from the society to make room for the vicious, accompanied by a vague projection that Communism will be defeated in the long haul. Thus, in contrast to its premodern counterpart, it focuses not on the triumph but on the failure of a regime's political and moral capacity to withstand evil. Under the novel's tentative promise of the return of orthodoxy lies a much darker subtext. Jiang Gui seems to ponder, in a way as if he were looking at the other side of the cyclical view of history, whether human folly and irrationality do not return just as regularly as justice and order.

There is yet another dimension beyond this discovery that a history can recycle its undesirable elements. If, following the May Fourth revolutionary discourse, history is that which has to be overthrown in favor of modernity, *A Tale of Modern Monsters* tells us a story full of contradictions. It recounts how modern Chinese, rightist and leftist alike, are eager to dispel the past by means of revolution, only to be twice haunted by the "pastness" of the past in the present. All of Jiang Gui's characters are seen as either victims or villains of a tradition that simply will not disappear in the wake of revolution, and Jiang Gui cannot exempt himself from the haunting past either.

It must be ironic for Jiang Gui, as a son of the martyr who died in the Republican Revolution and as a veteran Nationalist revolutionary in his own right, to speak with such nostalgia of a premodern, imperial notion of orthodoxy that he and his father had once fought to abolish. But if he were called a conservative, Jiang Gui would have retorted: aren't the leftist revolutionaries more self-contradictory when they vow to demolish the old history of evils, all the while proclaiming a new *zhengtong* that begets even more evils? There is something monstrous in China's search for modernity when reactionary and revolutionary are hardly distinguishable and the old dresses itself up as the new. If in ancient times *taowu* was embodied in individual monsters or evildoers, it has become an omnipresent style in which everyone bedevils everyone else. The violent and absurd consequences brought by the self-multiplying monster constitute the historicity—or its denial—in the modern age.

The final enigma is that *A Tale of Modern Monsters* was never duly recognized by the Nationalist government—the embodiment of Jiang Gui's orthodoxy—in the heyday of anti-Communism. Although Jiang Gui tried hard to articulate his Nationalist allegiance, the regime for which he wrote the novel failed to appreciate his efforts. As a matter of fact, Jiang Gui's situation only worsened after the publication of *A Tale of Modern Monsters*. By the time his second anti-Communist novel, *Chongyang* (Double suns, 1960), was published, his wife had died after a series of ailments and two of his three children had to be sent away for better care. Worse, Jiang Gui was mysteriously charged with having neglected his wife and caused her death, a case that almost drove him to commit suicide. Jiang Gui was eventually acquitted in controversial circumstances. One can only sigh when reading his reminiscences, which concluded that he must have been set up by "Communist spies" because of his firm anti-Communist works![35]

Whether paranoia or insight, Jiang Gui's "discovery" of a Communist plot against him was at one with the strange character of 1950s cultural politics. In any case, his unsolicited sensibility about his circumstances may well be part of the reason for his unpopularity within his own party. Compared to the multitude of novels endorsing anti-Communism, *A Tale of Modern Monsters* always appears to have had something more to offer. Because of his uncontrolled hatred of the evils of his time, Jiang Gui may have gone too far, recklessly exposing Nationalist as well as Communist evil. When the regime rewarded him by ignoring him, one wonders whether it never occurred to him to ask the obvious: how could a truly conscientious regime overlook contributions like his? Was it possible that the Nationalist regime was not after all anointed? And if not, for whom was he writing these histories of evil? We do not know the answers. Amid all his tribulations, Jiang Gui's persistent patriotism was either grotesquely quixotic or superbly adaptive to the spirit of the times. Perhaps this best illustrates a modern Chinese writer's response to the treacherous circumstances in which history is inscribed. After all, these conditions have their own legacy, as demonstrated almost two millennia earlier by the arch-historian, castrato, and singer of tales Sima Qian (145 or 135 B.C.–?).[36]

Modern Monstrosity and "Imperfect Villainy"

A Tale of Modern Monsters opens with Fang Xiangqian organizing an underground Communist cell in the city T (Tsi-nan [Jinan], the capital of Shandong). Despite his gentry background and Confucian training, Fang finds Marxist proletarian revolution the most promising remedy for China's malaise. In this pursuit, he has not only used up his fortune but also involved his family members, under the constant threat of Nationalist crackdown, imprisonment, and execution. While Fang Xiangqian supports the revolution owing to his firm belief in Communism, his nephew Fang Peilan joins the cell simply because of a chivalric bent and discontent with the family status quo. Peilan has won himself the reputation of being a strong man in avenging his father's execution by the local authorities. But his practice of gangster gallantry appears more and more dated. Before he meets Fang Xiangqian, he has already succumbed to co-optation by the local government and become a militia leader.

Revolving around the two Fangs' rise to power is a cluster of subplots, including the corruption and decline of four old houses of the Fang family; the continued confrontation and collaboration between bandits, underground society, warlord forces, Nationalist armies, and Japanese aggressors; the tragicomedy of a group of "new youth" in search of revolution and romance; and the sudden prosperity of two prostitutes, Pang Yuemei and her daughter Pang Jinlian, thanks to the political chaos. These plots constitute the mosaic of an early Republican Chinese community in drastic transformation.[37]

Even in such a sketchy summary, one can already perceive Jiang Gui's ambition to expose the complexities of traditional Chinese systems. Jiang Gui would have agreed with Lu Xun's charge that, behind its façade of propriety and civility, "cannibalism" prevails in Chinese society. This cannibalism had long infiltrated the most minute aspects of Chinese life, such that its victims end up becoming the accomplices of their victimizers. For instance, in the most prominent household of the Fang clan, the matriarch, Mistress Fang, turns out to be a sadist, taking nightly pleasure in maltreating her late husband's concubine, while her son, Ranwu, is an indiscriminate lecher.[38] Although Ranwu's wife is known for her feminine virtues, her way of edifying her husband is to condone and help plan the rape of a village girl, thereby making the girl a proper concubine.

Not unlike Lu Xun's madman, Fang Xiangqian bemoans the fate of the young descendents of these families because they have been brought up to become either cannibals or dishes to be served to cannibals. The most effective way to "save the children," Fang concludes, is to guide them toward the light of Communism. He thus sends his daughter and his cousin to study in the Soviet Union.

But Jiang Gui parts with Lu Xun by describing an even darker world of violence and irrationality. On the eve of the Literary Revolution, Lu Xun could still create a figure like the madman, who recognized traditional institutions as cannibalism. However ambiguous, the madman's critique contains a moral vision, which would be adopted by the new society. Despite his increasing cynicism, Lu Xun was tantalized by the vision of a postcannibalist society right up to his death in 1936. Writing *after* the Communist Revolution, Jiang Gui was convinced that the revolution had compounded rather than done away with social and personal insanity. In the name of overthrowing the old cannibalism, a higher cannibalism had been established, uplifted by technology to a new level of perpetrated violence.

As the novel develops, Fang Xiangqian manages to consolidate various local forces and makes the chamber of the two prostitutes, Pang Yuemei and Pang Jinlian, a hideout for his activities. The failure of the 1927 Communist Revolution temporarily thwarts Fang Xiangqian's plan, but he and his followers stage a comeback when the Second Sino-Japanese War breaks out. The Japanese occupation of Shandong creates a political vacuum in Fangzhen. While Fang Xiangqian and Fang Peilan form an antiaggression "Whirlwind Column" from their rural bands and local militia, they carry on a secret collaboration with the Japanese military, which enables them to annihilate a group of guerrillas loyal to the Nationalist regime. They even establish their own county government in rivalry with the puppet government and, oddly enough, they win the endorsement of both Japanese and Nationalist forces.

It is in this context that Jiang Gui observes the most chilling interplay between the old and new forms of cannibalism. A series of murders take place in Fang Ranwu's house. First, one of his ex-paramours is found murdered by Fang Peilan's militia. Mistress Fang's beloved servant is the next victim, and his death is followed by that of Fang Ranwu. After the new local government is established, all the members of the four Fang families are driven off their property and most of them die as a result of this persecution. At the end of the novel, the prostitute Pang Yuemei is honored as "Mother of the Revolution," and her daughter Pang Jinlian is appointed Director of the Revolutionary Women's Committee. Ranwu's wife is forced to marry a hooligan before she is reassigned as maid to the Pangs and a prostitute of the cheapest class.

While he never conceals his polemical aims, Jiang Gui's critique of Communism should not be taken as motivated merely by partisanship, for he spares no effort in mocking the rightist figures. Fang Zhen, the dedicated Nationalist and the spokeswoman for Confucian virtues in the novel, is a bigot and an unfilial daughter. She despises her natural mother because the latter was a concubine rather than the legal wife of her late father. Another character, county magistrate Cheng Shi (a homonym of *chengshi,* or honesty), makes his first appearance in a most modest manner: he arrives at his office by mule-drawn cart. Before the Japanese troops invade, however, Cheng abandons his post and flees, only to be captured and made the head of the puppet government. Jiang Gui above all has little confidence in the Chinese in general; he sees fanatics, perverts, opportunists, hypocrites, and cowards in both rightist and leftist parties, both high and low classes, and both younger and older generations.

I would argue that Jiang Gui derives his power not from his attack on the Chinese Communist Revolution as such, but rather from his apprehension in seeing any system, radical or conservative, malfunction in historical practice. As a social pathologist, he looks into the illnesses in Chinese society, of which the Communist revolution is only the most recent syndrome. Central to his story about modern Chinese revolution is a process of inevitable decadence, despite a promise of enlightenment and progress. In contrast with the linear, cause-and-effect description offered by most of his peers, Jiang

Gui offers a view of the rise of Chinese Communism in which political, moral, and libidinous forces, among others, cut across one another and generate a monstrosity that is beyond logical figuration. He may begin his novels with a clear historical/ideological agenda, but his narrative obeys a genealogy of deviation, in the best Foucauldian sense.[39]

I will have more to say in the next two sections about Jiang Gui's historiographical vision, in association with late Ming and late Qing *taowu* tales. What should be stressed here is the question that haunts *A Tale of Modern Monsters:* if the search for rationality constitutes a major part of China's modernity project, how does one come to terms with the plague of irrationalities that spread across China in the first half of the modern century? This leads us to rethink the way Jiang Gui depicts the novel's central figure, Fang Xiangqian. An eager student of the scientific formulation of Communism, Fang believes such endeavors are necessitated by history. Having witnessed the aftermath of the 1911 Republican Revolution and the aborted 1913 Second Revolution, he concludes that the revolution he is launching is socially rather than politically motivated, "a great revolution that will thoroughly destroy the old society both root and branch and then, according to the ideal, build a new society from the beginning."[40] He argues that before the "final" revolution comes, society is destined to sink to the lowest depths and that a revolutionary is entitled to help precipitate this fall so as to hasten the rejuvenation. He and his followers support themselves by banditry and by trafficking in heroin supplied by the Japanese.

Involved here is a strange combination of the Machiavellian reasoning of "the end justifies the means" and an apocalyptic faith in the leap of humanity from total fall to total salvation. But Fang Xiangqian is outwitted by the contingencies of history: the revolution simply does not unfold in accordance with his formula. Despite his wish to prove the scientific truth of Communist historicism, he stumbles once theory is put into practice. He can never convince his followers to follow his orders. Little surprise that when the local insurrection degenerates into chaos, he should find himself among the first group of counterrevolutionaries to be liquidated.

Here lies Jiang Gui's gravest warning about rationality and violence in modern Chinese revolution. Insofar as he is an enlightened intellectual ostracized by a callous society, Fang Xiangqian is a revolutionary in the vein of Lu Xun's heroic madman. Fang may even have been among the thousands of readers once enchanted by the madman's defiant stature and humanitarian concern. But whereas Lu Xun's madman is incarcerated and can only utter the futile cry "Save the children," Fang Xiangqian and his likes are determined to realize the lonely hero's dream. His adventure nevertheless exemplifies that, when Lu Xun's literary cry is taken literally, the dialectic of the madman's sanity/insanity may lose its enigmatic power and backfire. Fang Xiangqian boils Chinese modernity down to a simple choice between revolutionism and reactionism; in his own words, "Since the Taiping Rebellion, we have tried every possible kind of reform to no avail. We are left with the newest and last alternative, that is Communism."[41] Charged with a moral imperative and temporal urgency, Fang's commitment to Communism brings to light the hidden curse of Lu Xun's story. He and his followers replace the madman's paranoia with political fanaticism, and transform the lonely hero's anarchist impulse into a total(itarian) call to arms; as such they become the most dangerous readers of Lu Xun.

We can now better interpret the ambiguous characterization of Fang Xiangqian. Jiang Gui never makes Fang an archvillain in accordance with anti-Communist formulae; instead he portrays him as a mixture of shortsighted visionary and ineffective activist. Through such peculiar characterization, Jiang Gui examines the dilemmas and dangers hidden in revolutionary utopianism. Fang incites the rebellious impulses among his followers, yet fails to meld them into any coherent body. His eclectic approach collapses elements that previously did not interact into a grotesque conglomeration. *Taowu,* it will be recalled, is an anomaly. By making Fang Xiangqian the modern embodiment of *taowu,* Jiang Gui suggests a kind of evil and violence often overlooked by historians and literati. Fang Xiangqian is not a competent revolutionary, but he may cause society more harm precisely because of his imperfect villainy (or heroism). Above all, modern (Communist) revolution was made possible not by selected leaders but by hundreds and thousands of supporters like Fang Xiangqian, despite their individual limitations. With their contradictory attributes of dedication and fanaticism, vision and naïveté, altruism and "cannibalism," they constitute the enormous body of the modern monster.

The Erotics of Revolution

In his inquiry into the terms of revolution, Jiang Gui makes sexual politics the last site of ideological contestation. *A Tale of Modern Monsters* impresses one with its seemingly endless account of sexual deviation. Jiang Gui is highly critical of the way traditional society has instituted sexual mores, which result in both excessive license and inhuman oppression. Fang Xiangqian's grandfather, an honorable retired official and landlord, is known for his bizarre lust for nuns. His gallant public image aside, Fang Peilan is a man frustrated by an arranged marriage. He finds solace among local prostitutes, the older and uglier the better. Fang Ranwu's mother, Mistress Fang, has an addiction to opium as well as to her young servant, who in turn is involved with a lowly prostitute known for her large, unbound feet.

But Jiang Gui is equally cynical about the new generation's sexual encounters. The novel opens with the decapitation of the Communist leader Shi Shenzhi, a result of his affair with a local opera singer. The Bolshevik Ba Chengde is ambushed by rightist enemies at his wedding and beheaded by them. Another revolutionary, Dong Yinming, is jailed after his gun misfires and kills his father; the accidental patricide is interpreted as the result of an incestuous affair between Dong's father and his wife. To assert Communist egalitarianism, the daughter of a veteran Nationalist Party member, a four-time divorcee, gives herself to men of the lower depths. Despite their difference in class and upbringing, Fang Xiangqian's niece is persuaded to marry a battalion commander officer as a means of co-opting him. Among characters from the lower class, sleeping with ladies from noble households is their first wish after revolution, and Fang Ranwu's wife is their primary target. But none of these characters can surpass Fang Ranwu, whose insatiable and indiscriminate lust for women epitomizes the total abandon in the world of Fangzhen.

C. T. Hsia notices the thematic parallel between ideological craze and sexual fervor in *A Tale of Modern Monsters* and comments that, among Jiang Gui's characters, "the sensualists, like the revolutionaries, are impatient with the human condition, and demand unlimited scope for their appetites."[42] While Hsia's observation provides an important clue to Jiang Gui's moral scheme regarding sexuality, its scope is limited to a rather conventional stance. It is all too common in both leftist and rightist literature to demonize antagonists by first smearing them in their private life, particular their sexual life. To say that Jiang Gui equates revolutionaries with sex maniacs or vice versa would only reconfirm his image as a conservative ideologue. I am arguing that, his conservative ideology notwithstanding, Jiang Gui adopts a radical means of articulating his agenda. His idiosyncratic approach to sexual politics has to be read as a belated critique of the discourse of revolution plus love, or *geming jia lian'ai,* that prevailed in the first half of the twentieth century. To demonstrate the negative impact of revolution on Chinese mores, he depicts not a select group but almost all of his characters as overwhelmed by the power of desire.

As discussed in Chapter 3, revolution plus love constituted one of the major themes of post–May Fourth literature. Compared to a typical case of revolution plus love fiction in its heyday, such as *Eclipse, A Tale of Modern Monsters* may at first appear to be a parody. My reading suggests that beyond the parodic purpose, the novel leads us to examine the close ties between revolutionary desire and romantic libido, as well as Jiang Gui's dubious stance in unraveling these ties. With few exceptions, Jiang Gui's characters are unhappy men and women, and the immediate symptoms of their ressentiment are their sexual frustrations. One cannot find characters more different than Mistress Fang, the paragon of Confucian chastity, and Shi Shenzhi, the leader of Communist fraternity. But Jiang Gui intimates that when Mistress Fang indulges in her nightly sadistic pleasures, or when Shi Shenzhi is carried away by his fatal attraction to an opera singer, neither Confucianism nor Communism can be of any avail.

Mistress Fang and Shi Shenzhi are secondary characters in *A Tale of Modern Monsters*. When he takes pains to show that even these minor figures struggle to assuage their sexual discontent, Jiang Gui underlines the resistance of desire to rational social control. In the late 1950s, Gao Yang gave a Freudian analysis of Jiang Gui's characters as creatures driven by a "compensation mechanism." Irked by the inaccessibility of the desired object, they find in its perverse replacement a vicarious and ignominious satisfaction. Such a replacement can only intensify the characters' awareness of desires still unfulfilled.[43] The result is a proliferation of disorders ranging from incest to rape, from masochism to sadism, and from misogyny to nymphomania.

One may take *A Tale of Modern Monsters* as a showcase of the Marxian-Freudian interplay between the political unconscious and libidinous desire. From the perspective of the Bakhtinian carnival, Jiang Gui's parading of sexual absurdities may also be suggestive of the "bodily principle" that overthrows decorum in a moment of social upheaval.[44] One can quickly point out Jiang Gui's conservative bearings, however: he does not indicate enough confidence in the sublation of libido to a higher state of ideological and behavioral momentum, nor is he optimistic enough to embrace the total emancipation of the carnivalesque body. But one has to note that behind Jiang Gui's reservation about the revolutionary *élan vital*, there lies an unlikely fixation: the way he details the sexual transgressions betrays as much his abhorrence of as his fascination with the human's capacity to fall. Such a fixation propels Jiang Gui to explore the boundaries of *eros* and *polis* at their most treacherous.

If one agrees with Bataille and Freud that "violence is what the world of work excludes with its taboos,"[45] then the modern project of revolution, as Jiang Gui understands it, constitutes a disturbing attempt to reconcile the opposing poles of this binary. Revolution works through violence and violation. It provides a venue where the banishment of violence through taboo, in opposition to reason, can be subverted. In other words, violence is not opposed to reason; rather it is the completion of revolutionary logic.

In particular, the way Jiang Gui combines revolution, violence, and eroticism in *A Tale of Modern Monsters* brings to mind what Bataille calls the "erotics of dissolution."[46] To reread Bataille's notion in the interests of this study,[47] one can argue that, in the name of Communist solidarity, the revolutionaries view themselves as agents destined to overthrow established systems; their goal is to erect a socialist commonwealth, a "state of dissolution," by erasing all differences and disparities, from class to gender, of the old society. Dissolution can be achieved either through cold-bloodedly inflicting discipline, torture, and pain or through the sensuous imposition of pleasure, desire, and sexuality. When put into practice, these positions become ultimately exchangeable.

Thus, in Jiang Gui's treatment, corporeal eroticism is no longer a salacious interlude, but rather a violent and deleterious sacrificial theater. Placed on the border of discipline and desire, sexuality is at once a sign of the incommensurable difference between individuals and utterly dissoluble through revolutionary appropriation, thus catalyzing a mode of violation bordering on death, or murder. As the novel develops, more and more characters are involved in the macabre game of sensuality, as they are either aroused or disturbed by the call for revolution. From the murder of Fang Ranwu and his ex-paramour to the suicide of Lady Zhao and the licentiate's daughter, from the rape of Fang Ranwu's wife and his new concubine to the promiscuous practices of Pang Yuemei and Pang Jinlian, sexual deviation is the most immediate sign of revolution in Fangzhen.

It is small surprise that Jiang Gui's version of revolution and love should culminate in his portraits of the prostitutes Pang Yuemei and Pang Jinlian. Just as the two Fangs are committed to ideological force, so the Pangs exert sexual power. They contribute their bodies to reactionaries and revolutionaries, Japanese invaders and local bandits, merchants, scholars, and gentry. In between they also run a successful network of opium trafficking. The Pangs prosper even more after the leftists take over Fangzhen. In comparing politics to prostitution, Jiang Gui no doubt follows an old convention. But he is able to push such an analogy to the extreme, thereby laying bare the destructive power of sexuality over politics and vice versa. In their chamber, all sanctioned social relations are turned upside down. They bring together what should be kept ideologically and socially apart, and thus blur the contours of the social map. Their promiscuity provides the thematic matrix in the novel for linking the disparate worlds of commerce, politics, warfare, and romance.

As if he were determined to explore the boundaries of the erotics of dissolution, Jiang Gui sees revolutionary desire culminate in scenes where crowds are aroused to act out violence collectively. The last part of *A Tale of Modern Monsters* describes how the people in Fangzhen are organized by the new Communist regime to liquidate old feudal forces. There emerges an eerie carnival atmosphere that at any moment can turn into the chaos of mob hysteria. The orgiastic ecstasy of revolution will not be completed without the ritual of sacrifice, and women such as Fang Ranwu's wife are among the first victims. In describing this orgiastic ecstasy arising from revolution and the collective infliction of pain and suffering on the chosen underdogs, Jiang Gui reveals the ultimate horror behind the erotics of dissolution/revolution.

Through his assiduous pursuit of his characters' depravities, Jiang Gui becomes an unlikely chronicler of desires, his moral inquisition underscored by his uninhibited acquisition of forbidden knowledge. As a result, his sexual politics are more radical than most of his colleagues from both the Communist and Nationalist fronts. In this regard, he reminds us of the author of the pro-Communist novel *Hungry Guo Su'e,* Lu Ling.

AN IDLE COMMENTARY ON MONSTERS

Upon its publication in 1957, critics of *A Tale of Modern Monsters* were quick to point out Jiang Gui's indebtedness to classical Chinese fiction.[48] Cao Xueqin's *The Dream of the Red Chamber* was frequently cited as a comparison to the glory and decline of the four Fang families. On the other hand, Jiang Gui's satire of the pedantry and self-deception of intellectuals like Fang Xiangqian reminds one more of the disgruntled intellectuals in Wu Jingzi's *Rulin waishi* (The scholars). It has also been noted that the plot around Fang Peilan and his bandit followers, particularly his revenge of his father's death, may well be inspired by similar moments in the *Shuihuzhuan* (The water margin). Jiang Gui was aware of these influences. In an interview he stated that "before the age of twenty," he had been "interested in only three books, *The Dream of the Red Chamber, The Water Margin,* and *The Scholars.*"[49]

While these three classics manifest their impact on Jiang Gui in various ways, they do not constitute a coherent formal and thematic matrix for *A Tale of Modern Monsters.* I suggest that the missing clue lies in an obscure late Ming novel, *An Idle Commentary on Monsters.* These two novels, one published in the early seventeenth century and the other in the mid-twentieth century, appear at first glance to be different in a wide range of aspects, but the fact that they both refer to the same archaic image of *taowu* suggests that they have something in common. In his preface to *A Tale of Modern Monsters,* Jiang Gui traces the etymological origin of "taowu" and suggests that the late Ming novel and his are both meant to "recount evils so as to admonish." Close reading of the two novels show that, in addition to this didactic pretext, Jiang Gui may have been motivated by the late Ming novel in different ways than he wishes to admit. The Ming novel may be Jiang Gui's predecessor in exploring the genealogy of evil within the history of China.

The Genesis of a Modern Form of Evil

Published in 1629, *An Idle Commentary on Monsters* was one of a series of fictional indictments of the eunuch Wei Zhongxian after his suicide in 1627. Not until recent years was its author identified as Li Qing, a scholar-official who obtained his *jinshi* degree in 1621 and served the Chongzhen emperor (1628–1644) until the end of his reign.[50] Wei Zhongxian is the most notorious of the eunuchs of the late Ming. A gambler in his youth, he is said to have castrated himself when pursued by debtors. He rose to power during the Tianqi reign thanks to his connection with the emperor's wet nurse,

Madame Ke Yinyue. Together Wei and Ke manipulated the emperor, a fragile and weak-willed young man, taking control of the court. They accelerated the decline of a dynasty already mired in factional struggles, barbarian invasions, local riots, bureaucratic corruption, and eunuch manipulation. At the height of his power, Wei Zhongxian ran a pernicious network that watched and destroyed his opponents; meanwhile, hundreds of shrines were erected nationwide in his honor. Wei and Ke lost their power immediately after the Tianqi emperor's death and were quickly eradicated by Tianqi's successor, Emperor Chongzhen. But the dynasty had been damaged beyond repair. The Ming came to an end in less than two decades.[51]

In the wake of Wei Zhongxian's death there appeared a series of fictional accounts exposing Wei's evil doings and commemorating the virtuous suffering under his tyranny. Among the earliest are the anonymous novel *Huangming zhongxing shenglie zhuan* (Tales of the sage-like and virtuous in the restoration of the imperial Ming), *Jingshi yinyang meng* (Yin and yang dreams that admonish the world), by Changan daoren (Taoist monk of Changan), and *Wei Zhongxian xiaoshuo chijian shu* (Fiction that castigates the villainy of Wei Zhongxian), by Wuyue caomang chen (Exile in the wilderness of Wu and Yue), all published in 1628, one year prior to *An Idle Commentary on Monsters.* Insofar as historical discourse— discourse that validates the truthfulness of the narrated event by associating it with the distant past—constitutes one of the motivations of premodern Chinese vernacular fiction,[52] the fact that these works set out to chronicle and comment on a topical event still fresh in people's memory must be regarded as a breakthrough of the late Ming historical novel. It indicates not only the desire of the late Ming readers and writers to deal with a national disaster in its immediacy, but also their renewed concept of fiction as a way of registering the intelligibility of history. These novels about Wei Zhongxian help establish a subgenre of the late Ming historical novel, *shishi xiaoshuo,* or fiction on contemporary events.[53]

Two of the earliest novels on Wei Zhongxian, *Fiction That Castigates the Villainy of Wei Zhongxian* and *Yin and Yang Dreams That Admonish the World,* may represent two extreme options in the narrative spectrum of fiction on contemporary events. The first novel traces the ups and downs of Wei's life by consulting official and semiofficial records as well as the *dibao*—the "capital gazette" circulated by the central government among local administrators—from the late Wanli reign (late 1610s) to the early Chongzhen reign (1628), thereby achieving a high degree of journalistic credibility.[54] By contrast, the latter novel is derived largely from hearsay and fabrication framed by a morality tale of transmigration and retribution.[55] Both, however, are tangible ways by which late Ming audiences came to terms with the meaning of the immediate past. Whereas the novelistic interpretation of government documents responds to the increasing public demand to circulate a newsworthy event, the fantastic rendition of such an event reveals a different dimension of truth-claim and wish fulfillment that was equally popular among writers and readers. The supernatural and the religious fill in where factual report fails to fully explain human motives and historical movements.

In this context, *An Idle Commentary on Monsters* appears as an ambitious combination of the journalistic and the fantastic strains of fiction on contemporary events. The novel's faithfulness to historiographical accounts has impressed critics. Almost all the major events from the late Wanli reign through the Tianqi reign, including the "three cases" ("the attack with club case" [1615], "the red pill case" [1620], and "the change of palace case" [1620]),[56] the factional battles at court, peasant insurrections, and Wei Zhongxian and Madame Ke's horrific purge of their opponents, are woven into its narrative sequence.[57] Overlaid on this narrative sequence is a myth of karmic retribution that presumably lends the historical events a metaphysical layer of significance. It is said that Wei Zhongxian and Ke Yinyue are the embodiments of snake spirits taking revenge by disturbing the Ming fate.[58]

Beyond its historical and the fantastic discourses, *An Idle Commentary on Monsters* is notable for embracing many other subgenres of late Ming fiction. The first twenty chapters of the novel concentrate on Wei Zhongxian's personal life. We are told that Wei is the illegitimate son of a woman acrobat and a female impersonator. Mother and son fall into bandits' hands one year on their way north. They manage to run away ten years later, carrying with them three pearls. They take refuge with the Ke family, only to find out that the pearls used to belong to Master Ke's granddaughter, Yinyue. Zhongxian falls in love with Yinyue, and they are betrothed before Zhongxian departs to search for his natural father, who reportedly has become an official.[59]

In what follows, Wei Zhongxian takes an adventure with all the elements of the picaresque novel, including serving as a corrupt official's running dog, a eunuch's errand man, and a traveling merchant. He is briefly reunited with his father. By chance he marries Fu Ruyu after rescuing her from an accident, and the two have a son.

On a business trip, Wei stays in the home of a fellow merchant, whose wife turns out to be Ke Yinyue. Wei and Ke soon start an adulterous affair and are driven out of the household. Later, Wei becomes a beggar after squandering all his money in the capital. On his way home, he gets drunk with a group of hooligans and is robbed and thrown into water by them. When he comes to on the shore, he is in excruciating pain, hungry dogs having bitten off his genitalia.

I summarize the first part of the novel because it demonstrates Li Qing's changing strategies for representing history and evil. The adventure of Wei Zhongxian at different social strata reminds one of the genre of *faji biantai*, a saga about a nobody who becomes a hero.[60] Wei's case, however, must be read as one of the few premodern full-length narratives highlighting an antihero's life; his ascendance to power, even if bracketed within a predestined fall, serves as a powerful counterexample to the conventions of the heroic saga.[61] Compare *An Idle Commentary on Monsters* with a novel of the same time such as Yuan Yuling's *Suishi yiwen* (Forgotten tales of the Sui, 1633), which deals with Qin Shubao's heroic deeds in the founding days of the Tang, and one can see Li Qing's subversive intention. Whereas Qin Shubao is described as a man who "grows from teenage uncertainty to mature self-assurance against a background of suffering for the masses of people, court indulgence, widespread brigandage, and foreign and civil wars,"[62] Wei Zhongxian comes from a similar background and yet becomes the perpetrator of disasters that heroes such as Qin would have striven to avert. Wei acts out what Qin could have become. Where the saga of Qin Shubao, set in the remote late Sui and early Tang period, projects late Ming audience's yearning for a heroism believed lost,[63] Wei Zhongxian's story confirms everyone's acute awareness of an all too real crisis.

Moreover, episodes recounting Wei Zhongxian's romantic liaisons and domestic life reflect the influence of contemporary *renqing xiaoshuo,* or novel of manners, best illustrated by the *Jinpingmei* (The golden lotus).[64] Li Qing displays an almost naturalistic interest in relating Wei Zhongxian's base inclinations and the environment conducive to his degradation. Wei's marriage with Fu Ruyu brings the only hope of his redemption, but Fu's docility and virtue hardly have the power to rescue her husband from the world's temptations. In the arms of the adulterous Ke Yinyue, Wei's depraved nature thrives. As suggested by the legendary pearls that link them, Wei and Ke are a predestined match, and yet their romance is continuously beset by accidents, culminating in Wei's castration.

Li Qing treats Wei Zhongxian's castration as the beginning of his worldly success. An account follows of how, after a series of trials, Wei manages to enter the palace and encounters Ke Yinyue, who has become the emperor's wet nurse, after which the two join hands to create a clique in opposition to righteous officials. The second half of the novel concentrates on Wei and Ke's conspiracy to eliminate their enemies while rewarding their own families and cohorts. Li Qing deftly incorporates almost all the major events of the Tianqi reign, such as Wei's direction of the notorious eunuch security agency, the Eastern Depot *(dongchang);* his continued battle with opponents of the Donglin faction; his indictment by Yang Lian, the most vociferous of the Donglin members; the rise of the White Lotus cult; the insurrection in Suzhou; the expulsion of concerned aristocrats; and Wei Zhongxian and his followers' bloody purges, the most infamous being the killing of the "six men of superior virtue" *(liu junzi).*[65]

Odd as it may appear, a domestic ambiance lingers even during the most macabre moments of the court politics. Amid endless killings and schemes,

Wei and Ke show consistent concern for the welfare of their relatives and allies, as if they were the benign patriarchs of a Confucian family. One of Wei's nephews is made an earl and then a duke, and Wei later becomes a grand duke, a rank and title created expressly for him. Meanwhile, however disfigured or deprived, Wei and Ke carry on their mutual emotional attachment, punctuated by occasional misunderstandings and squabbles, like any ordinary couple.

Reading a novel that deplores dynastic decline due to devilish courtiers, one may be surprised by the fact that Wei Zhongxian and Ke Yinyue's private life should command so much attention, and that characters do not appear as total human demons. This leads one to rethink the tension between the novel's avowed goal of indicting the greatest villains of the time and its curiosity about daily life, even that of the villains. By injecting mundane, private details into its narrative, *An Idle Commentary on Monsters* domesticates, so to speak, the epic grandeur required of a novel of such scope.

One may suspect that Li Qing is incapable of imagining villainy on a greater scale. I disagree. As mentioned above, the burgeoning interest in secular reality among late Ming authors and readers of popular fiction must have encouraged Li Qing to consider the background, temperament, motives, and behavior of historical figures in a more comprehensive and material light.[66] He thus infiltrates the high mimetic world of the traditional historical novel, of the variety of *Sanguozhi yanyi* (The romance of the three kingdoms), with traits drawn from the low mimetic terrain.[67] History may still be presided over by figures who exert an immense impact on public lives, but these figures are shown to be no less occupied by the trivialities that concern ordinary men and women.

More challenging is the fact that such an approach to history and reality has given rise to a different fictional concept of evil. The early life of Wei Zhongxian impresses us by his mediocrity in both talent and judgment. Despite his inclination to pursue things low and unruly, he more often than not stumbles. His luck turns after he enters the palace and fends off an assassin in the "attack with a club" incident.[68] By the time of the Tianqi emperor's enthronement, he has become the most powerful person at court. However, Wei does not come across as a larger-than-life villain; rather he behaves more like an entrepreneur eager to enjoy and preserve newly-won power and fortune. As his ambition amplifies to a degree out of proportion with his new capacity, his flaws resurface. His lack of foresight leads him from one unexpected danger to another; his vanity demands compliments of the most superficial kind. Above all, his insatiable desire for power and blood suggests a twisted psyche that matches his deformed physique. Living shrines are built all over the nation, honoring him as the equal of Confucius and the emperor, and this eunuch dreams of attaining both cultural and political hegemony.

Saint or Beast?

The way Li Qing portrays Wei Zhongxian's villainy, or lack of sufficient villainy, should not be taken lightly. Precisely because the gap between Wei's mediocre character and the great disaster he causes is so obvious, one has to rethink Li Qing's notion of the human capacity to err. If he was not born with an extraordinary endowment for doing evil, what makes Wei Zhongxian such a monstrous being in later years? Wei in the middle of the novel brings to mind Ximen Qing of *The Golden Lotus*. Ximen Qing is a debauchee cum opportunist; thanks to good luck and shrewd maneuvering, he manages to gain wealth and power in a short time. Blinded by hubris, he immerses himself in sensual pleasure and thus rushes to his own destruction. Critics have suggested that for all its surface sensation, Ximen Qing's is a morality tale about an everyman who fails to curb his desires.[69] One finds a similar pattern in Wei Zhongxian's rise and fall, in that he allows himself to be consumed by excessive vanity. Wei is a flawed usurper just as Ximen is a flawed sensualist. Their defects, though all too human, make them no less susceptible to superhuman temptation. Once the machine of evil is set in motion, mediocrity proves just as efficient as any full-scale villainy in inducing monstrosity.

Li Qing's depiction of Wei Zhongxian displays the renewed interest of late Ming fiction writers in the genesis of evil. Evil does not necessarily appear as a mysterious given, nor does it have to be perpetrated by a great villain. Rather, with the right timing and agency, evil may stem from ordinary creatures and circumstances. This mundane view of evil is symptomatic of the changing discourse of realism in late Ming fiction, a discourse that approximates secular concerns, sensuous details of everyday life, conventional and unconventional wisdom, and competing narrative formats in order to bring out an effect of the real in its full complexity. The minute episodes of Wei's early adventures and life at court are nothing if not familiarization with a historical figure otherwise inaccessible to the imagination. This imaginary fabric of life must have helped redefine the temporal-spatial proximity of the narrated event or figure, thereby reinforcing the journalistic feeling conveyed by the novel. Thus, beyond the supernatural pretext, *An Idle Commentary on Monsters* actually demonstrates Li Qing's endeavor to naturalize evil—as well as narrative conventions of evil—into the continuum of lived experience.

Such a naturalized approach to evil can also be understood in terms of the debate over fate versus will, and natural endowment versus self-cultivation, issues that occupied late-sixteenth- and seventeenth-century elite fiction writers.[70] I cannot delve into these issues, but I want to suggest that by tracing the vicissitudes of Wei Zhongxian's life, *An Idle Commentary on Monsters* contributes to the debate. In response to the popular late Ming notion that even a commoner can transcend himself when enlightened by an innate call for edification, the novel gives it a decadent twist. It implies that once he is set free to mold his own subjectivity, a commoner is just as capable of evil as of virtue. This thought is not to be confused with Xunzi's theory that humanity is born evil, a theory taken up by David Roy in his interpretation of the moral thesis of *The Golden Lotus*.[71] The mercurial nature of Wei and the environment around him strongly suggests a flux of life beyond the calculus of conventional Confucian thought.

From a different perspective, scholars have already noticed that late Ming intellectuals' conviction of the attainability of the good by every man creates an unexpected moral anxiety. That is, insofar as he is endowed with an immense capacity to achieve virtue and is expected to do so, the individual is left with little room for mistakes in the pursuit of his goal.[72] Between the promised sainthood and default, the individual is thrown into a continual test of his moral integrity; any slight misstep is said to risk an irredeemable fall. The apparently free-spirited call for self-betterment is ironically underlain by a strict demand for self-rectification, thus engendering a grave tension between what one is and what one should be.[73] For a late Ming / early Qing scholar such as Chen Que (1604–1677), the stakes are such that humans are faced with an almost existential challenge of becoming "either saint or beast" *(rufei shengren, jishi qinshou)*.[74]

Sainthood or bestiality: Wei Zhongxian's story can be read as an allegory about the capricious terms through which one negotiates his own moral character. Li Qing may not have consciously played out the tortuous dialectic of late Ming Confucian discourse; research is yet to be done regarding his intellectual heritage. But at a more general level, one can say his novel registers, in the form of a negative dialectic, late Ming intellectuals' concern about historical turmoil, personal responsibility, and moral transcendence. When tested by external and internal stimuli, humanity is seen as responding on its own and will be held profoundly accountable for the consequences. Wei's story is about a man's degradation to the level of not just beast but monster. That he can seem understanding and generous to some people reminds us all the more of his potential for doing good and his failure to carry it out.

Li Qing, of course, never measures up to contemporaries such as Feng Menglong (1574–1646) in depicting a social and individual psychology in mutation. But through the fate of Wei and other characters, Li envisages life as a moral drama of individual destiny and choice. It will be recalled that Wei never received any fatherly guidance, and that despite Wei's deeds, his son Yingxing remains immune to all vicious influence. Together with his mother, Fu Ruyu, Yingxing articulates at the end of the novel the secular Daoist solution of relinquishing worldly attachments in favor of transcendence. Meanwhile, Wei's opponents, such as Yang Lian and Zuo Guangdou, demonstrate an insurmountable certitude, attacking the eunuch against all odds; their unconditional dedication is as astonishing as Wei's own determination to prevail at any expense.

That *An Idle Commentary on Monsters* was written in response to ongoing national crisis further intensifies the debate on selfhood and historical (ir)responsibility. Whereas Ximen Qing remains no more than a nouveau riche in a small city, Wei Zhongxian emerges as a formidable figure that threatens the dynasty's fate. At the end of the novel, Wei and his gang are brought down and justice is restored under the aegis of a new emperor. Moreover, we learn from the fantastic epilogue that the whole upheaval is attributable to the mystic cycle of retribution. This ending cannot but call attention to its tongue-in-cheek interpretation. The real mystery of the novel—the contingent eruption of evil and its uncontrollable dissemination in the course of history—remains to be solved. One cannot help asking whether, if Wei Zhongxian is to be condemned for his deeds, the Tianqi Emperor isn't more culpable for granting the eunuch such a power to do evil. The late Ming period, to be sure, is famous for a succession of weak or dim-witted rulers, and many a fictional piece was written as an implicit critique of the sovereign.[75] My point here is not to launch an anachronistic challenge of the imperial system as the real, hidden evil. Rather, I am questioning a technology of power that works despite weak emperors and mediocre but energetic courtiers and eunuchs.

Above all, in Li Qing's treatment of Wei Zhongxian, what is most impressive is not so much his conspiratorial capacity but rather the efficient way in which his will is carried out by his followers. Neither the spy network nor the surveillance system could have been invented solely by Wei or have functioned so well merely under his aegis. The real *taowu* cannot be identified with Wei Zhongxian, who is merely the human face on a monstrous regime, nor is the recounting of the evils of the late Ming exhausted by a litany of Wei Zhongxian's treachery and bloodthirstiness. My reading is that if the early Ming is known for its cruel, hegemonic rule and its meticulous implementation of coercive power, this sinister machine finally seems out of control—or rather, achieves its full, monstrous potential—when Wei Zhongxian is put in charge. If the Ming can be described as the first full manifestation of the modern state, administered rationally by ordinary men in service to absolute power, then the proof of this modernity must lie in revealing the ordinariness of Wei Zhongxian, before and after his assumption of the key position in the bureaucracy of terror

The above reading adds a polemical dimension to the issue of good and evil in *An Idle Commentary on Monsters*. While Li Qing may be quite sincere in his search for a balance point between the extremities of humanity, the way he conceives of contemporary affairs may have guided him to a different set of questions, questions that can no longer be answered at the level of intellectual debate. Accordingly, the moral tension between sainthood and bestiality described above can be expanded. It is a tension between the conventional approach to history, underlain by the periodic cycle of good versus evil and the articulation of orthodoxy, and the unconventional approach to history, marked first by a heightened anxiety about the feasibility of virtue and later by a premonition that something is looming beyond human reasoning. Li Qing could not have been fully aware of this tension, but his innovations, from the mixture of genres to the trivialization of villainy, are directed to a renewed set of questions about history. Reading *An Idle Commentary on Monsters* in the twentieth century, a writer such as Jiang Gui might finally be able to address what remains unsaid in Li's novel.

The "Sins" of Mediocrity and Anonymity

From the vantage point of *An Idle Commentary on Monsters,* one can now better understand Jiang Gui's description of modern villainy in terms of *taowu.* Unlike most writers in 1950s Taiwan, Jiang Gui treats Communism not merely as a contemporary political disaster, but as the latest transformation of an ancient monstrous force. His reference to *An Idle Commentary on Monsters* accordingly indicates more than acknowledgment of his literary inspiration. An impatient reader may find in *An Idle Commentary on Monsters* and *A Tale of Modern Monsters* a parallel between the late Ming days, when Wei Zhongxian and his gang almost ruined the Ming empire, and the mid-twentieth century, when the Chinese Communists turned the Republic upside down. But Jiang Gui's intention is not limited to invoking such a moralistic parallel. Three hundred years apart, the two moments are after all marked by very different sets of challenges and crises. However, when we look into Jiang Gui's survey of the Communist genealogy and the technology of evil, his indebtedness to the late Ming novel becomes clear.

Jiang Gui would have endorsed the comment by the late Qing scholar Wang Zhongqi (1880–1913): "Just as *The Golden Lotus* describes lust and *The Dream of the Red Chamber* deals with luxury, so *The Scholars* and *An Idle Commentary on Monsters* write about petty wickedness. . . . These works are all imbued with profound sorrows and drenched in blood."[76] In other words, the diversity of their thematic emphases notwithstanding, these novels share the same deep pathos and indignation in regard to human frailties and calamities. Wang Zhongqi brings home the moral trope of *An Idle Commentary on Monsters* when he defines it as a testimony to the "petty wickedness" *(beilie)* of human nature. In his usage of the term, "petty wickedness" indicates both a special kind of human defect and a changing narrative format capable of representing such a human defect.

Wang Zhongqi's comment on *An Idle Commentary on Monsters* may equally apply to the moral landscape of *A Tale of Modern Monsters.* Jiang Gui's is a world crowded by prostitutes, rascals, bandits, hooligans, opportunists, traitors, and imposters, characters representative of the "petty wickedness" of human nature. Two examples will suffice. Fang Xiangqian's nephew Fang Tianai is the ne'er-do-well of the family and a half-hearted follower of his uncle's revolution. Upon learning that his uncle is in disfavor with the party, he turns his back on him, pledging loyalty to the new leaders. Moreover, he volunteers to become the adopted son of the prostitute Pang Yuemei, although his mother was recently put to death by Pang and the Communists. He even discards the family name Fang and renames himself Pang Xiaomei ("Pang who is filial to Mei"). In another case, Fang Peilan is betrayed by his disciple Xu Dahai after Fangzhen falls into the Communists' hands—a familiar practice for Xu, as he sold out his former employer in a previous local struggle. Readers of *An Idle Commentary on Monsters* would find these characters remarkably familiar. For instance, after Wei Zhongxian attains power, both Tian Ergeng and Cui Chengxiu offer themselves to be Wei Zhongxian's sons, regardless of the fact that Tian is the cousin of Wei's wife, and Cui used to be Wei's bosom friend.

There is nevertheless a more subtle relation between *An Idle Commentary on Monsters* and *A Tale of Modern Monsters* in their authors' disposition of evil and moral responsibility. Jiang Gui may have learned from *An Idle Commentary on Monsters* in furbishing his world with unscrupulous opportunists and scoundrels, but unlike his predecessor, none of his characters are foregrounded on the scale of Wei Zhongxian. Mao Zedong and other Communist leaders remain only mysterious names in his novel. Mao's wife, Jiang Qing, is introduced as a local girl kidnapped and thrust into unlikely fortune as an actress, leftist cadre, and eventually Mao's woman.[77]

Instead of the centripetal structure of the late Ming novel, in which minor evil forces are drawn to the archvillain, one finds a looser configuration in *A Tale of Modern Monsters.* The two protagonists responsible for the Communist turmoil, Fang Xiangqian and Fang Peilan, are presented as self-deceiving idealists who fail to discern the fatal weakness of their plan; they have neither the charisma nor the leadership to unify the disparate forces. They instigate the local insurrection, but they can hardly control its rampageous outcome. Worse, in the end they become victims of their own campaigns.

I have pointed out that *An Idle Commentary on Monsters* offers a new, realistic view of evil by domesticating and humanizing it. This new form of evil is by no means less dangerous to dynastic stability; rather its "petty wickedness" circulates among social strata so efficiently as to aggregate into a force of unexpected magnitude. I also argued that beyond this realistic approach to villainy, Li Qing insinuated a machine at work in the absence of human agency. In *A Tale of Modern Monsters,* Jiang Gui radicalizes this concept of evil by relativizing it. Unlike the late Ming novel, in which corruption and conspiracy are associated in one way or another with Wei Zhongxian, evil amorphously disseminates throughout Jiang Gui's world. Fang Xiangqian and Fang Peilan mean to do good for their community and are dedicated practitioners of Communism, whatever their understanding of it; but their noble cause becomes the pretext for both old and new forms of abuse. All along, the two Fangs shuttle between the roles of incompetent villain and impractical idealist; as such, they show a vulnerability that can even win sympathy. When their progressive agenda brings out the primitive baseness of people in Fangzhen, or when their altruist dedication results in a cannibalistic circus, Jiang Gui calls attention to the paradox of the modernity of evil: the most spectacular horror can be carried out in the name of the most magnificent claims to rationality.

Jiang Gui's vision of evil includes a dimension of anonymity. This may at first sound like a paradox because throughout the novel he never hesitates to call the Communists the perpetrators of the chaos in modern China. But, as in the case of Li Qing's novel, Jiang Gui has to combat a far more mysterious force beyond the conventional, human dimension. His view of Communist anonymity can be interpreted in three ways. First, the Communist revolution initially billed itself a proletarian revolution, one by and for the "nobodies" of the old society. Once the revolution was mobilized, the power structure nevertheless assumed a posture of invisibility in the name of "the party." Secondly, Jiang Gui makes it clear that when villains and revolutionaries proliferate in his novel, it is increasingly hard to pin down a central figure in the chaos in the way that tradition holds Wei Zhongxian accountable for the fall of the Ming. Moreover, when the meek and virtuous reveal fatal foibles and the vicious and cruel show weakness, no one can be easily judged. This brings us to Jiang Gui's description of the Communist revolution at its most vicious: it blurs one's ability to name, to make a clear judgment of its nature. In a way, Jiang Gui has deliberately forsworn the Ming novel's technique of putting a single human face on the monster. By not allowing readers the luxury of centralizing blame, he shows that totalitarian evil can prevail only with the energetic participation of countless ordinary human beings. Coming to mind is the other title of *A Tale of Modern Monsters, The Whirlwind.* A whirlwind is a storm that blows violently in a spiral, with a vacuum at the center toward which floating objects are drawn.

To conclude this comparative reading of *An Idle Commentary on Monsters* and *A Tale of Modern Monsters,* I would address the different ways by which the two novels frame their moral inquiry into history in narrative form. In *An Idle Commentary on Monsters* one can identify three dimensions of agency through which the dynastic chaos is redeemed. In the ethical dimension, Li Qing introduces a long line of characters who stand up to the evildoers at the risk of their life and welfare. Through their sacrifice and suffering, a whole spectrum of values from loyalty to filial piety are tested and crystallized anew. Where the moral rationale fails to make sense of the injustice and cruelty inflicted on the innocent, the novel invokes a political discourse based on the sanctioned concept of orthodoxy. Li Qing, to be sure, deplores the Ming rulers' indulgence of vicious courtiers and eunuchs and their negligence of the state, but in the final analysis, he maintains that the dynasty will and should move on. Lastly, when even the mandate of Heaven cannot fully justify political aberrations, the power of the supernatural is called on, with its cycle of destiny, reincarnation, and retribution.

These three dimensions of action (ethical, political, and supernatural) interact throughout *An Idle Commentary on Monsters,* attaining only a superficial synthesis at the end of the novel. Writing in the late 1620s, Li Qing could not help but see that the national crisis did not subside with the fall of Wei Zhongxian and that a supernatural deus ex machina may fall short in justifying the unexplainable. However firm his belief in the continuation of the dynasty, he has to work hard to reconcile his claim to political orthodoxy and his awareness of political reality. In the novel's overeager effort to settle all inconsistencies, fissures become more apparent. This can hardly bring the novel to a satisfactory conclusion, and thus one encounters the same closure problem other contemporary novels face vis-à-vis a drastically changing political and intellectual climate.[78]

Jiang Gui sets out to challenge a more intransigent and arguably more invisible evil. Worse, he wrote at a moment when the evil showed no signs of being eradicated any time soon. Whereas Li Qing still pays lip service to established values, Jiang Gui deals only negatively with traditional ethical infrastructures. He begins his novel when all values are already bankrupt and ends with empty promises of restoration. Nor can he rely on any fantastic agency to intervene in human irrationality. Into this historical vacuity a modern machine branded "revolution" is called, with the promise of fixing the problems once and for all. Jiang Gui finds nevertheless in revolution a fiendish power working ever more efficiently to devour Chinese civilization. He tries to name those responsible for the brave new world, only to come to a more sullen recognition of the amorphism and anonymity of the monster.

It is here that Jiang Gui brings to the fore his most engaged dialogue with Li Qing. If Li Qing's world reveals the earliest signs of China's disintegration into the modern age, Jiang Gui reminds us that modern China has not proceeded too far from that moment of disintegration. Gone is the old, supernatural deus ex machina, but the modern political machine appears with a power more spellbinding than ever. Insofar as history is secularized to be associated with commonality, Fang Xiangqian and his cohorts act out the moral and political ambiguity already discernible in Wei Zhongxian's villainy.

What does the above observation mean to the premise of orthodoxy underlying Jiang Gui's novel? I suggested above that at a time when the Communists had occupied the mainland, Jiang Gui could best defend his party by viewing it as the bearer of orthodoxy, although in temporary eclipse. But Jiang Gui argues for this eclipsed orthodoxy in a most unconventional way. Unlike Li Qing in *An Idle Commentary on Monsters,* he introduces neither paradigmatic figures nor heroic actions in anticipation of the restoration of orthodoxy. As a matter of fact, it is the two arch-Communists, Fang Xiangqian and Fang Peilan, who articulate the thesis of the novel after they have been expelled by their fellow revolutionaries and put in jail. The novel ends with Fang Xiangqian's discourse:

> The future of the whole Communist Party will certainly be like that of a whirlwind. Although they rise at once, in the end they must pass away in the twinkling of an eye, vanishing without a shadow of a trace, and becoming a historical example. . . . The rise of the Communist Party is only an ebb that happens to occur within the tide. Going in the opposite direction, they will never have the possibility of reaching their goal, they have no reason to succeed.[79]

Rightist critics often contend that these two characters serve as the best critics of Communism because they were the masterminds of the revolution and eyewitnesses to its degradation. This may well be Jiang Gui's own interpretation too, but judging by the complex view of history and evil throughout his novel, one has to be alert to the equivocal undertone in its ending. Neither Fang Xiangqian nor Fang Peilan is a perceptive and capable Communist. If they have failed to predict the outcome of Communism and ended up in jail, on what grounds can one conclude that their disillusioned remarks about Communism prefigure a future victory of anti-Communism? The two Fangs are as much obtuse spectators of the Communist revolution as they are unreliable prophets of anti-Communist revolution. The novel's conclusion only opens up more questions.

A COMPENDIUM OF MONSTERS

For all its descriptions of irrationalities and cruelties, *A Tale of Modern Monsters* is couched in the peculiar narrative mode of laughter. In the corpus of anti-Communist literature shouting about Communist atrocities, the novel stands out for its determination to mock and ridicule. In his criticism of *A Tale of Modern Monsters,* C. T. Hsia likens the novel to Dostoevsky's *The Pos-*

sessed. He comments that as political novels, both contemplate "a humanity relentlessly selfish and relentlessly bent toward self-destruction" and that both adopt "the pose of derisive laughter to drive home the lesson of anarchy and help assert the claims of sanity."[80] Hence they share a style "drenched in buffoonery."[81] Hsia also notes Jiang Gui's continuation of a Chinese satirical tradition traceable to *The Scholars* and late Qing exposé, but he never elaborates on it. This indigenous vein of satire and exposé serves as the starting point of my discussion.

As far as the affective capacity of narrative is concerned, modern Chinese literature manifests itself best in two modes, tears and indignant cries. Liu E presented his theory of "weeping" in his preface to *The Travels of Lao Can,* and thus initiated the popularity of "tears and sniveling" in Chinese works.[82] Lu Xun, on the other hand, voiced his "call to arms" in the post–May Fourth days, calling for social critique and reformist radicalism. Both constitute the symptoms of what C. T. Hsia calls the "obsession with China." Along with tears and cries of indignation, however, there has existed a muffled tradition of laughter, which includes works by writers from Lao She to Zhang Tianyi, and from Lu Xun to Qian Zhongshu. Through laughter these writers mock political abuses, poke fun at social manners and morals, and insinuate a deep anxiety about the nation's fate. As argued elsewhere, while these writers are inspired by the satirical paradigm of *The Scholars,* they draw their immediate models from late Qing exposés.[83]

Jiang Gui's affiliation with the May Fourth politics of laughter can be traced back to his novel *Breaking Free* in the late 1930s. Hitherto little known to scholars, the novel features a group of petty bureaucrats of the Nationalist regime who are stranded in the ancient city of Luoyang when their office is relocated in the wake of the 1932 Japanese attack on Shanghai. Although the war is going on in the south, these characters have little time for patriotic campaigns; instead they indulge in a life of cheating, backbiting, falling in and out of love, and fighting for their boss's favor. The novel takes up where Lao She's *Lihun* (Divorce, 1932) leaves off, depicting the folly and triviality of modern Chinese officialdom, and anticipates Qian Zhongshu's *Weicheng* (Fortress besieged, 1947) in mocking the estrangement and self-deception of intellectuals trapped by national turmoil. Thus it provides a missing wartime link in the comic tradition.

A Tale of Modern Monsters carries on this tradition, charged with an even stronger impulse of radical laugher. With his excessive desire to deride and mock and his seemingly endless parading of profanities and perversities, Jiang Gui surpasses his May Fourth predecessors in emulating late Qing exposé writers.[84] He sees villainy as something not only horrible but absurd, so much so that one can only respond with laughter. Although Jiang Gui's reception of late Qing exposés has yet to be studied, one can hardly imagine that he could have created his circus of buffoonery without knowing works such as Li Boyuan's *Guchang xianxing ji* (Exposure of officialdom, 1905) or Wu Jianren's *Ershinian mudu zhi guaixiangzhuang* (Eyewitness report of strange things of the past twenty years, 1910). These are major works of the late Qing exposé, and they have been extensively analyzed by myself and other scholars.[85] For comparison, we adduce the obscure novel *A Compendium of Monsters* by Qian Xibao.

A Sinister Carnival

Although Jiang Gui may have never read Qian Xibao's novel, I have chosen to discuss it for two reasons. Since *taowu* is not a common image in the Chinese fictional vocabulary, any invocation of it calls attention to its historical legacy. That both *A Tale of Modern Monsters* and *A Compendium of Monsters* refer in their title to the same ancient monster suggests a shared tropic repertoire. As in the case of *A Tale of Modern Monsters,* Qian Xibao feels obliged to explain, at the end of his work, that his novel exhibits *taowu* because "it depicts no single good person throughout."[86] More importantly, when set next to Li Qing's *An Idle Commentary on Monsters* and Jiang Gui's *A Tale of Modern Monsters,* Qian's novel provides a unique late Qing perspective from which to examine the fictional metamorphosis of the monster in the course of history. By calling on *taowu* at different moments of social and political crisis, these authors bring the accumulated legendary burden to bear on the changeable monstrosities of history.

In twenty-four chapters, *A Compendium of Monsters* describes the absurd ways by which a group of literati and middle-ranking bureaucrats search for fame and fortune in late Qing society. The novel was completed in 1905 but not published until 1916, five years after the founding of the republic. Perhaps for this reason, it has fallen between the cracks of literary history and remained unknown until recent years. We know little about the author, Qian Xibao, except that he was a native of Hangzhou and held various clerical posts in the late Qing and early Republican era. Judged by his references to novels such as *The Travels of Lao Can, Huo diyu* (Living hell), and *Exposure of Officialdom,* Qian must have been quite familiar with the exposé tradition of the early 1900s. He divides the twenty-four chapters of his novel into twelve volumes, heading each with a character drawn from the phrase sequence "Yu zhu ding, Wen ran xi, jue yin fu, jing tan chi." Literally meaning "[The ancient sage king] Yu cast the images of good and evil in a tripod; [the Six Dynasty literatus] Wen Qiao brought light to the monsters' forms in water by burning a rhino's horn. Expose that which is hidden; warn those who are greedy and obsessed," this sequence of phrases succinctly reveals Qian's purpose.

In line with the episodic structure of late Qing exposés, *A Compendium of Monsters* contains a series of stories in which characters try every possible method to advance themselves in the bureaucratic hierarchy. In one case a junior official volunteers his wife as a "remedy" for his superior's mysterious illness; in another, an eager position seeker offers his stepmother, his sister, and his wife to a governor's assistant so as to win himself an office. When bribery is systemized into a routine enterprise, legal justice has become a euphemism for marketable opinion. These plots readily remind one of the plot of *Exposure of Officialdom* or *Eyewitness Report of Strange Things of the Past Twenty Years.* In particular, offering a wife to cure one's boss's ailment repeats similar episodes in *Eyewitness Report* (chapter 3) and Li Boyuan's *Wenming xiaoshi* (Modern times, chapter 58).

Nevertheless, *A Compendium of Monsters* distinguishes itself by foregrounding two major characters, Jia Duanfu and Fan Xingpu. Their ups and downs in the novel provide a narrative thread around which other episodes are organized. Jia Duanfu wins high esteem for his scholarship and moral cultivation. In his youth he is said to have once rejected the seduction of his master's concubine; his abstinence from any extramarital liaisons makes him a legend in an officialdom accustomed to extracurricular activities. However, for all his neo-Confucian discipline, Jia cannot keep his wife, mistress, and even children from falling into laxity. While he is being promoted to higher and higher posts as a result of his moral superiority, one family scandal after another besets him. By the end of the novel, Jia has been tricked out of his fortune by his butler and is left a penniless, retired moral emblem.

Jia Duanfu's friend Fan Xingpu is an unscrupulous opportunist who presents himself as an incorruptible judge-investigator. Wherever he is assigned, Fan launches bloody crackdowns on rioters and revolutionaries, so he soon becomes a rising star in the eyes of his conservative seniors. Meanwhile, he marries a member of the rich Hua family, then seduces his sister-in-law and his wife's maid. At a moment when the future looks more promising than ever, Fan finds himself charged with sexual misconduct and loses position, family fortune, wife, mistresses, and son. He finally dies a pathetic, lonely death. Jia Duanfu is the only person to concern himself with Fan's funeral.

Qian Xibao attacks his villains primarily by describing their sexual transgressions. This is where his novel provides a surprising parallel to Jiang Gui's *Tale of Modern Monsters,* which also is characterized by an unusual subtext of prurient sexuality. With clear ironic intent, Qian has Jia usher us into a dizzying network of perversities. While maintaining a saintly image in public, Jia is a sexual maniac in private. He abuses his wife in bed, forcing her to perform all the sexual acts, from oral to anal intercourse, that he denigrates in public. After the death of his wife, his butler's daughter occupies his sexual attentions, but he refuses to marry her even as a concubine because he wants to maintain his reputation as a man above desire. Jia's wife has her own lover, who in turn rapes Jia's daughter. Later on, Jia's daughter seduces her brother and eventually causes his death.

Incest is seen among other characters too. To console his widowed daughter-in-law, an officer of the Defense Ministry starts an affair with her, and Governor Quan Sizhuang loves his daughter so much that he shares the same bed with her. In another case, Zeng Langzhi, an assistant prefect, assists in a clerk's promotion and is rewarded by being invited to sleep with the clerk's concubine, daughter, and daughter-in-law. At the end of the novel, Zeng's wife carries on an intrigue with her cousin, who later marries Zeng's concubine. To protest her husband's imposture, the wife of the Grand Historian Wei gives herself to his cousin as his concubine. Meanwhile, the lonely wife of an official, keeping her identity secret, stages trysts with young scholars at home. Bisexuality, homosexuality, and transvestism constitute other important obsessions. One interlude describes an official's marriage to his fifth concubine, who turns out to be a young man trained as a courtesan. The servant who seduces Jia Duanfu's wife and daughter is equally interested in men. When he reappears at the novel's end, he becomes the lover of the father of Jia Duanfu's maid/mistress.

Chen Pingyuan suggests that such abundant references to sexual deviation point to a convergence of the two genres of late Qing fiction, the exposé *(qianze xiaoshuo)* and depravity fiction *(xiaxie xiaoshuo)*.[87] It should nevertheless be noticed that depravity fiction normally deals with sexual transactions within the pleasure quarters, a locus in which even the most licentious practice is taken for granted. What makes *A Compendium of Monsters* unique is its interest in sexual scandals in regular households and among upright personalities. When the cultural constructs fall apart, desire penetrates every texture of life and results in a collision of bodies and the functions supposedly regulating bodies. Qian Xibao thus describes a society that observes no boundaries, literary boundaries included.

"Disingenuous Gentleman" versus "Genuine Petty Man"

Read in the context of late Qing exposés, the stories of Jia Duanfu and Fan Xingpu sound familiar. They are hypocrites who climb to the top of the bureaucracy, only to collapse when the capricious wheel of fortune suddenly turns. But unlike other contemporary writers, who present their characters merely as laughable clowns, Qian Xibao follows Jia and Fan's fate to the end, even exploring their motives in a quasi-psychoanalytical manner. For instance, we are told that Jia works hard to become a neo-Confucian model partially because of his traumatic experience with snobbish courtesans and partially because of his cynical logic: if he cannot make himself a popular debauchee, he may as well go in the opposite direction by becoming a popular saint.

In my discussion of *An Idle Commentary on Monsters,* I suggested that the novel derives its theme from the late Ming debate over terms of virtue versus terms of evil. On the premise that even an ordinary person is eligible to achieve total goodness, any compromise with human weakness becomes a dangerous slip into the domain of evil. The line between the saint and the beast is so strict yet so slippery that it generates tremendous anxiety among those engaged in self-cultivation. At another level, I question whether such a rationale can fully explain Wei Zhongxian's villainy, in that he constitutes only part of the brutal late Ming political machine that runs haywire. It is historical reductionism to hold Wei Zhongxian responsible for the dynastic chaos at the expense of other, more invisible evils of the time. The competition between these two assumptions constitutes the historiographical tension of *An Idle Commentary on Monsters.*

In the case of Jia Duanfu, one sees an intricate twist. Whereas the late Ming dichotomy of sainthood and bestiality spells a perilous test of one's moral constitution, the late Qing dichotomy of morality and immorality, as Qian Xibao would have it, is no more than a pragmatic transaction. Jia Duanfu strives to become a moralist only *after* he has weighed the pros and cons of his options. In refraining from seducing his master's concubine in his youth, which establishes him as a Confucian gentleman, Jia is said to have been motivated not by any concern with decency but by a last-minute calculation. He knows what he may gain by temporarily curbing his desire; aware of a world of higher profitability, he invests a moment of frustration in the purchase of longtime political advantage.

What kind of historical view does such a plot imply? This question leads to the core of the novel's moral scheme. Throughout the novel, Qian Xibao distinguishes two types of evildoers: fraudulent gentlemen *(wei junzi)* and genuine petty crooks *(zhen xiaoren).* Whereas fraudulent gentlemen hide their disingenuous motives behind benign postures, petty crooks have no qualms in pursuing their base goals. But *xiaoren* has another layer of meaning in the Confucian tradition; it refers to commoners or ordinary people with limited moral resources, those who rely on the Confucian gentlemen to set standards for them and edify them.[88] For Qian, while both are equally despicable, hypocrites are more dangerous because one cannot see their true nature, as opposed to the petty crooks or commoners, who lay bare their motives. Thus Jia and Fan are contrasted with a group of characters who appear more likable, ironically owing to their visible unscrupulousness.

This is a quirky system that values not virtue over evil but one kind of evil over another. If the society is already beyond moral remedy, Qian seems to hint, one may as well settle for the less ambiguous form of evil, whose threat is at least visible from the outset. When hypocrites prevail, they switch from one role to another and upset a representational system already in ruins. Characters like Jia Duanfu and Fan Xingpu do not merely fool people around them. As they perfect the art of simulation, they become more and more convinced by the images they project. They literally turn a matter of morals into one of manners. Through these two characters, Qian Xibao vulgarizes the primary Confucian lesson of *xiushen*—literally, cultivating one's own body—at its base. He sees hypocrites who defend rationality, in either new or old form, most vehemently succumbing to carnal temptation. By contrast, the petty crooks who are not inhibited in their chase after desire are usually pardoned.[89]

If history is perceived in Li Qing's *An Idle Commentary on Monsters* as a continual confrontation between good and evil, it appears in Qian's *A Compendium of Monsters* to follow the principles that "evil always defeats good," and "the greater evil defeats the minor one," to quote Milená Doleželová.[90] As a result, the debate over man's choice between sainthood and bestiality, which was inherent in Li Qing's novel, has become gratuitous in Qian Xibao's world, and the tension between human agency and the invisible political machine does not induce any poignant deliberation. True, justice seems to be accomplished when both Jia Duanfu and Fan Xingpu suffer most horribly for their imposture. But this can only be a wayward justice when petty crooks are spared, in some cases even rewarded, in spite of their misdeeds. By normal standards these crooks' "honesty" about their base nature should not have exonerated them, not at least any more than the hypocrites' efforts to project honesty. Above all, Qian seems to be questioning whether the conventional differentiation between gentlemen and petty crooks has perhaps distracted from the "genuine" issue of his time, that time has passed and old institutions reveal their cracks.

What Qian aims at is not the moral inquiry into man's existence so much as its opposite. *A Compendium of Monsters,* as its pseudoencyclopedic format and mocking didactic tonality suggest, may as well be a manual for surviving a monstrous time when nothing seems to ring true anymore. In chapter after chapter, Qian meticulously lists the evils and absurdities his narrator and characters have encountered so as to caution readers against them. In this sense, Qian is in league with fellow writers such as Li Boyuan and Wu Woyao, proclaiming their insider's knowledge and survival skill. The best case in point is Wu Woyao's *An Eyewitness Report of Strange Events Seen in the Past Twenty Years,* in which the narrator is named *Jiusi yisheng,* or the man with nine lives.[91]

As I have argued elsewhere, the late Qing exposé writers' almost obsessive enumeration of evils generates a strong fear of moral anarchy and disillusion.[92] But it equally brings about complacency, a penchant for treating something despicable as palatable. They recount evils so as to show off. Thus these writers are part of the "strange things" they set out to laugh at; they are both eyewitnesses and participants in the age of decadence. At their most radical, their manuals/exposés constitute a necessary new evil to challenge the old evils; it takes their profane laughter to demythify the orthodoxy of political mandate and moral dictum. At their most cynical, their works amount to no more than a noncommittal observation of social absurdities and a playful parading of grotesques.

Usurpation and Duplication

Compared with Qian Xibao, who seems no longer convinced by any established value system, Jiang Gui may appear rather conservative because he does have a solemn commitment. I would suggest nevertheless that Jiang Gui's political commitment, which should have evoked the usual tears or "call to arms," and his posture—laughter—are so incompatible that they make his narrative all the more poignant. As a matter of fact, his modernity stems precisely from the mixture of traits drawn from his predecessors. He writes as if he was trying to mix the two types of *taowu* demonstrated by the late Ming and the late Qing novels discussed here. Whereas his vigilance about the susceptibility of everyman to evil recapitulates the tenor of *An Idle Commentary on Monsters,* his cynicism about multiple availability of evil is suggestive of the impact of late Qing exposés such as *A Compendium of Monsters.* That he strives to "recount evils so as to admonish" à la Ming never keeps him from posing the late Qing question on the murky boundaries of virtue and truth. Through mixing apparently disparate discourses of *taowu,* Jiang Gui reinscribes the monstrosity of history in a modern mode.

Let us revisit the thesis of Jiang Gui's novel that, in his time, history has come to a halt and orthodoxy has been usurped. To rescue history from its fall, he takes it as an obligation to recount evils so as to admonish in an unorthodox manner. While Wei Zhongxian of *An Idle Commentary on Monsters* showed how orthodoxy could easily be seized by conspirators and traitors, those clowns in *A Compendium of Monsters* demonstrate a less distant analogy by displaying the chicanery of more recent times. In the case of Wei Zhongxian, the eunuch's presumptuous plan to take over first the court and then the empire was treated as the cause of a dynastic crisis. The notion of usurpation was brought forth to explain Wei's deeds though the novel's subtext already points to factors that can hardly be subsumed by this notion. Wei would then be condemnable because he allowed himself to aspire to what he was not and could not be. His downfall is doomed, as imperial will reasserts its authenticity and again receives the mandate of heaven.

Qian Xibao's framework, or lack thereof, is that of a world whose value system has already been duplicated surreptitiously. Fragile legitimacy and its fictitious representation have been reduced to an endless game of exchange; any effort to improve the status quo is bound to become a (self-)parody. In other words, Qian concentrates on the metaphysics not of usurpation but of duplication. If usurpation in Li Qing's world still implies sacrilege for its violation of an orthodoxy that is irreplaceable, duplication, as Qian Xibao employs it, points to a circulatory system based on the principle of exchange. Like his fellow writers, Qian writes to mock, revere, and distort his subject so as to represent it. By presenting a world in moral and axiological disorder, it calls into question the writers' ability to represent values coherently as well as the legitimacy of any realist mode of narrative; hence it is an exercise of "phantom axiology."[93] Qian Xibao's vision leads us to rethink the image of *taowu* that constitutes part of the novel's title as a grotesque creature in ghostly form. There is no supernatural Ming framework here; the ghosts and devils that are described so well are recognizable inhabitants of Qing society.

Jiang Gui's novel still resonates with Li Qing's thesis in that he writes to retrieve a history almost lost to usurpation. But he also adheres to Qian Xibao's claim that orthodoxy has lost its "aura" and that we have been living in an age governed by phantom axiologies. Jiang Gui's fear of and fascination with the politics of duplication is articulated even by the title of his second anti-Communist novel, *Double Suns.*

In this perspective, Jiang Gui's ambivalent attitude toward Communism becomes clear. He treats the Communist revolution as a sham, something that may as well not have happened. By making all Communists either imposters or self-deceivers, he hints that the revolution is illusory, and thus he preempts its claim to ideological substance. But can he reconcile such a view with the facts that after the bloody civil war the immense mainland of China has changed hands, that thousands of lives, including his own, have been traumatically affected, and that the Nationalist Party is reduced to taking up residence in a province far from the capital, content to lob propaganda shells across the straits? When imposture inflicts real pain and masquerade turns into sacrificial theater, Jiang Gui reveals the other side of late Qing facetious satire. But he does not stop there. His is a voice crying out that the revolution is naked, its benefits as imaginary as the clothing of the old emperor and yet bought at the cost of great bloodshed. This is where Jiang Gui is at his most conservative—or most radical—regarding (Communist) revolution. Conservative because he still sees and names the outcome of revolution in light of historical authenticity; radical because he associates Communism with a phantom automaton, a modern simulacrum, that kills.[94]

One more note on Jiang Gui's observation of evil and clowning: as mentioned above, Jiang Gui sees his world as not only vicious but also absurd, so much so that it evokes laughter. Strangely enough in a novel crowded with grotesques, clowns, and perverts, its central figure, Fang Xiangqian, is an amazingly ordinary person. In contrast with Wei Zhongxian in *An Idle Commentary on Monsters* and those hypocrites and petty crooks in *A Compendium of Monsters,* Fang Xiangqian does not have the traits of a "bad" man. His ideological alliance aside, Fang is in effect one of the few upright, even uptight, characters in the novel. He wants to be a revolutionary because he is compelled to rescue China from the corrupt traditional system. He dedicates his wisdom and fortune to support local Communist activity, to the extent that his personal life seems almost blank. He is among the very few characters not troubled by sexual distractions. In short, Fang Xiangqian could be a *junzi,* or "genuine gentleman," in the Communist vein, a rarity even in the late Qing world, as Qian Xibao sees it.

Fang Xiangqian is depicted as the greatest villain in *A Tale of Modern Monsters* because of his overzealous and generous personality. Qian Xibao's *A Compendium of Monsters* teaches us that late Qing exposé writers no longer feel obliged to abide by established ways of thinking and seeing the real. In their comic world, everything is subject to capricious reevaluation; laughter at villainy and (innocent) suffering becomes one of the ambiguous means to confuse our sensibilities and dissipate any standards of decorum. Jiang Gui directs Qian Xibao's polemics of laughter toward a different dimension. If Fang Xiangqian is the most dangerous clown in *A Tale of Modern Monsters,* it is because his sincerity and good will disturb our judgment of him even more than a late Qing clown such as Jia Duanfu. His rise and fall compel one to ask why his altruism should induce the most selfish power struggle among his followers, why his self-sacrifice should cost the lives he aims to save.

This leads one to rethink the image Jiang Gui projects of himself in narrating his novel. *A Tale of Modern Monsters,* it will be recalled, starts with Jiang Gui's declaration to treat his novel as both confession and revelation. Once deeply involved in revolution and still struggling to maintain his belief in it, Jiang Gui is as much puzzled by the monstrous power of revolution as he is committed to it. And he surpasses his Ming and Qing predecessors in his willingness to explore this capricious monster that encompasses everyone's interiority, his own included.

Jiang Gui's account of evils thus contains a self-reflexive note. He depicts, if not defines, modern subjectivity as an agency beyond the deliberation of good and evil, as in the Ming novel, or its nullification in the form of ghostly double, as in the Qing novel. At his most polemical, nevertheless, Jiang Gui may have harbored a feeling of congeniality for Fang Xiangqian because, not unlike Fang, he dedicated the best part of his life to revolution while more often than not coming across as a misfit in his own party. Trapped by the contradictory forces of high and low, he could hardly avoid colliding with those who were more adaptable to the environment. He came out a loser, a butt of history's mischievous plan. One wonders if Jiang Gui has ever thought that at some treacherous twist of history, he, like Fang Xiangqian, might well have ended up becoming one of the monsters—a most unlikely duplicate.

I come to the conclusion of my survey by rethinking Spanish painter Francisco Goya's (1746–1828) caption to an engraving in the series *Los Capri-*

chos: "The dream of reason produces monsters." Completed in 1799, the plate is said to condense the postulates of the Enlightenment: "Where reason fails, the forces of the occult prevail."[95] The epigraph has nevertheless inspired much thought on the paradox of the human capacity to reason and reason's solicitation of its opposite, monstrosity. While it was meant to insinuate the shadowy aspect of a civilization otherwise known for its mastery of the unknown, Goya's epigraph takes on another dimension when interpreted in the perspective of Chinese history: that monstrosity may serve as the precondition of all civilized self-understanding.

With this in mind, I have looked into the question of the representation of monstrosity in connection with the genesis of modernity in late imperial and modern Chinese fiction. I argue that *An Idle Commentary on Monsters* contributes a unique view of history by revealing the relations between monstrosity and commonness. Following the late Ming moral discourse on the ordinary person's susceptibility to virtue, Li Qing nevertheless insinuates a counterargument regarding his equal susceptibility to evil. The story of Wei Zhongxian indicates that given the right historical environment and personal cultivation, an ordinary man can achieve as much vice as virtue. Thus to the late Ming intellectual debate on the attainability of sainthood Li Qing adds a sarcastic, decadent dimension. Even more polemical is Li's inquiry into personal responsibility and the imperial structure of power, which leads him to ponder not only the moral agency but also the political technology that makes a villain such as Wei Zhongxian possible.

When Qian Xibao takes up the image of the *taowu* almost three hundred years later, the Chinese dynastic cycle had almost completed its second turn and was about to break for good with the ancient autocracy, if not with autocrats. For Qian and his contemporaries, monstrosity can no longer be embodied by a single villain or a single set of negative values. Instead, it has been embodied in a whole society forced to rethink its axiological system. In contrast to *An Idle Commentary on Monsters,* which still longs for the battle of good versus evil as well as a recycling of the cosmic and moral universe, Qian Xibao's novel informs us, in the mock-authoritative manner of a compendia, that in the late Qing world, good and evil duplicate each other's traits in celebration of a world soon to be turned upside down.

In *A Tale of Modern Monsters,* Jiang Gui asks how it is that modern enlightenment and revolution set out to do away with historical irrationalities only to beget irrationalities on an even larger scale. He concludes that modern revolutionaries cannot circumscribe the old evil without first imagining and living it. They are monsters of their own reasoning. Jiang Gui shares in Qian Xibao's profane laugher, which threatens to bring down all established values, while at the same time cherishing moral schemata traceable to Li Qing's time. Communism is thus described both as a new, inscrutable automaton that bulldozes the old social body and as the return of a dark curse from the most ancient lore. Above all, Jiang Gui is not afraid of exposing and parodying either his apprehension of the increasing anonymity of modern evil or his illusory quest to retrieve lost orthodoxy as a corrective of evil. He makes his novel a testimonial to and an instance of a monstrous time called the Chinese modern.

Long gone are the days when monsters such as the *taowu* were said to roam the Chinese land and devour Chinese lives. Yet as late as the mid-twentieth century, a melancholy writer such as Jiang Gui still wrote as if guided by a deep-seated memory of this ancient monster. He did so by associating himself with his predecessors of the Ming and Qing eras and earlier times. Goya's words resound: "The dream of reason produces monsters," although by Jiang Gui's time it has become more and more difficult to tell dream from reason, and harder than ever to tell which dreams are monstrous and which are reasonable. Perhaps the difference is only obvious much later, but thinking so may be a dream of historians. If one of the functions of history is to record and therefore eschew irrationalities, the writers I have discussed have contributed a critique that is reserved not only for monsters per se but for history as a form of recollection. Should we really dream the dreams of a past if we must remember the past in order to want not to relive it?

The final irony of this study is perhaps that these three novels, which teach us not to forget history, have become forgotten titles in Chinese (literary) history. *An Idle Commentary on Monsters* and *A Compendium of Monsters* were rediscovered and reassessed only recently. And Jiang Gui's modern effort to "recount evils so as to admonish" has now been sent on its way into the realm of oblivion. *A Tale of Modern Monsters* was made known to readers under its own title for two years before it was renamed *The Whirlwind,* which in turn has long gone out of print.[96] Whither the monster? Whither the dream?

Chapter 7

The End of the Line

A poet is created by heaven out of a hundred calamities.
WANG GUOWEI[1]

In December 1933, Zhu Xiang (1904–1933), a modern Chinese poet, drowned himself in the Yangtze River. A member of the Xinyue (Crescent moon) school of poetry, Zhu had been praised by Lu Xun as the Keats of China for his passionate lyrics inspired by his European counterpart.[2] While the reasons for his death were never clear to his family and friends, it is believed that Zhu Xiang ended his own life because he could no longer cope with mounting personal problems, including an aborted overseas education, career frustrations, an unhappy family life, and an overall tendency to melancholy.[3]

In 1937, a second Chinese poet followed in the footsteps of Zhu Xiang and took his own life. But Chen Sanli (1852–1937) was a traditional-style poet, and he died during a patriotic hunger strike protesting the Japanese invasion of that year. Chen had been revered as a highly competent practitioner of Song-style poetry in the late Qing era, and he continued to practice the classical form after the May Fourth literary revolution. In his early days, Chen had been enthusiastic about political reform, but the Republican reality was such that he had chosen to become a "Chinese onlooker" *(Shenzhou xiushou ren).* Yet the old, reactionary poet died for this new China he had chosen to keep at a distance.[4]

Zhu Xiang and Chen Sanli's suicides are far apart, to be sure, in motivation and consequences, as were their poetic stances. But regardless of their distinct poetic postures, modern and traditional, they seem to have been struck by the same despair when their lives, built on exquisite language, began to fall apart. Suicide became the shared destiny of the two poets in an unpoetic age. However, the deeper significance of their suicides can only be understood if read against the suicide of Wang Guowei (1877–1927), one of the greatest scholars and connoisseurs of poetry of twentieth-century China.

On June 2, 1927, Wang Guowei drowned himself in a shallow pond of the Imperial Garden, Yihe Yuan. His brief will opens with this ambiguous statement: "After fifty years of living in this world, the only thing that has not yet happened to me is death; having been through such historical turmoil, nothing further can stain my integrity."[5] Wang's death has been attributed to, among other things, domestic and psychological turbulence, his immersion in Schopenhauer's philosophy, and his eschatological visions.[6] Above all, as a political conservative, Wang Guowei is said to have left behind him sufficient clues to connect his death with Qing loyalism. But there were other factors that made his suicide so compelling to Chinese readers then and now. As scholars have continuously speculated, Wang may have been acting out a death wish widely entertained by intellectuals when plunged into despair by historical and cultural crises.[7]

The enigma of Wang Guowei's suicide prods one to rethink Zhu Xiang and Chen Sanli's deaths. Could Zhu Xiang, like Wang Guowei, have drowned himself for reasons less trivial than apparent personal difficulties? Could Chen Sanli have starved himself to death for the old, elitist idealism and not the new patriotism? Or is it possible that Wang Guowei killed himself to express not so much belated Qing loyalism as an anticipatory mourning for all cultures, ancient and modern, on the verge of self-destruction?

One might reprove Zhu Xiang, Chen Sanli, and Wang Guowei for lagging behind the spirit of their times, which affirmed the life force and submitted to the discipline of self-renewal. But insofar as their "anachronisms" indicate a (deliberate) blurring of different temporalities and paradigms, they seem arguably more modern than most of the self-proclaimed modern literati of their time. For, at the beginning of the Chinese modern age, they had already discerned temporality as something more than the staged realization of enlightenment, revolution, and corporeal transcendence. Faced with radical incompatibilities between the public and private projects of modernity, they asserted their modern freedom negatively, in willful acts of self-annihilation. Thus their suicides paradoxically testify to the emergence of a new, post-traditional Chinese subjectivity.

Suicide never became a prominent emblem of early modern Chinese literary life, not at least in the sense in which it has allegedly constituted a national allegory for modern Japan.[8] Thanks to the abundant literary and historical accounts/acts, ranging from *seppuku* to *jisatsu*, from *junshi* to *sinju*, suicide has often been interpreted as an integral part of Japanese culture, a most inscrutable feature of what Roland Barthes calls "the empire of signs."[9] The Japanese mythology became all the more intriguing in the modern century when actual suicides were committed by an array of renowned writers, such as Akutagawa Ryûnosuke (1892–1927), Dazai Osamu (1909–

1948), Mishima Yukio (1925–1970), and Kawabata Yasunari (1899–1972). These cases lead one to contemplate not only the social and psychological causes that made Japanese writers susceptible to suicide but also the literary causes of the deaths. Between suicide and writing, between physical self-destruction and figural self-destruction *(littératuricide)*, there exists an inescapable dialectic.

Thus, Alan Wolfe uses Dazai's repeated suicide attempts and his final drowning in 1948 to illuminate the decadent turn in modern Japanese consciousness, and Roy Starrs takes up Mishima's spectacular *seppuku* in 1970 as the consummation of modern Japanese cultural and corporeal politics.[10] In both cases, where the writer's narrative may serve as a dress-rehearsal for self-annihilation, the actual suicide may enact a "final narrative" without which his fictive world remains incomplete. Hence Masao Miyoshi's comment, "if [there is] an essential relationship between literature and suicide, the Japanese novel and its authors are surely the most representative case."[11]

Beyond Wang Guowei, Zhu Xiang, and Chen Sanli, one finds few other cases from which to assemble a Chinese tradition of suicidal literati in the first half of the twentieth century.[12] But this does not mean that the macabre tradition of self-destruction exerted less power over Chinese writers and thinkers. In fiction, when Lu Xun ponders living among the dead in the Chinese world of cannibalism, when Yu Dafu writes about an overseas Chinese student walking into the sea in protest over thwarted pride, or when Shen Congwen recalls the romantic suicides of the young men and women of West Hunan, (literary) suicide serves as a powerful means of critiquing or probing the troubled Chinese soul trying to survive in a modern world.[13] Further examples would have to include works by Ding Ling (*Zisha riji* [Diary of suicide]), Mao Dun (*Shi* [Eclipse]), Lu Yin (1898–1934) (*Haibin guren* [Old acquaintances on the seashore]), and particularly Lao She (1899–1966) (*Yueya er* [The crescent moon], *Luotuo xiangzi* [Camel Xiangzi], *Huozang* [Cremation], and *Sishi tontang* [Four generations under one roof]).[14]

In the second half of the twentieth century, however, suicide—both biographical and imaginary—took on an intensified power over Chinese literary representation. Politics has often been cited as the main cause of the sudden surge in literary suicides. That Shen Congwen tried to kill himself in 1949, right after the Chinese Communist takeover, is an ominous prelude to the drama of suicides that followed, engulfing countless writers and thinkers in the decades to come.[15] Shen attempted to end his own life partly because he foresaw a bleak future for the creative imagination under a totalitarian regime. After his rescue, he forsook the novel and became an art historian. However reluctant, Shen's retreat into obscurity turned out to have been a wise move at the dawn of this age of struggles and purges. When the Cultural Revolution broke out, he saw many fellow writers choose, in the midst of humiliation and worse horrors, to end their own lives, including such famous names as Li Guangtian (1906–1968), Fu Lei (1908–1966), Wen Jie (1923–1971), and Lao She.

Lao She drowned himself on the night of August 24, 1966, after he had been publicly beaten and humiliated by the Red Guards earlier that day. A writer whole-heartedly dedicated to the new China, Lao She must have been devastated to find himself turned overnight from "people's artist," an honor conferred on him in 1951 by the Beijing government, into "people's enemy." Throughout his career Lao She pondered the social and political conditions of suicide. But as his son Shu Yi notes, "the real moment of self-sacrifice finally came, but at a time it should least have happened, in a place it should least have taken place, to a person who should least have deserved it, and in a plot that should least have been possible."[16] When he stepped into the water, one wonders if he felt an ironic relief in finally acting out what dozens of his characters had chosen for their own lives. Through suicide Lao She brought an ironic closure to his lifelong search for meaning in a world full of absurdities. One cannot fail to think of the famous line from his play *Chaguan* (Teahouse, 1957), which also uncannily ends with the protagonist's suicide, "I love my country. But does my country love me?"[17]

In his study of literature and suicide, Alfred Alvarez proposes two opposite types who seek "this dimension of death." One is what he calls the "totalitarian artist," by which he means the artist who has suffered under a dehumanizing and oppressive social system and been reduced to suicide, or to "silence, which amount to the same thing."[18] The other is the "extremist artist," in which destruction is internalized in the individual, who "deliberately explores in himself that narrow, violent area between the viable and the impossible."[19] Of these two opposite forms of suicide, Alvarez makes no secret of his preference. Whereas totalitarian art represents a language of deprivation, "of facts and images as depersonalized and deprived as the lives of the victims themselves," extremist art is defined as part of the heritage of the Romantic tradition. Indeed, it actually "completes the revolution that began with the first Romantics' insistence on the privacy of their subjective vision."[20] The link between art, creativity, death, and autobiography is made here in the strongest terms to assert the fulfillment of Romantic heroism.

Judged by Alvarez's definition, Shen Congwen and Lao She are perfect examples of the two options of life and death under totalitarian rule. Whereas Shen Congwen opts for silence in order to cope with Maoist censorship, Lao She kills himself in consummation of an ambivalent patriotism. But Alvarez's theory has its limitations; to see Lao She and Shen Congwen merely as typical victims of modern tyranny is to diminish their status as individuals. Insofar as suicide is a violent act committed by humanity against itself, overdetermined by private and public circumstances, there must be a multitude of gradations between, and within, the totalitarian and extremist types. This is where my inquiry starts.

As the following examples will indicate, thoroughly "political" suicides during the heyday of the Cultural Revolution could be occasioned by unabashedly romantic desire, and seemingly morbid suicides in the postmodern 1990s might well hide latent political traumas. Suicide, writing, and (post)modernity have formed an uneasy alliance in Chinese literature over the past four decades. The resultant phenomena cannot be reduced to any ready-made discursive formation; understanding their full significance demands both historical reflection and critical scrutiny.

Relevant cases in point are Wen Jie (1923–1971), a popular Maoist poet who killed himself during the Cultural Revolution by inhaling gas; Shi Mingzheng (1935–1988), a Taiwanese poet, painter, sculptor, and novelist who died from a hunger strike, purportedly in protest against the Nationalist government; Gu Cheng (1956–1993), a gifted Chinese poet and fiction writer of the New Era who hung himself in his home in New Zealand after killing his wife.

These three writers came from very different backgrounds, and they committed suicide for distinctly different reasons. But significantly enough, their suicides were either anticipated in their writings or written about posthumously by others. Hovering over these works is an enigma: was this writing in order to prepare for death? Or was the death in order to be able to write? In putting the three cases side by side, one suddenly recaptures the unlikely dialectic between late modern Chinese culture and body politics. Following in the wake of Wang Guowei, Zhu Xiang, and Chen Sanli from the early Republican era, these three new cases drive one to ponder all the more the gruesome price that Chinese literati paid in order to live—or die—in such a century.

WEN JIE

On August 25, 1996, the mutilated bodies of the renowned PRC writer Dai Houying (1938–1996) and her niece were found in Dai's Shanghai apartment.[21] The murder stunned the belles lettres circle and the nation because Dai Houying had been a prominent figure in PRC literature since the early 1980s. Dai's novels *Ren Ah! Ren* (Man ah! man, 1981) and *Shiren zhisi* (The death of a poet, 1982) were bestsellers in the 1980s, due to their reflection on the atrocities of the Cultural Revolution and their inquiry into the moral burden shared by a whole generation of Chinese. To that effect she had been regarded as a most noticeable voice in both the literature of the scarred and the literature of reflection.

Dai Houying is not the major figure of this section. Her tragic death nevertheless helps unravel an enigma of the Cultural Revolution that concerns me here: the suicide of the popular poet Wen Jie (a pen name of Zhao Wenjie) in 1971. In 1997, Dai's *Xinzhong de fen* (A tomb in my heart) was published posthumously; this book was based on Dai's fifty-thousand-character letter to her friend Gao Yun in 1978.[22] In the letter Dai described how she fell in love with Wen Jie against all likelihood in 1970 and how the romance led to Wen Jie's suicide early the next year. The romance had been a scandal during the Cultural Revolution and it was used by Dai Houying as raw material for her novel *The Death of a Poet*. Dai Houying had briefly mentioned the romance in her autobiography, *Xingge, mingyu* (Character, fate, 1994),[23] but not until the publication of the letter did we come to understand the tragic romance in detail, as well as the political violence underlying it.

The Rise and Fall of a Red Poet

Wen Jie was born into the family of a railroad-depot supervisor in Jiangsu in 1923. As a result of his father's untimely death, he was forced to drop out of school at fourteen to work in a coal retailer's shop in Nanjing. When the Second Sino-Japanese War broke out, Wen Jie joined the leftist patriotic campaign, traveling with a theater troupe around central China. He joined the Communist Party in 1938 and went to Yan'an in 1940. He spent the next decade in Yan'an as a journalist; during this time he tried his hand at creative writing.

Wen Jie's literary career did not take off until 1952, when he served as director of the Xinhua (New China) news agency in Xinjiang. The stunning landscapes of the northwest and the exotic ethnic cultures must have deeply moved him, as he wrote numerous poems about them. These poems, later collected in *Tianshan muge* (Ballads of Tianshan, 1956), feature a socialist-romantic poet at his most inspiring.[24]

Wen Jie is not content with idyllic motifs and balladic melodies, however. For him poetry is a most powerful tool in the service of political convictions. His poetry indicates the poet's effort to bring together lyricism and socialism, its light-hearted melodies resounding with the counterpoint of individual volition and party mandate.[25] Thus he writes in the epithet to his famous "Hexi zoulang xing" (Songs about the Northwest Corridor):

> I am living in such a place:
> Singing loud toward the sun every morning;
> Like a bird against the sunrise,
> Singing people's ideals and yearning.

I am giving all my passion,
Whereof is born my dearest nation.[26]

In "Wuhui jieshu yihou" (After the dance party), he directs the dynamism of romantic love toward the engines of socialist construction:

I made my choice this same day last year,
My fate had been decided at that time,
Arxi had taken away my heart,
To the power plant at Urumchi.[27]

A more conspicuous example is "Gucheng wantiao" (Lookout atop an ancient city at twilight), in which the poet transforms the celebrated motif of classic poetry, "huaigu," or "recollecting the past," into one of anticipatory vision, converting the lonely meditating voice in the opening line into the collective celebration of the climax.

At twilight, I stood atop an ancient gate looking out,
The last glamour of the setting sun
Like ten thousand hands reaching out from the sky,
Putting a golden cloak on Dunhuang.

Look, the gold is reflected in the water of the irrigation channels
Golden orchards embracing golden villages
On this land of shining gold,
Arise one after another golden factories . . .

Look, on the village path are running golden vehicles,
Roaming the pastures are flocks of golden cows and sheep,
In these shining golden days,
People sing loud their golden ideals.[28]

In the poem the poet visits Dunhuang, the desert city famous for its caves full of religious sculptures, wall paintings, and scriptures. When standing atop a gate of the ancient city, the poet does not feel nostalgia, as in any conventional poem on a similar subject, but instead looks at things far off with great enthusiasm. Before him, bathed in golden sunshine, is a landscape promising hope, abundance, and happiness. Is this a miracle or merely a mirage?

One can hardly miss the utopian tenor of the poem. Standing on the frontier of new ideological territory, Wen Jie embraces this new belief in a manner not unlike those pious Buddhist pilgrims and tradesmen of centuries before, when they too were ready to set out for the West. The poem's repetitive rhythm creates a litany reminiscent of the religious incantation of the remote past. The "golden" imagery of the sun is painted in such a way as to suggest the color of both ancient ruins and new construction, both empty desert and populated landscape, both Buddhist halos and Communist hymns. Thus the poem enacts a mystical exchange of religious fantasy and ideological wish-fulfillment, which underlines the cyclical nature of Wen Jie's vision of history.

As if echoing the escalating political tensions of late 1950s China, Wen Jie's poetry became increasingly contentious. After 1959, he published works whose titles suffice to indicate their content, such as *Women chapian hongqi* (We've erected red flags everywhere), *Fuchou de huoyan* (Fire of revenge), and "Dongdang de niandai" (A time of turmoil), followed by "Panluan de caoyuan" (A meadow in revolt). For these works he was honored as War Drum of the Great Leap Forward Movement.[29]

In the meantime, Wen Jie found himself more and more involved in power struggles because of his recalcitrant personality. When the Cultural Revolution broke out, Wen Jie was among the first group of "poisonous weeds" to be eradicated, a result of his antagonistic relationship with Zhang Chunqiao (b. 1917), then the czar of the Shanghai Circle of literature and the arts.[30] In 1968, Wen Jie was put into an "ox shed"—a detention center for antirevolutionaries—for intensified investigation of the charges against him. By then his wife had committed suicide and two of their three daughters had gone into exile in northeastern China. His manuscript in progress, *Wanli changjiang xing* (Song of the ten-thousand-mile Yangtze River), was confiscated and lost forever. But the worst was yet to come.

The last chapter of Wen Jie's life cannot be fully recounted without involving Dai Houying. A native of Anhui, Dai was a progressive student during her college days. By 1960, she was already a rising star in the left circle of Shanghai, owing to her Maoist fervor and inflammatory writing and oratory skills.[31] Most notorious among her feats at the time was her open denunciation of her mentor, the famous theoretician Qian Gurong, for his proclamation that "literature is about nothing but humanity" *(wenxue ji renxue).* This Maoist woman warrior nevertheless had a suspect personal background: both her father and uncle were condemned in the Anti-Rightist campaign, and the uncle subsequently committed suicide. With such a dubious family history, Dai could never be granted party membership. Dai also showed a vulnerable, romantic side when she married a classmate in 1961 despite his checkered political record. The couple never had a chance to live together; they were divorced in 1968.[32]

Dai Houying was among those most active in the early days of the Cultural Revolution, having served even as commander in chief of one of the numerous revolutionary factions. In March 1968, Dai, then the fourth most powerful person in the Shanghai Writers Association, was assigned to chair an investigation of Wen Jie, who had been in custody under charges of betraying the nation and the party. As the investigation went on, however, Dai became more and more sympathetic to the indicted poet. Fifteen years his junior, Dai had grown up reading Wen Jie's patriotic poetry; she could not comprehend how he could have been a traitor. It was at this time that Wen Jie learned that his wife had committed suicide and their three teenage daughters had been evicted from their house. In her memoir, Dai movingly describes how she brought the news to Wen Jie:

> Wen Jie covered his face with his hands; tears flew out between his fingers. I saw his jaw trembling drastically. I could not withhold my sympathy for him anymore. . . . Again and again I tried to convince him that he should "believe the People and the Party," and "take a correct attitude" toward his family tragedy. When I was about to leave, I suddenly felt a fear; I feared that in despair Wen Jie might take his own life. I turned my head and spoke to him loudly: "Wen Jie, you cannot die! You must live on."[33]

Ironically enough, Wen Jie eventually cleared himself of most of the charges and was put on probation, and it was Dai Houying who found herself trapped in the latest internecine power struggle. In late spring 1968, she was named a major conspirator against Zhang Chunqiao, and she became the subject of investigation and reeducation.

Such roller-coaster fates as befell Wen Jie and Dai Houying were nothing unusual in 1968, one of the more absurd moments of modern Chinese history. What makes their case more dramatic is that, regardless of the adverse circumstances, they madly fell in love. In 1970, both Dai and Wen were "sent-down" cadres at a farm turned cadre school near Shanghai. Now of equal status, they had more opportunity to know each other, and by late October of that year they had made their romance public.

The affair scandalized the cadre school, not only because love between a man and a woman was regarded as a bourgeois obscenity but also because Wen Jie was a recent widower and Dai Houying a recent divorcee. In addition, Wen Jie had long been the target of the Gang of the Four while until most recently Dai Houying had been an insider in the campaign against him. Despite their impressive resumés in the field of political practice, the two naïvely believed that love would and should prevail.

Wen Jie and Dai Houying underestimated the menace of the party machine. They duly applied for an approval to wed, only to be bluntly rejected; meanwhile Dai Houying was notified that she had been reassigned to the northeastern province of Jilin. The couple struggled to appeal the decisions amid mounting rumor, ridicule, and party pressure, but to no avail. When Wen Jie finally realized the hopelessness of their case, he broke off their relations and took the path Dai had once warned him against. He committed suicide by inhaling gas on January 10, 1971, exactly one hundred days after he and Dai first fell in love.[34]

The Politics of Suicide

Wen Jie, to be sure, is only one of numerous literati who chose suicide in reaction to the absurdities of the Cultural Revolution. As mentioned above, there were many cases far more brutal and unjust during the era when millions of Chinese were tortured to satisfy Mao's intellectual whims. Nevertheless, the suicide of Wen Jie is striking for its blatantly romantic, individualistic nature, a far cry from that of most other cases in the Cultural Revolution. One comes back to Alvarez's distinction between the totalitarian suicide and the extremist suicide. The suicide of Wen Jie, together with the suicides of Dai Houying's uncle and Wen Jie's wife, serve as the most chilling examples of Chinese literati living and writing under Maoist rule. When the external oppression became too monstrous for them to bear, suicide—eternal silence—presented itself as the last escape and protest.

Reading those enthusiastic "golden" poems Wen Jie wrote in the 1950s, one wonders if the poet felt irony that breathing gas was his only means of escaping from the new China, whose suffocating cruelty he had helped to create. One also wonders if Wen Jie had any second thoughts at the moment of his death, given his knowledge that suicide, like marriage, without party permission, was a revolutionary crime. Still, Wen Jie's death did not bring his usefulness to an end. Rallies and meetings were soon organized to attack him as a traitor, one who "killed himself to escape justice, thus deserving more than one death sentence."[35]

Even though he was indicted posthumously for "denying himself to the Party and People," Wen Jie may have obtained an unlikely justice on his own. However gratuitous, suicide served as a triumphant gesture against party rule. He enacted a kind of "extremist suicide" in that he "deliberately explores in himself that narrow, violent area between the viable and the impossible," to quote Alvarez again.[36] This extremist tendency is most emphatically demonstrated by his love for Dai Houying, a short-lived romance underscored by adolescent yearnings, frustrations, and death wishes. At a time when most literati could not soon enough eschew ideologically suspect behavior, Wen Jie, already found guilty by the party on other accounts, shocked everyone by daring to reach out for the forbidden fruit of romantic love. His passion was doomed from the outset and yet he was willing to risk all. Thus, when he perished, he left behind an image not of a Lao She or a Fu Lei, but rather of an anachronistic Chinese Werther. (*The Sorrows of Young Werther,* it will be recalled, had been translated by Guo Moruo [1892–1978] in his young and romantic days, long before he became an old and unscrupulous trumpeter of Maoist policies.)

One has to be cautious not to overromanticize Wen Jie's suicide. He may very well have derived his extremist motivation for death from the totalitarian dogma he once firmly believed, thus adding an ambiguous twist to Alvarez's dichotomy. Wen Jie was among the most vociferous celebrants of the Maoist vision, and his enthusiasm did not lessen during the Anti-Rightist campaign and the Great Leap Forward. His idyllic ballads and utopian hymns were written about, recited to, and paid for by the millions who suffered and died. One wonders whether it was not the same fanatical fervor that plunged him blindly into an impossible romantic attachment to his onetime interrogator.

Wen Jie's life and work exhibit a murky mixture of the selfish authoritarianism and unconditional romantic solipsism that pervades Maoist discourse. Wen Jie after all was writing in the shadow of Chairman Mao, who had been hailed as *the* poet of the New China since the 1950s.[37]

One can approach Wen Jie's suicide from yet another angle. In his genealogical study of power, Michel Foucault sees suicide as a significant indicator of the shifting structure of sovereignty in modern times. For him, the sovereign's right to impose death underwent a shift parallel to other transformations in the mechanisms of power. Whereas in premodern ages sovereign power demonstrated itself in terms of "essentially a right of seizure: of things, time, bodies, and ultimately life itself," in the modern age it has instead become an ability to generate, foster, and order growth. "The old power of death that symbolized sovereign power was now carefully supplanted by the administration of bodies and the calculated management of life."[38] It was in this context that suicide, which had been seen as a criminal act because it usurped the power of death exercised by the monarch and God, shifted into the private sphere. In Foucault's words, "it testified to the individual and private right to die, at the borders and in the interstices of power that was exercised over life. This determination to die was one of the first astonishments of a society in which political power had assigned itself the task of administering life."[39]

In the case of Wen Jie's suicide, one notices how the Maoist body politics significantly complicated the Foucauldian model. Insofar as it brutally claimed sole rights over the collective Chinese body, the Maoist regime exercised a power not unlike the feudal sovereign or deity. Thus suicide was deemed criminal behavior because it violated the Communist Party's privilege to oversee people's life and death. But the Maoist regime was also a modern political machine in that it imposed its power by means not only of "seizure" but also of "fostering." In a meticulous manner only possible in a modern technological society, it infiltrates into every texture of Chinese life, nurturing the national body as an orderly, apparently self-contained organism. The Cultural Revolution would not have been possible had it not been supported by hundreds and thousands of people like Wen Jie and Dai Houying. Mao's despotic will and the people's voluntary desire to follow his will interact.[40]

We can now better understand why Wen Jie's suicide posthumously became such a provocation to the party. Whereas "death is an ordinary event in the time of revolution," as the popular Maoist dictum expressed it, for Wen Jie to decide by himself when he should live and whether he should suffer is to defy the ancient principle of authority. It indicates a private act that mocks the feudal power from which the party derives its right to "foster" people's lives.

Once it has fallen through the holes in the party's network of somatic and semantic surveillance, Wen Jie's death unleashes a multiplicity of interpretations. It might represent drastic measures taken to demonstrate misjudged filiality—as in the historical accounts of the drowning of the ancient poet Qu Yuan (340 B.C.?–278 B.C.?). Or it might indicate a romantic attempt at individualistic volition, and self-assertion to the point of self-destruction. It is equally possible that Wen Jie might have been using suicide to erase all such meanings, including that of his own existence, as a critique of the teleology of history. Or, in the final analysis, he might have realized that he had to die so as to consummate the lethal mix of romantic whim and collectivist enthusiasm imbibed by both Mao and himself. It is hard to tell whether he died to defy the party line or to assert a peculiarly Communist vision. Choose, if you will, between romantic death wish and Marxist martyrdom, psychological despair and existentialist negation, but still Wen Jie's suicide refutes the clear-cut official version. In its resistance to the party's final say, Wen Jie's ambiguous suicide takes on its real significance.

The Death of a Poet

Our story does not stop here. Although Wen Jie's suicide seemed to many an enigma, its "textual" complexity was not fully borne out until it became a literary subject. Upon learning of the death of Wen Jie, Dai Houying was devastated. Having no official tie to her beloved, she was even denied the humble ritual of his cremation. She led a despondent life for the next few years, reconciling herself to the power of Zhang Chunqiao to the point of serving on a team of writers under Zhang's control. In the spring of 1978, barely a year after the downfall of the Gang of Four, Dai Houying was requested by her friend Gao Yun to write a few words in memory of Wen Jie, only to be engulfed again by the tremendous grief that had almost taken her life seven years before. To ease her pain, and perhaps also to better circumscribe the meaning of Wen Jie's suicide, she started to write a fictional version of their romance and tragedy. The result was the novel *The Death of a Poet.* Dai Houying was so driven by the subject that it took her only two weeks to complete the first, 300,000-character draft. The second draft, almost half a million characters in length, was finished in forty days in the summer of 1978.

Arguably the first full-length novel on the atrocities of the Cultural Revolution,[41] *The Death of a Poet* was nevertheless not published until 1982, due to the intervention of the censors. By then Dai Houying had become a celebrated representative of literature of the scarred for her bestseller *Man ah! Man.*[42] Much can be said about the drama of her fight for the publication of *The Death of a Poet.* What engages us here are two issues: first, the dialogic between the representability of suicide and the (im)mortality of poets, a dialogic to be found in the relay of writings between Wen Jie and Dai Houying; second, the tension between the Communist revolutionary agenda and the making of revolutionary subjectivity.

In a total of over six hundred pages, *The Death of a Poet* tells of three intellectual women's ideological pilgrimages during the Great Cultural Revolution, their successes and frustrations, and the ensuing emotional ups and downs. These three women, Xiang Nan, Duan Chaoqun, and Lu Wendi, grew up and attended school together like sisters, parting company after graduation. Both Xiang Nan and Duan Chaoqun become cadres in literary affairs, while Lu Wendi becomes an actress. When the Cultural Revolution breaks out, they are confronted with a series of tests. At the center of these tests is Yu Ziqi, a famous poet who, before the novel opens, has already come under investigation for his loyalty to a veteran party leader turned counterrevolutionary. Xiang Nan, a dedicated follower of the revolution, happens to be in charge of the investigation team for Yu Ziqi's case. Yu's archenemy is Di Huaqiao, a most vicious leader of the revolution.

Even from such a simple plot summary one can see the parallels between Yu Ziqi and Wen Jie, between Xiang Nan and Dai Houying, and between Di Huaqiao and Zhang Chunqiao. More biographical resemblances can be identified when Dai Houying describes Xiang Nan's miscalculated campaign against Di Huaqiao, which results in her own downfall, or the harsh life of Yu Ziqi and other literati and artists in the ox-shed. But the most striking resemblance is the party's search for and confiscation of Yu Ziqi's long poem *Bujin changjiang gungun liu* (Endlessly flows the Yangtze). Obviously modeled after Wen Jie's *Song of the Ten-Thousand-Mile Yangtze River,* this poem is alleged to celebrate those Communist veterans who turned out to be traitors, thus insinuating treachery against the party line. In a vain attempt to protect the manuscript, Yu Ziqi's wife kills herself by jumping from her apartment building, and their two daughters are thrown into disgrace.

This suicide nevertheless triggers Xiang Nan's curiosity about Yu and his poetry, and at the end of her investigation, she falls in love with him. Like the true story of Wen Jie and Dai Houying, Xiang and Yu are later sent to the same cadre school, but no sooner does their romance blossom than it is terminated by the party. While Di Huaqiao masterminds this persecution, the executioner is none other than Xiang Nan's bosom friend Duan Chaoqun, who has sold out to Di for self-advancement.

The novel derives its power from the poem Yu Ziqi never finishes, *Endlessly Flows the Yangtze.* Describing the heroism and dedication of Communist forerunners in the nation-founding days, the poem is conceived by Dai Houying as crystallizing what literature is all about in the People's Republic.

With its title derived from a famous line by the Tang poet Du Fu (712–770), *Endlessly Flows the Yangtze* is a modern salute to the notion of "writing poetry as history" *(shishi),* as Du Fu's oeuvre was famous for doing. But perhaps it equally suggests a Maoist commitment to making history of poetry. Consider the epic vision that a grand, self-sufficient utopia can be created, as prefigured by history, and that a poet's mission lies in bearing witness to the fusion of rhetoric and history, textuality and actuality. Mao's own poetry, as critics have suggested, best exemplifies this sublimation of the historical in the figural.[43] Judging by Wen Jie's works, one can imagine what kind of poetry Yu Ziqi (and Dai Houying) is engaged in. It is to such sanctioned dynastic labors that the poet, his wife and family, and his lover will all devote themselves, even at the cost of their lives.

But the poem is never completed. Ironically enough, because of its incompleteness, it becomes all the more tantalizing for both the poet and his persecutors. Whereas completing the poem becomes the collective wish of the poet, his fellow ox-shed inmates, and his new lover, the search for the manuscript on the party side amounts to an obsession, leading from one purge to another.

One can speak of a shared hermeneutic desire between the poet and his censors, the virtuous and the evil. But more uncanny is the fact that next to the poet, his dead wife, and a few censors, few have really read the poem, and yet everyone sounds as if he or she knew what the poem should, or should not, be like. At one point, the poet swears that he will piece together what he remembers in his mind with the assistance of his new lover and friends—easily one of the most touching romantic scenes.

At the end of the novel, Yu Ziqi chooses death to protect his and his poem's integrity. When he bids a silent farewell to his sleeping daughter and turns on the gas in the kitchen, the novel reaches its tragic climax. In his death note to Xiang Nan, Yu Ziqi writes:

> Good-by, little Xiang. I am not Pushkin, I won't die for the sake of love. Forgive me for not having told you the insoluble contradictions in my mind. But

> I have said it to the Party, to Chairman Mao. Thus I have nothing to fear. Don't believe that we got ourselves in trouble because of our love. No! It is all because of *Endlessly Flows the Yangtze.* I believe, for the sake of the poem, you will live on courageously. The time will come when heaven and earth will be back in their normal positions, and the sun and the moon will shine again.[44]

Rhetoric at its most sentimental, Yu Ziqi's words nevertheless pinpoint Maoist poetics and politics, as well as their dark subtexts. While the poet cannot lay bare to his lover his "insoluble contradiction," he is ever ready to confide his innermost secrets to his party and its chairman, and to die for this poem that embodies his love. For Dai Houying as for her characters, there must be an esoteric (and erotic?) tie between each and every loyal Communist writer and his or her beloved party and leader, and poetry, as the most exalted form of linguistic expression, can be the only medium for such communication. But Yu Ziqi's poem has to remain incomplete, not because he can never say enough about his love for his party and leader but because he has yet to find a format so transparent that it can be said without risking distortion.

The perfect poem, it seems, can be written only by the Poet of Poets, the Chairman himself. While awaiting the revelation of such a poem, accompanied by a cosmic renewal of heaven and earth, sun and moon, poets like Yu Ziqi can at best approximate its greatness, longingly gesturing toward the moment of its completion. Even so, chances are that they may misrepresent the irrepresentable and put their own career and life in jeopardy. This is where the "Maoist sublime" operates in full gear: an aesthetic effect that exudes an "overwhelming immensity and power of a life-crushing nature," in such a way that "the subject's imagination is faced with annihilation."[45]

To be sure, the Maoist sublime involves a series of emotive and cognitive transformations.[46] What concerns me now is that it works through the paradoxical mechanism of reflexivity, from self-denial to self-assertion, and from self-immolation to self-elevation. Shuttling between these poles, Maoist subjectivity is said to undergo both pain and pleasure in a spiral-like progression, to the point where self-annihilation becomes a most enticing climax.[47] Thus, for Yu Ziqi, to die for his unfinished poem is the last gesture to express the inadequacy of himself and his time before the Leader.[48]

I have described *The Death of a Poet* principally from the vantage point of Wen Jie and his fictional counterpart, Yu Ziqi. The fact that the novel is written by Dai Houying in memory of Wen Jie should be taken seriously, too. For Dai, seven years after Wen Jie's death, to write about the death of her beloved meant to reenact the traumatic scene and, more importantly, to resurrect buried words that should have been uttered by Wen Jie. In a way, Dai Houying plays the role of a medium, trying to speak on behalf of the dead. Where Wen Jie closed his life, Dai Houying reopens it; where Wen Jie chose to speak by means of eternal silence, Dai Houying responds with outbursts of sound and fury.

A closer reading, however, indicates a much more tortuous relation between the living and the dead. Insofar as suicide imposes itself as the conditioning factor for all writing, Wen Jie's has inscribed with his body the ultimate riddle, ever to be deciphered. In this sense his death is not unlike a literary act that must generate a posthumous narrative. As the survivor of the deadly romance, Dai Houying tries to relive Wen Jie's life and sort out on his behalf the reasons for his self-destruction. Whereas Wen Jie discards life in order to embody the impossibility of writing during the Cultural Revolution, Dai Houying tries to bridge the gap between writing and death while standing in the debris of the postrevolution. In her effort to "tell it all," however, she may have risked suppressing the enigma of Wen Jie's suicide.

One of the motifs of Dai's novel is writing. Almost everybody is busy writing: secret confessions, self-criticism, family histories, overheard secrets, conspiratorial strategies, ideological conversions and reconversions, indictments and verdicts. When all these written sources pile up, they contradict one another and therefore obscure what presumably might have been clear historiography. One no longer finds access to the truth that everyone subscribes to or pays lip service to.

Writing, either as a graphic text charged with information or as an act of communication, never becomes a problem for either the party or the poet and his friends. Nor does it bother Dai Houying as a writer. In like manner, they all seem to pursue a goal of "pure" writing—as encapsulated in the legendary *Endlessly Flows the Yangtze*—that should immaculately manifest both party line and historical truth. Accordingly, the party wants to destroy the manuscript because they believe that the poem will subvert the inevitability of what will happen, and the poet holds out because he believes that his work will outlast all temporary irrationalities, bearing witness to what really happened. For all their disputes over history, the heroes and villains share a belief in the immanence of history and in the power of poetry to delay it or to hurry it forward into their lives.

Dai Houying's novel presents a paradox in this sense. She sets out to describe a poet who wants to write a "superpoem," a poem subsuming all other literature and transcending all linguistic and ideological barriers. And the novel, in its turn, seeks to overcome the same limitations on behalf of the same impossible cause. But in fact this urge for truth in words gives rise only to lethal consequences. In addition to Yu Ziqi's death, Xiang Nan is made to witness four other suicides. Yu Ziqi's wife kills herself to protect her husband's manuscript; a neighbor's parents, a couple of respectable scholars, commit double suicide to protest unjust accusations by the party; and a weak-minded colleague of Xian Nan's ends his life because he is ashamed of betraying his family and friends.

Finally, while Dai Houying tries to recapture the utopian longing that once drove Wen Jie to suicide, she can scarcely duplicate the poetry that made it worthwhile. The poet is dead, and she is his belated mourner. However she tries, she can only invoke Wen Jie by means of the novel, a genre notoriously cacophonous and hybrid (in the Bakhtinian sense). As Xiang Nan declares in the novel's epilogue, *Endlessly Flows the Yangtze* is not just the title of Yu Ziqi's poem; rather, "having been through so much over the decade, each and every one of us can write novels under the universal title of *Endlessly Flows the Yangtze.*" Written at a time when Maoist poetry was giving way to Misty Poetry *(menglong shi),* Dai's novel about the death of a poet signals a shift from a literature of hymns to a literature of requiems.

SHI MINGZHENG

On August 22, 1988, a Taiwanese poet, painter, and fiction writer named Shi Mingzheng (1935–1988) died from lung failure in a hospital in Taipei. Outside the circle of nativist writers, Shi was not a well-known name. His death nevertheless captured the interest of the media, because of his younger brother Shi Mingde (b. 1941), arguably the most famous political dissident in 1980s Taiwan. Shi Mingde was one of the leaders of the proindependence demonstration held in 1979 in the southern port city of Gaoxiong. This demonstration resulted in a massive governmental crackdown and the arrest of Shi and other leaders. The failed demonstration, later named the Formosa Incident *(Meilidao shijian),* became a watershed in Taiwan's history of democracy, for it triggered a cluster of antigovernment campaigns over the next decade.[49]

In 1988, when the Nationalist regime lifted its forty-year martial law and paroled most of the prisoners from the Formosa Incident, She Mingde was kept in jail. In mid-April, to protest the government's denial of release, he launched a hunger strike, which soon drew national attention. No one noticed at the time that Shi Mingzheng had started a hunger strike of his own. Shi Mingzheng died four months later, while his brother, Mingde, survived and was eventually released.

Why did Shi Mingzheng end his own life? To his friends and sympathizers with Taiwan's independence movement, he had begun the hunger strike in support of his brother, although up to then he had kept a distance from Mingde's political causes. While the timing of the two brothers' parallel approaches to death seems to confirm such an assumption, ambiguity remains. The two brothers were never close (partially because Shi Mingde had spent most of his adult life in jail). As a matter of fact, Shi Mingde had called Shi Mingzheng "a coward" for his noncommittal attitude toward politics.[50] More notable was the fact that throughout the hunger strike Shi Mingzheng never said anything about his motives. He died a silent death while the country was transfixed by the drama of his brother's hunger strike. One would assume that if he had intended to make a political point with his suicide, he would have called public attention to it. Particularly at a time when the dissident movement in Taiwan had escalated to self-immolation, publicity was an integral part of political martyrdom.[51] Shi Mingzheng's quiet suicide was just the opposite, and his death shocked friends and media alike, precisely because of its apparent lack of shock value: his motives could only be determined by posthumous guesswork.

There is a series of ironies in the suicide of Shi Mingzheng: a "coward" who showed amazing tenacity in terminating his own life; a political outsider who achieved accidental martyrdom; and a brother who died a surrogate death for the sibling who was all too good at seeking fatal notoriety. While one may regard Shi Mingzheng's suicide as an irony of fate, a closer reading of his life and work indicates otherwise. Except for a five-year prison term during the White Terror of the early 1960s, Shi led a dissipated life devoted to wine and women. His poetry and fiction reveal a personality who flirted with extremes, and throughout his career he never ceased to play alternately the Byronic hero and the Dickensian ne'er-do-well. Thus his suicide leads one to ponder several questions: was his death a bitter testimonial to a life wasted by Taiwan politics or merely a macabre comedy of errors? Was it due to his self-destructive "devilism" or just deadly clowning? Most controversially, was it a rakish parody of his brother's heroic starvation or the gruesome fulfillment of a long-cultivated death wish?

The Bacchus of Taiwan

Shi Mingzheng started his literary career as a poet. He was involved in Taiwan's Modernist Poetry movement from its beginning in the 1950s. His good looks, debonair manners, and poetic talent must have impressed many leaders of the movement. In 1958, Ji Xian (b. 1913), an émigré Symbolist from Shanghai and founding father of Taiwan's *Xiandai shi,* or Modernist Poetry, was so delighted by Shi Mingzheng's romantic temperament and his amazing capacity for drink that on one occasion he wrote a onomatopoetic verse in his honor:

> If the orange liqueur doesn't utter a mute *é*
> And if all of us at the party were turned into kids
> I would be the little *ë*
> You are the long *ê*
> And the other *e*'s are already inverted
> An inverted *e* is universally silent
> Not even the minimum

Let us toss off the last bottle of Quemoy sorghum whiskey
And this will be the *è*.[52]

Inspired by poets such as Apollinaire and Rimbaud, Ji Xian used the variations of the French "e" sound to suggest the changing mood of inebriation among the poets at the party. The young poet became the Bacchus of Formosa, ushering everyone into the world of intoxication. For Ji Xian, Shi Mingzheng, "the long *ê*," was "truly outstanding among the younger native Taiwanese literati."[53]

Shi Mingzheng, however, came from a background that was a far cry from this world of "ë" and "ê." His father was a legendary figure in southern Taiwan of the 1930s, having made an enormous fortune as a martial artist, chiropractor, and herbal medicine physician, to say nothing of investing in real estate. The old Shi was also a pious Roman Catholic and a stubborn nonconformist under the Japanese. When at the age of fifty he was still without any offspring, he violated the Christian rule of monogamy to take a concubine thirty years his junior. The young woman gave birth to five boys and one girl, Shi Mingzheng being the oldest. From birth Shi Mingzheng enjoyed a life of luxury, while his parents trained him to take over the family businesses. He studied Chinese boxing and chiropractic medicine starting at age seven, and he was made to comply with Catholic teaching at home and at church until the age of sixteen.[54]

But deep in his mind the young Shi Mingzheng knew his interests lay elsewhere. As he later recalled, "I was so attracted to literature and the arts that I could never escape from their lure, even given ten more incarnations." When his father died, Shi, eighteen years old, was already "ferociously devouring the greatest legacies of humanity—poetry, painting, fiction, cinema—and was learning to create these forms of art as if in a frenzy of passion."[55] His domineering mother provided him with an excuse for keeping aloof from family duties: "As a coward unable to stand against my mother, I abandoned myself to the spiritual world of decadence, spending days and nights in painting, sculpture, and poetry."[56] By the late 1950s, Shi Mingzheng had become a well-known figure among the island literati, as indicated by Ji Xian's poem.

For all his indifference to politics up to this point, Shi Mingzheng was arrested in 1961 and charged as an accomplice in an anti-Nationalist conspiracy headed by his brother Mingde, and sentenced to five years' detention. Shi Mingde received a life sentence. This was typical of the White Terror: Shi Mingzheng was convicted primarily because of his familial ties to Shi Mingde. Because of his political troubles, his friends in the circle of belles lettres were forced to keep their distance. For instance, the poem by Ji Xian cited above was retitled when published in the mid-1960s, from "Zeng Mingzheng" (For

Mingzheng) to the more ambiguous "Jujiu yu Jinmen gaoliang" (Orange liqueur and Quemoy sorghum whiskey).[57]

However, Shi Mingzheng did not give up creative writing in jail. In 1967 he published his first short story, "Dayi yulei" (The overcoat and tears), which he had written while in prison. In the story a young artist has a chance encounter with an old couple while taking the train home on a wintry night. The old couple reminds him of his parents' expectations of him, his rebellious pursuit of art, and his despondent life. By "immersing himself in the abyss of lust and desire . . . he has become a shameful son who fails his father."[58] This prodigal son fails even to shed a tear at his father's funeral; he finally breaks down upon seeing a strange mourner who cries, almost surrealistically, like "a big candle steadily melting away."[59]

Shi Mingzheng (or his usual protagonist) seems perpetually haunted by his failure to fulfill his role as a filial son and a dependable man. But his guilty feeling drives him to indulge all the more in artistic and erotic revelry. Such contradictory impulses, to be sure, are typical of romantic characters in literary history. What enriches Shi's protagonist is his ability to poke fun at himself with dark humor, thereby deflating his egoistic inclinations. In "Baixian" (White line, 1969), a man is seen speeding on a motorcycle to meet his divorced wife and bid her farewell—in bed. Upon his arrival, he finds her in flagrante with another man. In "Wo, hongdayi, yu lingling" (I, red coat, and zerozero, 1970), a similar narrator recalls his romance with a dance hall girl. The romance evolves to include alcoholism, sadomasochist rivalry, mafia intervention, financial conspiracy, and family feuds, to the point where the seemingly vulnerable girl turns out to be a femme fatale. In both stories the narrator first appears cavalier and complacent, finally realizing that his machismo and romanticism are nothing but self-delusion.

Shi Mingzheng is quite self-conscious about the contradictory tendencies of this alter ego. He boasts that "perhaps in my personality the devilish surpasses the divine by more than a third. Since it is said that most women are more fond of men with a strong devilish bearing, I always like to pursue a woman with a few words of praise, followed by a barrage of playful sarcasm."[60] On the other hand, he also wrote:

> I am afraid of drawing a flower,
> I am afraid of loving a woman,
> I tend to mystify them in the course of work.
> This is unfortunate:
> That a poet drowns himself in the sea of his own words,
> And an actor kills himself
> In too convincingly playing the role of Romeo.[61]

In "Mogui de zihuaxiang" (Self-portrait of a devil, 1970) Shi Mingzheng fully described his self-confessed devilish hero. He tells of how he once lured his brother's girlfriend into his bed and then arranged for his bosom friend to get in with her. The story culminates in a sexual orgy shared by the narrator, his friend, and the girl. The girl eventually abandons herself to a life of prostitution. Though he should be held accountable for the girl's fall, Shi Mingzheng's protagonist shows no qualms. As a matter of fact, the "devilism" embodied by this character afterward became a key concept in many of his writings, and he even titled his most important poetry collection of the mid-1980s *Mogui de yaolian yu chunqing ji qita* (The devil's fiendish romance and innocent passion and other poems, 1984).[62]

A Man Longing for Death

One can trace a literary genealogy for Shi Mingzheng's "devilism." His Catholic training, together with an Oedipal complex, may have contributed the necessary repugnance to his diabolic imagination. His lifestyle contains traces of the Western Romantic-Symbolist tradition, from Byron to Baudelaire. Shi also describes how, as a teenager, he was fascinated with nineteenth-century Russian novels by Tolstoy, Gogol, and Dostoevsky. He was particularly fond of Dostoevsky, having read almost all of his works.[63] One easily discerns in Shi Mingzheng's heroes traits characteristic of a Raskolnikov or the Underground Man; they are souls torn between megalomania and an inferiority complex, desperately trying to define themselves by negating an oppressive external world. Finally, in view of Shi Mingzheng's interest in Japanese literature and the way he peppers his writing with erratic autobiographical experiences, he reminds one of writers such as Dazai Osamu and Mishima Yukio.

I will discuss Mishima momentarily. Dazai has been regarded as the spokesperson of the notorious Buraiha school of post–World War II Japanese literature—a style of life and writing involving "dissipation, debauchery, and irreverence."[64] Dazai derives his use of "buraiha" from the French "libertin," as in his famous 1946 manifesto, "I'm a libertine *(buraiha)*. I rebel against all constraints. I jeer at the opportunists."[65] Pushing the prewar tradition of the "I-novel" to a new extreme, his works dissect his depravities as if he were engaged in a cyclical exploration of a most decadent "heart of darkness." Evidence regarding Shi's indebtedness to the Japanese writer has yet to be discovered, but the resemblance between the two is striking. Both led a life of disturbances and debaucheries, and yet both reveal at the core of their writings what Shi calls "isolation, melancholy, and unfathomable loneliness."[66]

More pertinent to my concern is that the life and work of both Dostoevsky and Dazai are underscored by the leitmotif of suicide. Much ink has been spilled probing their shared desire for self-annihilation.[67] Whereas Dostoevsky may have contemplated suicide as an existentialist critique of and escape from the intellectual and spiritual decline of his time, Dazai continually wrote about and attempted suicide so as to live out his aesthetics and politics of self-negation.[68] Dazai eventually succeeded in killing himself in 1948. Compared with either Dostoevsky or Dazai, Shi Mingzheng admittedly had less talent, and never wrote enough to develop a full-blown philosophy of death. Still, questions can be raised, such as: if (literary and actual) suicide always posits a textual enigma about a self-terminated life, how then would one describe Shi Mingzheng's motives? If behind the suicidal desire of Dostoevsky and Dazai lay a single ressentiment that informed the psychology, politics, and art of their times, what can one say about Shi?

In 1972, in a story titled "Heniao zhe" (The man who drank his own urine), Shi Mingzheng for the first time wrote about his experience as a political prisoner. Among the chilling portraits of lives wasted behind bars, he focuses on an inmate nicknamed Quemoy Chen, who starts his day by drinking his own urine. Chen is said to have revealed the names of fellow dissidents in exchange for the Nationalist regime's favor. Because of his betrayal, many of his comrades were arrested, some even put to death. Ironically, Chen was also suspected of being a Communist spy who turned in his colleagues to protect his own revolutionary identity. Either way, he was put in jail and gradually lost his mind. He either brags about the lives he helped end or withdraws into silence. But it is his self-imposed morning ritual of urine-drinking that exhibits his moral and psychological chaos. By drinking what nature has eliminated, Chen displays not merely the malfunction of a metabolic system; he mimics humanity turning against its own nature.[69]

Although the urine drinker's story is replete with political innuendo, it fascinates us by its decadent overtones. There is an absurd quality in Chen's persistence, which makes him more than a mere traitor gone psychotic. Chen asserts his vanity and self-hatred through bodily self-debasement. Not unlike those he helped persecute, Chen the urine drinker is still a victim of the same national machine, his life doomed to be no more than waste recycling. From political betrayal to natural perversity, he embodies the confusion of body and politics in a time when eschatology is reduced to mere scatology.

Presumably for political reasons, "The Man Who Drank His Own Urine" was not published until 1981. By then Shi Mingzheng had already published another story about jail life, "Kesi zhe" (The man who hankered for death, 1980). This story is the antithesis of "The Man Who Drank His Own Urine." Put side by side, the two form a dialectic fully illuminating Shi Mingzheng's thought on death, politics, and self-negation.

In the story, Shi Mingzheng the I-narrator recalls his encounter in jail with a cellmate who later killed himself. This person, whose name Shi has forgotten, is from mainland China; he had joined the Chinese Youth Corps at the end of the Second Sino-Japanese War and later followed the Nationalist troops to Taiwan. "Perhaps due to his desolation over the lack of family and friends, and his arrogant personality as a poet, he could not adapt himself to the barracks community of green-uniformed soldiers."[70] He was sent to a country school to serve as a military training teacher, until one day when, "perhaps due to dizziness, having looked across the monotonous, immense sea at Red China bathed in the horror of the setting sun, he began shouting slogans in front of Taipei Railway Station."[71] He was charged with seven offenses, sentenced to a seven-year imprisonment, and became Shi Mingzheng's fellow prisoner.

By the standard of the legal system during the White Terror, a seven-year imprisonment would have been deemed lenient. The nameless hero nevertheless responds in a most vehement manner. He gives up his right to appeal; instead, one day he shocks his fellow prisoners by banging his head against the iron bars, as if "his skull were a drum and the iron bars were drumsticks." Moreover, Shi Mingzheng notices that "his front teeth, broken at the bottom, were compressed into the shape of a V"; he suspects that "his teeth were broken because, deep into the night, he had tried to gnaw at the iron bars."[72] When surrounded by wardens and inmates, the man quietly smiles.

The man's suicide attempts soon take on a compulsive pattern. In his repetitive search for death, he alienates himself more and more from the other inmates. In what is perhaps his most spectacular attempt, he devours more than a dozen hard, moldy steamed buns and drinks gallon after gallon of water. He seems bent on stuffing himself to death, "but the prison authorities who protected us so thoroughly succeeded in denying his decision to die." He eventually outwits them:

> The way he died was said to be very weird. As the prison laborer who had scabies on his head had gotten up and gone out to wash that day, he had availed himself of the opportunity to take off his own beltless blue underpants, slide the pant leg around his own neck, and knot it onto the handle of the iron door which was about the height of our belly button. Then, squatting, legs stretching, buttocks several inches above the ground, he resolutely hanged himself.[73]

If the urine drinker is a desperate life seeker *(kesheng zhe),* the nameless man is a determined death seeker *(kesi zhe).* Both men prove to be equally pathetic victims of the Nationalist machine. Why is the man so determined to kill himself? An immediate answer is that the political hegemony at the time was such that suicide was the individual's last avenue of protest or escape. But Shi Mingzheng seems more fascinated by this man's "entire dedication to the pursuit of death," so much so that he finds in it an "aesthetics." Shi ponders why the man is so determined to find a way, no matter how absurd, to terminate his life. The Chinese, he notes, are not a people prone to suicide. He asks ironically: wouldn't it have been easier and freer to kill oneself if one stayed out of jail? Shi then proposes two possible motives for the man's longing for death. His wish to die may have emerged only after those anti-Nationalist slogans had already been shouted; or his death wish might "exemplify the aesthetics of action endorsed by Mishima Yukio. But [the nameless suicide] died several years before Mishima Yukio, so it could not be that he meant to imitate Mishima."[74]

Shi Mingzheng's reference to Mishima Yukio is of particular significance here. Given his obsession with virile physique, dramatic lifestyle, and the incessant pursuit of "devilism," he must have found in Mishima's 1971 public *seppuku* a powerful instance of corporeal politics. There is a fundamental difference between the Japanese writer and Shi's nameless hero, however. Whereas Mishima committed a highly publicized ritual suicide after his failed coup, Shi's suicidal inmate dies a most obscure death, hanging himself while "squatting, legs stretching, buttocks several inches above the ground." Shi nevertheless calls attention to the fact that in both cases, political suicide is underlain by apolitical motivation—an "aesthetics of action." Mishima consummates his suicide with showmanship, whatever the cause. Similarly, Shi Mingzheng's inmate exhibits an obsession with suicide as if it were an end in itself, the uglier the better. Thus, as Shi speculates, perhaps his protagonist has all along been "seduced by nothing but the charm of death as such."[75]

This brings us to a most intriguing point, that the man longing for death had once been a poet. Himself a poet, Shi Mingzheng the narrator is naturally curious about the man's work, but he can never bring himself to talk to the man. To do so would have aroused suspicion among the wardens that they were engaged in some conspiracy. For the same reason, he evades the man's attempts to discuss poetry with him. In retrospect, Shi writes, "I deeply regret not having communicated with him at all to learn why he longed for death and what he thought about life, mankind, and the world. After all, the only one whom he had ever approached was myself, a poet."[76]

Conventional wisdom has it that Shi wrote a political allegory to indict the Nationalists for their crackdown on the dissidents. I suspect that he had another, more complex story to tell. Beyond the political allegory Shi Mingzheng sees in the man's longing for death a poetic allegory. And at his most polemical Shi equates poetics with politics. A poet is a dissident by nature. Thus prisoners like Shi and the nameless man suffer doubly. The nameless hero is put in jail for his offensive words against the government. As the story develops, one comes to realize that this man has always engaged in the "crazy language" of which politically subversive utterances are only one part. When he is locked up in jail by governmental authority, his desire for extraordinary lines is yet to emerge. The narrator, Shi Mingzheng, is his last hope for an outlet, and yet they failed to communicate with each other. And he at last fulfills (or fails?) his linguistic ecstasy through the eternal silence of suicide. In Shi's words, this man exerts his "will to action" *(youwei)* through "resignation" *(wuwei)*.[77]

The world of poetry is one of crystallized language and unalloyed human relations, and it is open only to a select few. Of the prisoners, the man chooses to talk only to Shi, perhaps because he recognizes in Shi a secret congeniality. In turn Shi is the only one who finds in the man's longing for death "a completely different prototype of misery in life . . . its origin has to do with a kind of suffering that verges on tragic beauty."[78] But Shi Mingzheng's political instinct makes him betray his poetic instinct, and he turns his back on the man.

The Lethal Art of Devilism

There is no doubt that in his younger days Shi already showed signs of decadence and despondency. The jail experience, however, ushered him into a world of irrationality and cruelty, so much so that upon his release he knew he could no longer be the same carefree poet he had once been. Instead, he was destined to live alternately with the spectres of the man who drinks his own urine and the man longing for death for the rest of his life. Devilism, as a style of living and writing, became a way for him to come to terms with his cowardice, humiliation, and overall ressentiment.

But devilism also provided Shi Mingzheng an entry point to a vision of life as a liaison with danger, paid for by an extravagant expenditure of taboos and inhibitions. Shi Mingzheng's poetry after the mid-1970s vividly exhibits a schizophrenic tendency. Writing poetry seems to have become both an exorcism—an attempt to expel the demons within—and a possession, a compulsion to welcome the demons that intrude upon his imagination. In a poem entitled "Tuomo" (Exorcism), he asks:

> Who says a devil is always a devil?
> Who has proven that a devil can never be transcended?
> Who can capture the traits of a devil?
> Who can freeze the figure of a devil?
> Who can congeal the metaphor of a devil?[79]

In "Kaige" (Victory song), he reiterates his desire to transcend temptation:

> For the sake of leaving something behind at death, Poet,
> No more devilish romance,
> Draw down your life before Death arrives.
> Poet, stop pounding like a carpenter
> Your woman's lustful bones,
> What do the echoes of the gravestone carver's work suggest?[80]

But Shi's craving for, and rejection of, devilism can only be completed by self-destruction. Shi is not unaware of the danger; death has always been his favorite theme.

> I tried continuously to withdraw, escape
> From the perils of life and love,
> Only I am a moth.
>
> Are you a candle? Do you want me to be your moth?
> All right, let me burn myself to death.
> Self-abuse, self-destruction, and everything else.
>
> I the moth who loves the candle—isn't this my nature? Sigh . . .
> Destruction and self-destruction—isn't this my fate? Mmm . . .
> If so, who needs a public cremation site?[81]

This poem was written in 1984, four years before his suicide. In the last years of his life Shi was a productive writer of both poetry and fiction. While his fiction reveals more and more of the political trauma and sexual fantasy of his early writings, his poetry betrays a soul increasingly torn by sensuous temptation and a yearning for apocalyptic salvation. Often he expresses his guilt at being a "shameful, weak, debased" survivor of the Nationalist crackdown that led to the imprisonment of his brother Shi Mingde and many other dissidents. Faced with the capricious politics in mid-1980s Taiwan, Shi must have felt more disoriented than ever. He seems to want to be a man ready for death, screaming protests but never able to do away with the fear that he is a traitor, a man who will someday drink his own urine.

In "Zhidao guan yu wo" (The inquisitor and I, 1985), one of the last stories Shi Mingzheng wrote, one again witnesses Shi's empty efforts to transcend his early traumas. The story recalls his early romantic adventures, followed by his conviction as an anti-Nationalist along with his two brothers, and his dissipated life after release. It ends with a lengthy description of the arrest of Shi Mingde in the wake of the 1979 Formosa Incident.

By now we are already quite familiar with Shi Mingzheng's autobiographical inclination; what makes this story interesting is that it introduces an antagonist, a military inquisitor, who has all along been working on the case of the Shi brothers. A suave bureaucrat and an archcynic, the inquisitor is a professional investigator of the thoughts as well as the soul of his culprits. Under his cross-examination, Shi gives away everything about himself: his literary favorites, familial members, political ties, romantic relations, predilections, fears, and so on. In the end the inquisitor has become intimately acquainted with all Shi's vulnerabilities; Shi's guilty conscience is projected onto an unlikely confidante of Shi's (forced) confession. The encounter between the inquisitor and Shi strikes one as a parody of the famous scene in Dostoevsky's *Brothers Karamazov,* in which the Grand Inquisitor meets with Ivan Karamazov and they debate religion, authority, belief, and moral and religious agency.

But Shi's story goes further. Even after his release from jail, he cannot keep away from the inquisitor. Because his family background is his sin, he is forced to suffer surprise visits from the inquisitor whenever the political wind blows in a new direction. The "hunter and his prey," as Shi puts it, are tied to one another in an endless cycle of investigations and confessions. As a result, "The Inquisitor and I" takes on a Kafkaesque dimension, telling a story of a political surveillance that turns into a spiritual nightmare.

Back to the spring of 1988, when Shi Mingzheng started his hunger strike in parallel with his brother's. The question can now be asked: why did he commit suicide? By choosing to wither away through fasting, he opts for a slow, persistent way of deforming the body and the face he had been so proud of—the greatest irony for someone who has always lived off attracting people's, especially women's, attention. His brother's hunger strike was greedily winning attention from the media, as during Mishima's final days. In contrast, Shi Mingzheng was determined to die a private death. Instead of martyrdom, he performed a rite of self-destruction full of ambiguities. One wonders: did he at last find a truly heroic act, one in which he could die for Taiwan's democratic movement? Did he "assert himself through resignation," like the "Man Who Hankered for Death"? Or did he bring devilism to its conclusion by negating all other romantic gestures—like a Byronic hero or an Underground Man—in a final demonic negation of his soul? But then perhaps Shi Mingzheng merely died a poet's death, a poet who wanted the world to stop interfering with his life.

GU CHENG

On October 8, 1993, the body of Gu Cheng, a PRC poet living in exile in New Zealand, was found hanging from a tree on Waiheke Island. Not far away was the body of his wife Xie Ye (1959–1993). It was reported that Gu Cheng had taken an axe and delivered the fatal blows to his wife's head before taking his own life. The news shocked Chinese readers both on the mainland and overseas, for Gu Cheng had been among the most celebrated of the younger generation of Chinese poets after the Cultural Revolution.

Gu Cheng was among the founding members of *Jintian* (Today) magazine, the first and foremost underground literary enterprise in late 1970s China. Together with writers such as Bei Dao, Mang Ke, Duoduo, and Yang Lian, he helped create the school of Misty Poetry, or *menglong shi.* They called for renewing the poetic language ossified by the Maoist style and experimented with obscure and bold themes and imagery that would have been unthinkable just a few years earlier.

Gu Cheng was an extremely sensitive and melancholy child; because of the perilous political circumstances and his own delicate constitution, he received no formal education beyond primary school. But he demonstrated talent as early as age six, and he continued to write even when he and his family were under persecution in the heyday of the Cultural Revolution. He wrote a short poem "Yidai ren" (One generation) in 1968, at the age of twelve:

> The dark night has given me dark eyes,
> Yet I use them to search for light.[82]

The poem is so simple and yet so suggestive that, one decade later, these became the most quoted lines among the younger generation.

During his formative years, Gu Cheng had the fortune to be encouraged by his father, Gu Gong (b. 1928), a famed PRC poet and movie scriptwriter. Gu Gong belonged to the generation of cadre-poets who wrote to celebrate the new republic and to endorse party policy. In many ways he reminds one of Wen Jie. Gu Cheng, however, came to drastically revise the idealism and utopian vision represented by his father's generation. There is an eerie otherworldly beauty in the young poet's works, as if he were enchanted by something apparent yet inscrutable. His pursuit of the primordial form of language, together with his imaginary return to an infantile existence, earned him the nickname "fairy-tale poet" *(tonghua shiren).*[83] In "Jin he yuan" (Near and far, 1980), he wrote:

> You are watching
> —me
> —a cloud
>
> gazing at me
> you are far away,
> watching the cloud
> I feel you near.[84]

In the next decade, Gu Cheng turned this ethereal style into a poetry charged with spectral power. In 1992, he wrote a cycle of poems entitled "Gui jincheng" (Ghost comes to the city), which begins,

> At 0 o'clock
> ghost
> walks very cautiously
> he is afraid of stumbling
> and becoming
> a man

In contrast to his father's generation, who embellished their language with a profusion of life forces, Gu Cheng opts for a "zero degree" of writing, minimalizing meaning and relevance to life. Death is his favorite subject. In "Shiwu" (Mistake, 1991), he writes:

> I should not have lived in this world
> I opened the small square box the first time
> And the bird flew away, flying to the dark fire
>
> I opened it the first time.[85]

The Ghost in a Fairy Tale

Gu Cheng had always indulged in thoughts of suicide, both in poetry and in life. In the last interview he gave, conducted only three weeks before the tragedy occurred, he confessed that he had seriously thought of ending his life since he was seventeen, and he had made numerous failed attempts. For him, such constant attempts at suicide "were actually of a great help to me whenever I was in despair, because they put me into new incarnations."[86]

His wife, Xie Ye, helped Gu Cheng repeatedly to survive his suicide attempts. The romance between the two was among the most popular fairy tales of PRC literature in the 1980s. Gu Cheng is said to have encountered Xie Ye, then a student, in 1979 on a train from Shanghai to Beijing. Over the next four years they developed an intense courtship, including an abundant exchange of love letters and poems, four major breakups, and, unsurprisingly, numerous threats of suicide on the part of Gu Cheng. After they married in 1983, Gu Cheng prevented Xie Ye from either working regularly or seeking advanced education. They carried on a bohemian life centered around Gu Cheng's writing. Gu Cheng depended on Xie Ye not as a wife but as a mother, so much so that he rejected the idea of having their own child. He wanted to be the only child of this mother/wife. Meanwhile, Gu Cheng's manic-depressive symptoms and abusive tendency gradually became known among his friends.

His personal problems notwithstanding, Gu Cheng enjoyed increasing popularity with readers and critics in China and overseas during the mid-1980s. The couple traveled to many countries; Gu Cheng's works and the chimney-shaped denim hat he had worn since 1984, even in bed, came to symbolize the talent and idiosyncrasy of a new generation of Chinese poets. In 1988, the couple was granted permanent residence in New Zealand. Gu Cheng had always dreamed of a life isolated from the world; when he and his wife finally settled on Waiheke Island, near Auckland, they seemed to have found a Peach Blossom Grove.

Behind the façade of an idyllic life, however, the poet was restless. "By accident" his wife got pregnant and gave birth to a baby boy.[87] Worse, before their immigration to New Zealand, Gu Cheng had fallen in love with a girl named Li Ying, one of his numerous fans. Gu Cheng corresponded with Li fervidly in the late 1980s, to the point that he became hysterical with lovesickness. In 1991 Xie Ye came to her husband's rescue by buying Li Ying an air ticket to come to New Zealand. What followed is unthinkable to most people. The three lived together in a ménage à trois, with the two women working to support the man. Xie's wifely generosity was indeed extraordinary. To alleviate her husband's jealousy, she even entrusted her son to a local native family. For a while, life could not appear better for Gu Cheng, a childlike grown-up ruling over what he called a "Country of Girls."

In the fall of 1992, when Gu Cheng and Xie Ye were participating in a writing program in Germany, word came that Li Ying, left alone in New Zealand, had disappeared with a neighbor twice her age. Upon hearing the news, Gu Cheng "went crazy," trying unsuccessfully to commit suicide.[88] Later on, he struggled to recover by writing the novel *Ying'er* (1993). It was during this time that Xie acquired a suitor, and Gu Cheng's relations with her, which had always been passionate and volatile, became estranged. Shortly after returning to New Zealand to finalize the divorce, the murderous incident happened.

I summarize Gu Cheng's story because, as in the cases of Wen Jie and Shi Mingzheng, his poetry is so intertwined with his life that we cannot decipher one without referring to the other. Neither Wen Jie nor Shi Mingzheng, however, can compete with Gu Cheng in terms of posthumous notoriety. One can attribute this to the fact that Gu Cheng enjoyed celebrity status in 1980s China and Europe, and his suicide was by far the most scandalous. Granting these factors, I would still argue that Gu Cheng's death captivated Chinese society because it unexpectedly dramatized the changing condition of literary politics.

No sooner had the news of Gu Cheng and Xie Ye's death been released than there erupted a virtual media frenzy over the case. Numerous essays, criticisms, interviews, and tabloid reports appeared, followed by heated debates about whether Gu Cheng was a talent gone mad or a cold-blooded male-chauvinist monster. While critics were busy offering interpretations of Gu Cheng's state of mind, including his childhood brain concussions, his Oedipal complex,[89] his clinically recorded paranoia,[90] and his "pathological narcissism,"[91] Gu Cheng's father and sister, Xie Ye's mother, and even Li Ying were all solicited to reminisce about the poet's past or write their opinions about the murder.[92] A complete collection of Gu Cheng's work was published with careful editing by his parents.[93] A spectacle developed, as if the death of the poet had temporarily revitalized a literary public demoralized by the Tian'anmen Incident and the burgeoning market economy.

In her essay on the "cult of poetry" in China, Michelle Yeh reminds us that Gu Cheng's suicide was not an isolated case; rather, it was preceded by at least two others, Haizi (1964–1989) and Ge Mai (1961–1990). At a time when poetry was ever more socially marginalized, these poets insisted on their poetic cause in a manner not unlike religious fanatics. Yeh sees in their dedication a paradoxical tendency in both avant-garde eccentricity and monolithic fixation. She asks, "Is the cult of poetry related to the cult of Mao, however remotely, as well as to the Chinese literary tradition and the Communist tradition in general? If it is indeed related to the cult of Mao, is avant-garde poetry in China both rebellious against and complicitous with the Maoist tradition?"[94] From a different angle, PRC critic Zhang Yiwu sees in Gu Cheng's death "the end of an epoch" in search of a new utopia amid the debris of Maoism. In view of the dissipating "cultural fever" of China in the 1980s, Zhang even suggests that Gu Cheng's death marks the demise of the last "national allegory."[95]

To be sure, Gu Cheng's image and poetry remind one of a spoiled, sullen poet in the romantic vein. But the way his death was received among his Chinese fans provides an unexpected perspective from which to view the conditions of Chinese (post)modernity. As mentioned above, Gu Cheng and Xie Ye's death induced not merely shock and mourning but also muted festivity among Chinese audiences. When the poet's life story was circulated and consumed by audiences across all social strata, and elite critics and tabloid reporters joined forces to treat the murder-suicide as something unbearably light, a new literary discourse was on the rise. More uncannily, Gu Cheng was not unconnected to this posthumous frenzy. Eternally silent, his ghost nevertheless oversaw the dissemination of his recordings. This ghost, I argue, appears in the form of the novel Gu Cheng completed just before his death, *Ying'er.*

Ying'er is the only full-length fictional work by Gu Cheng. As the novel puts it, it was written (partially in collaboration with his wife, Xie Ye, under the penname Lei Mi) both as a confession and as self-therapy; hence its subtitle, *Yibu ciru shengming lingsui de qingai chanhuilu,* or *A Romantic Confession Penetrating to the Essence of Life.*[96] In a tell-all mode, the novel recounts Gu Cheng's tumultuous relations with his girlfriend and his wife, respectively nicknamed Ying'er and Lei. It starts with Ying'er's arrival on Waiheke Island in 1990 and culminates in Gu Cheng's decision to terminate his life after Ying'er's disappearance in 1992. It should be pointed out that the manuscript was not discovered after Gu Cheng's death, as romantic cliché would demand. On the contrary, Gu Cheng submitted it to a "manuscript auction" held in Shenzhen in August, 1993. The first attempt of its kind in mainland China, this auction featured manuscripts by writers and celebrities.[97] That Gu Cheng had written a novel about his love story and his forthcoming suicide became a hot selling point in the auction, and as a result the manuscript was sold to an anonymous buyer at an excellent price. Thus, when Gu Cheng did commit suicide, his death confirmed the foreknowledge presumably shared by the novel's implied audience.

One might suggest that Gu Cheng was so cynical about his romance that he intended to cash in on it, even though he would eventually have to fulfill his part in the contract by taking his own life. One might also point out that, by rehearsing his suicide in fiction before enacting it in reality, Gu Cheng reaffirmed the convention that "life imitates art." Extenuating factors can be introduced, such as the fact that Gu Cheng had suffered from psychological problems throughout his life and that an inclination to extreme behavior was part of his clinical record. On top of these hypotheses, one might decide that *Ying'er* should be viewed as a death script, not by a poet who was about to die so much as by a poet who deemed himself *already* dead for most of his life. Gu Cheng was never shy about comparing himself to a ghost, and few ghosts succeed in dying twice. *Ying'er* comes across as a novel fashioned for the age of postnarrativity in that it preempts any narrative attempt to streamline the chronology of life to death. The novel does not foreshadow fatality any more than it narrates that which will have already happened.

Ying'er: *A Death Script*

Ying'er opens with an epithet, "You are my wives. I love you both, even up until this moment," followed by the poem quoted above:

> ghost
> walks very cautiously
> he is afraid of stumbling
> and becoming
> a man.[98]

So, from the outset, Gu Cheng suggests the two interrelated themes of the novel: the doubling of the object of his desire and the spectral context in which such a doubling takes place and fails. The novel is framed by the narrator's visit to Lei (Xie Ye), months after the suicide of the poet Lin Cheng (Gu Cheng), when he is given a box that contains various packets of writings. These writings constitute the four parts of the novel. In the first three parts, Lin Cheng describes his deep affection for Ying'er, their reunion on Waiheke Island with Lei's support, the pastoral life of the three together, and the sudden disappearance of Ying'er when Lin Cheng and Lei visit Germany. The fourth part reads like an appendix, in the form of letters and essays written by Xie Ye to her son.

Critics have noticed that the beginning of the novel, when Lin Cheng narrates how Ying'er first came to him, is the poet at his best.[99] Fragmentary sentences, elliptical pauses, sudden eruptions of pain and anger, lyrical vignettes, and erotic recollections are rendered in such a way as to dramatize a soul deeply hurt by his loss but all the while testing the possibilities of linguistic expression. As the story moves on, Lin Cheng's narration becomes more coherent, but he sounds increasingly vengeful. He even suspects Ying'er has fooled him from the beginning. One can only sigh when Lin Cheng rambles on about Ying'er using him to get overseas and still owing him rent and airfare.

While Gu Cheng may be behaving like any betrayed lover, his childish self-indulgence is not to be taken lightly. The novel's title is homophonic with the Chinese word "ying'er," or baby. For a writer who frequently writes about his reluctance to grow up, proclaiming that deep in his psyche he is "never more than eight years old,"[100] the invocation of *ying'er* may be more than a coincidence. It does not merely refer to Li Ying; it suggests Gu Cheng's own infantile alter ego. Throughout the novel, Lin Cheng repeatedly states that Ying'er is his soulmate; he even stresses that they bear similar birthmarks in similar areas. Little surprise that he should liken Ying'er and himself to the symbiotic pair Jia Baoyu and Lin Daiyu in the *Dream of the Red Chamber*. Ying'er's departure thus implies "his whole person being split into two."[101]

Unsurprisingly, Lin Cheng's wife, Lei, is compared to a mother. As in reality, Lei / Xie Ye treats her poet husband like a baby and takes the initiative to bring Ying'er to New Zealand and to send away her own child. The blatant Oedipal relationship between the two provides a vantage point from which to view the last part of the novel, a collection of essays written by Lei/Xie Ye to her son, Muer. At first glance this part may seem redundant. However, Gu Cheng cannot bring his narrative to an end without invoking Xie Ye's motherly tenderness. Only through Xie Ye's lullaby-like words can he complete his cycle of life and undergo the desired reincarnation of becoming a son—his wife's son.

In the first part of the novel, Gu Cheng / Lin Cheng regards Waiheke Island as a dreamland, comparing it to his castle, Peach Blossom Grove, the Country of Girls, and above all the Grand View Garden of the *Dream of the Red Chamber*. He sounds wishful when he says, "I like to see good girls get together . . . that is the only way to realize my love"; "I cannot love but I can hate, for the world has ruined girls"; "I am not in love; rather I am dreaming a world of girls. My love is nothing compared to this dream."[102] Ying'er's participation in his life with Lei / Xie Ye represents a dream come true. For a while, he feels Ying'er and his wife are becoming more alike, and he enjoys watching the two women as a spectator.

Even at the peak of this utopian life, however, Lin Cheng / Gu Cheng flirts with a death wish. "When we are deeply in love, death is a common call," he writes, and he praises Ying'er for "her understanding that love can only be consummated in death."[103] Paradoxically enough, Ying'er eventually helps fulfill his wish by betraying him. She "ruined not only my life but also the deepest root of my life, my dream."[104] Suicide is the only way out.

Gu Cheng's delirious ramblings about dreams, love, death, and a land of girls ready to do his pleasure have already drawn many feminist attacks. Chen Bingliang has analyzed Gu Cheng's narcissism from the perspective of Freudian psychoanalysis and myth criticism. He suggests that as a Chinese Narcissus, Gu Cheng cannot love anything but his own reflection. Just as in the Greek myth, his self-love cannot be materialized by any objective other, so he finds in death his last reunion with himself.[105] Death, accordingly, is the symbolic return to the mother's womb, the primordial site of darkness and rest.

While these theoretical analyses are well argued, what intrigues me is that Gu Cheng seemed to have anticipated his critics with his self-analysis, as if he meant to mock what would eventually be said about him. Thus from another character's viewpoint he writes about himself:

> He is a madman in a clever disguise. His fantasy and his capacity to realize his fantasy have reached the state of madness. He wants to do away with everything in the world, all men, all the male-controlled world, society, even procreation and nature, including himself. He challenges the world and destroys all rules on behalf of masquerading shyness and death. This reflects a mixture of rationality and madness, and it scares me. When he understands his own madness and absurdity, and uses his rationality in the service of his madness, pushing life to extremities, he is not merely mad. He is a devil![106]

In the epilogue, Gu Cheng again dissects himself by calling attention to his "immature personality, like a lonely and eccentric kid," his "fear of living a normal life," his fascination with "grotesque, outlandish, or licentious hallucinations," and his "irrational possessive desire." "He builds around himself a wall, cursing silently or loudly, hearing nothing but echoes of his own words." "He stubbornly isolates himself and ruins himself."[107]

Conventional wisdom tells us that a suicidal narrator cannot narrate his own death and the closure of such a story can only be expressed by his silence—death. Insofar as Gu Cheng always deems himself in living death, he enacts in his narrative a perception of the present viewed as the past from a future time. In other words, his suicide is to be viewed as a revisitation of the death that has always already informed his life. In contrast to the romantic discourse of suicide—self-assertion through self-annihilation—Gu Cheng's death does not bring so much an assertion of the romantic subject as the re-presentation of a phantom. His confessional narrative exudes a beguiling translucency, as if he had emptied out, on behalf of himself as well as his expected critics, whatever possessed him. His is a vision of nothingness:

Ghost has neither father nor mother
neither son nor grandson
ghost is neither crazy nor dumb

the raindrops that just fell
are contained in a bowl
ghost knows by merely a glance at them
they are the eyes he winked just now

Spectrality and specularity are intertwined in Gu Cheng's preview of his death. After the poet actually commits suicide, his novel serves as a post-narrative, unfolding what would in life remain unfinished. If this sounds familiar, it is because in a most unlikely manner Gu Cheng seems to have acted out postmodernist theories he did not care about. His narrative strongly suggests what Jean-François Lyotard calls a "future anterior" tense, seeing oneself with the world as having died yet still continuing to exist.[108] By making *Ying'er* the anticlimax of his career, he makes his poetry subject to metanarrativity and his death a simulacrum.[109] What ensues is the endless play of doubles of ghostly (self-)images. This game of doubling proliferates along with the progression—or regression—of the novel, with Ying'er and Gu Cheng, Gu Cheng and Xie Ye, Ying'er and Xie Ye, Gu Cheng and Muer, and Gu Cheng and his multiple selves each mirroring the other's image, voice, desire.

Nevertheless, that the real Xie Ye was murdered by the real Gu Cheng introduces an unwelcome aporia into the poet's prescripted meanings. This aporia brings us to a cluster of questions on the ethics of writing and reading Gu Cheng. By ethics I do not merely mean the differentiation of Xie Ye as the victim and Gu Cheng as the victimizer, a view held by the "moral majority." Rather I mean the heated debates that drive one to renegotiate the relations between poetics, individual fate, and social agency in the era of post-Mao-Dengism.[110] Immediately after Gu Cheng and Xie Ye's death, questions were raised such as: didn't Xie Ye plant the seeds of her own death by spoiling Gu Cheng all those years? Can't Gu Cheng be partially pardoned because he was a talented poet driven into despair by circumstances? Wasn't the audience complicitous by indulging Gu Cheng's eccentricity—even his death wish—during his lifetime and feasting upon the gory spectacle after his death?[111] Finally, is the violence in Gu Cheng's life and poetry any less suggestive of the breakdown of his personal psychological and moral make-up than it is of the outbreak of an inherited Maoist legacy, as hinted by Michelle Yeh? Each of these questions entertains a set of ambiguities; merely to circumscribe them would have been impossible within Maoist discourse. It is readers engaging themselves in these ambiguities, trying to come to terms with their consequences and reaching no absolute answer, that would mark the rise of an episteme that might be called the Chinese postmodern.

CODA

In June 1971, Gu Cheng, in exile with his father, wrote a short poem entitled "Wuming de xiaohua" (Nameless flowers):

> Wildflowers:
> starlight, here and there,
> fallen buttons
> scattered by the roadside
>
> Nameless flowers,
> my poems
> open quietly
> in the season's wind and rain
> amid the desolation of humanity . . .[112]

Earlier that year, Wen Jie had committed suicide because his poems were denigrated as poisonous weeds in disservice to the people. It was a tough time for Chinese literati, as thousands of writers and intellectuals were sent to cadre schools for reeducation. "Amid the desolation of humanity," the adolescent poet was cultivating his own works like "nameless flowers" that "open quietly/ in the season's wind and rain." The poem is admittedly immature, but it reminds us of the title of Lu Xun's collection of prose poetry, *Yecao* (Wild grass), particularly the prologue, where Lu Xun also compares his works to wildflowers. It reveals a lonely heart in search of a tranquility of its own. Thus, in both style and vision the poem cuts against the grain of the poetics of the sublime represented by the generation of Gu Gong and Wen Jie.

Wen Jie could not have conceived such a poetics; he was driven to write by his passion for the party and the people. In so doing he may not have thought any the less of his passion for poetry, but he believed in the immediate sublimation of personal vision into communal truth. Nevertheless, *because* of his forbidden love for Dai Houying and his subsequent suicide, Wen Jie managed to recast his own image after his death. His poems, even the most earnest pieces, take on a posthumous complexity. Still, Wen Jie's suicide can best be treated as a "classical" case in that he lived and died for a cause—a leader, a party, a beloved, or simply integrity as a poet. Suicide becomes one last sublime gesture laying claim to a unique and irreplaceable subjectivity; the only remaining way to preempt the usurpation of control by contingency.

Across the Taiwan Straits, in 1971, Shi Mingzheng was writing a series of works about his early life as a wanton poet, a life interrupted by imprisonment. Whereas Wen Jie was deeply involved in politicizing poetics and saw no conflict in his role as both cadre and poet, Shi Mingzheng tried to assert an autonomy for poetic creativity. He was, however, tricked by fate in that he ended up becoming an unlikely paragon of the political poet-martyr. Shi's case represents both the blossoming of Taiwanese modernism and its historical predicament. For years he tried to take shelter in dandyism—devilism, in his expression—only to realize that the practice of pure erotics could not redeem a passion for pure poetry. Once contaminated by political coercion, poetry seemed to become only a pretext for the recollection of trauma. When he died from a "belated" suicide, he still was enacting a double role as stubborn modernist and Christian (im)moralist, his ressentiment leading him to a most dubious ending.

In 1971, Gu Cheng could not have been fully aware of the reasons for Wen Jie's fatal choice, much less of Shi Mingzheng's one-man campaign for devilism. He grew up to inscribe a very different type of poetry and lived out his own kind of devilry. Partially because of his personality and partially because of his place in history, Gu Cheng's poetry pits itself against Wen Jie's while it shows a much more introverted romanticism than Shi Mingzheng's. However, if both Wen Jie and Shi Mingzheng can be said to have died to achieve a plenitude of their own, in Gu Cheng one finds an anachronistic pastiche of wishes. He can be read as a poet mortgaging his death so as to live, like a living dead; a post-Mao Chinese man dreaming the pre-Mao (or Mao's own) dream of polygamy and the male-centered household;[113] a publicity maker gaining fame by shunning the crowd; a late-twentieth-century Werther come back from his fictional suicide to murder his beloved before committing a second, "real" suicide; a modernist who by chance ushers us into a postmodernist world.[114] Although he proclaimed his philosophy of nothingness throughout his life, Gu Cheng was inundated by the multiple images he, by accident or by design, created for himself by the time he took his life.

Gu Cheng's death thus seemed to signal the end of a poetics of suicide begun by literati like Zhu Xiang, Chen Sanli, and Wang Guowei at the beginning of the twentieth century. But this poetics could not really come to an end without canceling its own logic. Think again of Xie Ye, who died an unexpected death in tandem with Gu Cheng's suicide, thereby spoiling the poet's otherwise neat plan of self-annihilation.

Still, when speaking of gratuitous circumstances in the death of a poet, can there be a case more poignant than the murder of Dai Houying in 1996? Twenty-five years after the suicide of her beloved Wen Jie, Dai lost her life—but purely by accident, as a result of a quarrel with a remote relative over a matter of money. The leading promoter of *The Death of a Poet* after the Cultural Revolution, Dai Houying served as a witness to the ebb and flow of Cultural Fever through the 1980s. By the mid-1990s, she had watched the kind of writings she was popular for lose their market in the post-Tian'anmen cultural economy. Little could she have foreseen, however, that she would conclude her own historical role by dying in a manner so apparently irrelevant to the poetic death of Wen Jie. But this is where history makes itself acutely manifest: precisely because Dai's death was in no way a part of a scenario of historic significance, it marked the final dissipation of the early century's discourse of death and poetry. One might therefore argue, following a Baudrillardian logic, that Dai Houying's death added the crucial, authentic touch of accidentalism to post-Mao/Deng, and so to postmodern, poetics.

Chapter 8

Second Haunting

The meaning of ghost *is "that which returns."*

ERYA

In his *huaben* (storytelling) collection *Yushi mingyan* (Illustrious tales to instruct the world, 1620), Feng Menglong (1574–1646) relates a story, "Yang Siwen Yanshan feng guren" (An encounter of Yang Siwen and old acquaintances in Yanshan), which takes place three years after the fall of the Northern Song dynasty to the Nüzhen Tartars (1129 A.D.). On the night of the Lantern Festival that year, the protagonist Yang Siwen runs into a familiar woman. Like many northerners who failed to flee to the south after the fall, Yang has submitted to Tartar rule and is making a modest living in Yanshan, the new capital. The woman he encountered at the Lantern Festival turns out to be Zheng Yiniang, the wife of his sworn-brother Han Sishou. Yang learns from Yiniang that she and her husband were separated on their way south and she ended up becoming a maid in an aristocratic household. It then happens that Han Sishou comes to Yanshan as part of a diplomatic mission from the Southern Song court. When by coincidence Yang and Han meet, to Yang's great amazement Han confides that his wife Yiniang has died.

What is related next confirms one's suspicions. After falling into the hands of a Tartar general, Yiniang committed suicide. The reunion of Yiniang and Han Sihou marks the most touching moment of the story. Death could not prevent her from returning to the world in the form of a ghost to rejoin Yang Siwen and her husband.[1] Asked by Yang Siwen about the true nature of her Yanshan companions, Yiniang sighs,

> In the times of peace, men and ghosts are kept apart,
> In a world like ours, men and ghosts mingle freely.[2]

Zheng Yiniang's words touch on one of the most important motifs of the classical Chinese ghost tale, whether in the vernacular or in literary tradition: at times of chaos or *luanshi,* the world is so disturbed as to unleash the forces of both social and cosmological transgression. "An Encounter of Yang Siwen and Old Acquaintances" is based on the Song *huaben* story "Huigujia" (Casket of ashes), which in turn is based on Hong Mai's (1123–1202) "Taiyuan Yiniang" (Yiniang of Taiyuan) in the *Yijianzhi*.[3] As scholars point out, this story gives a highly realistic account of life in northern China after the Tartar takeover.[4] Through numerous references to the old days in Bianliang (Dongjing), the capital of the Northern Song, it evokes the nostalgia for a lost era and a fallen dynasty.[5] What immediately strikes one is that critics could term "realistic" a world that is most emphatically populated with ghosts. This puts into question the supposed opposition between the realistic and the fantastic.

After Yiniang's return to the human world, we are told, the two male protagonists are painfully awakened to an irredeemable loss. The reality they now inhabit is to them but a phantom existence in comparison to the memory of things forever lost. Indeed, the Chinese title of the story, "Yang Siwen Yanshan feng guren," contains a pun: "guren" can be understood as "old acquaintances," but it is also a homonym for *guren,* "the dead." At the very least, the role of the supernatural in history is its subjective reality, as the dead are mourned by the living.

Given Zheng Yiniang's comment that ghosts return to and haunt the human world especially at times of chaos, one may make a rather ironic observation with regard to ghosts and their historicity in premodern Chinese narrative. The profusion of ghost stories throughout the whole of Chinese literature must indicate that how rare are times of peace and how rarely human beings and ghosts have been kept apart. The continued reappearance of ghosts in Chinese literature is then a reminder of the incessant calamities of Chinese history. Across corporeal and temporal-spatial barriers, ghosts reappear like vanishing memories and perished relations, "disembodying" the hiatus between the dead and the living, the unreal and the real, the unthinkable and the admissible. Thus, instead of serving merely as an index to ancient superstition, the ghost story brings itself directly to bear upon the contested issue of history and realism in premodern Chinese narrative. The historical validity of ghost stories forces a reevaluation of the intricate relations between the modes of verisimilitude and conceptions of history and historicity.

The ghost tale reached its first climax as early as the Six Dynasties period,[6] and it underwent several major transformations in the following centuries.[7] The Ming and Qing eras witnessed a revived interest among literati and popular raconteurs alike in narrating the ghostly. In the classical narrative tradition, one can trace out a genealogy that includes tales from at least as far back as *Jiandeng xinhua* (New stories written while trimming the wick, ca.

1378), *Jiandeng yuhua* (More stories written while trimming the wick, 1420), *Mideng yihua* (Stories written while searching for a lamp, 1592), *Liaozhai zhiyi* (Liaozhai's record of the strange, 1679), *Zibuyu* (What the master [Confucius] would not discuss, ca. 1781), *Yuewei caotang biji* (Jottings from the thatched abode of close observations, 1798), and *Yeyu qiudenglu* (Writings done in the rainy nights and under the autumn lamp, 1895). In the vernacular tradition, one can find even more examples, ranging from the collections of the *Sanyan* (*Yushi mingyan, Jingshi tongyan* [Comprehensive tales to admonish the world, 1624], and *Xingshi hengyan* [Lasting tales to awaken the world, 1627]) to the *Erpai* (*Chuke paian jingqi; Erke paian jingqi* [Striking the table in amazement at the wonders; first and second editions], 1628, 1632) and from the bulk of *shenmo* fiction (fiction about gods and demons) and late Qing fantasies. Granting the manifest diversity in style, theme, plotting, discursive rationale, and worldview, scholars have noticed in these works an increasing tendency to "mingle the human and the ghostly." The conflation of the nonhuman and all-too-human qualities in Ming and Qing narrative accounts about ghosts even furnished the necessary repertoire for writers' configuration of this-worldly affairs. As Lu Xun noticed, Ming fiction about gods and demons *(shenmo xiaoshuo)* thrived alongside fiction about social manners *(shiqing xiaoshuo);* and in the late Ming and early Qing ghost novellas, there arose a remarkable confluence of ghostly and human motifs.[8] Ghost fiction, in Lu Xun's opinion, was a precursor of Qing social satire.[9]

This tradition nevertheless came to a halt in the modern era. In the wake of the May Fourth movement, authentic modern literature was expected to highlight themes such as enlightenment and revolution, and "art for the sake of *life*" became the guideline for progressive writers. In a discourse largely modeled after nineteenth-century European canons of realism, ghosts, together with other supernatural beings, find no place.[10] Ghosts were associated with obsolete superstition, feudal practices, or merely a decadent imagination, and were thus impediments to modern epistemological and ideological advancement. In a poem to Mei Guangdi (1890–1945) in 1915, Hu Shi (1891–1962), then studying in the United States, had already envisaged the revival of Chinese literature in terms of exorcism: "Chinese literature has withered for too long . . . let us summon like-minded friends . . . flogging and expelling the whole carriage of ghosts, and welcome the arrival of the new era."[11] With an equal fervor, Guo Moruo (1892–1978) wrote to Zong Baihua (1897–1986) in Japan in 1920 that "I used to live like a ghost in Hell; I will live in a bright world from now on, as a human being."[12] Guo may have been inspired by Ibsen's *The Ghosts,* which had been translated into Chinese the year before.[13]

It was nevertheless Zhou Zuoren (1885–1967) who summarized the intellectual ethos of the time when he proclaimed the importance of "Ren de wenxue" (Literature of the human) in 1921.[14] In the following years Zhou would doggedly launch attacks on anything related to the ghostly. "Who are our enemies," asked Zhou in 1924, "but the beasts and ghosts—the beasts and ghosts that have lived off us human creatures?"[15] And speaking of life-and-death war against the spectral world, one can find no more dramatic a statement than this one made by Hu Shi:

> Let me rip open my heart and explain to the world: it is only because I believed perfectly well that in the "pile of rotten paper" are numberless old ghosts who can eat people and cast a spell over people. For the harm they can do, they are much more deadly than the germs discovered by Pasteur. But it is also because I believe that though I am powerless against the germs, I take pride in my ability to "chain the demons and subdue the ghosts."[16]

Hu Shi's antighost theory was to culminate in his condemnation of the "five ghosts" in 1930—poverty, disease, ignorance, corruption, and chaos. With this imagery he epitomized the agenda of the Chinese Enlightenment.[17]

The modern campaign to exorcise the ghosts haunting China was charged with even more power in the period of revolutionary literature. The most remarkable manifesto is perhaps from the climax of the play *Bai Maonü* (White-haired girl, 1946): "The old society turned human beings into ghosts; the new society turns ghosts into human beings."[18] But despite Communist crackdowns, ghosts kept creeping back into China, and worse, they seem to have multiplied in number after the founding of the new republic. *Bupagui de gushi* (Stories defying the superstition of ghosts), edited by He Qifang (1912–1977), was a popular compilation in the 1950s. In 1963, when Meng Chao's (1902–1976) new Beijing opera, *Li Huiniang* (1961), was banned by Jiang Qing, the charge was that the play inculcated the dangerous principle that "ghosts do humanity no harm" *(yougui wuhai)*.[19] The banning of *Li Huiniang*, it will be recalled, was a prelude to the Great Cultural Revolution; during that time, the resounding slogan was "Down with ox-ghosts and snake-spirits."

This context causes one to pay special attention to the vigorous return of ghosts to elite and popular Chinese culture in the 1980s. The ghostly malady broke out first in Taiwan and Hong Kong, as illustrated by the immense popularity of fiction about the bizarre and the otherworldly by writers such as Sima Zhongyuan and Ni Kuang.[20] Ghosts and ghost-related subjects—possession, haunting, exorcism, predestination, retribution, visits to Hell, and so on—are preferred subjects of popular media, from television soap operas to movies, and from radio talk shows to newspaper columns. Most notably, the last decade of the twentieth century saw the return of various kinds of ghost narratives on the mainland, which had reportedly been cleansed of all nonhuman and inhuman creatures. Among the top-ranking writers, whereas Can Xue and Han Shaogong insinuate in many of their works fantastic elements by means of eerie symbolism and unearthly settings, Su Tong, Mo Yan, Jia Pingwa, Lin Bai, Wang Anyi, and Yu Hua, among others, simply use ghosts. The landscape of fin-de-siècle Chinese fiction is once again haunted by goblins, spirits, apparitions, and phantoms; and one can hear echoes of Zheng Yiniang's words from almost eight hundred years before: "In a world like ours, human beings and ghosts mingle freely."

One may argue that the recent ghost fever corresponds to the importation of Western fantastic discourse from the Gothic romance to magical realism, or more generally, that it reflects a global outburst of the fin-de-siècle imaginary. But it is perhaps more apropos to note that the premodern Chinese ghost narrative tradition has made a comeback in the postmodern literary scene. In particular, as writers enthusiastically borrow characters, themes, and plots from works ranging from the *Sanyan* collections to *Liaozhai's Records of the Strange,* they find themselves mingling with the literary ghosts of the Ming and Qing. While this borrowing again vividly demonstrates the literary recapitulation of tradition, what concerns me is the changing aesthetics and politics of fantasy and realism behind such a recapitulation. From the vantage point of the interplay between ghost narrative and historical memory in premodern narrative tradition, one must ask certain questions: to what extent can specters of the past be summoned back to bear witness to the atrocities of the present? How does the late twentieth-century ghost story testify to the capricious link between violence and corporeality? If ghosts thrive in a time of troubles, a *luanshi,* why then did they fail to appear more frequently in the first eight decades of the twentieth century, a time so full of man-made and natural disasters in comparison to our own time? Can there be a homeland so menacing that it even frightens away its ghosts? The disappearance and return of ghosts in twentieth-century Chinese fiction makes us want to amend Zheng Yiniang's words:

> In a time when war is called peace, even ghosts fear to mingle with men,
> In a world like ours, men and ghosts can mingle freely again.

WRITING AS REVENANT

Etymologically, the Chinese character for "ghost," or *gui,* partakes of the connotation of "return," or *gui;* hence the interpretation in *Erya:* "the meaning of *ghost* is 'that which returns.'"[21] "Return" in this context indicates "return home"; but, contrary to common wisdom, "home" refers not to an abode in the human world but to the site of eternal rest. If life is seen as a temporary sojourn among the living, death represents a return to the source from which all creatures have come. References to the relations between "ghost" and "that which returns" can be found in *Zuozhuan* ("If ghosts have an abode to return to, they will not cause terror") and *Liji* ("All creatures are destined to die; they return to the earth after death, and that is what 'ghost' means").[22]

While death indicates a "homecoming," what remains understated here is that this "return" presupposes a departure—departure from all those human traits that came with living. Ghosts have not yet returned to this home of all things, simply because they have not put off all their humanity. Ghosts reappear because they still long for home: they retain the human meaning of "returning." Between the condition we are all destined to return to and the home we are reluctant to leave, there is a paradox that cannot be more emphatically presented than in the numerous stories about the return of ghosts. It is natural to die, but it is also natural not to want to be dead. When the order of nature is put in question, then there will be more traffic between men and ghosts, who in their natures question Nature.

In the case of "An Encounter of Yang Siwen with Old Acquaintances," Zheng Yiniang comes back to the human world because she cannot let go of her passion for her husband and the life they had shared in the last glorious days of the Northern Song. But we are soon reminded that Yiniang can return neither to her home nor to her home country, both ruined during the Tartar wars, and that she is reunited with Han Sishou in the "barbarian" capital Yanshan rather than in the old Song capital Bianliang (or the new Song capital in the south). In addition, forever underscored by the line that cuts between the world of life and that of death, her reunion can only be a phantom reenactment of the good old days, a ghostly revisitation of a world that is no longer extant. Yiniang's return thus indicates not so much a moment of wish fulfillment as its default. Between the world of the living and that of the dead, a fold in time has occurred, and it is in that parallel time that the unspeakable catastrophe—the loss of nation, capital, home, and the beloved—has taken place. Time has been considered in such a way that it alienates both nature and the individual's search for plenitude in the way of nature.

What happens when the old theme, "the ghost is 'that which returns,'" returns in late-twentieth-century Chinese fiction? Take a look at Hang Shaogong's (b. 1956) acclaimed story "Guiqulai" (Homecoming, 1983). Situated after the Great Cultural Revolution, the story relates a man's visit to a village he believes he has never been in before. Yet the village looks familiar to him; its natural and cultural setting, residents, customs, and even animals remind him of the place where he was exiled as *zhiqing* (educated youth) during the revolution. Had the local people not addressed him using the wrong name, the protagonist might well have brought himself to treat this strange encounter as an actual homecoming event. A sense of déjà vu abounds. The climax is the protagonist's encounter with a girl who claims to be his beloved's sister. She tells this man that his old sweetheart has died.

"Homecoming" has often been discussed either as a climax of the literature of the scarred *(shanghen wenxue)* or as a harbinger of root-seeking *(xungen)* fiction. What has been ignored is that it is narrated within the conventions of the ghost story. The Chinese title of the story, "Guiqulai," is a pun on the famed poem "Guiqulai ci" (Homecoming) by Tao Qian (365–427). But for someone writing in the aftermath of the Great Cultural Revolution, "Homecoming" does not evoke ancient, reclusive withdrawal into a familial refuge; rather it indicates a nightmarish withdrawal into a locus of memory utterly familiar and yet utterly strange. Playing with the instruments of Freudian analysis, one might read the story as recapturing an uncanny experience, a horrific sensation that results from the confusion of homely and unhomely memories.[23]

Across the Taiwan Straits, Zhu Tianxin (b. 1958) wrote a novella entitled *Gudu* (Ancient capital, 1997), in which a woman writer (not unlike Zhu herself) returns from a trip to Kyoto to Taipei, only to realize that if looked at from the perspective of a Japanese tourist, the city so familiar to her could feel threateningly foreign. Roaming the streets and alleys by following a city map from the Japanese colonial period, the woman is struck by an eerie feeling that fin-de-siècle Taipei is no more than a dumping ground for its fragmented pasts, a place where ghosts find no resting place. Her homecoming has become a voyage into the heart of darkness.

Zhu Tianxin has been known for creating galleries of characters called *lao linghun,* or "old souls"—jaded city dwellers who see through everything at too young an age to carry on their lives into maturity as they should. Zhu, an "old soul" par excellence, has an agenda of her own, however. Born into a mainland Chinese émigré family, she comes to realize that the Nationalist orthodoxy she and her family believed in might have been illusory from the outset, when Nativist forces were increasingly denigrating all that was not "pure" and indigenous. Doubly alienated, she thus sees in Taipei a space where memory has failed and history has been derailed. All that remains is vacuity, breeding amnesia as much as anamnesis.

In contrast to Zhu's modern-day Taipei are her continued references to the Peach Blossom Grove, a utopian site conceived by (again) Tao Qian. But on examination one wonders: wouldn't the Peach Blossom Grove prove to be an equally false promise, because it too is a site outside of history and remembrance? Zhu Tianxin's "old souls" are thus creatures harboring memories of "home" yet finding nowhere to return.[24]

Neither "Homecoming" nor *Ancient Capital* introduces any ghost characters, but no reader could fail to notice their miasmic ambiance. While no ghost returns to the human world to witness the passage of time, as in the case of a premodern story like "An Encounter of Yang Siwen," neither protagonist can help but be drawn down into the sunken passageways of a bygone world, a world of the absent. Through his or her involuntary revisitation of the past, images of what may have been and what used to be are called upon to form a momentary illusion of the palpable—a phantom dimensionality, like the illusion of depth in a stereoscope. This scopic duplicity, when coupled with the protagonist's incapacity for naming and being named, further accentuates the breakdown of the representational system in Han's and Zhu's works. As their respective narratives become increasingly inscrutable, the protagonists are trapped in a limbo of sensory and cognitive uncertainty—the very atmosphere in which ghostly illusions can be expected to appear.

This observation leads us to rethink the issue of writing as revenant in late-twentieth-century Chinese fiction. Take Yu Hua's (b. 1960) "Gudian aiqing" (Classical romance, 1987), for example. As its title suggests, this story is inspired by classical talent and beauty *(caizi jiaren)* fiction, and Yu Hua lavishes the clichés one is expected to find in the genre: a chance encounter between a talented scholar and a beautiful girl, a nocturnal liaison, and a romance that seems to promise a happy ending. But what happens next is anything but a faithful recapitulation of the conventions. Three years after their separation, the scholar is reunited with his beauty in the midst of a famine. The beauty is found in a tavern, not as a guest to be served but as a dish to be prepared, her limbs chopped off to order. No sooner does the scholar purchase the dying beauty than she asks him to terminate her existence, and their romance is consummated in a mercy killing.

Yu Hua parodies the *caizi jiaren* convention by literally mutilating its idealized characters and conventions.[25] Through such radical appropriation, he may be indicating the gruesome force of violence that can erupt at any historical time and the absurdity of any human making sense of such an eruption. However, the ultimate violence in his story derives not from the presentation of the ghoulish action as such, but from the lack of any affective consequence. Yu Hua is said to have been fascinated with the concept of eroticism in George Bataille's *The Tears of Eros,* particularly the tie between eroticism and violence, which culminates in death.[26] While Yu Hua may reveal his indebtedness to the French writer by invoking an unlikely festivity in the scholar's killing of the beauty, this bloody scene is not shocking, for by this time his story is so loaded with irrationality that even the most gruesome episode has become routine.[27]

This is where the conventions of the ghost tale are brought to bear on a paradox: the unpredictable is already implicated in the all-too-predictable. The scholar becomes so obsessed with his beloved that he gives up his career to remain by her tomb. Then, to no one's surprise, the beauty returns and offers herself to the scholar, thus resuming their affair. Driven by curiosity, the scholar opens the beauty's tomb, where he finds the flesh of her body almost as fresh as when she was alive. But the ghost girl is now forced to leave the scholar for good because he has fatally interrupted the process of restoration.

My purpose, however, is not merely to point out that Yu Hua recapitulates a classical gothic tale. In calling upon the apparitions of the past, I argue, Yu Hua's narrative is itself a half-hearted revival of a genre pronounced dead by Maoist literary history. A genealogical survey of Yu Hua's story brings us to "Li Zhongwen nü" (The daughter of Li Zhongwen) in Tao Qian's *Soushen houji* (Sequel to "In search of the supernatural"), in which the dead daughter of Li Zhongwen returns to life and falls in love with the young man Zhang Shizhi.[28] The couple's affair ends abruptly when the girl's tomb is exhumed (by her father), and thus her chance of resurrection is denied forever. "The Daughter of Li Zhongwen," it will be recalled, is a source of Tang Xianzu's (1550–1617) *chuanqi* play *Mudanting* (Peony Pavilion, 1599), which in turn served as a protomodel of the talent/beauty genre.[29]

More polemically, through reviving the convention by parodying—ghosting—it, Yu Hua's writing prods one to ponder the spectral dimension of narrativity, which calls attention to the ties between narrative, the repetition impulse, and the death wish.[30] I have in mind the psychoanalytical mechanism that makes narrative a ploy to preempt death—a precondition of all humanity—by rehearsing it.[31] A warp in time is said to have occurred in such a narrative endeavor, for its preemptive effort is based on an unlikely foreknowledge of posteriority. Accordingly, writing can no longer be seen as an affirmation of life force and plenitude, as conventional (Maoist) realism would have it, but rather is an elegiac anticipation, a haunted mimicry, of the desired state of reality that is nullification. Thus, before any actual ghost makes its appearance, a ghostly discontent permeates Yu Hua's writing. No surprise that his romance, in the sense both of the narrated love affair and of the narration of the love affair, should evaporate into the vacuity of formulaic melancholy.

Speaking of describing and thus enacting the return of a revenant, can writers of other Chinese communities ever emulate those in Hong Kong at the end of the last century who bore witness to Hong Kong's *Return* (or *huigui*)? In writings by Li Bihua (Lillian Lee), one of the most popular Hong Kong romance writers, "return" is treated both as a gothic motif and as an uncanny effect of writing,[32] both as historical inevitability and as supernatural doom. In *Yanzhi kou* (Rouge, 1985), later made popular by Stanley Kwan's 1988 film adaptation,[33] the ghost of Fleur, a courtesan of the 1930s, returns to 1980s

Hong Kong to look for her lover who survived their double suicide attempt half a century before. Not unlike Yiniang of the Song dynasty, Fleur crosses the gap between life and death, hoping to be reunited not only with her beloved but with the time and space in which their romance thrived. Nevertheless, her return ends more bleakly than that narrated in the Song story, not because she can no longer retrieve her lost love—she does locate him in the end—but because an attempted retrieval, even when it works, no longer matters in the new historical context.[34]

This sense of gratuitous achievement underscores the novel's logic of imaginary nostalgia, homesickness for an object that is already suspected of inauthenticity.[35] With her death and spectral return, Fleur paradoxically "personifies" love and trust over time as imagined virtues, ghostly gifts. In the context of 1980s Hong Kong, where the official promise that "nothing will change for fifty years" only reminded the reluctant colony of its uneasy expectations, *Rouge* may even beg a political reading: thriving by living on borrowed time in a borrowed place, was Hong Kong likely to prosper by submitting to historical inevitability and demographic insignificance?

Li Bihua's treatment of the ghostly return was followed by a cluster of works that appeared after the 1997 Return. In Chen Guanzhong's (b. 1952) *Shenmo dou meiyou fasheng* (Nothing has happened at all, 1999), the narrator looks back at his business adventures and romantic rendezvous on the first anniversary of Hong Kong's Return, and comes to realize the emptiness of both. "Nothing has happened at all," sighs this man whose life story parallels Hong Kong's history of the preceding half century. Even the Return has not brought any changes. What he does not make clear until the end of the novel, however, is that at the moment his recollection starts, he has already been fatally wounded in a gangster accident on July 1, 1998, and that before his narrative reaches its end, he will be dead. The novel therefore turns out to be a Hong Kong ghost's commemoration of his life story in the post-Return era, which amounts to the return to, and of, nothingness.[36]

The spectrality of the Return strikes a more menacing note in Huang Biyun's (b. 1961) fiction. Her indulgence in violence and sadomasochistic drama recalls Yu Hua.[37] For our purposes here, she is at her most chilling when she pictures the demise of Hong Kong even before the Return. Huang draws her inspiration freely from diverse periods, genres, and national traditions, showing no qualms about yoking them together to create bizarre doublings. Thus, characters borrowed from the fiction of Lu Xun and Eileen Chang mingle in front of an anachronistic backdrop, and Western masters from Sartre to Fellini act as muses to a Chinese Theater of the Absurd.[38] But the most striking feature of Huang's stories is their recycling of the same group of characters throughout her writing, regardless of their fate at the end of individual stories, as if they were going through repeated reincarnations. The eternal return of these characters induces the reader to muse about repetitions and hauntings, in which the present is ominously independent of the past.

I have discussed the way writers from Taiwan and mainland China at the end of the twentieth century have presented the ghostly effects of déjà vu, of uncanny re-visions of the past. Hong Kong writers, by contrast, create a ghostly effect of *déjà disparu,* an uncanny pre-vision of the future. This effect of *déjà disparu,* as Ackbar Abbas argues, via theories taken from Paul Virilio and others, refers to a "feeling that what is new and unique about the situation is always already gone, and we are left holding a handful of clichés, or a cluster of memories of what has never been."[39] If history is an invisible power that forestalls any difference between human and nonhuman constructs, it does not matter whether the ghost returns or not. These Hong Kong writers, like the Hong Kong critic Abbas, thus cast a revenant-like shadow of Return, nay, of Eternal Return, that for them darkens their fate, and Hong Kong's.[40]

THE GHOST IN REALISM

The return of the ghosts to late-twentieth-century fictional narrative leads us to rethink the problematic of realism, which constitutes the most powerful narrative format in modern Chinese literature. Realism, as defined in terms of nineteenth-century European models by such writers as Balzac, Dickens, Tolstoy, and Zola, was once hailed as the key to representing Chinese culture in search of the modern. I have argued elsewhere that this valorization of realism does not merely indicate a paradigm shift regarding narrative format; rather it forms a crucial part of the literati's cultural-intellectualist approach to Chinese crises: a conviction that China's problem stemmed solely from the break in cultural/intellectual coherence and could be solved only in immanent, holistic terms.[41] Both rhetorically and conceptually, a renovated narrative paradigm like realism was regarded as a prerequisite for reflecting and rectifying reality. In Roland Barthes's words, "a mode of writing is an act of historical solidarity."[42]

At the center of this modern realist discourse is the imperative of exorcism. As mentioned above, Hu Shi's famous call to "chain the demons and subdue the ghosts" encapsulates the ethos of the enlightened literati. But if one looks into what the demons and ghosts are exactly, ambiguous ramifications surface. The enlightened literati's continued need to designate and exclude "demons and ghosts" of the past and present forms an integral part of realist discourse across the century. This trend of laying a realist claim to the territory of the imaginary realm of the ghostly can be traced as far back as the Qing period. I have in mind a group of late Ming and early Qing works, including *Pingyao zhuan* (Quelling the ghosts, ?), *Zhangui zhuan* (A romance of devil-killing, 1688), and *Pinggui zhuan* (A romance of cracking down on ghosts, 1785?),[43] as well as *Hedian* (What sort of book is this? 1820?). These works, mostly novellas, inherit the traits of the earlier *shenmo* novels, featuring monstrous figures, supernatural props, and fantastic episodes. But compared with familiar examples such as *Xiyou ji* (Journey to the west) and *Fengshen zhuan* (Investiture of the gods), they are characterized by a degradation of fantastic motivation to the human or subhuman level, whether in characterization, plot, setting, or symbolism, and by a distinct penchant for black humor focused on human foibles.[44] These comic ghost novellas are intended less to generate an autonomous world of the supernatural than to evoke macabre and humorous parallels between the other world and this one. Human fixations, vanity, injustice, and corruption are supposedly examined through the prism of mortality in order to induce sardonic laughter. Hence Lu Xun's discussion of these works under the category of "the novel of satire."

Literally a "ghostly" genre, comic ghost fiction drifts somewhere between social satire and supernatural fantasy. Its capacity to conjure up a nonhuman world with all-too-human motifs nevertheless anticipates many of the traits of late Qing fictional realism. In my discussion in *Fin-de-siècle Splendor* of the changing mode of late Qing narrative, I suggested that to communicate their grotesque vision of social absurdities and corruption, exposé writers such as Li Boyuan (1867–1906) and Wu Jianren (1866–1910) must have taken their inspiration from fiction about the strange and the supernatural. By comparing the human world to that of ghosts, monsters, and other supernatural beings, these writers encourage their readers to approach their works as if they derived from the fantastic tradition, although the settings suggest otherwise. Wu Jianren's preface to *Ershinian mudu zhi guaixianzhuang* (Eyewitness reports of strange things from the past twenty years, 1910) demands that one see contemporary society as inhabited by monsters and ghosts. Not surprisingly, *Eyewitness Reports* has another title, *Renjian wangliang zhuan* (A tale of demons and devils in the human world). In the last chapter of his novel *Guanchang xianxing ji* (Exposure of officialdom, 1905), Li Boyuan concludes that his book "unleashes all the monsters, devils, ghosts, and ogres."[45]

The late Qing exposé writers' play with the ghostly quality in human subjects brought to the fore the crisis in representation of their time. When things are seen as having lost their "nature," whether called ontological belief, episteme, ideology, or merely sensory objectivity, it is difficult to achieve "an effect of the real" without at the same time undermining the credibility of the entire representational system. To the extent that they appear unfailingly as impostors, frauds, charlatans, and con men, the characters of late Qing exposés, however energetic, act out, not their "bodily potential" in the Bakhtianian sense, but their ghostly potential.[46] Assuming a "phantom axiology," they are no longer familiarly human; they are "dead souls" who thrive because of their visible insubstantiality.

The late Qing writers have traditionally been denigrated by scholars under the May Fourth influence as failing to grapple with social malaise in a "realistic" way. In fact, by collapsing conventions such as satire and ghost fiction into something unprecedented, these writers create a narrative format that not only questions the established boundaries of verisimilitude but also preempts the complacent closure of realism to be established by writers to come. The narrative of reality fashioned by late Qing exposé writers refuses to adopt a fixed notion of social evil or to genuflect before fixed icons of innocence and worth. They have far more terrifying demons to fight and far less confidence about anyone's sanctity. In contrast to the mainstream May Fourth writers, whose negative critique of society reinforced their desire for the lost plenitude of the Real, late Qing exposé writers inscribe "strange things" in a manner of "eyewitness account," only to conclude that, between what one sees and what one believes, there is always a specter of contingency. The most threatening aspect of their vision of the real comes from their and their characters' comprehension of the historical condition in which they live: they are staring at an axiological void, of which visible villainy is only a part.

The shifting perspective cultivated in late Qing exposés was pinned down in May Fourth fiction, when clairvoyant explanations of social ills and vociferous calls to arms became the hallmarks of the real. The ghosts, in their rare appearances in realist fiction of this time, serve only as counterexamples to those in traditional works. In Wang Luyan's (1901–1943) "Juying de chujia" (The wedding of Ju Ying), for instance, a funereal wedding between two dead persons is treated as a quaint relic of local superstition. In Peng Jiahuang's (1898–1933) "Huogui" (Living ghost), a haunting by a male ghost turns out to be a hoax staged by a man to cover his illicit affair with a widow. Similarly, Wu Zuxiang's "Luzhu shanfang" (Bamboo cottage) describes a female ghost who is actually a lonely widow incarcerated in an isolated building. And in Ba Jin's (b. 1904) "Gui" (Ghost), the ghost is invoked to refer to those who succumb to fate and live a life of the walking dead; in Luo Shu's (1903–1938) "Rengui he tade qi de gushi" (A story about a human ghost and his wife), a poor man is compared to a ghost when he is forced to pawn his wife to make a living.

In view of the rarity of "actual" ghosts in mainstream realist fiction, one feels doubly appreciative of works such as Xu Xu's (1908–1980) "Guilian" (Ghost love), in which a woman in the guise of a ghost arouses a writer's decadent romantic desire; Shen Congwen's (1902–1988) "Shangui" (Mountain ghost), in which a surreal story is related in the vein of the *Chuci* and the mythical beliefs of West Hunan; and Qian Zhongshu's (1910–1998) "Linggan" (Inspiration), in which a second-rate novelist's ghost is chased and chastised by the characters he created but failed to enliven with flesh and blood.

By contrast, ghosts and ghostly images are dealt with more skillfully in modern Chinese drama despite the limited number of examples. Hong Shen's (1894–1955) *Zhao Yanwang* (Yama Zhao, 1922), for instance, explores its protagonist's "heart of darkness" by mixing elements drawn from both Western Expressionist theater and traditional Chinese ghost imagery. Bai Wei's *Dachu youling ta* (Fight out of the ghost tower) likens feudal patriarchy to a haunting in a Chinese version of Ibsen's *Ghosts*. A rehashing of the familiar May Fourth formula, the play nevertheless reveals a Bai Wei who is as much repulsed as she is intrigued by the motifs of incest, madness, and death. And one wonders if Cao Yu (1910–1996) took up where Bai Wei left off when he peppered his famous melodrama *Leiyu* (Thunderstorm, 1934) with references to both Chinese and Ibsenian ghosts.

Although ghosts appear to have been kept at bay by enlightened literati, chances are that they still lurked not far behind the façade of the new literature. More intriguingly, modern Chinese writers and intellectuals cannot carry on their enlightened discourse without invoking, or even inventing, new ghosts. The most prominent case in point is Lu Xun, the bugler of Chinese literary modernity. Critics from T. A. Hsia to Leo Lee, Wang Xiaoming, and Wang Hui have repeatedly argued that, for all his efforts to redraw the boundary of the rational world, Lu Xun is fascinated with the dark domain he himself rules out, a domain haunted by funeral rites, graves, executions, ghosts, demons, and death wishes.[47] Lu Xun's fascination with the macabre and the deadly can be frequently discerned in his stories, ranging from the madman's hallucination of a cannibalistic banquet in "Kuangren riji" (The diary of a madman) to the illusory light that leads the old scholar to drown himself in "Biaguang" (White light), from the corpse with a grim smile in "Guduzhe" (The misanthrope) to Xianglin's wife's dubious question, "Is there life after a man is dead?" in "Zhufu" (New Year's sacrifice) and the specter-like characters' mourning over past passion in "Shangshi" (mourning) and "Zai jiulou shang" (In the tavern). In the wake of T. A. Hsia's study, the Japanese scholar Maruo Tuneki has even dedicated a book-length study to Lu Xun's ghostly obsession.[48] One of his controversial arguments is that the letter *Q* of "A True Story of Ah Q" refers to "gui," or ghost, and that by extension, the story describes a stereotypical Chinese as a living dead.[49]

Lu Xun's ghostly obsession is particularly evident in *Yecao* (Wild grass, 1927), a collection of prose poetry filled with surreal settings, nightmarish encounters, and "lost souls" *(yuhun),* and in *Zhaohua xishi* (Morning flowers plucked at the sunset, 1927), an essay collection permeated with reminiscences about the ghostly ambiance—including family deaths, haunted gardens, exorcism rituals, and gothic theaters—in which he grew up. Both works give an impression of Lu Xun living life retrospectively, as if he could define his existence only from the perspective of posterity. To quote Sartre out of context, Lu Xun "became [his] own obituary."[50]

Lu Xun once wrote, "I feel very unhappy about the ancient ghosts that I carry on my back. I cannot shake them off. So often do I feel a heavy weight that it depresses me."[51] He reiterates this feeling in a letter to his friend Li Bingzhong, "I have always felt that my soul is filled with something poisonous and ghostly *(guiqi).* I hate it and want to get rid of it, but I cannot."[52] Moreover, in the preface to the Russian translation of "The True Story of Ah Q," Lu Xun indicates that "layers of black clouds have always teemed before my eyes, in the midst of which are old ghosts, new ghosts, wandering ghosts, ox-headed monsters, condemned animals, and numerous incarnations. The way they are screaming or not screaming is beyond my tolerance."[53]

Thus, behind his premonition of ideological and epistemological exclusion for the unreal and the irrational, there always lurks Lu Xun's ambivalent desire to embrace what he denounces, to transgress what he confirms. In particular, T. A. Hsia calls attention to the resemblance between the world created by the master and the world of the *Mulian xi* (Mulian drama cycle), a popular folk theater dating to the Song dynasty.[54] This drama combines Buddhist teachings with hellish superstitions, festive performances with religious rituals—it is a theater that entertains through its "horror and humor."[55] Hsia notices that in his accounts of the *Mulian* drama cycle, Lu Xun holds an attitude of "doting fondness" in spite of the element of sheer absurdity in its performance. In Hsia's opinion, Lu Xun acknowledges the terror and beauty of death and the mystery of life embodied by ghost figures on and off the stage; though he could not construe the mystery of the ghosts, he never denies their power. He started his career with the hope of expelling these ghosts, only to fall so spellbound by them that with his pen "he has recreated them, and they have lived a charmed life ever since."[56]

Lu Xun is not the only modern writer who flirts with the ghostly, however. At the other end of the spectrum represented by Lu Xun stands Eileen Chang, priestess of the Shanghai decadent cult in the 1940s. Partially because of her family heritage and partially because of her personal bent in the aesthetics of desolation, Chang is at her best in recounting tales of moral aberration against the background of a stale society. These tales, though couched in realist rhetoric, constantly suggest a chilling gothic world, a world in which

> People only sense, to the point of terror, that things are not quite right in all aspects of their daily lives. People live in an era, but this era sinks like a shadow and they feel they have been abandoned. In order to prove their existence and grasp a bit of something real and quite elemental, they have no choice but to draw on their ancient memories for help, memories lived by all humanity in all eras. . . . Thus a strange feeling emerges toward surrounding reality, a suspicion that this is an absurd, ancient world, dark and shadowy, and yet bright and clear.[57]

Thus, in "Chenxiang xie: Diyilu xiang" (Ashes of sandalwood: The first incense burner), Zhang's first story, the girl Ge Weilong is seen visiting her aunt's grand mansion in Hong Kong, feeling as if she had stumbled into an "ancient, imperial tomb."[58] A naturalist account of the fall of an innocent girl in the demimonde of Hong Kong, "The First Incense Burner" nevertheless invites a reading in the vein of the ghost story. In the late critic Tang Wenbiao's words, it deals with "how a young girl steps into a haunted house, attracted to a vampire, and ends up becoming a new ghost. Ghosts hang around only with ghosts, because this is a rich, self-sufficient world, which has nothing to do with the human world."[59]

Eileen Chang's gothic imagination is equally demonstrated by works such as *Jinsuoji* (The story of the golden cangue), in which the aging female protagonist, Cao Qiqiao, behaves like a vampiress; *Yangge* (The rice-sprout song), in which the aftermath of Communist land reform is reinforced by a dance parade in celebration of a harvest year—a danse macabre; and *Chidi zhilian* (Naked earth), in which Shanghai after the Communist seizure takes on the aspect of a ghost town, with all its residents walking about like lost souls.[60]

But Chang's ultimate flirtation with the representation of the dead and the ghostly appeared in the publication of her family photo album in 1993, almost thirty years after the beginning of her life as a recluse and just two years before her death. In the album she features not only pictures of herself from childhood to middle age but also those of her parental and grandparental generations. As she puts its, "Their blood flows in me, and they will die once more when I die."[61] Zhang's remarks bring to mind Roland Barthes's observations about photographic and elegiac representation, though I doubt if Chang would have known the French critic's works. "Whether or not the subject is already dead, every photograph is a catastrophe that has already occurred,"[62] writes Barthes, uncannily anticipating Chang. "At the end of this first death, my own death is inscribed; between, nothing more than waiting."[63]

In contrast to Lu Xun, who is agonized by the unlikely temptation of the ghosts, Chang welcomes, almost in a style of jubilant nonchalance, the doomsday of the world and thus indulges in a premature eschatology. While the ghosts of Lu Xun's world were temporarily suppressed between the 1950s and the 1980s as a result of the Communist crackdown, Eileen Chang's traveled freely in other Chinese communities, so much so that one can talk about a trend of gothic writing, particularly among women writers, à la Chang. In my 1988 survey, I pointed out that this trend includes writers such as Li Ang (b. 1952), Shi Shuqing (b. 1945), Xixi (b. 1938), Li Li (b. 1948), Zhong Xiaoyang (b. 1962), and Su Weizhen (b. 1954). I asked what the ghosts and ghostlike beings in these writers' works are: are they "memories and desires quelled by the masculine power? Are they the dark forces, madness, and taboos ever rejected by the discourse of rationality? Are they ironic self-projections of modern Chinese women writers? Are they apparitions of the unnamable 'evil' as defined by Bataille?"[64] In view of the continued strength of this trend, one can add to the list more names, Zhong Ling (b. 1945), Yuan Qiongqiong (b. 1950), Lin Bai (b. 1957) and Li Zishu (b.1972), Hong Ling (b. 1971), and, as mentioned, Li Bihua and Huang Biyun.[65]

AN AESTHETICS OF PHANTASMAGORIA

Insofar as realism has gradually lost its predominant position in late-twentieth-century Chinese literature, one may question the extent to which the resurgence of the ghost and ghost-related fiction has contributed to our reconfiguration of the real. I suggest that the ghostly narrative has introduced a phantasmagoric dimension to the Chinese fin-de-siècle discourse of the real. I derive my definition of the phantasmagoric partially from "phantasmagoria," the term for a specific Western type of magic-lantern performance of the 1790s and 1800s; this device used back projection to keep the audience unaware of the lanterns, thus creating an illusion of the real.[66] Critics such as Walter Benjamin and Theodor Adorno have used the term to critique forms of inauthentic representation after 1850. Benjamin sees Paris of the Second Empire as a "modern" space in which the ordinary is turned into the spectacular and the exterior mixes with the interior, producing a figurative surplus of meaning. This urban civilization is built above all on a parade of spectral images and illusory sensations that, for Benjamin, may well be a modern magic lantern show, a phantasmagoria.[67] Taking Wagner's operas as his case in point, Adorno criticizes the composer for having turned his works into phantasmagoric ploys by "reproducing the dream world of commodity in the form of myth."[68] As commodity form begins to invade all aspects of modern life, argues Adorno, all aesthetic appearance is in danger of being transformed into "the illusion of the absolute reality of the unreal."[69]

Granting their different theoretical premises, the way Benjamin and Adorno critique the phantasmagoric condition of early modern European society reminds one of the gothic veins of Marxist discourse. This gothic vein of Marxism, in one critic's words, is "fascinated with the irrational aspects of society's processes and takes seriously a culture's ghosts and phantoms as a significant and rich field of social production rather than a mirage to be expelled."[70] Jacques Derrida added a polemical twist to this tradition in the 1990s, when he called on the "specters of Marx" amid global trends declaring the death of Marxism. Derrida holds that traditional scholarship approaches the ghost by ontologizing it, bypassing the issue of spectrality in history. "Haunting is historical . . . but it is not dated, it is never docilely given a date in the chain of precedents . . . according to the instituted order of the calendar."[71] Ghosts—"revenants," in Derrida's favored terminology—do not merely arrive from the past, but rather anticipate a repeated return in the future. One way to engage with claims of the death of Marxism, therefore, is to live on with the return of the ghosts of Marx. Instead of ontology, one acquires a "hauntology," a ghostly deconstruction of history, identity, and origin. Like a double-edged knife, Derrida's critique helps conjure up the spirit of Marxism while emptying out its own ontological infrastructure.[72]

For my part, the course of the debate from phantasmagoria to hauntology provides an additional perspective from which to unveil the reified construct of Chinese reality and realism in the twentieth century. Phantasmagoric realism—a realism ironically deriving its effect of verisimilitude from the incantation of apparitions, phantoms, hallucinations, and so on—can be regarded as a special discourse with which late-twentieth-century Chinese writers lay bare "the illusion of the absolute reality of the unreal."

Modern Chinese realism, to be sure, has been discussed in a multitude of theories and manners;[73] what I would like to stress here is its inherent assertion of a body politics of re-forming China at both national and personal levels. When early modern Chinese writers engage themselves in the realist project, they see in it a tool crucial to reconstructing the national body, and they consolidate their project by accumulating tangible social data and sensory stimuli. History presumably can be embodied as the full representation of reality.

Along with such a realist agenda arose an aesthetics of corporeality that exerts its power on the forming of the national and nationalist community. The formation of a new Chinese body was a shared cause among late Qing and early Republican enlightened literati and revolutionaries, as evinced by the strong physical premise in such campaigns as "military Chinese" *(jun guomin),* "new people" *(xinmin),* and "citizen" *(gongmin).*[74] Particularly in the tradition of revolutionary literature, from Mao Zedong's "Tiyu zhi yanjiu" (A study of physical culture, 1917) of his early days to the massive campaign for rehabilitation through labor during the Cultural Revolution, one finds a recurrent logic that links ideological correctness and physical fitness.[75]

This call for massive reform of the Chinese body finds an echo in the rightist camp too. Chiang Kai-shek and his followers launched the New Life movement *(xin sheng huo yundong)* in 1934 as a way to rejuvenate China from the circumstances of "ghostly life" *(gui shenghuo)*. As Chiang proclaimed, "modern Chinese life is one full of filth, decadence, laziness and despondency; this is not a life of humanity and it can only be called a 'ghostly life.'"[76] For Chiang and his followers, the New Life movement was aimed at fashioning a Chinese body based on the notions of "militancy, productivity, and aestheticization."[77]

The paradox implied in both the rightist and leftist campaigns for a new national body is no doubt a ghostly replacement and displacement of somatic constitution with semantic conviction. Behind the call for bodily strength lies a yearning for spiritual transformation. Hence Lu Xun's famous conclusion in his preface to *A Call to Arms* that a sturdy Chinese body needs to substantiate a sturdy Chinese soul.[78] Critics from Liu Chi-hui (Joyce Liu) to Jing Tsu have pointed out how such a yearning had become completely politicized in the 1930s, when both rightist and leftist art workers pursued a representation of the national spirit as validated by a strong body.[79] Despite their ideological antagonism, Liu argues, there existed a similar fascist impulse in both camps to aestheticize the body in the service of a superstructural premise.[80] Ban Wang describes this aestheticization of the sensuous and the physical in terms of the "figure of the sublime," which means "a discursive dynamic, a psychic mechanism, a stunning figure, a grand image of the body, or a crushing or uplifting experience from the lowest depression to the highest picture."[81]

It is in response to such a sublime discourse that phantasmagoric realism becomes both a critique and a parody. The orthodox modern Chinese realist narrative secretly entertained an illusory dimension in the concrete configuration of the real and the sublime, and the late-twentieth-century writer's exercise of the phantasmagoric calls attention to this "unrealistic" dimension by reactivating the ghost narrative. I am suggesting that among late-twentieth-century writers there is a rigorous endeavor to replace modern realism with a discourse about the "materiality of incorporeal things,"[82] which is in line with Foucault's "phantasm." For Foucault, phantasm "must be allowed to function at the limits of bodies; against bodies, because they stick to bodies and protrude from them, but also because they touch them, cut them, break them into sections, regionalize them, and multiply their surfaces; and equally, outside of bodies, because they function between bodies according to laws of proximity, torsion, and variable distance."[83]

Writing after the fall of the sublime tradition, late-twentieth-century Chinese writers find themselves roaming the ruins of history. Their wish for "homecoming"—an ontological desire for the lost origins of revolution, reality, and so on—quickly degenerates into a ghostly journey, just as in Han

Shaogong and Zhu Tianxin's works discussed above. These writers stumble before the "gate of darkness," a gate said to have been forever shut by Lu Xun and his followers, and they reopen it. Across the threshold, they enter "an absurd, ancient world" of "ancient memories" once enjoyed by Eileen Chang, and they are spellbound by the sensation that they may have never left there. Through such an encounter with the past, these writers exchange the "order of mimesis" handed down by their modern forerunners for the "seduction of simulacra."[84]

In "Zhuogui dadui" (Mission: Ghost hunt, 1997) by the Taiwanese writer Lin Yiyun (b. 1963), a small city is disturbed by the appearance of a ghost. A police squad is formed to track down the ghost, and suspects are turned in by volunteer informants: neurotics, "Communist spies," con men, deserted wives, juvenile delinquents, homeless people, and even sleepwalkers. Meanwhile, in response to public hysteria, social and cultural critics are solicited to give the media their theories about the ghost, ranging from the "oppression of women in a patriarchal society" to a "projection of the collective unconscious."

By now it is clear that this is a satire about society's enforcement of totems and taboos in response to a ghost hunt. One also suspects Lin must mean to ridicule and preempt the pomposity of any scholarly effort to "theorize" the ghost, including this research. The story nevertheless takes a new twist when a "real" ghost named Babbit turns up in the city and is amazed at its residents' pursuit of an imaginary ghost. Babbit intervenes in this chase by demonstrating "authentic" haunting, and scares no one. He eventually sees a public parade celebrating the capture of the ghost—the ghost being ghosted by an employee of the police office as it has failed to arrest the genuine one.

One can read the story as deflating society's complacency about its rational power. What makes it more interesting, however, is that Lin Yiyun may have been inspired as much by the Ming and Qing comic ghost fiction, in which ghosts have all-too-human foibles, as by the late Qing exposé, in which the human beings are more ghastly than the ghosts. But the story does not merely repeat these conventions; rather it hints that in a time like ours, the imaginary ghost is needed more than the "real" one, though by definition the ghost is already a phantasmal existence. A phantom of a phantom, this imaginary ghost seems to come from nowhere, but it substantiates the haunted reality everyone inhabits.

A similar argument applies to "Yishi de wancheng" (The completion of a ritual, 1988) by the mainland writer Su Tong (b. 1963), in which an anthropologist travels to a village to observe a vanishing ritual of exorcism. The ritual, when fully carried out, has the villagers draw straws to select a "ghost king"; whoever assumes the role of the ghost king will be killed as a scapegoat. The anthropologist requests the villagers to reinstate the ritual for his sake, and as a result, he finds himself the new ghost king.

What happens next is a series of mysterious coincidences. Carried away by the lifelike staging of the ritual, the villagers almost beat the anthropologist to death. The anthropologist survives the mock ritual of exorcism, but on his way out of the village he is run over by a car. Although the anthropologist dies accidentally, the likelihood is that through an artificial incantation, he has brought back to life a dead, and deadly, ritual. However belated and beguiling his (academic) pursuit, he meets his predestined fate. At a time when the ghost is no longer traceable, the anthropologist, inspired by an imaginary haunting, has created his own sequence of exorcism and made himself both the executor and victim of the ritual.

The two stories represent two related approaches by which phantasmagoric realism defies the paradigm of modern Chinese realism. It may introduce fantastic elements to the text and treat them as if they were an integral part of the real, as in the case of Lin Yiyun's story. As a result, the reader is compelled to rethink the multiple possibilities of delineating the limits of the real. More intriguing is Su Tong's approach. This approach does not necessarily feature anything unthinkable or unknown on the surface of narrative. Rather it follows the realist formula in such a way as to generate its chiasmatic replica, as demonstrated by the anthropologist's desire to reproduce the lost ritual in Su Tong's story. When the presumably monolithic image of the real multiplies, one is faced with the dilemma that the world one so confidently inhabits may already be part of a chain of ghostly reflections.[85] Both approaches threaten the aesthetics of corporeality and the politics of agency on which the conventional mimetic realism is based, and the threat is most emphatically expressed by the subversion of the two dominant sensory faculties underlying such a realist paradigm: the invocatory (*call* to arms) and the scopic (*seeing* is believing).[86]

My point here is not merely to use these Chinese cases to endorse contemporary theory. The more challenging task is to ask, at a time when the Chinese sublime figure of the real has been replaced by the phantasmagoric, how history is (dis)embodied by the return of fictional ghosts. Yang Lian's (b. 1959) "Guihua" (Ghost talk, 1991), Wang Anyi's "Tianxian pei" (Heavenly match, 1997), and Mo Yan's novella *Zhanyou chongfeng* (Reunion of fellow fighters, 1998), all dealing with themes of heroism, martyrdom, and mourning—arguably the most blatant subjects in the aesthetics of corporality—can be cited as examples.

In "Ghost Talk," a lonely soul is heard murmuring in an empty house; the response is a series of echoes of his own voice. Whose is this voice? Why is he deprived of authentic existence? One of the most talented among the younger generation of mainland Chinese poets, Yang Lian went into exile after the Tian'anmen Incident, and the story may very well have been inspired by his own experience of expatriatism as a result of the incident in particular and the Communist regime in general. But the narrative of "Ghost Talk" bears no apparent historical imprint; the causal link between the world and the words seems missing. To mourn over the thousands who were eternally muted under Mao-Deng discourse, public indictment is no longer sufficient.

Yang Lian inscribes the loss and the concomitant work of mourning that accompanies such a refusal of vociferous utterance. In a way it brings to mind what Michel de Certeau writes about the impossible "quest for lost and ghostly voices" in modern, scriptual societies.[87] Yang Lian's story explores the possibility of the phantasmatic "insinuation" of fugitive voices within Mao-Deng discourse: hence fragments, marginalities, traces—signs of the heteroglossia in Chinese (post)modernity.

Wang Anyi's "Heavenly Match" tells of a ghost marriage in the pre-1949 period. A wounded young Communist woman soldier is left to die in a village after a bloody defeat. After her death, the villagers find her a spirit husband so that she can have a happy afterlife marriage. Decades later, the woman soldier's lover, now a senile cadre, comes to the village and asks to have the body of his beloved exhumed and moved to another cemetery.

The dispute over the ownership of the woman soldier's relics is rooted in the clash of two discourses about memory and mourning. Despite the fact that the woman soldier died for the cause of revolution, the villagers commemorate her in a "reactionary" fashion. The cadre, however, wants to relocate the woman soldier to where she "should" belong, because her remains are part of national history. While the two parties are engaged in circuitous negotiation over the woman soldier's body, Wang Anyi poses a question: granted that the woman soldier's ghost marriage is nonsense, does it make any more sense to have her body enshrined in honor of the myth of revolutionary history? Lost somewhere between folkloric belief and the national imaginary is the young woman soldier's lonely soul, half a century after her death, still with no "home" to return to.

In Mo Yan's *Reunion of Fellow Fighters,* the first-person narrator, a lieutenant commander on his way home, is forced to take shelter in a tree from a mysterious flood. In the tree he is reunited with fellow combatants from the Sino-Vietnamese war, all supposedly dead. One after another, the ghosts of the dead reminisce about their pasts, to the point that the I-narrator begins to doubt his own status. He then realizes that he is already dead, too, and the body of a drowned military man he saw earlier in the water was in fact his own.

Rarely can one find in contemporary Chinese fiction a tale about war as perplexing and moving as *Reunion of Fellow Fighters.* Not unlike Yang Lian, Mo Yan indicates that the brutalities and casualties of the war are such that they can be conveyed only by "talk among the ghosts." The soldiers in Mo

Yan's *Reunion of Fellow Fighters* have sacrificed their lives to safeguard a national myth. Little did they know that instead of glory, their afterlife would be one filled with unfulfilled dreams, fear, and loneliness in the underworld. Worse yet, some of them died an even more meaningless death from trivial accidents after the war. A sense of absurdity permeates the novella as the ghosts exchange afterlife stories, stories that do not add up to any heroic magnitude.

Mo Yan's narrator at first appears like a medium through whose account the other ghosts' stories are heard. But midway through the novella, more and more clues betray his shadowy role as an unreliable narrator. When the narrator eventually comes to recognize that he too is a ghost, his mourning over the war bounces back onto himself and is turned into a self-mourning. The novella's realistic format thus calls attention to its own duplicitous nature: the "history" the narrator tries to relate proves to be nothing more than a lifelike simulacrum relayed among ghosts. Moreover, if official history is made possible by those who survive the war, fiction is the genre that solicits ghosts' voices.

GHOSTS OF HISTORY

Returning to the ambiguities of the ancient citation "ghost is 'that which returns,'" we can now trace with more care the trajectories through which premodern ghost fiction (and drama) return to haunt the work of late-twentieth-century Chinese writers. I ask: what does it take to make a late-twentieth-century ghost story as intelligible as its premodern predecessors? How can a fantastic mode be taken as part of this renewed realistic vision? In other words, when they appropriate motifs, plots, and characters of premodern Chinese ghost narrative to inscribe the real, these writers are obliged to renegotiate the law of verisimilitude of both realism and fantasy in a way hitherto unseen in the tradition. The second haunting of the premodern ghosts, therefore, does not bring us any closer to the arguable primal scene of the real, but it nevertheless showcases the changeable norms of realism and fantasy alike in depicting the past in the present.

I turn to four examples, each demonstrating the "return" of premodern Chinese ghost fiction or drama. Through their second haunting in the fin-de-siècle, premodern ghosts help undo the myth of mimetic realism and usher us into the phantasmagoric sphere of Chinese postmodernity. Take Taiwanese writer Zhong Ling's novella *Shengsi yuanjia* (Life-and-death partners, 1991) as a first example. The work is inspired by the famous Song *huaben* story "Nianyü Guanyin" (Carved jade Guanyin [Avalokiteshvara]) and its rewrite by Feng Menglong, "Cui daizhao shengsi yuanjia" (Artisan Cui and his life-and-death romantic partner).[88] In the original story, the jade carver Cui Ning is promised by his master, Prince Xian'an, an arranged marriage with Xiuxiu, the prince's maidservant, in recompense for his excellent craftsmanship of a jade Guanyin statue. Xiuxiu persuades Cui Ning to elope with her one night in the midst of a fire at the prince's residence. They start a jade-carving business in Tanzhou but before long are apprehended by the prince's guard. Cui Ning is sentenced to exile, and on the road he is joined by Xiuxiu. Later on, Cui is rehabilitated and the couple reopen their business in the capital, until the same prince's guard runs into them and is shocked by the presence of Xiuxiu. She was supposed to have been killed by the prince when Cui was exiled.

Although faithfully based on the Song original, Feng Menglong's version shifts its focus to human concerns, as reflected by the change of the title from "Carved Jade Guanyin" to "Artisan Cui and His Life-and-Death Romantic Partner." In both versions, nevertheless, the storyteller is able to modulate the audience's expectation in such a way as to create suspense and surprises. As such, when the "truth" is told and "reality" unveiled, we are shocked to recognize anew the reciprocal relations between life and death, and between phantom and humanity. A story about a ghostly romance, it also marks a triumphant moment, in which premodern Chinese vernacular fiction touches on the complex motivations behind the depiction of the real.

In Zhong Ling's treatment, the foremost change is that she drops the storyteller's voice and instead lets Xiuxiu narrate the story. While this rearrangement may indicate to feminist critics a ghost *woman*'s acquisition of narrative power,[89] the flip side of the argument applies too: the story may sound like a powerless woman's "ghost talk" about her fantasy in a closed, narcissistic context. Equally noticeable is the way Zhong Ling invests erotic symbolism in the fatal attraction between Xiuxiu and Cui Ning. Whereas the original ends with Cui Ning abruptly killed by Xiuxiu after he discovers her identity, Zhong Ling has the jade carver lured to death by his beloved as if in lovemaking. The returned ghost Xiuxiu serves as the executor of the completion of her and Cui Ning's desire.

But Zhong Ling's is more than a story of eros and thanatos. She foregrounds the fact that Xiuxiu is as much a first-rate embroiderer as Cui Ning is a superb jade carver, and that it is her passion for artifacts that enables her to appreciate Cui Ning in the first place. A jade connoisseur in her own right, Zhong Ling demonstrates a keen interest in jade in Chinese cultural symbolism, including on the one hand the homonymity in Chinese of jade *(yu)* with desire *(yu)*,[90] and on the other the funereal association of jade with death. Xiuxiu is able to maintain her human shape after death, we are told, thanks to an ancient jade pendant. It is through the fantastic mediation of jade that her will to life/love and death wish become interchangeable. Similarly, Cui Ning, the carver of jade/desire, is by potential and profession a practitioner of the arts of love and death. As the jade imagery becomes increasingly dominant, one is tempted to read Cui Ning and Xiuxiu's life-

and-death story as an erotic romance about, and with, the mysterious stone. Indeed, insofar as she makes jade the motivation for Xiuxiu's romantic account, Zhong Ling has transformed a story about a couple's deadly love into one about jade fetishism; and fetishism is nothing if not a phantom replacement of that which is forever lost, an obsession with a thing as if it were the return of the originary.[91] When the Song dynasty ghost Xiuxiu returns to Zhong Ling's story, she has entered into a world tapestried with postmodernist decadence.

My second example is the PRC writer Jia Pingwa's (b. 1952) novel *Baiye* (White night, 1995). Jia aroused a national controversy in 1993 for his erotic romance cum satire *Feidu* (Abandoned city). *White Night* in a sense continues Jia's panoramic sketch of the changing social manners in *Abandoned City,* an aspect too often overlooked by prudish critics. But instead of the theme of lust underlying *Abandoned City,* in *White Night* Jia Pingwa explores the theme of death. As Jia Pingwa puts it, the novel was inspired by his experience of watching performances of the *Mulian* drama cycle in Sichuan in 1993. He deeply appreciates the ancient theater that crosses the boundaries between "the world of the dead and the world of the living, history and reality, performers and audience, theatre and life,"[92] so much so that he wants to give a novelistic interpretation of the theater.

The history and production of the *Mulian* drama is too complex to be summarized here.[93] What can be addressed for our purposes is that, whatever its variations in different periods and locales, the themes, characters, and plots of the *Mulian* drama cycle revolve around the monk Mulian's rescue of his mother, who has been condemned to hell for sacrilege during her lifetime, and his consequent interaction with other ghosts in hell. In the novel, the male protagonist, Yelang, is a literatus turned actor in a *Mulian* drama troupe. Through his performance tours, he enters a social network where all values, social identities, and emotive capacities are turned upside-down, and as such he can no longer judge the legitimacy of his own professional and emotional adventures.

The novel evolves with Yelang's performances in various cities, his changing stage roles of men and ghosts, and his romance with two women. In between, Jia Pingwa introduces a sequence of interludes depicting various northwestern folk cultures from fortune-telling to paper-cutting—all dying forms in a rapidly modernizing society. A ghost play that absorbs a multitude of bygone folk theatrical forms and religious beliefs, the *Mulian* drama generates its own incarnations across history, a "living fossil" as Jia Pingwa calls it.[94] In other words, this is a theater that presupposes the posthumous status of all forms of humanity, a theater that comes to life only on account of the death of others. It has insinuated itself into the layered texture of lived Chinese experience and charmed audiences with its "horror and humor." The romance of Yelang and his two women, though apparently separate from the drama cycle, proves at the end to be only part of a continually transforming, and transmigrating, life as drama.

At this juncture, one recalls Lu Xun's ambivalent record of his experience with local *Mulian* theater almost seventy years before. For Lu Xun, the theater is a haunting model of the terror and charm of the old China, and his attempt to conjure away his fascination with it by writing is to no avail. In the 1990s, the *Mulian* drama stages a comeback to post-Mao-Deng China, its gothic appeal taking on a postmodernist dimension. As one character has it, ours is a time when "all the forbidden words have been said aloud, all the forbidden clothes have been made into fashion, all the forbidden deeds have been done everywhere . . . men are now not afraid of anything but their own kind, plus ghosts. This is why the *Mulian* drama should be a marketable entertainment nowadays."[95] The *Mulian* drama, accordingly, has become a fin-de-siècle spectacle informing the nature of our existence. The novel, straddling past and present, day and night, as its title suggests, manifests itself as a footnote to this amorphous theater, which in the final analysis is a ghostly (forbidden?) dramatization of life.

My third and fourth examples pertain to late-twentieth-century writers' revision of *Liaozhai zhiyi* or *Liaozhai's Records of the Strange,* the paramount Qing collection of fantastic tales in literary Chinese. Since its publication in the mid-eighteenth century, *Liaozhai* has served as arguably the most important spring of inspiration for writers and readers of the fantastic. As Judith Zeitlin argues, the collection provides clues not only to how the discourse of the strange undergoes transformation at a specific historical moment, in this case, the late Ming and early Qing, but also to how the discourse of the normal—and the real—develops as a result of the depiction of the strange.[96] Calling himself a "historian of the strange," Pu Songling is quite aware that he is engaged in a history of alterity; with ghosts and demons, fox spirits and monstrous creatures, he has created a heterological account in remembrance of the past. He thus challenges the orthodoxy of traditional historiography, turning it into a haunted text.

When late-twentieth-century writers work on phantasmagoric realism, they are inevitably drawn to Pu Songling's fantastic and yet historical view of humanity. Mo Yan's collection of short stories, *Shenliao* (Fantastic talk, 1993), even shares part of the *Liaozhai*'s title. Mo Yan established himself with works such as *Hong Gaoliang jiazu* (Red sorghum, 1987), which have been likened to Western magical realism. In a biographical essay entitled "Haotan guiguai shenhu" (My penchant for ghosts, demons, gods, and fox spirits, 1994), he states that one of his creative models is the fiction of Pu Songling, and that he and Pu even come from the same region in Shandong Province.[97] When one reads Mo Yan's sketches about a fisherman's romantic nocturnal encounter with a woman ghost ("Yeyu" [Nocturnal fishing]), or a strange boy who lives by eating iron ("Tiehai" [Iron kid]), or others in *Fantastic Talk,* it brings to mind tales by the early Qing historian of the strange. Nevertheless, perhaps because it is written with too much "anxiety of influence," *Fantastic Talk* reads like a pale mimicry of the *Liaozhai* in format and thematics; it fails to impress on its own.

The enchanting power of *Liaozhai* has also had an influence on the Hong Kong writer Li Bihua's *Yanhua sanyu* (The red string, 2001). A "reportage," as Li calls it, *Red String* relates the search of an aged Chinese comfort woman for her beloved, an ex-Nationalist policeman and former worker in a Communist concentration camp, thirty-eight years after their forced divorce during the Great Leap Forward. With Li Bihua's assistance, an international manhunt is launched using the postmodern technology of computer networking as well as the premodern technology of deciphering mystical signs from the *I Ching,* and it leads to a happy outcome. The old woman and her long lost ex-husband, who has remarried, are finally reunited at a place named Zibo, which just happens to be the hometown of Pu Songling! As Li Bihua writes, "If a legend could start with the *I Ching* and end with the *Liaozhai,* it would be a good legend."[98]

What intrigues us more is Li Bihua's own role. Compelled by the old couple's story, Li vows to help them find each other and, judging by the way she mobilizes her connections—scientific and magical alike—she may well have acted the role of a modern-day medium. At the climax of the book, Li escorts the old comfort woman to Zibo, meets the woman's ex-husband and his current wife, and gives a firsthand report of the reunion. But as witness to "the saddest reunion story in modern Chinese history," as her book's cover proclaims, Li is technically "invisible." This is not only because she takes a transparent perspective from which the story will appear to unfold on its own, but also because she is bound to find herself having no part to play within other people's romances—however much she has fallen in love with the romance itself.

As a Hong Kong writer writing after the Return, Li may have wanted to produce something more rooted in the Chinese earth, something more human and realistic, as a way of doing penance for her gothic style. But she ends up telling a love story haunted by truncated memory and irretrievable time, which allows no "return" except in a ghostly manner. Finally, Li Bihua may be not unlike those women ghosts of her early works in that she is searching for a way to vindicate her love (or imaginations of love) on native soil, only to further expose her suspect identity, both as the storyteller and as a character in the story, traveling as she does to Zibo, the home of classical Chinese literary ghosts.

I conclude my survey by looking into the works by the Chinese Malaysian writer Huang Jinshu (Kim-chu Ng, b. 1967), now based in Taiwan. Compared with Mo Yan or Li Bihua, Huang is more inventive in coming to terms with the impact of Pu Songling. In "Xinliu" (New willow, 1997), Huang gives a dazzling rendition of stories drawn from the *Liaozhai.* The book follows the dream adventures of Ju Yaoru in a mysterious land, where he enters the lives of Liu Zigu, Ah Zhu, Peng Yugui, Gong Mengbi, and others—all characters drawn from tales of the *Liaozhai.*[99] The way Huang Jinshu mixes their fates and capacities creates a vertiginous sequence of stories within stories. In the final episode, Ju Yaoru falls back into the first dream context and meets an old man named Pu Songling.

Whether called a parody, an homage, a metafiction, or a pastiche, "New Willow" impresses one above all as a tour de force in the postmodernist spirit. This is nothing original. The truly compelling moment comes when the character Pu Songling talks about his frustrated career, and Pu's "Liaozhai zizhi" (Liaozhai's own record) is quoted in full. In this "Record," Pu describes his writing of the *History of the Strange* as an involuntary and compulsive action: he cannot help himself but let the ghosts and fox spirits occupy his text as if he were possessed. Moreover, he delineates a genealogy of writing the strange in which he is but a late comer; this genealogy dates as far back as Qu Yuan, Gan Bao, and Li He.[100] Through "strange" writings by these writers, a phantom history has been inscribed in parallel to authentic history.

We can now see Huang Jinshu's ambition. Beyond the fanciful postmodernist language play, he wants to reopen the problematic of phantom history and makes himself the latest successor to the tradition of the history of the strange. Writing in the late twentieth century, Huang finds that the strange worthy of his account happens neither in mainland China nor in Taiwan but in his hometown region, the Chinese communities in Southeast Asia. The descendents of the Chinese immigrants to these areas are destined to be outcasts of the Middle Kingdom despite their fervent but often anachronistic attempt to maintain their cultural legacy. Spatially and temporally displaced, as Huang suggests in most of his fiction, they are the forlorn souls overseas. And at a time when the natives' calls for assimilation become increasingly urgent, their obsession with China partakes of an even more ghostly nature.

Thus in his prize winning short story "Yuhai" (Fish relics, 1996),[101] Huang depicts a young Chinese Malaysian scholar's fantastic search for his roots and his horrific discoveries. Relocated in Taiwan, this scholar is doubly deprived of his cultural heritage, and yet deep in his mind he still entertains the dream of ancient China. The scholar specializes in deciphering the enigmatic signs and languages of ancient Chinese civilizations. Along with his research interest, he develops a bizarre hobby of killing turtles and preparing the shells for augury reading, just as his forebears did during the ancient Yin and Shang dynasties; he even discovers that as far back as four thousand years ago, turtles available only in the Malay Peninsula area were sent to the Middle Kingdom as tribute. When left alone, this sinologist "eats turtle, listens to turtle language, deciphers the oracular messages for familiars in the dark . . . carves out the ancient languages on oracle bones, retrieving the feelings of ancient China."[102]

In Chinese, turtle, or *gui,* it will be recalled, is a homonym for *gui,* or return. Again, if "the ghost means 'that which returns,'" it returns to Huang Jinshu's story by way of the ritual of killing the turtle. With every oracular incantation, the apparitions of China come back to the scholar through the burning of the turtle shells, including the apparition of his brother who died in a local riot in Malaysia years before in the name of his "homeland." My questions are: at the end of the twentieth century, can this young Chinese Malaysian scholar in Taiwan still return to his imaginary China? If a mainland writer like Han Shaogong has already found his "homecoming" to be a literary trip to a dead(ly) end, what is a chance for Huang Jinshu as an overseas revenant? In acting out his own anachronistic ritual of killing turtles in invocation of an ancient ghost, isn't Huang's sinologist like the anthropologist of Su Tong's "Completion of a Ritual," who plays a fatal game at the cost of his own life? While his protagonist carves tortoise shells in pursuit of a mythical telos, Huang Jinshu, who too has no home country to return to, inscribes in fiction an oracular message about the nostalgia for a lost promised land and his diasporic position in history. Is such carving/inscribing a fetishistic gesture, like what happens to the artisans in Zhong Ling's "Life-and-Death Partners," or is it a fantastic act, like what happens to the "historian of the strange," Pu Songling, in "New Willow"?

As a way of restating the theme of this chapter, we now return to where we began. Our story of the Ming dynasty retelling of the story of the Song dynasty ghost woman Zheng Yiniang has so far not revealed her second haunting. During their moment of reunion, her husband Han Sishou promises her that he will bring the casket with her ashes to the South and that he will remember her forever. Han later meets a beautiful widow turned nun who claims to have quit the world of the Red Dust in honor of a husband killed in the Tartar invasions. Han falls in love with the nun and marries her. But just one month after their marriage, the newlyweds find themselves haunted again. At the suggestion of a Daoist exorcist, Han Sihou has the casket of his ex-wife's ashes taken out of her tomb and dumped into the Yangtze River. The haunting subsides. Years later, the couple are boating on the river when two ghosts, one male and one female, shoot up from the water, each grabbing a victim and pulling them under the waves to drown them. Where men forget, ghosts remember.

NOTES

INTRODUCTION

1. I am referring to Marston Anderson's succinct analysis of the moral dilemma in modern Chinese realism. See Anderson, *The Limits of Realism: Chinese Fiction in the Revolutionary Period* (Berkeley: University of California Press, 1990), ch. 1. Also see Wei Chee Dimock, *Residues of Justice, Literature, Law, Philosophy* (Berkeley: University of California Press, 1997).
2. These figures vary, to be sure, thanks to an insufficiency of data. But even the most conservative estimate already points to a huge loss of Chinese lives during the past century. For a detailed account of the death toll of Chinese related to political and military events during the twentieth century, see, for example, Rudolph J. Rummel, *China's Bloody Century: Genocide and Mass Murder since 1900* (New Brunswick, N.J.: Transaction Publishers, 1991); Ho Ping-ti, *Studies on the Population of China: 1368–1953* (Cambridge, Mass.: Harvard University Press, 1957). Jasper Baker estimates that around thirty million Chinese perished during the Great Leap Forward; see *Hungry Ghosts: Mao's Secret Famine* (New York: Free Press, 1996), esp. part 2. Ling Feng estimates that more than thirty million Chinese were killed in the Second Sino-Japanese War and that around forty million lost their lives during the Great Leap Forward and its aftermath; see *Zhonggong fengyu bashi nian* (A stormy history of the Chinese communist revolution) (Edison: Epoch Publication Co., 2001), 33. One of the more moderate and up-to-date estimates of the number of deaths resulting from PRC government action is six to ten million, in Jean-Louis Margolin, "China: A Long March into Night," in *The Black Book of Communism: Crimes, Terror, Repression*, ed. Stephane Courtois et al., trans. Jonathan Murphy (Cambridge, Mass: Harvard University Press, 1999), 463. See also the discussion by Philip Williams and Yenna Wu in the first chapter and conclusion of *The Great Wall of Confinement: The Contemporary Prison Camp through Fiction and Reportage* (Berkeley: University of California Press, forthcoming); part of my bibliographical information is derived from this study.

3. I am referring in particular to the book edited by Nancy Armstrong and Leonard Tennenhouse, *The Violence of Representation: Literature and the History of Violence* (London and New York: Routledge, 1989).
4. Literature, of course, babbles on about injustice and revolution, but these are just terms in the new master narrative. The silences are about actual cruelties and actual repetitions, and the worst silence is the one about literary complicity, because it does representational violence to representation itself.
5. Zheng Zhenduo, "Xue he lei de wenxue" (Literature of blood and tears), in *Zheng Zhenduo xuanji* (Works of Zheng Zhenduo) (Fuzhou: Fujian renmin chubanshe, 1984), 1097.
6. Liu Shaoming (Joseph S. M. Lau), *Tilei jiaoling de xiandai zhongguo wenxue* (Modern Chinese literature in tears and snivelling) (Taipei: Yuanjing chubanshe, 1980).
7. C. T. Hsia, "Closing Remarks," in *Chinese Fiction from Taiwan: Critical Perspectives*, ed. Jeannette L. Faurot (Bloomington: Indiana University Press, 1980).
8. Liu Zaifu and Lin Gang, "Zhongguo xiandai xiaoshuo de zhengzhishi xiezuo: Cong 'Chuncan' dao *Taiyang zhaozai Sanggan heshang*" (The politics of writing in modern Chinese literature: From "Spring Silkworms" to *The Sun Shines over the Sanggan River*), in *Fangzhu zhushen: Wenlun tigang he wenxueshi chongping* (Exiling gods: Outlines of literary theory and rereadings of literary history) (Hong Kong: Tiandi tushu gongsi, 1994), 133–34, 140.
9. For late Ming testimonials to the fall of the dynasty and subsequent atrocities, see, from example, Lynn Struve, ed. and trans., *Voices from the Ming-Qing Cataclysm* (New Haven, Conn.: Yale University Press, 1993). By "the history of pain," I am thinking of the title of a novel by the late Qing writer Wu Jianren, *Tongshi*, or, *A History of Pain* (1905).
10. One finds examples in works by Tongling Lu, *Mysogyny, Nihilism, and Oppositional Politics: Contemporary Chinese Experimental Fiction* (Stanford, Calif.: Stanford University Press, 1995); and Gang Yue, *The Mouth That Begs* (Durham, N.C.: Duke University Press, 1999).
11. Theodor Adorno, "After Auschwitz," in *Negative Dialectics*, trans. E. B. Ashton (New York: Continuum, 1973), 362.
12. Conscientious writers are thus seen as being ruled by two forces: compelled to write continuously on behalf of the dead and the inarticulate, they can best do so by writing instead about the "irrepresentability" of the pain and death they refrain from representing. See Shoshana Felman and Dori Laub, *Testimony: Crises of Witnessing in Literature, Psychoanalysis, and History* (New York: Routledge, 1992), 12–56; esp. 33–34.
13. René Girard, *Violence and the Sacred*, trans. Patrick Gregory (Baltimore, Md.: Johns Hopkins University Press, 1977).
14. Walter Benjamin, "Critique of Violence," in *Reflections: Essays, Aphorisms, Autobiographical Writings*, trans. Edmund Jephcott (New York: Schocken, 1986), 279–300. For a succinct summary of Benjamin's concept of violence, see, for example, Beatrice Hanssen, "On the Politics of Pure Means: Benjamin, Arendt, Foucault," in *Violence, Identity, and Self-Determination*, ed. de Vries and Weber, 236–46.

15. Mikhil Bakhtin, *Rabelais and His World,* trans. Helene Iswolsky (Cambridge, Mass.: MIT Press, 1968).
16. Hannah Arendt, *On Violence* (San Diego: Harcourt Brace Jovanovich, 1970); Jean Baudrillard, "On Theater of Cruelty," *Semiotext(e)* 4 (1982): 108–109. Also see Anthony Kubiak, *Stages of Terror: Terrorism, Ideology, and Coercion as Theatre History* (Bloomington: Indiana University Press, 1991), 158–59.
17. See, for example, Michel Foucault, *Discipline and Punish: The Birth of the Prison,* trans. Alan Sheridan (New York: Pantheon, 1977).
18. Jacques Derrida, *Specters of Marx: The State of the Debt, the Work of Mourning, and the New International,* trans. Peggy Kamuf (London and New York: Routledge, 1994), 4.
19. *Mengzi zhushu* (Annotated *Mencius*) "Tengwengong zhang ju" xia, juan 6, xia, 5a, in *Runkan Shisanjing zhushu* (Annotated Thirteen Classics, the Ruan edition; a reprint of the 1815 Jiangxi Nanchangfuxue chongkan edition of *Shisanjing zhushu*) (Taipei: Yiwen yinshuguan, 1993), 118.
20. *Lunyu zhushu* (Annotated *Analects*), "Zilu," juan 13, 5a, in *Runkan Shisanjing zhushu* (Annotated Thirteen Classics, the Ruan edition; a reprint of the 1815 Jiangxi Nanchangfuxue chongkan edition of *Shisanjing zhushu*) (Taipei: Yiwen yinshuguan, 1993), 117.
21. *Chunqiu Zuozhuan zhengyi* (Annotated *Chunqiu Zuozhuan* with commentary), "Xianggong ershiwunian," juan 36, 6b, in *Runkan Shisanjing zhushu* (Annotated Thirteen Classics, the Ruan edition; a reprint of the 1815 Jiangxi Nanchangfuxue chongkan edition of *Shisanjing zhushu*) (Taipei: Yiwen yinshuguan, 1993), 619.
22. I am grateful to Wai-yee Li's succinct argument in "The Idea of Authority in the *Shih chi* (Records of the Historian)," *Harvard Journal of Asiatic Studies* 54, no. 2 (Dec. 1994): 345–405.
23. *Shenyi jing,* in *Biji xiaoshuo daguan* (Compendium of biji fictional narratives), 38 bian (Taipei: Xinxing shuju, 1985), juan 1, 226.
24. Sima Qian, *Shiji,* "Wudi benji" (Chronicles of the five emperors), in *Shiji huizhu kaozheng* (An annotated edition of the *Shiji*) (Taipei: Hongye shuju, 1980), juan 1, 31.
25. *Shangshu zhengyi* (Annotated *Shangshu* with commentary), "Yushu," "Shundian," juan 3, 4a, in *Runkan Shisanjing zhushu* (Annotated Thirteen Classics, the Ruan edition; a reprint of the 1815 Jiangxi Nanchangfuxue chongkan edition of *Shisanjing zhushu*) (Taipei: Yiwen yinshuguan, 1993), 35; *Chunqiu Zuozhuan zhengyi,* "Wengong shiba nian," juan 20, 17a–19b, 354–55, in *Runkan Shisanjing zhushu* (Annotated Thirteen Classics, the Ruan edition; a reprint of the 1815 Jiangxi Nanchangfuxue chongkan edition of *Shisanjing zhushu*) (Taipei: Yiwen yinshuguan, 1993), 354–55.
26. Zhang Jun, *Chuguo shenhua yuanxing yanjiu* (A study of the mythological archetypes of the Chu) (Taipei: Wenjin chubanshe, 1994), 71.
27. Ibid.
28. Ibid.
29. Ibid.
30. Mencius, *Mencius,* "Lilou" xiapain; I am using D. C. Lau's translation, in *Mencius* (London: Penguin, 1970), 131.

31. *Chunqiu Zuozhuan zhengyi,* xu, juan 1, chunqiu xu.
32. Walter Benjamin, "Theses on the Philosophy of History," in *Illuminations,* trans. Harry Zohn (New York: Schocken, 1969), 256.
33. See below, Chapter 6 note 95.

CHAPTER 1: INVITATION TO A BEHEADING

1. Youhuan Yusheng, *Lingnüyu* (Women's words overheard), in *Wanqing xiaosshuo daxi* (A compendium of late Qing literature) (Taipei: Guangya chubanshe, 1984), 45. The novel was first serialized in *Xiuxiang xiaoshuo* (Illustrated fiction) from 1903 to 1904, totaling twelve chapters. Like many other late Qing novels, it remains unfinished. Commercial Press (Shangwu yinshu guan) first published it in book form in 1913.
2. Ibid.
3. Ibid.
4. Ah Ying mentions this episode in *Wanqing xiaoshuoshi* (A history of late Qing fiction) (Hong Kong: Taiping shuju, 1961), 46–47; see also Guo Yanli, *Zhongguo jindai wenxue fazhanshi* (History of early modern Chinese literature) (Jinan: Shangdong jiaoyu chubanshe, 1991), 1369.
5. For a full account of Lu Xun seeing the slide show, see, for example, Leo Oufan Lee, *Voices from the Iron House: A Study of Lu Xun* (Bloomington: Indiana University Press, 1987), 17–18.
6. However, this structure is maintained only in the first six chapters of the novel.
7. Interestingly enough, by pointing fingers at the Qing rulership and Confucian pedagogy, Jin Bumo downplays the foreign invaders' nefarious deeds and the colonial interests they represent. His argument tends to either integrate the foreigners—barbarians—into the conventional Chinese cosmology, therefore validating the formula of Confucian edification, or to bracket them as that which is inscrutable and therefore beyond the reach of the current Chinese episteme.
8. C. T. Hsia, "Obsession with China: The Moral Burden of Modern Chinese Literature," appendix 1 of *A History of Modern Chinese Fiction* (New Haven, Conn.: Yale University Press, 1971), 533–54.
9. See Liu Dashen, "Guanyu *Laocan you ji*" (On *The Travels of Lao Can*), in *Liu E ji* Lao Can youji *ziliao* (Liu E and research materials on *The Travels of Lao Can*), ed. Liu Delong, Zhu Xi, and Liu Deping (Chengdu: Sichaun renmin chubanshe, 1985), 391–92.
10. See *Fin-de-siècle Splendor,* chap. 3.
11. Lu Xun, "Zixu" (Preface to *Nahan* [A Call to Arms]), in *Lu Xun quanji* (Complete works of Lu Xun) (Beijing: Renmin wenxue chubanshe, 1981), 1: 417.
12. Yü-sheng Lin, *The Crisis of Chinese Consciousness: Radical Antitraditionalism in the May Fourth Era* (Madison: University of Wisconsin Press, 1979), 26.
13. See Wang Hui's analysis in "Sihuo chongwen" (A rekindled dead fire), in *Sihuo chongwen* (A rekindled dead fire) (Beijing: Renmin wenxue chubanshe, 2000), 413–34.
14. See my discussion in *Fictional Realism in Twentieth-Century China: Mao Dun, Lao She, Shen Congwen* (New York: Columbia University Press, 1992), chap. 1.

15. Lee, *The Iron House,* 18.
16. In light of the Lacanian model, the continued invocation of severed heads (and the kinds of affective attachment that they inspire) lends itself to a psychological reading in terms of their status as "objets petit a," or partial objects. These "partial objects" are loci that "originally" were perceived as being associated with the subject, but which have subsequently become disassociated from it, and have entered a circulatory economy at the margins of the Self as Chinese subjectivity, standing as necessarily impossible objects of desire. I want to thank Carlos Rojas for this suggestion.
17. T. A. Hsia, *The Gate of Darkness: Studies of the Leftist Literary Movement in China* (Seattle: University of Washington Press, 1968), 146–62.
18. One thinks of Paul de Man's comment that "writing always includes the moment of dispassion in favor of an arbitrary power play of the signifier and from the point of view of the subject, this can be experienced as a dismemberment, a beheading or a castration." Paul de Man, *Allegories of Reading: Figural Language in Rousseau, Nietzsche, Rilke, and Proust* (New Haven, Conn.: Yale University Press, 1979), 296.
19. Lu Xun, "Changong daguan" (A spectacle of chopping communists), in *Lu Xun zawenxuan* (Selections of Lu Xun's essays) (Shanghai: Renmin chubanshe, 1972), 124.
20. Michel Foucault, *Discipline and Punish: The Birth of the Prison,* trans. Alan Sheridan (New York: Pantheon, 1977), 24–95.
21. Ibid. For a detailed discussion of Foucault's concept of "discipline and punish," see, for instance, Frank Lentricchia, *Ariel and the Police: Michel Foucault, William James, Wallace Stevens* (Madison: University of Wisconsin Press, 1988), 29–102.
22. Marston Anderson, *The Limits of Realism: Chinese Fiction in the Revolutionary Period* (Berkeley: University of California Press, 1990), 76–92.
23. Shen Congwen, *Congwen zizhuan* (Autobiography of Congwen), in *Shen Congwen wenji* (Works of Shen Congwen) (Hong Kong: Sanlian Shudian, 1984), 9: 100–219.
24. Ibid., 165.
25. Wang Luyan, "Youzi" (Grapefruit), in *Youzi* (Shanghai: Shenghuo shudian, 1937).
26. Shen Congwen, "Wode jiaoyu" (My Education), in *Shen Congwen wenji* (Works of Shen Congwen) (Hong Kong: Sanlian Shudian, 1984), 3:130.
27. In haste to rejoin head and body—to restore China to its proper self—Lu Xun overlooks the possibility that there are many alternatives to his pharmaceutical imperative (to effect a "cure" for China's spiritual "malaise"). Shen Congwen's moral concern about China is the equal of Lu Xun's, but this moral concern does not give him the guilty conscience that haunts Lu Xun and his followers, sending them in search of desperate remedies. A moralizing realism has no prior claim to moral realism. Had Lu Xun lived long enough to write as many novels and stories as Shen Congwen did, he would surely have found his way into other realisms.
28. Ivan Turgenev, *Sketches from a Hunter's Album,* trans. Richard Freeborn (Baltimore: Penguin, 1967), 129–44.

29. Wuhe, *Yusheng* (Remains of life) (Taipei: Maitian chuban gongsi, 2000), 251.
30. Ibid.
31. See my discussion of "Shigu zhe Wuhe" (Wuhe, the bone collector) in Wuhe, *Yusheng,* 7–40.
32. For a more detailed account in English, see Leo T. S. Ching, *Becoming Japanese: Colonial Taiwan and the Politics of Identity Formation* (Berkeley: University of California Press, 2001), 133–51. For more information in Chinese, see Deng Xiangyang, *Wushe shijian* (Musha incident) (Taipei: Yushanshe, 1999); *Fengzhong feiying: Wushe shijian zhenxiang ji huagang chuzi de gushi* (Red cherry blossoms in the wind: The truth of the Musha Incident) (Taipei: Yushanshe, 2000); Wang Zhiheng, "Wushe shijian mianmian guan" (The multifaceted aspects of the Musha Incident), *Zhongwai zazhi* (Chung-wai monthly) 15, no. 6 (1974): 13–17.
33. See Ching, *Becoming Japanese,* 161–68.
34. See, for example, Deng Xiangyang, *Wushe shijian,* chaps. 3–4.
35. Deng Xiangyang, *Fengzhong feiying,* 107.
36. Ching, *Becoming Japanese,* 161–73.
37. Ibid. Also see my essay, "Wuhe, The Bone Collector," in Wuhe, *Yusheng,* 7–40.
38. Deng Xiangyang, *Fengzhong feiying,* 152.
39. Wuhe, *Yusheng,* 46.
40. Ibid., 81.
41. Theodor W. Adorno, "A Portrait of Walter Benjamin," in *Prisms,* trans. Samuel Weber and Shierry Weber (Cambridge, Mass.: MIT Press, 1981), 277.
42. See Deng, *Fengzhong feiying,* 109–13.
43. Wuhe, *Yusheng,* 52.
44. See Leo Ching's discussion, *Becoming Japanese,* 151–60.
45. Michael Taussig, *Mimesis and Alterity: A Particular History of the Senses* (New York: Routledge, 1992).
46. Lu Xun, "Zixu," 3.
47. Jeffery Kinkley, *The Odyssey of Shen Congwen* (Stanford, Calif.: Stanford University Press, 1987), chap. 1. Also see Hsiao-yen Peng's discussion of Shen Congwen's ethnic romanticism, in *Chaoyue xieshi* (Beyong realism) (Taipei: Lianjing chuban gongsi, 1993), chaps. 1–2.
48. For an in-depth discussion of Shen Congwen's regionalism in his fiction, see Hsiao-yen Peng, *Antithesis Overcome: Shen Tsung-wen's Avant-gardism and Primitivism* (Taipei: Academia Sinica, 1994), chaps. 4–5.
49. See my discussion in *Fictional Realism,* chap. 6.
50. See my discussion in *Fictional Realism,* chap. 7.
51. Quoted from Shen Congwen, "Three Men and One Woman," trans. Jeffery Kinkley, in *Modern Chinese Short Stories and Novellas, 1919–1949,* ed. Joseph S. M. Lau, C. T. Hsia, and Leo Ou-fan Lee (New York: Columbia University Press, 1981), 265.
52. Wuhe, *Yusheng,* 47.
53. This refers to the Nationalist troops' bloody crackdown on the Taiwanese rioters on February 28, 1947.
54. Wuhe, *Yusheng,* 71.
55. Ibid., 43.

CHAPTER 2: CRIME OR PUNISHMENT?

1. For more discussion of the political and cultural significance of the appearance of *Xin Xiaoshuo*, see my *Fin-de-siècle Splendor: Repressed Modernities of Late Qing Fiction, 1849–1911* (Stanford, Calif.: Stanford University Press, 1977), chap. 1.
2. See Fan Mingxin and Lei Chengsheng, *Zhongguo jindai fazhi shi* (A history of the modern Chinese legal system) (Xian: Shanxi renmin chubanshe, 1988), chap. 1; Xiao Yongqing, ed., *Zhongguo fazhishi jianbian* (A short history of the Chinese legal system) (Taiyuan: Shanxi renmin chubanshe, 1982), 2: 18–55. Also see Laszlo Ladany, *Law and Legality in China: The Testament of a China Watcher*, ed. Marie-Luise Näth (Honolulu: University of Hawaii Press, 1992), 35–55. For general background information on the Qing legal system, see, for example, Derk Bodde and Clarence Morris, *Law in Imperial China: Exemplified by 190 Ch'ing Dynasty Cases* (Cambridge, Mass.: Harvard University Press, 1967).
3. Despite the social and political turmoil in the wake of the founding of the Republic of China, the Nationalist regime undertook the task of legal codification during the more settled times of the 1920s. It completed China's new criminal code and civil code in 1928 and 1929, respectively. Inspired by the late Qing Revised Code as well as Japanese and Western models, the new codes separated the judicial and executive arms of the government and reduced the gap between China's criminal justice and that of the West. See Ladany, *Law and Legality in China*, 50. Also see Philip Williams and Yenna Wu, *The Great Wall of Confinement: The Contemporary Prison Camp through Fiction and Reportage* (Berkeley: University of California Press, forthcoming), 30.
4. Richard H. Weisberg and Jean-Pierre Barricelli, "Literature and the Law," in *Interrelations of Literature*, ed. Joseph Gibaldi and Jean-Pierre Barricelli (New York: MLA, 1982), 150.
5. See Robert M. Cover, "*Nomos* and Narrative," *Harvard Law Journal* 95 (1986): 1609. Also see Clifford Geertz, *Local Knowledge: Further Essays in Interpretive Anthropology* (New York: Basic Books, 1983), particularly his discussion of the interplay between law and fact in the making of local knowledge, 197; Pierre Bourdieu, "The Force of Law: Toward a Sociology of the Juridical Field," *Hasting Law Journal* 38 (1987), 838, quoted in Kieran Dolin, *Fiction and the Law: Legal Discourse in Victorian and Modernist Literature* (New York: Cambridge University Press, 1999), 11. The first two chapters of Dolin's discussion of "narrative forms and normative worlds" and the rise of modern Western *nomos* illuminate my argument.
6. The most blatant example in this regard is perhaps the continued invention of cruel penal forms throughout Chinese history. See Wang Yongkuan, *Zhongguo gudai Kuxing* (Cruel forms of punishment in premodern China) (Taipei: Yunlong chubanshe, 1991). Also see Jonathan N. Lipman and Stephen Harrell, eds., *Violence in China: Essays in Culture and Counterculture* (Albany: State University of New York Press, 1990).
7. See, for example, Bodde and Morris, *Law in Imperial China*; Hugh T. Scogin Jr., "Civil 'Law' in Traditional China: History and Theory," in *Civil Law in Qing and Republican China*, ed. Kathryn Bernhardt and Philip C. C. Huang (Stanford, Calif.: Stanford University Press, 1994), 13–41; Geertz, *Local Knowledge*, 167–235. In her study of the relationship between literature, law, and philosophy in eigh-

teenth- and nineteenth-century American literature, Wai Chee Dimock describes four forms that constitute the "program of justice": corrective, distributive, compensatory, and revolutionary. Dimock's argument is based on rethinking justice as an ontological given and justice as a historical praxis subject to the debate of "commensurability." See *Residues of Justice: Literature, Law, Philosophy* (Berkeley: University of California Press, 1997), chap. 1.

8. I am referring in particular to the book edited by Nancy Armstrong and Leonard Tennenhouse, *The Violence of Representation: Literature and the History of Violence* (New York: Routledge, 1989). See their introduction, 1–26.
9. Chen Duxiu, "Wenxue geming lun" (On literary revolution), in *Duxiu wencun* (Writings of Chen Duxiu) (Shanghai: Yadong tushuguan, 1931), 1: 135–40.
10. Lu Xun, "Kuangren riji" (Diary of a madman), in *Lu Xun quanji,* (Complete works of Lu Xun) (Beijing: Renmin wenxue chubanshe, 1981), 1: 420.
11. Liu Zaifu, "Zhongguo xiandai xiaoshuo de zhengzhishi xiezuo: Cong 'Chuncan' dao *Taiyang zhaozai Sanggan heshang*" (The politics of writing in modern Chinese literature: From "Spring Silkworms" to *The Sun Shines over the Sanggan River*), in *Fangzhu zhushen: Wenlun tigang he wenxueshi chongping* (Exiling gods: Outlines of literary theory and rereadings of literary history) (Hong Kong: Tiandi tushu gongsi, 1994), 133–34, 140.
12. See Armstrong and Tennenhouse, *Violence,* 1–26.
13. Ibid., 9.
14. Zhang Taiyan published "Ruxia pian" (On the scholarly knight) in *Yadong shibao* (East Asian times) in 1899, arguing that the concept and practice of traditional chivalric knight-errantry, or *xia,* is derived from the Confucian scholarly tradition. See Wang Yue's discussion in "Zhang Taiyan de ruxia guan jiqi lishi yiyi" (Zhang Taiyan's concept of the scholarly knight and its historical significance), in *Xia yu Zhongguo wenhua* (Knight-errantry and Chinese culture), ed. Department of Chinese, Tamkang University (Taipei: Xuesheng shuju, 1993), 269–86. Also see Wendy Larson's discussion in *Literary Authority and the Modern Chinese Writer: Ambivalence and Autobiography* (Durham, N.C.: Duke University Press, 1991), 31–59.
15. Of course, literature babbles on about injustice and revolution, but these are just terms in the new master narrative. The silences are about actual cruelties and actual repetitions, and the worst silence is the one about literary complicity, because it does representational violence to representation itself.
16. Zheng Zhenduo, "Xue he lei de wenxue" (Literature of blood and tears), in *Zheng Zhenduo xuanji* (Works of Zheng Zhenduo) (Fuzhou: Fujian renmin chubanshe, 1984), 1097.
17. Ibid., 245. Throughout the chapter I will use the term "incorruptible" to mean specifically "not bribable."
18. This appears in chapter 6 of *Laocan youji.* See C. T. Hsia's discussion in "*The Travels of Lao Ts'an:* An Exploration of Its Arts and Meaning," *Tsing Hua Journal of Chinese Studies* 7, no. 2 (1969): 40–66.
19. See C. T. Hsia, "Travels," 50–52 and n. 31.
20. The Yellow River in this area is less than a mile wide and is rimmed by small dikes built and maintained by the farmers whose land they protect. The government-built dikes are massive embankments twenty feet high and are up to three miles

away from the water. The land between the two dikes is fertile and densely populated. See Harold Shadick's note in his translation of *Travels* (Ithaca, N.Y.: Cornell University Press, 1952), 262.

21. See Liu E's commentary at the end of chapter 13 of *Travels*, ibid., 124.
22. Ibid., 259–66.
23. Liu E may not have been aware of the potential for this ironic reading. Schematically, however, his novel encourages us to apply on the celestial level the same rules he has been applying to terrestrial justice. By mentioning the bureaucracy of Hell in the context of the failures of human bureaucracy, Liu E sets up the comparison.
24. Li Boyuan, *Huo diyu* (Living hell) (Taipei: Guangya shuju, 1984), 1. I am using Douglas Lancashire's translation, quoted in Lancashire, *Li Poyuan* (Boston: Twayne Publishers, 1978), 64–65.
25. It was the second of Li Boyuan's novels, serialized in his magazine *Xiuxiang xiaoshuo* (Illustrated fiction). The novel comprises forty-three chapters; like most novels by Li Boyuan, it remains incomplete. Li died after finishing chapter 39. Chapters 40 to 42 were added by his friend, the novelist Wu Jianren. The last chapter is said to have been written by Ouyang Juyuan (1883–1907), Li's friend and the assistant editor of *Illustrated Fiction*. The novel was only published in book form in 1956 in Shanghai, under the auspices of the well-known scholar Zhao Jingshen.
26. Lancashire, *Li Poyuan*, 63.
27. Here I am partially indebted to Lyotard's concept of justice. See Jean-François Lyotard and Jean-Loup Thébaud, *Just Gaming*, trans. Brian Massumi (Minneapolis: University of Minnesota Press, 1979), 25–26.
28. Li Boyuan, *Huo diyu*, 72.
29. The first is a long aluminum pipe wrapped around the prisoner's body. The attendants inject boiling water at one end of the pipe and let it flow slowly to the other end. The second is a form of capital punishment, where five nails are inserted into the four limbs and the chest of the prisoner. In the third, three iron sticks are used to beat the prisoner. By pressing one iron stick on the prisoner's chest and the other on his legs, the courtroom attendants stop the prisoner's breath at the two ends of his body and force it to accumulate in his stomach. They then use the third stick to beat the prisoner's stomach, and with one loud sound, the intestines explode.
30. Michel Foucault, *Discipline and Punish: The Birth of the Prison*, trans. Alan Sheridan (New York: Pantheon, 1977), 24–85.
31. Lao Can is compared to Sherlock Holmes in chapter 18 for his investigation of the aforementioned murder case.
32. Lu Xun, "Zixu," in *Lu Xun quanji* (Complete works of Lu Xun) (Beijing: Renmin wenxue chubanshe, 1981), 1: 417.
33. See also my discussion in "Lu Xun, Shen Congwen, and Decapitation," in *Politics, Ideology, and Literary Discourse in Modern China: Theoretical Interventions and Cultural Critique*, ed. Liu Kang and Tang Xiaobing (Durham, N.C.: Duke University Press, 1993), 174–87.
34. Lu Xun, "Zixu," 417.
35. T. A. Hsia, *The Gate of Darkness: Studies of the Leftist Literary Movement in China* (Seattle: University of Washington Press, 1968), 146.

36. Lu Xun seems to have understood the full meaning of late Qing intellectual chivalry; one cannot always say this for the writers after him, who too often thought they had passed through the gate and left the late Qing far behind them.
37. For a discussion of the rise and development of Chinese court-case drama, see Zeng Yongyi, *Zhongguo gudian xiju de renshi yu xinshang* (An introduction to and appraisal of classical Chinese drama) (Taipei: Zhengzhong shuju, 1991), 55.
38. Ouyang Yuqian, "Pan Jinlian," in *Ouyang Yuqian wenji* (Works of Ouyang Yuqian) (Beijing: Renmin wenxue chubanshe, 1984), 1: 90.
39. Ibid., 93.
40. Lu Xun, "Lun Leifeng ta de daodiao" (On the collapse of Leifeng tower), in *Lu Xun quanji,* 1: 74–77.
41. Bai Wei, *Dachuyouling ta* (Fight out of the ghost tower), in *Zhongguo xinwenxue daxi: 1927–1937, xiju juan* (A compendium of Modern Chinese literature: 1927–1937, drama), ed. Zhao Jiabi (Shanghai: Shanghai wenyi chubanshe, 1982) 1: 64.
42. Ibid., 75.
43. Zhu Yiqui, *Zhongguo xiandai xijushi* (History of modern Chinese drama) (Guilin: Guangxi renmin chubanshe, 1981), 234–36.
44. See, for example, Meng Yue and Dai Jinhua, *Fuchu lishi dibiao: Zhongguo xiandai nüxing wenxue yanjiu* (Voices emerging from the foreground of history: A study of contemporary Chinese women's literature) (Taipei: Shibao wenhua chuban gongsi, 1993), 227–30.
45. Bai Wei, "*Dachu youling ta* houji" (Afterword to *Dachu youling ta* [Breaking out of the tower of ghosts]), in *Bai Wei zuopinji* (Works of Bai Wei) (Changsha: Hunan renmin chubanshe, 1985), 77.
46. Marston Anderson, *The Limits of Realism: Chinese Fiction in the Revolutionary Period* (Berkeley: University of California Press, 1990), 44.
47. T. A. Hsia, *Gate of Darkness,* 55–59.
48. Jiang Guangci, *Paoxiao de tudi* (The roaring earth), in *Jiang Guangci wenji* (Selected works of Jiang Guangci) (Shanghai: Shanghai wenyi chubanshe, 1982), 2: 374.
49. Ibid.
50. Ibid. See also Leo Ou-fan Lee, *The Romantic Generation of Modern Chinese Writers* (Cambridge, Mass.: Harvard University Press, 1973), 201–21.
51. Wu Zuxiang, "Young Master Gets His Tonic," trans. Cyril Birch, in *Modern Chinese Short Stories and Novellas: 1919–1949,* ed. C. T. Hsia, Joseph S. M. Lau, and Leo Ou-fan Lee (New York: Columbia University Press, 1981), 381.
52. Part of the plot summary is derived from Marston Anderson, *Limits,* 198.
53. C. T. Hsia, *A History of Modern Chinese Fiction* (New Haven, Conn.: Yale University Press, 1971), 284–85; Philip Williams, *Village Echoes: The Fiction of Wu Zuxiang* (Boulder: Westview Press, 1993), 82–84.
54. C. T. Hsia, *History,* 286.
55. Wu Zuxiang, "Yiqian babai dan" (Eighteen hundred piculs of rice), in *Wu Zuxiang* (Taipei: Haifeng chubanshe, 1990), 158–59.
56. See, for example, Merle Goldman, *Literary Dissent in Communist China* (Cambridge, Mass: Harvard University Press, 1967), 1–50. Few literary historians have noticed that, right after Mao delivered his talks, the Nationalist Party retaliated by commissioning Zhang Daofan, a playwright and literary propagandist, to ad-

vocate a literature based on Sun Yat-sen's *Three Principles of the People.* This policy would eventually become the backbone of the anti-Communist literature that the Nationalist Party promoted in Taiwan in the 1950s and 1960s. A comparative reading of both Nationalist and Communist literary policies indicates, ironically, a parallel between them in theory and practice, despite the fact that they were meant as antagonistic discourses. See Cheng Ming-lee, "Dangdai Taiwan wenyi zhengce de fazhan, yingxiang, yu jiaotao" (On the development, impact, and consequences of the literary policy in contemporary Taiwan), in *Dangdai Taiwan zhengzhi wenxue lun* (Politics and contemporary Taiwanese literature), ed. Cheng Ming-lee (Taipei: Shibao chuban gongsi, 1994), 1–20. See also Chapter 5 below.

57. See my paper "Reinventing National History."
58. C. T. Hsia, *History,* 326–60. Also see Theodore Huters, "Hu Feng and the Critical Legacy of Lu Xun," in *Lu Xun and His Legacy,* ed. Leo Ou-fan Lee (Berkeley: University of California Press, 1985), 129–52.
59. See David E. Apter and Tony Saich's discussion in *Revolutionary Discourse in Mao's Republic* (Cambridge, Mass: Harvard University Press, 1994), 243–92.
60. Yi-tsi Mei Feuerwerker, *Ding Ling's Fiction* (Cambridge, Mass: Harvard University Press, 1982), 114. Also see Tani E. Barlow and Gary J. Bjorge, eds., *I Myself Am a Woman: Selected Writings of Ding Ling* (Boston: Beacon Press, 1989), 34–45.
61. Ding Ling, "When I Was in Hsia Village," trans. Gary J. Bjorge, in *Modern Chinese Stories and Novellas,* 1919–1949, ed. Joseph S. M. Lau, C. T. Hsia, and Leo Ou-fan Lee (New York: Columbia University Press, 1981), 274.
62. This argument can be read in light of Apter and Saich's recent discussion, where they borrow Baudrillard's theory to describe an effect of simulacrum in the production of the revolutionary discourse and revolutionary site, *Revolutionary Discourse,* 224–62.
63. See Huang Ziping's succinct discussion in "Bing de yinyu yu wenxue shengchan: Ding Ling de 'Zai yiyuan zhong' ji qita" (The metaphor of illness and literary production: Ding Ling's "In the Hospital" and other works), in *Zaijiedu: Dazhong yu yishi xingtai* (Rereading: Mass literature and ideology), ed. Tang Xiaobing (Hong Kong: Oxford University Press, 1993), 51–67.
64. Ding Ling, "When I Was in Hsia Village," 268.
65. Merle Goldman, *Literary Dissent,* 67–86.
66. Lu Ling, *Ji'e de Guo Su'e* (Hungry Guo Su'e) (Beijing: Beijing renmin wenxue chubanshe, 1988), 103.
67. Ibid., 104.
68. See Feuerwerker, *Fiction,* 136–46.
69. Ibid., 139–40. Also see Apter and Saich, *Revolutionary Discourse,* 263–332.
70. Liu Zaifu and Lin Gang, "Zhongguo xiandai xiashuo," 130.
71. Fan Mingxin and Lei Chengsheng, *Zhongguo jindai fazhi shi,* 420–28.
72. Ibid., 124–25.
73. Roland Barthes, *Writing Degree Zero,* trans. Annete Lavers and Colin Smith (New York: Hill and Wang, 1978), 71.
74. Ding Ling, "Taiyang zhaozai Sanggan heshang" (The sun shines over the Sanggan River), in *Ding Ling xuanji* (Selected works of Ding Ling) (Chengdu: Sichuan renmin chubani, 1984), 1: 300. English translation from C. T. Hsia, *History,* 486.

75. Zhou Libo, *Baofeng zouyu* (Hurricane) (Changsha: Hunan renmin chubanshe, 1983), 174. See Tang Xiaobing's discussion in "Baoli de bianzheng fa" (The dialectic of violence), in *Zaijiedu: Dazhong wenyi yu yishi xingtai* (Rereading: Mass literature and ideology), ed. Tang Xiaobing (Hong Kong: Oxford University Press, 1993), 122.
76. Fan Mingxin and Lei Chengsheng, *Zhongguo jindai fazhi shi,* 421.
77. Writers like Liu E criticize the way incorruptible judges abuse their power, torturing innocent people, but they rarely criticize the habit of torturing people who are not innocent. Lao Can the dreamer condones the most horrible punishments imposed on condemned souls in Hell, just as Liu E applauds the edifying power of horrible punishments imposed on condemned criminals on Earth.
78. Also see Li Yang's discussion in *Kangzheng summing zhilu: Shehui zhuyi xianshi zhuyi (1942–1976) yan jiu* (A path to challenge fatalism: A study of socialist realism, 1942–1976) (Changchun: Shidai wenyi chubanshe, 1993). Inspired by the Foucauldian "bio-power" of discourse, Li argues that the rural violence perpetrated by the peasants has been legitimated not so much because of the mounting of a new justice system as because of the introduction of a new narrative discourse in the name of peasant revolution. See 96–114.
79. See Apter and Saich's description of Foucault's so-called paradox involved here: "The inversionary discourse that appears offers an unlimited prospect of freedom and proposes to free people from constraints of power, to break the hegemony of the discourse through which it is represented; but it, in turn, becomes hegemonic, all the more as it cleaves to its original intent," *Revolutionary Discourse,* 331.
80. Tang Xiabing, "Baoli de bianzheng fa," 120.
81. Ibid., 121.
82. Apter and Saich, *Revolutionary Discourse,* chaps. 8, 9.
83. Ding Ling, *Taiyang zhaozai Sanggan heshang,* 247–48.

CHAPTER 3: AN UNDESIRED REVOLUTION

1. Quoted in Shen Weiwei, *Jianxin de rensheng* (A hard life) (Taipei: Yeqiang chubanshe, 1993), 80–81. Dated August 12, 1927, the poem was published on August 19. Chen Yu-shih translated part of this poem in her book, *Realism and Allegory in the Early Fiction of Mao Tun* (Bloomington: Indiana University Press, 1986), 39–40. The current translation is based on hers with modifications.
2. See C. Martin Wilbur, *The Nationalist Revolution in China: 1923–1928* (New York: Columbia University Press, 1984); Immanuel C. Y. Hsu, *The Rise of Modern China* (New York: Oxford University Press), 530. See also Guo Tingyi, *Jindai zhongguo shigang* (A history of modern China) (Hong Kong: Chinese University of Hong Kong Press, 1986), 537–70; William G. Rosenberg and Marilyn B. Young, *Transforming Russia and China: Revolutionary Struggle in the Twentieth Century* (Oxford: Oxford University Press, 1982), 112–19.
3. Rosenberg and Young, *Transforming Russia and China,* 117.
4. For the general information about the Shanghai workers' riot, followed by the massacre launched by Chiang Kai-shek, see, for example, Wilbur, *Nationalist Revolution,* esp. 95–165.

5. Mao Dun, *Wo zouguo de daolu* (The road I have taken) (Hong Kong: Sanlian shudian, 1981), 1: 292–98.
6. According to his autobiography, *Wo zouguo de daolu,* Mao Dun was not informed beforehand of the Nanchang Uprising, and he learned of the incident from the waiters of the hotel where he stayed. See *Wo zouguo,* 296. Shen Weiwei suggests instead that Mao Dun was hiding from the uprising, *Jianxin de rensheng,* 78.
7. Ibid.
8. See Chen Yu-shi, *Realism and Allegory,* chap. 2; Shen Weiwei, *Jianxin de rensheng,* 80–82.
9. For a detailed discussion of the rise and development of "revolution" as a modern Chinese political and cultural project, see Jianhua Chen's comprehensive survey in *Geming de xiandaixing: Zhongguo geming huayu kaolun* (The modernity of revolution: A genealogical study of Chinese revolutionary discourse) (Shanghai: Shanghai guji chubanshe, 2000), 1–182. Also see Jianhua Chen, "Chinese 'Revolution' in the World Syntax of Revolution," in Lydia Liu, *Tokens of Exchange: The Problem of Translation in Global Circulations* (Durham, N.C.: Duke University Press, 1999), 33–354.
10. See also Marston Anderson's close reading of selected novels produced at this time by Mao Dun and other writers, in *The Limits of Realism: Chinese Fiction in the Revolutionary Period* (Berkeley: University of California Press, 1990).
11. Chingkiu Stephen Chan, "The Problematics of Modern Chinese Realism: Mao Dun and His Contemporaries (1919–1937)" (Ph.D. diss., University of California at San Diego, 1986).
12. Ibid, 146.
13. Peter Brooks, *Reading for the Plot: Design and Intent in the Narrative* (Cambridge, Mass: Harvard University Press, 1992).
14. The check was never cashed because it was made payable only to a designated recipient. Mao Dun was obviously very concerned about the way people thought of him in handling the check. In his memoir, he described in detail that the money was eventually reclaimed by the Communist Party. See *Wo zoguo de daolu,* 295. Wan Shuyu, *Mao Dun nianpu* (Biographical chronology of Mao Dun) (Hangzhou: Zhejiang wenyi chubanshe, 1986), 124–25.
15. Mao Dun considered *Eclipse* a chronicle of the1927 revolution in three stages, "first, young revolutionaries' exuberance on the eve of revolution and the disillusionment when coming face to face with it; second, their vacillation during the intensification of the revolutionary struggle; and third, their unwillingness to accept the desolation and despair after the revolution, and their desire to make a final search for the ideal." Mao Dun, "Cong Guling dao Dongjing" (From Kuling to Tokyo), in *Mao Dun pingzhuan* (Critical and biographical essays on Mao Dun), ed. Fu Zhiying (Shanghai: Xiandai shuju, 1931), 342.
16. For a recent analysis of *Eclipse,* see, for example, Jianhua Chen, "Geming de nüxing hua yu nüxing de geminghua," in *"Geming" de xiandaixing: Zhongguo geming huayu kaolun* (The modernity of revolution: A genealogical study of Chinese revolutionary discourse) (Shanghai: Shanghai guji chubanshe, 2000), 286–333.
17. David Der-wei Wang, *Fictional Realism in Twentieth-Century Chinese Fiction: Mao Dun, Lao She, Shen Congwen* (New York: Columbia University Press, 1992), chaps. 2–3.

18. Chen Yu-shi, *Realism and Allegory,* chaps. 3–5; Anderson, *Limits,* chap. 3. See also John Berninghausen, "The Central Contradiction in Mao Dun's Earliest Fiction," in Merle Goldman, ed., *Modern Chinese Literature in the May Fourth Era* (Cambridge, Mass: Harvard University Press, 1976), 233–59.
19. Fu Zhiying's *Mao Dun pingzhuan* illustrates well the debate over Mao Dun's fiction.
20. Mao Dun, "Cong Guling dao dongjing," 357–67.
21. Qian Xingcun, "Cong Dongjing huidao Wuhan" (From Tokyo back to Wuhan), in *Mao Dun pingzhuan,* 258.
22. Ibid, 269–71; see also Qian's "Mao Dun yu xianshi" (Mao Dun and Reality), in *Mao Dun pingzhuan,* 159–69, and esp. 189.
23. Ibid., 286.
24. Qian, "Mao Dun yu xianshi," 310–11.
25. See Wang-chi Wong, *Politics and Literature in Shanghai: The Chinese League of Left-Wing Writers, 1930–1936* (Manchester: Manchester University Press, 1991), 19; Kuang Xinnian, *1928: Geming wenxue* (1928: Revolutionary literature) (Jinan: Shandong jiaoyu chubanshe, 1998), 128–42; Liao Chaohui, *Zhongguo xiandai wenxue sichao lunzheng shi* (A history of the debates over literary thoughts in modern China) (Wuhan: Wuhan chubanshe, 1997), chap. 5.
26. Quoted in Leo Ou-fan Lee, *Voices from the Iron House: A Study of Lu Xun* (Bloomington: Indiana University Press, 1987), 163. See also Jiang Wenqi, *Sulian ershi niandai wenxue gailun* (Introduction to Soviet literature of the 1920s) (Shanghai: Shanghai waiyu jiaoyu chubanshe, 1990), 1–84.
27. See, for example, Mao Dun, "Ziran zhuyi yu zhongguo xiandai xiaoshuo" (Naturalism and modern Chinese fiction), in *Mao Dun wenyi zalun ji* (Critical essays by Mao Dun), ed. Zhang Liaomin (Shanghai: Shanghai wenyi chubanshe, 198), 92–93.
28. Mao Dun, "Du *Ni Huanzhi*" (Reading *Ni Huanzhi*), in *Mao Dun quanji,* 19: 197–217.
29. Mao Dun, *Wo zoguo de daolu,* 2: 11. See also Liao Chaohui, *Zhongguo xiandai wenxue sichao lunzheng shi,* 445–54.
30. Lu Xun, *Lu Xun quanji,* 3: 418; Wang-chi Wong's translation, *Politics and Literature,* 15. See also Liu Kang's discussion in *Aesthetics and Marxism: Chinese Aesthetic Marxists and Their Western Contemporaries* (Durham, N.C.: Duke University Press, 2000), 57–60.
31. Lu Xun, "Geming wenxue" (Revolutionary literature), in *Lu Xun quanji* (Beijing: Renmin chubanshe, 1981), 3: 544; Wong's translation, *Politics and Literature,* 15.
32. This certainly refers to Lu Xun's famous short story *Zai jiulou shang* (In the tavern). Feng Naichao, "Yishu yu shehui shenghuo" (Art and social life); quoted in Kuang, *1928,* 116.
33. Kuang, *1928,* 169–71.
34. Wong, *Politics and Literature,* 22.
35. Lee, *Iron House,* 156.
36. Wong, *Politics and Literature,* 23; Liao Chaohui, *Zhongguo xiandai wenxue sichao lunzheng shi,* 451–52; Liu Kang, *Aesthetics and Marxism,* 60–71.
37. Wong, *Politics and Literature,* 158; Liao Chaohui, *Zhongguo xiandai wenxue sichao lunzheng shi,* 451–54.

38. Mai Keang, "Yingxiong shu" (Tree of heroism), *Chuangzao yuekan* (Creation monthly) 1: 8; quoted in Qian Xingcun, "Cong donjing huidao Wuhan," 290.
39. Wu Tenghuang, *Jiang Guangci zhuan* (Biography of Jiang Guangci) (Hefei: Anhui renmin chubanshe, 1982), 75.
40. Ibid., 93. Lu Xun's and Jiang Guangci's names appeared side by side in the announcement of the renewed issuance of *Chaungzao zhoubao* (Creation weekly), a major channel of leftist literature, later that year. History took a twist at this juncture, however. The weekly never came out, owing to the internecine conflict among editors. As a result, Jiang left the Creation Society to found the even more radical Sun Society in early 1928. Meanwhile, Lu Xun had changed from Jiang's ally to his and his colleagues' enemy.
41. Leo Ou-fan Lee, *The Romantic Generation of Modern Chinese Writers* (Cambridge, Mass: Harvard University Press, 1973), 208–209.
42. Jiang Guangci conceded that *The Youthful Tramp* was a "crude and violent" work that might violate many readers' refined tastes. But he insisted that, living at a chaotic time, he had no other choice but "utterly crude and violent cries." Aesthetic defects notwithstanding, *The Youthful Tramp* was a bestseller. Its mixture of maudlin narcissism and Byronic martyrdom captured the hearts of numerous young readers. Above all, the novel derived its power from invoking *youth and untimely death,* the time-honored romantic motif, in the new context of Chinese revolution. Precisely because the historical moment was "crude and violent," Jiang's youthful tramp appeared doubly vulnerable, and his undeserved suffering and heroic sacrifice became a larger-than-life critique of the capricious environment. Jiang Guangci, *Shaonian paiopozhe* (The youthful tramp), in *Jiang Guangci wenji* (Selected works of Jiang Guangci) (Shanghai: Shanghai wenyi chubanshe, 1982), 1: 4.
43. Jiang Guangci, "Yeji" (A sacrifice in the wild), *Jiang Guangci wenji,* 1: 371.
44. Wu Tenghuang, *Jiang Guangci zhuan* (Biography of Jiang Guangci) (Heifei: Anhui renmin chubanshe, 1982).
45. Jiang Guangci, *Chongchu yunwei de yueliang* (The moon forces its way through the clouds), in *Jiang Guangci wenji,* 2: 48.
46. Qu Qiubai, "Geming de langman dike" (Revolutionary romanticism), in *Qu Qiubai wenji: Wenxuebian* (Works of Quqiubai: Literature) (Beijing: Renmin wenxue chubanshe, 1985), 1: 456–60. Mao Dun, "*Diquan* duhougan" (Thoughts after reading *Earth Spring*), in *Jiang Guangci yanjiu ziliao* (Research materials on Jiang Guangci), ed. Fang Ming (Yinchuan: Ningxia renmin chubanshe, 1983), 207. See also Jianmei Liu's discussion in "Engaging with Revolution and Love" (Ph.D. diss., Columbia University, 1998), 103–14.
47. Years later, Hua Han would admit the limitation of revolutionary romanticism in that "it cannot reflect the materialistic dialectic of society; instead it treats the cruel social struggle in terms of idealism, mysticism, elitism, and romanticism." Kuang, *1928,* 106.
48. Mao Dun, "Geming yu lianai de gongshi" (On the formula of revolution and love), *Mao Dun quanji,* 20: 337–53.
49. Hong Ruizhao, *Geming yu lianai* (Revolution and love) (Shanghai: Minzhi shuju, 1928), 2.
50. Hong, *Geming yu lianai,* 51.

51. Anderson, *Limits,* chap. 3. See also my discussion in *Fictional Realism,* chaps. 2–3.
52. Fang Gu, "Geming wenxue yu ziran zhuyi" (Revolutionary literature and naturalism); quoted in Kuang, *1928,* 108.
53. Jiang Guangci, "Shiyue geming yu elouosi wenxue" (October revolution and Russian literature), in *Jiang Guangci wenji,* 4: 68. Also see Kuang's discussion, *1928,* 112.
54. Jiang Guangci, *Jiang Guangci wenji,* 4: 68.
55. Ibid., 65; Kuang, *1928,* 111.
56. T. A. Hsia, *The Gate of Darkness: Studies of the Leftist Literary Movement* (Seattle: University of Washington Press, 1968), 60.
57. Ibid., 71.
58. See T. A. Hsia's discussion, *Gate of Darkness.* See also Wu Tenghuang, *Jiang Guangci zhuan,* 146–51.
59. See Chen Yu-shi, *Realism and Allegory.*
60. Hong, *Geming yu liamai,* 80.
61. Ibid., 83–84.
62. Quoted in Bai Shurong, *Bai Wei pingzhuan* (Critical biography of Bai Wei) (Changsha: Hunan renmin chubanshe, 1983), 51.
63. Ibid.
64. Bai Shurong, *Bai Wei pingzhuan,* 77–79.
65. The play was later rewritten and retitled *Letu* (Happy land).
66. Bai Wei, *Beiju shengya* (Shanghai: Shenghuo shudian, 1936), 217.
67. Ibid, 247.
68. Chan, "Problematics," 36.
69. Liu Jianmei, "Engaging with Revolution and Love" (Ph.D. diss., Columbia University, 1998), 132.
70. Shen Weiwei, *Jianxin de rensheng,* 109–15. See also Shen Weiwei, "Yiwei cenggei Mao Dun de shenghuo yu chuangzuo yi henda yingxiang de nuxing: Qin Dejun duihua lu" (A woman who exerted great impact on Mao Dun's life and writing: A dialogue with Qin Dejun), *Xuchang shizhuan xuebao* (Journal of Xuchang Teachers' College) 2 (1990), 48–81.
71. See, for example, Mao Dun, *Wo zouguo de daolu,* 2: 17–27.
72. For more information about the marriage, see Mao Dun, *Wo zouguo de daolu,* 1: 120–28. For a biographical account of Mao Dun and Kong Dezhi's marital life, see Ding Ergang, *Mao Dun, Kong Dezhi* (Beijing: Zhongguo qingnian chubanshe, 1995). Ding displays a sympathetic attitude toward the couple, unlike Shen Weiwei in his biography of Mao Dun.
73. Shen Weiwei, *Jianxin de rensheng,* 52; Ding Ergang, *Mao Dun,* 103. Mao Dun's attitude is also reflected in his endorsement of the remarriage of his colleague Yun Daiying. Yun argued, in response to his colleagues' criticism that he married his late wife's sister for convenience, that his decision was made in terms not of "free love" but of a love motivated by a "revolutionary goal." "If we revolutionaries cannot make even those who are close to us happy, what is the purpose of revolution?" See Mao Dun, *Wo zouguo de daolu,* 1: 280.
74. Mao Dun, *Wo zouguo de daolu,* 2: 10. See also my discussion in *Fictional Realism,* 80–82.
75. See Shen Weiwei's interview with Qin Dejun, "Yiwei cenggei Mao Dun." See also

Qin Dejun and Liu Huai, *Huo fenghuang: Qin Dejun he tade yige shiji* (Phoenix in the fire: Qin Dejun and her century) (Beijing: Zhongyang bianyi chubanshe, 1999), 23.

76. See Shen Weiwei, "Yiwei cenggei Mao Dun."
77. Ibid.
78. Shen Weiwei is among the very few Chinese scholars working in the 1990s on Qin's romance. In Japan, Shirinaga Jun has made an extensive study of Mao Dun's stay in Japan. Qin Dejun's autobiography, *Huo fenghuang,* though available in manuscript form as early as the late 1980s, was not published until 1999. According to Shen Weiwei, upon its publication, the autobiography was boycotted by Mao Dun's family and scholars of Mao Dun studies. Part of an early version of Qin's autobiography was published in 1988 in Japan; see Qin Dejun, "Yingshi" (Cherry blossoms in eclipse), *Yecao* (Wild grass), 41, 42 (1988): 63–76, 1–22. The part of Ding Ergang's book about the triangle between Mao Dun, Kong Dezhi, and Qin Dejun relies much on Qin Dejun's materials. When *Mao Dun, Kong Dezhi* was published in 1995, Qin's autobiography was not yet available. Ding's book clearly takes a critical attitude toward Qin. See chaps. 5, 6.
79. See Raoul David Findeisen, "Two Works—*Hong* (1930) and *Ying'er* (1993)—As Indeterminate Joint Adventures," in *Essays, Interviews, Recollections, and Unpublished Material of Gu Cheng, Twentieth-Century Chinese Poet: The Poetics of Death,* ed. Xia Li (Lewiston: Edwin Mellen, 1999), 135–78.
80. Mao Dun, "Cong Guling dao Donjing," 368.
81. In a letter to Zhuang Zhongqing dated June 15, 1961, Mao Dun made it clear that by the Scandinavian Goddess of Fate he meant the Soviet Union. See Sun Zhongtian and Zhou Ming, eds., *Mao Dun Shuxinji* (Correspondence of Mao Dun) (Beijing: Wenhua yishu chubanshe, 1988), 195–96.
82. Shen Weiwei, *Jianxin de rensheng,* 113–14; Qin, "Yingshi," 67; Ding Ergang, *Mao Dun,* 156–59. There has been a dispute among Mao Dun biographers as to whether Mao Dun really meant Qin Dejun to be his "Scandinavian goddess of fate." Ding Ergang points out that by the time Mao Dun invoked the image in "Cong Guling dao Donjing," he had known Qin for no more than half a month and therefore logically could not have conferred this honorable name on Qin. Ding Ergang, *Mao Dun,* 124. One could easily challenge this point by arguing that, be that as it may, Mao Dun could have retroactively identified Qin with the goddess after having fallen in love with her. In the absence of further evidence, this issue will remain arguable in the foreseeable future.
83. Xin Yi, "*Zhuiqiu* zhongde Zhang Qiuliu" (Zhang Qiuliu in *Zhuiqiu*), quoted in Fu Zhiying, *Mao Dun pingzhuan,* 103–104.
84. See Shen Weiwei's interview with Qin Dejun, "Yiwei cenggei Mao Dun," 53–55. Also see Qin, "Yingshi," 93.
85. Shen Weiwei, *Jianxin de rensheng,* 131–32; Ding Ergang, *Mao Dun,* chapter 6.
86. Shen Weiwei, *Jianxin de rensheng,* 176.
87. See my discussion in *Fictional Realism,* 89–100.
88. Shen Weiwei's interview with Qin Dejun, "Yiwei cenggei Mao Dun," 2, 79. For a different interpretation, see Ding Ergang, *Mao Dun,* 222–23. Ding insists that the novel is based on historically verifiable figures and therefore has nothing to do with Mao Dun and Qin Dejun's aborted romance.

89. Mao Dun, *Fushi* (Putrefaction), in *Mao Dun quanji* (Complete works of Mao Dun) (Beijing: Renmin wenxue chubanshe, 1984–97), 5: 5.
90. Jiang Guangci, "Shiyue geming yu eluosi wenxue," 4: 68.
91. "You address me as a beloved friend—this, honestly, I doubt somewhat, because I feel in the present world no one loves me," wrote Jiang in one letter. Song responded with letters replete with equally strong romantic provocations: "My Xiasheng! Why can't I stop loving you? I wish I could sincerely and everlastingly love only you. . . . Can you love me forever?" Quoted in Leo Ou-fan Lee, *The Romantic Generation,* 214.
92. Ibid., 215.
93. Wu Tenghuang, *Jiang Guangci zhuan,* 77.
94. Jiang Guangci, "Guling yihen"(Everlasting regrets in Guling), in *Jiang Guangci wenji,* 3: 433.
95. Huang Ziping, "Bing de yinyu he wenxue shengchan" (The metaphor of disease and the production of literature), in *Geming, lishi, xiaoshuo* (Revolution, history, fiction) (Hong Kong: Niujin daxue chubanshe, 1996), 141–58; Su Wei, "The School and the Hospital: On the Logics of Socialist Realism," in *Chinese Literature in the Second Half of the Modern Century: A Critical Survey,* ed. Pang-yuan Chi and David Der-wei Wang (Bloomington: Indiana University Press, 2000), 65–75; Andrew Schonebaum, "The New Commerce: The Venereal Disease in Modern Chinese Literature," conference paper at AAS, March 10, 2000; Xiaobing Tang, "The Last Tubercular," in *Chinese Modern: The Heroic and the Quotidian* (Durham, N.C.: Duke University Press, 2000), 131–60.
96. Karatani Kojin, "Sickness As Meaning," in *Origins of Modern Japanese Literature,* trans. and ed. Brett de Bary (Durham, N.C.: Duke University Press, 1993), 108–10. See also Susan Sontag's *Illness As Metaphor, and, AIDS and Its Metaphors* (New York: Farrar, Straus & Giroux, 1978), chaps. 1–5.
97. See Xiaobing Tang's discussion of Ba Jin's wartime novel *Hanye* (Cold night), in *Chinese Modern,* 131–60.
98. Wu Tenghuang, *Jiang Guangci zhuan,* 143.
99. Bai Wei, *Zuoye* (Last night), quoted in Bai Shurong, *Bai Wei pingzhuan,* 40–41.
100. Bai Shurong, *Bai Wei pingzhuan,* 117.
101. Ibid., 118
102. Amy Dooling, "Feminism and Narrative Strategies in Early Twentieth-Century Chinese Women's Writing" (Ph.D. diss., Columbia University, 1998). See also Meng Yue and Dai Jinhua, *Fuchu lishi dibiao: Zhongguo xiandai nüxing wenxue yanjiu* (Voices emerging from the foreground of history: A study of contemporary Chinese women's literature) (Taipei: Shibao wenhua chuban gongsi, 1993), 231–35.
103. Ibid., 726.
104. Ibid.
105. Ibid., 729.
106. Ibid., 738.
107. Bai Shurong, *Bai Wei pingzhuan,* 149–52.
108. Ibid., 748.
109. Ibid., 855.
110. Ibid., 746–47.

111. For Bai Wei's life from the 1940s to the 1980s, see veteran woman writer Zhao Qingge, "Huang Baiwei yu Xie Bingying" (Huang Baiwei and Xie Bingying), in *Chang xiangyi* (Remembrances forever) (Shanghai: Xuelin chubanshe, 1999), 5–11.
112. Shen Weiwei, *Jianxin de rensheng,* 276.
113. For a detailed description of Qin's involvement in Communist underground activities during wartime, see Qin, "Yingshi," 121–30.

CHAPTER 4: THREE HUNGRY WOMEN

1. For a comprehensive description of food shortages and their political and economic consequences in early-twentieth-century China, see, for instance, Walter Hampton Mallory, *China, Land of Famine* (New York: American Geographical Society, 1926); John Lossing Buck, Owen L. Dawson, and Yuan-li Wu, *Food and Agriculture in Communist China* (Stanford, Calif.: Hoover Institution Publications, 1966).
2. See, for example, Gang Yue's succinct analysis in "Hunger, Cannibalism, and the Politics of Eating: Alimentary Discourse in Chinese and Chinese American Literature" (Ph.D. diss., University of Oregon, 1993), which came to my attention after I wrote this chapter. Also see Yue's book, *The Mouth That Begs: Hunger, Cannibalism, and the Politics of Eating in Modern China* (Durham, N.C.: Duke University Press, 1999).
3. Lu Hsun [Xun], "The New Year's Sacrifice," in *Selected Stories of Lu Hsun,* trans. Yang Hsien-yi and Gladys Yang (Beijing: Foreign Language Press, 1978), 127.
4. James W. Brown, *Fictional Meals and Their Function in the French Novel, 1789–1848* (Toronto: University of Toronto Press, 1984), 12–13; Gang Yue, "Hunger, Cannibalism, and the Politics of Eating," 16; and Louis Marin, *Food for Thought,* trans. Mette Hjort (Baltimore, Md.: Johns Hopkins University Press, 1989), 35–38.
5. See Gang Yue's discussion in *Mouth,* chap. 1.
6. Lu Ling is the pseudonym of Xu Sixing. For more biographical information, see Zhang Huan, Wei Lin, Li Zhiyuan, and Yang Yi, eds., *Lu Ling yanjiu ziliao* (Research materials on Lu Ling) (Beijing: Beijing shiyue wenyi chubanshe, 1993); Zhu Hengqing, *Lu Ling: Weiwancheng de tiancai* (Lu Ling: An unaccomplished talent) (Jinan: Shandong wenyi chubanshe, 1997); Zhang Yesong, ed., *Lu Ling yinxiang* (Impressions of Lu Ling) (Shanghai: Xuelin chubanshe, 1997).
7. Originally from Lu Ling's letter to Hu Feng on May 12, 1942, this statement was nevertheless misquoted by Hu Feng when writing his preface to *Ji'e de Guo Su'e.* "Langfeide" (wastefully) should have been "langmande" (romantically). See Xiaofeng, ed., *Hu Feng, Lu Ling wenxue shujian* (Correspondance on literature between Hu Feng and Lu Ling) (Hefei: Anhui wenyi chubanshe, 1994), 37. While acknowledging his oversight, I see in Hu Feng's misquote of "langfeide" an intriguing Freudian slip, which brings to the fore Lu Ling's compulsion to excess in both form and content.
8. Lu Ling, *Ji'e de Guo Sue* (Hungry Guo Su'e) (Beijing: Beijing renmin wenxue chubanshe, 1988), 103.
9. Hu Feng, "*Ji'e de Guo Su'e* xu" (Preface to *Hungry Guo Sue*), in *Lu Ling yanjiu ziliao* (Research materials on Lu Ling), ed. Zhang Huan, Wei Lin, Li Zhiyuan,

and Yang Yi (Beijing: Beijing shiyue wenyi chubanshe, 1993), 60. I am using Kirk Denton's translation, in "Mind and the Problematic of Self in Modern Chinese Literature: Hu Feng's Subjectivism and Lu Ling's Psychological Fiction" (Ph.D. diss., University of Toronto, 1992), 235.

10. See Yunzhong Shu's detailed discussion in *Buglers on the Home Front: The Wartime Practice of the Qiyue School* (Albany: State University of New York Press, 2000). See also C. T. Hsia, *A History of Modern Chinese Fiction* (New Haven, Conn.: Yale University Press, 1971), 326–60; Theodore Huters, "Hu Feng and the Critical Legacy of Lu Xun," in *Lu Xun and His Legacy,* ed. Leo Ou-fan Lee (Berkeley: University of California Press, 1985), 129–52; Kirk Denton, *The Problematic of Self in Modern Chinese Literature: Hu Feng and Lu Ling* (Stanford, Calif.: Stanford University Press, 1998), part 1, esp. chap. 2.
11. I am referring to the famous statement about the urgency of reforming Chinese souls instead of Chinese bodies.
12. Hu Feng, "*Ji'e de Guo Su'e* xu," 60.
13. Shao Quanlin, "Ji'e de Guo Su'e" *(Hungry Guo Su'e),* in *Lu Ling yanjiu ziliao,* ed. Zhang Huan et al., 66.
14. Yang Yi, "Lu Ling: Linghun aomi de tansuozhe" (Lu Ling: An explorer of the mystery of the soul), in *Lu Ling yanjiu ziliao,* ed. Zhang Huan et al., 175–203; Qian Liqun, "Tansuozhe de de yu shi" (Gains and losses of an explorer), in *Lu Ling yanjiu ziliao,* ed. Zhang Huan et al., 156–72.
15. Rey Chow, *Primitive Passions: Visuality, Sexuality, Ethnicity, and Contemporary Chinese Cinema* (New York: Columbia University Press, 1997). Chow bases her observation on the arguably underprivileged experience of (filmic) visuality, in contrast to that of literary textuality. But insofar as "primitive passions" can be seen as a rhetorical trope and emotive deployment foregrounding the absent cause of Modernity, they can find an equally powerful manifestation in writing. For a discussion along similar lines, see my definition of "imaginary nostalgia" in regard to Shen Congwen's nativist writings, in *Fictional Realism in Twentieth-Century China: Mao Dun, Lao She, Shen Congwen* (New York: Columbia University Press, 1992), chap. 7.
16. Chow, *Primitive Passions,* 21.
17. See Kirk Denton, "Lu Ling's Literary Art: Myth and Symbol in *Hungry Guo Su'e,*" *Modern Chinese Literature* 2, no. 2 (fall 1986): 197–209; Denton, "Mind," 202–37, and *The Problematic of Self,* 243–53; Liu Kang, "The Language of Desire, Class, and Subjectivity in Lu Ling's Fiction," in *Gender and Sexuality in Twentieth-Century Chinese Literature and Society,* ed. Tongling Lu (Albany: State University of New York Press, 1993), 67–84; and Shu Yunzhong, *Buglers,* 20–123.
18. See Mallory, *China, Land of Famine;* and Buck, Dawson, and Wu, *Food and Agriculture.*
19. Zhonggong zhongyang wenxian yanjiushi, ed., *Mao Zedong wenji* (Works of Mao Zedong) (Beijing: Renmin chubanshe, 1981) 1: 5–7, 15–16, 33, 44–45.
20. See Gang Yue's discussion in "Hunger, Cannibalism, and the Politics of Eating," 160–61.
21. Denton, "Mind," 129, and *The Problematic of Self,* chap. 1. The neo-Confucians had assimilated the language of Buddhist salvationism; Russian Marxists were

assimilating the language of Orthodox Christianity into similar metaphors of revolutionary holiness.

22. Mencius, *Mencius,* trans. D. C. Lau (London: Penguin, 1970), 181.
23. Ban Wang, *The Sublime Figure of History: Aesthetics and Politics in Twentieth-Century China* (Stanford, Calif: Stanford University Press, 1997), 1.
24. Mao Zedong, *Mao Zedong wenji,* 2: 700.
25. See Yue, *The Mouth That Begs,* 152; see also his analysis of the increase in the use of the hunger motif in Yan'an literature, chap. 4.
26. Lu Ling, *Ji'e de Guo Su'e,* 37.
27. C. T. Hsia, "Closing Remarks," in *Chinese Fiction from Taiwan: Critical Perspectives,* ed. Jeannette L. Faurot (Bloomington: Indiana University Press, 1980), 240.
28. I am using Liu Kang's translation in "The Language of Desire," 79–80.
29. Lu Ling, *Ji'e de Guo Su'e,* 37.
30. Ibid., 48.
31. Sun Lung-Kee, *Zhongguo wenhua de shenceng jiegou* (The deep structure of Chinese culture) (Taipei: Tangshan chubanshe, 1990).
32. See my discussion in *Fictional Realism,* chap. 3.
33. See Meng Yue's discussion in "*Baimao nü* yanbian de qishi: Jian lun Yan'an wenyi de lishi duozhi xing" (The transformations of *The White-Haired Girl* and its significance: On the polyphony of history in Yan'an literature), in *Zaijiedu: Dazhong wenyi yu yishi xingtai* (Reinterpretation: Mass literature and ideology), ed. Tang Xiaobing (Hong Kong: Oxford University Press, 1993), 68–89.
34. A statement made by He Jingzhi, one of the coauthors of the Yan'an version of *Baimao nü,* quoted in Meng Yue, "*Baimao nü* yanbian de qishi," 76.
35. Lu Ling, *Ji'e de Guo Su'e,* 22.
36. Also see Denton's discussion in *The Problematic of Self,* chap. 4.
37. See Ban Wang, *The Sublime Figure of History,* chap. 1.
38. See Liu Kang, "The Language of Desire."
39. Robert D. Newman, *Transgressions of Reading: Narrative Engagement As Exile and Return* (Durham, N.C.: Duke University Press, 1993), 141; Julia Kristeva, *Powers of Horror: An Essay on Abjection,* trans. Leon S. Roudiez (New York: Columbia University Press, 1982); and Victor Burgin, *In/Different Spaces: Place and Memory in Visual Culture* (Berkeley: University of California Press, 1996), 47–56.
40. Newman, *Transgressions of Reading,* 140.
41. Lu Ling, *Ji'e de Guo Su'e,* 81.
42. Ibid., 89. For Denton's translation, see "Mind," 231.
43. See note 7.
44. Georg Lukács, *Studies in European Realism: A Sociological Survey of the Writings of Balzac, Stendhal, Zola, Tolstoy, Gorki and Others,* trans. Edith Bone (New York: Grosset and Dunlap, 1964). Hu Feng was heavily influenced by Lukacs's *History and Class Consciousness* through reading its Japanese translation by the Communist literatus Fukumoto Kazuo, as early as the 1930s. See Yunzhong Shu, *Buglers,* 30–32.
45. Shi Shu, *Lixiang zhuyizhe dejianying* (The silhouette of an idealist) (Taipei: Xindi chubanshe, 1990), 142–59.
46. I am referring to the starvation that occurred during the Great Leap Forward

movement, from 1959 to 1962, in which millions of people perished. On the practice of cannibalism during the Great Leap Forward, see Jasper Becker, *Hungry Ghosts: Mao's Secret Famine* (New York: Free Press, 1996), chap. 14.

47. See, for example, Zhang Yesong and Xu Lang, eds., *Lu Ling wannian zuopinji* (Works by Lu Ling in his last years) (Shanghai: Dongfang chuban zhongxin, 1998).
48. See also my preface to the new edition of Eileen Chang's *The Rice-Sprout Song* (Berkeley: University of California Press, 1998).
49. Zhao Shuli, *Li Jiazhuang de bianqian* (Changes of the Li village) (Beijing: Renmin wenxue chubanshe, 1962); Zhou Libo, *Baofeng zouyu* (Hurricane) (Changsha: Hunan renmin chubanshe, 1983); Ding Ling, *Taiyang Zhaozai Sanggan heshang* (The sun shines over the Sanggang river), in *Ding Ling xuanji* (Selected works of Ding Ling) (Chengdu: Sichuan renmin chubani, 1984).
50. Hu Shi's letter to Eileen Chang, in *Zhang Ailing quanji* (Complete works of Eileen Chang) (Taipei: Huangguan chubanshe, 1995), 1: 4.
51. C. T. Hsia, *A History,* 357–67; Long Yingtai, *Long Yingtai pingxiaoshuo* (Fiction criticism by Long Yingtai) (Taipei: Erya chubanshe, 1985), 108.
52. Becker, *Hungry Ghosts,* 53.
53. C. T. Hsia, *A History,* 357–67.
54. Eileen Chang, *Zhang Ailing quanji,* 3: 87.
55. Eileen Chang, *Yangge* (The rice-sprout song), in *Zhang Ailing quanji,* 1: 189–90.
56. Becker, *Hungry Ghosts,* chap. 1.
57. Eileen Chang, preface to *Chuanqi* (Romance), in *Zhang Ailing quanji,* 5: 6.
58. Chen Yingzhen, "Shanlu" (Mountain path), in *Chen Yingzhen zuopinji* (Works of Chen Yingzhen) (Taipei: Renjian chubanshe, 1988), 9: 53.
59. Chen Yingzhen, "Shanlu," 38.
60. Leslie Heywood, *Dedication to Hunger: The Anorexic Aesthetic in Modern Cultures* (Berkeley: University of California Press, 1995), 61–88; and Mark Anderson, "Anorexia and Modernism, or How I Learned to Diet in All Directions," *Discourse* 11, no. 1 (1988–89): 28–41.
61. Joan Jacobs Brumberg, *Fasting Girls: The History of Anorexia Nervosa* (Cambridge, Mass.: Harvard University Press, 1988), 61–99; see also Heywood, *Dedication to Hunger,* 72–73.
62. Brumberg, *Fasting Girls,* 99; Haywood, *Dedication to Hunger,* 73.
63. See Denton's succinct analysis in "Mind," 129, where he points out the link between Lu Ling and Song and Ming neo-Confucian thought.
64. See Zhong Caijun's discussion in "Er Cheng shengren zhixue de yanjiu" (A study of the theory of sainthood by Cheng Yi and Cheng Hao) (Ph.D. diss., National Taiwan University, 1990), 234–43.
65. Chen Yingzhen, "Mountain Path," trans. Nicholas Koss, in *Death in a Corn Field and Other Stories from Contemporary Taiwan,* ed., Ching-hsi Perng and Chiu-kuei Wang (Hong Kong: Oxford University Press, 1994), 9.
66. Ibid., 9–10.
67. Ibid., 20.
68. Ibid., 21.
69. Ibid.
70. Shi Shu, "Taiwan de youyu: Lun Chen Yingzhen zaoqi xiaoshuo jiqi yishu" (The

melancholy of Taiwan: On the art of Chen Yingzhen's early fiction), in *Liang'an wenxue lunji* (Critical essays on Chinese literature across the Taiwan Straits) (Taipei: Xindi chubanshe, 1997), 149–65.

71. Manfred M. Fichter, "The Anorexia Nervosa of Franz Kafka," *International Journal of Eating Disorders* 2 (1987): 367–77; and Mark Anderson, "Anorexia and Modernism," 28–41.
72. See Rey Chow's discussion in "We Endure, Therefore We Are: Survival, Governance, and Zhang Yimou's *To Live*," *South Atlantic Quarterly* 95, no. 4 (fall 1996): 1039–64.
73. Hongying, *Ji'e de nüer* (The daughter of hunger) (Taipei: Erya, 1997), 322.
74. Ibid., 339.

CHAPTER 5: OF SCARS AND NATIONAL MEMORY

1. Odysseus's scar, therefore, is treated as that which motivated the mimetic discourse of Western realist narrative in Auerbach's classic study. See Erich Auerbach, *Mimesis: The Representation of Reality in Western Literature,* trans. Willard R. Trask (Princeton, N.J.: Princeton University Press, 1953), chap. 1.
2. Luo Guangbin and Yang Yiyan, *Hongyan* (Red rock) (Beijing: Renmin chubanshe, 1961), 71–73.
3. Ibid., 220.
4. Ibid.
5. Liang Qichao, "Lun xiaoshuo yu qunzhi zhi guanxi" (On the relationship between fiction and ruling the people), in *Wanqing wenxue congchao: Xiaoshuo xiqu yanjiu juan* (Compendium of late Qing literature: Fiction and drama), ed. A Ying (Taipei: Xuesheng shuju, 1971), 12–15.
6. See my article on Chinese writers' effort to reinterpret history in the early 1980s, "Dai Houying, Feng Jicai, A. Cheng: Three Approaches to the Historical Novel," in *Asian Pacific Quarterly* 16, no. 2 (1988): 71–88.
7. Both Communist and Nationalist literary historians have tended to see 1949 as a distinct breaking point in modern Chinese literature. See, for example, Wang Yao, *Zhongguo xinwenxue shigao* (Manuscript of modern Chinese literature) (Beijing: Renmin wenxue chubanshe, 1962); and Liu Xinhuang, *Xiandai zhongguo wenxue shihua* (History of modern Chinese literature) (Taipei: Zhengzhong shuju, 1977). Questions about how to periodize modern Chinese literature have been emphatically raised by critics, such as Sima Changfeng in *Zhongguo xinwenxue shi* (History of modern Chinese literature) (Taipei: Zhuanji wenxue chubanshe, 1991), 9–14.
8. See, for example, Merle Goldman, *Literary Dissent in Communist China* (Cambridge, Mass.: Harvard University Press, 1967); Rudolf G. Wagner, *Inside a Service Trade: Studies in Contemporary Chinese Prose* (Cambridge, Mass.: Council on East Asian Studies, Harvard University, 1992).
9. For the invocation of a Promethian image of modern Chinese intellectuals and literati, see Benjamin Schwartz's discussion in *In Search of Wealth and Power: Yan Fu and the West* (Cambridge, Mass.: Harvard University Press, 1964), chap. 6. In his interpretation of Lu Xun, T.A. Hsia interprets this Promethian image by referring to the heroic figure who sacrificed himself so as to rescue other chival-

ric knights in the classical Chinese military romance, *Shuo Tang* (The Tang saga, or *Suitang yanyi,* the saga of the Sui and the Tang). See *The Gate of Darkness* (Seattle: University of Washington Press, 1968), 146–62.

10. C. T. Hsia, *A History of Modern Chinese Fiction* (New Haven, Conn.: Yale University Press, 1971), 533–54.
11. Liang, "Lun xiaoshuo yu qunzhi zhi guanxi," 12–15.
12. Chen Duxiu, "Wenxue geming lun" (On literary revolution), in *Duxiu wencun* (Writings of Chen Duxiu) (Shanghai: Yadong tushuguan, 1931), 1: 135–40; Hu Shi, "Jianshe de wenxue geming lun" (On a constructive revolution in Chinese literature), *Xin qingnian* (New youth) 4, no. 4 (Apr. 1918): 289–306; Lu Xun, "Zixu" (Preface to *Nahan* [A call to arms]), *Lu Xun quanji* (Complete works of Lu Xun) (Beijing: Renmin chubanshe, 1981), 1: 417.
13. See, for example, Paul G. Pickowicz, *Marxist Literary Thought in China: The Influence of Chu Chiu-pai* (Berkeley: Center for Chinese Studies, University of California, 1980); Marian Gálik, *Mao Dun and Modern Chinese Literary Criticism* (Wiesbaden: Franz Steiner Verlag, 1969).
14. See Marston Anderson, *The Limits of Realism: Chinese Fiction in the Revolutionary Period* (Berkeley: University of California Press, 1990); and David Der-wei Wang, *Fictional Realism in Twentieth-Century China: Mao Dun, Lao She, Shen Congwen* (New York: Columbia University Press, 1992).
15. See Merle Goldman's classic study of the Yan'an Talks and the literary and political practice inspired by the talks, *Literary Dissent,* 1–50.
16. "Zhongguo zuojia xiehui zhangcheng" (Guidelines of the Chinese Writers' Association), quoted in Lin Manshu, Hai Feng, and Cheng Hai, *Zhongguo dangdai wenxue shigao, dalu bufen 1949–1965* (A manuscript of contemporary Chinese literature, the mainland section, 1949–1965) (Paris: Center for East Asian Studies, University of Paris VII, 1978), 25.
17. See, for example, Goldman, *Literary Dissent;* and Wagner, *Inside a Service Trade.* See also D. W. Fokkema, *Literary Doctrine in China and Soviet Influence, 1956–1960* (The Hague: Mouton, 1965).
18. Mao Dun, "Wenxue yishu zhong de guanjianxing wenti" (The key problem concerning literary and art work), *Weiyi bao* (Gazette of literature and arts) 12, no. 3 (1956); quoted in C. T. Hsia, *History of Modern Chinese Fiction,* 338.
19. See, for example, Goldman's analysis in *Literary Dissent,* chaps. 5–7.
20. See my discussion on Mao Dun in *Fictional Realism,* chap. 2.
21. For a survey of the "modern" dimensions of the ideological novel, see Susan Rubin Suleiman, *Authoritarian Fictions: The Ideological Novel as a Literary Genre* (Princeton, N.J.: Princeton University Press, 1992), 1–23, esp. 22–23.
22. See, for example, Rudolf Wagner's analysis in *Inside a Service Trade,* 17–70.
23. Stephen Greenblatt, *Shakespearean Negotiations: The Circulation of Social Energy in Renaissance England* (Berkeley: University of California Press, 1984), 5–18.
24. By this, I have in mind publications such as Liu Kang and Xiaobin Tang, eds., *Politics, Ideology, and Literary Discourse in Modern China: Theoretical Interventions and Cultural Critique* (Durham, N.C.: Duke University Press, 1993). As they fluently talk about "theoretical intervention" and "cultural critique," magical words in current Western literary criticism, the editors and (some of) the contributors sound as if they did not know that these neologisms could have struck

a bitter note in the Chinese context. Modern Chinese literature, especially that produced from the late 1940s to the 1970s, was burdened with too much "intervention" and "critique" from concerned parties. Are the ghosts of the midcentury being suppressed by the critics of the end of the century? Or are they looming ever larger behind modern-day Chinese critical discourse?

25. For a definition of "Maoist discourse" *(Mao wenti),* see Li Tuo, "Xuebeng hechu" (Where is the avalanche?), the preface to Yu Hua's collection of stories, *Shibasui chumen yuanxing* (Going out for a travel at the age of eighteen) (Taipei: Yuanliu chuban gongsi, 1991), 3–7.
26. In 1956 to 1957, Ba Ren published a series of essays on the necessity of writing about humanity, for which he was purged in the Anti-Rightist movement. See Lin Manshu, Hai Feng, and Cheng Hai, *Zhongguo dangdai wenxue shigao,* 73–77.
27. Liu Xinhuang, "Ziyou zhoongguo wushi niandai de sanwen" (Prose in free China of the 1950s), *Wenxun* (Literary message) 9, no. 3 (1984): 60.
28. Zhang Suzhen, "Wushi niandai xiaoshuo gaunkui" (A preliminary examination of fiction of the 1950s), *Wenxun* (Literary message) 9, no. 3 (1984): 84.
29. The Ministry of National Defense sponsored a literary prize for "military service writers" from 1954 to 1958. More than 260 writers were awarded the prize; most of the winners were men and women in the service or their family members. See Wei Ziyun, preface to *Dangdai zhongguo wenxue daxi* (Compendium of contemporary literature of ROC) (Taipei: Tianshi chuban gongsi, 1979), 1: 150.
30. A few established writers followed the Nationalist government to Taiwan; among them, Liang Shiqiu, Tai Jingnong, and Xie Bingying were the better known names. Hu Shi went to Taiwan in 1952, as did the woman writer Su Xuelin, who once waged war with Lu Xun in the 1930s.
31. See Huang Jichi, "Wushi niandai nanlai zuojia" (Writers coming to the south in the 1950s), in *Sishi nianlai de zhongguo wenxue: 1949–1993* (Four decades of Chinese literature: 1949–1993), ed. Yuming Shao (Taipei: Lianhe wenxue, 1994), 411–22; Nanguo, "Xianggang de nanmin wenxue" (Hong Kong's refugee literature), *Wenxun* (Literary message) 20 (Oct. 1985): 32–37.
32. See Yu Qing, *Zhang Ailing zhuan: Cong Li Hong Zhang zeng wai sun nü dao xian dai* (A Biography of Eileen Chang) (Taipei: Shijie shuji, 1993), 221–35.
33. Ye Shitao, *Taiwan wenxue shigang* (An outline of the history of Taiwanese literature) (Gaoxiong: Wenxuejie, 1987), 88–89; Huang Chongtian, Zhuang Mingxuan, Que Fengling, Xu Xue, and Zhu Shuangyi, *Taiwan xinwenxue gaiguan* (A general view of the new literature of Taiwan) (Taipei: Daohe chubanshe, 1992), 69.
34. Works by these May Fourth writers were not allowed to be published before the government abolished martial law in 1987.
35. "The path by which the new literary movement took over the past three decades may be described as one of military combat. Its first mission was to fight old literature; this was an anti-feudal powers war. Second came its mission to awaken the nation to struggle against imperialist oppression. The following mission was to wrestle with the evil leftist forces of literature. The anti-Japanese aggression has been the most powerful and intense performance to date of the militant literature. The militant literature of the current stage should inherit the

honorable militant tradition of the May Fourth new literary tradition and march forward." Situ wei, "Zhandou wenyi de renshi yu tuixing" (The learning and promotion of war literature), in *Zhandou wenyi yu ziyou wenyi* (Literature for war and literature for freedom), ed. Chen Jiying (Taipei: Wentan she, 1955), 62.

36. Ge Xianning, "You wusi de wenxue geming lun dangqian de zhandou wenyi" (On the contemporary literature for war from the perspective of the May Fourth Literary Revolution), in Mu Mu, *Zhandou wenyi yu ziyou wenyi,* 26–43.
37. For a detailed discussion of the rise of the modernist poetry movement in Taiwan and Ji Xian's role, see, for example, Ke Qingming, "Liushi niandai xiandai zhuyi wenxue?" (Modernist literature in the 1960s?), in *Sishinian lai zhongguo wenxue* (Modern Chinese Literature from the 1940s to the 1990s), ed. Shao Yuming, Zhang Baoqin, and Yaxian (Taipei: Lianhe wenxue chubanshe, 1994), 85–146.
38. Critics have argued that the Nationalist government deliberately encouraged writers to take a "dissipated," modernist stance so that they would not meddle with the mainstream propaganist literary discourse. See, for example, Yang Zhao, "Wuliu shi niandai de taiwan wenxue" (Taiwanese literature of the 1950s and 1960s), *Lianhe wenxue* (Unitas) 5 (1994): 73–78.
39. In the words of a postcolonialist such as Timothy Brennan, it seemed to be the novel that "historically accompanied the rise of nations by objectifying the 'one, yet many' of national life, and by mimicking the structure of the nation, a clearly bordered jumble of languages and styles." Timothy Brennan, "The National Longing for Form," in *Nation and Narration,* ed. Homi K. Bhabha (London: Routledge, 1990), 44. See also Benedict R. O. Anderson, *Imagined Communities: Reflections on the Origin and Spread of Nationalism* (London: Verso and New Left Books, 1983), 35. Brennan is as blind to the imperialist ideology as the May Fourth literati were: there is no necessary connection between the historical rise of nations and their possession of epics (the Romantic version) or nineteenth-century realist novels (the Victorian version).
40. See my discussion in *Fictional Realism,* chap. 2.
41. Yi-tsi Mei Feurwerker, *Ding Ling's Fiction: Ideology and Narrative in Modern Chinese Literature* (Cambridge, Mass.: Harvard University Press, 1982), 139–40.
42. See Li Chi, "Communist War Stories," *China Quarterly* 13 (1963): 139–57.
43. See Lu Xun, *Lu Xun quanji* (Complete works of Lu Xun) (Beijing: Renmin wenxue chubanshe, 1981), 18: 265–74, 603–13.
44. For a recent discussion regarding the borrowing of premodern popular literary material by early Chinese communist writers, see, for example, Chen Sihe, *Huanyuan minjian* (Going back to the people) (Taipei: Sanmin shudian, 1997).
45. T. A. Hsia, "Heroes and Hero-Worship in Chinese Communist Fiction," *China Quarterly* 13 (1963): 113–38.
46. I am referring to Eve Sedgwick's concepts in *Between Men: English Literature and Male Homosocial Desire* (New York: Columbia University Press, 1985), 83–96.
47. Du Pengcheng, *Baowei Yan'an* (Guarding Yan'an) (Beijing: Renmin wenxue chubanshe, 1954), 29.
48. See Huang Ziping's discussion of the genre of the revolutionary historical novel in "Geming lishi xiaoshuo: Shijian yu xushu" (The revolutionary historical novel:

Temporality and narration), in *Xincunzhe de wenxue* (The literature of a survivor) (Taipei: Yuanliu chuban gongsi, 1991), 229–45.

49. Du Pengcheng, "*Baowi Yan'an* de chuangzuo wenti" (Questions about the writing of *Guarding Yan'an*), in *Du Pengcheng yanjiu zhuanji* (Research materials on Du Pengcheng), ed. Chen Shu and Yu Shuqing (Fuzhou: Fujian renmin chubanshe, 1983), 27–41.
50. See C. W. Shih, "Co-operatives and Communes in Chinese Communist Fiction," *China Quarterly* 13 (1963): 195–211.
51. C. T. Hsia, *History of Modern Chinese Fiction,* 480–90.
52. Liu Zaifu and Lin Gang, "Zhongguo xiandai xiaoshuo de zhengzhishi xiezuo: Cong 'Chuncan' dao *Taiyang zhozai Sanggan heshang*" (The politics of writing in modern Chinese literature: From "Spring Silkworns" to *The Sun Shines over the Sanggan River*), in *Zai jiedu* (Interpreting again), ed. Tang Xiaobin (Hong Kong: Oxford University Press, 1993), 90–107; Tang Xiaobin, "Baoli de bianzheng fa" (The dialectic of violence), in *Zaijiedu: Dazhong wenyi yu yishi xingtai* (Rereading: Mass literature and ideology), ed. Tang Xiaobing (Hong Kong: Oxford University Press, 1993), 108–26.
53. Rudolf Wagner, "The Chinese Writer in His Own Mirror: Writer, State, and Society—The Literary Evidence," in *China's Intellectuals and the State: In Search of a New Relationship,* ed. Merle Goldman, Timothy Cheek, and Carol Lee Hamrin (Cambridge, Mass.: Harvard University Press, 1987), 192–94.
54. Lu Xun, "Xiao zagan" (Small miscellaneous thoughts), in *Lu Xun quanji* (Complete works of Lu Xun) (Beijing: Renmin wenxue chubanshe, 1981), 13: 532. See Leo Lee's discussion in *Voices from the Iron House: A Study of Lu Xun* (Bloomington: Indiana University Press, 1987), 139.
55. Wang, *Fictional Realism,* 252.
56. Huang Chongtian et al., *Taiwan xinwenxue gaiguan,* 285.
57. Chang Ailing, *Chidi zhilian* (Naked earth) (Taipei: Huangguan chubanshe, 1991), 253.
58. Chang, of course, published *Yuannu,* or *Rouge of the North,* in 1967, which was nevertheless a rewrite of her 1943 novella, *Jinsuo ji,* or *The Story of a Golden Cangue.*
59. Marian Gálik, *Milestones in Sino-Western Literary Confrontation: 1898–1979* (Wiesbaden: Otto Harrassowitz, 1986), 235–47.
60. Zhang Daofan, "Baxunzhang xu" (Preface to *Ba xunzhang* [The badge of scars]) (Taipei: Zhengzhong shuju, 1951), 3.
61. See my discussion in "*Lianyi biaomei:* Jianlun sanling dao wuling niandai de zhengzhi xiaoshuo" (*Cousin Lianyi* and the political novel from the 1930s to the 1950s), in *Xiaoshuo zhongguo: Wanqing dao dangdai de zhongwen xiaoshuo* (Narrating China: Chinese fiction from the late Qing to the contemporary era) (Taipei: Maitian chuban gongsi, 1993), 71–94.
62. Hu Feng, "*Ji'i de Guo Su'e* xu" (Preface to *Hungry Guo Sue*), in *Lu Ling yanjiu ziliao* (Research materials on Lu Ling), ed. Zhang Huan et al. (Beijing: Beijing shiyue wenyi chubanshe, 1993), 60. The issue of whether Chinese people suffer from "spiritual scars" was much debated among leftist literati in the late 1940s. See Lu Ling, "Lun wenyi chuangzuo di jige jiben wenti" (On several basic issues of literary creation), in *Lu Ling piping wenji* (Collection of critical es-

says by Lu Ling), ed. Zhang Yesong (Guangzhou: Zhuhaichu banshe, 1998), 97–100.

63. C. T. Hsia, *History of Modern Chinese Fiction,* 303–305.
64. C. T. Hsia, "Closing Remarks," in *Chinese Fiction from Taiwan: Critical Perspectives,* ed. Jeannette L. Faurot (Bloomington: Indiana University Press, 1980), 240.
65. Tang Xiaobing, "Baoli de bianzheng fa," 51–67.
66. Zhou Libo, *Baofeng zouyu* (Hurricane) (Changsha: Hunan renmin chubanshe, 1983), 174.
67. Zhao Shuli, *Li Jiazhuang de bianqian* (Changes of the Li Village) (Beijing: Renmin chubanshe, 1962), 211.
68. Ding Ling, *Taiyang zhaozai sanggan heshang* (The sun shines over the Sanggan River) (Beijing: Renmin wenxue chubanshe, 1979), 285. English translation in C. T. Hsia, *History of Modern Chinese Fiction,* 486.
69. Theodor Adorno, "After Auschwitz," in *Negative Dialectics,* trans. E. B. Ashton (New York: Continuum, 1973), 362.
70. See Shoshana Felman and Dori Laub, *Testimony: Crises of Witnessing in Literature, Psychoanalysis, and History* (New York: Routledge, 1992), 12–56, esp. 33–34.
71. See my discussion in "Fangong fuguo xiaoshuo: Yizhong shiqu de wenxue?" (Anti-communist fiction: A dead literature?), in *Ruhe xiandai, zenyang wenxue* (Taipei: Ryefield Publications, 1997), 141–58.
72. *Du Pengcheng yanjiu ziliao* (Research materials on Du Pengcheng); Zhou Yangzhi, "Yeye Zhou Libo zai haojie zhong de rizi" (Life of my grandfather Zhou Libo during the days of the holocaust), in *Zhou Libo yanjiu ziliao* (Research material on Zhou Libo), ed. Li Huasheng and Hu Guangfan (Changsha: Hunan renmin chubanshe, 1983), 190–96.
73. *Zhao Shuli yanjiu ziliao* (Research materials on Zhao Shuli) (Beijing: Renmin wenxue chubanshe, 1981).

CHAPTER 6: THE MONSTER THAT IS HISTORY

1. For a thorough discussion of the rise of the anticommunist literature in Taiwan of the 1950s, see my article, "Yizhong shiqu de wenxue? Fangong xiaoshuo xinlun" (A deceased literature? New perspectives on anticommunist fiction), in *Ruhe xiandai, zenyang wenxue? Shijiu, ershi shiji zhongwen xiaoshuo xinlun* (The making of the modern, the making of a literature: New perspectives on nineteenth- and twentieth-century Chinese fiction) (Taipei: Maitian chuban gongsi, 1998), 141–59.
2. Jiang Gui, "Zixu" (preface), in *Jin taowu zhuan* (A tale of modern monsters) (Tainan: Chunyulou, 1957), 4.
3. For more details about the publication of the novel, see Timothy A. Ross, *Chiang Kuei* (Boston: Twayne, 1974), 76–86.
4. Jiang Gui, "Zizhuan" (Autobiography), in *Wuwei ji* (Not against my wishes) (Taipei: Youshi wenyi chubanshe, 1974), 242.
5. See Jiang Menglin's letter to Jiang Gui and Hu Shi's reference to *A Tale of Modern Monsters,* in *Huaixiu shu: "Xuanfeng" pinglunji* (A book of one's own: a collection of critical articles on *The Whirlwind*), ed. Chunyu lou (Tainan: Chunyulou, 1960), 18–19, 20–21.
6. Wang Jicong, "Pin *Xuanfeng*" (A critique on *The Whirlwind*), and Liu Xinhuang

"Ping Jiang Gui zhu *Xuanfeng*" (On Jiang Gui's *Whirlwind*), both in *Huaixiu shu,* 87–96, 111–15.

7. Gao Yang, "Guanyu *Xuanfeng* de yanjiu" (A study on *The Whirlwind*), in *Huaixiu shu,* 40–86.
8. C. T. Hsia, "The Whirlwind," in *A History of Modern Chinese Fiction* (New Haven, Conn.: Yale University Press, 1971), 555–62.
9. Ibid.
10. Ibid., 556.
11. Jiang Gui, "Zixu," 3.
12. Ibid.
13. Ibid.
14. *Shenyi jing,* in *Biji xiaoshuo daguan* (Compendium of biji fictional narratives), 38 bian (Taipei: Xinxing shuju, 1985), juan 1, 226.
15. Sima Qian, *Shiji,* "Wudi benji" (Chronicles of the five emperors), in *Shiji huizhu kaozheng* (An annotated edition of the *Shiji*) (Taipei: Hongye shuju, 1980), juan 1, 31.
16. For references to *taowu* as one of the four major evils in ancient China, see, for example, *Shangshu,* "Xiashu," juan 6, "yugong"; *Chunqiu zuozhuan zhengyi,* Wengong, juan 20, zhuan year 18.
17. Chunqiu zuozhuan zhengyi, "xu," juan 1, Chunqiuxu.
18. *Mencius,* "Lilou" xiapian; I am using D. C. Lau's translation, in *Mencius* (London: Penguin, 1970), 131.
19. Zhang Jun, *Chuguo shenhua yuanxing yanjiu* (A study of the mythological archetypes of the Chu) (Taipei: Wenjin chubanshe, 1994), 71.
20. Ibid.
21. Ibid.
22. Tu Cheng-sheng, "Gudai wuguai zhi yanjiu: Yi zhong xintaishi he wenhuashi de tansuo" (Wu-Kuai as a reflection of the mentality and culture of ancient China) (1), *Dalu zazhi* 104, no. 1 (Jan. 2002): 1–14. I wish to thank Professor Tu for allowing me to cite part of the conclusions from the manuscript.
23. Jiang Gui, "Zixu," 3.
24. As discussed in the following, Jiang Qing plays a small role in the novel.
25. For Jiang Gui's family background, see *Wuwei ji,* 72–76. See also Ross, *Chiang Kuei,* chaps. 1–3.
26. Ibid.
27. Ibid., 227–33.
28. See Ba Ren, "Houji" (Afterword), in *Tuwei* (Breaking free) (Shanghai: Shijie shuju, 1939), 150.
29. Jiang Gui, "Zixu," 2.
30. See, for example, Rao Zongyi, *Zhongguo shixue shang zhi zhengtong lun: Zhong guo shi xue guan nian tan tao zhi yi* (The theory of orthodoxy in Chinese historiography: An approach to Chinese historiographical concepts) (Taipei: Zongqing tushu chuban gongsi, 1979).
31. Ibid., 3–5.
32. I am referring to Peter Brooks's terminology. See *The Melodramatic Imagination: Balzac, Henry James, Melodrama, and the Mode of Excess* (New York: Columbia University Press, 1985), chaps. 1–3.

33. See Rao Zongyi, *Zhongguo shixue shang zhi zhengtong lun,* 56–57.
34. To be sure, among the mainland émigré writers of Jiang Gui's time, many were equally eager to extract a morality tale from the recent Nationalist fiasco. As discussed in Chapter 5, Chen Jiying's *Dicun zhuan* (Fools in the reeds, 1951), Pan Renmu's *Lianyi Biaomei* (Cousin Lianyi, 1952), and Wang Lan's *Lan yu hei* (Blue and black, 1957) serve as good examples. While they share with Jiang Gui a similar anticommunist agenda, few can surpass him in pursuing the dialectic between politics and ethics underneath the national crisis, to say nothing of inquiring into its historiographical relevance. Because of his historical bearings, Jiang Gui is able to look beyond immediate anti-Communist formulas and find inspiration in a classical novel such as *An Idle Commentary on Monsters.* From the vantage point of the late Ming novel, which details how Wei Zhongxian and his cohorts almost ruined the Ming, he relates a story about how Communist evils almost brought down the Nationalist regime.
35. Jiang Gui, "Zizhuan."
36. I am grateful to Waiyee Li's argument in "The Idea of Authority in the *Shih chi* (Records of the Historian)," *Harvard Journal of Asiatic Studies* 54, no. 2 (Dec. 1994): 345–405.
37. See *Wuwei ji,* 5–120. Judged by his biographical accounts, many of the characters and episodes in the novel may derive from Jiang Gui's personal experience. Fang Xiangian, for example, may well be modeled after Jiang Gui's uncle, Wang Xiangqian, a self-styled reformer whose idealism brought his hometown grave disasters. Fang Peilan may also find his counterpart in reality, a remote relative of Jiang Gui's known for his bandit heroism and vengeful spirit.
38. She has the sliding weight of a steelyard hung atop her bed, and swings it with her foot onto the face of Lady Ximen, who has been ordered to kneel upright before her all night long. She pricks Lady Ximen with a gold hairpin, leaving half-inch-deep wounds all over her body. In winter, she beats her with red-hot stove irons.
39. For a critical introduction to Foucault's genealogical view of history, see, for example, Hubert L. Dreyfus and Paul Rabinow, *Michel Foucault: Beyond Structuralism and Hermeneutics* (Chicago: University of Chicago Press, 1982), part 2.
40. Jiang Gui, *Jin Taowu zhuan,* 104–105. I am using Ross's translation with modification, *Chiang Kuei,* 86.
41. Ibid., 70.
42. C. T. Hsia, *A History of Modern Chinese Fiction,* 560.
43. Gao Yang, "Guanyu *Xuanfeng* de yanjiu," 51–62.
44. Mikhail Bakhtin, *Rabelais and His World,* trans. Helene Iswolsky (Cambridge: MIT Press, 1968). For more discussion of the political implication of the Bakhtinian "bodily principle," see Peter Stallybrass and Allon White, *The Politics and Poetics of Transgression* (Ithaca, N.Y.: Cornell University Press, 1986).
45. Georges Bataille, *Eroticism: Death and Sensuality,* trans. Mary Dalwood (San Francisco: City Lights, 1986), 42. See also Sigmund Freud, *Totem and Taboo: Some Points of Agreement between the Mental Lives of Savages and Neurotics,* trans. James Strachey (London: Hogarth Press, 1955).
46. Bataille distinguishes three kinds of eroticism, the corporeal, the emotional, and the sacrificial. All the three forms involve a movement toward dissolution

as the ultimate state of continuity, having initially situated in a state of separation. The locus of such a movement can be the body, the heart (emotions), and the spirit (sacred practice). Whereas the eroticism of the body is more cynical and sinister, the eroticism of heart and sacred eroticism are said to be less constrained and more "intellectual." See *Eroticism,* 19–23. Also see his *Tears of Eros* (San Francisco: City Lights, 1989), particularly the last section where he discusses corporal and sacred eroticism in the light of the Chinese penal form of public mutilation *(linchi).*

47. I am inspired by criticism on Bataille's theory of eroticism by critics such as Jonathan Dillimore and Ali Behdad. See Dillimore, *Desire, Death, and Loss in Western Culture* (New York: Routledge, 1998), 257–58; Ali Behdad, "Eroticism, Colonialism, and Violence," in *Violence, Identity, and Self-Determination,* ed. Hent de Vries and Samuel Weber (Stanford, Calif.: Stanford University Press, 1997), 201–8.

48. See, for example, Wang Jicong, "Pin *Xuanfeng,*" 88; Ji Wuwei, "Haoshu chutou" (Let a good book stand out), in *Huaixiu shu,* 37–38; Gao Yang, "Xuanfeng, Jiang Gui, wo" (The Whirlwind, Jiang Gui and myself), *Huaixiu shi,* 137. At the most conspicuous level, the titles of all the chapters are formed in poetic couplets modeled after those of classical Chinese vernacular fiction. These titles have been taken out in the new edition of *The Whirlwind.*

49. Quoted from Gao Yang, "*Xuanfeng,* Jiang Gui, wo," 137. Jiang Gui best presents his vision of *lived history* as a grotesque existence through a distorted version of *literary history.* He yokes together mutually exclusive elements from these novels and brings into play a new narrative amalgam. As a frustrated intellectual fascinated with the modernizing classicism of Marx, Fang Xiangqian is a figure reminiscent of intellectuals nurtured on the wistful classicism of Confucius in *The Scholars.* Fang Peilan, the gangster-turned-militia-chieftain, appears to be drawn from the world of *The Water Margin.* While the two Fangs are eager to promote Communist revolution as "the last and newest alternative for saving China," the way they act on behalf of their cause reminds one of the famous campaign, "Carrying out the Way on behalf of Heaven," of *The Water Margin,* with the "Way" replaced by Marxism. Nevertheless, for Fang Xiangqian the scholar, the path to the Communist commonwealth proves to be a nightmarish and anarchic game; and for the strongman Fang Peilan, a modern adaptation of premodern chivalric gallantry brings him nothing but betrayal and imprisonment.

The declining Fang families are often compared to the declining Jia families in *The Dream of the Red Chamber.* With the fate of the Fang families, Jiang Gui seems to ask what would have happened to a noble household like the Jia had they been thrown into the maelstrom of modernization? After the May Fourth movement, almost all the descendents of the Fang families leave home to pursue the new learning. They end up becoming characters with mixed traits: a monk full of sensual attachments, a leftist warrior inclined to decadent thoughts, a new woman dreaming of old-fashioned romance, a Confucian daughter who denies her own mother, and a self-righteous son who forsakes his own name. In the new as in the old regimes, the women of the Fang families suffer equally. They are ignored, humiliated, raped, incarcerated, commit suicide, or get killed. While Mistress Fang dies from starvation, Fang Ranwu's wife is sent to the whorehouse. Whereas *The Dream of the Red Chamber* attains a certain philosophical understanding of women's fate, *A Tale of Modern Monsters* ends with no redemption at all for women.

50. Li Qing became a recluse after the Ming fell and dedicated himself to intellectual and literary studies. In Robert Hegel's recent paper "Conclusions: Judgements on the Ends of Times," presented at the symposium "From the Late Ming to the Late Qing: Dynastic Decline and Cultural Innovation" (Columbia University, November 6–7, 1998), he holds that Li Qing only wrote the novel after the fall of the Ming. His argument is based on Liu Wenzhong's research, in Liu's edited version of Li Qing, *Taowu xianping* (An idle commentary on monsters) (Beijing: Renmin wenxue chubanshe, 1983), 570.
51. For a more detailed account of Wei Zhongxian in English, see Frederick W. Mote and Denis Twitchett, *The Cambridge History of China,* vol. 7 (New York: Cambridge University Press, 1988), 596–613.
52. See my article "Fictional History / Historical Fiction," *Studies in Language and Literature* 1 (1985): 64–76.
53. The term was first coined by the PRC scholar Luan Xing and has since been referred to by scholars such as Cheng Dakang, Chen Dadao, and Qi Yukun. See Luan Xiang, "Ming Qing zhiji de sanbu jiangshi xiaoshuo" (Three historical novels in the late Ming and early Qing), in *Ming Qing xiaoshuo luncong* (Compendium of criticism on Ming and Qing fiction), vol. 3, ed. Chunfeng wenyi chubanshe (Shenyang: Chunfeng wenyi chubanshe, 1986), 146; Chen Dakang, *Tongsu xiaoshuo de lishi guiji* (The historical trajectories of popular fiction) (Changsha: Hunan chubanshe, 1993), 126; Chen Dadao, "Mingmo qingchu 'shishi xiaoshuo' de tese" (Characteristics of "fiction on contemporary events"), *Xiaoshuo xiqu yanjiu* (Studies of fiction and drama) 3 (1987): 219. Luan Xing defines "fiction on contemporary events" as fiction "written by writers about events contemporaneous to their own time." In Chen Dadao's opinion, "fiction on contemporary events" has three characteristics: it is completed in a short span of time, it depends largely on historical materials, and it has a very loose structure. Ouyang Jian calls *Taowu xianping* a "novel on contemporary events," or *dangdai xiaoshuo.* See Ouyang Jian, "*Taowu xianping* de sixiang qingxiang he xingxiang tixi" (The intellectual inclination and figural system of *An Idle Commentary on Monsters*), in *Ming Qing xiaoshuo caizheng* (Rereading Ming and Qing fiction) (Taipei: Guanya chubanshe, 1992), 138–71. Also see Xu Zhiping, *Qingchu qianqi huaben xiaoshuo zhi yanjiu* (A study of storytelling fiction in the first phase of early Qing) (Taipei: Xuesheng shuju, 1998), 183–210.
54. Ouyang Jian, "*Taowu xianping* de sixiang qingxiang he xingxiang tixi," 139.
55. Ibid. See also Robert Hegel's discussion in "Conclusions," 11–13.
56. For a detailed account of these cases, see Mote and Twitchett, *The Cambridge History of China,* 1.
57. Ibid.
58. It is said in the prelude that in the Jiajing reign, governmental officials Huang Da and Zhu Heng were ordered to cope with the flood on the Huai River. Instructed by a mysterious old man, the embodiment of a snake spirit, on the condition that they should never harm any of the river creatures, they build a

series of dikes by following a trail of purple bamboo groves. It just happens that the dike project is obstructed by a pair of red snakes in Red Silk Village. To facilitate his work, Zhu Tong sets a fire to kill the snakes, thus violating his promise. By the end of the novel, the narrator informs us that Wei Zhongxian and Madame Ke are none other than transformations of the two red snakes and that they have returned to avenge their death by taking the lives of righteous governmental officials, such as Yang Liang (1571–1625) and Zuo Guangdou (1575–1625), who are reincarnations of Huang Da and Zhu Heng, respectively.

59. Thanks to the romance between Zhongxian and Yinyue and the legendary loss and return of the three pearls, the novel is also called *Mingzhu yuan* (A romance of pearls).

60. For a recent study of the genre, see, for example, Kang Laixin, *Faji biantai: Songren xiaoshuo xue lungao* (The making of a hero: A study of the narratology of Song fiction) (Taipei: Da'an chubanshe, 1996).

61. See Robert Hegel's discussion in *The Novel in Seventeenth-Century China* (New York: Columbia, 1980), chap. 4.

62. Ibid., 119.

63. Ibid.

64. See Lu Hsun, *A Brief History of Chinese Fiction,* trans. Hsien-yi Yang and Gladys Yang (Beijing: Foreign Language Press, 1976), chap. 14.

65. For a more detailed account of these events, see Mote and Twitchett, *The Cambridge History of China,* 7: 596–613.

66. This, of course, has something to do with the general social and economic ethos of the late Ming. See Hegel's discussion in *The Novel,* chap. 1.

67. I am referring to Northrop Frye's terminology. See his *Anatomy of Criticism: Four Essays* (New York: Antheneum, 1968).

68. This is a good example of how Li Qing mixes fact with imagination. For a more detailed description of the incident, see note 53 above.

69. See, for example, Sun Shuyu's analysis of Ximen Qing as an Everyman in *Jin Pingmei de yishu* (The art of Jin Pingmei) (Taipei: Shibao chuban gongsi, 1977), chap. 7. Andrew H. Plaks approaches the characterization from the late Ming literati's call for self-cultivation and their ironic approach to humanity. See *The Four Masterworks of the Ming Novel* (Princeton, N.J.: Princeton University Press, 1987), chap. 3.

70. See Yue Hengjun, *Yizhi yu mingyun: Zhongguo gudian xiaoshuo shijieguan zonglun* (Fate and will: A general study of the world view in classical Chinese fiction) (Taipei: Da'an chubanshe, 1992), 131–274. See also Plaks, *Four Masterworks,* chap. 1; and Hegel, *The Novel,* chap. 4.

71. See David Tod Roy's introduction to his translation of Xiaoxiaosheng, *Jinpingmei (The Plume in the Golden Vase)* (Princeton, N.J.: Princeton University Press, 1995).

72. See, for example, Wang Fansen's discussion in "Mingmo Qingchu de renpu yu xiingguohui" (The journal of humanity and the society of moral edification in the late Ming and early Qing), *Zhongyang yanjiuyuan lishi yuyan yanjiusuo jikan* (Journal of the Institute of History and Philology, Academia Sinica) 63, no. 3 (July 1993): 695–712.

73. See Zhao Yuan's succinct discussion of the ambivalent distinction between *ren,*

or benevolence, and *bao,* or violence, in late Ming society, in *Ming Qing zhiji shidafu zhi yanjiu* (A study of the intelligentsia of the late Ming and early Qing) (Beijing: Beijing daxue chubanshe, 1999), 3–22.

74. *Chen Que ji* (Collection of Chen Que's works); quoted in Wang Fan-sen, "Mingmo Qingchu de renpu yu xingguohui" (The journal of humanity and the society of moral edification in the late Ming and early Qing), *Zongyang yanjiuyuan lishi yuyan yanjiusuo jikan* (Journal of the Institute of History and Philology, Academia Sinica) 63, no. 3 (Jul. 1993): 682. Also see Zhang Hao, *Youan yishi yu minzhu chuantong* (Dark consciousness and democratic tradition) (Taipei: Lianjing chuban gongsi, 1989), 21–27, 69–73.
75. See Robert Hegel's succinct discussion in *The Novel,* chap. 4, and "Conclusions."
76. Wang Zhongqi, *Zhongguo lidai xiaoshuo shilun* (A critical history of Chinese fiction), quoted in Liu Wenzhong, afterword to Li Qing, *Taowu xianping,* 574.
77. The most fascinating is the case of Jiang Qing, the wife of Mao Zedong. Referred to only as the Big Daughter of the Li family, she makes her first appearance at the beginning of the novel as a girl who returns home years after being abducted and sold to a Beijing opera theater. Since Fang Xiangqian knows her grandfather well and likes her looks and talent, he arranges to take her as his goddaughter. By the end of the novel, she is said to have tried to break into films but to have made her best career move when she became Mrs. Mao.
78. See Hegel's discussion in "Conclusions."
79. Jiang Gui, *Jin taowu zhuan,* 519.
80. C. T. Hsia, *A History of Modern Chinese Fiction,* 560.
81. Ibid.
82. Liu E, *Lao Can youji* (The travels of Lao Can) (Taipei: Lianjing chuban gongsi, 1983), 1–2. See my discussion in *Fin-de-siècle Splendor: Repressed Modernities in Late Qing Fiction, 1849–1911* (Stanford, Calif.: Stanford University Press, 1997), 36–42.
83. David Wang, *Fin-de-siècle Splendor,* 251.
84. By blending the generic conventions of classical novels, Jiang Gui presents a narrative no longer intelligible in terms of any prefigured formula. When "talents and beauties" are converted to bandits and prostitutes, or when scholars join hands with rascals, one witnesses in *A Tale of Modern Monsters* an unlikely reconstellation of classical fictional motifs, actions, and figures. Jiang Gui casts an equally doubtful look at May Fourth discourse. He discovers that the avant-garde call for reform can be based on an amazingly conservative idea of revolt, and that a compassionate political movement is never too far from self-serving motives. If many of his characters look one-dimensional, perhaps it is because they *are* embodiments of superficial contemporary thoughts and stereotypes. Meanwhile, he problematizes the representability of history by creating fiction from topical events and figures. Echoing the subtrend of late Qing exposés, romans à clef, and *yinshe xiaoshuo,* Jiang Gui introduces a large number of historically verifiable characters. Fang Xiangqian and Fang Peilan, it will be recalled, are derived from two members of Jiang Gui's family. Among other examples, Fang Tongsan, a literatus without firm political grounds, is modeled after the May Fourth writer Wang Tongzhao, and Zhang Jia, an opportunistic

new-style poet who eventually marries the conservative Nationalist Fang Zhen, is a fictional double of the leftist poet Zang Kejia. Fang Zhen is in turn based on a local celebrity in Jiang Gui's hometown, Wang Shenting. One also comes across Zhang Zongchang and Han Fuqu, the two major warlords of Shandong Province, who are involved in various events.

85. See my discussion in *Fin-de-siècle Splendor,* chap. 4. Milena Doleželová-Velingerová, ed., *The Chinese Novel at the Turn of the Century* (Toronto: University of Toronto Press, 1980).
86. Qian Xibao, *Taowu cuibian* (A Compendium of Monsters) (Tianjin: Baihua wenyi chubanshe, 1989), 397.
87. Chen Pingyuan, "Qianze xiaoshuo yu xiaxie xiaoshuo: Shuo *Taowu cuibian*" (Exposé and depravity fiction: On *A Compendium of Monsters*), in *Chen Pingyuan xiaoshuoshi lunji* (Collection of critical essays on Chinese fiction by Chen Pingyuan) (Shijiazhuang, Hebei renmin chubanshe, 1996), 3: 1428–36.
88. The *Analects,* for example, is full of examples contrasting the Confucian gentleman, or *junzi,* with commoners, or *xiaoren.*
89. Qian has to deal with his own ambivalence and wavering attitude toward different cases, however. While he endorses Grand Historian Wei's wife, who gives herself in concubinage to Wei's cousin to protest her husband's hypocrisy, he shows no sympathy for a widow who runs away with her brother-in-law and ends up being sold to a house of prostitution, assuming the professional name *Ziyou hua,* or Liberated Flower.
90. Doleželová-Velingerová, *The Chinese Novel at the Turn of the Century,* 53.
91. See my discussion in *Fin-de-siècle Splendor,* 192–94.
92. Ibid., chaps. 1, 4.
93. David Wang, *Fin-de-siècle Splendor,* 191–209. As the preface to *A Compendium of Monsters* states, the novel is at its most intriguing in its approximation of human perversities: "It is not difficult to describe a ghost in terms of a wolf's head and hairy face, red hair and a snake's body. But it is difficult even for a painter such as Luo Liangfeng, known for his vivid portraits of devils, to draw a man harboring a devilish mentality, or someone called human but actually a ghost. . . . *A Compendium of Monsters* is a novel which manages to carry out this task [of representing ghosts]." See Qianyi Ciren, "*Taowu cuibian* xu" (Preface to *Taowu cuibian*), in *Tawowu cuibian* (A compendium of monsters), ed. Dansou (Wian Xibao) (Tianjin: Baihua wenyi chubanshe, 1989), 1.
94. See David E. Apter and Tony Saich's discussion of Maoism as a simulacrum in *Revolutionary Discourse in Mao's Republic* (Cambridge, Mass.: Harvard University Press, 1994), chap. 7.
95. On February 6, 1799, Francisco Goya published a series of eighty aquatint plates titled *Los Caprichos.* Plate 43 is the only one that contains a title, "El sueño de la razón produce monstruos" or "The dream of reason produces monsters." The plate is said to have been conceived as the first of the series, only to be renumbered for political reasons. "In principle, *Capricho* 43 seems to condense the postulates of the Enlightenment: where reason fails, the forces of the occult prevail." See José B. Monleón, *A Specter Is Haunting Europe: A Sociohistorical Approach to the Fantastic* (Princeton, N.J.: Princeton University Press, 1990), 22; also see 40–42.

96. The novel was reprinted in 2000, as a result of its being recognized as a canonical work in Taiwanese literary history, by Juge chuban she.

CHAPTER 7: THE END OF THE LINE

1. Wang Guowei, "Huifeng qinqu" (Fragrant wind and pleasant sound of zither), quoted in *Wang Guowei wenji* (Works of Wang Guowei), ed. Wu Wuji (Beijing: Beijing Yanshan chubanshe, 1997), 49. The "poet" in the original refers to a composer of "ci"—a special genre of Chinese poetry.
2. Quoted in Xue Ruiyue and Xu Rongjie, eds., *Zhongguo xiandai wenxue cidian* (Dictionary of modern Chinese literature) (Xuzhou: Zhongguo kuangye daxue chubanshe, 1988), 64.
3. See, for instance, Wang Wei, *Zhuxing, Nijun* (Zhu Xiang and Ni Jun) (Beijing: Zhongguo qingnian chubanshe, 1995).
4. The cause of Chen Sanli's death has been much debated, although the general assumption is that he died on hunger strike protesting the Japanese invasion. For instance, Liu Yazi, the renowned early Republican poet, refers to Chen's death as a suicide in his 1941 poem; see Liu Yazi, *Mojianshi shiciji* (Sharpening sword studio collection of poetry) (Shanghai: Shanghai renmin, 1983), 2: 893; I want to thank Wu Shengqing for his advice on this issue. See also Huang Lin's discussion in *Jindai wenxue piping shi* (A history of early modern Chinese literary criticism) (Shanghai: Shanghai guji chubanshe, 1993), 129.
5. For a succinct analysis of Wang Guowei's will, see, for example, Ye Jiaying, *Wang Guowei jiqi wenxue piping* (Wang Guowei and his literary criticism) (Taipei: Yuanliu, 1982), chap. 2.
6. See Joey Bonner, *Wang Kuo-wei: An Intellectual Biography* (Cambridge, Mass.: Harvard University Press, 1986), chaps. 5–8.
7. For more discussion of Wang's career and his suicide, see Ye Jiaying, *Wang Guowei.*
8. Alan Stephen Wolfe, *Suicidal Narrative in Modern Japan: The Case of Dazai Osamu* (Princeton, N.J.: Princeton University Press, 1990), chap. 1.
9. Roland Barthes, *The Empire of Signs,* trans. Richard Howard (New York: Hill and Wang, 1982), see esp. 88–94.
10. Roy Starrs, *Deadly Dialectics: Sex, Violence, and Nihilism in the World of Yukio Mishima* (Folkestone: Japan Library, 1994).
11. Masao Miyoshi, *Accomplices of Silence,* quoted in Wolfe, *Suicidal Narrative,* epigraph.
12. Wu Mi (1894–1978), a poet and advocate of post–May Fourth intellectual conservatism who in his early years seriously contemplated suicide (but never carried it out). See, for example, Shen Weiwei, *Wu Mi zhuan* (The biography of Wu Mi) (Taipei: Li Xu wenhua chubanshe, 2000), chap. 14.
13. See, for example, Yu Dafu's "Chenlun" (Sinking) and Shen Congwen's "Meijin, baozi yu" (Meijng, baozi, and the white kid); see Jeffrey Kinkley's discussion, in *The Odyssey of Shen Congwen* (Stanford, Calif.: University of Stanford Press, 1987), 155.
14. David Der-wei Wang, *Fictional Realism in Twentieth-Century China: Mao Dun, Lao She, Shen Congwen* (New York: Columbia University Press, 1992), chap. 5.

15. Shen Congwen tried to commit suicide in late March of 1949 (perhaps March 28). He was then sent to an asylum for treatment and rest. Earlier that year, he had already shown signs of a nervous breakdown, one of the reasons being the attack by Gu Moruo at the end of 1948. See Zhang Zhaohe, ed., *Shen Congwen jiashu* (Correspondence between Shen Congwen and Zhang Zhaohe) (Taipei: Shangwu yinshuguan, 1998), 152; see also Ling Yu, *Shen Congwen zhuan* (A biography of Shen Congwen) (Beijing: Shiyue wenyi chubanshe, 1988), 425.
16. Shu Yi, *Lao She de zuihou liangtian* (The last two days of Lao She) (Guangzhou: Huacheng chubanshe, 1987), 221.
17. See my discussion in *Fictional Realism,* chap. 5, esp. 159–68.
18. A. (Alfred) Alvarez, *The Savage God: A Study of Suicide* (New York: Random House, 1972), 238. Part of the wording in this argument is derived from Wolfe, *Suicidal Narrative,* 71.
19. Ibid.
20. Ibid., 245.
21. See Wu Zhongjie and Gao Yun, eds., *Dai Houying ah Dai Houying* (Dai Houying, ah, Dai Houying) (Haikou: Hainan Guoji xinwen chuban zhongxin, 1997).
22. The letter was published posthumously as *Xinzhong de fen: Zhi youren de xin* (Grave in my mind: A letter to my friend) (Shanghai: Fudan daxue chubanshe, 1996).
23. Dai Houying, *Xingge, mingyun, wode gushi* (Character, fate, my story) (Xian: Taibai wenyi chubanshe, 1994), chap. 6.
24. For more information, see Jia Zhifang et al., eds., *Wen Jie zhuanji* (A critical reader of Wen Jie) (Fuzhou: Fujian renmin chubanshe, 1982), 3–66.
25. For a recent discussion of the lyrical manifestation of socialist realist literature, see Li Yang's discussion in *Kangzheng summing zhilu: Shehui zhuyi xianshi zhuyi (1942–1976) yan jiu* (A path to challenge fatalism: A study of socialist realism, 1942–1976) (Changchun: Shidai wenyi chubanshe, 1993), 229.
26. *Wen Jie zhuanji,* 174.
27. Ibid.,162.
28. Ibid.,183.
29. Ibid., 4.
30. At the head of the charges brought against him was an accusation that when he was arrested by Nationalist troops in 1939, he wrote a "confession" betraying the party. See Dai Houying, *Xingge,* 139–47.
31. Dai Houying, *Xingge,* chap. 7.
32. Ibid., 85–90.
33. Ibid., 127.
34. Ibid., 143–44; see also Dai Houying, *Xinzhong,* 79–85.
35. Dai Houying, *Xingge,* 144.
36. Alvarez, *The Savage God,* 237.
37. See, for example, Hu Weixiong, *Shiguo mengzhu Mao Zedong* (Mao Zedong: The hegemon in the kingdom of poetry) (Beijing: Dangdai zhongguo chubanshe, 1996); Gong Guoji, *Mao Zedong yu shi* (Mao Zedong and poetry) (Beijing: Zhongguo wenlian chuban gongsi, 1998); Li Yang, *Kangzheng summing zhilu,* 170–92. See also Ban Wang's discussion in *The Sublime Figure of History: Aesthetics and Politics in Twentieth-Century China* (Stanford, Calif.: Stanford University Press, 1997), 108–9.

38. Michel Foucault, *The History of Sexuality,* vol. 1 (New York: Vintage, 1980), 139–40.
39. Ibid., 139.
40. See Ban Wang's discussion in *The Sublime Figure,* chap. 6.
41. Dai Houying, *Xingge,* 189.
42. See my "Dai Houying, Feng Jicai, and Ah Cheng: Three Approaches to the Historical Novel," *Asian Culture Quarterly* 16, no. 2 (1988): 71–88; Wendy Larson, *Literary Authority and the Modern Chinese Writer: Ambivalence and Autobiography* (Durham, N.C.: Duke University Press, 1991).
43. Ban Wang, *The Sublime Figure,* 108–10.
44. Dai Houying, *Shiren zhisi* (The death of a poet) (Fuzhou: Fujian renmin chubanshe, 1982), 565–66.
45. Ban Wang, *The Sublime Figure,* 225.
46. Ibid.
47. Ibid.
48. While such a scenario applies to the suicide of Yu Ziqi, it does not fully spell out its complexity. One has to look at the flip side of the Maoist sublime. Instead of signaling an unfolding of meaning in escalating progression, it may hint at an involuted turn, a move that expands and curls in such a way as to turn inward upon itself. It should be recalled that even before the fortification of the Maoist discourse, there had already existed among Chinese communists a dialectic of interiority. The numerous campaigns of rectification and confession throughout the 1940s and 1950s were always premised on the continued discovery of the unspeakable, dark nexus in revolutionary subjectivity. And one can never try hard enough to explore this heart of darkness. In this regard, personal motives aside, Yu Ziqi's enemies are entitled to suspect the impurity hidden in his poem and his personality alike, and to take it upon themselves to help him diagnose his malaise. Thus when Yu Ziqi commits suicide with his own presumed innocence, he is deemed to have committed an even greater crime by turning down the opportunity of self-purging. Hence the necessity of critical rallies after his death. As such, the revolutionary poetics Yu Ziqi embraces at the moment of death posits itself as a closure both self-contained and self-contaminated. The intended effect of the Maoist sublime appears undercut by its decadent threat from the outset. Suicide is no more a climax of self-elevation thorough self-elimination than it is the beginning of an eternal fall into the opacity of selfhood. See, for example, David E. Apter and Tony Saich, *Revolutionary Discourse in Mao's Republic* (Cambridge, Mass.: Harvard University Press, 1994); Kirk A. Denton, *The Problematic of Self in Modern Chinese Literature: Hu Feng and Lu Ling* (Stanford, Calif.: Stanford University Press, 1998).
49. For more information about the Formosa Incident, see, for example, Zhang Jianlong et al., *Lishi de ningjie: Taiwan minzhu yundong yingxiang shi, 1977–1979* (Frozen history: A photo history of Taiwan's democratic movement, 1977–1979) (Taipei: Shibao chuban gongsi, 1999).
50. Quoted in Huang Juan, "Zhengzhi yu wenxue zhijian: Lun Shi Mingzheng *Dao shang ai yu si*" (Between literature and politics: On Shi Mingzheng's *Love and death on an island*), in *Shi Mingzheng ji* (A collection of works by Shi Mingzheng), ed. Lin Ruiming and Chen Wanyi (Taipei: Qianwei chubanshe, 1993), 317.

51. The self-immolations of Zheng Nanrong and Zhan Yihua happened around this time, and the two were regarded as martyrs for the Taiwanese independence movement.
52. Quoted in Li Kuixian, "Wosuo zhidao de Shi Mingzheng" (The Shi Mingzheng I know), in *Shi Mingzheng shihua ji* (A collection of poetry and painting by Shi Mingzheng) (Taipei: Qianwei chubanshe, 1985), 3.
53. Ibid., 4.
54. Huang Juan, "Zhengzhi yu wenxue zhijian," 327–28.
55. See Shi Mingzheng, "Chilai de chulian jiqi lianxiang" (A belated first love and its associations), in *Shi Mingzheng ji*, 142.
56. Ibid.
57. Li Kuixian, "Wosuo zhidao de Shi Mingzheng," 4.
58. Shi Mingzheng, "Dayi yulei" (The overcoat and tears), in *Shi Mingzheng ji*, 5.
59. Ibid., 6.
60. Ibid., 60.
61. Ibid., 98.
62. This is the subtitle of *Shi Mingzheng shihua ji.*
63. Shi Mingzheng, "Zhidao guan yu wo" (The inquisitor and I), *Shi Mingzheng ji*, 194.
64. Wolfe, *Suicidal Narrative*, 87.
65. Ibid., 88.
66. *Shi Mingzheng ji*, 320.
67. See Wolfe, *Suicidal Narrative.*
68. See N. N. Shneidman, *Dostoevsky and Suicide* (New York: Mosaic Press, 1984); Wolfe, *Suicidal Narrative*, chap. 5.
69. Shi Mingzheng, "Heniao zhe"(The man who drank his own urine), in *Shi Mingzheng ji*, 115–32.
70. Shi Mingzheng, "Kesi zhe" (The man who hankered for death, 1980), in *Shi Mingzheng ji*, 171.
71. Ibid.
72. Ibid., 173.
73. Ibid., 178.
74. Ibid.
75. Ibid.
76. Ibid.
77. Ibid., 176.
78. Ibid., 175.
79. *Shi Mingzheng ji*, 73.
80. Ibid., 96.
81. Shi Mingzheng, "Feie" (Moth), in *Shi Mingzheng ji*, 30.
82. Gu Cheng, *Selected Poems*, ed. Sean Golden and Chu Chiyu (Hong Kong: Research Centre for Translation, Chinese University of Hong Kong, 1990), 1.
83. Shu Ting once wrote a poem for Gu Cheng entitled "Tonghua shiren" (Fairy-tale poet); for more discussion of the "loss" of the fairy-tale quality in Gu Cheng's world, see Zhang Yiwu, "Yige tonghua de zhongjie" (The end of a fairy tale), in *Gu Cheng qi cheng*, ed. Xiao Xialin (Beijing: Tuanjie chubanshe, 1994), 296–97.
84. Gu Cheng, "Jin he yuan" (Near and far), *Selected Poems*, 26.

85. Gu Gong, ed., *Gu Cheng shi quanbian* (Complete collection of Gu Cheng's poetry) (Shanghai: Shanghai Sanlian shudian, 1995), 837.
86. Zeng Huiyan, "Gu Cheng, Xie Ye tan *Ying'er* yu Ying'er," in *Gu Cheng qi cheng,* 155.
87. Ibid., 157.
88. Ibid., 154.
89. Kong Qingdong, "Gu Cheng, shiren de beiju zhicheng" (Gu Cheng, a city of a poet's tragedy), in *Gu Cheng qi cheng,* ed. Xiao Xialin (Beijing: Tuanjie chubanshe, 1994), 311.
90. See, for example, Wang Xiaoyu's interview with Xie Ye's mother, in *Gu Cheng qicheng,* 36–45; Jiji, "Gu Cheng zhaobu dao tade cheng" (Gu Cheng cannot find his own city), in *Gu Cheng qi cheng,* 55–56.
91. Chen Bingliang, "Gu Cheng xiandai shuixianzi" (Gu Cheng, the modern Narcisscus), in *Gu Cheng qi cheng,* 161–63.
92. Gu Cheng's father, Gu Gong, may not have written anything immediately after his son's death. But he must have granted permission to publishers to reissue some of his earlier essays about Gu Cheng to publicize his son's posthumous works. See Raoul David Findeisen, "Two Works—Hong (1930) and Ying'er (1993)—As Indeterminate Joint Adventures," in *Essays, Interviews, Recollections, and Unpublished Material of Gu Cheng, Twentieth-Century Chinese Poet: The Poetics of Death,* ed. Li Xia (Lewiston: Edwin Mellen Press, 1999), 145–58. See also Wang Xiaoyu's interview with Xie Ye's mother, in *Gu Cheng qi cheng,* 36–45; Gu Xiang (Gu Cheng's sister), *Wo miandui de Gu Cheng zuihou shisitian: Yi jiu jiu san nian jiu yue er she si ri zhi shi yue ba ri* (The last fourteen days of Gu Cheng's life I was faced with: September 24–October 8, 1993) (Beijing: Guoji wenhua chuban gongsi, 1994). Li Ying published her love story as *Hunduan jiliu dao: Gu Cheng, Xie Ye, and Ying'er* (Death on the island of torrents [Waiheke]: The story of Gu Cheng, Xie Ye, and Ying'er) (Hong Kong: Mingbao chubanshe, 1995).
93. Gu Gong took charge of editing a complete collection of Gu Cheng's poetry, *Gu Cheng shi quanbian.* Gu Cheng's mother, a script writer in her own right, allegedly supervised the editing of the preface—an interview between Suizi Zhang-Kubin and Gu Cheng—to make sure that Xie Ye, rather than Gu Cheng, was responsible for the family tragedy. See Wolfgang Kubin, "Gu Cheng: Beijing. I," in Li Xia, ed., *Essays, Interviews, Recollections,* 22.
94. Michelle Yeh, "Death of the Poet: Poetry and Society in Contemporary China and Taiwan," in *Chinese Literature in the Second Half of a Modern Century: A Critical Survey,* ed. Pang-yuan Chi and David Wang (Bloomington: Indiana University Press, 2000), 216–38.
95. Zhang Yiwu, "Yige tonghua de zhongjie," 304–306. See also Wang Yuechuan, "A Perspective on the Suicide of Chinese Poets in the 1990's," in Li Xia, ed., *Essays, Interviews, Recollections,* 61–76.
96. The novel appears under the names Gu Cheng and Lei Mi (pen name of Xie Yeh). It has at least three official editions. The first version, published by Zuojia chuban she (Writers' Publications, Beijing), claims to be the "only legal, complete version of authorized by the writers. It was a gift to the press from an anonymous person who professes to have bought the script for 33,000 renminbi at

a Shenzhen manuscript auction one day after Gu Cheng axed his wife to death and then committed suicide." The second version, published by Huayi chubanshe (Huayi publications, Beijing), was presented to the publisher by Liu Zhenyun, a friend of Gu Cheng and a writer in his own right, who had met Gu Cheng and Xie Ye at a conference in Berlin in June 1993. The two versions are different in narrative structure and style, though the content remains largely the same. It is assumed that Gu Cheng may have given the second version, based on an earlier script, to Liu Zhenyun without Xie Ye's agreement. See Li Xia, "Gu Cheng's *Ying'er:* A Journey to the West," in Li Xia, ed. *Essays, Interviews, Recollections,* 61–75. Li Xia is the English translator of the first version of the novel. See also Raoul David Findeisen, "Two Works," 145–58. The third version, in complicated Chinese characters, is published by Yuanshen chubanshe (Yuanshen publications, Taipei); it is based on the Zuojia chubanshe edition. I am using the Taiwan edition as my reference.

97. Wen Quanxin et al., "Gu Cheng, Jiliudao tucheng" (Gu Cheng, murder and suicide on Waiheke Island), in *Gucheng qi cheng,* 50,
98. Gu Cheng, *Ying'er* (Yiner) (Taipei: Yuanshen chubanshe, 1993).
99. See, for example, Shi Ming, "Ying'er," in *Gu Cheng qi cheng,* 151.
100. Gu Cheng, *Ying'er,* 388.
101. Ibid., 394.
102. Ibid., 168.
103. Ibid., 16.
104. Ibid., 218.
105. Chen Bingliang, "Gu Cheng xiandai shuixianzi."
106. Gu Cheng, *Ying'er,* 178.
107. Ibid., 439–40.
108. Jean-François Lyotard, *The Postmodern Condition: A Report on Knowledge,* trans. Geoffrey Bennington and Brian Massumi (Minneapolis: University of Minnesota Press, 1984), 37.
109. See Su Ying, "Gu Cheng fangsi, piandi *Ying'er*" (*Ying'er* is everywhere right upon Gu Cheng's death), in *Gu Cheng qi cheng,* 146–48.
110. See, for example, discussions by critics such as Luo Changlu, Zhang Yiwu, Hang Yuhai, and Kong Qingdong, in *Gu Cheng qi cheng,* section 9.
111. Luo Changlu, "Shihua zuie: Gu Cheng zhisi de yulun fengxiang" (Making poetry of the evil: On the consensual responses to the death of Gu Cheng), in *Shiren Gu Cheng zhisi* (The death of Gu Chen, a poet), ed. Chen Zishan (Shanghai: Shanghai renmin chubanshe, 1993), 90–92.
112. Gu Cheng, "Wuming de xiaohua" (Nameless flowers), *Gu Cheng shi quanbian,* 40–41. I use the translation in *Selected Poems,* 2.
113. See Zhou Mai, "Shiren, baojun" (Poet, tyrant), in *Gu Cheng qi cheng,* 323–24; Lü Dianwen, "Shiren de siwang he daode" (The death of the poet and morality), in *Gu Cheng qi cheng,* 320–22. Also see Shanlin, "Ye tan Gu Cheng de Jiating beiju" (Also a talk on Gu Cheng's family tragedy), *Lianhe wenxue* (Unitas) 13, no. 9 (July 1997): 176–80.
114. See Liu Zhe, "Hei yanjing chuantou buliao heiye: Shiren zisha yu wenhua jiegou" (Black eyes cannot pierce through the dark night: The suicide of the poet and the deconstruction of culture), in *Gu Cheng qi cheng,* 325–28.

CHAPTER 8: SECOND HAUNTING

1. "Gui," translated as "ghost" in this essay, is a complex concept in Chinese history. While this chapter does not delve into the various etiological and archaeological origins of *gui,* my discussion is based at least on the following sources. In his study of "gui," Shen Jianshi concludes, "(1) 'Gui,' like 'yu,' first referred to a strange creature which looks like humanity; (2) the meaning of 'gui' was then expanded, pointing to the mankind of different tribal origins; (3) the meaning of 'gui' underwent a change from something concrete to something abstract, such as 'wei' and other adjectives, indicating the fantastic and the strange; (4) finally 'gui' was borrowed to describe the imaginary soul after the death of mankind." See Shen Jianshi, "Gui zi yuanshi yiyi zhi shitan" (A preliminary survey of the original meaning of gui), *Guoxue jikan* (Chinese studies quarterly) 5, no. 3 (1935): 45–60. For an overview of the Chinese concept of afterlife, see Ying-shih Yu, "Zhongguo gudai sihou shijieguan de yanbian" (The changing view of afterlife in ancient China), in *Zhongguo sixiang chuantong de xiandai quanshi* (A modern interpretation of traditional Chinese thoughts) (Taipei: Lianjing chuban gongshi, 1987), 123–43; Tu Cheng-sheng, "Xingti, jingqi, yu hunpo: Zhongguo chuantong dui 'ren' renshi de xingcheng" (Body, essence, and soul: The formation of the concept of humanity in Chinese tradition), *Xin shixue* (New historiography) 2, no. 3 (Sept. 1991): 1–35; Arthur P. Wolf, "Gods, Ghosts, Ancestors," in *Religion and Ritual in Chinese Society* (Stanford, Calif.: Stanford University Press, 1974), 131–82. For general studies of death, death rituals, and concepts of the afterlife in China, see James I. Watson and Evelyn S. Rawski, eds., *Death Ritual in Late Imperial and Modern China* (Berkeley: University of California Press, 1988); C. K. Yang, *Religion in Chinese Society: A Study of Contemporary Social Functions of Religion and Some of Their Historical Factors* (Berkeley: University of California Press, 1970), 28–57; Guo Yuhua, *Side kunrao yu sheng de zhizhuo: Zhongguo minjian sangzang yili yu chuantong shengsi guan* (The trouble of death and the fixation of life: The death ritual in Chinese popular society and traditional concepts of life and death) (Bejing: Zhongguo renmin daxue chubanshe, 1992); Xu Jijun "Lun zhongguo minjian sangsu linghun xinyang de yanbian" (Transformations of funeral customs and beliefs regarding the soul in Chinese popular society), in *Minjian xinyang yu zhongguo wenhua guoji yantaohui lunwenji* (Compendium of international conference on popular beliefs and Chinese culture), ed. Hanxue zhongxin (Taipei: Hanxue yanjiu zhongxin, 1994), 885–902; Lin Fu-shih, *Guhun yu guixiong de shijie: Bei Taiwan de ligui xinyang* (The world of lonely souls and ghosts: Beliefs in vicious ghosts in northern Taiwan) (Banqiao: Taipei xianli wenhua zhongxin, 1995), chaps. 1–2. I wish to thank Dr. Lin Fu-shih for bibliographical information on ghosts and funereal customs in China and Taiwan.
2. Feng Menglong, *Yushi mingyan* (Illustrious tales to lecture the world) (Hong Kong: Gudian wenxue chubanshe, 1974), 376. The story originated in Hong Mai's *Yijian zhi,* entitled "Taiyuan Yiniang" (Yiniang of Taiyuan). It was already made into a popular *huaben* story in the Southern Song under the title "Huigujia" (Casket of ashes). Shen He wrote a *zhaju* play in the Yuan dynasty, entitled "Zheng Yu'e Yanshan feng guren" (An encounter of Zheng Yu'e in Yanshan).

See Hu Shiying, *Huaben xiaoshuo gailun* (A general study *of huaben xiaoshuo*) (Taipei: Danqing tushu, 1983), 222–23, 243–44. My translation of the quotation is based on Stephen Chingkiu Chan's in "The Return of the Ghostwoman: A Critical Reading of Three Sung Hua-pen stories," *Asian Culture Quarterly* 15, no. 3 (1987): 47.

3. *Yijianzhi* is the largest collection of tales after the *Taiping guangji*. It originally contained 420 volumes and nearly 2,700 stories; only a little over 200 volumes are extant. These stories were written by Hong Mai over the period 1161–1198. They deal with dreams, the human and superhuman worlds, origins of poems, etc. See William H. Nienhauser, Jr., ed., *The Indiana Companion to Traditional Chinese Literature* (Bloomington: Indiana University Press, 1986), 457.
4. Hu Shiying, *Huaben xiaoshuo gailun,* 223; Stephen Chan, "The Return of the Ghostwoman," 47–51.
5. For Southern Song literati's nostalgic accounts of life in the Northern Song capital, Bianliang, see Pei-yi Wu's discussion in "Memories of K'ai-feng," *New Literary History* 25, no. 1 (1994): 47–60. With Meng Yuanlao's *Dongjing menghua lu* (A record of the dreams of the eastern capital's splendor) as his case in point, Wu makes a specific reference to the glory of the Lantern Festival in Bianliang before its fall.
6. For the fantastic tradition in ancient Chinese literature and its variations, see Yang Yi, *Zhongguo gudian xiaoshuo shilun* (History of classical Chinese fiction) (Beijing: Zhongguo shehui kexue chubanshe, 1995), chaps. 4, 8; Li Jianguo, ed., *Tangqian zhiguai xiaoshuo jishi* (Annotated collection of pre-Tang *zhiguai* fiction) (Taipei: Wenshizhi chubanshe, 1987). Also see Karl S. Y. Kao, "Introduction," in *Classical Chinese Tales of the Supernatural and the Fantastic: Selections from the Third to the Tenth Century* (Bloomington: Indiana University Press, 1985). Kenneth DeWoskin, "The Six Dynasties *Chih-kuai* and the Birth of Fiction," in *Chinese Narrative: Critical and Theoretical Essays,* ed. Andrew H. Plaks (Princeton, N.J.: Princeton University Press, 1977), 21–52. Also see Liu Yuanru's new book, *Liuchao zhiguai de changyi lunshu yu xiaoshuo meixue: Shenti, xingbie, jieji* (The discourse of normalcy and anomaly in Six Dynasties tales and its narrative aesthetics: Body, gender, class) (Taipei: Zhongyang yanjiuyuan wenzhesuo, 2002).
7. See Yang Yi, *Zhongguo gudian xiaoshuo shilun,* chaps. 4, 8, 12, 20. Also see Chen Pingyuan, "Zhongguo xiaoshuo shilun" (A history of Chinese fiction), in *Chen Pingyuan xiaoshuoshi lunji* (Collection of works on Chinese fictional history by Chen Pingyuan) (Shijiazhuang: Hebei renmin chubanshe, 1996), 3: 1495–506, 1533–41; Cheng Yizhong, ed., *Shenguai qingxia de yishu shijie: Zhongguo gudai xiaoshuo liupai man hua* (The world of the supernatural, the romantic, and the chivalric) (Beijing: Zhonggong zhongyang dangxiao chubanshe, 1994); Wang Guoliang, "Liuchao yu suitang de xiaoshou gui" (Ghosts in Six Dynasties and Sui-Tang fiction), in *Lianhe wenxue* (Unitas) 16, no. 10 (Aug. 2000): 47–48.
8. Lu Xun, *Zhongguo xiaoshuo shilui* (A brief history of Chinese fiction) (rpt. Hong Kong: Qingwen shuwu, 1972), 230. See also Liao Yuhui, "Cong sheng juanshu dao si yuanjia: Song huaben zhong de rengui hunlian gushi" (Romantic couples from life to death: On ghostly love and marriage in Song *huaben* stories), *Lianhe wenxue* 16, no. 10 (Aug. 2000): 49–52.
9. Lu Xun, *Zhongguo xiaoshuo shilui,* 230. In his study, Maruo Tsuneki has pointed

out Lu Xun's comments on *Hedian* (What sort of book is this?), a major late Qing novel on ghostly themes. See *Ren yu gui de jiuge: Lu Xun xiaoshuo lunxi* (The entanglements between ghosts and humanity: An analysis of Lu Xun's fiction), trans. Qin Gong (Beijing: Renmin wenxue chubanshe, 1995), 162.

10. To be sure, nineteenth-century European realist fiction "contains" numerous elements of the supernatural in forms ranging from tales within tales to dream sequences and narrated hallucinations. Realistic portrayal of primitive peoples, women, children, madness, dreams, daydreams, hallucinations, science fiction, and ideology—the ghostly by a positivist standard—constitutes the rule of verisimilitude. A superb example can be found in *The Temptation of St. Anthony,* by the archrealist Flaubert, in which one gets the Christian myth of saintly self-torture as imagined by a deluded disciple of historicism.
11. Quoted in Maruo Tuneki, *Ren yu gui de jiuge,* 214.
12. Guo Moruo's letter to Zong Baihua quoted from Maruo Tuneki, 213.
13. Maruo Tuneki, *Ren yu gui de jiuge,* 105.
14. Zhou Zuoren also said that he did not believe in the immortality of soul. See "Tangguilun" (On gossiping about ghosts), in his volume of essays, *Guadouji* (Melons and beans) (Shanghai: Yuzhou fengshe, 1937), 21.
15. Quoted in Maruo Tuneki, *Ren yu gui de jiuge,* 215–16. Zhou Zuoren is arguably the most prolific among the May Fourth writers on the subject of the ghostly. See Qian Liqun, *Zhou Zuoren lun* (A study of Zhou Zuoren) (Shanghai: Shanghai renmin chubanshe, 1991), chap. 9.
16. Hu Shi made the statement in 1921. Hu Shi, "Zhengli guogu yu 'dagui'" (Sinological learning and subduing the ghosts), in *Hu Shi wencong* (Works of Hu Shi); quoted in T. A. Hsia, *The Gate of Darkness: Studies of the Leftist Literary Movement in China* (Seattle: University of Washington Press, 1968), 159. For more information about the attitude of the post–May Fourth literati and intelligentsia toward the ghostly and the supernatural, see Zeng Yu, ed., *Mingrenbi congshu: Liaokan gui yu shen* (Compendium of renowned literati writings: Random notes on ghosts and gods) (Changchun: Jilin renmin chubanshe, 1996).
17. Quoted in Maruo Tuneki, *Ren yu gui de jiuge,* 215.
18. A statement made by He Jingzhi, one of the cowriters of the Yan'an version of *Baimao nü;* see Meng Yue's discussion in "*Baimao nü* yanbian de qishi: Jian lun Yan'an wenyi de lishi duozhi xing" (The transformations of the *The White-Haired Girl* and its significance: On the polyphony of history in Yan'an literature), in *Zaijiedu: Dazhong wenyi yu yishi xingtai* (Rereading: Mass literature and ideology), ed. Tang Xiaobing (Hong Kong: Oxford University Press, 1993), 68–89.
19. Dai Jiafang, *Yangban xi de fengfeng yuyu: Jiang Qing, yangbanxi ji neimu* (The stormy history of the model drama: Jiang Qing, model theater, and the stories behind the scenes) (Beijing: Zhishi chubanshe, 1995), 7–8. The essay "Yougui wuhai lun" (Ghosts do humanity no harm) was written by Liao Mosha.
20. Both writers deserve more notice, particularly in the context of popular culture.
21. *Erya zhushu* (Annotated *Erya*) "Shixun disan," juan 4, 14a, in *Runkan Shisanjing zhushu* (Annotated Thirteen Classics, the Ruan edition; a reprint of the 1815 Jiangxi Nanchangfuxue chongkan edition of *Shisanjing zhushu*) (Taipei: Yiwen yinshuguan, 1993), 61.

22. *Chunqiu Zuozhuan zhengy* (Annotated *Chunqiu Zuozhuan* with commentary) "Zhaogong qinian," juan 44, 12a; 13a–13b, in *Runkan Shisanjing zhushu* (Annotated Thirteen Classics, the Ruan edition; a reprint of the 1815 Jiangxi Nanchangfuxue chongkan edition of *Shisanjing zhushu*) (Taipei: Yiwen yinshuguan, 1993), 763, 764; *Liji zhushu,* "jiyi," juan 47, 14b, in *Runkan Shisanjing zhushu* (Annotated Thirteen Classics, the Ruan edition; a reprint of the 1815 Jiangxi Nanchangfuxue chongkan edition of *Shisanjing zhushu*) (Taipei: Yiwen yinshuguan, 1993), 813.
23. Sigmund Freud, "The Uncanny," *The Standard Edition of the Complete Psychological Works of Sigmund Freud,* ed. and trans. James Strachey, vol. 17 (London: Hogarth Press, 1955), 219–56. For a discussion of the "uncanny" from a modern spatial point of view, see Anthony Vidler, *The Architectural Uncanny: Essays in the Modern Unhomely* (Cambridge, Mass.: MIT Press, 1992). To this, Han Shaogong's story adds a twist, that a home by Chinese Communist definition is no longer a nuclear, private space, as understood in modern Western terms, but instead a space dedicated to collective fulfillment. The strange village the protagonist returns to is therefore a "home" only in the sense that it is now twice removed from the homely image of prerevolutionary nostalgia.
24. For a detailed discussion, see my article, "Lao linghun qianshi jinsheng: Zhu Tianxin de xiaoshuo meixue" (The previous lives and the current incarnation of the old soul: the novelistic aesthetics of Zhu Tianxin), in Zhu Tianxin, *Gudu* (Ancient capital) (Taipei: Maitian chubanshe, 1997), 3–37.
25. Wang Dewei (David Wang), "Shanghen jijing, baoli qiguan: Yu Hua de xiaoshuo" (A tableau vivant of scar, a spectacle of violence: Yu Hua's fiction), in *Xu Sanguan maixue ji* (Xu Sanguan the blood donor) (Taipei: Maitian chuban gonsi, 1997), 1–23.
26. Xiaobin Yang, *The Postmodern / Post-Mao-Deng History and Rhetoric in Chinese Avant-Garde Fiction* (Ph.D. diss., Yale University, 1996), 90.
27. As Xiaobin Yang puts it, in Yu Hua's world, "all the past events are dispersed as ruins, discontinuities or collages in an instant. . . . There is no temporal duration in this moment, no rational development of history; everything is conjured up in the Now." Ibid., 205.
28. Tao Qian, "Li Zhongwen nu" (The daughter of Li Zhongwen), in *Tangqian zhiguai xiaoshuo jishi,* ed. Li Jianguo, 429.
29. Tang Xianzu, "*Mudanting* tici" (Preface to *Peony Pavilion*), in *Tangqian zhiguai xiaoshuo jishi,* ed. Li Jianguo, 433.
30. See, for example, Peter Brooks, *Reading for the Plot: Design and Intervention in the Narrative* (Cambridge, Mass.: Harvard University Press, 1992).
31. Ibid.
32. A considerable portion of Li Bihua's fiction is based on existing legends, drama, or even historical accounts. Among the most prominent examples are *Farewell, My Concubine,* which was made into a film, and *Qing She* (Green snake, 1986), a rewrite of the famous legend of the White Snake.
33. For criticisms on *The Rouge* and the movie based on the novel, see Ackbar M. Abbas, *Hong Kong: Culture and the Politics of Disappearance* (Minneapolis: University of Minnesota Press, 1997), 40–47; Rey Chow, *Ethics after Idealism: Theory, Culture, Ethnicity, Reading* (Bloomington: Indiana University Press, 1998),

133–48; Xiaoliang Li, "Wending yu buding: Li Bihua sanbu xiaoshuo zhongde wenhua rentong yu xingbie yishi" (Certainty and uncertainty: Cultural identification and gender consciousness in three novels by Li Bihua), *Xiandai zhongwen wenxue pinglun* (Review of modern Chinese literature) 4 (Dec. 1995): 101–11; Ye Si, *Xianggang wenhua* (Hong Kong culture) (Hong Kong: Xianggang yishu zhongxi, 1995), chap. 6.

34. Li Bihua's contemplation of the pact between historical memory and the ghost finds an equally poignant presentation in the novel *Pan Jinlian zhi qianshi jinsheng* (The previous and present lives of Pan Jinlian, 1989). This work takes the leading *femme fatale* of premodern Chinese fiction, *Jinpingmei* (Golden Lotus), and asks what it would be like if her story happened in contemporary Hong Kong. In contrast to other rewritings of Pan Jilian in the twentieth century, Li's version does not relate Pan Jinlian's "life" story anew, as in Ouyang Yuqian's play (see Chapter 2), but rather starts when she dies, an adulteress and murderer. When the novel opens, the ghost of Pan Jinlian is seen undergoing its latest incarnation as Song Yulian, an ex–ballet dancer specialized in *White-Haired Girl,* who is about to encounter yet another love triangle set in Hong Kong. As if parodying the historical dialectic in that play, Li Bihua hints that the new society, be it Communist China or capitalist Hong Kong, can "turn a human being into a ghost" just as efficiently as it can "turn a ghost into a human being." Residual, ghostly traits are found in modern human shape, as in the case of Jinlian and other characters.

Insofar as Pan Jianlian's fatal search for love and revenge has fallen into routine repetition, the endless cycle of *The Previous and Present Lives of Pan Jinlian* tends to "turn her tragedy into an absurdist comedy," in Li Bihua's own words. Li Bihua, *Pan Jilian zhi qianshi jinsheng* (The previous and present lives of Pan Jinlian) (Hong Kong: Tiandi tushu gongsi, 1989), 218.

35. For an extensive discussion of "imaginary nostalgia," see my book, *Fictional Realism in Twentieth-Century China: Mao Dun, Lao She, Shen Congwen* (New York: Columbia University Press, 1992), chap. 7.

36. A comparable example is Chen Hui's *Shixiangji: 1974–1996* (A tale of Shixiang: 1974–1996) (Hong Kong: Tiandi tashu, 2000), a novel about a Hong Kong family's ups and downs from the late 1940s to the eve of the Return. This novel is narrated by a girl named Shixiang who, as the novel's subtitle indicates, has died before the narration starts. Unlike Chen Guanzhong, however, Chen Hui finds love in both the ethical and religious sense, a possible redemption for the decay of life.

37. See my discussion in "Baolie de wenrou: Huang Biyun de xiaoshuo" (Violent tenderness: Huang Biyun's fiction), in Huang Biyun, *Shier nüse* (Twelve female colors) (Taipei: Maitian chubanshe, 2000), 9–36.

38. See ibid., 22–28.

39. Abbas, *Hong Kong,* 25.

40. Of course, this does not have to be the only vision contemporary Hong Kong writers have projected onto their hometown. See my discussion in "Love and Passion in Hong Kong," presented at South China Lecture series, the University of Science and Technology, Hong Kong, November 7, 2001.

41. Yü-sheng Lin, *The Crisis of Chinese Consciousness: Radical Antitraditionalism in the*

May Fourth Era (Madison: University of Wisconsin Press, 1979), 26–33. See my argument in *Fictional Realism,* chap. 1.

42. Roland Barthes, *Writing Degree Zero,* trans. Annette Lavers and Colin Smith (New York: Hill and Wang, 1968), 14.
43. See Hu Wanchuan, *Zhong Kui shenhua yu xiaoshuo zhi yanjiu* (A study of the myth and fiction about Zhong Kui) (Tiapei: Wenshizhe chubanshe, 1980), 127–55.
44. See my argument in *Fin-de-siècle Splendor: Repressed Modernities of Late Qing Fiction 1849–1911* (Stanford, Calif.: Stanford University Press, 1998), 191–209.
45. Ibid., 200.
46. Ibid., 200–209.
47. T.A. Hsia, "The Gate of Darkness," in *The Gate of Darkness;* Leo Ou-fan Lee, *Voices from the Iron House: A Study of Lu Xun* (Bloomington: University of Indiana Press, 1987), chaps. 3–4; Wang Xiaoming, *Wufa zhimian de rensheng: Lun Xun zhuan* (A life that cannot be faced up to) (Taipei: Yeqiang chubanshe, 1992); Wang Hui, "Sihuo chongwen" (A rekindled dead fire), in *Sihuo chongwen* (Beijing: Renmin wenxue chubanshe, 2000), 413–34.
48. Maruo Tuneki, *Ren yugui de jiuge.*
49. Ibid., 84–100.
50. Jean Paul Sartre, *Les Mots* (Paris: Gallimard, 1986), 171; quoted in Peter Brooks, "Freud's Masterplot," in *Contemporary Literary Criticism,* ed. Robert Con Davis and Ronald Schleifer (New York: Longman, 1989), 289.
51. Lu Xun, postword to *Fen* (Grave); quoted in T. A. Hsia, *The Gate of Darkness,* 148.
52. The letter is dated September 24, 1924, in *Lu Xun shuxin ji (shang)* (Lu Xun's correspondence, part 1) (Beijing: Renmin wenxue chubanshe, 1976), 61.
53. Lu Xun, "E yiben 'Ah Q zhengzhuan xu' ji zhuzhe zixu zhuanlue" (Preface to the Russian translation of "The True Story of Ah Q" and the author's autobiographical notes), in *Lu Xun quanji,* 7: 81.
54. For more information about the origin and development of the *Mulian* legend and drama, see, for example, Chen Fangying, *Mulian jiumu gushi zhi yanji ji qi youguan wenxue zhi yanjiu* (A study of the evolution of the legend of Mulian's rescue of his mother and its related literary variations) (Taipei: National Taiwan University , 1984); Hunan sheng xiju yanjiu suo and Zhong guo yishu yanjiu yuan Xiqu yanjiu bianjibu, eds., *Mulianxi xueshu zuotanhui lunwenxue* (Collection of articles on *Mulian* drama) (Hunan: Huanan yinshua, 1985).
55. T.A. Hsia, *The Gate of Darkness,* 160.
56. Ibid., 162.
57. Eileen Chang, "My Writing," trans. Wendy Larson, in *Modern Chinese Literary Thought: Writings on Literature, 1893–1945,* ed. Kirk Denton (Stanford, Calif.: Stanford University Press, 1997), 438.
58. Eileen Chang, "Chenxiang xie: Diyilu xiang" (Ashes of sandalwood: The first incense burner), in *Chuanqi* (Romance), *Zhang Ailing wenji* (Works of Eileen Chang) (Taipei: Huangguan chubanshe, 1992), 8.
59. Tang Wenbiao, *Zhang Ailing yanjiu* (A study of Eileen Chang) (Taipei: Lianjing chuban gonsi, 1976), 56.
60. See my article "Chongdu Zhang Ailing de *Yangge* yu *Chidi zhilian*" (Rereading Eileen Chang's *Rice-Sprout Song* and *Naked Earth*), in *Ruhe xiandai, zenyang wenxue? Shijiu, ershi shiji zhongwen xiaoshuo xinlun* (The making of the modern, the

making of a literature: New perspectives on nineteenth- and twentieth-century Chinese fiction) (Taipei: Maitian chuban gongsi, 1998), 337–62.

61. Eileen Chang, *Duizhao ji: Kan lao zhao xiang bu* (A volume of reciprocal spectatorship: Reading an old photo album) (Taipei: Huangguan chubanshe, 1994), 52.
62. Roland Barthes, *Camera Lucida: Reflections on Photography,* trans. Richard Howard (New York: Hill and Wang, 1981), 96. The translation has been modified.
63. Ibid., 92–93.
64. "Nü'zuojia de xiandai 'gui' hua: Cong Zhang Ailing dao Su Weizhen" (Modernist ghost talk by Chinese women writers: From Eileen Chang to Su Weizhen), in *Zhongsheng xuanhua: Sanling yu baling niandai de zhongguo xiaoshuo* (Heteroglossia: Chinese fiction of the 1930s and the 1980s) (Taipei: Yuanliu chuban gongsi, 1988), 227–38.
65. See my review essay, "Nüzuojia de houxiandai guihua" (Postmodernist "ghost talk" by Chinese women writers), *Lian he bao, du shu ren* (United Daily News), Oct. 19, 1998.
66. See Jonathan Crary, *Techniques of the Observer: On Vision and Modernity in the Nineteenth Century* (Cambridge, Mass.: MIT Press, 1992), 132–34. See also Terry Castle, "Phantasmagoria: Spectral Technology and the Metamorphosis of Modern Reverie," *Critical Inquiry* 15, no. 1 (1988): 26–61.
67. Walter Benjamin, *Charles Baudelaire: A Lyric Poet in the Era of High Capitalism,* trans. Harry Zohn (London: Verso, 1983), 67–101. See also Christina Britzolakis, "Phantasmagoria: Walter Benjamin and the Poetics of Urban Modernism," in *Ghosts: Deconstruction, Psychoanalysis, History,* ed. Peter Buse and Andrew Stott (New York: St. Martin, 1999), 72–91.
68. Andreas Huyssen, *After the Great Divide: Modernism, Mass Culture, Postmodernism* (Bloomington: Indiana University Press, 1986), 40.
69. Theodor Adorno, *In Search of Wagner,* trans. Rodney Livingstone (New York: Verso, 1981), 85. The original quote is: "Its [the phantasmagoria's] perfection is at the same time the perfection of the illusion that the work of art is reality *sui generis* that constitutes itself in the realm of the absolute without having to renounce its claim to image the world." I am using Huyssen's translation, *After the Great Divide,* 41. Harry Harootunian, echoing Anthony Giddens, uses the term "phantasmagoric" to describe the "experience of everydayness" in Japan as "the locale—place was penetrated and shaped by practices and knowledges distant and distinct from those received from an immediate history and culture." Harry Harootunian, *History's Disquiet: Modernity, Cultural Practice, and the Questions of Everyday Life* (New York: Columbia University Press, 2000), 63; Anthony Giddens, *The Consequences of Modernity* (Stanford, Calif.: Stanford University Press, 1990), 18–19.
70. Margaret Cohen, *Profane Illumination: Walter Benjamin and the Paris of Surrealist Revolution* (Berkeley: University of California Press, 1993), 2, 12.
71. Jacques Derrida, *Specters of Marx: The State of the Debt, the Work of Mourning, and the New International,* trans. Peggy Kamuf (London and New York: Routledge, 1994), 4.
72. See Peggy Kamuf, "Violence, Identity, Self-Determination and the Question of Justice: On *Specters of Marx,*" in *Violence, Identity, and Self-Determination,* ed. Hent

de Vries and Samuel Weber (Stanford, Calif.: Stanford University Press, 1997), 271–83; Nigel Mapp, "Specter and Impurity: History and the Transcendental in Derrida and Adorno," in *Ghosts,* ed. Buse and Stott, 92–124. For more criticism on Derrida's book, see Michael Sprinker, ed., *Ghostly Demarcations: A Symposium on Jacques Derrida's "Spectres of Marx"* (London: Verso, 1999).

73. For recent studies of Chinese realism, see, for example, Marston Anderson, *The Limits of Realism: Chinese Fiction in the Revolutionary Period* (Berkeley: University of California Press, 1990); Wang, *Fictional Realism.*
74. See Huang Jinlin, *Lishi, shenti, guojia: Jindai zhongguo shenti de xingcheng, 1895–1937* (History, body, nation: The formation of the modern Chinese body, 1895–1937) (Taipei: Lianjing chuban gongsi, 2001), chap. 2.
75. See Ban Wang's discussion in *The Sublime Figure of History: Aesthetics and Politics in Twentieth-Century China* (Stanford, Calif.: Stanford University Press, 1997), chaps. 2 and 6.
76. Chiang Kai-shek, "Xin shenghuo yundong gangyao" (Guidelines of new life movement), in *Xin shenghuo yundong shiliao,* ed. Xiao Jizong (Taipei: Zhongyang wenwu gongyingshe, 1975), 30–32.
77. Ibid., 33–34.
78. Lu Xun, Preface to *Nahan* (A call to arms), trans. Hsien-yi Yang and Gladys Yang (Beijing: Foreign Languages Press, 1978), 7.
79. Chi-hui Liu, "Sanshi niandai zhongguo wenhua lunshu zhong de faxisi wangxiang jiqi yayi: Cong jige wenben zhengzhuang tanqi" (Fascist fantasy and its repression in the cultural discourse of 1930s China: Textual symptoms), paper presented at the Institute of Chinese Literature and Philosophy, Academia Sinica, Taipei, March 21, 2000; Jing Yuen Tsu, "Failure: Nation, Race, and Literature in China, 1895–1937" (Ph.D. diss., Harvard University, 2001), chap. 3.
80. See Chi-hui Liu, "Sanshi niandai zhongguo wenhua lunshu zhong de faxisi wangxiang jiqi yayi."
81. Ban Wang, *Sublime Figure of History,* 1.
82. Michel Foucault, "Theatrum Philosophicum," in *Language, Counter-Memory, Practice: Selected Essays and Interviews,* trans. Donald F. Bouchard and Sherry Simon (Ithaca, N.Y.: Cornell University Press, 1981), 170.
83. Ibid., 169–70.
84. I am referring to Christopher Prendergast's book, *The Order of Mimesis: Balzac, Stendhal, Nerval, Flaubert* (Cambridge: Cambridge University Press, 1986), chaps. 1–2.
85. This can be associated with Gilles Deleuze's observation of the phantasm in narrative in *Logique du sens,* quoted in J. Hillis Miller, *Fiction and Repetition: Seven English Novels* (Cambridge, Mass.: Harvard University Press, 1982), 4.
86. See, for example, Gérard Genette's classic study in *Narrative Discourse.* For Genette, voice in (realist) narrative functions more powerfully than a statement made by the narrator or another character. Closely related to viewpoint, voice regulates the relation between narrative and its instance. *Narrative Discourse: An Essay in Method,* trans. Jane E. Lewin (Ithaca, N.Y.: Cornell University Press, 1980), 212–14.
87. Michel de Certeau, *The Practice of Everyday Life,* trans. Steven F. Rendell (Berkeley: University of California Press, 1988), 131–32.

88. For the origin and development of the story, see Hu Shiying, *Huaben xiaoshuo gailun,* 200–201.
89. See Chen Bingliang, "Xu" (preface), in *Shengsi yuanjia* (Life-and-death partners), ed. Zhong Ling (Taipei: Hongfan chubanshe, 1991), 1–7.
90. I am of course referring to Wang Guowei's famous interpretation of *yu* (jade) and *yu* (desire) in "Hongloumeng pinglun" (A commentary on *The Dream of the Red Chamber*), in *Ershi shiji Zhongguo xiaoshuo lilun ziliao* (Critical materials on the Chinese novel by twentieth-century Chinese scholars), ed. Chen Pingyuan and Xia Xiaohong (Beijing: Beijing daxue chubanshe, 1989).
91. Sigmund Freud, "Three Essays on the Theory of Sexuality," in *The Freud Reader,* ed. Peter Gay (New York: Norton, 1989), 249–50.
92. Jia Pingwa, *Baiye* (White night) (Taipei: Fengyun shidai chubanshe, 1996), 3.
93. See Chen Fangying, "Mulian jiumu gushi."
94. Jia, *Baiye,* 3.
95. Ibid., 7.
96. Judith T. Zeitlin, *Historian of the Strange: Pu Songling and the Chinese Classical Tale* (Stanford, Calif.: Stanford University Press, 1993), chap. 1.
97. Mo Yan, "Haotan guiguai shenmo" (My penchant for ghosts, monsters, deities, and fox spirits), in *Cong Sishi niandai dao jiushi niandai: Liangan sanbian Huawen xiaoshuo yantaohui lunwenji* (From the 1940s to the 1990s), ed. Yang Ze (Tiapei: Shibao chuban gongsi, 1994), 345.
98. Li Bihua, *Yanhua sanyue* (The red string) (Taipei: Lianpu, 2001), 285.
99. The character Ju Yaoru appears in "Ju Yaoru," vol. 12 of *Liaozhai;* Liu Zigu appears in "Ah Xiu," vol. 9.
100. See Zeitlin's discussion, *Historian of the Strange,* chap. 2.
101. The story won first prize in the fiction contest sponsored by *Zhongguo shibao* (China times) in 1996. See Yang Ze, ed., *Yuhai* (Fish relics), (Taipei: China Times, 1997), 18–46.
102. Ibid., 34–35.

BIBLIOGRAPHY

ENGLISH

Abbas, M. Ackbar. *Hong Kong: Culture and the Politics of Disappearance.* Minneapolis: University of Minnesota Press, 1997.

Adorno, Theodor W. "After Auschwitz." In *Negative Dialectics,* translated by E. B. Ashton. New York: Continuum, 1973.

———. "A Portrait of Walter Benjamin." In *Prisms,* translated by Samuel Weber and Shierry Weber. Cambridge, Mass.: MIT Press, 1981.

———. *In Search of Wagner.* Translated by Rodney Livingstone. New York: Verso Books, 1991.

Ahmad, Aijaz, "Jameson's Rhetoric of Otherness and the 'National Allegory.'" *Social Text* 17 (1987): 3–25.

Alvarez, A. [Alfred]. *The Savage God: A Study of Suicide.* New York: Random House, 1972.

Anderson, Benedict R. O. *Imagined Communities: Reflections on the Origin and Spread of Nationalism.* London: Verso and New Left Books, 1983.

Anderson, Mark. "Anorexia and Modernism, or How I Learned to Diet in All Directions." *Discourse* 11, no. 1 (1988–89): 28–41.

Anderson, Marston. *The Limits of Realism: Chinese Fiction in the Revolutionary Period.* Berkeley: University of California Press, 1990.

Apter, David E., and Tony Saich. *Revolutionary Discourse in Mao's Republic.* Cambridge, Mass.: Harvard University Press, 1994.

Arendt, Hannah. *On Violence.* San Diego: Harcourt Brace Jovanovich, 1970.

Armstrong, Nancy, and Leonard Tennenhouse, eds. *The Violence of Representation: Literature and the History of Violence.* London and New York: Routledge, 1989.

Auerbach, Erich. *Mimesis: The Representation of Reality in Western Literature.* Translated by Willard R. Trask. Princeton, N.J.: Princeton University Press, 1953.

Bakhtin, Mikhail M. *Rabelais and His World.* Translated by Helene Iswolsky. Cambridge, Mass.: MIT Press, 1968.

Balzac, Honoré de. "Sarrasine." Appendix of Roland Barthes, *S/Z,* translated by Richard Miller. New York: Hill and Wang, 1973.

Barbier, Patrick. *The World of the Castrati: The History of an Extraordinary Operatic Phenomenon.* Translated by Margaret Crosland. London: Souvenir Press, 1996.

Barlow, Tani E., and Gary J. Bjorge, eds. *I Myself Am a Woman: Selected Writings of Ding Ling.* Boston: Beacon Press, 1989.

Bärthelein, Thomas. "'Mirrors of Transition': Conflicting Images of Society in Change from Popular Chinese Social Novels, 1908 to 1930." *Modern China* 25, no. 2 (1999): 204–27.

Barthes, Roland. *Writing Degree Zero.* Translated by Annete Lavers and Colin Smith. New York: Hill and Wang, 1978.

———. *Camera Lucida: Reflections on Photography.* Translated by Richard Howard. New York: Hill and Wang, 1981.

———. *The Empire of Signs.* Translated by Richard Howard. New York: Hill and Wang, 1982.

Bataille, Georges. *Eroticism: Death and Sensuality.* Translated by Mary Dalwood. San Francisco: City Lights Books, 1986.

———. *The Tears of Eros.* Translated by Peter Connor. San Francisco: City Lights Books, 1989.

Baudrillard, Jean. "On Theater of Cruelty." *Semiotext(e)* 4 (1982).

Becker, Jasper. *Hungry Ghosts: Mao's Secret Famine.* New York: Free Press, 1996.

Behdad, Ali. "Eroticism, Colonialism, and Violence." In *Violence, Identity, and Self-Determination,* edited by Hent de Vries and Samuel Weber. Stanford, Calif.: Stanford University Press, 1997.

Benjamin, Walter. "Theses on the Philosophy of History." In *Illuminations,* translated by Harry Zohn. New York: Schocken, 1969.

———. *Charles Baudelaire: A Lyric Poet in the Era of High Capitalism.* Translated by Harry Zohn. London: Verso, 1983.

———. "Critique of Violence." In *Reflections: Essays, Aphorisms, Autobiographical Writings,* translated by Edmund Jephcott. New York: Schocken, 1986.

Berninghausen, John. "The Central Contradiction in Mao Dun's Earliest Fiction." In *Modern Chinese Literature in the May Fourth Era,* edited by Merle Goldman. Cambridge, Mass.: Harvard University Press, 1976.

Bodde, Derk, and Clarence Morris. *Law in Imperial China: Exemplified by 190 Ch'ing Dynasty Cases.* Cambridge, Mass.: Harvard University Press, 1967.

Bonner, Joey. *Wang Kuo-wei: An Intellectual Biography.* Cambridge, Mass.: Harvard University Press, 1986.

Brennan, Timothy. "The National Longing for Form." In *Nation and Narration,* edited by Homi K. Bhabha. London: Routledge, 1990.

Britzolakis, Christina. "Phantasmagoria: Walter Benjamin and the Poetics of Urban Modernism." In *Ghosts: Deconstruction, Psychoanalysis, History,* edited by Peter Buse and Andrew Stott. New York: St. Martin, 1999.

Brooks, Peter. *The Melodramatic Imagination: Balzac, Henry James, Melodrama, and the Mode of Excess.* New York: Columbia University Press, 1985.

———. *Reading for the Plot: Design and Intention in the Narrative.* Cambridge, Mass.: Harvard University Press, 1992.

Brown, James W. *Fictional Meals and Their Function in the French Novel, 1789–1848.* Toronto: University of Toronto Press, 1984.

Brumberg, Joan Jacobs. *Fasting Girls: The History of Anorexia Nervosa.* Cambridge, Mass.: Harvard University Press, 1988.

Buck, John Lossing, Owen L. Dawson, and Yuan-li Wu. *Food and Agriculture in Communist China.* Stanford, Calif.: Hoover Institution Publications, 1966.

Bullough, Vern L., and Bonnie Bullough. *Cross-Dressing, Sex, and Gender.* Philadelphia: University of Pennsylvania Press, 1993.

Burgin, Victor. *In/Different Spaces: Place and Memory in Visual Culture.* Berkeley: University of California Press, 1996.

Butler, Judith P. *Gender Trouble: Feminism and the Subversion of Identity.* New York: Routledge, 1990.

Castle, Terry. "Phantasmagoria: Spectral Technology and the Metamorphosis of Modern Reverie." *Critical Inquiry* 15, no. 1 (1988): 26–61.

Chan, Chingkiu Stephen. "The Problematics of Modern Chinese Realism: Mao Dun and His Contemporaries (1919–1937)." Ph.D. diss., University of California at San Diego, 1986.

———. "The Return of the Ghostwoman: A Critical Reading of Three Sung Hua-pen Stories." *Asian Culture Quarterly* 15, no. 3 (1987).

Chang, Eileen, "My Writing." Translated by Wendy Larson. In *Modern Chinese Literary Thought: Writings on Literature, 1893–1945,* edited by Kirk A. Denton. Stanford, Calif.: Stanford University Press, 1997.

Chen, Jianhua, "Chinese 'Revolution' in the World Syntax of Revolution." In *Tokens of Exchange: The Problem of Translation in Global Circulations,* edited by Lydia H. Liu. Durham, N.C.: Duke University Press, 1999.

Chen Yingzhen, "Mountain Path." Translated by Nicholas Koss. In *Death in a Corn Field and Other Stories from Contemporary Taiwan,* edited by Ching-hsi Perng and Chiu-kuei Wang. Hong Kong and New York: Oxford University Press, 1994.

Chen Yu-shi. *Realism and Allegory in the Early Fiction of Mao Tun.* Bloomington: Indiana University Press, 1986.

Ching, Leo T. S. *Becoming Japanese: Colonial Taiwan and the Politics of Identity Formation.* Berkeley: University of California Press, 2001.

Chow, Rey. *Woman and Chinese Modernity: The Politics of Reading Between West and East.* Minneapolis: University of Minnesota Press, 1990.

———. "We Endure, Therefore We Are: Survival, Governance, and Zhang Yimou's *To Live.*" *South Atlantic Quarterly* 95, no. 4 (fall 1996): 1039–64.

———. *Primitive Passions: Visuality, Sexuality, Ethnography, and Contemporary Chinese Cinema.* New York: Columbia University Press, 1997.

———. *Ethics after Idealism: Theory, Culture, Ethnicity, Reading.* Bloomington: Indiana University Press, 1998.

Cohen, Margaret. *Profane Illumination: Walter Benjamin and the Paris of Surrealist Revolution.* Berkeley: University of California Press, 1993.

Cover, Robert M. "*Nomos* and Narrative." *Harvard Law Journal* 95 (1986): 1609.

Crary, Jonathan. *Techniques of the Observer: On Vision and Modernity in the Nineteenth Century.* Cambridge, Mass.: MIT Press, 1992.

Deleuze, Gilles. *Logique du sens.* Paris: Editions de Minuit, 1969.

———. "Coldness and Cruelty." In *Masochism: Coldness and Cruelty,* edited by Gilles Deleuze and Leopold Ritter von Sacher-Masoch, translated by Jean McNeil. New York: Zone Books, 1989.

De Man, Paul. *Allegories of Reading: Figural Language in Rousseau, Nietzsche, Rilke, and Proust.* New Haven, Conn.: Yale University Press, 1979.

Denton, Kirk A., "Lu Ling's Literary Art: Myth and Symbol in *Hungry Guo Su'e.*" *Modern Chinese Literature* 2, no. 2 (1986): 197–209.

———. "Mind and the Problematic of Self in Modern Chinese Literature: Hu Feng's Subjectivism and Lu Ling's Psychological Fiction." Ph. D. diss., University of Toronto, 1992.

———. *The Problematic of Self in Modern Chinese Literature: Hu Feng and Lu Ling.* Stanford, Calif.: Stanford University Press, 1998.

Derrida, Jacques. *Specters of Marx: The State of the Debt, the Work of Mourning, and the New International.* Translated by Peggy Kamuf. London and New York: Routledge, 1994.

De Vries, Hent, and Samuel Weber, eds. *Violence, Identity, and Self-Determination.* Stanford, Calif.: Stanford University Press, 1997.

DeWoskin, Kenneth J. "The Six Dynasties *Chih-kuai* and the Birth of Fiction." In *Chinese Narrative: Critical and Theoretical Essays,* edited by Andrew H. Plaks. Princeton, N.J.: Princeton University Press, 1977.

Dimock, Wei Chee. *Residues of Justice, Literature, Law, Philosophy.* Berkeley: University of California Press, 1997.

Ding Ling, "When I Was in Hsia Village." In *Modern Chinese Stories and Novellas, 1919–1949,* edited by Joseph S. M. Lau, C. T. Hsia, and Leo Ou-fan Lee, translated by Gary J. Bjorge. New York: Columbia University Press, 1981.

Doleželová-Velingerová, Milená, ed. *The Chinese Novel at the Turn of the Century.* Toronto: University of Toronto Press, 1980.

Dolin, Kieran. *Fiction and the Law: Legal Discourse in Victorian and Modernist Literature.* New York: Cambridge University Press, 1999.

Dollimore, Jonathan. *Death, Desire and Loss in Western Culture.* New York: Routledge, 1998.

Dooling, Amy. "Feminism and Narrative Strategies in Early Twentieth-Century Chinese Women's Writing." Ph.D. diss., Columbia University, 1998.

Dreyfus, Hubert L., and Paul Rabinow. *Michel Foucault: Beyond Structuralism and Hermeneutics.* Chicago: University of Chicago Press, 1982.

Felman, Shoshana, and Dori Laub. *Testimony: Crises of Witnessing in Literature, Psychoanalysis, and History.* New York: Routledge, 1992.

Ferris, Lesley, ed. *Crossing the Stage: Controversies on Cross-Dressing.* New York: Routledge, 1993.

Feuerwerker, Yi-tsi Mei. *Ding Ling's Fiction: Ideology and Narrative in Modern Chinese Literature.* Cambridge, Mass.: Harvard University Press, 1982.

Fichter, Manfred M. "The Anorexia Nervosa of Franz Kafka." *International Journal of Eating Disorders* 2 (1987): 367–77.

Findeisen, Raoul David. "Two Works—*Hong* (1930) and *Ying'er* (1993)—As Indeterminate Joint Adventures." In *Essays, Interviews, Recollections, and Unpublished Material of Gu Cheng, Twentieth-Century Chinese Poet: The Poetics of Death,* edited by Xia Li. Lewiston, N.Y.: Edwin Mellen Press, 1999.

Fokkema, D. W. *Literary Doctrine in China and Soviet Influence, 1956–1960.* The Hague: Mouton, 1965.
Foucault, Michel. *Discipline and Punish: The Birth of the Prison.* Translated by Alan Sheridan. New York: Pantheon, 1977.
———. *The History of Sexuality.* Vol. 1. New York: Vintage, 1980.
Freud, Sigmund. *Totem and Taboo: Some Points of Agreement between the Mental Lives of Savages and Neurotics.* Translated by James Strachey. London: Hogarth Press, 1955.
———. "The Uncanny." In *The Standard Edition of the Complete Psychological Works of Sigmund Freud,* edited and translated by James Strachey, vol. 17. London: Hogarth Press, 1955.
———. "Theatrum Philosophicum." In *Language, Counter-Memory, Practice: Selected Essays and Interviews,* translated by Donald F. Bouchard and Sherry Simon. Ithaca, N.Y.: Cornell University Press, 1981.
———. "Three Essays on the Theory of Sexuality." In *The Freud Reader,* edited by Peter Gay. New York: W. W. Norton, 1989.
Frye, Northrop. *Anatomy of Criticism: Four Essays.* New York: Atheneum, 1968.
Furth, Charlotte, ed. *The Limits of Change: Essays on Conservative Alternatives in Republican China.* Cambridge, Mass.: Harvard University Press, 1976.
Gálik, Márian. *Mao Tun and Modern Chinese Literary Criticism.* Wiesbaden: Franz Steiner Verlag, 1969.
———. *Milestones in Sino-Western Literary Confrontation: 1898–1979.* Wiesbaden: Otto Harrassowitz, 1986.
Garber, Marjorie B. *Vested Interest: Cross-Dressing and Cultural Anxiety.* New York: Routledge, 1992.
Geertz, Clifford. *Local Knowledge: Further Essays in Interpretive Anthropology.* New York: Basic Books, 1983.
Genette, Gérard. *Narrative Discourse: An Essay in Method.* Translated by Jane E. Lewin. Ithaca, N.Y.: Cornell University Press, 1980.
Giddens, Anthony. *The Consequences of Modernity.* Stanford, Calif.: Stanford University Press, 1990.
Girard, René. *Violence and the Sacred,* translated by Patrick Gregory. Baltimore, Md.: Johns Hopkins University Press, 1977.
Goldberg, Jonathan. *Sodometries: Renaissance Texts, Modern Sexualities.* Stanford, Calif.: Stanford University Press, 1992.
Goldman, Merle. *Literary Dissent in Communist China.* Cambridge, Mass.: Harvard University Press, 1967.
Greenblatt, Stephen J. *Shakespearean Negotiations: The Circulation of Social Energy in Renaissance England.* Berkeley: University of California Press, 1984.
Hanan, Patrick. *The Chinese Vernacular Story.* Cambridge, Mass.: Harvard University Press, 1981.
———. *The Invention of Li Yu.* Cambridge, Mass.: Harvard University, 1988.
Harootunian, Harry D. *History's Disquiet: Modernity, Cultural Practice, and the Questions of Everyday Life.* New York: Columbia University Press, 2000.
Hegel, Robert E. *The Novel in Seventeenth-Century China.* New York: Columbia University Press, 1981.
———. "Conclusions: Judgements on the Ends of Times." Presented at the sympo-

sium "From the Late Ming to the Late Qing: Dynastic Decline and Cultural Innovation," Columbia University, November 6–7, 1998.

Heriot, Angus. *The Castrati in Opera.* New York: Da Capo, 1974.

Heywood, Leslie. *Dedication to Hunger: The Anorexic Aesthetic in Modern Cultures.* Berkeley: University of California Press, 1996.

Hinsch, Bret. *Passions of the Cut Sleeve: The Male Homosexual Tradition in China.* Berkeley: University of California Press, 1990.

Ho Ping-ti. *Studies on the Population of China: 1368–1953.* Cambridge, Mass.: Harvard University Press, 1957.

Hsia, C. T. "Aspects of the Power of Darkness in Lu Hsun," In *The Gate of Darkness: Studies on the Leftist Literary Movement in China,* edited by Hsia Tsi-an. Seattle: University of Washington Press, 1968.

———. "*The Travels of Lao Ts'an:* An Exploration of Its Arts and Meaning." In *Tsing Hua Journal of Chinese Studies* 7, no. 2 (1969): 40–66.

———. *A History of Modern Chinese Fiction.* New Haven, Conn.: Yale University Press, 1971.

———. "Obsession with China: The Moral Burden of Modern Chinese Literature." Appendix 1 of *A History of Modern Chinese Fiction.* New Haven, Conn.: Yale University Press, 1971.

———. "The Whirlwind." Appendix 2 of *A History of Modern Chinese Fiction.* New Haven, Conn.: Yale University Press, 1971.

———. "Closing Remarks." In *Chinese Fiction from Taiwan: Critical Perspectives,* edited by Jeannette L. Faurot. Bloomington: Indiana University Press, 1980.

Hsia, T. A. "Heroes and Hero-Worship in Chinese Communist Fiction." In *The China Quarterly* 13 (1963): 113–38.

———. *The Gate of Darkness: Studies of the Leftist Literary Movement in China.* Seattle: University of Washington Press, 1968.

Hsu, Immanuel C. Y. *The Rise of Modern China.* New York: Oxford University Press.

Huters, Theodore. "Hu Feng and the Critical Legacy of Lu Xun." In *Lu Xun and His Legacy,* edited by Leo Ou-fan Lee. Berkeley: University of California Press, 1985.

Huyssen, Andreas. *After the Great Divide: Modernism, Mass Culture, Postmodernism.* Bloomington: Indiana University Press, 1986.

Jameson, Fredric. "Third World Literature in the Era of Multinational Capitalism." *Social Text* 15 (1986): 65–87.

Kamuf, Peggy. "Violence, Identity, Self-Determination and the Question of Justice: On *Specters of Marx.*" In *Violence, Identity, and Self-Determination,* edited by Hent de-Vries and Samuel Weber. Stanford, Calif.: Stanford University Press, 1997.

Kao, Karl S. Y. "Introduction." In *Classical Chinese Tales of the Supernatural and the Fantastic: Selections from the Third to the Tenth Century.* Bloomington: Indiana University Press, 1985.

Kinkley, Jeffery C. *The Odyssey of Shen Congwen.* Stanford, Calif.: Stanford University Press, 1987.

Kojin Karatani. *Origins of Modern Japanese Literature.* Translated and edited by Brett de Bary. Durham, N.C.: Duke University Press, 1993.

Kristeva, Julia. *Powers of Horror: An Essay on Abjection.* Translated by Leon S. Roudiez. New York: Columbia University Press, 1982.

Kubiak, Anthony. *Stages of Terror: Terrorism, Ideology, and Coercion As Theatre History.* Bloomington: Indiana University Press, 1991.

Ladany, Laszlo. *Law and Legality in China: The Testament of a China-Watcher,* edited by Marie-Luise Näth. Honolulu: University of Hawaii Press, 1992.

Lancashire, Douglas. *Li Poyuan.* Boston: Twayne Publishers, 1978.

Lang, Olga. *Pa Chin and His Writings: Chinese Youth between the Two Revolutions.* Cambridge, Mass.: Harvard University Press, 1967.

Larson, Wendy. *Literary Authority and the Modern Chinese Writer: Ambivalence and Autobiography.* Durham, N.C.: Duke University Press, 1991.

Lee, Leo Ou-fan. *The Romantic Generation of Modern Chinese Writers.* Cambridge, Mass.: Harvard University Press, 1973.

———. *Voices from the Iron House: A Study of Lu Xun.* Bloomington: Indiana University Press, 1987.

———. *Shanghai Modern: The Flowering of a New Urban Culture in China, 1930–1945.* Cambridge, Mass.: Harvard University Press, 1999.

Lentricchia, Frank. *Ariel and the Police: Michel Foucault, William James, Wallace Stevens.* Madison: University of Wisconsin Press, 1988.

Li Chi. "Communist War Stories." *China Quarterly* 13 (1963): 139–57.

Li, Waiyee, "The Idea of Authority in the *Shih chi* (Records of the Historian)." *Harvard Journal of Asiatic Studies* 54, no. 2 (Dec. 1994): 345–405.

Li, Xia, ed. *Essays, Interviews, Recollections, and Unpublished Material of Gu Cheng, Twentieth-Century Chinese Poet: The Poetics of Death.* Lewiston, N.Y.: Edwin Mellen Press, 1999.

Lin, Yü-sheng. *The Crisis of Chinese Consciousness: Radical Antitraditionalism in the May Fourth Era.* Madison: University of Wisconsin Press, 1979.

Link, E. Perry. *Mandarin Ducks and Butterflies: Popular Fiction in Early Twentieth-Century Chinese Cities.* Berkeley: University of California Press, 1981.

Lipman, Jonathan N., and Steven Harrell, eds. *Violence in China: Essays in Culture and Counterculture.* Albany: State University of New York Press, 1990.

Liu E. *The Travels of Lao Ts'an.* Translated by Harold Shadick. Ithaca, N.Y.: Cornell University Press, 1952.

Liu, Jianmei. "Engaging with Revolution and Love." Ph. D. diss., Columbia University, 1998.

Liu Kang. "The Language of Desire, Class, and Subjectivity in Lu Ling's Fiction." In *Gender and Sexuality in Twentieth-Century Chinese Literature and Society,* edited by Tong-ling Lu. Albany: State University of New York Press, 1993.

———. *Aesthetics and Marxism: Chinese Aesthetic Marxists and Their Western Contemporaries.* Durham, N.C.: Duke University Press, 2000.

Liu Kang and Xiaobing Tang, eds. *Politics, Ideology, and Literature Discourse in Modern China: Theoretical Interventions and Cultural Critique.* Durham, N.C.: Duke University Press, 1993.

Liu, Lydia He. *Translingual Practice: Literature, National Culture, and Translated Modernity—China, 1900–1937.* Stanford, Calif.: Stanford University Press, 1995.

———. *Tokens of Exchange: The Problem of Translation in Global Circulations.* Durham, N.C.: Duke University Press, 1999.

Lu Hsun (Lu Xun). *A Brief History of Chinese Fiction.* Translated by Yang Hsien-yi and Gladys Yang. Beijing: Foreign Language Press, 1976.

———. "The New Year's Sacrifice." In *Selected Stories of Lu Hsun,* translated by Yang Hsien-yi and Gladys Yang. Beijing: Foreign Language Press, 1978.

———. Preface to "Nahan" [A Call to Arms]. In *Selected Stories of Lu Hsun,* translated by Yang Hsien-yi and Gladys Yang. Beijing: Foreign Languages Press, 1978.

Lu, Tongling. *Misogyny, Cultural Nihilism and Oppositional Politics: Contemporary Chinese Experimental Fiction.* Stanford, Calif.: Stanford University Press, 1995.

Lukács, Georg. *Studies in European Realism: A Sociological Survey of the Writings of Balzac, Stendhal, Zola, Tolstoy, Gorki and Others.* Translated by Edith Bone. New York: Grosset and Dunlap, 1964.

Lyotard, Jean-François, and Jean-Loup Thébaud. *Just Gaming.* Translated by Brian Massumi. Minneapolis: University of Minnesota Press, 1979.

———. *The Postmodern Condition: A Report on Knowledge.* Translated by Geoffrey Bennington and Brian Massumi. Minneapolis: University of Minnesota Press, 1984.

Mallory, Walter Hampton. *China, Land of Famine.* New York: American Geographical Society, 1926.

Mapp, Nigel. "Spectre and Impurity: History and the Transcendental in Derrida and Adorno." In *Ghosts: Deconstruction, Psychoanalysis, History,* edited by Peter Buse and Andrew Stott. New York: St. Martin, 1999.

Margolin, Jean-Louis. "China: A Long March into Night." In *The Black Book of Communism: Crimes, Terror, Repression,* edited by Stephane Courtois et al., translated by Jonathan Murphy. Cambridge, Mass.: Harvard University Press, 1999.

Marin, Louis. *Food for Thought.* Translated by Mette Hjort. Baltimore and London: Johns Hopkins University Press, 1989.

Mencius. *Mencius.* Translated by D. C. Lau. London: Penguin, 1970.

Miller, Joseph Hillis. *Fiction and Repetition: Seven English Novels.* Cambridge, Mass.: Harvard University Press, 1982.

Monleón, José B. *A Specter Is Haunting Europe: A Sociohistorical Approach to the Fantastic.* Princeton, N. J.: Princeton University Press, 1990.

Mote, Frederick W., and Denis Twichett. *The Cambridge History of China.* Vol. 7. New York: Cambridge University Press, 1988.

Newman, Robert D. *Transgressions of Reading: Narrative Engagement as Exile and Return.* Durham, N.C.: Duke University Press, 1993.

Nienhauser, William H. Jr., ed. *The Indiana Companion to Traditional Chinese Literature.* Bloomington: Indiana University Press, 1986.

Peng, Hsiao-yen. *Antithesis Overcome: Shen Tsung-wen's Avant-gardism and Primitivism.* Taipei: Academia Sinica, 1994.

Pickowicz, Paul G. *Marxist Literary Thought in China: The Influence of Chu Chiu-pai.* Berkeley: Center for Chinese Studies, University of California, 1980.

———. "Melodramatic Representation and the 'May Fourth' Tradition of Chinese Cinema." In *From May Fourth to June Fourth: Fiction and Film in Twentieth-Century China,* edited by Ellen Widmer and David D. Wang. Cambridge, Mass.: Harvard University Press, 1993.

Plaks, Andrew H. *The Four Masterworks of the Ming Novel.* Princeton, N. J.: Princeton University Press, 1987.

Prendergast, Christopher. *The Order of Mimesis: Balzac, Stendhal, Nerval, Flaubert.* New York: Cambridge University Press, 1986.

Ramet, Sabrina Petra, ed. *Gender Reversals and Gender Cultures: Anthropological and Historical Perspectives.* New York: Routledge, 1996.

Rosenberg, William G., and Marilyn B. Young. *Transforming Russia and China: Revolutionary Struggle in the Twentieth Century.* New York: Oxford University Press, 1982.

Ross, Timothy A. *Chiang Kuei.* New York: Twayne, 1974.

Roy, David Tod. "Introduction." In Xiaoxiaosheng, *Jinpingmei* (The Plume in the Golden Vase), translated by David Tod Roy. Princeton, N.J.: Princeton University Press, 1995.

Rummel, Rudolph J. *China's Bloody Century: Genocide and Mass Murder since 1900.* New Brunswick, N.J.: Transaction Publishers, 1991.

Sacher-Masoch, Leopold von. "Venus in Furs." In *Masochism: Coldness and Cruelty,* edited by Gilles Deleuze and Leopold von Sacher-Masoch, translated by Jean McNeil. New York: Zone Books, 1989.

Santner, Eric L. *Stranded Objects: Mourning, Memory, and Film in Postwar Germany.* Ithaca, N.Y.: Cornell University Press, 1990.

Sartre, Jean-Paul. *Les Mots.* Paris: Gallimard, 1986.

Schonebaum, Andrew. "The New Commerce: The Venereal Disease in Modern Chinese Literature." Paper presented at AAS, March 10, 2000.

Schwartz, Benjamin Isadore. *In Search of Wealth and Power: Yen Fu and the West.* Cambridge, Mass.: Harvard University Press, 1964.

Scogin, Hugh T. Jr. "Civil 'Law' in Traditional China: History and Theory." In *Civil Law in Qing and Republican China,* edited by Kathryn Bernhardt and Philip C. C. Huang. Stanford, Calif.: Stanford University Press, 1994.

Sedgwick, Eve Kosofsky. *Between Men: English Literature and Male Homosocial Desire.* New York: Columbia University Press, 1985.

Shen, Congwen. "Three Men and One Woman." In *Modern Chinese Stories and Novellas, 1919–1949,* edited by Joseph S. M. Lau, C. T. Hsia, and Leo Ou-fan Lee, translated by Jeffery C. Kinkley. New York: Columbia University Press, 1981.

Shih, C. W. "Co-operatives and Communes in Chinese Communist Fiction." *The China Quarterly* 13 (1963): 195–211.

Shneidman, N. N. *Dostoevsky and Suicide.* Oakville, Ontario, and New York: Mosaic Press, 1984.

Shu, Yunzhong. *Buglers on the Home Front: The Wartime Practice of the Qiyue School.* Albany: State University of New York Press, 2000.

Sprinker, Michael, ed. *Ghostly Demarcations: A Symposium on Jacques Derrida's* Spectres of Marx. London: Verso, 1999.

Sontag, Susan. *Illness As Metaphor: and, AIDS and Its Metaphors.* New York: Farrar, Straus and Giroux, 1978.

Stallybrass, Peter, and Allon White. *The Politics and Poetics of Transgression.* Ithaca, N.Y.: Cornell University Press, 1986.

Starrs, Roy. *Deadly Dialectics: Sex, Violence, and Nihilism in the World of Yukio Mishima.* Sangate, Folkestone: Japan Library, 1994.

Struve, Lynn, ed. and trans. *Voices from the Ming-Qing Cataclysm.* New Haven, Conn.: Yale University Press, 1993.

Su Wei. "The School and the Hospital: On the Logics of Socialist Realism." In *Chinese Literature in the Second Half of the Modern Century: A Critical Survey,* edited by

Pang-yuan Chi and David Der-wei Wang. Bloomington: Indiana University Press, 2000.

Suleiman, Susan Rubin. *Authoritarian Fictions: The Ideological Novel As a Literary Genre.* Princeton, N.J.: Princeton University Press, 1992.

Tang, Xiaobing. *Chinese Modern: The Heroic and the Quotidian.* Durham, N.C.: Duke University Press, 2000.

Taussig, Michael. *Mimesis and Alterity: A Particular History of the Senses.* New York: Routledge, 1992.

Tsu, Jing Yuen. "Failure: Nation, Race, and Literature in China, 1895–1937." Ph.D. diss., Harvard University, 2001.

Turgenev, Ivan. *Sketches from a Hunter's Album.* Translated by Richard Freeborn. Baltimore: Penguin, 1967.

Vidler, Anthony. *The Architectural Uncanny: Essays in the Modern Unhomely.* Cambridge, Mass.: MIT Press, 1992.

Wagner, Rudolf G. "The Chinese Writer in His Own Mirror: Writer, State, and Society—The Literary Evidence." In *China's Intellectuals and the State: In Search of a New Relationship,* edited by Merle Goldman, Timothy Cheek, and Carol Lee Hamrin. Cambridge, Mass.: Harvard University Press, 1987.

———. *Inside a Service Trade: Studies in Contemporary Chinese Prose.* Cambridge, Mass.: Council on East Asian Studies, Harvard University, 1992.

Wang, Ban. *The Sublime Figure of History: Aesthetics and Politics in Twentieth-Century China.* Stanford, Calif.: Stanford University Press, 1997.

Wang, David Der-wei. "Fictional History/Historical Fiction." In *Studies in Language and Literature* 1 (1985): 64–76.

———. "Dai Houying, Feng Jicai, and Ah Cheng: Three Approaches to the Historical Novel." *Asian Culture Quarterly* 16, no. 2 (1988): 71–88.

———. *Fictional Realism in Twentieth-Century China: Mao Dun, Lao She, Shen Congwen.* New York: Columbia University Press, 1992.

———. "Lu Xun, Shen Congwen, and Decapitation." In *Politics, Ideology, and Discourse in Modern China: Theoretical Interventions and Cultural Critique,* edited by Liu Kang and Tang Xiaobing. Durham, N.C.: Duke University Press, 1993.

———. *Fin-de-siècle Splendor: Repressed Modernities of Late Qing Fiction, 1849–1911.* Stanford, Calif.: Stanford University Press, 1997.

———. "*The Rice-Sprout Song* preface." In *The Rice-Sprout Song,* by Eileen Chang. Berkeley: University of California Press, 1998.

———. "Love and Passion in Hong Kong." Paper presented at South China Lecture series, the University of Science and Technology, Hong Kong, November 7, 2001.

Wang, Yuechuan. "A Perspective on the Suicide of Chinese Poets in the 1990's." In *Essays, Interviews, Recollections, and Unpublished Material of Gu Cheng, Twentieth-Century Chinese Poet: The Poetics of Death,* edited by Xia Li. Lewiston, N.Y.: Edwin Mellen Press, 1999.

Watson, James L., and Evelyn S. Rawski, eds. *Death Ritual in Late Imperial and Modern China.* Berkeley: University of California Press, 1988.

Weisberg, Richard H., and Jean-Pierre Barricelli. "Literature and the Law." In *Interrelations of Literature,* edited by Joseph Gibaldi and Jean-Pierre Barricelli. New York: MLA, 1982.

Wexler, Alice. *Emma Goldman in Exile: From the Russian Revolution to the Spanish Civil War.* Boston: Beacon Press, 1984.

Wilbur, C. Martin. *The Nationalist Revolution in China: 1923–1928.* Cambridge and New York: Cambridge University Press, 1984.

Williams, Philip. *Village Echoes: The Fiction of Wu Zuxiang.* Boulder: Westview Press, 1993.

Williams, Philip, and Yenna Wu. *The Great Wall of Confinement: The Contemporary Prison Camp through Fiction and Reportage.* Berkeley: University of California Press, forthcoming.

Wolf, Arthur P. "Gods, Ghosts, Ancestors." In *Religion and Ritual in Chinese Society,* edited by Arthur P. Wolf. Stanford, Calif.: Stanford University Press, 1974.

Wolfe, Alan Stephen. *Suicidal Narrative in Modern Japan: The Case of Dazai Osamu.* Princeton, N.J.: Princeton University Press, 1990.

Wong, Wang-chi. *Politics and Literature in Shanghai: The Chinese League of Left-Wing Writers, 1930–1936.* Manchester: Manchester University Press, 1991.

Wu, Pei-yi. "Memories of K'ai-feng." *New Literary History* 25, no. 1 (1994): 47–60.

Wu, Zuxiang. "Young Master Gets His Tonic." In *Modern Chinese Stories and Novellas, 1919–1949,* edited by Joseph S. M. Lau, C. T. Hsia, and Leo Ou-fan Lee, translated by Cyril Birch. New York: Columbia University Press, 1981.

Yang, C. K. *Religion in Chinese Society: A Study of Contemporary Social Functions of Religion and Some of Their Historical Factors.* Berkeley: University of California Press, 1970.

Yang, Xiaobin. *The Postmodern/Post-Mao-Deng History and Rhetoric in Chinese Avant-Garde Fiction.* Ph.D. diss., Yale University, 1996.

Yeh, Michelle. "Death of the Poet: Poetry and Society in Contemporary China and Taiwan." In *Chinese Literature in the Second Half of a Modern Century: A Critical Survey,* edited by Pang-yuan Chi and David Wang. Bloomington: Indiana University Press, 2000.

Yue, Gang. "Hunger, Cannibalism, and the Politics of Eating: Alimentary Discourse in Chinese and Chinese American Literature." Ph.D. diss., University of Oregon, 1993.

———. *The Mouth That Begs: Hunger, Cannibalism, and the Politics of Eating in Modern China.* Durham, N.C.: Duke University Press, 1999.

Zarrow, Peter. *Anarchism and Chinese Political Culture.* New York: Columbia University Press, 1990.

Zeitlin, Judith T. *Historian of the Strange: Pu Songling and the Chinese Classical Tale.* Stanford, Calif.: Stanford University Press, 1993.

CHINESE

Erya (爾雅), "Shixun" (釋訓). Shanghai: Shanghai guji chubanshe, 1977.

Liji (禮記), "Jiyi" (祭義). Taipei: Xuesheng shuju, 1981.

Zuozhuan (左傳). Taipei: Guangwen shuju, 1963.

Ba, Ren (巴人), "Houji" (afterword to *Tuwei* [Breaking free]) (後記), in *Tuwei* (Breaking free) (突圍). Shanghai: Shijie shuju, 1939.

Bai, Shurong (白舒榮). *Bai Wei pingzhuan* (Critical biography of Bai Wei) (白薇評傳). Changsha: Hunan renmin chubanshe, 1983.

Bai, Wei (白薇). *Beiju shengya* (悲劇生涯). Shanghai: Wenxue chubanshe, 1936.

———. "*Dachu youling ta* houji" (afterword to *Dachu youling ta* [Breaking out of the tower of ghosts]) (《打出幽靈塔》後記), in *Bai Wei zuopinji* (Works of Bai Wei) (白薇作品集). Changsha: Hunan renmin chubanshe, 1985.

Bai, Wei (白薇) and Yang Sao(楊騷). *Zuoye* (Last night) (昨夜). Shanghai: Nanqiang shuju, 1933.

———. *Zuoye* (Last night) (昨夜). Shijiazhuang: Hebei jiaoyu chubanshe, 1994.

Chang, Ailing (張愛玲) (Eileen Chang). *Chidi zhilian* (Naked earth) (赤地之戀). Taipei: Huangguan chubanshe, 1991.

———. *Yangge* (The rice-sprout song) (秧歌). Taipei: Huangguan chubanshe, 1991.

———. *Duizhao ji: kan lao zhao xiang bu* (A volume of reciprocal spectatorship: reading an old photo album) (對照記：看老照相簿). Taipei: Huangguan chubanshe, 1994.

Chen, Bingliang (陳炳良). "Xu" (Preface to *Shengsi yuanjia*) (序), in Zhong Ling (鍾玲), *Shengsi yuanjia* (Life-and-death partners) (生死冤家). Taipei: Hongfan chubanshe, 1991.

———. "Gu Cheng: xiandai shuixianzi" (Gu Cheng, the modern Narcisscus) (顧城：現代水仙子), in *Gu Cheng Qi Cheng* (Gu Cheng loses his city) (顧城棄城), ed. Xiao Xialin (蕭夏林). Beijing: Tuanjie chubanshe, 1994.

Chen, Dadao (陳大道), "Mingmo qingchu 'shishi xiaoshuo' de tese" (Characteristics of "fiction on contemporary events") (明末清初「時事小說」的特色), in *Xiaoshuo xiqu yanjiu* (Studies of fiction and drama) (小說戲劇研究), 3, 1987.

Chen, Dakang (陳大康). *Tongsu xiaoshuo de lishi guiji* (The historical trajectories of popular fiction) (通俗小說的歷史軌跡). Changsha: Hunan chubanshe, 1993.

Chen, Duxiu (陳獨秀), "Wenxue geming lun" (On literary revolution) (文學革命論), in *Duxiu wencun* (Writings of Chen Duxiu) (獨秀文存). Shanghai: Yadong tushuguan, 1931.

Chen, Fangying (陳芳英), *Mulian jiumu gushi zhi yanji ji qi youguan wenxue zhi yanjiu* (A study of the evolution of the legend of Mulian's rescue of his mother and its related literary variations) (目連救母故事之演進及其有關文學之研究). Taipei: National Taiwan University, 1984.

Chen, Jianhua (陳建華). *"Geming" de xiandai xing: Zhongguo geming huayu kaolun* (The modernity of revolution: a genealogical study of Chinese revolutionary discourse) (「革命」的現代性：中國革命話語考論). Shanghai: Shanghai guji chubanshe, 2000.

Chen, Jiying (陳紀瀅). *Dicun zhuan* (Fools in the reeds) (荻村傳). Taipei: Congguang wenyi chubanshe, 1951.

Chen, Pingyuan (陳平原). "Qianze xiaoshuo yu xiaxie xiaoshu: Shuo *Taowu cuibian*" (Eopose and depravity fiction; on *A Compendium of Monsters*) (譴責小說與狹邪小說：說《檮杌萃編》), in *Chen Pingyuan xiaoshuoshi lunji* (Collection of Critical essays on Chinese fiction by Chen Pingyuan) (陳平原小說史論集). Vol. 3. Shijiazhuang: Hebei renmin chubanshe, 1996.

———. "Zhongguo xiaoshuo shilun" (A history of Chinese fiction) (中國小說史論), in *Chen Pingyuan xiaoshuoshi lunji* (Collection of works on Chinese fictional history by Chen Pingyuan) (陳平原小說史論集). Vol. 3. Shijiazhuang: Hebei renmin chubanshe, 1996.

Chen Sihe(陳思和). *Huanyuan minjian* (Going back to the people) (還原民間) (Taipei: Sanmin shudian, 1997).

Chen, Yingzhen(陳映真). "Shanlu" (Mountain path) (山路), in *Chen Yingzhen zuopinji* (Works of Chen Yingzhen) (陳映真作品集). Vol. 9. Taipei: Renjian Chubanshe, 1988.

Cheng, Yizhong (程毅中) ed. *Shenguai qingxia de yishu shijie: zhongguo gudai xiaoshuo liupai man hua* (The world of the supernatural, the romantic, and the chivalric) (神怪情俠的藝術世界：中國古代小說流派漫話). Beijing: Zhonggong zhongyang dangxiao chubanshe, 1994.

Chiang, Kai-shek (蔣介石), "Xin shenghuo yundong gangyao" (Guidelines of new life movement) (新生活運動綱要), in *Xin shenghuo yundong shiliao* (新生活運動史料), ed. Xiao Jizong(蕭繼宗). Taipei: Zhongyang wenwu gongyingshe, 1975.

Dai, Houying (戴厚英). *Shiren zhisi* (The death of a poet) (詩人之死). Fuzhou: Fujian renmin chubanshe, 1982.

———. *Xingge, mingyun, wode gushi* (Character, fate, my story) (性格·命運·我的故事). Xian: Taibai wenyi chubanshe, 1994.

———. *Xinzhong de fen: zhi youren de xin* (Grave in my mind: a letter to my friend) (心中的憤：致友人的信). Shanghai: Fudan daxue chubanshe, 1996.

Dai, Jiafang (戴嘉枋). *Yangban xi de fengfeng yuyu: Jiang Qing, yangbanxi ji neimu* (The stormy history of the model drama: Jinag Qing, Model theater and the stories behind the scene) (樣板戲的風風雨雨：江青·樣板戲及內幕). Beijing: Zhishi chubanshe, 1995.

Dansou (誕叟) [Qian, Xibao{錢錫寶}]. *Taowu zuibian* (A Compendium of Monsters) (檮杌萃編). Tianjin: Baihua wenyi chubanshe, 1989.

Deng, Xiangyang (鄧相揚). *Wushe shijian* (Musha incident) (霧社事件). Taipei: Yushanshe, 1999.

———. *Fengzhong feiying: wushe shijian zhenxiang ji huagang chuzi de gushi* (Red cherry blossoms in the wind: the truth of the Musha Incident) (風中緋櫻：霧社事件真相及花岡初子的故事). Taipei: Yushanshe, 2000.

Ding, Ling (丁玲), "Taiyang zhaozai Sanggan heshang (The sun shines over the Sanggan River) (太陽照在桑乾河上), in *Ding Ling xuanji* (Selected works of Ding Ling) (丁玲選集). Vol. 1. Chengdu: Sichuan renmin chubani, 1984.

Du, Pengcheng (杜鵬程). *Baowei Yan'an* (Guarding Yan'an) (保衛延安). Beijing: Renmin wenxue chubanshe, 1954.

———. "Baowei Yan'an de chuangzuo wenti" (Questions about the writing of Guarding Yan'an) (保衛延安的創作問題), in *Du Pengcheng yanjiu zhuanji* (Critical materials on Du Pengcheng) (杜鵬程研究專集), eds. Chen Shu (陳紓) and Yu Shuqing (余水清). Fuzhou: Fujian Renmin chubanshe, 1983.

Fan, Boqun (范伯群). *Minguo tongsu xiaoshuo yuanyang hudie pai* (Mandarin Ducks and Butterfly school: the popular fiction in the Republican China) (民國通俗小說鴛鴦蝴蝶派). Taipei: Guowen tiandi zazhishe, 1990.

Fan, Boqun (范伯群) ed. *Zhongguo jinxiandai tongsu wenxueshi* (A history of popular literature in late Qing and modern China) (中國近現代通俗文學史). Nanjing: Jiangsu jiaoyu chubanshe, 2000.

Fan, Mingxin (范明辛) and Lei, Chengsheng (雷晟生). *Zhongguo jindai fazhi shi* (A history of modern Chinese legal system) (中國近代法制史). Xian: Xiaxi renmin chubanshe, 1988.

Feng, Menglong (馮夢龍). *Yushi mingyan* (Illustrious tales to lecture the world) (喻世明言). Hong Kong: Gudian wenxue chubanshe, 1974.

Gao, Yang (高陽). "Guanyu *Xuanfeng* de yanjiu" (A study on *The Whilrwind*) (關於《旋風》的研究), in *Huaixiu shu: "Xuanfeng" pinglunji* (A book of one's own: criticism on The *Whirl wind*) (懷袖書：《旋風》評論集), ed. Chunyu lou (Spring rain pavilion) (春雨樓). Tainan: Chunyu lou, 1960.

———. "*Xuanfeng,* Jiang Gui, wo" (*The Whirlwind,* Jiang Gui, and myself) (《旋風》·姜貴·我), in *Huaixiu shu: "Xuanfeng" pinglunji* (A book of one's own) (懷袖書：《旋風》評論集), ed. Chunyu lou (Spring rain pavilion) (春雨樓). Tainan: Chunyu lou, 1960.

Ge, Xianning (葛賢寧), "You wusi de wenxue geming lun dangqian zhandou wenyi" (On the contemporary literature for war from the perspective of the May Fourth Literary Revolution) (由五四的文學革命論當前戰鬥文藝), in *Zhandou wenyi yu ziyou wenyi* (Literature for war and literature for freedom) (戰鬥文藝與自由文藝), Chen Jiying (陳紀瀅) et. al. Taipei: Wentan she, 1955.

Gong, Guoji (龔國基). *Mao Zedong yu shi* (Mao Zedong and poetry) (毛澤東與詩). Beijing: Zhongguo wenlian chuban gongsi, 1998.

Gu, Cheng (顧城). *Selected Poems,* eds. Sean Golden and Chu Chiyu. Hong Kong: Research Centre for Translation, the Chinese University of Hong Kong, 1990.

Gu, Cheng (顧城) and Lei, Mi (雷米[謝燁]). *Ying'er* (Yiner) (英兒). Taipei: Yuanshen chubanshe, 1993.

Gu, Gong (顧工) ed. *Gu Cheng shi quanbian* (Complete collection of Gu Cheng's poetry) (顧城詩全編). Shanghai: Shanghai Sanlian shudian, 1995.

Gu, Xiang (顧鄉). *Wo miandui de Gu Cheng zuihou shisitian: yi jiu jiu san nian jiu yue er shi si ri zhi shi yue ba ri* (The last fourteen days of Gu Cheng's life I was faced with: September 24–October 8, 1993) *(我面對的顧城最後十四天：1993年9月24日–10月8日).* Beijing: Guoji wenhua chuban gongsi, 1994.

Guo, Tingyi (郭廷以). *Jindai zhongguo shigang* (A history of modern China) (近代中國史綱). Hong Kong: Chinese University of Hong Kong Press, 1986.

Guo, Yanli (郭延禮). *Zhongguo jindai wenxue fazhanshi* (History of early modern Chinese literature) (中國近代文學發展史). Jinan: Shangdong jiaoyu chubanshe, 1991.

Guo, Yuhua (郭于華). *Side kunrao yu sheng de zhizhuo: zhongguo minjian sangzang yili yu chuantong shengsi guan* (The trouble of death and the fixation of life: the death ritual in Chinese popular society and traditional concepts of life and death) (死的困擾與生的執著：中國民間喪葬儀禮與傳統生死觀). Bejing: Zhongguo renmin daxue chubanshe, 1992.

Han, Yuhai (韓毓海), "Turu yu yuhui: dui yi ge ren de huainian" (Breaking through and circumventing: in memory of a person) (突入與迂迴：對一個人的懷念), in *Gu Cheng Qi Cheng* (Gu Cheng loses his city) (顧城棄城), ed. Xiao Xialin (蕭夏林). Beijing: Tuanjie chubanshe, 1994.

Hong, Ruizao (洪瑞釗). *Geming yu lianai* (Revolution and love) (革命與戀愛). Shanghai: Minzhi shuju, 1928.

Hongying (虹影). *Ji'e de nüer* (The daughter of hunger) (饑餓的女兒). Taipei: Erya, 1997.

Hu, Feng (胡風). "*Ji'e de Guo Su'e* xu" (preface to Hungry *Guo Su'e)* (《饑餓的郭素娥》序), in *Lu Ling yanjiu ziliao* (Research materials on Lu Ling) (路翎研究資料), eds. Zhang Huan (張環), Wei Lin (魏臨), Li Zhiyuan (李志遠), and Yang Yi (楊義). Beijing: Beijing Shiyue Wenyi Chubanshe, 1993.

Hu, Jinzhao (胡金兆). *Cheng Yanqiu* (程硯秋). Changsha: Hunan wenyi chubanshe, 1987.

Hu, Shi (胡適). "Jianshe de wenxue geming lun" (On a constructive revolution in Chinese literature) (建設的文學革命論), in *Xin qingnian* (New youth) (新青年), 4.4/1918.4: 289–306.

———. "Zhengli guogu yu 'dagui'" (Sinological learning and subduing the ghosts) (整理國故與「打鬼」), in *Hu Shi wencun* (Works of Hu Shi) (胡適文存). Vol. 3. Taipei: Yuanliu chuban gongshe, 1986.

Hu, Shiying (胡士瑩). *Huaben xiaoshuo gailun* (A general study of huaben xiaoshuo) (話本小說概論). Taipei: Danqing tushu, 1983.

Hu, Wanchuan (胡萬川). *Zhong Kui shenhua yu xiaoshuo zhi yanjiu* (A study of the myth and fiction about Zhong Kui (鍾馗神話與小說之研究). Taipei: Wenshizhe chubanshe, 1980.

Hu, Weixiong (胡偉雄). *Shiguo mengzhu Mao Zedong* (Mao Zedong: The hegemon in the kingdom of poetry) (詩國盟主毛澤東). Beijing: Dangdai zhongguo chubanshe, 1996.

Huang, Chongtian (黃重添), Zhuang, mingxuan (莊明萱), Que, fengling (闕豐齡), Xu, xue (徐學) and Zhu, Shuangyi (朱雙一). *Taiwan xinwenxue gaiguan* (A general view of new literature of Taiwan) (台灣新文學概觀). Taipei: Daohe chubanshe, 1992.

Huang, Jinlin (黃金麟). *Lishi, shenti, guojia: jindai zhongguo shenti de xingcheng, 1895–1937* (History, body, nation: the formation of the modern Chinese body, 1895–1937) (歷史、身體、國家：近代中國身體的形成). Taipei: Lianjing chuban gongsi, 2001.

Huang, Jinshu (黃錦樹). "Xinliu" (New willow) (新柳), in *Wuanming* (Dark night) (烏暗暝). Taipei: Jiuge chubanshe, 1997.

Huang, Juan (黃娟). "Zhengzhi yu wenxue zhijian: lun Shi Mingzheng *Dao shang ai yu si*" (Between literature and politics: on Shi Mingzheng's *Love and Death on an Island*) (政治與文學之間：論施明正《島上愛與死》), in *Shi Mingzheng ji* (A collection of works by Shi Mingzheng) (施明正集), eds. Lin Ruiming (林瑞明) and Chen Wanyi (陳萬益). Taipei: Qianwei chubanshe, 1993.

Huang, Ziping (黃子平). "Bing de yinyu yu wenxue shengchan: Ding Ling de 'Zai yiyuan zhong' ji qita" (The metaphor of illness and literary production: Ding Ling's "In the Hospital" and other works) (病的隱喻與文學生產—丁玲的《在醫院中》及其他), in *Zaijiedu: Dazhong wenyi yu yishi xingtai* (Rereading: mass literature and ideology) (再解讀：大眾文藝與意識形態), ed. Tang Xiaobing (唐小兵). Hong Kong: Oxford University Press, 1993.

———. "Bing de yinyu he wenxue shengchan" (The metaphor of disease and the production of literature) (病的隱喻和文學生產), in *Geming, Lishi, Xiaoshuo* (Revolution, history, fiction) (革命・歷史・小說). Hong Kong: Niujin daxue chubanshe, 1996.

———. "Geming lishi xiaoshuo: shijian yu xushu" (The revolutionary historical novel: temporality and narration) (革命歷史小說：時間與敘事), in *Xincunzhe de wenxue* (The literature of a survivor) (倖存者的文學). Taipei: Yuanliu chuban gongsi, 1991.

Hunan sheng xiju yanjiu suo and Zhong guo yishu yanjiu yuan Xiqu yanjiu bianjibu (湖南省戲劇研究所，中國藝術研究院戲曲研究部) eds. *Mulianxi xueshu zuotanhui lunwenxuan* (Collection of articles on *Mulian* drama) (目連戲學術座談會論文選). Hunan: published by the editor, 1985.

Jia, Pingwa (賈平凹). *Baiye* (White night) (白夜). Taipei: Fengyun shidai chubanshe, 1996.

Jiang, Guangci (蔣光慈). *Chongchu yunwei de yueliang* (The moon forces its way through the clouds) (衝出雲圍的月亮), in *Jiang Guangci wenji* (Selected works of Jiang Guangci) (蔣光慈論文集). Vol. 2. Shanghai: Shanghai wenyi chubanshe, 1982.

———. *Paoxiao liao de tudi* (The roaring earth) (咆哮了的土地), in *Jiang Guangci wenji* (Selected works of Jiang Guangci) (蔣光慈文集). Vol. 2. Shanghai: Shanghai wenyi chubanshe, 1982.

———. *Shaonian piaopozhe* (The youthful tramp) (《少年漂泊者》), in *Jiang Guangci wenji* (Selected works of Jiang Guangci) (蔣光慈文集). Vol. 1. Shanghai: Shanghai wenyi chubanshe, 1982.

———. "Shiyue geming yu eluosi wenxue" (October revolution and Russian literature) (十月革命與俄羅斯文學), in *Jiang Guangci wenji* (Selected works of Jiang Guangci) (蔣光慈文集). Vol. 4. Shanghai: Shanghai wenyi chubanshe, 1982.

———. "*Yeji*" (A sacrifice in the wild) (野祭), in *Jiang Guangci wenji* (Selected works of Jiang Guangci) (蔣光慈文集) Vol. 1. Shanghai: Shanghai wenyi chubanshe, 1982.

Jiang, Gui (姜貴), "Zixu" (preface to *Jin taowu zhuan* [A tale of modern monsters]) (自序), in *Jin taowu zhuan* (A tale of modern monsters) (今檮杌傳). Tainan, Chunyulou, 1957.

———. "Zizhuan" (Autobiography) (自傳), in *Wuwei ji* (Not against wishes) (無違集). Taipei: Youshi wenyi chubanshe, 1974.

———. (姜貴). *Wuwei ji* (Not against wishes) (無違集). Taipei: Youshi wenyi chubanshe, 1974.

Jiang, Menglin (蔣夢麟). "Jiang Menglin xiansheng zhi Jian Gui han" (A letter to Jinag Gui from Jinag Menglin) (蔣夢麟先生致作者函), in *Huaixiu shu: "Xuanfeng" pinglunji* (A book of one's own) (懷袖書：《旋風》評論集), ed. Chunyu lou (Spring rain pavilion) (春雨樓). Tainan: Chunyu lou, 1960.

Jiang, Wenqi (江文琦). *Sulian ershi niandai wenxue gailun* (Introduction to Soviet literature of the twenties) (蘇聯二十年代文學概論). Shanghai: Shanghai waiyu jiaoyu chubanshe, 1990.

Jiji (季季). "Gu Cheng zhaobu dao tade cheng: Gu Cheng shengqian youren kan Gu Cheng de huimie qingjie" (Gu Cheng cannot find his own city) (顧城找不到他的城：顧城生前友人看顧城的毀滅情結), in *Gu Cheng Qi Cheng* (Gu Cheng loses his city) (顧城棄城), ed. Xiao Xialin (蕭夏林). Beijing: Tuanjie chubanshe, 1994.

Kang, Laixin (康來新). *Faji biantai: songren xiaoshuo xue lungao* (The making of a hero: a study of the narratology of Song fiction) (發跡變泰：宋人小說學論稿). Taipei: Da'an chubanshe, 1996.

Kong, Qingdong (孔慶東). "Shengming shibai de weimiao" (The subtlety of a failed life) (生命的失敗的微妙), in *Gu Cheng Qi Cheng* (Gu Cheng loses his city) (顧城棄城), ed. Xiao Xialin (蕭夏林). Beijing: Tuanjie chubanshe, 1994.

Kongzi (孔子). *Lunyu* (The *Analects*) (論語).

Kuang, Xinnian (曠新年). *1928: Geming wenxue* (1928: Revolutionary literature) (*1928*: 革命文學). Jinan: Shandong jiaoyu chubanshe, 1998.

Li, Bihua (李碧華). *Qing She* (Green Snake) (青蛇). Hong Kong: Tiandi tushu gongsi, 1986.

———. *Pan Jinlian zhi qianshi jinsheng* (The previous and present lives of Pan Jinlian) (潘金蓮之前世今生). Hong Kong: Tiandi tushu gongsi, 1989.

———. *Yanhua sanyue* (The red string) (煙花三月). Taipei: Lianpu, 2001.

Li, Boyuan (李伯元). *Huo diyu* (Living hell) (活地獄). Taipei: Guangya shuju, 1984.

Li Huasheng (李華盛) and Hu Guangfan (胡光凡), eds. *Zhou Libo yanjiu ziliao* (Research material on Zhou Libo) (周立波研究資料), eds. Changsha: Hunan renmin chubanshe, 1983.

Li, Jianguo (李劍國) ed. *Tangqian zhiguai xiaoshuo jishi* (Annotated collection of pre-Tang *zhiguai* fiction) (唐前志怪小說輯釋). Taipei: Wenshizhi chubanshe, 1987.

Li, Kuixian (李魁賢). "Wosuo liaojie de Shi Mingzheng" (The Shi Mingzheng I know of) (我所瞭解的施明正), in *Shi Mingzheng shihua ji* (A collection of poetry and painting by Shi Mingzheng) (施明正詩畫集). Taipei: Qianwei chubanshe, 1985.

Li Qing (李清). *Taowu xianping* (An idle commentary on monsters) (檮杌閒評). Beijing: Renmin wenxue chubanshe, 1983.

Li, Tuo (李陀), "Xu: Xuebeng hechu?" (Preface: Where is the avalanche?) (序：雪崩何處), in Yu Hua, *Shibasui chumen yuanxing* (Going out for a travel at the age of eighteen) (十八歲出門遠行). Taipei: Yuanliu chuban gongsi, 1990.

Li, Xiaoliang (李小良). "Wending yu buding: Li Bihua sanbu xiaoshuo zhongde wenhua rentong yu xingbie yishi" (Certainty and uncertainty: Cultural identification and gender consciousness in three novels by Li Bihua) (穩定與不定：李碧華三部小說中的文化認同與性別意識), in *Xiandai zhongwen wenxue pinglun* (Review of modern Chinese literature) (現代中文文學評論), 4/1995.12: 101–11.

Li, Yang (李楊). *Kangzheng suming zhilu: shehui zhuyi xianshi zhuyi (1942–1976) yan jiu* (A path to challenge fatalism: a study of socialist realism, 1942–1976) (抗爭宿命之路：社會主義現實主義*[1942–1976]*研究). Changchun: Shidai wenyi chubanshe, 1993.

Li, Ying (李英). *Hunduan jiliu dao: Gu Cheng, Xie Ye, Ying Er de gu shi* (Death on the island of torrents; i.e. Waiheke: the story of Gu Cheng, Xie Ye, and Ying'er) (魂斷激流島：顧城、謝燁、英兒的故事). Hong Kong: Mingbao chubanshe, 1995.

Liang, Qichao (梁啓超). "Lun xiaoshuo yu qunzhi zhi guanxi" (On the relationship between fiction and ruling the people) (論小說與群治之關係), in *Wanqing wenxue congchao: xiaoshuo xiqu yanjiu juan* (Compendium of late Qing literature: volume of fiction and drama) (晚清文學叢鈔：小說戲曲研究卷), ed. A Ying (阿英). Taipei: Xuesheng shuju, 1971.

Liao, Chaohui (廖超慧). *Zhongguo xiandai wenxue sichao lunzhengsh* (A history of the debates over literary thoughts in modern China) (中國現代文學思潮論爭史). Wuhan: Wuhan chubanshe, 1997.

Liao, Yuhui (廖玉蕙). "Cong sheng juanshu dao si yuanjia: Song huaben zhong de rengui hunlian gushi" (Romantic couples from life to death: on ghostly love and marriage in Song *huaben* stories) (從生眷屬到死冤家：宋話本中的人鬼婚戀故事), in *Lianhe wenxue* (Unitas) (聯合文學), 16.10/2000.8: 49–52.

Lin, Fushih (林富士). *Guhun yu guixiong de shijie: bei Taiwan de ligui xinyang* (The world of lonely souls and ghosts: beliefs in the vicious ghosts in northern Taiwan) (孤魂與鬼雄的世界：北台灣的厲鬼信仰). Banqiao: Taipei xianli wenhua zhongxin, 1995.

Ling, Feng (凌鋒). *Zhonggong fengyu bashi nian* (A stormy history of Chinese communist revolution) (中共風雨八十年). Edison: Epoch Publication Co., 2001.

Ling Yu (凌宇), *Shen Congwen zhuan* (沈從文傳) (A biography of Shen Congwen). Beijing: Shiyue wenyi chubanshe, 1988.

Liu, Dashen (劉大紳). "Guanyu *Laocan you ji*" (On *The Travels of Lao Can*) (關於《老殘遊記》), in *Liu E ji Lao Can youji ziliao* (Liu E and research materials on *The Travels of Lao Can*) (劉鶚及《老殘遊記》資料), eds. Liu Delong (劉德隆), Zhu xi (朱禧), and Liu deping (劉德平). Chengdu: Sichuan renmin chubanshe, 1985.

Liu, E (劉鶚). *Lao Can youji* (The travels of Lao Can) (老殘遊記). Taipei: Lianjing chuban gongsi, 1983.

Liu, Jihui (劉紀蕙). "Sanshi niandai zhongguo wenhua lunshu zhong de faxisi wangxiang yiji yayi: cong jige wenben zhengzhuang tanqi" (Fascist fantasy and its repression in the cultural discourse of the thirties' China: textual symptoms) (三十年代中國文化論述中的法西斯妄想以及壓抑：從幾個文本徵狀談起), in *Zhongguo wenzhe yanjiu jikan* (Bulletin of Modern Chinese Literature and Philosophy) (中國文哲研究集刊), 16/2000.3: 95–149.

Liu, Shaoming (Joseph S. M. Lau) (劉紹銘). *Tilei jiaoling de xiandai zhongguo wenxue* (Modern Chinese literature in tears and sniveling) (涕淚交零的現代中國文學). Taipei: Yuanjing chubanshe, 1980.

Liu, Xinhuang (劉心皇). "Ziyou zhongguo wushi niandai de sanwen" (The prose in free China of the fifties) (自由中國五十年代的散文), in *Wenxun* (Literary message) (文訊), 9/1984.3: 54–82.

———. *Xiandai Zhongguo wenxue shihua* (History of modern Chinese literature) (現代中國文學史話). Taipei: Zhengzhong shuju, 1977.

———. "Ping Jiang Gui zhu *Xuanfeng*" (On Jiang Gui's *The Whirlwind*) (評姜貴著《旋風》), in *Huaixiu shu: "Xuanfeng" pinglunji* (A book of one's own) (懷袖書：《旋風》評論集), ed. Chunyu lou (Spring rain pavilion) (春雨樓). Tainan: Chunyu lou, 1960.

Liu, Zaifu (劉再復) and Lin Gang (林崗). "Zhongguo xiandai xiaoshuo de zhengzhishi xiezuo: cong 'Chuncan' dao *Taiyang zhaozai Sanggan heshang*" (The politics of writing in modern Chinese literature: From "Spring Silkworms" to *The Sun Shines over the Sanggan River*) (中國現代小說的政治式寫作：從〈春蠶〉到《太陽照在桑乾河上》), in *Fangzhu zhushen: Wenlun tigang he wenxueshi chongping* (Exiling gods: outlines of literary theory and rereadings of literary history) (放逐諸神：文論提綱和文學史重評). Hong Kong: Tiandi tushu gongsi, 1994.

Liu, Zhe (劉哲). "Hei yanjing chuantou buliao heiye: shiren zisha yu wenhua jiegou" (Black eyes cannot pierce through the dark night: the suicide of the poet and the deconstruction of culture) (黑眼睛穿透不了黑夜：詩人自殺與文化解構), in *Gu Cheng qi cheng* (Gu Cheng loses his city) (顧城棄城), ed. Xiao Xialin (蕭夏林). Beijing: Tuanjie chubanshe, 1994.

Long, Yingtai (龍應台). *Long Yingtai pingxiaoshuo* (Fiction criticism by Long Yingtai) (龍應台評小說). Taipei: Erya Chubanshe, 1985.

Lu, Ling (路翎). *Ji'e de Guo Su'e* (Hungry Guo Su'e) (饑餓的郭素娥). Beijing: Beijing renmin wenxue chubanshe, 1988.

———. *Lu Ling piping wenji* (Collection of critical essays by Lu Ling) (路翎批評文集), ed. Zhang Yesong (Guangzhou: Zhuhaichu banshe, 1998).

Lu, Xun (魯迅). "Changong daguan" (A spectacle of chopping communists) (鏟共

大觀), in *Lu Xun Zawenxuan* (Selections of Lu Xun's essays) (魯迅雜文選). Shanghai: Renmin chubanshe, 1972.

———. *Zhongguo xiaoshuo shilui* (A brief history of Chinese fiction) (中國小說史略). Hong Kong: Qingwen shuwu, 1972.

———. "Geming shidai de wenxue" (History of the revolutionary era) (革命時代的文學), in *Lu Xun Quanji* (Complete works of Lu Xun) (魯迅全集). Vol. 3. Beijing: Renmin wenxue chubanshe, 1981.

———. "Kuangren riji" (Diary of a madman) (狂人日記), in *Nahan* (A Call to Arms) (吶喊), in *Lu Xun Quanji* (Complete works of Lu Xun) (魯迅全集). Vol. 1. Beijing: Renmin wenxue chubanshe, 198l.

———. "Lun Leifeng ta de daodiao" (On the collapse of the Leifeng tower) (論雷峰塔的倒掉), in *Nahan* (A Call to Arms) (吶喊), in *Lu Xun Quanji* (Complete works of Lu Xun) (魯迅全集). Vol. 1. Beijing: Renmin wenxue chubanshe, 1981.

———. "Zixu" (Preface to *Nahan* [A Call to Arms]) (自序), in *Nahan* (A Call to Arms) (吶喊), in *Lu Xun Quanji* (Complete works of Lu Xun) 魯迅全集. Vol. 1. Beijing: Renmin wenxue chubanshe, 1981.

———. "Zai jiulou shang" (In the wine shop) (在酒樓上), in *Panghuang* (Wandering) (徬徨), in *Lu Xun Quanji* (Complete works of Lu Xun) 魯迅全集. Vol. 2. Beijing: Renmin wenxue chubanshe, 1981.

———. "Xiao zagan" (Small miscellaneous thoughts) (小雜感), in *Lu Xun Quanji* (Complete works of Lu Xun) (魯迅全集). Vol. 13. Beijing: Renmin wenxue chubanshe, 1981.

———. "Guafu zhuyi" (Widowhood) (寡婦主義), in *Nahan* (A Call to Arms) (吶喊), in *Lu Xun Quanji* (Complete works of Lu Xun) (魯迅全集). Vol. 1. Beijing: Renmin wenxue chubanshe, 1981.

Lü, Dianwen (呂滇雯), "Shiren de siwang he daode" (The death of the poet and morality) (詩人的死亡和道德), in *Gu Cheng Qi Cheng* (Gu Cheng discards his city) (顧城棄城), ed. Xiao Xialin (蕭夏林). Beijing: Tuanjie chubanshe, 1994.

Luan, Xing (欒星), "Ming Qing zhiji de sanbu jiangshi xiaoshuo" (Three historical novels in the late Ming and early Qing) (明清之際的三部講史小說), in *Ming Qing xiaoshuo luncong* (Compendium on criticism on Ming and Qing fiction) (明清小說論叢), Vol. 3, ed. Chunfeng wenyi chubanshe. Shenyang: Chunfeng wenyi chubanshe, 1986.

Luo, Changlu (羅長祿), "Shihua zuie: Gu Cheng zhisi de yulun fengxiang" (Making poetry of the evil: on the consensual responses to the death of Gu Cheng) (詩化罪惡：顧城之死的輿論風向), in *Shiren Gu Cheng zhisi* (The death of Gu Chen, a poet) (詩人顧城之死), ed. Chen zishan (陳子善). Shanghai: Shanghai renmin chubanshe, 1993.

Mai, Keang (麥克昂), "Yingxiong shu" (Tree of heroism) (英雄樹), in *Chuangzao yuekan* (*Creation* monthly) (創造月刊), 1, 8.

Mao, Dun (茅盾). *Shi* (Eclipse) (蝕). Beijing: Kaiming shudian, 1929.

———. "Cong Guling dao Dongjing" (From Kuling to Tokyo) (從牯嶺到東京), in *Mao Dun pingzhuan* (Critical and biographical essays on Mao Dun) (茅盾評傳), ed. Fu Zhiying(伏志英). Shanghai: Xiandai shuju, 1931.

———. "Wenxue yishu zhong de guanjianxing wenti" (The key problem concerning literary and art work) (文學藝術中的關鍵性問題), in *Weiyi bao* (Gazette of literature and arts) (文藝報), 1956.3: 12.

———. *Wo zouguo de daolu* (The road I have taken) (我走過的道路). Hong Kong: Sanlian shudian, 1981.

———. "Ziran zhuyi yu zhongguo xiandai xiaoshuo" (Naturalism and modern Chinese fiction) (自然主義與中國現代小說), in *Mao Dun wenyi zalun ji* (Critical essays by Mao Dun) (茅盾文藝雜論集), ed. Zhang Liaomin (張遼民). Shanghai: Shanghai wenyi chubanshe, 1981.

———. "*Diquan* duhougan" (Thoughts after reading "Earth Spring") (《地泉》讀後感), in *Jiang Guangci yanjiu ziliao* (Research materials on Jiang Guangci) (蔣光慈研究資料), ed. Fang Ming (方銘). Yinchuan: Ningxia renmin chubanshe, 1983.

Meng, Yue (孟悦) and Dai Jinhua (戴錦華). *Fuchu lishi dibiao: zhongguo xiandai nüxing wenxue yanjiu* (Voices emerging from the foreground of history: a study of contemporary Chinese women's literature) (浮出歷史地表：中國現代女性文學研究). Taipei: Shibao wenhua chuban gongsi, 1993.

Meng, Yue (孟悦), "*Baimao nü* yanbian de qishi: Jian lun Yan'an wenyi de lishi duozhi xing" (The transformations of *The White-Haired Girl* and its significance: on the polyphony of history in Yan'an literature) (《白毛女》演變的啓示：兼論延安文藝的歷史多質性), in *Zaijiedu: Dazhong wenyi yu yishi xingtai* (Rereading: mass literature and ideology) (再解讀：大眾文藝與意識形態), ed. Tang Xiaobing (唐小兵). Hong Kong: Oxford University Press, 1993.

Mo, Yan (莫言). "Haotan guiguai shenmo" (My penchant for ghosts, monsters, deities, and fox spirits) (好談鬼怪神魔), in *Cong Sishi niandai dao jiushi niandai: liangan sanbian Huawen xiaoshuo yantaohui lunwenji* (From the forties to the nineties) (從四0年代到九0年代：兩岸三邊華文小說研討會論文集), ed. Yang ze (楊澤). Taipei: Shibao wenhua chuban gongsi, 1994.

Nanguo (南郭). "Xianggang de nanmin wenxue" (Hong Kong's refugee literature) (香港的難民文學), in *Wenxun* (Literary message) (文訊), 20/1985.10: 32–37.

Ouyang, Jian (歐陽健). "*Taowu xianping* de sixiang qingxiang he xingxiang tixi" (The Intellectual inclination and Figural system of An Idle Commentary on Monsters) (《檮杌閒評》的思想傾向和形象體系), in *Ming Qing xiaoshuo caizheng* (Rereading Ming and Qing fiction) (明清小說采正). Taipei: Guanya chubanshe, 1992.

Ouyang, Yuqian (歐陽予倩). "Pan Jinlian" (Pan Jinlian) (潘金蓮), in *Ouyang Yuqian wenji* (Works of Ouyang Yuqian) (歐陽予倩文集). Vol. 1. Beijing: Renmin wenxue chubanshe, 1984.

Pan, Renmu (潘人木). *Lianyi Biaomei* (Cousin Lianyi) (蓮漪表妹). Taipei: Wenyi chuangzuo chubanshe, 1952.

Peng, Hsiao-yen (彭小妍). *Chaoyue xieshi* (Beyong realism) (超越寫實). Taipei: Lianjing chuban gongsi, 1993.

Qian, Liqun (錢理群). "Tansuozhe de de yu shi" (Gains and losses of an explorer) (探索者的得與失), in *Lu Ling yanjiu ziliao* (Research materials on Lu Ling) (路翎研究資料), eds. Zhang Huan (張環), Wei Lin (魏臨), Li Zhiyuan (李志遠), and Yang Yi (楊義). Beijing: Beijing Shiyue Wenyi Chubanshe, 1993.

Qian, Xingcun (錢杏邨). "Cong Dongjing huidao Wuhan" (From Tokyo back to Wuhan) (從東京回到武漢), in *Mao Dun pingzhuan* (Critical and biographical essays on Mao Dun) (茅盾評傳), ed. Fu Zhiying (伏志英). Shanghai: Xiandai shuju, 1931.

Qianyi, ciren (纖綺詞人). "*Taowu cuibian* xu" (Preface to *Taowu cuibian*) (《檮杌萃編》序), in Dansou (誕叟) (Qian, Xibao[錢錫寶]), *Taowu zuibian* (A Compendium of Monsters) (檮杌萃編). Tianjin: Baihua wenyi chubanshe, 1989.

Qin, Dejun (秦德君), "Yingshi" (Cherry blossoms in eclipse) (櫻蝕), in *Yecao* (Wild grass) (野草), 41, 42/1988: 63–76; 1–22.

Qin, Dejun (秦德君) and Liu, Huai (劉淮). *Huo fenghuang: Qin Dejun he tade yige shiji* (Phoenix in the fire: Qin Dejun and her century) (火鳳凰：秦德君和她的一個世紀). Beijing: Zhongyang bianyi chubanshe, 1999.

Qu, Qiubai (瞿秋白). "Geming de langman dike" (Revolutionary romanticism) (革命的浪漫底克), in *Qu Qiubai wenji: wenxuepian* (Works of Quqiubai: Literature) (瞿秋白文集：文學篇). Vol. 1. Beijing: Renmin wenxue chubanshe, 1985.

Rao, Zongyi (饒宗頤). *Zhongguo shixue shang zhi zhengtong lun: zhong guo shi xue guan nian tan tao zhi yi* (The theory of orthodoxy in Chinese historiography: an approach to Chinese historiogrpahical concepts) (中國史學上之正統論：中國史學觀念探討之一). Taipei: Zongqing tushu chuban gongsi, 1979.

Shanlin (山林), "Ye tan Gu Cheng de Jiating beiju" (Also a talk on Gu Cheng's family tragedy) (也談顧城的家庭悲劇), in *Lianhe wenxue* (Unitas) (聯合文學), 13.9/1997.7: 176–80.

Shao, Quanlin (邵荃麟). "Ji'e de Guo Su'e" (*Hungry Guo Su'e*) (饑餓的郭素娥), in *Lu Ling yanjiu ziliao* (Research materials on Lu Ling) (路翎研究資料), eds. Zhang Huan (張環), Wei Lin (魏臨), Li Zhiyuan (李志遠), and Yang Yi (楊義). Beijing: Beijing Shiyue Wenyi Chubanshe, 1993.

Shen, Congwen (沈從文). 從文自傳 (Autobiography of Congwen), in *Shen Congwen wenji* (Works of Shen Congwen) (沈從文文集). Vol. 9. Hong Kong: Sanlian Shudian, 1984.

———. "Wode jiaoyu" (My Education) (我的教育), in *Shen Congwen wenji* (Works of Shen Congwen) (沈從文文集). Vol. 3. Hong Kong: Sanlian Shudian, 1984.

Shen, Jianshi (沈兼士). "gui zi yuanshi yiyi zhi shitan" (A preliminary survey of the original meaning of gui) (鬼字原始意義之試探), in *Guoxue jikan* (Chinese Studies Quarterly) (國學集刊), 5.3 (1935): 45–60.

Shen, Weiwei (沈衛威). *Jianxin de rensheng* (A hard life) (艱辛的人生). Taipei: Yeqiang chubanshe, 1993.

———. *Wu Mi zhuan* (A biography of Wu Mi) (吳宓傳). Taipei: Li Xu wenhua chubanshe, 2000.

Shi, Ming (史明). "Dui daojie 'wubuwei' dao 'heiyanjing': Shiren Gu Cheng zhi si shixi" (對道家「無不為」到「黑眼睛」：詩人顧城之死試析), in *Gu Cheng Qi Cheng* (Gu Cheng loses his city) (顧城棄城), ed. Xiao Xialin (蕭夏林). Beijing: Tuanjie chubanshe, 1994.

Shi, Mingzheng (施明正). "Chilai de chulian jiqi lianxiang" (A belated first love and its associations) (遲來的初戀及其連想), in *Shi Mingzheng ji* (A collection of works by Shi Mingzheng) (施明正集), eds. Lin Ruiming (林瑞明) and Chen Wanyi (陳萬益). Taipei: Qianwei chubanshe, 1993.

———. "Dayi yulei" (The overcoat and tears) (大衣與淚), in *Shi Mingzheng ji* (A collection of works by Shi Mingzheng) (施明正集), eds. Lin Ruiming (林瑞明) and Chen Wanyi (陳萬益). Taipei: Qianwei chubanshe, 1993.

———. "Zhidaoguan yu wo" (The inquisitor and I) (指導官與我), in *Shi Mingzheng ji* (A collection of works by Shi Mingzheng) (施明正集), eds. Lin Ruiming (林瑞明) and Chen Wanyi (陳萬益). Taipei: Qianwei chubanshe, 1993.

———. "Heniao zhe" (The man who drank his own urine) (喝尿者), in *Shi Mingzheng ji* (A collection of works by Shi Mingzheng) (施明正集), eds. Lin Ruiming (林瑞明) and Chen Wanyi (陳萬益). Taipei: Qianwei chubanshe, 1993.

———. "Kesi zhe" (The man hankering for death) (渴死者), in *Shi Mingzheng ji* (A collection of works by Shi Mingzheng) (施明正集), eds. Lin Ruiming (林瑞明) and Chen Wanyi (陳萬益). Taipei: Qianwei chubanshe, 1993.

———. "Feie" (Moth) (飛蛾), in *Shi Mingzheng ji* (A collection of works by Shi Mingzheng) (施明正集), eds. Lin Ruiming (林瑞明) and Chen Wanyi (陳萬益). Taipei: Qianwei chubanshe, 1993.

Shi, Shu (施淑). *Lixiang Zhuyizhe dejianying* (The silhouette of an idealist) (理想主義者的剪影). Taipei: Xindi Chubanshe, 1990.

———. "Taiwan de youyu: Lun Chen Yingzhen zaoqi xiaoshuo jiqi yishu" (The melancholy of Taiwan: On the art of Chen Yingzhen's early fiction) (台灣的憂鬱：論陳映真早期小說及其藝術), in *Liang'an wenxue lunji* (Critical essays on Chinese literature across the Taiwan Strait) (兩岸文學論集). Taipei: Xindi chubanshe, 1997.

Shu, Yi (舒乙). Lao She de zuihou liangtian (The last two days of Lao She's life) (老舍的最後兩天). Guangzhou: Huacheng chubanshe, 1987.

Sima, Changfeng (司馬長風). *Zhongguo xinwenxue shi* (History of modern Chinese literature) (中國新文學史). Taipei: Zhuanji wenxue chubanshe, 1991.

Sima, Qian (司馬遷), *Shiji* (史記).

Situ, Wei (司徒衛). "Zhandou wenyi de renshi yu tuixing" (The learning and promotion of war literature) (戰鬥文藝的認識與推行), in *Zhandou wenyi yu ziyou wenyi* (Literature for war and literature for freedom) (戰鬥文藝與自由文藝), ed. Chen Jiying (陳紀瀅). Taipei: Wentan she, 1955.

Su, Ying (蘇英). "Gu Cheng fangsi, piandi *Ying'er*" (*Ying'er* is everywhere right upon Gu Cheng's death) (顧城方死，遍地《英兒》), in *Gu Cheng Qi Cheng* (Gu Cheng loses his city) (顧城棄城), ed. Xiao Xialin (蕭夏林). Beijing: Tuanjie chubanshe, 1994.

Sun, Lung-Kee (孫隆基). *Zhongguo wenhua de shenceng jiego* (The deep structure of Chinese culture) (中國文化的深層結構). Taipei: Tangshan chubanshe, 1990.

———. *Wei duannai de minzu* (China: a people yet to be weaned) (未斷奶的民族). Taipei: Juliu tushu gongsi, 1995.

Sun, Shuyu (孫述宇). *Jin Pingmei de yishu* (The art of Jinpingmei) (金瓶梅的藝術). Taipei: Shibao chuban gongsi, 1977.

Tang, Wenbiao (唐文標). *Zhang Ailing yanjiu* (A study of Eileen Chang) (張愛玲研究). Taipei: Lianjing chuban gongsi, 1976.

Tang, Xianzu (湯顯祖). "*Mudanting* tici" (Preface to *Peony Pavilion*) (《牡丹亭》題記), in *Tangqian zhiguai xiaoshuo jishi* (Annotated collection of pre-Tang *zhiguai* fiction) (唐前志怪小說輯釋), ed. Li Jianguo (李劍國). Taipei: Wenshizhi chubanshe, 1987.

Tang, Xiaobing (唐小兵). "Baoli de bianzheng fa" (The dialectic of violence) (暴力的辯證法), in *Zaijiedu: Dazhong wenyi yu yishi xingtai* (Rereading: mass literature and ideology) (再解讀：大眾文藝與意識形態), ed. Idem. Hong Kong: Oxford University Press, 1993.

Tao, Qian (陶潛). "Li Zhongwen nü" (The daughter of Li Zhongwen) (李仲聞女), in *Soushen houji* (Sequel to in search of the supernatural) (搜神後記), in *Tangqian zhiguai xiaoshuo jishi* (Annotated collection of pre-Tang *zhiguai* fiction) (唐前志怪小說輯釋), ed. Li Jianguo (李劍國). Taipei: Wenshizhi chubanshe, 1987.

Tu, Chengsheng (杜正勝). "Xingti, jingqi, yu hunpo: zhongguo chuantong dui 'ren' renshi de xingcheng" (Body, essence, and soul: the formation of the concept of humanity in Chinese tradition) (形體、精氣與魂魄：中國傳統對「人」認識的形成), in *Xin shixue* (New historiography) (新史學), 2.3/1991.9: 1–65.

———. "Gudai wuguai zhi yanjiu: yi zhong xintaishi he wenhuashi de tansuo" (Wu-Kuai as a reflection of a mentality and culture of ancient China) (古代物怪之研究：一種心態史和文化史的探索) (1), in *Dalu zazhi* (大陸雜誌), 104.1/ 2002.01: 1–14.

Wan, Shuyu (萬樹玉). *Mao Dun Nianpu* (Biographical chronology of Mao Dun) (茅盾年譜). Hangzhou: Zhejiang wenyi chubanshe, 1986.

Wang, Der-wei (David Wang) (王德威), "'Nü'zuojia de xiandai 'gui'hua: Cong Zhang Ailing dao Su Weizhen" (Moderist ghost talk by Chiense women writers: from Eileen Chang to Su Weizhen) (「女」作家的現代「鬼」話：從張愛玲到蘇偉貞), in *Zhongsheng xuanhua: Sanling yu baling niandai de zhongguo xiaoshuo* (Heteroglossia: Chinese fiction of the thirties and the eighties) (眾聲喧嘩：三0與八0年代的中國小說). Taipei: Yuanliu chuban gongsi, 1988.

———. "Lianyi biaomei—Jianlun sanling dao wuling niandai de zhengzhi xiaoshuo" (*Cousin Lianyi* and the political novel from the thirties to the fifties) (蓮漪表妹—兼論三0到五0年代的政治小說), in *Xiaoshuo zhongguo: wanqing dao dangdai de zhongwen xiaoshuo* (Narrating China: Chinese fiction from late Ching to the contemporary Era) (小說中國：晚清到當代的中文小說). Taipei: Maitian chuban gongsi, 1993.

———. "Wushiniandai fangong xiaoshuo xinlun: yizhong shiqu de wenxue?" (Anti-communist fiction: a dead literature?) (五十年代反共小說新論：一種逝去的文學？), in *Sishinian lai zhongguo wenxue* (Modern Chinese literature from the forties to the nineties) (四十年來中國文學), eds. Shao Yuming (邵玉銘), Zhang Baoqin (張寶琴), and Yaxian (瘂弦). Taipei: Lianhe wenxue chubanshe, 1994.

———. "Lao linghun qianshi jinsheng: Zhu Tianxin de xiaoshuo" (The previous lives and the current incarnation of the old soul: the novelistic aesthetics of Zhu Tianxin) (老靈魂前世今生：朱天心的小說), in Zhu Tianxin (朱天心), *Gudu* (Ancient capital) (古都). Taipei: Maitian chuban gongsi, 1997.

———. "Shanghen jijing, baoli qiguan: Yu Hua de xiaoshuo" (A tableau vivant of scar, a spectacle of violence: Yu Hua's fiction) (傷痕即景，暴力奇觀：余華的小說), in Yu Hua (余華), *Xu Sanguan Maixue ji* (Xu Sanguan the blood donor) (許三觀賣血記). Taipei: Maitian chuban gongsi, 1997.

———. "Yizhong shiqu de wenxue?: fangong xiaoshuo xinlun" (A deceased literature? New perspectives on anti-communist fiction) (一種逝去的文學？：反共小說新論), in *Ruhe xiandai, zenyang wenxue?: shijiu, ershi shiji zhongwen xiaoshuo xinlun* (The making of the modern, the making of a literature: new perspectives on nineteenth- and twentieth-century Chinese fiction) (如何現代，怎樣文學？：十九、二十世紀中文小說新論). Taipei: Maitian chuban gongsi, 1998.

———. "Chongdu Zhang Ailing de *Yangge* yu *Chidi zhilian*" (Rereading Eileen Chang's *Rice-Sprout Song* and *Naked Earth*) (重讀張愛玲的《秧歌》與《赤地之戀》), in *Ruhe xiandai, zenyang wenxue?: shijiu, ershi shiji zhongwen xiaoshuo xinlun* (The making of the modern, the making of a literature: new perspectives on nineteenth- and twentieth-century Chinese fiction) (如何現代，怎樣文學？：十九、二十世紀中文小說新論). Taipei: Maitian chuban gongsi, 1998.

———. "Nüzuojia de houxiandai guihua" (Postmodernist "ghost talk" by Chinese women writers) (女作家的後現代鬼話), in Lian he bao, Du shu ren (*United Daily*

News, edition of book review weekly) (聯合報・讀書人), 1998.10.19.

———. "Shigu zhe Wuhe" (The bone collector) (拾骨者舞鶴), in Wuhe (舞鶴), *Yusheng* (Remains of life) (餘生). Taipei: Maitian chuban gongsi, 2000.

———. "Baolie de wenrou: Huang Biyun de xiaoshuo" (Violent tenderness: Huang Biyun's fiction) (暴烈的溫柔：黃碧雲的小說), in Huang Biyun (黃碧雲), *Shier nüse* (Twelve female colors) (十二女色). Taipei: Maitian chuban gongsi, 2000.

Wang, Fansen (王汎森). "Mingmo Qingchu de renpu yu xingguohui" (The journal of humanity and the society of moral edification in the late Ming and early Qing) (明末清初的人譜與省過會), in *Zhongyang yanjiuyuan lishi yuyan yanjiusuo jikan* (Journal of the Institute of History and Philology, Academia Sinica) (中央研究院歷史語言研究所集刊), 63.3/1993.7: 679–712.

Wang, Guoliang (王國良), "Liuchao yu suitang xiaoshou gui" (Ghosts in Six-Dynasties and Sui-Tang fiction) (六朝與隋唐小說鬼), in *Lianhe wenxue* (Unitas) (聯合文學), 16.10/2000.8: 47–8.

Wang, Guowei (王國維), "Hongloumeng pinglun" (A commentary of *The Dream of the Red Chamber*) (《紅樓夢》評論), in *Ershi shiji Zhongguo xiaoshuo lilun ziliao* (Critical materials on the Chinese novel by twentieth-century Chinese scholars) (二十世紀中國小說理論資料), eds. Chen pingyuan (陳平原) and Xia Xiaohong (夏曉虹). Beijing: Beijing daxue chubanshe, 1989.

———. "Huifeng qinqu" (Fragrant wind and pleasant sound of zither) (蕙風琴趣), in *Wang Guowei wenji* (Works of Wang Guowei) (王國維文集), ed. Wu Wuji (吳無忌). Beijing: Beijing Yanshan chubanshe, 1997.

Wang, Hui (汪暉). "Sihuo chongwen" (A rekindled dead fire) (死火重溫), in *Sihuo chongwen* (A rekindled dead fire) (死火重溫). Beijing: Renmin wenxue chubanshe, 2000.

Huang, Jichi (黃繼持). "Xianggang wenxue zhutixing de fazhan" (The development of Hong Kong's literary subjectivity) (香港文學主體性的發展), in *Sishinian lai zhongguo wenxue* (Chinese literature from the fifties to the nineties) (四十年來中國文學), eds. Shao Yuming (邵玉銘), Zhang Baoqin (張寶琴), and Yaxian (瘂弦). Taipei: Lianhe wenxue chubanshe, 1994.

Wang, Jicong (王集叢). "Pin *Xuanfeng*" (A critique on *The Whirlwind*) (評《旋風》), in *Huaixiu shu: "Xuanfeng" pinglunji* (A book of one's own) (懷袖書：《旋風》評論集), ed. Chunyu lou (Spring rain paivilion) (春雨樓). Tainan: Chunyu lou, 1960.

Wang, Lan (王藍). *Lan yu hei* (Blue and black) (藍與黑). Taipei: Honglan chubanshe, 1957.

Wang, Luyan (王魯彥). "Youzi" (Grape fruit) (柚子), in *Youzi* (Grapefruit) (柚子). Shanghai: Shenghuo shudian, 1937.

Wang, Xiaoming (王曉明). *Wufa zhimian de rensheng: Lun Xun zhuan* (A life that can not be faced up to) (無法直面的人生：魯迅傳). Taipei: Yeqiang chubanshe, 1992.

Wang, Xiaoyu (王曉玉). "Na futou, tiantian kan wo de xin: Xie Ye mu qing Xie Wene de tongsu" (That ax axing my heart everyday: Xieye's mother Xie Wenye's heartbreaking report) (那斧頭，天天砍我的心：謝燁母親謝文娥的痛訴), in *Gu Cheng Qi Cheng* (Gu Cheng loses his city) (顧城棄城), ed. Xiao Xialin (蕭夏林). Beijing: Tuanjie chubanshe, 1994.

Wang, Yao (王瑤). *Zhongguo xinwenxue shigao* (Manuscript of modern Chinese literature) (中國新文學史稿). Beijing: Renmin wenxue chubanshe, 1962.

Wang, Yue (王樾). "Zhang Taiyan de ruxia guan jiqi lishi yiyi" (Zhang Taiyan's concept of the scholarly knight and its historical significance) (章太炎的儒俠觀及其歷史意義), in *Xia yu Zhongguo wenhua* (Knight-errantry and Chinese culture) (俠與中國文化), ed. Department of Chinese, Tamkang University (淡江大學中文系). Taipei: Xuesheng shuju, 1993.

Wang, Yongkuan (王永寬). *Zhongguo gudai Kuxing* (Cruel forms of punishment in premodern China/Brutal forms of punishment in ancient China) (中國古代酷刊). Taipei: Yunlong chubanshe (雲龍出版社), 1991.

Wang, Zhiheng (王志恆). "Wushe shijian mianmian guan" (The multifaceted aspects of the Musha Incident) (霧社事件面面觀), *Zhongwai zazhi* (Chung-wai monthly) (中外雜誌), 15/1974.6: 13–7.

Wei, Shaochang (魏紹昌). *Wokan yuanyang hudie pai* (My view of Mandarin Ducks and Butterflies fiction) (我看鴛鴦蝴蝶派). Taipei: Taiwan Shangwu yinshu guan, 1992.

Wei, Ziyun (魏子雲). "*Dangdai zhongguo wenxue daxi* xu" (Preface to *Dangdai zhongguo wenxue daxi* [Compendium of contemporary literature of ROC]) (《當代中國文學大系》序), Taipei: Tianshi chuban gongsi, 1979.

Wen, Jie (聞捷), Jia Zhifang (賈植芳), and others, eds. *Wen Jie Zhuanji* (A critical reader of Wen Jie) (聞捷專集). Fuzhou: Fujian renmin chubanshe, 1982.

Wu, Tenghuang (吳騰凰). *Jiang Guangci zhuan* (Biography of Jiang Guangci) (蔣光慈傳). Hefei: Anhui renmin chubanshe, 1982.

Wu, Zhongjie (吳中傑) and Gao, Yun (高雲) eds. *Dai Houying ah Dai Houying* (Dai Houying, ah, Dai Houying) (戴厚英啊，戴厚英！). Haikou: Hainan Guoji xinwen chuban zhongxin, 1997.

Wu, Zuxiang (吳組緗). "Yiqian babai dan" (Eighteen hundred piculs of rice) (一千八百擔), in *Wu Zuxiang* (Wu Zuxiang) (吳組緗). Taipei: Haifeng chubanshe, 1990.

Wuhe (舞鶴). *Yusheng* (Remains of life) (餘生). Taipei: Maitian chuban gongsi, 2000.

Xiao, Yongqing (蕭永清), ed. *Zhongguo fazhishi jianbian* (A short history of Chinese legal system) (中國法制史簡編). Taiyuan: Shanxi renmin chubanshe, 1982.

Xiaofeng (曉風) ed. *Hu Feng, Lu Ling wenxue shujian* (Correspondeces on literature between Hu Feng and Lu Ling) (胡風，路翎文學書簡). Hefei: Anhui wenyi chubanshe, 1994.

Xin, Yi (辛夷). "*Zhuiqiu* zhongde Zhang Qiuliu" (Zhang Qiuliu in *Zhuiqiu*) (追求中的章秋柳), in *Mao Dun pingzhuan* (Critical and biographical essays on Mao Dun) (茅盾評傳), ed. Fu Zhiying (伏志英). Shanghai: Xiandai shuju, 1931.

Xu, Jijun (徐吉軍). "Lun zhongguo minjian sangsu linghun xinyang de yanbian" (Transformations of funeral customs and beliefs of the soul in Chinese popular society) (論中國民間喪俗靈魂信仰的演變), Appendix , *Minjian xinyang yu zhongguo wenhua guoji yantaohui lunwenji* (Compendium of international conference on popular beliefs and Chinese culture) (民間信仰與中國文化國際研討會論文集), ed. Hanxue yanjiu zhongxin (漢學研究中心). Vol. 2. Taipei: Hanxue yanjiu zhongxin, 1994.

Xu, Ruiyue (徐瑞岳) and Xu, Rongjie (徐榮街) eds. *Zhongguo xiandai wenxue cidian* (Dictionary of modern Chinese literature) (中國現代文學辭典). Xuzhou: Zhongguo kuangye daxue chubanshe, 1988.

Xu, Zhiping (徐志平). *Qingchu qianqi huaben xiaoshuo zhi yanjiu* (A study of storytelling fiction in the first phase of early Qing) (清初前期話本小說之研究). Taipei: Xuesheng shuju, 1998.

Yang, Yi (楊義). "Lu Ling: linghun aomi de tansuozhe" (Lu Ling: an explorer of the mystery of soul) (路翎：靈魂奧祕的探索者), in *Lu Ling yanjiu ziliao* (Research materials on Lu Ling) (路翎研究資料), eds. Zhang Huan (張環), Wei Lin (魏臨), Li Zhiyuan (李志遠), and Yang Yi (楊義). Beijing: Beijing Shiyue Wenyi Chubanshe, 1993.

———. *Zhongguo gudian xiaoshuo shilun* (History of classical Chinese ficiton) (中國古典小說史論). Beijing: Zhongguo shehui kexue chubanshe, 1995.

Yang, Zhao (楊照). "Shenhua de wenxue, Wenxue de shenhua: Wuling, liuling niandai de taiwan wenxue" (A myth of literature, a literature about myth—Taiwan literature of the fifties and sixties) (神話的文學・文學的神話：五0、六0年代的台灣文學), in *Lianhe wenxue* (Unitas) (聯合文學), 10.7/1994.5: 99–104.

Ye, Jiaying (葉嘉瑩). *Wang Guowei jiqi wenxue piping* (Wang Guowei and his literary criticism) (王國維及其文學批評). Taipei: Yuanliu, 1982.

Ye, Shitao (葉石濤). *Taiwan wenxue shigang* (An outline of the history of Taiwan literature) (台灣文學史綱). Gaoxiong: Wenxuejie, 1987.

Ye Si (也斯), *Xianggang wenhua* (Hong Kong culture) (香港文化). Hong Kong: Xianggang yishu zhongxi, 1995.

Youhuan, Yusheng (憂患餘生). *Lingnüyu* (Women's words overheard) (鄰女語), in Wanqing xiaoshuo daxi (A compendium of late Qing literature) (晚清小說大系). Taipei: Guangya chubanshe, 1984.

Yu, Dafu (郁達夫), *Chen lun* (Sinking) (沉淪). Taipei: Wunan tushu chuban youxian gongshi, 1979.

Yu, Qing (于青). *Zhang Ailing Zhuan: Cong Li Hong Zhang zeng wai sun nü dao xian dai Cao Xue Qin* (A Biography of Eileen Chang) (張愛玲傳). Taipei: Shijie shuji, 1993.

Yu, Ying-shih (余英時). "Zhongguo gudai sihou shijieguan de yanbian" (The changing world view of afterlife in ancient China) (中國古代死後世界觀的演變), in *Zhongguo sixiang chuantong de xiandai quanshi* (A modern interpretation of traditional Chinese thoughts) (中國思想傳統的現代詮釋). Taipei: Lianjing chuban gongshi, 1987.

Yue, Hengjun (樂蘅軍). *Yizhi yu mingyun: zhongguo gudian xiaoshuo shijieguan zonglun* (Fate and will: a general study of the world view in classical Chiense fiction) (意志與命運：中國古典小說世界觀綜論). Taipei: Da'an chubanshe, 1992.

Zeng, Huiyan (曾慧燕). "Gu Cheng, Xie Ye tan *Ying'er* yu Ying'er" (Gu Cheng, Xie Ye on Ying'er of Ying'er) (顧城，謝燁談《英兒》與英兒), in *Gu Cheng Qi Cheng* (Gu Cheng loses his city) (顧城棄城), ed. Xiao Xialin (蕭夏林). Beijing: Tuanjie chubanshe, 1994.

Zeng, Yongyi (曾永義). *Zhongguo gudian xiju de renshi yu xinshang* (An introduction to and appraisal of classical Chinese drama) (中國古典戲劇的認識與欣賞). Taipei: Zhengzhong shuju, 1991.

Zeng, Yu (曾煜) ed. *Mingrenbi congshu: liaokan gui yu shen* (Compendium of renowned literati's writings: random notes on ghosts and gods) (名人筆叢書：聊侃鬼與神). Jilin: Jilin renmin chubanshe, 1996.

Zhang, Daofan (張道藩). "Baxunzhang xu" (Preface to *Ba xunzhang* [The badge of scars]) (《疤勳章》序), in 疤勳章. Taipei: Zhengzhong shuju, 1951.

Zhang, Hao (張灝). *Youan yishi yu minzhu chuantong* (Dark consciousness and democratic tradition) (幽暗意識與民主傳統). Taipei: Lianjing chuban gongsi, 1989.

Zhang Huan (張環), Wei Lin (魏臨), Li Zhiyuan (李志遠), and Yang Yi (楊義) eds. *Lu Ling yanjiu ziliao* (Research materials on Lu Ling) (路翎研究資料). Beijing: Beijing Shiyue Wenyi Chubanshe, 1993.

Zhang, Jianlong (張建龍) and others. *Lishi de ningjie: Taiwan minzhu yundong yingxiang shi, 1977–1979* (Frozen history: A photo history of Taiwan's democratic movement, 1977–1979) *(歷史的凝結：1977–79 台灣民主運動影像史)*. Taipei: Shibao chuban gongsi, 1999.

Zhang Jun (張軍). *Chuguo shenhua yuanxing yanjiu* (A Study of the mythological archetypes of the Chu) (楚國神話原型研究). Taipei: Wenjin chubanshe, 1994.

Zhang, Suzhen (張素貞). "Wushi niandai xiaoshuo gaunkui" (A preliminary examination of fiction of the fifties) (五十年代小説管窺), in *Wenxun* (Literary message) *(文訊)*, 9/1984.3: 83–110.

Zhang, Taiyan (章太炎), "Ruxia pian" (On the scholarly knight) (儒俠篇), in *Yadong shibao* (East Asian times) (亞東時報), 1899.

Zhang, Yesong (張業松) ed. *Lu Ling Yinxiang* (Impressions of Lu Ling) (路翎印象). Shanghai: Xuelin Chubanshe, 1997.

Zhang Yesong (張業松)and Xu Lang (徐朗), eds. *Lu Ling wannian zuopinji* (Works by Lu Ling in his last years) (路翎晚年作品集). Shanghai: Dongfang chuban zhongxin, 1998.

Zhang, Yiwu (張頤武). "Yige tonghua de zhongjie" (The end of a fairy tale) (一個童話的終結), in *Gu Cheng Qi Cheng* (Gu Cheng loses his city) (顧城棄城*)*, ed. Xiao Xialin (蕭夏林). Beijing: Tuanjie chubanshe, 1994.

Zhang Zhaohe (張兆和), ed., *Shen Congwen Jiashu* (Correspondences between Shen Congwen and Zhang Zhaohe) (沈從文家書). Taipei: Shangwu yinshuguan, 1998.

Zhao, Qingge (趙清閣). "Huang Baiwei yu Xie Bingying" (Huang Baiwei and Xie Bingying) (黃白薇與謝冰瑩), in *Chang xiangyi* (Remembrances forever) (長相憶). Shanghai: Xuelin chubanshe, 1999.

Zhao, Shuli (趙樹理). *Li Jiazhuang de bianqian* (Changes of the Li Village) (李家莊的變遷). Beijing: Renmin wenxue chubanshe, 1962.

Zhao, Yuan (趙園). *Ming Qing zhiji shidafu zhi yanjiu* (A study of the intelligentsia of the late Ming and early Qing) (明清之際士大夫之研究). Beijing: Beijing daxue chubanshe, 1999.

Zheng, Minglee (鄭明娳). "Dangdai Taiwan wenyi zhengce de fazhan, yingxiang yu jiaotao" (On the development, impact, and consequences of the literary policy in contemporary Taiwan) (當代台灣文藝政策的發展，影響與檢討), in *Dangdai Taiwan zhengzhi wenxue lun* (Politics and contemporary Taiwanese literature) (當代台灣政治文學論), ed. Zheng Minglee (鄭明娳). Taipei: Shibao wenhua chuban gongsi, 1994.

Zheng, Zhenduo (鄭振鐸), "Xue he lei de wenxue" (Literature of blood and tears) (血和淚的文學), in *Zheng Zhenduo xuanji* (Works of Zheng Zhenduo) (鄭振鐸選集). Fuzhou: Fujian renmin chubanshe, 1984.

———. *Zheng Zhenduo xuanji* (Works of Zheng Zhenduo) (鄭振鐸選集). Fuzhou: Fujian renmin chubanshe, 1984.

Zhong, Caijun (鍾彩鈞). "Er Cheng shengren zhixue de yanjiu" (A study of the theory of sainthood by Cheng Yi and Cheng Hao) (二程聖人之文學的研究), Ph. D. Dissertation, National Taiwan University, 1990.

Zhonggong zhongyang wenxian yanjiushi (中共中央文獻研究室) ed. *Mao Zedong wenji* (Works of Mao Zedong) (毛澤東文集). Beijing: Renmin chubanshe, 1981.

Zhou, Libo (周立波). *Baofeng zouyu* (Hurricane) (暴風驟雨). Changsha: Hunan renmin chubanshe, 1983.

Zhou, Zuoren (周作人). "Tangguilun" (On gossiping about the Ghosts) (談鬼論), in *Guadouji* (Melons and beans) (瓜豆集). Shanghai: Yuzhou fengshe, 1937.

Zhu, Hengqing (朱珩青). *Lu Ling: Weiwancheng de tiancai* (Lu Ling: An unaccomplished talent) (路翎：未完成的天才). Jinan: Shandong wenyi chubanshe, 1997.

GLOSSARY

Ah Cheng 阿城
Ah Q zhengzhuan 阿Q正傳
Ah Zhu 阿朱
Ai Zhongguo 哀中國
Aina 艾衲
Aiqing sanbuqu 愛情三部曲

Ba Jin 巴金
Ba Ren 巴人
Ba xunzhang 疤勳章
Bai Hua 白樺
Bai Maonü 白毛女
Bai Wei 白薇
Bai Xianyong 白先勇
Baiguang 白光
Baixian 白絃
Baiye 白夜
Banxialiu shehui 半下流社會
Baofengzhouyu 暴風驟雨
Baowei Yenan 保衛延安
Bayue de xiangcun 八月的鄉村
Bei Cun 北村
Bei Dao 北島
Beiju shengya 悲劇生涯
Beilie 卑劣
Bianliang 汴梁
Boyi 伯夷
Bujin changjiang gungun liu 不盡長江滾滾流
Buneng zou zhetiaolu 不能走這條路
Bupagui de gushi 不怕鬼的故事

Cai Qianhui 蔡千惠
Cairen 菜人
Caizhu de ernü men 財主的兒女們
Caizi jiaren 才子佳人
Can Xue 殘雪
Canghai zhi yisu 滄海之一粟
Cao Xueqin 曹雪芹
Cao Yu 曹禺
Chaguan 茶館
Chang, Eileen 張愛玲
Changan daoren 長安道人
Changong daguang 鏟共大觀
Changshun 常順
Chen Duxiu 陳獨秀

Chen Guanzhong	陳冠中
Chen Hui	陳慧
Chen Jiying	陳紀瀅
Chen Qixia	陳企霞
Chen Que	陳確
Chen Sanli	陳三立
Chen Yingzhen	陳映真
Cheng Ren	程仁
Cheng Yi	程頤
Chenxiang xie: diyilu xiang	沉香屑：第一爐香
Chi dahu	吃大户
Chi ku	吃苦
Chidi	赤地
Chidi zhilian	赤地之戀
Chimei	魑魅
Chongchu yunwei de yueliang	衝出雲圍的月亮
Chongyang	重陽
Chu	楚
Chu sanhai	除三害
Chuangzao	創造
Chuangzao she	創造社
Chuci	楚辭
Chuke paian jingqi	初刻拍案驚奇
Chulu	出路
Chunqiu	春秋
Cong baicaoyuan dao sanwei shuwu	從百草園到三味書屋
Cong Guling dao Dongjing	從牯嶺到東京
Cong Guling huidao Wuhan	從牯嶺回到武漢
Congwen zizhuan	從文自傳
Cui daizhao shengsi yuanjia	崔待詔生死冤家
Cui Ning	崔寧
Dachu youling ta	打出幽靈塔
Dai Houying	戴厚英
Dao Mosike qu	到莫斯科去
Daya	達雅
Dayi mieqin	大義滅親
Dayi yu lei	大衣與淚
De	德
Dibao	邸報
Dicun zhuan	荻村傳
Ding Ling	丁玲
Diquan	地泉
Dongchang	東廠
Dongdang de niandai	動蕩的年代
Dongjing	東京
Donglin	東林
Dongyao	動搖
Doupeng xianhua	豆棚閒話
Du Fu	杜甫
Du Pengcheng	杜鵬程
Du Quan	杜荃
Duangmu Fang	端木方
Duanku dang	短褲黨
Dunhuang	敦煌
Duo Duo	多多
Erke paian jingqi	二刻拍案驚奇
Ernü yingxiong zhuan	兒女英雄傳
Erpai	二拍
Ershinian mudu zhi guaixianzhuang	二十年目睹之怪現狀
Erya	爾雅
Faji biantai	發跡變泰
Fang Peilan	方培蘭
Fang Xiangqian	方祥謙

Fangong dalu, shoufu shidi	返攻大陸，收復失地
Fanji'e	反饑餓
Fanjia pu	樊家鋪
Feng Deying	馮德英
Feng Fangmin	馮放民
Feng Menglong	馮夢龍
Feng Naichao	馮乃超
Fengshen zhuan	封神傳
Fengzi	鳳子
Fenshu	焚書
Fuchou de huoyan	復仇的火焰
Fushi	腐蝕
Gan Bao	干寶
Gangbi	剛愎(弼)
Gao Yang	高陽
Gao Yun	高雲
Ge Fei	格非
Ge Mai	戈麥
Ge Weilong	葛薇龍
Ge Xianning	葛賢寧
Geming de langman dike	革命的浪漫蒂克
Geming jia lian'ai	革命加戀愛
Geming lishi xiaoshuo	革命歷史小說
Geming shen shounan	革命神受難
Geming wenxue	革命文學
Geming yu lian'ai	革命與戀愛
Geming yu lian'ai de gongshi	革命與戀愛的公式
Gengzi guobian tanci	庚子國變彈詞
Gong Mengbi	宮夢弼
Gongmin	公民
Gongshi xing	共時性
Gu Cheng	顧城
Gu Gang	顧岡
Gu Gong	顧工
Guanchang xianxing ji	官場現形記
Guanguan de bupin	官官的補品
Gucheng wantiao	古城晚眺
Gudian aiqing	古典愛情
Gudu	古都
Guduzhe	孤獨者
Guen	鯀
Gui	鬼
Gui	龜
Gui	歸
Gui jincheng	鬼進城
Guibing	鬼病
Guihua	鬼話
Guilian	鬼戀
Guiqi	鬼氣
Guiqulai	歸去來
Guiqulai ci	歸去來辭
Guling yihen	牯嶺遺恨
Gundong de toulu	滾動的頭顱
Guo Moruo	郭沫若
Guo Quanhai	郭全海
Guomin ribao	國民日報
Guren	古人
Guren	故人
Haibin guren	海濱故人
Haizi	海子
Han Laoliu	韓老六
Han Shaogong	韓少功
Han Sishou	韓思壽
Hangzhou	杭州

Haotan guiguai shenhu 好談鬼怪神狐
He Qifang 何其芳
Hedian 何典
Henhai 恨海
Heniao zhe 喝尿者
Hexi zoulang xing 河西走廊行
Hong 虹
Hong gaoliang jiazu 紅高粱家族
Hong Ling 洪凌
Hong Mai 洪邁
Hong Ri 紅日
Hong Ruizhao 洪瑞釗
Hong Shen 洪深
Hong Yan 紅岩
Honghe sanbuqu 紅河三部曲
Hongloumeng 紅樓夢
Hongyan 紅岩
Hongying 虹影
Hsia, C. T. 夏志清
Hu Feng 胡風
Hu Lanqi 胡蘭畦
Hu Shi 胡適
Hua Han 華翰
Huaben 話本
Huaigu 懷古
Huang Biyun 黃碧雲
Huang Chunming 黃春明
Huang Jinshu 黃錦樹
Huang Juan 黃娟
Huang Zhang 黃彰
Huang Zhenbo 黃貞柏
Huangming shenglie zhuan 皇明聖烈傳
Huanghun 黃昏
Huanmie 幻滅
Huigui 回歸
Huigujia 灰骨匣
Hunan nongmin yundong kaocha baogao 湖南農民運動考察報告
Huo diyu 活地獄
Huogui 活鬼
Huozang 火葬
Huozhe 活著

I-ching 易經

Ji Xian 紀弦
Ji'e de Guo Su'e 飢餓的郭素娥
Ji'e de nüer 飢餓的女兒
Ji'e sanbuqu 饑餓三部曲
Ji'e yiwei jie 紀惡以為戒
Jia 家
Jia Duanfu 賈端甫
Jia Pingwa 賈平凹
Jiandeng xinhua 剪燈新話
Jiandeng yuhua 剪燈餘話
Jiang Guangci 蔣光慈
Jiang Gui (Wang Yijian) 姜貴 (王意堅)
Jiang Menglin 蔣夢麟
Jiang Qing 江青
Jiang Ruheng 蔣如恆
Jiangjun de tou 將軍的頭
Jiangsu 江蘇
Jiao 教
Jin Bumo 金不磨
Jin he yuan 近和遠
Jin taowu zhuan 今檮杌傳
Jingen 金根
Jingshen shiliang 精神食糧
Jingshi tongyan 警世通言
Jingshi yinyang meng 警世陰陽夢
Jinianbei 紀念碑
Jinpingmei 金瓶梅

Jinsuoji	金鎖記
Jintian	今天
Jiudi gongshen	就地公審
Jiuguo	酒國
Jixia	季俠
Juezhan	決戰
Jujiu yu Jinmen gaoliang	橘酒與金門高粱
Julian	劇聯
Jun Guomin	軍國民
Juying de chujia	菊英的出嫁
Kaige	凱歌
Ke Yinyue	客印月
Kesheng zhe	渴生者
Kesi zhe	渴死者
Kong Dezhi	孔德沚
Kong Jue	孔厥
Ku caihua	苦菜花
Kuangren riji	狂人日記
Langfeide	浪費的
Lao linghun	老靈魂
Lao She	老舍
Laocan youji	老殘遊記
Lei Feng	雷峰
Lei Mi	雷米
Leiyu	雷雨
Li Ang	李昂
Li Bihua	李碧華
Li Boyuan	李伯元
Li Chao	李超
Li Chuli	李初梨
Li Guangtian	李廣田
Li He	李賀
Li Huiniang	李慧娘
Li Li	李黎
Li Qing	李清
Li Rui	李銳
Li Ruzhen	李汝珍
Li Ying	李英
Li Zhi	李贄
Li Zhongwen nü	李仲聞女
Li Zhun	李準
Li Zishu	黎紫書
Lian Mengqing	連夢青
Liang Qichao	梁啓超
Liang Shiqiu	梁實秋
Lianyi biaomei	蓮漪表妹
Liaozhai zhiyi	聊齋志異
Liaozhai zizhi	聊齋自志
Lihun	離婚
Liji	禮記
Lin Bai	林白
Lin Yiyun	林宜澐
Linggan	靈感
Linnü yu	鄰女語
Lishi de zuiren	歷史的罪人
Liu Bingyan	劉賓雁
Liu E	劉鶚
Liu junzi	六君子
Liu Quan	劉荃
Liu Shaotang	劉紹唐
Liu Xinhuang	劉心皇
Liu Zaifu	劉再復
Liu Zhenyun	劉震雲
Liu Zongzhou	劉宗周
Liubie	留別
Long Yingtai	龍應台
Lu Ling	路翎
Lu Wenfu	陸文夫
Lu Xiaoman	陸小曼
Lu Xinhua	盧新華
Lu Xun	魯迅
Lu Yin	盧隱

Luanshi 亂世
Lühua shu sanbuqu 綠化樹三部曲
Lüliang yingxiong zhuan 呂梁英雄傳
Lun leifeng ta de daodiao 論雷峰塔的倒掉
Luo Guangbin 羅廣斌
Luo Shu 羅淑
Luotuo xiangzi 駱駝祥子
Lushan 盧山
Luzhu shanfang 菉竹山房

Ma Feng 馬烽
Mahebo 馬赫坡
Mai Keang 麥克昂
Mang Ke 芒克
Mao Dun 茅盾
Mei guangdi 梅光迪
Mei Jianchi 眉間尺
Meilidao shijian 美麗島事件
Meishijia 美食家
Meng Chao 孟超
Menglong shi 朦朧詩
Miao 苗
Mingdeng yinhua 明燈因話
Miewang 滅亡
Minsheng zhuyi yule liangpian bushu 民生主義育樂兩篇補述
Minzu bao 民族報
Mo Yan 莫言
Mogui de yaolian yu chunqing ji qita 魔鬼的妖戀與純情及其他
Mogui de zihuaxiang 魔鬼的自畫像
Monarudao 莫那魯道
Mudanting 牡丹亭
Mujie wen 墓碣文
Mulian xi 目蓮戲

Nahan 吶喊
Nanlai zuojia 南來作家
Ni Huanzhi 倪煥之
Ni Kuang 倪匡
Nianyü Guanyin 碾玉觀音
Nizhao zhong de toulu 泥沼中的頭顱
Nüzhen 女真

Ouyang Yuqian 歐陽予倩

Pan Jinlian 潘金蓮
Pan Lei 潘壘
Pan Renmu 潘人木
Pan Zinian 潘梓年
Pang Yuemei 龐月梅
Panluan de caoyuan 叛亂的草原
Paoxiao lede tudi 咆哮了的土地
Peng Dehuai 彭德懷
Peng Jiahuang 彭家煌
Pinggui zhuan 平鬼傳
Pingyao zhuan 平妖傳
Pu Songling 蒲松齡

Qian Gurong 錢谷融
Qian Liqun 錢理群
Qian Wengui 錢文貴
Qian Xiaojing 黔小景
Qian Xibao 錢錫寶
Qian Xingcun 錢杏邨
Qian Zhongshu 錢鍾書
Qianze xiaoshuo 譴責小說
Qin Dejun 秦德君
Qin Shubao 秦叔寶
Qin Zhaoyang 秦兆陽
Qingchun zhige 青春之歌
Qingdang 清黨
Qiqiao 七巧
Qiu Jin 秋瑾

Qiwang	棋王
Qiyue	七月
Qu Qiubai	瞿秋白
Qu Yuan	屈原
Qunzhong gongshen	群眾公審
Ren Ah! Ren	人啊！人
Ren de wenxue	人的文學
Rengui he tade qi de gushi	人鬼和他的妻的故事
Renjian wangliang zhuan	人間魍魎傳
Renqing xiaoshuo	人情小說
Renrou	人肉
Rongsheng	榮生
Rou Shi	柔石
Rufei shengren, jishi qinshou	如非聖人，即是禽獸
Rulin waishi	儒林外史
Ruxia	儒俠
San Liwan	三里灣
Sange nanren yu yige nuren	三個男人與一個女人
Sanguozhi yanyi	三國志演義
Sanqianli jiangshan	三千里江山
Sanxia wuyi	三俠五義
Sanyan	三言
Shafu	殺夫
Shandong	山東
Shang	商
Shanghai	上海
Shanghai daxue	上海大學
Shanghen wenxue	傷痕文學
Shangshi	傷逝
Shangshu	尚書
Shangui	山鬼
Shanlu	山路
Shao Quanlin	邵荃麟
Shaonian piaobozhe	少年漂泊者
Shen Congwen	沈從文
Shen Yanbing	沈雁冰
Sheng	乘
Shengsi chang	生死場
Shengsi yuanjia	生死冤家
Shenliao	神聊
Shenmo	神魔
Shenmo dou meiyou fasheng	什麼都沒有發生
Shenmo xiaoshuo	神魔小說
Shenwu zhiai	神巫之愛
Shenyi jing	神異經
Shenzhou xiushou ren	神州袖手人
Shi	蝕
Shi Mingde	施明德
Shi Mingzheng	施明正
Shi Shuqing	施叔青
Shi yanzhi	詩言志
Shi Zhecun	施蟄存
Shiba chun	十八春
Shigu zhe	拾骨者
Shiji	史記
Shijing	詩經
Shiqing xiaoshuo	世情小說
Shiren zhi si	詩人之死
Shishi tongtang	四世同堂
Shishi xiaoshuo	時事小說
Shu	檮
Shu Yi	舒乙
Shui	水
Shuihu zhuan	水滸傳
Shujun	淑君
Shun	舜
Shuqi	叔齊
Sima Qian	司馬遷

Sima Zhongyuan	司馬中原
Sister Jiang	江姐
Situ Wei	司徒衛
Song Ruoyu	宋若瑜
Soushen houji	搜神後記
Su Tong	蘇童
Su Weizhen	蘇偉貞
Su Xuelin	蘇雪林
Suishi yiwen	隋史遺文
Suitang yanyi	隋唐演義
Sun Ling	孫陵
Taiyang she	太陽社
Taiyang yuekan	太陽月刊
Taiyang zhaozai Sanggan heshang	太陽照在桑乾河上
Taiyuan yiniang	太原意娘
Tan Yuexiang	譚月香
Tan Zhongdao	譚中道
Tang Wenbiao	唐文標
Tang Xianzu	湯顯祖
Tang Xiaobing	唐小兵
Tao Qian	陶潛
Taowu	檮杌
Taowu cuibian	檮杌萃編
Taowu xianping	檮杌閒評
Tayal	泰雅
Tian'anmen	天安門
Tianshan muge	天山牧歌
Tianshi	天史
Tianxian pei	天仙配
Tiedao youjidui	鐵道游擊隊
Tiehai	鐵孩
Tiyu zhi yanjiu	體育之研究
Tonghua shiren	童話詩人
Tujia	土家
Tuwei	突圍
Wang Anyi	王安憶
Wang Guowei	王國維
Wang Hui	汪暉
Wang Jicong	王集叢
Wang Jingzhi	汪靜之
Wang Luyan	王魯彥
Wang Manying	王曼英
Wang Meng	王蒙
Wang Ruowang	王若望
Wang Tongzhao	王統照
Wang Xiaoming	王曉明
Wang Yingxia	王映霞
Wang Yuanjian	王願堅
Wang Zhenhe	王禎和
Wang Zhongqi	王鍾麒
Wei Haiqing	魏海清
Wei junzi	偽君子
Wei nuli de muqin	為奴隸的母親
Wei Zhongxian	魏忠賢
Wei Zhongxian xiaoshuo chijian shu	魏忠賢小說斥奸書
Weicheng	圍城
Weihu	韋護
Wen Jie	聞捷
Wengu 1942	溫故一九四二
Wenming xiaoshi	文明小史
Wenxue ji renxue	文學即人學
Wenxue yanjiuhui	文學研究會
Wenxue zazhi	文學雜誌
Wo, hongdayi, yu lingling	我，紅大衣與零零
Wode jiaoyu	我的教育
Wode putishu	我的菩提樹
Women chabian hongqi	我們插遍紅旗
Wozai xiacun de shihou	我在霞村的時候

Wu Jianren	吳研人
Wu Jingzi	吳敬梓
Wu Qiang	吳強
Wu Sihong	吳似鴻
Wu Woyao	吳沃堯
Wu Zuxiang	吳組緗
Wufeng zhishu	無風之樹
Wuguai	物怪
Wuhe	舞鶴
Wuhui jieshu yihou	舞會結束以後
Wuming de xiaohua	無名的小花
Wushe shijian	霧社事件
Wuwei	無為
Wuyue caomang chen	吳越草莽臣
Xi Rong	西戎
Xi Xi	西西
Xiandai shi	現代詩
Xiandai shishe	現代詩社
Xiang Peiliang	向培良
Xiangdong jiwen	湘東紀聞
Xiangxi	湘西
Xiao Ai	小艾
Xiao Hong	蕭紅
Xiao Jun	蕭軍
Xiaoshuo geming	小說革命
Xiaxie xiaoshuo	狹邪小說
Xie Bingying	謝冰瑩
Xie Ye	謝燁
Ximen Qing	西門慶
Xin ernü yingxiong zhuan	新兒女英雄傳
Xin xiaoshuo	新小說
xin xieshi zhuyi	新寫實主義
Xin yu jiu	新與舊
Xingge Mingyun	性格 命運
Xingshi hengyan	醒世恆言
Xinjiang	新疆
Xinliu	新柳
Xinmeng	新夢
Xinmin	新民
Xinsheng	新生
Xinsheng bao	新生報
Xinzhong de fen	心中的墳
Xiuding falü guan	修訂法律館
Xiushen	修身
Xiushou pangguan lun	袖手旁觀論
Xiyou ji	西遊記
Xu Xu	徐訏
Xu Zhimo	徐志摩
Xuanfeng	旋風
Xungen	尋根
Xunzi	荀子
Yalu jiangshang	鴨綠江上
Yan'an	延安
Yang Hansheng	陽翰笙
Yang Lian	楊煉
Yang Mo	楊沫
Yang Sao	楊騷
Yang Shuo	楊朔
Yang Siwen Yanshan feng guren	楊思溫燕山逢故人
Yang Xi'er	楊喜兒
Yang Yi	楊義
Yang Yiyan	楊益言
Yangge	秧歌
Yanhua sanyu	煙花三月
Yanzhi kou	胭脂扣
Yao	藥
Yaofande	要飯的
Ye Shaojun	葉紹鈞
Ye Ting	葉挺
Yecao	野草

Yeji 野祭
Yelang 夜郎
Yeyu 夜漁
Yeyu qiudenglu 夜雨秋燈錄
Yibu ciru shengming lingsui de qingai chanhuilu 一部刺入生命靈髓的情愛懺悔錄
Yidairen 一代人
Yijianzhi 夷堅志
Yin 殷
Ying'er 英兒
Yinong liguo 以農立國
Yiqian babai dan 一千八百擔
Yishi de wancheng 儀式的完成
Youhuan Yusheng 憂患餘生
Youwei 有為
Youzi 柚子
Yu Dafu 郁達夫
Yu Hua 余華
Yu zhu ding, wen ran xi, jue yin fu, jing tan shi 禹鑄鼎,溫燃犀,掘隱伏,警貪癡
Yu Ziqi 余子期
Yuan Jing 袁靜
Yuan Qiongqiong 袁瓊瓊
Yuan Shikai 袁世凱
Yuan Yuling 袁于令
Yuan zhumin 原住民
Yuelin 月林
Yuewei caotang biji 閱微草堂筆記
Yueya er 月牙兒
Yuhai 魚骸
Yusheng 餘生
Yusheng jinian bei 餘生紀念碑
Yushi mingyan 喻世明言
Yuxian 玉賢
Zai Haidebao zhuiru qingwang 在海德堡墜入情網
Zai jiulou shang 在酒樓上
Zai tielian zhong 在鐵鏈中
Zang Kejia 臧克家
Zeng Mingzheng 贈明正
Zeng Pu 曾樸
Zhadan yu zhengniao 炸彈與征鳥
Zhandou wenyi 戰鬥文藝
Zhang Ailing (Eileen Chang) 張愛玲
Zhang Chunqiao 張春橋
Zhang Daofan 張道藩
Zhang Qiuliu 章秋柳
Zhang Taiyan 章太炎
Zhang Tianyi 張天翼
Zhang Xianliang 張賢亮
Zhang Yiwu 張頤武
Zhang Zhenshan 張振山
Zhangui zhuan 斬鬼傳
Zhanyou chongfeng 戰友重逢
Zhao Huiming 趙惠明
Zhao Shuli 趙樹理
Zhao Wenjie 趙文節
Zhao Yanwang 趙閻王
Zhao Yulin 趙玉林
Zhao Zifan 趙滋蕃
Zhaohua xishi 朝花夕拾
Zhen xiaoren 真小人
Zheng Boqi 鄭伯奇
Zheng Yiniang 鄭意娘
Zheng Zhenduo 鄭振鐸
Zhengtong 正統
Zhenzhen 貞貞
Zhidao guan yu wo 指導官與我
Zhiqing 知青

Zhong Ling 鍾玲
Zhong Xiaoyang 鐘曉陽
Zhongguo gongxue 中國公學
Zhongguo ribao 中國日報
Zhongguo shehui jieji de fenxi 中國社會階級的分析
Zhou Dayong 周大勇
Zhou Libo 周立波
Zhou Zuoren 周作人
Zhouli 周禮
Zhu Tianxin 朱天心
Zhu Xiang 朱湘
Zhuanxu 顓頊
Zhucheng 諸城
Zhufu 祝福
Zhuiqiu 追求
Zhuiqiu zhongde Zhang Qiuliu 追求中的章秋柳
Zhujian 鑄劍
Zhuogui dadui 捉鬼大隊
Zibo 淄博
Ziibuyu 子不語
Zuo Guangdou 左光斗
Zisha 自殺
Zisha riji 自殺日記
Ziye 子夜
Ziyou zhongguo 自由中國
Zong Baihua 宗白華
Zong Pu 宗璞
Zuoye 昨夜
Zuozhuan 左傳

INDEX

Abandoned Capital (Jia Pingwa), 286
Abbas, Ackbar, 272
abjection, 127
aborigines: Miao, 25, 36; Tayal, 9, 17, 30–34, 37–39, 40; Tujia, 36
Adorno, Theodor, 4, 32, 178–79, 278, 340n69
adultery, 44, 49, 55, 69, 120, 146, 202–3
aesthetic imperative, 83–84
Ah Cheng, 145
"Ah Q zengzhuan." *See* "True Story of Ah Q, The" (Lu Xun)
Ah Ying, 296n4
Ah Zhu (in *Liaozhai*), 289
Aina, 6
Aiqing sanbuqu (Trilogy of love; Ba Jin), 88
Ai zhongguo (Lamenting China; Jiang Guangci), 109
Akutagawa Ryûnosuke, 225
Alvarez, Alfred, 227, 233–34
Analects (Confucius), 327n88
Ancient Capital (Zhu Tianxin), 268–69
Anderson, Marston, 24, 59, 82, 91, 293n1, 302n52, 305n10
anorexic logic, 138–42, 143
aporia, 21, 27, 29, 258
Apter, David E., 74, 303n62, 304n79, 327n94
Arendt, Hannah, 5
arranged marriage, 67–68, 94–95, 98, 100, 111, 146, 196, 284
"Artisan Cui and his Life-and-Death Romantic Partner" (Feng Menglong), 284–85
Association of Chinese Literature, 157
Association of Literary Workers, 153–54
Auerbach, Erich, 315n1
Autobiography of Congwen, 25–26
avant-garde hunger narratology, 128–31

Babbit (in "Mission: Ghost hunt"), 281
Badge of Scars, The (Duanmu Fang), 149–50, 174–75
"Baiguang" (White light; Lu Xun), 275
Bai Hua, 156
Bai, Judge (in *The Travels of Lao Can*), 44
Baimao nü (The white-haired girl; Lu Ling), 125–26, 265, 336n18
Bai Wei: dialectic of justice and, 10, 54, 56–59, 64; ghost tales and, 275; "revolution plus love" fiction and, 79–81, 88, 94–99, 105, 110–16, 308n65, 311n111
"Baixian" (White line; Shi Mingzheng), 243
Bai Xianyong, 160
Baiye (White night; Jia Pingwa), 286–87
Ba Jin, 17, 79, 88, 157, 158, 274
Bakhtin, Mikhail, 5, 122, 198, 273, 322n44
Ban Wang, 123, 280
Banxialiu shehui (Semi-lower class society; Zhao Zifan), 179
Baofeng zouyu. See *Hurricane* (Zhou Libo)
Baowei Yan'an (Guarding Yan'an; Du Pengcheng), 163–65
Ba Ren, 156–57, 189, 317n26
Barthes, Roland, 71, 225, 272, 277

Bataille, Georges, 4, 198, 269, 278, 322–23nn46,47
Baudrillard, Jean, 5
Ba xunzhang (The badge of scars; Duanmu Fang), 149–50, 174–75
Bayue de xiangcun (August in the village; Xiao Jun), 163
Becker, Jasper, 137
beheading. *See* decapitation syndrome
Bei Cun, 131
Bei Dao, 250
Beiju shengya. See *My Tragic Life* (Bai Wei)
benevolent kingship, 18–19, 296n7
Benjamin, Walter, 4, 8, 32, 278, 294n14
Between Men: English Literature and Male Homosocial Desire (Sedgwick), 318n46
Bitter Endive Flower, 164–65, 177
"bitter love," 156
"blood and tears," literature of, 4, 9, 43, 59–65, 66
body politics, 108, 124, 143–44, 174, 178, 181, 234
Bomb and the Expeditionary Bird, The (Bai Wei), 79, 88, 98–99, 110
Boxer Rebellion (1900), 8–9; dialectic of justice and, 41; in *Fool in the Reeds* (Chen Jiying), 169; in *The Travels of Lao Can* (Liu E), 45–46; in *Women's Words Overheard* (Youhuan Yusheng), 15–19, 35, 296n7
Boyi, 140
Breaking Free (Jiang Gui), 213
Brennan, Timothy, 318n39
Brooks, Peter, 80, 321n32
Brothers Karamazov (Dostoevsky), 250
Brumberg, Joan, 140
Buddhism, 63, 230, 276, 312–13n21
Bujin changjiang gungun liu. See *Endlessly Flows the Yangtze* (in *The Death of a Poet*)
Buneng zou zhetiaolu (Do not take this path; Li Zhun), 167–68
Bupagui de gushi (Stories defying the superstition of ghosts; He Qifang), 265
Buraiha school, 244
Bureau of International Information, 81
Byron, George Gordon, Lord, 87, 106, 241, 244, 250, 307n42

Cai Qianhui (in "Mountain Path"), 119, 137–44
Caizhu de ernü men (Children of the rich; Lu Ling), 158, 176
caizi jiaren (talent/beauty genre), 269–70
Call to Arms, A (Lu Xun), 20, 24, 121, 280, 312n11
"Canghai zhi yisu" (A tiny grain in the world; Tan Zhongdao), 145
cannibalism: Bai Wei and, 56; during Great Leap Forward (1959–1962), 131, 313–14n46; hungry woman image and, 119, 128, 145, 147; in *Hurricane* (Zhou Libo), 72; Lu Xun and, 21, 35, 43, 51–54, 64, 118, 180, 193, 226; in "scar writing," 178, 180; Shen Congwen and, 26–27; in *The Sun Shines over the Sanggan River* (Ding Ling), 71–73, 75; in *A Tale of Modern Monsters* (Jiang Gui), 193–94, 210, 322n38; Wu Zuxiang and, 62–63
Can Xue, 266
Cao Qiqiao (in "The story of the golden cangue"), 277
Cao Xueqin, 186–87, 200
Cao Yu, 59, 275
Los Caprichos (Goya), 12, 221–22, 327n95
"Carved Jade Guanyin," 284–85
censorship, 3, 43, 114, 137, 154, 227, 236, 237, 300n15
Chaguan (Teahouse; Lao She), 227
Chang, Eileen: fin-de-siècle writers and, 158; ghost tales and, 276–78, 281; Huang Biyun and, 271; hungry woman image and, 9, 11, 119, 131–37, 142, 144–45; land reform movement and, 175–76; "scar writing" and, 171–73, 180, 319n58
Changan daoren, 201
Changes in Li Village (Zhao Shuli), 177–78
"Changong daguan" (A spectacle of chopping Communists; Lu Xun), 22
Changshun the Fool (in *Fool in the Reeds*), 169
Chan, Stephen, 80, 98
Chaungzao zhoubao (Creation weekly), 109, 307n40
Chen Bingliang, 257
Chen Dadao, 324n53
Chen Duxiu, 42, 152
Cheng Dakang, 324n53
Cheng Ren (in *The Sun Shines over the Sanggan River*), 74–75
Cheng Shi (in *A Tale of Modern Monsters*), 194
Chen Guanzhong, 271, 338n36
Chen Guocheng. *See* Wuhe
Cheng Yi, 140

UNIVERSITY
BOOK STORE
RETAIN THIS RECEIPT
2006-2007

1 20 162676 STEPHEN Sale

6438900 CINDERELLAS SISTERS	29.95
6439078 MONSTER THAT IS HISTO	24.95
726584811015 / 41	
UW EXAM BOOK LARGE 24PG	0.40
726584811015 / 41	
UW EXAM BOOK LARGE 24PG	0.40
726584811015 / 41	
UW EXAM BOOK LARGE 24PG	0.40
Subtotal	56.10
Total Tax	4.94

Total	61.04 *
Bankcard Online	61.04

Account: XXXXXXXXXXXX0765
Expiration Date:# 1010
Authorization: 01473A
Reference: 27910011
Control#: 1..20.162676.37427.3278
10:22 10/27/06
ALL 2006 AUTUMN QUARTER TEXTBOOK
SALES ARE FINAL.

Chen Hui, 338n36
Chen Jiying, 157, 169–70, 175, 322n34
Chen Pingyuan, 216
Chen Qixia, 154
Chen Que, 206
Chen Quemoy (in "The man who drank his own urine"), 245
Chen Sanli, 224–26, 228, 260, 328n4
"Chenxiang xie: Diyilu xiang" (Ashes of sandalwood: The first incense burner; Eileen Chang), 277
Chen Yingzhen, 9, 11, 119, 137–44
Chen Yu-shi, 82
Chiang Kai-shek, 78–79, 84–85, 138, 156–57, 279–80, 304n4
Chidi (Red land; Chen Jiying), 157–58, 169
Chidi zhilian. See *Naked Earth* (Eileen Chang)
Children of the Rich (Lu Ling), 158, 176
Chimei, 186
Chinese Communist takeover. *See* Great Divide (1949)
Chinese Public College (Zhongguo Gongxue), 110
Chinese Writers' Association, 154
chivalry, 43, 48–49, 52, 163, 300n14, 315–16n9
Chongchu yunwei de yueliang. See *Moon Forces Its Way through the Clouds, The* (Jiang Guangci)
Chongyang (Double suns; Jiang Gui), 191, 220
Chongzhen reign, 201
Chow, Rey, 121, 312n15
"Chuangzao" (Creation; Mao Dun), 100
Chuci, 275
Chuke paian jingqi, 264
Chunqiu (Confucius), 5
Chu Sanhai campaign, 157
Committee of Chinese Literature and the Arts, 157
Communist hunger discourse, 119–31, 138, 140–41, 144
Communist revolution (1927), 8, 10–11, 77–116, 305n9; Bai Wei and, 94–99, 110–15; dialectic of justice and, 71; Jiang Guangci and, 86–93, 106–10; Jiang Gui and, 220; love stories "in reality" and, 99–116; Mao Dun and, 77–86, 100–106, 305n15; spiritual hunger and, 122–23
Communist United Front, 67
Communist Youth League, 87
Compendium of Monsters, A (Qian Xibao), 11, 188, 212–23, 327n89, 327n93
"Completion of a Ritual" (Su Tong), 281–82, 290
Comte, Auguste, 90
Confucianism: in *A Compendium of Monsters* (Qian Xibao), 216–18, 327nn88,89; dialectic of justice and, 43, 300n14; in *An Idle Commentary on Monsters* (Li Qing), 204, 206; Lu Xun and, 35; in *A Tale of Modern Monsters* (Jiang Gui), 192, 194, 197–98, 323–24n49; Youhuan Yusheng and, 18–20, 35, 39–40, 296n7
Confucius, 5, 16, 19
"Cong baicaoyuan dao sanwei shuwu" (From Baicao Garden to Sanwei Study; Lu Xun), 24
"Cong Dongjing huidao Wuhan" (From Tokyo back to Wuhan; Qian Xingcun), 83
"Cong Guling dao Dongjing" (From Guling to Tokyo; Mao Dun), 82–83, 102, 309n82
Congwen zizhuan (Autobiography of Congwen), 25–26
corporeality, aesthetics of, 279–82
corruption: in *Living Hell* (Li Boyuan), 48–49, 51; in *The Travels of Lao Can* (Liu E), 45–47, 50–51, 73, 300n17, 304n77
courtroom drama, 54–56, 72–73, 75, 302n37
Cousin Lianyi (Pan Renmu), 158, 170, 175, 322n34
Creation Society (Chuangzao she), 82, 85, 86, 307n40
Creation Weekly, 109, 307n40
crime and punishment, 41–76
criminal law, 41, 299n3
Cui Chengxiu (in *An Idle Commentary on Monsters*), 209
"Cui daizhao shengsi yuanjia" (Artisan Cui and his life-and-death romantic partner; Feng Menglong), 284–85, 342n88
Cuihuan (in *The Travels of Lao Can*), 46
Cui Ning (in "Carved Jade Guanyin"), 284–85
Cultural Revolution (1966–76): Bai Wei and, 116; Chen Yingzhen and, 11, 138–39; Dai Houying and, 231, 235, 236, 239, 260; Du Pengcheng and, 182; ghost tales and, 265, 267–68, 279–80; Gu

Cultural Revolution (1966–76) *(continued)*
Cheng and, 250–51; Hongying and, 146; literary suicide and, 227–29; in *The Scar* (Lu Xinhua), 173–75; "scar writing" and, 4, 8–9, 150, 156; Wen Jie and, 12, 231, 233, 235, 239, 329n30

Dachu youling ta. See *Fight Out of the Ghost Tower* (Bai Wei)
Dai Houying, 228–29, 231–33, 235–40, 259–61, 329n22
Daoist dynamics, 122
Dao Mosike qu (Go to Moscow; Hu Yepin), 88
Dasai Osamu, 225–26, 244–45
Daughter of Hunger, The (Hongying), 145–47
"Daughter of Li Zhongwen, The" (Tao Qian), 270
Daya (in *Remains of Life*), 38
"Dayi yulei" (The overcoat and tears; Shi Mingzheng), 243
Death of a Poet, The (Dai Houying), 228–29, 235–40, 260
"Death" (Turgenev), 28
decapitation syndrome, 9, 10, 15–40, 297nn16,18; Jiang Gui and, 197; Lu Xun and, 20–25, 34–36; Shen Congwen and, 25–30; Wuhe and, 30–34, 37–39; Youhuan Yusheng and, 15–21, 34–35, 296n4
de Certeau, Michel, 283
dèjá disparu, 272
Deleuze, Gilles, 341n84
De Man, Paul, 297n18
Denton, Kirk, 122, 314n63
depravity fiction *(xiaxie xiaoshuo),* 215–16
Derrida, Jacques, 5, 279
despair, discourse of, 98–99, 113, 115
devilism, 243–44, 248–50, 260
"Diary of a Madman" (Lu Xun), 24, 52, 58, 193, 195–96, 275
Dickens, Charles, 241, 272
Dicun zhuang. See *Fool in the Reeds* (Chen Jiying)
Di Huaqiao (in *The Death of a Poet*), 236–37
Dimock, Wai Chee, 299–300n7
Ding Ling: dialectic of justice and, 66–75; hungry woman image and, 122, 131, 132; literary suicide and, 226; "revolution plus love" fiction and, 80–81, 88; "scar writing" and, 153–54, 156, 166, 177–78, 182
Ding Yaokang, 6
Diquan (Earth spring; Hua Han), 89
"discourse of despair," 98–99, 113, 115
Disillusionment (Mao Dun), 81–82, 89
Doleželová, Milená, 218
"Dongdang de niandai" (A time of turmoil; Wen Jie), 231
Dong Hu of the Jin, 6
Dongjing menghua lu (A record of the dreams of the eastern capital's splendor; Meng Yuanlao), 335n5
Donglin faction, 203
Dongyao. See *Vacillation* (Mao Dun)
Dong Yinming (in *A Tale of Modern Monsters*), 197
Do Not Take This Path (Li Zhun), 167–68
Dooling, Amy, 113–14
Dostoevsky, 212, 244–45, 250
Double Suns (Jiang Gui), 191, 220
Doupeng xianhua (Casual talks under the bean arbor; Aina), 6
Dream of the Red Chamber, The (Cao Xueqin), 186–87, 200, 208, 256, 323–24n49
Duan Chaoqun (in *The Death of a Poet*), 236–37
Duanku dang. See *Sans-culottes* (Jiang Guangci)
Duanmu Fang, 149, 174
Du Daxin (in *Xinsheng*), 17
Du Fu, 4, 237
Duoduo, 250
Du Pengcheng, 163–65, 182
Du Quan, 85

East Asia Bookstore, 108
Eastern Depot, 203
"eat bitterness" *(chiku),* 138–39, 141–42
"eat the rich" *(chi dahu),* 122
Eclipse (Mao Dun), 81–83, 85, 88, 89, 99–100, 102–4, 226, 305n15
Eighteen Hundred Piculs of Rice (Wu Zuxiang), 63–65, 72, 122
"eight-legged" literature, 158–60
"Encounter of Yang Siwen and Old Acquaintances, An" (Feng Menglong), 262–63, 267, 268, 290–91
"Encounter of Zheng Yu'e in Yanshan" (Shen Ye), 334–35n2
Endlessly Flows the Yangtze (in *The Death of a Poet*), 236–40
Erke paian jingqi, 264

Ernü yingxiong zhuan (Tale of heroes and lovers), 163
Erpai (Striking the table in amazement at the wonders), 264
Ershinian mudu zhi guaixiangzhuang. See *Eyewitness Report of Strange Things of the Past Twenty Years* (Wu Jianren)
Erya, 266
evil, 5–8; in *A Compendium of Monsters* (Qian Xibao), 217–19; in *The Death of a Poet* (Dai Houying), 237; in "Diary of a Madman" (Lu Xun), 52; ghost tales and, 278; in *Hungry Guo Su'e* (Lu Ling), 70; in *An Idle Commentary on Monsters* (Li Qing), 200, 204–10, 216–18; "scar writing" and, 180; in *A Tale of Modern Monsters* (Jiang Gui), 209–12, 219–23; taowu and, 186–88, 190–91, 196, 200; in *The Travels of Lao Can* (Liu E), 45–46
exorcism, 264, 272
exposé *(qianze xiaoshuo),* 213–23, 273–74, 326–27n84
Exposure of Officialdom (Li Boyuan), 214–15
extremist suicide, 227–28, 233–34
Eyewitness Report of Strange Things of the Past Twenty Years (Wu Jianren), 214–15, 218, 273

Fahai (monk), 56
"fairytale poet" *(tonghua shiren),* 251, 331n83
faji biantai, 202–3, 325n60
Fan Denggao (in *Three-Mile Bay*), 167
"Fan Family Village" (Wu Zuxiang), 63–64, 72, 119, 302n52
Fang Luolan (in *Vacillation*), 104
Fang, Mistress (in *A Tale of Modern Monsters*), 193–94, 196–98, 322n38, 323–24n49
Fang Peilan (in *A Tale of Modern Monsters*), 183, 192, 194, 196, 200, 209–12, 322n37, 323–24n49, 326–27n84
Fang Ranwu (in *A Tale of Modern Monsters*), 193–94, 196, 199, 323–24n49
Fang Tianai (in *A Tale of Modern Monsters*), 209
Fang Tongsan (in *A Tale of Modern Monsters*), 326–27n84
Fang Xiangqian (in *A Tale of Modern Monsters*), 183, 192–97, 200, 209–12, 220–21, 322n37, 323–24n49, 326–27nn77,84
Fang Zhen (in *A Tale of Modern Monsters*), 194, 326–27n84
"Fanjia pu." *See* "Fan Family Village" (Wu Zuxiang)
Fantastic Talk (Mo Yan), 287–88
Fan Xingpu (in *A Compenium of Monsters*), 215–18
"Farewell" (Mao Dun), 77–78, 83, 100, 304n1
Farewell, My Concubine (Li Bihua), 337n32
Fathers and Sons (Turgenev), 62
Feidu (Abandoned capital; Jia Pingwa), 286
feminists, 58, 67, 88, 94–99, 101, 121–22, 135, 143, 285
Feng Deying, 164
Feng Fangmin, 157
Feng Menglong, 206, 262–63, 284–85, 334–35n2
Feng Naichao, 85, 306n32
Fengshen zhuan (Investiture of the gods), 273
Fengzi (Shen Congwen), 36
Fenshu (Burning books; Li Zhi), 6
feudalism, 62, 70, 126, 127, 163, 264, 275
Feuerwerker, Yi-tsi Mei, 67, 71, 162
Fiction That Castigates the Villainy of Wei Zhongxian (Wuyue caomang chen), 201
Fight Out of the Ghost Tower (Bai Wei), 54, 56–59, 64, 95, 110, 275
filicide, 57
fin-de-siècle discourse, 12, 132, 158, 266, 278
Fin-de-siècle Splendor (Wang), 273
"First Incense Burner, The" (Eileen Chang), 277
Flaubert, Gustave: *The Temptation of St. Anthony,* 336n10
Fleur (in *Rouge*), 270–71
food shortages, 117, 124, 133, 135–37, 311n1
Fool in the Reeds (Chen Jiying), 157, 169, 175, 322n34
Forbidden City, 18, 32
forensic discourse, 10, 44, 56, 59–60, 64, 76
Formosa Incident *(Meilidao shijian),* 240, 249, 330n49
Foucault, Michel, 5, 23, 50, 195, 234, 280, 297n21, 304nn78,79, 322n39
fraudulent gentlemen *(wei junzi),* 217–18, 220, 327n88
French Revolution, 71
Freud, Sigmund, 90, 118, 129, 198, 257, 268, 337n23
"From Guling to Tokyo" (Mao Dun), 82–83, 102, 309n82

"From Tokyo Back to Wuhan" (Qian Xingcun), 83
Frye, Northrop, 325n67
Fuchou de huoyan (Fire of revenge; Wen Jie), 231
Fu Kexing, 83
Fukumotoism, 83
Fu Lei, 227, 233
Fu Ruyu (in *An Idle Commentary on Monsters*), 202–3, 206
Fushi (Putrefaction; Mao Dun), 105–6, 309n88

Gálik, Marian, 174
Gan Bao, 289
Gangbi, Prefect (in *The Travels of Lao Can*), 44–47
Gang of Four, 232, 235
Gao Yang, 184, 198
Gao Yun, 229, 235, 329n22
Ge Fei, 131
Ge Mai, 254
Geming shen shounan (The revolutionary god is in danger; Bai Wei), 95–96, 308n65
"Geming wenxue" (Revolutionary literature; Lu Xun), 85
Geming yu lianai (Revolution and love; Hong Ruizao), 90
"Geming yu lian'ai de gongshi" ("On the formula of revolution and love"; Mao Dun), 89
gender politics, 11, 75, 94–99
Genette, Gérard, 341n86
Gengzi guobian tanci (A ballad about the national calamity of the Boxer Rebellion; Li Boyuan), 19
Ge Weilong (in "Ashes of Sandalwood: The First Incense Burner"), 277
Ge Xianning, 159
ghosts, 12, 258, 262–91, 334–35nn1–3; aesthetics of, 278–84; Gu Cheng and, 254–55; realism and, 263–65, 272–78, 279–80, 336n10; revenant, writing as, 266–72; writing of, 284–91
Ghosts, The (Ibsen), 264, 275
"Ghost Talk" (Yang Lian), 282–83
Giddens, Anthony, 340n69
Girard, René, 4
Girl (in *Remains of Life*), 30, 38–39, 40
Golden Lotus, The, 203, 205–6, 208, 325n69
Gong Mengbi (in *Liaozhai*), 289
gongshi xing, 34
gonorrhea, 112–14
Gouzi (in "Fan Family Village"), 63–64
Goya, Francisco, 12, 221–23, 327n95
Grand Inquisitor (in *Brothers Karamazov*), 250
"Grapefruit" (Wang Luyan), 17, 25
Great Divide (1949), 8, 148–60, 184, 188–90, 220, 315n7, 322n34, 329n15
Great Famine, 2, 145–46
Great Leap Forward (1959–1962), 2, 131, 146, 231, 234, 288, 313–14n46
Guanchang xianxing ji (Exposure of officialdom; Li Boyuan), 214–15, 273
"Guanguan de bupin" (Young master gets his tonic; Wu Zuxiang), 62–63
Guarding Yan'an (Du Pengcheng), 163–64, 177, 182
Gu Cheng, 12, 228, 250–61, 331n83, 332–33nn90,92,93,96
"Gucheng wantiao" (Lookout atop an ancient city at twilight; Wen Jie), 230–31
"Gudian aiqing" (A classical love story; Yu Hua), 145, 269–70
Gudu (Ancient capital; Zhu Tianxin), 268–69
"Guduzhe" (The misanthrope; Lu Xun), 275
Guen, 6, 185
Gu Gang (in *The Rice-Sprout Song*), 135–37, 144
Gu Gong, 251, 259, 332nn92,93
gui, 266, 290, 334n1
"Gui" (Ghost; Ba Jin), 274
"Guihua" (Ghost talk; Yang Lian), 282–83
"Gui jincheng" (Ghost comes to the city; Gu Cheng), 251
"Guilian" (Ghost love; Xu Yu), 274
"Guiqulai ci" (Homecoming; Tao Qian), 268
"Guiqulai" (Homecoming; Hang Shaogong), 267–68, 337n23
"Guling yihen" (Everlasting regrets in Guling; Jiang Guangci), 108
Gu Moruo, 329n15
"Gundong de toulu" (Rolling heads; Jiang Xun), 17
Guo Chuntao, 105
Guomin ribao (Citizens' news), 81
Guo Moruo, 85, 86, 87, 157, 233, 264
Guo Quanhai (in *Hurricane*), 167
Guo Su'e (in *Hungry Guo Su'e*), 69–70, 119–31, 139, 142, 144, 146

Haibin guren (Old acquaintances on the seashore; Lu Yin), 226
Haizi, 254
Han Chinese, 30–34, 36, 37
Han Fuqu, 326–27n84
Hang Shaogong, 267
Hang Yuhai, 333n110
Han Laoliu (in *Hurricane*), 72, 178
Han Shaogong, 266, 280–81, 290, 337n23
Han Sishou (in "An Encounter of Yang Siwen and Old Acquaintances"), 262–63, 267, 290–91
"Haotan guiguai shenhu" (My penchant for ghosts, demons, gods and fox spirits; Mo Yan), 287–88
"hard-core" realism, 177, 181
Harootunian, Harry, 340n69
hauntology, writing of, 5, 279, 284–91
Haywood, Leslie, 140
headhunting, 17, 32–34, 37, 38–39, 40
"Heavenly Match" (Wang Anyi), 282–83
Hedian (What sort of book is this?), 273
Hegel, Robert, 324n50
Heini (in *The Sun Shines over the Sanggan River*), 74–75
He Jingzhi, 336n18
hell: in *Living Hell* (Li Boyuan), 47–49, 51, 52, 53, 65; Lu Xun and, 52–53; in *The Travels of Lao Can* (Liu E), 47, 52, 53, 65, 301n23, 304n77
Henhai (The sea of regret; Wu Jianren), 19
"Heniao zhe" (The man who drank his own urine; Shi Mingzheng), 245
He Qifang, 265
heteroglossia, 122
"Hexi zoulang xing" (Songs about the Northwest Corridor; Wen Jie), 229–30
historiography, 6, 82, 162, 165, 168, 186–87, 190, 217
History of Modern Chinese Fiction, A (C.T. Hsia), 184
History of the Strange (Pu Songling), 289
Holocaust, 4, 178, 294n12
"Homecoming" (Hang Shaogong), 267–68, 337n23
homosocial bonding, 164, 318n46
Hong. See *Rainbow* (Mao Dun)
Hong Gaoliang jiazu (Red sorghum; Mo Yan), 287
Honghe sanbuqu (Red river trilogy; Pan Lei), 158, 170
Hong Ling, 278
Hongloumeng. See *Dream of the Red Chamber, The* (Cao Xueqin)
Hong Mai, 263, 335n3
Hongri (Red sun; Wu Qiang), 164
Hong Ruizhao, 90, 94, 96
Hong Shen, 275
Hongyan (Red rock: Luo Guangbin and Yang Yiyan), 17, 149–50
Hongying, 145–47
"Hougui" (Living ghost; Peng Jiahuang), 274
Hsia, C. T., 4, 9, 19, 63–64, 124, 134, 165, 177, 184, 197, 212–13, 300n18
Hsia, T. A., 52, 62, 93, 160, 164, 275–76, 315–16n9
huaben stories, 263, 284–86, 334–35n2
Hua Han, 89, 104, 307n47
Huai River flood, 324–25n58
Huang Biyun, 271, 278
Huang Chunming, 160
Huang Da (in *An Idle Commentary on Monsters*), 324–25n58
"Huanghun" (Twilight; Shen Congwen), 25, 27–28
Huang Jinshu, 289–90
Huang Juan (in *Naked Earth*), 172
Huangming zhongxing shenglie zhuan (Tales of the sage-like and virtuous in the restoration of the imperial Ming), 201
Huang Zhang. *See* Bai Wei
Huang Zhenbo (in "Mountain Path"), 139, 141–42
Huang Ziping, 108
Huanmie (Disillusionment; Mao Dun), 81–82, 89
Hu Feng, 66, 120–22, 124, 128–31, 144, 154, 176, 311n7, 313n44
"Huigujia" (Casket of ashes), 263, 334–35n2
Hu Lanqi, 102
"Hunan nongmin yundong kaocha baogao" (Report on an investigation of the peasant movement in Hunan; Mao Zedong), 122
Hundred Flowers Movement, 154, 160
"Hunger Artist" (Kafka), 143
Hungry Guo Su'e (Lu Ling), 69–70, 119–31, 142, 200

hungry woman image, 11, 117–47; in *Hungry Guo Su'e (Lu Ling)*, 69–70, 119–31; in "Mountain Path" (Chen Yingzhen), 119, 137–44; in *The Rice-Sprout Song* (Eileen Chang), 119, 131–37
Huo Diyu. See *Living Hell* (Li Boyuan)
Huozang (Cremation; Lao She), 226
Huozhe (To live; Yu Hua), 145
Hurricane (Zhou Libo), 72, 74, 166–67, 177–78, 182
Hu Shi, 106, 133, 152, 184, 264–65, 272, 317n30, 336n16
Hu Yepin, 88
hyperbole, 178–80
hypocrisy, 217–18, 220, 327n89

Ibsen, Henrik, 264, 275
I Ching, 288
Idle Commentary on Monsters, An (Li Qing), 11, 185, 188, 200–212, 214, 216–20, 222–23, 322n34, 324–25nn53,58,68
Illustrated Fiction, 301n25
imaginary nostalgia, 36, 169–70, 271, 312n15, 338n35
"Inquisitor and I, The" (Shi Mingzheng), 249–50
Institute for Legal Revision (Xiuding Falü Guan), 41

Jewish mysticism, 4, 143
Jia Baoyu (in *The Dream of the Red Chamber*), 256
Jia Duanfu (in *A Compenium of Monsters*), 215–18, 221
Jia (Family; Ba Jin), 158
Jia family (in *The Dream of the Red Chamber*), 323–24n49
Jiandeng xinhua (New stories written while trimming the wick), 263
Jiandeng yuhua (More stories written while trimming the wick), 264
Jiang Guangci: dialectic of justice and, 60–62, 64, 72; hungry woman image and, 122; "revolution plus love" fiction and, 10, 79–81, 86–94, 96–98, 104, 106–10, 112, 115–16, 307nn40,42, 310n91
Jiang Gui: monster symbolism and, 7–8, 11, 183–200, 208–14, 219–23, 321n25, 322nn34,37, 323–24n49, 326–27n84; "scar writing" and, 158, 171
"Jiang jun de tou" (The general's head; Shi Zhecun), 17
Jiang Mengling, 184
Jiang Qing, 188, 209, 265, 321n24, 326n77
Jiang, Sister (in *Red Rock*), 149
Jiang Xun, 17
Jian of the Qi, 6
Jia Pingwa, 266, 286–87
Jia Wei (in *The Travels of Lao Can*), 44–46
Ji'e sanbuqu (A trilogy of hunger; Wang Ruowang), 145
Ji'e de Guo Su'e. See *Hungry Guo Su'e* (Lu Ling)
Ji'e de nüer (The daughter of hunger; Hongying), 145–47
Jin Bumo (in *Women's Words Overheard*), 15, 17–19, 40, 296n7
Jingshi tongyan, 264
Jingshi yinyang meng (Yin and yang dreams that admonish the world; Changan daoren), 201
Jing Tsu, 280
Jin'gen (in *The Rice-Sprout Song*), 133–34
"Jin he yuan" (Near and far; Gu Cheng), 251
Jinianbei (Monument; Jiang Guangci), 108–9
Jinpingmei (The golden lotus), 203, 205, 338n34
Jinsuoji (The story of the golden cangue; Eileen Chang), 277
Jin taowu zhuan. See *Tale of Modern Monsters, A* (Jiang Gui)
Jintian (Today) magazine, 250
Jiuguo (The wine republic; Mo Yan), 145
Jixia (in *A Sacrifice in the Wild*), 88, 89
Ji Xian, 160, 241–42, 318n37
July (Qiyue) school, 121
justice, dialectic of, 10, 41–76, 299–300nn5–8; Ding Ling and, 66–75, 166; in *Fight Out of the Ghost Tower* (Bai Wei), 54, 56–59; in *Living Hell* (Li Boyuan), 47–51, 301n27; Lu Xun and, 51–54; in *Pan Jinlian* (Ouyang Yuqian), 54–56; in *Roaring Earth* (Jiang Guangci), 60–62; in *The Travels of Lao Can* (Liu E), 44–47; Wu Zuxiang and, 62–65
Ju Yaoru (in "New Willow"), 289
"Juying de chujia" (The wedding of Ju Ying; Wang Luyan), 274

Kafka, Franz, 143, 250
"Kaige" (Victory song; Shi Mingzheng), 248–49
Kang Sheng, 188
Karamazov, Ivan (in *Brothers Karamazov*), 250
Karatani Kojin, 108
Kawabata Yasunari, 226
"Kesi zhe." *See* "Man Who Hankered for Death, The" (Shi Mingzheng)
Ke Yinyue, Madame (in *An Idle Commentary on Monsters*), 185, 201–4, 324–25nn58,59
Kim-chu Ng. *See* Huang Jinshu
Kong Dezhi, 100, 103–5, 116, 308n72, 309n78
Kong Jue, 177
Kong Qingdong, 333n110
Korean War, 132, 163, 171–73, 180
Korehito, Kurahara, 83, 86
Kristeva, Julia, 127
"Kuangren riji." *See* "Diary of a Madman" (Lu Xun)
Ku caihua (Bitter endive flower; Feng Deying), 164–65, 177
Kwan, Stanley, 270

Lacan, Jacques, 122, 297n16
land reform movement, 70–74, 132–36, 162, 165–68, 169, 277
Lantern Festival, 262, 335n5
Lan yu hei (Black and blue; Wang Lan), 322n34
Lao Can (in *The Travels of Lao Can*), 44–47, 301n29, 304n77
Lao Can youji. See *Travels of Lao Can, The* (Liu E)
lao linghun ("old souls"), 268
Lao She, 29, 213, 226, 227, 233
Last Night (Bai Wei and Yang Sao), 114
laughter, politics of, 213, 219–22
Lau, Joseph, 4
League of Drama Workers, 114
League of Left-Wing Writers, 86, 93, 104, 110, 114
Lee, Leo, 21, 86, 107, 275
Lee, Lillian. *See* Li Bihua
legal justice, 3, 10, 42–43, 76, 215
legal reform, 41–42, 299n3
Lei Feng, 164
Leifeng Tower, 56–57
Lei (in *Ying'er*), 254–56
Lei Mi. *See* Xie Ye
Leiyu (Thunderstorm; Cao Yu), 59, 275
Letu (Happy land; Bai Wei), 308n65
Li Ang, 145, 278
Liang Qichao, 41, 150, 152
Liang Shiqiu, 151, 317n30
Lian Mengqing. *See* Youhuan Yusheng
Lianyi biaomei. See *Cousin Lianyi* (Pan Renmu)
Liaozhai zhiyi (Liaozhai's record of the strange), 264, 266, 287–89
Li Bihua, 270–71, 278, 288–89, 337n32, 338n34
Li Bingzhong, 276, 339n52
Li Boyuan, 19, 47–51, 52, 53, 73, 75, 214, 218, 273, 301n25
Li Chao, 106
Li Chuli, 85
Life-and-Death Partners (Zhong Ling), 284–86, 290, 342n90
Li Guangtian, 227
Li Guokun (in "Mountain Path"), 139, 141
Li Guomu (in "Mountain Path"), 137
Li He, 289
Li Huiniang (Meng Chao), 265
Lihun (Divorce; Lao She), 213
Liji, 267
Li Jie (in *Roaring Earth*), 60–62, 64
Li Li, 278
Lin Bai, 266, 278
Lin Cheng (in *Ying'er*), 255–56
Lin Daiyu (in *The Dream of the Red Chamber*), 256
"Linggan" (Inspiration; Qian Zhongshu), 275
Lingnüyu. See *Women's Words Overheard* (Youhuan Yusheng)
Linli (Bai Wei), 97
Lin Yiyun, 281–82
Li Qing, 185, 188, 200, 202–12, 214, 222, 324n50, 325n68
Li Ruchen (in *Changes in Li Village*), 178
Li Rui, 145
Li Shangzhi (in *The Moon Forces Its Way through the Clouds*), 89
Literary Revolution, 3, 193
"Little Scene in Guizhou" (Shen Congwen), 25–26
"Liubie." *See* "Farewell" (Mao Dun)
Liu Binyan, 160
Liu Bojian, 101

Liu Chi-hui, 280
Liu E, 19, 44–49, 50–53, 73, 75, 213, 301n23, 304n77
Liu Jianmei, 99
Liu, Joyce, 280
Liu Kang, 122
Liu Quan (in *Naked Earth*), 171–73, 180
Liu Shaotang, 160
Liu Shouchun (in *Hungry Guo Su'e*), 120, 124
Liu Wenzhong, 324n50
Liu Xinhuang, 184
Liu Yazi, 328n4
Liu Zaifu, 4, 43, 71, 166
Liu Zhenyun, 145, 332–33n96
Liu Zigu (in *Liaozhai*), 289
Liu Zongzhou, 140
Living Hell (Li Boyuan), 47–51, 52, 53, 65, 70, 72, 214, 301n25
Li Yang, 304n78
Li Ying, 252–53, 256
Li Zhi, 6
"Li Zhongwen nü" (The daughter of Li Zhongwen; Tao Qian), 270
Li Zhun, 167–68
Li Zishu, 278
Logique du sens (Deleuze), 341n84
Long Yingtai, 17
love stories "in reality," 99–116; Bai Wei and Yang Sao, 110–15; Jiang Guangci and Song Ruoyu, 106–10, 310n91; Mao Dun and Qin Dejun, 100–106
Lühua shu sanbuqu (Mimosa trilogy; Zhang Xianliang), 145
Lukács, Georg, 129–30, 176, 313n44
Lüliang Yingxiong zhuan (Heroes of Lüliang Mountain), 162
Lu Ling: dialectic of justice and, 66, 69–70, 73; hungry woman image and, 9, 11, 119–31, 142, 144–45, 311nn6,7, 314n63; Jiang Gui and, 200; "scar writing" and, 158, 176
Lunacharsky, 86
"Lun leifeng ta de daodiao" (On the collapse of Leifeng Tower; Lu Xun), 56
Luo Changlu, 333n110
Luo Guangbin, 17, 149
Luo Shu, 274
Luotuo xiangzi (Camel Xiangzi; Lao She), 226
Lu Wendi (in *The Death of a Poet*), 236
Lu Wenfu, 145
Lu Xiaoman, 106
Lu Xinhua, 173–75
Lu Xun: Bai Wei and, 58, 110; cannibalism and, 64, 118, 180, 193, 226; Chen Jiying and, 157; Chen Yingzhen and, 142; decapitation syndrome and, 2, 16–17, 20–25, 43, 51–52, 74, 148, 296n5; dialectic of justice and, 52–54, 56, 59, 73; Eileen Chang and, 131; Fadeyev and, 163; ghost tales and, 264, 273, 275–76, 277, 281, 339n52; Gu Cheng and, 259; Huang Biyun and, 271; hungry woman image and, 11, 117–19, 121, 145, 312n11; Jiang Guangci and, 64, 87, 93, 108–10, 307n40; Mao Dun and, 84–86, 306n32; Mulian theatre and, 287; Nationalist banning of, 157; nativist fiction and, 169; physical fitness and, 280; politics of laughter and, 213; revolutionary poetics and, 152, 155, 167; "scar writing" and, 74, 148, 173, 179–80; Shen Congwen and, 10, 26, 29, 297n27; Su Xuelin and, 317n30; Wuhe and, 9–10, 30, 32–33, 34–36, 39; Wu Zuxiang and, 62–64; Youhuan Yusheng and, 9, 10, 20–21; Zhu Xiang and, 224
Lu Yin, 226
"Luzhu shanfang" (Bamboo cottage; Wu Zuxiang), 274
Lyotard, Jean-François, 258, 301n27
lyricism, 26–27, 29–30, 36, 39–40, 229, 329n25

Ma Feng, 153
Mahebo tribe, 31
Mai Keang, 86
Man ah! Man (Dai Houying), 228, 236
Mang Ke, 250
"Man Who Hankered for Death, The" (Shi Mingzheng), 245–47, 250
"Man Who Drank His Own Urine, The" (Shi Mingzheng), 245
Mao-Dengism, 258, 261, 283, 287
Mao Dun, 77–86, 305nn6,10,14; Bai Wei and, 96–98; Eileen Chang and, 131; hungry woman image and, 122; Jiang Guangci and, 86–93, 106, 109–10; Jiang Gui and, 189; Kong Dezhi and, 100, 103–5, 116, 308nn72,73, 309n78; literary suicide and, 226; nationalized history and,

162; PRC and, 154; Qin Dejun and, 98–106, 116, 309nn78,81,82,88; realism and, 82–86, 91–92, 102, 104–6, 305n10, 306n19; revolutionary poetics and, 81–99, 152, 155; "revolution plus love" fiction and, 10, 125
maodun (contradiction), 104
Maoist hunger discourse, 119–31, 138, 140–41, 144
Maoist literary tradition, 24, 69, 151–56, 162, 254, 258, 270
Maoist sublime, 237–40, 330n48
Mao Zedong: Hundred Flowers Movement and, 160; land reform movement and, 133; revolutionary romanticism and, 93, 115, 233–35; in *A Tale of Modern Monsters* (Jiang Gui), 209, 326n77; Ya'an talks of, 42, 66, 129, 153, 160, 163, 176, 302–3n56, 316n15
Maruo Tsuneki, 275
Masao Miyoshi, 226
master narratives, 4, 43, 121, 155, 181, 294n4, 300n15
matricide, 63–64, 119
May Fourth Movement, 8, 10; anti-Communist literature and, 157–60, 317–18nn34,35; Bai Wei and, 98, 113–14; Chen Sanli and, 224; dialectic of justice and, 42, 44, 51, 54; ghost tales and, 264, 274–75, 336nn15,16; Jiang Guangci and, 87–88, 106; Jiang Gui and, 189, 191, 323–24n49; Mao Dun and, 79, 82, 87, 103; nationalized history and, 318n39; politics of laughter and, 213, 326–27n84; Qin Dejun and, 100; revolutionary poetics and, 87, 154–56; "scar writing" and, 151–52, 176, 177, 181; Shen Congwen and, 29–30; Wang Luyan and, 25
May Thirtieth Incident, 82, 103
Mei Guangdi, 264
Mei (in *Rainbow*), 103
Mei Jianchi, 22
"Meishijia" (The gourmet; Lu Wenfu), 145
Mencius, 7, 123, 186
Meng Chao, 109, 265
Meng Yuanlao, 335n5
metaphoric actions, 11, 119, 127
Miao aborigines, 25, 36
Mideng yihua (Stories written while searching for a lamp), 264
Miewang (Destruction; Ba Jin), 17, 79
mimesis, 24, 204, 281, 315n1, 325n67, 341n84
Ming period, 4, 6; ghost tales and, 263–64, 266, 272, 281, 287; in *An Idle Commentary on Monsters* (Li Qing), 11, 185, 188, 200–210, 217, 219–23, 322n34, 324nn50,53, 325–26nn66,69,73
Mingzhu yuan (A romance of pearls; Li Qing), 325n59
Ministry of National Defense, 317n29
Minzu Bao (People's News), 157
Mishima Yukio, 226, 244, 247
"Mission: Ghost hunt" (Lin Yiyun), 281–82
Misty Poetry *(menglong shi)*, 250
modernist poetry movement, Taiwanese, 160, 318nn37,38
Modernist Poetry Society (Xiandai Shishe), 160, 241, 318n37
Mogui de yaolian yu chunqing ji qita (The devil's fiendish romance and innocent passion and other poems; Shi Mingzheng), 244
"Mogui de zihuaxiang" (Self-portrait of a devil; Shi Mingzheng), 244
Monamahong, 38
Monarudao, 30–32, 34, 38
monsters, 183–223; *A Compendium of Monsters* (Qian Xibao), 212–23; *An Idle Commentary on Monsters*, 200–212; *A Tale of Modern Monsters* (Jiang Gui), 188–200. See also *taowu*
Monument (Jiang Guangci), 108–9
Moon Forces Its Way through the Clouds, The (Jiang Guangci), 88–89, 109, 112
"moral occult," 190, 321n32
"Mountain Path" (Chen Yingzhen), 119, 137–44
Mo Yan, 145, 266, 282–84, 287–89
Mudanting (Peony Pavilion; Tang Xianzu), 270
Muer (in *Ying'er*), 256, 258
Mu Jibo, 101
"Mujie wen" (Tomb tablet; Lu Xun), 24
Mukden Incident, 114
Mulian xi (Mulian drama cycle), 276, 286–87, 339n54
Musha Incident (1930), 9, 17, 34, 37–39
My Education (Shen Congwen), 25–26
My Tragic Life (Bai Wei), 96, 113–16

Nahan (A call to arms; Lu Xun), 20, 24
Naked Earth (Eileen Chang), 131, 158, 171–73, 176, 180, 277
Nanchang Uprising, 78, 81, 82, 101, 305n6, 305n14
narcissism, 60, 62, 92, 107, 257, 307n42
Narrative Discourse (Genette), 341n85
narrators, 36–37, 53–54, 59, 67–68, 117–18, 245–48, 255, 283, 285
National Conference of Writers and Artists (Beijing), 153
nationalized history, 11, 160–73, 318nn39,44
National Taiwan University, 160
nativism, 31–32, 169–70, 240, 268
neo-Confucianism, 123, 140, 312–13n21, 314n63
New Fiction, 41, 299n1
New Fourth Army, 105
New Life Daily, 156–57
New Life movement, 279–80
"new realism," 83, 86, 91–92, 97
New Tale of Heroes and Lovers (Yuan Jing and Kong Jue), 163, 177
"New Willow" (Huang Jinshu), 289–90
"New Year's Sacrifice" (Lu Xun), 2, 23–24, 53, 117–19, 127, 179–80, 275
"Nianyü Guanyin" (Carved jade Guanyin [Avalokiteshvara]), 284–85
nihilism, 29, 82, 88
Ni Huanzhi (Ye Shaojun), 84
Ni Kuang, 265, 336n20
"Nizhao zhong de toulu" (Heads in the mire; Zong Pu), 17
noble savage, 34, 36
nomos, 42, 299–300nn5–8
Northern Expedition, 79, 82, 188
Northern Song dynasty, 262–63, 267, 271, 335n5
nostalgia, 36, 69, 158, 169–70, 191, 271, 312n15, 338n35
Nüzhen Tartars, 262

Odysseus's scar, 174, 315n1
"Old and New, The" (Shen Congwen), 25–26
orality, 118, 125, 128
Oriental University (Moscow), 87
orthodoxy, reinstatement of, 190–92
Ouyang Juyuan, 301n25
Ouyang Yuqian, 54–56, 57, 59, 338n34

Pang Jinlian (in *A Tale of Modern Monsters*), 193–94, 199
Pang Yuemei (in *A Tale of Modern Monsters*), 193–94, 199, 209
Pan Jinlian (Ouyang Yuqian), 54–56, 57, 72, 338n34
Pan Jinlian zhi qianshi jinsheng (The previous and present lives of Pan Jinlian; Li Bihua), 338n34
Pan Lei, 158, 170
"Panluan de caoyuan" (A meadow in revolt; Wen Jie), 231
Pan Renmu, 158, 170, 175, 322n34
Pan Zinian, 83
Paoxiao lede tudi. See *Roaring Earth* (Jiang Guangci)
parricide, 57, 60–64, 119, 197
partial objects, 297n16
patriarchy, 95, 275
patricide, 57, 60–62, 197
"peach-blossom grove," 15–16, 17, 19, 40, 296n4
Peach Blossom Grove, 36, 252, 256, 268
peasant rebellion: in *Eighteen Hundred Piculs of Rice* (Wu Zuxiang), 65; in land-reform novels, 165–67, 178; Li Yang on, 304n78; in *The Rice-Sprout Song* (Eileen Chang), 135–36; in *Roaring Earth* (Jiang Guangci), 60–61; in *The Sun Shines over the Sanggan River* (Ding Ling), 71–74; in *The Water Margin,* 163
Peng Dehuai, 163, 165, 182
Peng Jiahuang, 274
Peng Yugui (in *Liaozhai*), 289
People's News, 157
People's Republic (1949), 2; in *The Death of a Poet* (Dai Houying), 237; Eileen Chang and, 131–32, 171; in *Fool in the Reeds* (Chen Jiying), 169; in *Hungry Guo Su'e,* 146; nationalized history and, 11, 161; revolutionary poetics and, 151–53; "revolution plus love" fiction and, 115–16
petty crooks *(zhen xiaoren),* 217–18, 220
"petty wickedness," 208–10
phantasmagoria, aesthetics of, 12, 278–84, 340n69, 341nn84,85
physical fitness, 279–82
Pinggui zhuan (A romance of cracking down on ghosts), 273
Pingyao zhuan (Quelling the ghosts), 272
Plaks, Andrew H., 325n69

poetic justice, 3, 76; dialectic of justice and, 10, 42–43, 59; in *The Travels of Lao Can* (Liu E), 20, 45, 47, 51
Possessed, The (Dostoevsky), 212–13
Prendergast, Christopher, 341n84
Previous and Present Lives of Pan Jinlian, The (Li Bihua), 338n34
primitivism, 34, 36, 121, 312n15
"Principle of Livelihood" (Sun Yat-sen), 157
Promethian symbolism, 152, 315–16n9
Pursuit (Mao Dun), 81–82, 88–89, 102, 112
Pu Songling, 287–90
Putrefaction (Mao Dun), 105–6, 116, 309n88

Qian Gurong, 231
Qian Liqun, 121
Qian Wengui (in *The Sun Shines over the Sanggan River*), 71–72, 73, 74–75, 178
"Qian xiaojing" (Little scene in Guizhou; Shen Congwen), 25–26
Qian Xibao, 188, 214–22
Qian Xingcun, 83–86, 90, 96, 104
Qian Zhongshu, 157, 213, 275
Qiaoming (in *Fight Out of the Ghost Tower*), 56–57
Qin Dejun, 100–106, 116, 309nn78,82,88, 311n113
Qingchun zhige (The song of youth; Yang Mo), 164
Qing period, 4, 6; in *Autobiography of Congwen*, 25; in *A Compendium of Monsters* (Qian Xibao), 11, 214–20, 222; dialectic of justice in, 41, 42–44, 52–53, 65, 73–76; exposé tradition in, 213–23, 326–27n84; ghost tales and, 263–64, 266, 272–74, 281, 287–88; in *Living Hell* (Li Boyuan), 47–51; nationalized history and, 163; in *Remains of Life* (Wuhe), 30–34; "scar writing" and, 148, 150–52, 181; in *The Travels of Lao Can* (Liu E), 44–47; Wang Guowei and, 225; in *Women's Words Overheard* (Youhuan Yusheng), 9, 10, 15–19
Qing She (Green snake; Li Bihua), 337n32
Qinlan (in *Linli*), 97
Qin, Prince of, 22
Qin Shubao, 203
Qin Zhaoyang, 160
Qiu Jin, 22
"Qiwang" (The chess king; Ah Cheng), 145
Qi Yukun, 324n53
Qu Qiubai, 86, 87, 89, 152
Qu Yuan, 235, 289

Rainbow (Mao Dun), 89, 102–4, 116
RAPP (All Russian Association of Proletarian Writers), 83
rationality, 195, 198, 210, 222–23
realism: Anderson, Marston, and, 2, 293n1; Bai Wei and, 96–99; in *A Compendium of Monsters* (Qian Xibao), 220; fin-de-siècle writers and, 12; ghost tales and, 263–65, 272–78, 279–80, 336n10; in *Hungry Guo Su'e* (Lu Ling), 124, 128–30; in *An Idle Commentary on Monsters* (Li Qing), 205, 209; Lu Xun and, 21, 23–25, 29, 297n27; Mao Dun and, 82–86, 91–92, 102, 104–6, 305n10; revolutionary poetics and, 152–54; "scar writing" and, 177; in "When I Was in Xia Village" (Ding Ling), 68; Wuhe and, 17
Red Land (Chen Jiying), 157–58, 169
Red River Trilogy (Pan Lei), 158, 170
Red Rock (Luo Guangbin and Yang Yiyan), 149–50, 165
Red String, The (Li Bihua), 288–89
Remains of Life (Wuhe), 17, 30–34, 37–39, 40
re-membering China, 25–30, 39
Ren Ah! Ren. See *Man ah! Man* (Dai Houying)
"Ren de wenxue" (literature of the human), 264–65
"Rengui he tade qi de gushi" (A story about a human ghost and his wife; Luo Shu), 274
Renjian wangliang zhuan (A tale of demons and devils in the human world; Wu Jianren), 273
renqing xiaoshuo (novel of manners), 203
"Renrou" (Human flesh; Wang Jingzhi), 119
Republican Revolution (1911), 25, 41, 94, 195, 214, 224, 299n3
the Return (Hong Kong, 1997), 9, 271–72, 288, 338nn36,40
Reunion of Fellow Fighters (Mo Yan), 282–84
revenant, writing as, 266–72, 279
Revolution and Love (Hong Ruizhao), 90
revolutionary historical novel (geming lishi xiaoshuo), 163–65, 318–19n48
revolutionary poetics, 150; implosion of, 152–56, 316–17nn21–25

"revolution plus love" fiction, 9, 10–11, 77–116; Bai Wei and, 94–99, 110–15; gender politics and, 94–99; Jiang Guangci and, 60, 86–93, 106–10; Jiang Gui and, 197; love stories "in reality" and, 99–116; Lu Ling and, 125; Mao Dun and, 77–86, 100–106; realism and, 82–86; romanticism and, 86–93, 307nn42,47
Rice-Sprout Song, The (Eileen Chang), 119, 131–37, 158, 171, 175–76, 180, 277
Roaring Earth (Jiang Guangci), 60–62, 64, 72, 109, 122
Rojas, Carlos, 297n16
romanticism, revolutionary, 86–93, 110, 116, 129, 227, 233–35, 307nn42,47
Rongsheng (in *Fight Out of the Ghost Tower*), 56–58
Rouge (Li Bihua), 270–71
Rou Shi, 118
Rout, The (Fadeyev), 162
Roy, David, 206
Rulin waishi (The scholars; Wu Jingzi), 200

Sacrifice in the Wild, A (Jiang Guangci), 87–88, 89
Saich, Tony, 74, 303n62, 304n79, 327n94
"Sange nanren yu yige nüren" (Three men and one woman; Shen Congwen), 25
Sanguozhi yanyi (The romance of the three kingdoms), 204
Sanli wan (Three-mile bay; Zhao Shuli), 167–68
Sanqianli jiangshan (Three-thousand-mile mountain; Yang Shuo), 163, 172
Des Sans-culottes (Jiang Guangci), 87, 109
Sanxia wuyi (Three knights-errant and five sworn brothers), 48, 163
Sanyan (Comprehensive tales to admonish the world), 264, 266
Sartre, Jean-Paul, 271, 276
satire, 213, 220, 273
savagery, 10, 17, 19, 31, 34, 35, 39
Scandinavian goddess of fate, 102, 104, 116, 309nn81,82
Scar, The (Lu Xinhua), 173–75
the scarred, literature of, 4, 66, 74, 148–51, 173–82, 229, 236, 268, 315n1, 319–20n62
schadenfreude, 49
"scholarly knight-errant" (ruxia), 43, 48, 52, 300n14
Scholars, The (Wu Jingzi), 200, 208, 213, 323–24n49
Schonebaum, Andrew, 108
Schopenhauer, 225
Schwartz, Benjamin, 315–16n9
Second Musha Incident, 33–34
Second Sino-Japanese War, 2, 8, 11, 105, 115, 149, 159, 194, 224, 229, 246
Sedgwick, Eve, 318n46
self-immolation, 241, 331n51
sexual politics, 55, 196–200
Shafu (The butcher's wife; Li Ang), 145
Shanghai College (Shanghai Daxue), 86
Shanghai massacre, 78, 85, 87, 88, 109, 304n4
Shanghai Writers Association, 231
"Shanghen" (The scar; Lu Xinhua), 173–75
shanghen wenxue. See the scarred, literature of
Shang mythological tradition, 6
"Shangshi" (Mourning; Lu Xun), 275
Shangshu, 6, 186
"Shangui" (Mountain ghost; Shen Congwen), 274–75
"Shanlu." *See* "Mountain Path" (Chen Yingzhen)
Shaofang (in *The Bomb and the Expeditionary Bird*), 98
Shaonian piaopozhe. See *Youthful Tramp, The* (Jiang Guangci)
Shao Quanlin, 121
Shen Congwen: Bai Wei and, 110; decapitation syndrome and, 10, 16–17, 25–30, 36–37, 39–40; ghost tales and, 274–75; literary suicide and, 226–27, 329n15; Lu Xun and, 297n27; Nationalist banning of, 157; nativist fiction and, 169, 312n15; regionalism and, 298n48
Shengsi chang (The field of life and death; Xiao Hong), 119
Shengsi yuanjia (Life-and-death partners; Zhong Ling), 284–86
Shen Jiaben, 41
Shen Jianshi, 334n1
Shenliao (Fantastic talk; Mo Yan), 287–88
Shenmo dou meiyou fasheng (Nothing has happened at all; Chen Guanzhong), 271
shenmo fiction, 264, 273
Shen Weiwei, 309n78
Shenwu zhiai (The romance of a shaman; Shen Congwen), 36
Shen Yanbing. *See* Mao Dun

Shen Ye, 334–35n2
Shenyi jing (Classic of the supernatural and the strange), 6, 185
Sherlock Holmes techniques, 51, 301n29
Shi. See *Eclipse* (Mao Dun)
Shiba chun (Eighteen springs; Eileen Chang), 158
Shifu (in *The Bomb and the Expeditionary Bird*), 98
"Shigu zhe" (The bone collector; Wuhe), 37
Shiji, 5–6, 185
Shijing, 4
Shi Mingde, 240–42, 249
Shi Mingzheng, 12, 228, 240–50, 253, 259–60
Shi Mingzheng shihua ji, 333n62
Shiren zhisi. See *Death of a Poet, The* (Dai Houying)
Shi Shenzhi (in *A Tale of Modern Monsters*), 197–98
Shi Shuqing, 278
"Shiwu" (Mistake; Gu Cheng), 252
Shixiang ji (A tale of Shixiang; Chen Hui), 338n36
Shi Xun (in *Pursuit*), 82, 88, 112
Shi Zhecun, 17
"Shui" (Flood; Ding Ling), 122
Shuihu zhuan (The water margin), 163, 200
Shujun (in *A Sacrifice in the Wild*), 88
Shuqi, 140
Shu Ting, 331n83
Shu Yi, 227
silence, 3, 43, 227, 233, 239, 254, 257, 294n4, 300n15
Sima Qian, 6, 192
Sima Zhongyuan, 265, 336n20
simulacrum, 220, 258, 284, 303n62, 327n94
Sino-Japanese War (1936–1945). *See* Second Sino-Japanese War
Sino-Vietnamese war, 283
Sishi tontang (Four generations under one roof; Lao She), 226
Sister Cloud, 77–78
Situ Wei, 159, 317–18n35
Six Dynasties period, 263
Sketches from a Hunter's Album (Turgenev), 28
slide show of decapitation, 16, 20–22, 32, 51–52, 54, 296n5
snake spirits, 202, 265, 324–25n58
socialist realist literature, 229–31, 329n25
social justice: Communist literature and, 73; hungry woman image and, 119; in *Living Hell* (Li Boyuan), 50; in 1930s, 59; in *The Travels of Lao Can* (Liu E), 45–47
Society of Literary Studies (Wenxue Yanjiuhui), 87
Song clan (in *Eighteen Hundred Piculs of Rice*), 65
Song Laoding (in *Do Not Take This Path*), 167
Song of the Ten-Thousand-Mile Yangtze River (Wen Jie), 231, 236
Song Ruoyu, 106–10, 112, 310n91
Song Yulian (in *The Previous and Present Lives of Pan Jinlian*), 338n34
Sorrows of Young Werther, The (Goethe), 233, 260
Soushen houji (Sequel to "In search of the supernatural"; Tao Qian), 270
spectacle: Foucault and, 23, 50; in *Hungry Guo Su'e* (Lu Ling), 70; Jiang Guangci and, 62; Li Boyuan and, 49–50; Lu Xun and, 22–23, 39, 54; Shen Congwen and, 26
spiritual food, 120–25, 135, 144, 313n28
spiritual hunger, 120–25, 312n11, 313n25
Stalin Literary Prize, 70, 166
Starrs, Roy, 226
Story of the Golden Cangue, The (Eileen Chang), 277
subjectivity: Chinese, 108, 121, 225, 297n16; collective, historical, 66, 121, 135; gendered, 119, 122; individual, 135, 206; revolutionary, 87, 91, 221, 236, 238, 330n48; socialist, 156; tribal, 33–34; wounded, 176
Sugano Masae, 31
suicide, 224–61; Gu Cheng and, 250–61; politics of, 233–35; Shi Mingzheng and, 240–50; Wen Jie and, 228–40, 330n48
Suishi yiwen (Forgotten tales of the Sui; Yuan Yuling), 203
Suitang yanyi (The saga of the Sui and Tang dynasties), 161
Suizi Zhang-Kubin, 332nn92,93
Sun Ling, 157
Sun Longki, 125
Sun Monthly, 109
Sun Shines over the Sanggan River, The (Ding Ling), 70–75, 166, 177–78
Sun Shuyu, 325n69
Sun Society (Taiyang she), 82, 85–87, 109–10, 307n40

Sun Yat-sen, 157, 302–3n56
Sun Yat-sen University, 94
"Supplemental Treatises on Education and Recreation" (Chiang Kai-shek), 157
surveillance, 114, 154, 168, 235
surviving China, 30–40
Su Tong, 266, 281–82, 290
Su Wei, 108
Su Weizhen, 278
Su Xuelin, 151, 317n30
Suzhou insurrection, 203
symbolic justice, 61
Symbolists, 241–42, 244
"synchronic" view (gongshi xing) of history, 34, 36
syphilis, 82, 88–89, 112–13

Taichushu Police Bureau, 31
Tai Jingnong, 317n30
Taiping guangji, 335n3
Taiwanese independence movement, 12, 240–41, 331n51. *See also* Great Divide (1949)
Taiyang yuekan (Sun monthly), 109
Taiyang zhaozai Sanggan heshang. See *Sun Shines over the Sanggan River, The* (Ding Ling)
"Taiyuan Yiniang" (Yiniang of Taiyuan), 263
Tale of Modern Monsters, A (Jiang Gui), 7, 11, 158, 171, 183–200, 209–15, 219–23, 320n3, 322n37, 323–24nn48,49, 326–27n84
Tang Wenbiao, 277
Tang Xianzu, 270
Tang Xiaobing, 74, 166
Tan Yuexiang (in *The Rice-Sprout Song*), 119, 131–37, 139, 144, 146
Tan Zhongdao, 145
Tao Qian, 268, 270
taowu, 6–8, 11–12, 185–87, 190, 196, 200, 207–8, 214, 219–20, 222–23, 321n16, 327n93
Taowu cuibian. See *Compendium of Monsters, A* (Qian Xibao)
Taowu xianping. See *Idle Commentary on Monsters, An* (Li Qing)
Taussig, Michael, 35
Tayal aborigines, 9, 17, 30–34, 37–39, 40
"tears and blood" literature, 4, 9, 43, 59–65, 66, 133
Tears of Eros, The (Bataille), 269
Temptation of St. Anthony, The (Flaubert), 336n10
Theater of the Absurd, 271
Three-Mile Bay (Zhao Shuli), 167–68
Three Principles of the People (Sun Yat-sen), 302–3n56
Three-Thousand-Mile Mountain (Yang Shuo), 163, 172
Thunderstorm (Cao Yu), 59, 275
Tian'anmen Incident, 9, 116, 260, 282
Tian Ergeng (in *An Idle Commentary on Monsters*), 209
Tianqi reign, 185, 200–204, 207, 325n65
Tianshan muge (Ballads of Tianshan; Wen Jie), 229
Tianshi (History of heaven; Ding Yaokang), 6
"Tianxian pei" (Heavenly match; Wang Anyi), 282–83
Tiedao youji dui (Railroad guerrillas), 177
"Tiehai" (Iron kid; Mo Yan), 288
"Tiyu zhi yanjiu" (A study of physical culture; Mao Zedong), 279
Toda tribe, 33–34
Tolstoy, Leo, 104, 244, 272
Travels of Lao Can, The (Liu E), 19–20, 44–53, 65, 70, 73, 213, 214, 301n23
"True Story of Ah Q, The" (Lu Xun), 2, 22, 54, 72, 85, 157, 169, 275–76
tuberculosis, 82, 107–10, 112
Tu Cheng-sheng, 186
Tujia aborigines, 36
"Tuomo" (Exorcism; Shi Mingzheng), 248
Tuwei (Breaking free; Jiang Gui), 189
"Twilight" (Shen Congwen), 25, 27–28

uncanny, 268, 272, 337n23
Underground Man (in *Notes from Underground*), 244, 250
United Association of Chinese Literature and the Arts, 153
U.S. Information Service, 131, 158, 184

Vacillation (Mao Dun), 81–82, 104
venereal disease, 82, 88–89, 112–15
verisimilitude, 56, 97, 113, 263, 274, 279, 284, 336n10
Village Trilogy (Mao Dun), 105, 122, 133
violence of representation, 3–4, 43–44, 294n4, 300n15
Virilio, Paul, 272

Wagner, Rudolf, 166
Waiyee Li, 322n36
Wanderer (in *Remains of Life*), 37
Wang Anyi, 266, 282–83
Wang Guowei, 224–26, 228, 260, 328nn5,7, 342n90
Wang Hui, 275
Wang Jicong, 184
Wang Jingzhi, 119
Wang Lan, 322n34
Wang Luyan, 17, 25, 274
Wang Manying (in *The Moon Forces Its Way through the Clouds*), 88–89, 112–13
Wang Meng, 160
Wang Mengzou, 108
Wang Mingzhao, 188
Wang Ruowang, 145
Wang Shenting, 326–27n84
Wang Tongzhao, 188, 326–27n84
Wang Xiangqian, 322n37
Wang Xiaoming, 275
Wang Xiaoyu, 332n90
Wang Yijian. *See* Jiang Gui
Wang Yingxia, 106
Wang Yuanjian, 188
Wang Zhenhe, 160
Wang Zhongqi, 208
Wanli changjiang xing. See *Song of the Ten-Thousand-Mile Yangtze River* (Wen Jie)
Wanli reign, 201–2
Wanqing xiaoshuoshi (Ah Ying), 296n4
War Drum, 231
Water Margin, The, 163, 200, 323–24n49
Weicheng (Fortress besieged; Qian Zhongshu), 213
Wei Haiqing (in *Hungry Guo Su'e* , 120
Weihu (Ding Ling), 88
"Wei nuli de muqin" (A slave's mother; Rou Shi), 118–19
Weirdo (in *Remains of Life*), 37
Wei Zhongxian (in *An Idle Commentary on Monsters*), 185, 200–212, 217, 219–20, 324–25nn58,59
Wengu 1942 (Remembering 1942; Liu Zhenyun), 145
Wen Jie, 12, 227, 228–40, 251, 253, 259–61, 329n30
Wenming xiaoshi (Modern times; Li Boyuan), 215
Wenxue Zazhi (Literary magazine), 160
Werther (in *The Sorrows of Young Werther*), 233, 260
West Hunan (Shen Congwen), 25–26
Whampoa Military Academy, 84, 87
"When I Was in Xia Village" (Ding Ling), 67–69, 70, 75
Whirlwind, The (Jiang Gui), 158, 171, 183–85, 210, 223, 323n48, 328n96
White-Haired Girl, The (Lu Ling), 125–26, 338n34
White Lotus cult, 203
White Night (Jia Pingwa), 286–87
White Snake, 56–57, 337n32
White Terror, 137, 139, 241–42, 246
Wie Zhongxian xiaoshuo chijian shu (Fiction that castigates the villainy of Wei Zhongxian; Wuyue caomang chen), 201
Williams, Philip, 63
Wode jiaoyu (My education; Shen Congwen), 25–26
Wo de putishu (My own Bodhi tree; Zhang Xianliang), 145
"Wo, hongdayi, yu lingling" (I, red coat, zerozero; Shi Mingzheng), 243
Wolfe, Alan, 226
Women chapian hongqi (We've erected red flags everywhere; Wen Jie), 231
women's liberation, 58, 94, 302n44
Women's Words Overheard (Youhuan Yusheng), 15–20, 32, 35, 40, 296nn1,6,7
"Wozai xiacun de shihou" (When I was in Xia village; Ding Ling), 67–69, 70
Wu Da (in *Pan Jinlian*), 55
Wu Feng, 34
Wufeng Zhishu (Trees without wind; Li Rui), 145
wuguai, 186
Wuhan regime, 78, 81, 90, 94–95, 98, 101, 104, 111, 115
Wuhe, 9, 10, 17, 30–34, 36–40
"Wuhui jieshu yihou" (After the dance party; Wen Jie), 230
Wu Jianren, 19, 214, 273, 301n25
Wu Jingzi, 200
Wu Mi, 328n12
"Wuming de xiaohua" (Nameless flowers; Gu Cheng), 259
Wu Pei-yi, 335n5
Wu Qiang, 164
Wu Shengqing, 328n4
Wushe shijian. See Musha Incident (1930)

Wu Sihong, 109–10, 112
Wu Song (in *Pan Jinlian*), 55
Wu Woyao, 218
Wuyue caomang chen, 201
Wu Zuxiang, 62–65, 72, 119, 122, 274

Xian'an, Prince (in "Carved Jade Guanyin"), 284–85
Xiangdong jiwen (Accounts of the eastern Hunan region), 186
Xianglin's wife (in "New Year's Sacrifice"), 53, 117–19, 127, 146–47, 179–80, 275
Xiang Nan (in *The Death of a Poet*), 236–40
Xiang Peiliang, 58
Xiangxi (West Hunan; Shen Congwen), 25–26
Xianzi (in "Fan Family Village"), 63–64
Xiao Ai (Little Ai; Eileen Chang), 158
Xiaobing Tang, 108
Xiaobin Yang, 337n27
Xiao Hong, 119
Xiao Jun, 163
Xiao Sen (in *Fight Out of the Ghost Tower*), 56–58
Xiao Xiang (in *Hurricane*), 166–67
Xie Bingying, 81, 151, 317n30
Xie Ye, 250, 252–58, 260, 332–33nn90,93,96
Ximen Qing (in *Pan Jinlian*), 55
Ximen Qing (in *The Golden Lotus*), 205, 207, 325n69
Xin ernü yingxiong zhuan (New tale of heroes and lovers), 162
Xingge, mingyu (Character, fate; Dai Houying), 229
Xingshi hengyan (Lasting tales to awaken the world), 264
"Xinliu" (New willow; Huang Jinshu), 289–90
Xinmeng (New dream; Jiang Guangci), 87
Xinsheng (New birth; Ba Jin), 17
Xinsheng Bao (New life daily), 156–57
Xin xiaoshuo (New Fiction), 41, 299n1
Xinyi. *See* Qin Dejun
Xinyue (Crescent moon) school of poetry, 224
"Xin yu jiu" (The old and new; Shen Congwen), 25–26
Xinzhong de fen (A tomb in my heart; Dai Houying), 229, 329n22
"Xiou'shou panngguan lun" (On the theory of noncommital spectatorship; Ba Ren), 156–57
Xi Rong, 153
Xiuding Falü Guan (Institute for Legal Revision), 41
Xiuxiang xiaoshuo (Illustrated fiction), 301n25
Xiuxiu (in "Carved Jade Guanyin"), 285–86
Xixi, 278
Xiyou ji (Journey to the west), 273
Xuanfeng. See *Whirlwind, The* (Jiang Gui)
Xu Dahai (in *A Tale of Modern Monsters*), 209
Xunzi, 206
Xu Sixing. *See* Lu Ling
Xu Yu, 274
Xu Zhimo, 106, 151

Yalu jiangshang (On the Yalu River; Jiang Guangci), 109
Yama (in *The Travels of Lao Can*), 47, 51
Yan Fu, 152
Yan'an, battle of, 163–65
Yan'an period (1940s), 8, 10, 44, 229
Yang Cunren, 109
Yangge. See *Rice-Sprout Song, The* (Eileen Chang)
Yang Hansheng. *See* Hua Han
Yang Lian, 250, 282–83
Yang Liang (in *An Idle Commentary on Monsters*), 203, 206, 324–25n58
Yang Mo, 164
Yang Sao, 81, 95, 96, 97, 110–16
Yang Shuo, 163, 172
"Yang Siwen Yanshan feng guren." *See* "Encounter of Yang Siwen and Old Acquaintances, An" (Feng Menglong)
Yang Xi'er (in *The White-Haired Girl*), 125–26
Yang Yi, 121
Yang Yiyan, 17, 149
Yanhua sanyu (The red string; Li Bihua), 288–89
Yanzhi kou (Rouge; Li Bihua), 270–71
"Yao" (Medicine; Lu Xun), 22
Yecao (Wild grass; Lu Xun), 259, 275
Yeh, Michelle, 253–54, 258
Yeji (A sacrifice in the wild; Jiang Guangci), 87, 89
Yelang (in *Mulian xi*), 286–87
Yellow River flood, 46, 300–301n20
Ye Shaojun, 84
Ye Ting, 149
"Yeyu" (Nocturnal fishing; Mo Yan), 288
Yeyu qiudenglu (Writings done in the rainy nights and under the autumn lamp), 264

"Yidai ren" (One generation; Gu Cheng), 251
Yijianzhi (Hong Mai), 263, 335n3
Yin and Yang Dreams That Admonish the World (Changan daoren), 201
Ying'er (Gu Cheng), 253–58, 332–33n96
Yiniang (in "An Encounter of Yang Siwen and Old Acquaintances in Yanshan"), 262–63, 266–67, 271, 290
Yiqian babai dan (Eighteen hundred piculs of rice; Wu Zuxiang), 63, 64–65
"Yishi de wancheng" (The completion of a ritual; Su Tong), 281–82, 290
Youhuan Yusheng, 15–21; Lu Xun and, 9–10; Shen Congwen and, 26, 29; Wuhe and, 30, 32–33, 34–35, 39–40
"Young master gets his tonic" (Wu Zuxiang), 62–63
Youth Corps, 246
Youthful Tramp, The (Jiang Guangci), 87, 109, 307n42
"Youzi" (Grapefruit; Wang Luyan), 17, 25
Yuan Jing, 177
Yuan Qiongqiong, 278
Yuan Shikai (in *Women's Words Overheard*), 9, 15, 18–19
Yuan Yuling, 203
Yu Bin (in *The Bomb and the Expeditionary Bird*), 98–99
Yu Dafu, 87, 106, 108, 151, 226
Yuelin (in *Fight Out of the Ghost Tower*), 56–58
Yuewei caotang biji (Jottings from the thatched abode of close observations), 264
Yueya er (The crescent moon; Lao She), 226
"Yuhai" (Fish relics; Huang Jinshu), 289–90, 342n101
Yu Hua, 131, 145, 266, 269–70, 271, 337n27
Yu Liansan, 41
Yun Daiying, 308n73
Yunzhong Shu, 122
Yü-sheng Lin, 21, 24
Yusheng (Remains of life; Wuhe), 17, 30–34, 37–39, 40
Yushi mingyan (Illustrious tales to instruct the world; Feng Menglong), 262, 264, 334–35n2
Yuxian (in *A Sacrifice in the Wild*), 88
Yuxian (in *The Travels of Lao Can*), 45–47, 300n18
Yu Yue (in *The Bomb and the Expeditionary Bird*), 98–99
Yu Ziqi (in *The Death of a Poet*), 236–39, 330n48

"Zai Haidebao duoru qingwang" (Falling in love in Heidelberg; Long Yingtai), 17
"Zai jiulou shang" (In the tavern; Lu Xun), 24, 275, 306n32
Zai tielian zhong (In the midst of the shackles; Lu Ling), 176
Zang Kejia, 188, 326–27n84
Zeitlin, Judith, 287
Zeng Langzhi (in *A Compenium of Monsters*), 216
"Zeng Mingzheng" (For Mingzheng; Ji Xian), 242–43
Zeng Pu, 108
"Zen of Bushido," 37
Zhadan yu zhengniao. See *Bomb and the Expeditionary Bird, The* (Bai Wei)
Zhang Ailing. *See* Chang, Eileen
Zhang Chunqiao, 231–32, 235–36
Zhang Daofan, 157, 174, 302–3n56
Zhang Qiuliu (in *Pursuit*), 82, 88–89, 102, 112–13
Zhang Shizhi (in "Li Zhongwen nu"), 270
Zhang Taiyan, 43, 300n14
Zhang Tianyi, 213
Zhangui zhuan (A romance of devil-killing), 272–73
Zhang Xianliang, 145
Zhang Yiwu, 254, 333n110
Zhang Yousong, 111
Zhang Zhenshan (in *Hungry Guo Su'e*), 120, 125
Zhang Zongchang, 326–27n84
Zhan Yihua, 331n51
Zhanyou chongfeng (Reunion of fellow fighters; Mo Yan), 282–84
Zhaohua xishi (Morning flowers plucked at the sunset; Lu Xun), 276
Zhao Huiming (in *Putrefaction*), 105
Zhao Jingshen, 301n25
Zhao Shuli, 132, 153, 167–68, 177, 182
Zhao Wenjie. *See* Wen Jie
Zhao Yanwang (Yama Zhao; Hong Shen), 275
Zhao Yulin (in *Hurricane*), 166–67
Zhao Zifan, 179
Zheng Boqi, 87

Zheng Nanrong, 331n51
zhengtong, 189–91, 321n32
Zheng Yiniang (in "An Encounter of Yang Siwen and Old Acquaintances in Yanshan"), 262–63, 266–67, 271, 290–91
"Zheng Yu'e Yanshan feng guren" (An encounter of Zheng Yu'e in Yanshan; Shen Ye), 334–35n2
Zheng Zhenduo, 4, 9
Zhenzhen (in "When I Was in Xia Village"), 67–69, 70, 75
"Zhidao guan yu wo" (The inquisitor and I; Shi Mingzheng), 249–50
"Zhongguo shehui jieduan de fenxi" (Analysis of class in Chinese society; Mao Zedong), 122
Zhongguo shibao (China times), 342n101
Zhong Ling, 278, 284–86, 290
Zhong Xiaoyang, 278
Zhou Dayong (in *Guarding Yan'an*), 163–65
Zhou dynasty, 186
Zhouli, 186
Zhou Libo, 72, 74, 132, 153, 156, 166–67, 177, 182
Zhou Zuoren, 264–65, 336nn14,15
Zhuang, Governor (in *The Travels of Lao Can*), 44, 46–47
Zhuang Zhongqing, 309n81
Zhuanxu, Prince, 6, 185
"Zhufu." *See* "New Year's Sacrifice" (Lu Xun)
Zhu Heng (in *An Idle Commentary on Monsters*), 324–25n58
Zhuiqiu. See *Pursuit* (Mao Dun)
"*Zhuiqiu zhongde* Zhang Qiuliu" (Zhang Qiuliu in Pursuit; Qin Dejun), 102
"Zhujian" (Forging swords; Lu Xun), 22
"Zhuogui dadui" (Mission: Ghost hunt; Lin Yiyun), 281–82
Zhu Tianxin, 268–69, 281
Zhu Xiang, 224–26, 228, 260
Zibuyu (What the master [Confucius] would not discuss), 264
Zisha Riji (Diary of suicide; Ding Ling), 226
"Zisha" (Suicide; Mao Dun), 101
Ziye (Midnight; Mao Dun), 105
Ziyou Zhongguo (Liberal China), 160
Zola, Emile, 104, 129–30, 272
Zong Baihua, 264
Zong Pu, 17
Zuo Guangdou (in *An Idle Commentary on Monsters*), 206, 324–25n58
Zuoye (Last night; Bai Wei and Yang Sao), 114
Zuozhuan, 5, 6–7, 186, 267

Compositor: Integrated Composition Systems
Text: 10/12 Baskerville
Display: Baskerville
Printer and binder: Maple-Vail Manufacturing Group